Shifting Forms of Continental Colonialism

Dittmar Schorkowitz · John R. Chávez ·
Ingo W. Schröder
Editors

Shifting Forms of Continental Colonialism

Unfinished Struggles and Tensions

Editors
Dittmar Schorkowitz
Max Planck Institute for Social
Anthropology
Halle (Saale), Germany

John R. Chávez
Southern Methodist University
Dallas, TX, USA

Ingo W. Schröder
Department of Cultural and Social
Anthropology
Philipps University of Marburg
Marburg, Germany

ISBN 978-981-13-9816-2   ISBN 978-981-13-9817-9   (eBook)
https://doi.org/10.1007/978-981-13-9817-9

This Palgrave Macmillan imprint is published by the registered company Springer Nature Singapore Pte Ltd.
The registered company address is: 152 Beach Road, #21-01/04 Gateway East, Singapore 189721, Singapore

ACKNOWLEDGEMENTS

This volume has received support from many sides for which the editors wish to express their sincere gratefulness. First of all we would like to thank the contributors for their patience, cooperation, and suggestions. Special thanks goes to Wolfgang Reinhard for his stimulating keynote lecture as well as to Bruce Grant and Michael Khodarkovsky for their thought-provoking discussions at the conference *Forms of Continental Colonialism: The 'Other' Colonialism* that took place in Halle (Saale) in July 2016. We gratefully acknowledge their comments and recommendations. We likewise feel indebted to Sara Crowley and Connie Li of Palgrave Macmillan Publishers for keeping things rolling and to the publisher's anonymous reader who noted ways of improvement. Last, but not least, we thank the Max Planck Institute for Social Anthropology in Halle (Saale) for funding and organizing the conference.

CONTENTS

NOTES ON CONTRIBUTORS

James Olusegun Adeyeri Department of History and International Studies, Lagos State University, Lagos, Nigeria

Epp Annus Department of Slavic and East European Languages and Cultures, Ohio State University, Columbus, OH, USA

Carole Blackburn Department of Anthropology, University of British Columbia, Vancouver, BC, Canada

John R. Chávez Clements Department of History, Southern Methodist University, Dallas, TX, USA

Dipankar Dey Guest Faculty, Department of Business Management, University of Calcutta, Kolkata, India

Wolfgang Gabbert Institute of Sociology, Leibniz University Hannover, Hannover, Germany

John Mwangi Githigaro Faculty of Social Sciences, St. Paul's University, Limuru, Kenya

Stefan Krotz Universidad Autónoma de Yucatán, Mérida, Mexico; Universidad Autónoma Metropolitana, Mexico City, Mexico

Orhon Myadar School of Geography and Development, The University of Arizona, Tucson, AZ, USA

Wolfgang Reinhard Department of History, University of Freiburg, Freiburg im Breisgau, Germany

David Z. Scheffel Department of Sociology and Anthropology, Thompson Rivers University, Kamloops, BC, Canada

David Schimmelpenninck van der Oye Department of History, Brock University, St. Catharines, Canada

Dittmar Schorkowitz Max Planck Institute for Social Anthropology, Halle (Saale), Germany

Ingo W. Schröder Department of Cultural and Social Anthropology, Philipps University of Marburg, Marburg, Germany

Ute Schüren Department of History, University of Münster, Münster, Germany

Willard Sunderland Department of History, University of Cincinnati, Cincinnati, OH, USA

Lili Zhu Faculty of History, Bielefeld University, Bielefeld, Germany

LIST OF FIGURES

CHAPTER 1

Empires, Modern States, and Colonialism(s): A Preface

Wolfgang Reinhard

Years ago, when I told a French friend that I was writing a book on colonialism, her remarkable comment was: *are you also going to include the colonization of women by men?* At about the same time I had to refuse the offer to write a paper on the colonization of the Ex-German Democratic Republic by the Federal Republic of Western Germany. Of course, both perspectives are possible and *colonization*, as well as *colonialism*, can easily be employed as a kind of universally applicable invective. As a historian, however, I feel obliged to make a narrower and more precise use of terminology. On the other hand, my use of terminology may sometimes look not extremely professional because I am no addict of extreme theorizing German style. For my part as historian of the expansion of Europe, I prefer a practical approach to the *imperial turn* (Hirschhausen 2015). But in doing this, I remain to some extent confined to general and West European perspectives because I lack expertise in the Russian and Chinese languages (but see Schorkowitz 2015, 2017). Nevertheless, my approach from outside may still help to sharpen

W. Reinhard (✉)
Department of History, University of Freiburg,
Freiburg im Breisgau, Germany
e-mail: wolfgang.k.w.reinhard@web.de

© The Author(s) 2019
D. Schorkowitz et al. (eds.), *Shifting Forms of Continental Colonialism*,
https://doi.org/10.1007/978-981-13-9817-9_1

1

our analytical instruments, and a general view of the *longue durée* may demonstrate the "powerful impact of trans-epochal path-dependencies" (Schorkowitz 2015, 2) of continental colonialism even more easily.

In short, in this chapter I intend to prove two propositions which should contribute to a better understanding of the *other colonialism* which is essentially continental and not maritime as usual. My first thesis claims that modern colonialism succeeded only because the hard core of every colonial empire was a modern national power state, whereas the colonial empire itself was not a state but something of different pre-modern political structure. In German, this is the difference between *Staat* and *Reich*, which unfortunately has been blurred in research. Secondly, I have every reason to believe that a convincing distinction between colonial empires and empires in general is not possible (Reinhard 2016).

EMPIRE VS. STATE—REICH VS. STAAT

Starting with the first proposition, we are immediately in trouble because of the implicit terminological difference between German *Reich* and English *empire*. Whereas *empire* just designates a particularly large state or polity, *Reich* in addition covers the structural difference between modern and pre-modern polities. It is a matter of quality not just of quantity. A *Reich* needed not be large at all. Instead of an *Imperium* in Latin terminology, it could also be a mere *Regnum* or even a small territorial unit like the *Aachener Reich* which covered not more than 8.7 square kilometers (Brecher 1957). But in any case, a *Reich* lacked essential qualities of the *Staat* in German or of the *modern state* in English. Therefore, if we want to be exact, we have to translate the simple German contrast of *Reich* and *Staat* into the complicated English terminology of *pre-modern polity* versus *modern state*. However, we are lucky because the Eurasian empires I am going to analyze were all pre-modern polities. Therefore, when additionally defining *state* just for once as the *modern state*, I can contrast *empire* with *state* in the same way as I would do it in German.

But is it still the state of the art to insist upon the historical development of structural differences between empire and state? Does this approach not pay tribute to an outdated modernization theory which considered the unitary national state superior to a plural empire, where different peoples lived peacefully together, a kind of polity we are inclined to prefer after so many ethnic and national excesses

(Hirschhausen 2015, 724, 742)? But the insistence upon such structural differences between state and empire does not automatically imply an evaluation. The modern state's superiority in power politics does not necessarily include a higher political morality or a better life for the subjects. Quite the opposite can be true. Just remember that the *Holocaust* was the ultimate performance of a modern power state.

My intention could not be more different. I simply want to use the concepts of *empire* and *state* in the sense of Max Weber as ideal types of political organization without any implicit evaluation. I have a reason to believe that they may prove useful instruments for analyzing colonialism in general and Eurasian colonialism in particular, because the success of modern colonialism is based upon the ambiguous European invention of the modern nation state and this is the most outstanding accumulation of power in the history of mankind (Reinhard 1999, 2007).

Expanding Europeans were organized as modern power states or at least they practiced forms of social and political life which produced an organization of that type. In contrast, even highly developed polities such as China remained pre-modern empires. Such an empire might deploy remarkable power but in the long run could not compete with the European power state. As long as this difference of power subsisted, European states remained superior and were able to add colonial empires to the nation state they had at home. Of course, the other side tried at once to imitate the European power state. The Japanese did it with immediate success. Others had to wait until decolonization. In the meantime, almost all polities of the world have become modern states, at least in theory, with the consequence that together with different political structure European superiority started to disappear.

STATENESS: TERRITORY AND POPULATION

But why are modern states stronger than other polities? The essential difference is the unity and uniformity of the modern state in contrast to the notorious plurality inside pre-modern empires. Unity and uniformity do not only produce power, they are also the very essence of modernity, whereas plurality is an attribute of pre-modern as well as of post-modern societies. Because of similar pre-modern political structure, ancient European polities could serve as contrasting examples as well as extra-European ones. During early modern times not only Spain and Britain were so-called *composite monarchies* consisting of several countries with unequal status but even such a small country as Tuscany. Accordingly, the official designation of Spain was *las Españas*. Down to 1918 neither Austria-Hungary nor the German Empire were modern states. The first consisted of two different groups of countries whereas the latter was in fact a confederation of semi-sovereign princes. It is not by chance that in our post-modern age of plurality Great Britain and Spain tend to disintegrate again. Just think of Scotland or Catalonia!

In contrast according to the traditional doctrine of German jurisprudence, the first and basic attribute of the modern state is the unity of territory. Not only composite empires, which consist of different countries with different status and territorially overlapping authorities such as con-dominions, contradict the nature of the modern state but any territorial difference of authority at all. Well defined linear borders outside and inside the country are essential. In contrast, quite often the intermediate level offices of the branches of pre-modern government such as administration, law courts, revenue, the military or the church resided in different towns with overlapping districts. In addition, political control tended to decrease together with the distance from the center. Between France and Germany and in Northern Italy the political membership of some territories was uncertain, others belonged to both domains. The town of Mulhouse (Mülhausen) remained a German island in French Alsace because it happened to be not only a free city of the Empire but also an associate member of the Swiss Confederation at the same time.

Spatial plurality could correspond to a different legal status of the inhabitants. In contrast, the modern state has a uniform and stationary population as a second basic quality. Nomads can create an empire but never a state. Therefore, Russia's rulers down to Stalin have always tried to make the nomads of their steppe regions sedentary, often by force. As far as I know, the Chinese are still busy with that. Beyond territorial plurality, an empire's population could also be divided into groups or strata with different status, with different relations to the central authority, and in addition speaking different languages. Besides local languages and dialects, the elites of Western Europe used Latin, later French, England's lawyers *Law French* whereas China's political class spoke Mandarin Chinese.

The inhabitants of a modern state are considered and consider themselves as only one *people*, a *Staatsvolk* in German, after the French Revolution as a *nation*. They identify themselves with their polity, enjoy or sometimes even lack the same rights and have the same obligations, they speak the same language and believe to be of the same ethnic origin. In reality, however, this is almost never the case (Anderson 1983; Gellner 1983). Therefore, states are inclined to enforce homogeneity, beginning with the language. In extreme cases, they proceed to murderous ethnic cleansings.

In contrast, the power of an empire is based upon a select part of its population only, upon one of its peoples, the *Reichsvolk* in German, such as the Castilians in Spain, the English in Britain or the Han in China. For the rest of the inhabitants this could result in discrimination, but also in toleration, and the protected existence of a minority with a culture and a language of its own, a status which China's 55 minorities are supposed to enjoy. In other cases, all inhabitants were transformed into one single people, the *Reichsvolk* became a *Staatsvolk* or nation, either directly by linguistic, ethnic and cultural assimilation or indirectly and formally through a federal constitution. Russia tried both models. But successful integration of all inhabitants does still not transform a pre-modern empire into a modern state which is characterized by about a dozen of different attributes.

COLONIALISM

At this point, we touch the problem of colonialism for the first time. Does the rule of one people, of the core group, over other peoples inside an empire amount to colonialism? Were Egypt and Greece in antiquity Roman colonies although their cultures were much older and even idealized by the Romans? Or should this quality be reserved for *Gallia* and *Germania* which lived under the cultural impact of Rome?

Formally, Mexico and Peru enjoyed the same status of secondary domains of the Castilian monarchy as Aragon or Naples, governed by their own council at Madrid and by a viceroy as delegate of the monarch. In theory, their inhabitants were subjects of the same right. Therefore, they were called *las Indias* as the kingdoms of the Iberian Peninsula were called *las Españas*. It was not before the eighteenth century when the central authorities intensified their control that the designation *colonies* became common usage. This brings us closer to a solution of our problem. For in reality, an equal status of the different European and American countries and their inhabitants was always out of the question. But it was not so much the extraction of American silver by Spain that amounts to exploitation. The tax revenue of the Kingdom of Naples was also spent by the Castilian kings for their own purpose just like the church of Naples had to finance the papacy and the Roman Curia. Therefore, Naples has recently been characterized as duplex colony (Metzler 2004). The essential difference was the inferior legal, social, and economic status of the Amerindians. Whereas a single Aragonese or Neapolitan was not discriminated personally, all *indigenas* were exposed to legal tutelage, social humiliation, and economic exploitation. But confronted with such gradually differentiated dependency of peoples and countries, we are no longer able to define where colonialism begins and ends.

According to Jürgen Osterhammel (Osterhammel and Jansen 1995, 20; cf. Osterhammel 1999, 16)

> Colonialism is a relationship of domination between an indigenous (or forcibly imported) majority and a minority of foreign invaders. The fundamental decisions affecting the lives of the colonized people are made and implemented by the colonial rulers in pursuit of interests that are often defined in a distant metropolis. Rejecting cultural compromises with the colonial populations, the colonizers are concerned of their own superiority and of their ordained mandate to rule.

I prefer a less complicated definition: "I will use 'colonialism' to mean one people's control over another people through the economic, political and ideological development gap between the two" (Reinhard 2011, 1).

Both of us agree that colonialism means foreign rule in the interest of those foreigners. Nevertheless, not every kind of foreign rule is colonial, especially a mere hegemony or an *informal empire* as characterized by Osterhammel elsewhere (Osterhammel and Jansen 1995, 22–24). Today, despite supposed German hegemony Europe is no German colony. And for the former informal control of China and the Ottoman Empire by the great powers, a terminological compromise such as *semi-colony*, in German *Halbkolonie*, was necessary to account for the fact, that despite foreign control, the respective governments still enjoyed remarkable political options. It should also be evident that ancient Egypt and Greece under Roman rule were no colonies.

Therefore, the necessary condition of imperial foreign rule has to be completed by another sufficient condition if an empire should be considered as a colonial empire. Obviously, this essential condition demands the ranking of the groups involved. According to the recent tendency of historiography to turn the significance of history into a history of significance, Osterhammel locates this difference in the culture of the ruling group and identifies it as their feeling of superiority and their missionary impetus. But I think it is empirically necessary to go beyond this definition and to attribute this obvious state of mind of the ruling foreign group to the historical reality of a different level of development of both groups. Because if we would instead assume only different levels of this or that power this could apply to any empire and the specific contents of the colonial situation would disappear.

Of course, this approach is of excessive political incorrectness. Firstly, because from a synchronous perspective, the evident superiority of one part implies the inferiority of the other and any real inferiority is no longer acceptable in our age of supposed equality. Secondly, because from a diachronic point of view, it apparently assumes again a general path of development of mankind where only the ruling colonialists have achieved the final objectives. However, I think that two empirical statements provide sufficient contradicting evidence against this denigration of my argument. Firstly, the obvious superior killing capacity of atomic bombs does not imply in every respect a higher value compared with bow and arrow. Secondly, even if most probably a general path of development of mankind does not exist, path-dependency of the development of different groups can still be identified. Today, instead of one general modernity, we assume multiple particular modernities.

In contrast to former concepts, I consider as essential the political development which leads to the modern nation state and not so much the military and economic achievements connected with it. Therefore, in order to understand the decisive organizational development, it is necessary to analyze all different attributes of the modern state. For recent research tends to resolve the monolithic category *state* into its components which in more or less complete combination constitute different levels of *stateness*.[1] The ideal type of the complete modern state was rarely or probably never present in real history. But nevertheless or perhaps for this very reason, it provides an excellent analytical tool.

---

[1] For the original German term *Staatlichkeit* see Schuppert (2010).

STATENESS AGAIN: AUTHORITY, POWER, THE RULE OF LAW, AND SOME OTHER ATTRIBUTES

In the third place, this modern state with a unified territory and population as first and second qualities is governed by one single authority whereas in most empires local lords claim power of their own right, sometimes with an authority which is older than the central one. Quite often they are former independent rulers who have been subdued by the empire. In modern states, however, local administrators are just delegates of the central government. Autonomous rule of nobles has disappeared and communal self-administration, if it exists at all, is authorized by the state. Since 1787 former plural empires have sometimes been unified by transformation into a federal commonwealth. Their government may be decentralized but the state is unitary.

In this respect, Russian and other Eurasian monarchies were right from the beginning more modern than the Europeans because their rulers enjoyed unlimited power (cf. Torke 1974). But were they able to profit from this advantage?

In the fourth place, the central authority of a modern state holds sovereignty and that means complete independence of any overlordship as claimed by pope and emperor during the European Middle Ages. Once again, their unlimited power made Russian and Asian rulers more modern than their European counterparts. Today, in contrast, the sovereignty of most states is limited by international treaties and organizations. Only very few of them are free to wage war as they like, whereas this competence had once been the essence of sovereignty. Therefore, sovereignty implied the complete control of the armed forces. Under the modern state, however, no malcontent vassal could withdraw his men from the king's army or pass over to the enemy.

In the fifth place, the state holds the monopoly of legitimate physical violence covering the whole territory and exercised by the police force. In extreme cases, in contrast to the U.S. and Switzerland, subjects are completely disarmed. Nobody is any longer entitled to enforce justice in his own right or to wage a private war such as the medieval feud. But it took a long time to suppress this practice, because in pre-modern Europe violent resistance against authorities was considered at least as legitimate if not as legal. Russia and China had a similar tradition of popular uprisings. In China, a natural catastrophe could be interpreted as proof that the *mandate of heaven* had been withdrawn from the ruling dynasty.

The European Enlightenment and the French Revolution added important further attributes to the five 'classical' ones mentioned so far. In the sixth place, they secularized the state. All pre-modern empires had been founded upon religious or quasi-religious legitimacy. From this point of view, the Chinese emperor's *mandate of heaven* was rather the rule and not an exception. During World War I, the Ottoman sultan still remembered that one of his predecessors had assumed the role of the caliph, the successor of the prophet Muhammad. But in this respect, Latin Europe differed from the standards of world history because it had to live with a dualism of religious and secular authorities, in institutional terminology of church and state. When European monarchs emancipated themselves from ecclesiastical tutelage, they still insisted on their legitimation *by the grace of God*. This provided them with immunity as long as they did not break the law of God or nature. On the other hand, this unique fundamental separation of God and world made a secular concept of politics possible. As a consequence, the modern state after the Revolution could refuse any legitimation from outside, because from now on it was able to legitimize itself through the fiction of the sovereignty of the people. From now on it was competent to define its own competence, to limit it by a declaration of fundamental rights or to repeal this limit at discretion.

This contrast between legitimation by a transcendent authority from outside and self-legitimation from inside had consequences for the relation of state and law. Because in the seventh, eighth, and ninth places, the modern state is characterized by the rule of law, by a constitution, and by democracy. That is, government should be regulated and limited by law, in particular by a fundamental law called constitution. This guarantees human rights and establishes the regular election of a legislative body as well as of the holders of authority.

Pre-modern European monarchies have been named *States of Justice* (*Justizstaaten*) because firstly, law and order were the chief task of the ruler and secondly, the king had anyhow to rule by administration of justice owing to the lack of bureaucracy. But pre-modern European law was based upon the transcendent idea of divine or natural justice. Therefore, in some way the king was subject to the law whereas in China law was just another instrument of imperial rule. The European state also achieved a similar unlimited control of the law but not before the time of the enlightenment, when law was re-created systematically in new codifications and autonomous lawyers were transformed into obedient state servants. In this way, the legal plurality of traditional polities was replaced by the uniform law of the modern state.

In such a situation, for example in the case of ancient Prussia, rule of law could even work without constitution and democracy. And where the state controls the law without limits no constitution is irreversible. But today very few states can afford not to have the appearance of being democracies. Nevertheless, a working modern state does not even need a constitution and democracy to exert full power. Perhaps it works even better without democracy and rule of law. Totalitarian regimes of the twentieth century and authoritarian ones of the twenty-first century demonstrate this. In any case, on the one hand a constitution is the guarantee for the rule of uniform law, but on the other hand legal uniformity is also the precondition of democracy and of any constitutional regime. Therefore, the term *constitution* applies to European and extra-European pre-modern polities only by analogy. A 'constitutional history' of the European Middle Ages is correctly considered as anachronistic, as a mere re-projection of the modern state of affairs. And in manuals of Chinese, Indian, Persian, Ottoman, and Russian pre-modern history this word is even missing. The absolute power of Asian and Russian rulers was too obvious to be noticed and debated by historians!

In the tenth place, the modern nation state was another achievement of the French Revolution. The established uniformity of the state's population becomes activated where rulers legitimate themselves as executors of the will of the politically organized people, because exactly this is the nation. To be a *nation state* is the extreme opposite of the pre-modern polity and also the most sanguinary attribute of the modern state. The ideological power of nationalism induces subjects to sacrifice life and property and legitimates suppression and even extermination of national minorities as well as an aggressive foreign policy against 'foreign devils'. European nations usually refer to their countries and peoples and claim to be 'natural' because they developed from the ancient kingdoms (*regna*) during a long historical process in an almost self-evident way. But the short-cut state building in decolonized Latin America and Africa produced some completely artificial polities which have their problem to become nations. Such cases demonstrate the basic artificiality of nations which have always to be 'invented'. On the other hand, the handling of nationalities or national minorities has always been a fundamental problem of the Chinese and Russian empires (Schorkowitz 2001, 2017). It is the key problem of continental colonialism.

In the eleventh place, the French Revolution produced first concepts of the welfare state. This in fact did not start before the late nineteenth century. Besides war itself, social security became the largest part of the modern state's budget after World War II because of the social consequences of that war.

This implies that, in the twelfth and final place, the modern state is and always has been a ruthless power state. Increase of power was the purpose of the activities which generated the state, in particular of the endless wars of European history. From its very origin, the modern European state was a war state and power was its *raison d'être*. State power claims to increase the power of the nation and inversely employs the nation for this same purpose. Even the expanding responsibility of the state for social security has an increase of state power as a consequence. Therefore, I maintain that the fully developed welfare state is just a soft variety of the totalitarian state. This politically incorrect statement does not intend to minimize the difference between rule of law and arbitrary power. Nobody should do that. Nevertheless, it is obvious that the state starts to regulate our life before we are born and still disposes of our dead body with profit.

Of course, pre-modern empires were likewise created through sanguinary expansion processes because of the lust of power of their founders. But none of them ever reached the intensity of control and the extent of mobilization of resources which are the characteristics of the modern national power state—once again: the most powerful creation of mankind! In comparison with pre-modern empires the superiority of the modern state can be summarized in three points: first, the tremendous increase of competence with the totalitarian state of the twentieth century as the final consequence—second, the strict unification of the polity as a nation—third, the unlimited mobilization of resources as a consequence of both, in particular for war and armament culminating in two World Wars and the Cold War afterwards.

CONTINENTAL AND MARITIME COLONIALISM(S)

We used twelve basic attributes of *stateness* to contrast pre-modern with modern states. However, in history these attributes emerge in different combinations and 'dosages'. Therefore, our analysis has to start with using the ideal types for the differing historical realities of pre-modern and modern empires according to their respective temporal and spatial conditions. For both China and Russia differ from other colonial empires because of their pulsatile but nevertheless continuous presence in time and space.

At first sight, this is the main difference between maritime and continental colonialism, the very essence of the *other colonialism*. European historiography always used to treat colonial history as overseas history, abruptly beginning with the Portuguese and the Castilians in the late fifteenth century and to be continued by the Dutch, the English and the French in the later sixteenth and the early seventeenth centuries.[2] In contrast, already in the 1980s, I included the continental expansion of Russia and the U.S. in my history of European expansion. Their pulsatile continuity, however, is to some extent always political, whereas in maritime empires quite often economic interests are more important than the activities of the states.[3]

Russian expansion starts in the high Middle Ages, Chinese expansion even before our era. Both result in contiguous extension of the respective cultural space. Nevertheless, both processes do not show teleology and not even linear continuity. Neither contradictory tendencies are missing, nor changes of direction. Just remember Mongol rule over Russia and China when in Russia the focus was moved from Kiev to Moscow, or the different foreign dynasties in China down to the Qing, or the abandoned Chinese attempts of maritime expansion in the early fifteenth century. The mere change of dynasty or rule might result in changes as in the cases of Peter the Great and Catherine the Great in Russia and of Kangxi and Qianlong in China. Nevertheless, considered in the aggregate, there was a continuous expansion of Russia toward East and South, of China toward North and West for hundreds or even thousands of years.

At a closer look, however, also the maritime expansion of Western Europe on the one hand had a medieval tradition and on the other hand sometimes resulted in continental colonialism as a consequence. Beginning in the high Middle Ages, Portugal, and Castile had been expanding on the Iberian Peninsula as England did on the British Isles. The Iberian *Reconquista* continued in North Africa and via the

---

[2] Therefore, the German journal founded by Eberhard Schmitt in 2001 was still called *Jahrbuch für europäische Überseegeschichte*.

[3] But this difference is overstressed by Ulrike von Hirschhausen (2015, 740).

Canary Islands became the *Conquista* of the New World. The English subdued the Irish 'savages', 'the black Irish', founded settlements in their country and tried to civilize them. In both cases, the cut-throats of the *Reconquista* and Irish wars continued with their activities in America.

On the other hand, maritime primary expansion quite often produced secondary continental expansion in most cases through settlement. The Spanish *Conquista* followed that rule but the 'classic' case was the occupation of North America by the British maritime colonies, the U.S. and Canada. But mention should at least also be made of Argentina, Chile, South Africa, and Australia in the nineteenth century and Brazil from the seventeenth century until today.

Finally, primary or secondary continental expansion might in the end change into maritime expansion again. When Russians occupied Alaska and roamed over the Pacific Ocean, they met U.S.-American activities, because after the conquest of their continent, the U.S. started to transform the Pacific into an American lake with the Philippines as an overseas colony.

If we compare the modes of procedure, the difference between maritime and colonial expansion shrinks further and that between imperial and colonial expansion almost disappears. Quite often in the beginning there was no initiative of an empire or a state, but the activities originated with informal networks of discoverers, businessmen, soldiers, missionaries, and other adventurers who managed to involve their governments or were engaged by them. Russia's Stroganovs and Alaska shareholders despite all obvious differences were structurally close relatives of the participants of Spanish *entradas*, of the shareholders of British and French North America companies, of Brazilian *bandeirantes*, and of the different chartered colonial companies of the age of imperialism. Catholic, orthodox, and protestant missionaries swarmed to save souls and were in similar ways used as instruments of legitimation and rule until the enlightenment transformed their impulse into a secular civilizing mission.

China did not send out missionaries but the propagation of Chinese culture to civilize the barbarians was an axiomatic program too. Chinese networks are less known but the behavior of Chinese settlers and businessmen in the Ussuri area under Russian rule resembles very much that which we know from other colonies (Arsenjew 1926).

TYPES OF COLONIES

Maritime expansion created three types of colonies with several sub-va-
rieties (Osterhammel and Jansen 1995, 14–16; Reinhard 2011, 3). The
Roman *colonia*, the prototype of the concept, as former Phoenician and
Greek settlements combined two of these types. On the one hand, it was
a settlement, on the other hand a stronghold in a foreign country which
originally belonged to an enemy but later became subdued.

The first type, the settler colony, usually lived on agriculture. The
necessary land could be acquired through displacement of the natives as
in Russia, North America, and Australia. In Algeria, Kenya, South and
Southwest Africa native farmers were dispossessed. Displacement might
result in extermination, whereas by dispossession natives could be trans-
ferred into the labor force of the new lords. A third variety was re-settle-
ment through forced migration of African slaves in plantation colonies in
America, of convicts in Australia and Siberia.

Strongholds, the second type, usually are considered exclusively as an
element of maritime expansion. Most were of commercial origin, beginning with trading bases in a foreign city, but later on autonomous, sometimes even fortified trading post colonies constructed on foreign soil. Or
they were naval bases (strategic colonies). In the end, the Royal Navy
maintained hundreds of them worldwide. A combination of both was
the infrastructure of the Portuguese, Dutch, and English commercial
empires in Asia. But similar commercial and military strongholds were
also a necessary element of continental empires under construction in
Siberia or North America, in particular the network of forts of the US
army in the Far West.

Colonies of rule, in German *Herrschaftskolonien* (Reinhard) or
Beherrschungskolonien (Osterhammel), the third type, controlled an
entire country without subjecting it to the comprehensive new settlement. The Hispano-American variety includes settlement, but the settlers
based their subsistence primarily on the domination of an indigenous
majority which is, for this purpose, usually left largely alone to pursue its
own economic way of life. The characteristic feature of the more recent
Asian-African type, the pattern being British India, is the domination of
a huge majority of indigenous people by a tiny minority of colonial rulers, who are not even permanently resident in the colony. Both variants
depend on the collaboration of indigenous helpers for survival. However,
this type was also the original one in the South of Russian Central Asia,

in Caucasia, in Tibet, in Xinjiang and in Manchuria. As the essential character of imperial rule, this does away with the supposed difference between colonial and non-colonial empires.

But the temporal sequence of types of colonies in continental empires is inverted compared with maritime colonialism. This is one of the two really important differences between the maritime and the colonial modes of expansion. Whereas maritime expansion usually starts with strongholds or settlements to be followed later by true colonies of rule, continental expansion begins with the imperial, in old-fashioned terminology: imperialistic conquest of the whole foreign country. But in contrast to maritime empires, the consequence is not the establishment of a permanent colony of rule but increasing colonial penetration. Obviously, territorial contiguity of metropolis and periphery does not allow permanent rule at distance. Therefore, in continental empires conquest is followed by the establishment of a network of strongholds, next by trickling immigration, *Sickerwanderung* in German (Goehrke 2010, 33–43), and ends with mass settlement, cultural assimilation of the indigenous population and final political integration of the conquered territory into the conquerors' polity.

INTERNAL COLONIALISM AND FRONTIER

As in the famous case of the conquest, exploitation and at least intended assimilation of Britain's *Celtic fringe*, the concept of *internal colonialism* can be applied. For continental empires are also characterized by an uneven pattern of development with different cultural prestige of participating groups (González-Casanova 1965; Hechter 1975; Hind 1984). But often the spatial, ethnic, and historic distance of these groups is smaller than in maritime empires (Kappeler 1992, 56).

Under such circumstances, the 'frontier' phenomenon is emerging. This is a particularly dynamic border zone but not necessarily with the outstanding political and ideological importance which has been ascribed to it by U.S.-American historiography (Waechter 1996). It is 'no man's land' according to Carsten Goehrke (2010, 43–47) "where no one has an enduring monopoly on violence" (Weaver 2003, 73). But whereas in other empires the frontier was continuously moving because of the settlers' pressure, ancient empires tried to stabilize it through fortifications again and again. The Romans had their *limes* or Hadrian's Wall, the Chinese the Great Wall to protect them against nomad invasions from the north. Finished under the Ming dynasty, it became superfluous under the Qing who came from beyond and in addition through imperialist expansion pushed the empire's outer borders much further. In the eighteenth century also the Russians constructed border fortifications against the nomads of Central Asia and these became superfluous after further expansion of the empire.

A particular advantage of the Russian empire was the exceptional frontier population of Cossacks. Of course, the squatters, trappers, and cowboys of the Far West contributed to the expansion of the U.S.A. and the missionaries stabilized the Hispano-American empire when they established their settlements on the frontier. But Russia's expansion depended to a much larger extent on the Cossacks. They served as spearhead of the conquest of Siberia and within few decades reached the Pacific Ocean. Like other frontiersmen, they adopted to some extent the economic and military way of life of their enemies and this contributed to their success. But in contrast to others, they became a closed group with a pronounced identity. Finally, membership was no longer acquired but ascribed, which means that it was inherited. Perhaps Cossacks might even have developed their own ethnicity. But when the political structure of the empire became gradually more stable and modern, it could do without them.

STATE BUILDING, NATION BUILDING, AND THE INTEGRATION OF MINORITIES

This particular process of political integration is the second essential difference between maritime and continental empires. Whereas the building of Western maritime empires was prepared by state building and nation building at home, in China and Russia the empire preceded the state. Until the present day, the structural consequences of this historical fact remain a special challenge for these empires. Have they really become modern nation states or at least is this their intention, or are they still plural empires despite their unwillingness to admit their imperial reality?

Western colonial powers were complete and unitary modern nation states when they started to build additional colonial empires around these hard political cores, empires which were loosely structured and all but uniform. Certainly, Germany and Italy were slightly unfinished national states in the late nineteenth century and early modern Castile and England were just proto-modern nation states. But they profited from the enormous technological and organizational difference between themselves and the peoples which they met in the New World.

In contrast, Russia did not start to become a modern state before the eighteenth century and did not achieve this end before the nineteenth or perhaps twentieth century. China had slowly embarked on that development since the late nineteenth century and had become a modern state in the second half of the twentieth century. However, the complete *stateness* of both polities is still doubtful today because they suffer from their unmastered imperial heritage. As everywhere, state building and nation building also in their case necessarily imply linguistic, cultural and to some extent ethnic assimilation and organizational centralization. From time to time, even the great colonial powers of Britain and France tried to transform their colonial empires into federations with a common *stateness* to stabilize them. But they failed very soon because of the spatial and ethnic distance between the metropolis and the empire and the consequential differing regional interests. Russia and China, however, because of their coherent imperial territories, had no choice but to include their 'colonies' in their state and nation building at a time when this process had not yet achieved its end in the imperial centers. In contrast to maritime powers, they had somehow to assume the identity of empire and state.

In 1897, 130 different languages were spoken in the Russian empire whereas only 45% of the population were proper Russians. But 70% were Orthodox Christians. From the beginning to the end, the Russian empire had comparatively co-opted the indigenous elites successfully into the Russian nobility. It is well-known that in most cases colonialist rule is based upon an alliance of foreign rulers and native elites to exploit the indigenous subjects. It was not before the mid-nineteenth century that Russian nationalists started an intensive Russification of language and culture. However, this policy was neither continuous nor coherent. In a pragmatic way, different groups were treated differently. Muslim cultures were respected, provided the eleven percent Muslims did not attempt resistance or develop a nationalism of their own (Kappeler 1992; Goehrke 2010).

After the monarchy had disappeared and Lenin had liquidated for some time the 'prison of nations', the new empire of Soviet Russia solved the problem of integration through a multi-level ethnic federalism. In reality, however, owing to the communist party, Soviet Russia was a more or less strictly centralized modern state and a multi-ethnic empire at the same time. The breakdown of 1989 came by surprise. In Central Asia and Transcaucasia this was just a final process of decolonization when several member-republics of the Soviet Union, simply for the first time, seriously claimed their sovereign rights to leave the union as permitted by the constitution. In contrast, peoples inside the closer Russian Federation, the former RSFSR, like the Chechens were not allowed to do so. However, the separation of the European Soviet republics in exactly the same way demonstrates once again the lack of difference between categories from the linguistic fields of 'colonialism' and of 'empire'.

In the eighteenth century, the Qing dynasty increased the Chinese empire by expansion from four to eleven million square kilometers and stabilized it in a similar way by co-option of the elites of the subject peoples respecting their cultural traditions and religious identities. Nevertheless, demographic pressure from the core of the empire resulted in economic penetration of parts of Mongolia and of Xinjiang by Han-Chinese. Ethnic resistance movements, sometimes directed against their own ethnic elites, who co-operated with the Chinese, was the consequence. But only northern Mongolia could achieve independence with Russia's assistance after the breakdown of the Manchu dynasty in 1911. Tibet tried in vain to escape internal colonialism, whereas Xinjiang experienced administrative autonomy and several attempts to found independent republics.

The precondition of this development was the impotence of the Chinese Republic between 1912 and 1949. Nevertheless, the republic claimed to be the Chinese national state. However, as in the French Revolution the unity of the nation was in the first place defined spatially and only in the second place ethnically. Only four peoples, the Tibetans, the Mongols, the Manchus, and the Hui-Muslims were recognized as minorities but submitted to a rigid assimilation policy. The exploding nationalism of the Han-Chinese reduced them anyhow to mere subgroups of the Chinese race.

Similar to their Russian comrades, the Chinese communists started with a liberal minority policy but as early as 1938 turned to the concept of a historically legitimated unitary state with limited cultural rights of minorities. But not more than 55 of the about 400 groups which applied for this status were recognized as minorities. Independence movements of Tibet and Xinjiang were brutally broken. Aspirations to ethnic autonomy were doomed as counter-revolutionary, cultural peculiarities as reactionary. The Cultural Revolution was meant to destroy them by violence. Tibetan monasteries were attacked and destroyed. After 1979 the new policy restored the status of cultural autonomy and the present regime makes every effort to present folkloristic cultural diversity. But in political reality, it insists upon the unitary character of the state. Independence movements in Tibet and Xinjiang are still suppressed without mercy. Islamic terrorism provides a welcome legitimation of this repressive policy. As a result, all marginal territories of Tibet, Xinjiang and Inner Mongolia became effectively assimilated by massive immigration and planned economic development (Dabringhaus 1995, 2006). For in contrast to tsarist and Soviet Russia, China could and can rely upon the mere numeric preponderance of an imperial people which has become a nation. Whereas in Russia *continental colonialism* resulted in decolonization or in minority problems in successor states, in China the unity of the nation state is apparently going to be enforced successfully.

Obviously, it is no longer of any historical consequence where we stick the label of 'colonialism' and where not. In contrast, however, the ideal types of *pre-modern empire* and *modern state* allow an exact analysis of the different levels of 'stateness' and therefore a better understanding for the shifting colonial forms in Eurasia.

References

Anderson, Benedict. 1983. *Imagined Communities: Reflections on the Origin and Spread of Nationalism*. London: Verso.

Arsenjew, Wladimir K. 1926. *Russen und Chinesen in Ostsibirien*. Berlin: August Scherl.

Brecher, August. 1957. *Die kirchliche Reform in Stadt und Reich Aachen von der Mitte des 16. bis zum Anfang des 18. Jahrhunderts*. Münster: Aschendorff.

Dabringhaus, Sabine. 1995. „Ethnische Identitäten im modernen China." In *Die fundamentalistische Revolution: Partikularistische Bewegungen der Gegenwart und ihr Umgang mit der Geschichte*, edited by Wolfgang Reinhard, 69–110. Freiburg: Rombach.

Dabringhaus, Sabine. 2006. *Territorialer Nationalismus in China: Historisch-geographisches Denken 1900–1949 (Menschen und Kulturen 2)*. Köln: Böhlau.

Gellner, Ernest. 1983. *Nations and Nationalism*. Oxford: Blackwell.

Goehrke, Carsten. 2010. *Russland: Eine Strukturgeschichte*. Paderborn: Schöningh.

González-Casanova, Pablo. 1965. "Internal Colonialism and National Development." *Studies in Comparative International Development* 1(4): 27–37.

Hechter, Michael. 1975. *Internal Colonialism: The Celtic Fringe in British National Development, 1536–1966*. London: Routledge and Kegan Paul.

Hind, Robert J. 1984. "The Internal Colonial Concept." *Comparative Studies in Society and History* 26(3): 543–68.

Hirschhausen, Ulrike von. 2015. "A New Imperial History? Programm, Potenzial, Perspektiven." *Geschichte und Gesellschaft* 41(4): 718–57.

Kappeler, Andreas. 1992. *Russland als Vielvölkerreich: Entstehung, Geschichte, Zerfall*. München: C.H. Beck.

Metzler, Guido. 2004. „Die doppelte Peripherie: Neapel als römische Kolonie und als spanische Provinz." In *Römische Mikropolitik unter Papst Paul V. Borghese (1605–1621) zwischen Spanien, Neapel, Mailand und Genua*, edited by Wolfgang Reinhard, 179–334. Tübingen: Max Niemeyer.

Osterhammel, Jürgen. 1999. *Colonialism: A Theoretical Overview*. 3rd ed. Princeton: Markus Wiener Publishers.

Osterhammel, Jürgen, and Jan C. Jansen. 1995. *Kolonialismus: Geschichte, Formen, Folgen*. 7th ed. München: C.H. Beck.

Reinhard, Wolfgang. 1999. *Geschichte der Staatsgewalt: Eine vergleichende Verfassungsgeschichte von den Anfängen bis zur Gegenwart*. München: C.H. Beck.

Reinhard, Wolfgang. 2007. *Geschichte des modernen Staates: Von den Anfängen bis zur Gegenwart*. München: C.H. Beck.

Reinhard, Wolfgang. 2011. *A Short History of Colonialism*. Manchester: University Press.

Reinhard, Wolfgang. 2016. *Die Unterwerfung der Welt: Globalgeschichte der europäischen Expansion 1415–2015*. München: C.H. Beck.

Schorkowitz, Dittmar. 2001. *Staat und Nationalitäten in Rußland: Der Integrationsprozeß der Burjaten und Kalmücken, 1822–1925*. Stuttgart: Franz Steiner.

Schorkowitz, Dittmar. 2015. *Imperial Formations and Ethnic Diversity: Institutions, Practices, and Longue Durée Illustrated by the Example of Russia*. Halle/Saale: Max Planck Institute for Social Anthropology.

Schorkowitz, Dittmar. 2017. "Dealing with Nationalities in Imperial Formations: How Russian and Chinese Agencies Managed Ethnic Diversity in the 17th to 20th Centuries." In *Managing Frontiers in Qing China: The Lifanyuan and Libu Revisited*, edited by Dittmar Schorkowitz and Chia Ning, 389–434. Leiden: Brill.

Schuppert, Gunnar Folke. 2010. *Staat als Prozess: Eine staatstheoretische Skizze in sieben Aufzügen*. Frankfurt am Main: Campus Verlag.

Torke, Hans-Joachim. 1974. *Die staatsbedingte Gesellschaft im Moskauer Reich: Zar und Zemlja in der altrussischen Herrschaftsverfassung, 1613–1689*. Leiden: E.J. Brill.

Waechter, Matthias. 1996. *Die Erfindung des amerikanischen Westens: Die Geschichte der Frontier-Debatte*. Freiburg: Rombach.

Weaver, John C. 2003. *The Great Land Rush and the Making of the Modern World, 1650–1900*. Montreal: McGill-Queen's University Press.

CHAPTER 2

The Shifting Forms of Continental Colonialism: An Introduction

Dittmar Schorkowitz

Recent studies of modern colonialism have focused on path dependencies of overseas colonialism in the developing and the developed world establishing a comprehensive body of literature which helped to form distinct approaches and patterns in the disciplines involved.[1] Students of global and colonial history like Christopher Bayly, Jane Burbank, David Fieldhouse, Jürgen Osterhammel, or Wolfgang Reinhard dealt either with the interdependencies of empire and overseas colonialism in general or with the complexities of settlers' lives. Historically minded anthropologists like Susan Bayly, Nicholas Dirks, John Comaroff, David Scott, and Ann Laura Stoler as well as anthropologically informed historians like Urs Bitterli and Frederick Cooper have proceeded similarly. Many scholars have engaged with settler colonialism as a "global and genuinely transnational phenomenon" (Veracini [2010] 2014, 2) including its inherent genocidal ('indigenocidal') implications (Churchill 2002;

---

[1] I am grateful to my co-editors and the volume contributors for their comments on various versions of this chapter. Needless to say, the editors and contributors do not agree on all points regarding the colonial paradigm.

D. Schorkowitz (✉)
Max Planck Institute for Social Anthropology, Halle (Saale), Germany
e-mail: schorkowitz@eth.mpg.de

D. Schorkowitz et al. (eds.), *Shifting Forms of Continental Colonialism*,
https://doi.org/10.1007/978-981-13-9817-9_2

23

Docker 2008; Wildcat 2015; Woolford and Benvenuto 2015). Others stress particular national experiences: the influence of the French colonial lobby (Chafer and Sackur 2002), the supremacy of the British colonial currency system (Narsey 2016), North America's complex colonial patchworks (Taylor 2013), or Italy's belated and short-lived colonialism (Ben-Ghiat and Fuller [2005] 2008). How relevant such studies are for contemporary integration strategies and social healing is revealed by public reconciliation projects in "liberal democratic settler nations" which feel "compelled to make [...] urgent political compacts between indigenous and non-indigenous peoples to address the legacy of violent pasts" (Edmonds 2016, 1; cf. Niezen 2013; Green 2015).

Postcolonial studies, while analyzing the cultural legacy of colonialism and imperialism, have been particularly preoccupied with modes of textual and discursive representations. Inquiring into the manner in which a culture is viewed in the social sciences and the humanities, they have invented a profound critique of the 'constructedness' of anthropological knowledge and colonizer-centered narratives emerging under and after colonial rule. This 'literary turn' resulted in a body of classical works on the social construction of the *other* and the *subaltern* (Guha 1982; Bhabha 1984; Spivak [1985] 2006; Chakrabarty 1992) who experienced discrimination in the hegemonic discourses of colonial and nationalistic histories reflecting what Edward Said called a long "crisis in representation" (1989, 205). The initial praise for this fresh approach was, however, followed by later concerns over "certain deconstructive and psychoanalytical approaches" (Thomas 1994, 19), that the "trope of otherness or alterity has become a cliché" and that the metaphorical use of colonization "risks making colonialism appear everywhere-and hence nowhere" (Cooper 2005a, 47).[2] While refining this critique in different directions, colonial studies on the other hand have often limited their scope to particular units of analysis, such as power and government (Scott 1995), identities and identification (Cooper 2005a), race and difference, hybridity and gender (Stoler and Cooper 1997), or colonial imaginations of the 'civilized savage', and socio-cultural repercussions for the postcolonial metropolis and for those "to 'come home' to the mother country" (Hall 2002, 3).

---

[2] For a critical summary of postmodern and postcolonial writing and the irony of confusions of ideas, see also Reinhard (2010).

For anthropologists the 'colonial situation' appeared to be a thorny, though productive debate ever since Georges Balandier introduced this notion, which was accompanied by a clear critique on 'cultural' and 'applied' anthropology criticizing the former for rejecting this complex "as being a disturbing factor or [...] seen as only one of the causes of cultural change" and the latter for being "viewed only in certain aspects" and never "as a force acting in terms of its own totality" ([1951] 1966, 35; cf. Hechter [1975] 1999, 30, 69). Suggesting a holistic approach for the 'colonizer and colonized' instead, Balandier's critique was taken seriously though with delay and not always directly. Some identified the "colonial connections of anthropology" as a major obstacle to and the decolonization of African nations as a pushing factor for changing anthropological attitudes and "radically subversive forms of understanding" (Asad [1973] 1998, 13, 17). Others were more explicit, pointing to the double ambivalence in relation to "official authority" and the "growing nationalist and revolutionary movements" (James [1973] 1998, 42–43), which gave anthropology, a markedly colonial-state and semi-governmental sponsored branch in academia, a conservative twist. The criticism of methods quickly developed into a crisis of general confidence in the discipline itself spurring further criticism of 'embedded anthropology' in theaters of war and the "failure of anthropologists to come to terms with and accept responsibility for the political implications of their work" (Lewis 1973, 581; cf. Bayly 2000, 602–604). The critique of British, American, and French colonial anthropology was soon backed by emic voices and a growing self-awareness among those 'colonial subjects' in Africa, Latin America, and Southeast Asia whom anthropologists had studied before and who were instrumental for their career-making afterwards.

Anthropology survived this crisis (as many others) transforming the debate into a new sub-field. Yet, the 'anthropology of colonialism' turned the focus away from the actual 'colonial situation' and diverted the political concerns to the "problem of colonialist representation [...] and discourse in the making of anthropological knowledge" (Scott [2001] 2015, 218). Moreover, the initial shift to anthropological self-reflection, epistemology, semiotics, and the 'linguistic turn' (Clifford Geertz) led somehow away from methodical basics of textuality (ethnography) and empirical evidence (fieldwork), toward studies on postcolonial nation-building and nationalism (Ernest Gellner, Benedict Anderson), colonial governmentality (Scott 1995), and 'nonverbal' practices. Under the conditions of accelerated modernity the anthropologists' cascading responses to the colonial legacies of their discipline were, however, not always productive or convincing. They also paved the way for a new wave of empiro-criticism, contextualist epistemology (opposing invariant knowledge), blind presentism (bypassing temporalities and historicity), and a too hasty deconstruction (sanitation) of useful classifications, dichotomies and notions such as 'Enlightenment', 'Europe', 'modernity', 'colonial state' or 'culture' and 'ethnography' "criticized for their contribution to colonial and postcolonial essentializations of ethnic entities" as justified repeatedly by one prominent advocate (Pels 1997, 166; 2008, 281; cf. Comaroff 2002, 108). However, while some anthropologists found themselves trapped in the jungle of ontological snares, literary theorems, displacement activities, and collective control over politically correct speech, colonial studies experienced another upsurge of scholarship. Instrumental for this renewal was a still critical awareness "translated into various forms of Marxist or anti-imperialist anthropology" (Said 1989, 208), a considerable cross-fertilization of "literature, anthropology, and history" (Cooper 2005a, 3), and a growing critique over recent decades against "ahistorical tendencies of story plucking, leapfrogging legacies, and time flattening" (Schorkowitz 2012, 53 referring to Cooper 2005b) that became an "important stimulus" for the "study of the history of colonization" (Gagné 2012, 114; cf. Scott 1995).

Against this background of historical and anthropological engagement with essentially Anglo-Saxon and French entanglements of the 'colonizer and the colonized', an imagery introduced by Albert Memmi (1957) to exemplify the enduring psychomental complex of the two (cf. Stoler 2009, 62), one is surprised by the minimal discussion on continental and internal colonialism in current debates. Only very few studies on these variants exist although they promise "great challenges to theories of comparative colonialism and imperialism" (Osterhammel [1995] 2010, 118) particularly, but not exclusively, with regard to Russia and China. The paradox is striking, since in the wake of the shifting politico-intellectual climate after World War II and the "increasing numerical strength of the United Nation's anti-colonial membership" (Twitchett 1965, 307) when the "retreat from empire changed from a measured crawl to an uncontrolled gallop" (Fieldhouse [1965] 1982, 404) overseas colonies have become a rare phenomenon as indicated by the adoption of the UN Resolution 1514 in December 1960 (United Nations List 2017).

Whereas continental, internal, neo- and crypto-colonialism still prevail in many parts of the world, despite enhanced decolonization triggered by the break-up of the Soviet Union which, following common numbering, we may call the 'Fourth Wave' of decolonization. The silence on this particular colonial past, due as some suggest "to the excessive pride of Western Europe in its own achievements" (Marquard 1957, 2), continues perhaps because these forms are "less spectacular than expansion overseas, and therefore often ignored by historians of colonialism" (Reinhard 2015, 225). Other factors, such as uncritical adoptions of obsolete assumptions and ideologies, arguing for instance that the concept of internal colonialism is not applicable to socialist countries and "only suitable for an analysis of capitalism" (Goodman 1983, 107; cf. Gladney 1998, 2; Myadar 2017, 6–7), may have furthered the situation. Terrestrial expansion into allegedly "vacant or semi-vacant land masses […] of the United States across the North American continent and that of Russia across much of Siberia and Central Asia", to add another blind alley, was long considered as "morally superior to western European 'colonialism'" (Twitchett 1965, 308). Thus, national leaders from decolonized Africa and Asia for a long time advocated in favor of the Communist regimes in the Soviet Union and China, perceiving the two not as protagonists, but as victims of western colonialism and imperialism. Indeed, this silence is not simply an academic problem. The scholarly failure to develop and the public failure to apply such colonial thought undermine practical efforts to rectify ethno-racial inequality. A native group's continued political under-representation, for example, may be viewed as a result of its small population when in fact the colonizers' historic practice of racial gerrymandering has caused the problem.

The Colonial Situation: The Colonizers and Colonized and What Class Has to Do with It

In principle, a racial or ethnic group that experiences subordination in its own homeland at the hands of a foreign group—arriving not necessarily from another continent—is colonized; the colonizer is of a separate ethno-racial group. Usually, a colonized status develops from "military conquest, typically followed by political, economic, cultural, and complete social and even psychological subordination" (Chávez 2011, 786). As a result, the situation of a colonized society, which itself may have a complex class structure, is under rigid external control and maintained to satisfy the needs of the colonizer, where the latter is not willing to acculturate with the former. The colonial subordination thus usually cuts across all races, classes, and genders as moving categories, and is likely to be reflected in the class structure of the colonizers' society. Also, people (predominantly white males in most modern cases) in the service of the colonizing state "came from different classes" and the military "depended on soldiers who were simultaneously coerced and coercing" (Stoler and Cooper 1997, 24).

When characterizing a particular situation as colonial, we define a specific historical trajectory as relevant for understanding contemporary power structures within a society. Understanding a situation's distinct roots (colonial, class, caste) has the potential to help rectify inequality. For example, to marshal ethical and other resources to revive a native language, the colonial causes of its decline, due perhaps to an educational system's use of the dominant language, must be recognized. In contrast to class or caste dependencies, colonialism creates colonial societies and unique colonial cultures that are, "in varying degrees, in a state of latent crisis [...] involved to some extent in a kind of social pathology" (Balandier [1951] 1966, 37). Such societies show a particular and diverse colonial experience of dominance and subordination that reflect specific social practices and mixed cultural representations, despite and beyond close ties between capitalism and colonial expansion.

> Colonial cultures are not simply ideologies that mask, mystify or rationalize forms of oppression that are external to them; they are also expressive and constitutive of colonial relationships in themselves. (Thomas 1994, 2)

A colonial situation and the struggle against it (Churchill 2002, 26) are thus different from a class situation in origins, composition, and consequences (e.g. decolonization) even if we take into account that many colonies produced a considerable number of 'poor whites'. Accordingly, the objectives of decolonial activists may not necessarily be the same for anti-capitalist campaigners. Similarly, not all the problems of postcolonial societies are inevitably legacies of colonialism.

It is thus essential to be more specific about what makes the unequal and exploitive relationship colonial. Otherwise, the notion of colonialism is at risk of becoming a catch-all term for any form of discrimination and the question "in what way does internal colonial exploitation differ from class exploitation" (Wolpe [1975] 2013, 233) has always had to be addressed by those who engaged in this debate. Indeed, the analysis of internal colonialism "does not replace the class analysis but, rather, complements it" (Chaloult and Chaloult 1979, 87). Exploitation and inequality are universal human phenomena, often better understood in class terms as the outgrowth of the particular internal characteristics and contradictions of a given society, rather than external colonial legacies. When it is a society's own elite or state doing the exploitation while sharing language and ethnicity with the oppressed, then other terms and frameworks are needed—such as class exploitation, authoritarian rule, or gender inequality (Gabbert 2007). In many cases, the oppressed are indeed of the same ethno-racial group as the oppressor, for instance when the region of the former has been economically or otherwise subordinated by the latter. Though this relationship is sometimes figuratively addressed as a colonial situation or as 'regional colonialism', we would rather call this 'political regionalism' to avoid unnecessary confusion. Such clarifications of terms and relations are of particular importance when discussing internal colonialism. Because this represents a concept that is often mistakenly employed as a placeholder for class debates, typically in core (colonizer)—periphery (colonized) analogies, whereas the "expansion of the core responds to the interests of a class" and the "character of this expansion depends [...] on the strength of this class and [...] of the ruling class in the periphery" and has nothing or little to do with ethno-racial antagonism (Palloni 1979, 363; cf. Brown [1994] 2001, 159–61).

Given the massive collaboration with changing colonial empires and the co-optation of indigenous elites, groups, and individuals by the colonial management in British India, Russia, and the Americas, the dichotomy of 'colonizer-colonized' seems somehow simplistic and tends to gloss over power, legal, and marriage dynamics within and across both categories. Of course, there was always a middle ground where the "makers of metropole policies become conflated with its local practitioners", as Ann Stoler reminds us (1992, 320). Imperial, colonial, and class interests (poor whites), though keeping their characteristic features, became intertwined, and the boundaries of categories often blurred so that 'resistance' and 'collaboration' appear to be too value-laden for changing options under changing conditions. It might be more appropriate, therefore, to discuss the focal points of this relationship as structural positions within the colonial matrix of power—Frederick Cooper speaks of different "truth regimes" (2005b, 414)—where both positions maintain their explanations of their situation and develop ideologies that justify strategies of either maintaining or resisting the status quo. It goes without saying, though, that the colonizers might have changed and vanished over time, whereas the colonial situation stayed behind as a multi-layered legacy of (self-)integration strategies and resistance experiences, of stereotyped behavior, images, and ideologies.

EMPIRE AND COLONY, IMPERIALISM AND COLONIALISM: SOME LINES DRAWN

When speaking of empire we employ a political term that refers to a large multiethnic state in modern and early modern times. The implicit dualism of pre-modern vs. modern empire should not oversimplify the complexities of the evolving modern state replacing the pre-modern empire, but is considered to be a helpful differentiation applicable for most cases discussed in this book. Representing multinational empires, the *Pax Mongolica* as well as pre-Petrine Russia, for example, employed 'politics of difference' following a model of inclusive ethnicity and 'integration by difference' as opposed to 'integration by sameness' typical for the modern nationalizing state (Burbank and Cooper 2010; Schorkowitz 2015; Schlee 2018). Cultural and ethnic diversity as well as imperial habitus are factors that determine the ways empires—large ones but also multiethnic *empires in miniature*, such as Georgia or Yugoslavia—reproduce social inequality and spatial difference resulting in various strategies of integration.

A colony or colonial state is not merely a foreign possession with "its own legislature" (Finley 1976, 168), a socio-political network of individuals, and central agencies within such an empire. More than that, it embraces a "series of institutional mechanisms" and a "specific form of governance" being also a "cultural construct", a "work-in-progress", and thus a process of becoming an "ideological project" (Comaroff 2002, 108, 125). The colonial state is, however, not a constitutional copy of its respective motherland representing rather an executive variation of the latter and it "made no de facto distinction between the executive and legislative branches and did not recognize an independent judicial branch" (Osterhammel [1995] 2010, 58; cf. González-Casanova 1965, 29). In this sense, a colony means a land occupied by outsiders without self-government, but also the society resulting from that occupation and expropriation. Common wisdom holds that colonies are situated in or being part of an empire's overseas dominions (plantations). Sometimes, however, they are located within its territorial confines as was the case with tsarist Russia, Qing China, and the Ottoman Empire ruling over large parts of Siberia, Central and Inner Asia, the Middle East, and Southeast Europe, respectively.

Imperialism for our purposes is the beliefs, practices, and politics associated with such a state. Its imperial system can be regarded as *formal* colonialism representing a colonial empire. Because empires, such as the Spanish, Portuguese, British, French, and American, defined their own national interests as imperial interests in order to legitimize foreign interventionist policies, their colonial policy almost always had global repercussions leading to worldwide conflict and imperialistic warfare. Besides, imperialism has been frequently treated as a particular (highest) stage of developed capitalism (Lenin)—a category in political economy and world-systems analysis (André Gunder Frank, Immanuel Wallerstein) that, despite its obvious financial and technical relationship with 'new imperialism' (1870–1914), is not within the scope of this volume.

Imperialism and colonialism, provoking "emotional images" (Twitchett 1965, 307) to this day, are not the same. Though the value-laden term colonialism "became a political slogan in the twentieth century" (Reinhard 2011, 1), and was indeed "closely linked, and often interchangeable, with imperialism [...], it is a particular form of the latter" (Hodder-Williams 2001, 2237). In other words, "colonial imperialism is but one form of economic imperialism" (Balandier [1951] 1966, 39). Yet, we acknowledge that this definition cannot apply to early modern colonialism when "colonial empires without imperialism" were rather the rule (Osterhammel [1995] 2010, 22). Modern colonialism, on the other hand, is a much broader term because it includes *informal* types, such as semi-colonialism or crypto-colonialism maintained usually by economic, not political control.

CONTINENTAL AND INTERNAL COLONIALISM: A SYNTHESIS OF THOUGHT

Colonialism is not simply, or even mainly, an overseas phenomenon. Yet, in what ways continental colonialism differs from overseas colonialism in terms of domination strategies, power structures, crude exploitation, state building, or legacies for the colonizer and colonized in a postcolonial world seems to be one of the most intriguing questions. While scholars arguing in favor of functional convergences may have good reason to doubt that there is any significant difference between the two forms, others would refer to their divergent trajectories and developments without neglecting common features. Perhaps most interesting are the similarities because we have often ignored them and thus failed to apply the *colonial paradigm* to huge landmasses and their peoples.

Historically, with the disintegration of the land-based Silk Road and the discovery of the New World, commerce moved more frequently by water, making economic exploitation easier for Britain, France, Portugal, Spain, and the Netherlands. These seaborne empires always faced the troubles of maintaining long-distance communication with and continuous control over their colonies which they lost essentially because their fleets, merchants, soldiers, and colonial officials could no longer sustain either their customers' loyalty or the marginalization of the colonized and oppose their strife for economic and political independence. The situation was slightly different for modern (Russia, China, Ottoman Turkey, North America) and pre-modern (e.g. Mongol, Mughal, Oyo, Inca) land-based empires which, unless they remained unified, developed different ways of expansion and cultural integration (or rather assimilation) of the indigenous groups they once conquered. Because their armies and peasants moved more readily by land and administrative infrastructures were better maintained (particularly with the invention of railways and telegraphs), continental empires held most of their 'internal' colonies.

Continental colonialism—as a process and outcome of territorial expansion, land-based economic underdevelopment, and center-periphery dependency on a mainland—displays some distinctive characteristics that we must consider to arrive at a fuller understanding of colonialism as a "heterogeneous and historically specific set of phenomena" (Dirks 1992, 12). Representing the pre-maritime predecessor of colonial exploitation, continental colonialism—sometimes also referred to as 'continental imperialism' (Reinhard 2011, 130–47)—developed within empires varying greatly in size. Large imperial formations like tsarist Russia, Qing China, the Ottoman Empire, and their successor states have controlled ethnically diverse, partly integrated areas, while others—over centuries of domination—were turned into internally colonized spaces. This is true for great parts of the Caucasus, the Baltic countries, and the

Balkans; for Central Asia, Xinjiang, Tibet, and Mongolia; but also for the Indian reservations in the United States and Canada. Thus, Qing China's "territorial contiguity" with her Inner and Central Asian peripheries can hardly be an argument against classifying her rule as colonial as Nicola Di Cosmo (1998, 290) has illustrated; and the same can be said for two other Eurasian empires—Russia and Ottoman Turkey—and, to a somewhat lesser extent also for Austria-Hungary. There is, thus, good reason to compare their forms and "colonial patterns of reproducing difference" with overseas variations, despite alleged "geographic possibilities of absorption" (Stoler and Cooper 1997, 23).

Maritime empires, located overseas and continuously separated from the metropoles, are problematic to govern. They usually unfold as 'colonies of exploitation' with commercial strongholds or as settler colonies and end up as 'colonies of rule'. The trajectories of continental empires point in a reverse direction. They start with expansion and conquest of new territories as 'colonies of rule' only later to be penetrated by settlers of the empire's major group and dominant culture. Hence, the trajectories of continental and overseas colonialism are in some way 'counterrotating'—they start and end up differently. For the colonized this makes a difference, too. In continental colonialism they are spared much of the horrors of early settler colonialism and, though undergoing significant assimilation, survived as ethno-cultural entities. The picture is slightly different for overseas colonies where the natives are more easily targeted, dispersed, and turned into objects of cultural genocide, given the lack of control or a blunt partisanship by governmental agencies (Logan 2015; Hirschhausen 2015, 726). While *terra nullius* doctrines regularly employed by advocates of both forms (for Central Asia see the Gorchakov Memorandum of 1864), the notion of 'unoccupied' (virgin) territories or 'no-one's land' (*vacuum domicilium*) is obviously based "on a commitment to annihilate native or indigenous peoples" particularly "in settler colonial contexts" (Bateman and Pilkington 2011, 1; cf. Levene 2008, 189; Sen 2017).

The Russian, Chinese, and Ottoman Empires started with continental expansion and 'colonies of rule' at their peripheries, though indirect and with lesser state interference in the beginning, but with a tendency toward direct rule on a later stage. Agrarian settlers appeared late, indeed very late in Siberia, Central and Inner Asia, and economic exploitation ranked second after geopolitical and prestige gains in an arena of competing empires, contrary to the profits made in overseas colonies and maritime trade with spices, sugar, gold, silver, slaves, weaponry, textiles, tea, and coffee. In a nutshell, one can say that maritime empires are more driven by economic, and continental empires by political interests. As Russia and China "transformed their newly acquired frontiers step-by-step into internal colonies" (Schorkowitz 2017, 419), the shift from indirect to direct rule eventually resulted in a more rigid integration and domination. Methods of indirect rule were dominant at an early stage when administrative and military hegemony was still weak. With the spread of enhanced infrastructure and intensified control, however, forms of direct rule began to dominate accompanied by efforts at establishing cultural sameness—labeled as Russification, Sinicisation, and Osmanisation—and the standardization of the legal, administrative, and economic spheres. The French and British Empires in their overseas territories, by contrast, seem to have employed varying methods of direct and indirect rule interchangeably from early times right into the twentieth century following pragmatic considerations and the political culture in their metropoles which over time developed from social Darwinism to governmentality (Dimier 2002; Howe 2002, 15–16).

However, the two colonial forms do not simply differ, they also interrelate and may occasionally shift from maritime to continental as illustrated by the Americas, Australia, and New Zealand. North America was not simply an instance of the "English becoming Americans" (Taylor 2013, 7) but, given the presence of British, French, and Russian colonizers, represented a broad arena of alliance building with the indigenous societies across different ethno-racial boundaries and sometimes against the respective motherlands. When this situation changed with the political independence of the colonies from their European overlords, colonialism took another—a continental form aggressively promoting western settlements (Churchill 2002, 93). The new freedom paved the way for internal colonialism vis-à-vis indigenous groups of the Americas now dominated by a national 'white' elite and Europeanized mestizos. This change of forms is even mirrored by a division of labor in today's humanities where

> 'Atlantic historians' examine the interdependence of Europe, Africa, and the Americas through the transatlantic flow of goods, people, plants, animal, capital, and ideas [and] 'continental historians' seek to restore the importance of native peoples to the colonial story. (Taylor 2013, 5)

Analyzing forms of domination in their complexity and ambivalence, **internal colonialism**, if "appropriately amended" (Williams 1983, 5–6), is a sensitizing concept and most applicable when it refers to native people in their own country and cases of reactive ethnicity offering a "positive theory of nationalism" (Hechter 1983, 32; cf. Goodman 1983, 109; Corbridge 1987, 250; Brown [1994] 2001, 159; Gabbert 2015). The concept which has been applied in various contexts and criticized for offering "too many explanations", making "too many deductions" (Hind 1984, 553; cf. Love 1989, 905) and for its "diverse sets of variables" (Chaloult and Chaloult 1979, 87) is employed here in its literal and strict sense. It is related to "certain categories of people" in "specific spaces," generally though not necessarily "within self-governing territories", but not metaphorically as some scholars do "to denote extremes of categorization and discrimination of people in a polity that is formally national" (Cooper 2005a, 249). More precisely, this form refers to the subordination of an ethno-racial group "in its own homeland within the boundaries of a larger state dominated by a different people" (Chávez 2011, 786; cf. Das 1978; Dey 2015). Admittedly, this concept loses its sharp focus when applied to later in-migrating groups, such as African-Americans in the United States or the Roma people in Europe, when territoriality and the question of a nation's 'homeland' become critical (cf. Blauner 1969; but see Hechter [1975] 1999, 33).

Internal colonialism should therefore not be confused with what is sometimes figuratively called '**regional colonialism**', where a macroregion like Italy's *Mezzogiorno* is economically underdeveloped and its population oppressed relative to a country's core, but the people of both regions are of the same ethno-racial stock. White Southerners before the U.S. Civil War, to give another example, increasingly saw themselves as colonized by the North and then by the U.S. government (Stone 1979, 255). Since Southerners were from the same ethno-racial group as Northerners this, again, would be a case of 'regional colonialism', though better referred to as '**political regionalism**' (Williams 1983; Cooke 1984; Corbridge 1987). The link between such examples of regional disparities is the exploitation of rural communities by an "urban-centered power elite" (Hind 1984, 544, 546) and industrialized centers, a long-disputed subject in social sciences that takes its origins from Russia's prerevolutionary *Narodniks* and Marxist thinkers (Lenin, Gramsci) from which Michael Hechter ([1975] 1999, XIII–XIV, 8–9; cf. Hicks 2004, 1; Etkind 2011) seized much of his inspiration. However, the exploitation of a Russian (serfdom) and subsequently Soviet (collectivization) peasantry belongs rather to the category of class contradictions, transformed by socialist thought and disguised as bureaucratic hegemony (planned economy). In other words, political domination alone does not constitute colonialism "even if it might be politically correct today to consider Scotland or Catalonia or the late GDR as colonies"[3] unless it assumes "a racial or ethnic and, therefore, a colonial rather than a class form" (Wolpe [1975] 2013, 250). If still uncritically applied, the concept of internal colonialism represents rather a "political catchword [...] connecting the fight against capitalism and centralism with revolutionary intent" (Blaschke 1985, 127) than an analytical category in social sciences. It converts into inflationary currency and becomes meaningless.

Internal colonialism is a global and diverse phenomenon not restricted to modern states, and it overlaps with continental colonialism as the core state incorporates surrounding territories. Because of their expansion into contiguous territory, the continental empires usually develop forms of internal colonialism, unlike their maritime counterparts. In general, one may say that continental and internal colonialism do the exploitation from within the core state in contrast to overseas and modern neo-colonialism. However, being continental in nature does not exclude internal colonialism from temporal overlaps with its overseas equivalent and vice versa. Pablo González-Casanova already considered "colonialism as an integral phenomenon, changeable from an international to an internal category" (1965, 28). In the case of Britain's relationship with the *Celtic fringe*, for example, the phenomenon coexisted under both the pre-modern and later maritime frameworks. Celtic Cornwall, was kept as an internal colony by the Kingdom of England well before Ireland was forced into the Kingdom in 1603. Another case in point is Brittany, the neighboring Celtic nation across the Channel being an independent Duchy until 1532, which became an internal colony of the French kingdom at a time when France took possession of her first colonies in the New World (Hechter [1975] 1999, 64–65; Weber 1976, 489–90; Reece 1979, 275;

---

[3] I am grateful to Wolfgang Reinhard for bringing this to my attention—personal communication from September 29, 2017. Hechter himself raised doubts on the colonial nature of Scotland calling the situation "somewhat more complex" ([1975] 1999, 342) and comparing this "overdeveloped peripheral region" (1983, 33) with Catalonia in later writings. See also Blaschke (1985, 154–56) on Catalonian regionalism.

Blaschke 1985, 145–49). Similarly, the U.S. has simultaneously exploited both continental American Indians and overseas native Hawaiians (1898) within the same national state and helped to found Liberia, a colonial-like state (1821–47), to resettle a growing mass of free Black Americans (Whyte 2016). The cases of colonial Puerto Rico (1898) and the Philippines (1898–1946) can only be mentioned in passing here. Also Russia, while pursuing an imperialist agenda toward China, Turkey, and Europe, was transforming large parts of her empire, particularly Siberia, into internal colonies from the seventeenth century onward though maintaining temporary control over parts of Alaska and California (Fort Ross) hence oppressing Siberian peoples as well as Native Americans (Vinkovetsky 2011). But these are just a few examples suitable for comparison and contrast placed within the same analytical frame as "sometimes mutually constitutive and sometimes conspicuously disjoined formations" (Goldstein 2014, 4). They prove the rule that expansion into contiguous, as opposed to overseas, territory increases the likelihood that colonialism exists within the core state.

FORMS AND TYPES OF COLONIALISM: AN ATTEMPT AT A DEFINITION

There is no blueprint in history for colonial expansion and because colonialism comprises so many forms across ages and places embedding different realities and aspects on the spot, "colonization is […] a phenomenon of colossal vagueness" (Osterhammel [1995] 2010, 4). The difficulties in defining, classifying and describing types of expansion and colonies, as discussed by most students of colonialism, are obvious (cf. Horvath 1972; Hind 1984). However, though "a convincing theory of colonization and colonialism […] does not exist […] scholars have still to define the concepts they use" (Reinhard 2015, 223). In this sense we see colonialism as a set of ideas, beliefs, practices, and politics of a given people (nation, state, empire) emanating from a habitus of cultural superiority (neither always eurocentric nor white race based) and compressed as structural hegemony that builds on extractive economy, civilizing mission, and military conquest to control other ethno-racially different peoples. Bound to economic, administrative, military, and territorial criteria, colonialism involves the settling and appropriating of foreign, especially occupied land, resulting often in a competitive race among 'colonial powers' for preventive occupation. It is not confined to a specific era, but a form of dominance and a phenomenon with changing meanings that has occurred and can occur at any time.

Though often used interchangeably in corresponding literature, for the sake of preciseness and heuristic purposes, we draw a line between **colonization and colonialism** and treat them as different concepts. Colonization we regard as the concrete process of doing colonialism reflecting its practical and cultural sides, particularly the physical settling of a land—an empty place or an already occupied place. Colonization treated almost synonymously with the establishment of settlements is thus more concerned with migration and culture (etymologically sharing the same Latin root—*colere*). It describes an ongoing development, whereas colonialism is the abstract correspondent referring to structures of domination, unequal relationships among ethno-racial groups not encompassed or classified exclusively by class exploitation.

When we speak of **forms** we mean those that have developed into theories addressed usually as overseas-, crypto-, post-, or neo-colonialism. They are briefly discussed in this book in relation to continental and internal colonialism in order to emphasize these hitherto neglected forms and discuss the distinction between maritime and continental empires, if there is any. In addition, loosely identifiable **types**, known as conquest-, trading-post-, settler-, and predatory colonialism are mentioned and contrasted with each other, again, in an attempt to show how and why they differ (cf. Reinhard 2011, 3–4).

The notion of **crypto-colonialism**, also referred to as **semi-colonialism** or the rule of informal empire, is usually applied to colonial conditions in countries that are nominally sovereign, but economically dependent and thus under political control of foreign nations. This form is a timeless and global, but temporary phenomenon surfacing, for instance, under neo-colonial conditions in countries like present-day Greece and Thailand which, while separated by distance, "religion and language, display some common elements" (Herzfeld 2009, 343) of the colonial matrix.[4] Other examples that are frequently mentioned include

---

[4] But see Brown's study of Thailand ([1994] 2001, 158–205) where he, apart from addressing Thailand's neo-colonial situation vis-à-vis an "international economy" (ibid., 166), applies the internal colonialism concept for the relationships between a lowland Thai (Khon Muang) dominated urban elite (Bangkok) and upland tribal communities (Hmong) particularly in the North as well as Lao speaking groups (Isan) in Northeastern Thailand.

independent Cuba before Castro, Qing China under foreign rule, the Ottoman Empire and the 'veiled protectorate' of Egypt at the end of the nineteenth century, or Liberia as well as South Vietnam under U.S. American influence. Conversely, one may also add cases where countries "without having been classical colonial powers" (Lüthi et al. 2016, 1) benefited from the engagement of and the proximity to 'real' colonial empires. In fact, external control over indigenous inhabitants—practiced no more by permanent settlements or (in)direct rule—seems to be a characteristic of modern colonialism, based on the Great Powers' claim to rule over vast parts of the world. However, given the long distances and limitations in resources and personnel, remote control of local administration is sometimes as difficult to maintain in crypto-colonialism as in overseas colonialism.

Despite the decolonization drive after World War II ('Third Wave') that was succeeded by the 'Fourth Wave' of the disintegrating Soviet Union, the colonial situation did not always end with the new nations' declaration of independence, but took other forms guided by a particular dependency on the former metropolitan state (Reinhard 2011, 265–66; Maldonado-Torres 2016, 67). This ongoing though transformed relation is a common phenomenon characteristic of those empires that lost their colonies due to their own weakness as well as of those that emerged more powerful from the war and either let their colonies go voluntarily or were forced to do so after violent independence struggles. The burdensome heritage of colonial rule is still manifest in present culture and institutions, in the economy and ecological systems of many 'postcolonial' societies as has been emphasized by 'postcolonial' scholars, social scientists, and historians alike who argue that colonialism is not a thing of the past, hence making the notion of 'postcolonialism' indeed meaningless (Thomas 1994, 1; Howe 2002, 25–26; de L'Estoile 2008; Pinderhughes 2011, 235). Colonial traces are abundant in political thought and daily practices, in natural landscapes and catalogues of imported plants and diseases. They are present not only in the colonized mind or as ethnic fragmentation resulting from imperial 'divide and conquer', but persist as European perceptions of the Orient ideologically expressed as *Orientalism*, "a way of coming to terms with the Orient [...], a Western style for dominating [...], and having authority over the Orient" (Said [1978] 2008, 213–14). Decolonizing is thus a process far from completion even after many waves of political and recent economic decolonization, "whereas mental and cultural decolonization has not even begun" (Reinhard 2015, 227). On the contrary, parallel to the discreet life of colonial legacies, a new form of dominance developed in many decolonized nation-states based on economic, technological, intellectual, and cultural control or privileges maintained by a non-indigenous group (e.g. the former colonizer, an international organization) widely seen as **neo-colonialism**. Being one possible model to explain decolonization, this form abandons the colonial format and "coercive colonial structures that have become obsolete," but retains the exploitive nature and techniques of governmentality to "retain geopolitical and economic influence" (Jansen and Osterhammel 2017, 30; cf. Twitchett 1965, 318–19).

Early modern **trading-post colonialism** and **conquest colonialism** manifested as distinct or mixed types were intrinsically tied to the discovery of the New World and the European expansion into parts of Africa and Asia particularly in the early sixteenth and seventeenth centuries resulting in the establishment of maritime hubs and control over contested ocean routes. Their colonial institutions (factories, chartered companies) were of private nature sometimes backed by governmental or military support, their agents driven by a desire for profit, prestige, or missionary zeal—not farming. These outposts later developed into a system of military bases and a dominion of foreign assets under more or less strict territorial rule governed as overseas colonies by the imperial powers until the twentieth century.

The arrival of settlers in the New World, Australia, South Africa, and elsewhere is, if we disregard the precursors of ancient times, a later phenomenon resulting often, but not exclusively from conquest colonialism though sharing much of its violent and genocidal aspects (MacDonald 2015). In fact, among the various types **settler colonialism**, subdivided further into 'mixed' and 'pure' colonies (Fieldhouse [1965] 1982, 11–14), is probably the best-studied type of all and in many cases related to occupation by **frontier societies**, hungry for land and ready to kill the locals. Settlers are not to be confused with migrants who are willing to adapt and integrate more easily into their host society, while settlers "are founders of political orders" (Veracini [2010] 2014, 3) who carry their culture with them which they import, plant, and disseminate in their new home colony. Another characteristic relates to the foundational and enduring structural violence in settler societies which, "unlike other colonial societies, have not been transformed by the dramatic rupture of decolonization and the move to a postcolonial state, but rather are marked by settler colonialism's historical continuity" (Edmonds 2016, 1–2). Indeed, they have given reason to argue that settler colonialism "has been resistant to decolonization" (Veracini 2011, 204). Such distinctions between a locally and collectively based settler colonialism, with farm household or cash-crop economies on the one hand and a centrally organized and state-run non-settler colonialism on the other, are thus often seen as the most important colonial typology—perhaps more important than the distinction between maritime and continental empires. However, a certain coincidence of state-run and continental colonialism vs. settler-driven overseas colonialism cannot be discarded.

In addition to the two types mentioned, the origins and domination modes of which are related either to the maintenance of bases or the arrival of settlers, a third type is well-known purely exploitative in nature and thus aptly called **predatory colonialism**. In this case, a tiny and often changing foreign elite—with or without the help of the locals—extracts the colony's natural resources and labor forces without any intention to baptize or civilize the colonized. This form was practiced in the plantation economies in parts of Latin America, the West Indies, British India, and Africa.

What have been described so far as ideal forms appear in reality sometimes more blurred and mixed. Thus, in the case of post-, crypto-, and neo-colonialism the boundaries of definition may become fuzzy depending on which aspect of the colonial situation is highlighted. In fact, the similarities between the various types of colonialism well exceed their differences, if seen not from the angle of class-based but ethno-racial exploitation. The methods of domination and techniques of direct or indirect rule are likely to be most similar under formal colonialism where colonizers exercise military and police power with little restraint resulting in a particular imperial habitus and legitimizing ideologies known as civilizing missions and conversions to modernity from the days of Thomas More to John Major (Finley 1976, 179–80). However, these methods and techniques probably vary most under informal colonialism where colonizers exercise power more subtly through culture, legislation, education, and economics (Howe 2002, 24–25).

INTERNAL COLONIALISM(S) WORLDWIDE: MANIFESTATIONS AND MISNOMERS

Ever since Michael Hechter published his seminal work on the Celtic Fringe in 1975, the concept of internal colonialism grew in popularity, particularly in the late 1970s and 1980s. Preserving much of the political atmosphere of the 1960s, it has become a reference point for colonial, political, and economic studies around the globe, though debates on its theoretical dividends are still underway. Thus, in an early attempt to specify the notion of internal colonialism and its alternative conceptions, it was noticed that the discourse on "intra-national exploitation of cultural distinct groups" turned out to be the "most influential" and "most well developed" (Williams 1983, 7) characterization of the concept. But cultural difference alone—or Hechter's notion of "cultural division of labor" therefore—has proved to be insufficient as a defining quality, suggesting rather the inclusion of all kinds of exploitation in class and dual societies or along regional underdevelopment. Besides, 'culture' is, as has often been noted, "yet another of those large, baggy, rather shapeless words" (Howe 2002, 18). To make the concept a precise analytical tool other characteristics should be added, particularly ethnic or racial difference between the colonizer and the colonized and the belonging to a historical homeland of the latter. In this modified form internal colonialism "as a particular type of exploitation" (Williams 1983, 18) is not only a useful tool to analyze the colonial situation of those who are exploited by the dominant, but ethno-racially different group of the core state. But also the applicability of the concept to "states that once had empires and to those that were once colonies, [...] to entire political entities as well as to some of their constituent parts, [...] is incontrovertible" (Hind 1984, 552).

In Europe this was for instance the case in pre-modern Wales and Ireland whose people differed not only culturally (language, religion), but also in their social organization (economy, inheritance system) and by ethnic origin from the English state that expanded into their ancestral territories in the sixteenth and seventeenth centuries. English cultural dominance was imposed on Wales following the Act of Union in 1536 (Hechter [1975] 1999, 57–59, 102–4; Blaschke 1985, 133–35). In Ireland where "currency manipulations [...] preceded those in other colonies by three centuries", England demonetized all currencies and issued a new one in 1598 "which was debased by 25% but declared to be full legal tender for the old unit of account" in order to gain the seigniorage profits of issue and the control of money flows, "to limit the market for colonial possessors of currency" (Narsey 2016, 55–56) and thus to keep the rebellious Irish underfinanced. Cromwell's subsequent plantation regime, "whereby land was taken away from the Irish, Catholics could hold no land, positions, nor could they vote" (Docker 2008, 86), was, if we ignore the 'Blue-Water-Thesis' for a moment, a "clear example of internal colonial development [...] a precursor of apartheid" (Hechter 1983, 31; cf. Blaschke 1985, 135–40) and settler colonialism particularly after the Cromwellian Settlement of 1642.

In the wake of Hechter's study of the Celtic Fringe, other regions in Europe came under the scrutiny of students with a combined interest in nationalism, separatism, and colonialism. The concept was, for example, applied for Savonia and Karelia, two East Finnish provinces appropriated by the expanding Swedish kingdom in medieval times (Alapuro 1979). A similar case, that of Sweden's relationship with the Sami, "Europe's only recognized indigenous people", was discussed as "colonialism without colonies", a notion introduced by Gunlög Fur to explain the Swedish "discourse of innocence in relation to colonialism and settler expansion" (2016, 12; cf. Lantto 2005) that helped to avoid responsibilities for the colonizing nation. However, while it would be correct to speak of internal—and indeed continental—colonialism as long as the Savonia-Karelian territories populated by Finnish speaking groups were part of the Swedish Empire, this seems no more fitting when Sweden lost Finland in 1809 which then became a Grand Duchy within the Russian Empire enjoying a high degree of autonomy. With this shift in sovereignty also the forms of dependency changed from previous formal continental colonialism within the Swedish Empire to regional under-development as part of Finland. Regional disparities between coastal market forces and hinterland peasant economy continued in peripheral Eastern Finland, resulting in peasant pauperization and finally political regionalism with a distinctive party system pushed by a landless proletariat before and after the October Revolution.

Similarly, a mushrooming industrialization and capitalist transformation since the late nineteenth century are regarded as driving forces behind the enduring discrepancies between Italy's mercantile-industrial core in the north and an agricultural periphery in the *Mezzogiorno*. However, though being predominantly either under Spanish or French foreign rule until the *Risorgimento*, this macroregion was never turned into a colony and never experienced a colonial situation by these two empires. The diversity of Northern and Southern Italy which, by the way, has an analogy in Northern and Southern France regarding Occitania—*Le midi*—was neither induced nor enshrined by colonial rule, but is historically based on distinct trajectories in economy, infrastructure, political institutions, and knowledge transfer on the one hand and by a still incomplete national integration on the other (Palloni 1979; Lafont 1971; Blaschke 1985, 142–45). Cases of national malintegration and economic underdevelopment are, indeed, abundant and often seen as an invitation to colonial reinterpretations. Thus, though sometimes argued by leftist authors (e.g. Dümcke and Vilmar 1995), the situation in reunited Germany, where Germans (East) were allegedly discriminated against or oppressed by Germans (West), can hardly be described, even metaphorically, as a colonial relationship—for two substantial reasons. First, thirty years of isolation behind the Iron Curtain did not ultimately transform East Germans into a distinct ethnic group, despite existing differences in political thinking, collective identity, taste, and dress (but see Bierschenk 2010). And secondly, grave regional inequalities in economy, infrastructure, and education aggravated over a long period of planned economy were swiftly met with tailored reconstruction programs that successfully fostered the diffusion of national development (Hertog 2004, 273–75).

Brittany in Northwest France is, on the contrary, a striking example of the internal colonial model leading to devastating consequences for Bretons particularly in the "heavily Gallicized coastal zones" (Reece 1979, 279) where living conditions (poverty, alcoholism, suicide) resemble much of the colonial situation in other parts of the French colonial empire. Also the multiethnic Habsburg Empire, expanding into East Central Europe and including large non-Austrian populations until World War I, offers various cases of internal colonialism not only with regard to Bosnia and Herzegovina occupied in 1878 (Wendland 2010, 213–15). Hungary, for instance, was turned into the "Empire's chief producer of agricultural commodities" and showed a "dependent economic development" from the early nineteenth century, while Transylvania reacted to "new exploitative relations among ethnic groups" (Verdery 1979, 383, 388) even decades earlier with a political movement for civil and religious rights mobilized by Romanian peasants, the clergy, and intellectuals.

Equally influential as Hechter's Celtic Fringe for the understanding of reactive ethnicity in Europe were two essays on the colonial situation in the New World by Pablo González-Casanova and by Robert Blauner at the peak of the Civil Rights Movement. Given the racial segregation and urban riots in the United States, the 'colonial analogy' was widely used by political activists and regularly employed to analyze racial conflicts in the 1960s (Das 1978, 93; Hicks 2004, 2). Yet, this approach was cautiously criticized as too artificial by Blauner who differentiated between "colonization as a process [...] that Afro-Americans share" as set apart from "the situation of classical colonialism" as a "social, economic, and political system" (1969, 393) in which they did not partake. African-Americans who may have experienced even worse oppression than African groups by their colonizers are not in their own native land and their pattern of colonization is different from the classic form: "they constitute a minority, they are less autonomous, they are more dispersed, and [...] less developed" (Hind 1984, 546–47; cf. Blauner 1969, 398). In fact, though even Blauner perceives African-Americans as victims of colonization, their situation is that of peoples deported to a foreign land, exploited by a different race and culturally undermined—what we could call perhaps an 'imported quasi-colonial situation' that is indeed different from internal (domestic) colonialism (but see Pinderhughes 2011, 235–36). Tellingly and aside from some activists' claims, the African-Americans' reference point of grievance focuses predominantly on equal rights, treatment, and participation within the dominant society, not territorial autonomy (reconstitution), or independence outside of it.

The point of departure could be no more different for Native Americans and Canada's First Nations. Here, territory and natural resources (fur, coal, oil, gas, uranium, water), native homeland and ethnicity were highly contested at all times "especially as settlers aspire to extinguish indigenous peoples and variously affirm and naturalize their own status as native to America" (Goldstein 2014, 3). In fact, the natives' struggle for the land in North America has always been a "struggle against internal colonialism" as Ward Churchill (2002, 15) illustrates with striking examples drawn from different American Nations, such as the Iroquois (Haudenosaunee), Lakota, Cree, Navajo (Diné), and Shoshone. This list of internally colonized peoples is of course far from being complete and does not include, for instance, Mexicans in the U.S. "indigenous to the region and not imported" (Moore 1970, 465), but often portrayed as 'alien immigrants to the Southwest' (New Mexico,

Texas, California). Deriving from "Anglo-Americans' perceptions of themselves as natives of the region despite their own historically late arrival as a people", this myth worsened the situation of undocumented Mexicans who had to hide "in order to work and live in areas that were once part of Mexico" (Chávez 2011, 785). Such unfinished struggles caused by Anglo occupation of Mexican ranches and towns after 1848 are making waves in the Southwest even today (Oropeza 2014).

Farther north in Alaska, sold to the U.S. by Russia in 1867, a "culturally diversified indigenous population [...] was penetrated by raw resource exploiting colonizers in the eighteenth and nineteenth centuries" to be followed by "settlers who brought with them the instruments and values of industrial modernization" (Ritter 1979, 320). Until the 1970s, however, industrialization neither led to a significant diversification in higher occupations among the indigenous population nor to a related decline in ethnic solidarity among culturally distinct groups as many modernization theories predicted. On the contrary, as the hierarchical settler-indigenous divide and struggles over territory continue, the cultural and ethno-racial division of labor (occupational specialization) persists. This colonizer-colonized relationship corresponds well with the core-periphery paradigm of underdevelopment and strict political control in almost all parts of neighboring Canada. As for the First Nations in British Columbia and the Yukon Territory for example "who did not own the land where their villages were located" (Smyth 2005, 187) as well as for the Inuit societies of the Northwest Territories, it took the central government decades to enter into treaty negotiations and give way to land claim and self-government agreements after many years of 'history wars' over colonial legacies (Cairns [2002] 2008; Hicks 2004; MacDonald 2015). However, establishing Indian nationhood in the 1980s and 1990s was not really an escape from internal colonialism, while full citizenship perhaps is. Like the First Nations and Inuit, the Métis are "one of the three officially recognized groups of Aboriginal peoples in Canada" (Logan 2015, 433) according to the Constitution Act of 1982. Being descendants of indigenes and European settlers, but sharing a distinct language (*Michif*) and identity, they too have experienced forced removal from their homes, the deprivation of Indian status rights, forced sterilization, and, until recently, the forced transfer of their children into the Indian Residential Schools system. The Métis are thus frequently, though not uncontroversially, portrayed as victims of colonial 'cultural genocide' (Niezen 2013, 18–20, 127–29; Wildcat 2015,

392–94; Woolford and Benvenuto 2015, 373–75). Whereas *Québécois*, a term that refers to Francophone Catholic inhabitants of Quebec province which started "not as an internal colony, but as an overseas colony" (McRoberts 1979, 296) that came under British control rather late (i.e. 1759), is a typical case of political regionalism reflecting a lasting French Canadian nationalism within an Anglo-Saxon culturally, economically, and politically dominated state.

Based on a combination of regional traditions and Marxist thought, González-Casanova developed a distinct and influential critique of the concept of internal colonialism and underdevelopment with reference to Mexico. Prior to Blauner's colonization hypothesis and Hechter's cultural division of labor theory, he argued that "the exploitation of the Indians continues, having the same characteristics it had before independence" (González-Casanova 1965, 27), meaning that despite the expulsion of Spaniards mestizo and "creole Mexicans continued to dominate Indians" (Chávez 2011, 789). Remarkably, the mestizos' historical integration, generally led by creole elites in the "various revolutions in Latin America" (Maldonado-Torres 2016, 69), developed in a different direction compared to the Métis in Canada. Questioning the analytical value of the concept to explain exploitation vis-à-vis commonly used categories such as class, social strata, and the rural(feudal)-urban(capitalist) divide of dual societies, González-Casanova treated "the problem of internal colonialism in a nation as a stage of industrial process" (1965, 28) supplemented by the effects of ethno-racial segregation as being "essential in the colonial exploitation of some peoples by others" (32). For Mexico he confirmed that Indians were not only discriminated against culturally and politically, but deprived of their lands and turned into peons by a dominant Ladino population, thus underlining the viability of the concept. It was immediately applied to Guatemala (Stavenhagen 1965), Peru (Cotler 1967; Epstein 1971), Colombia (Havens and Flinn 1970), and idiosyncratically with a focus on class, world economy, and peripheries to Latin America as a whole that "suffers from a colonial underdevelopment" (Frank 1969, IX; cf. Chávez 2011, 790).

There are striking similarities in the colonial experiences between Africa and Latin America, particularly in that former colonizers left the continent in the course of revolution, decolonization, and nation-building, but retaining much of their economic, legalistic, and cultural influence, kept many of the newly independent nations in a state of neo-colonial dependency. As Mohamed Salih assures us: "Most post-in-dependent African states were no less cruel towards their indigenous populations than the colonialists" (1993, 271). Of course, non-white forms of continental colonialism had appeared in Africa at least since the Yoruba Empire (1608–1800) and recurred when in the mid-nineteenth century Americo-Liberians settlers "implemented colonial systems of control over indigenous inhabitants of the area, established themselves as leaders of an expansionist civilizing mission, and continually sought to expand Monrovia's reach beyond Liberia's borders" (Whyte 2016, 84). Another example of non-white continental colonialism that resulted in an internal colonial system would be Sudan which saw and still is expe-riencing "Northern Arab Sudanese hegemony over the Negroid Africans of the South" with a systemic discrimination based "upon racial, cultural, religious, and regional differences" against the South (Wai 1984, 172; cf. Salih 1993, 285).

Today it is black or white Africans dominating other Africans with physical and structural violence, sometimes performing as proxies for their old colonial motherlands. Having gained its independence from Britain in 1910, South Africa was a white settler state that exploited and oppressed black Africans in their own homelands until the end of apart-heid in 1994 (Wolpe [1975] 2013, 249–50; Comaroff 2002, 111–13; Reinhard 2011, 265), a situation that shows striking analogies at the northern edge of the continent regarding Arabs (Palestinians) in Israeli society (Zureik 1979, 16–17). In his presidential address at the annual meeting of the Council of the South African Institute of Race Relations in January 1957, liberal politician Leo Marquard has made it very clear that "South Africa was in reality a colonial power [...] disguised by the circumstance that her colonial subjects lived within the physical bound-aries of the mother country" where "no ocean separates ruler from sub-ject" (Marquard 1957, 1). Bantu speaking Tswana people, for instance, were in no position even in the 1960s to prevent the Dutch Reformed Church from erecting a building—an icon of internal colonial control—on their land against their will (Comaroff and Comaroff 1991, 1–4). Nineteenth century's Tsonga speakers, a "distinctly separate group" (Harries 1991, 83) who only later became classified as a people, were deprived of their land in Transvaal and economically marginalized by white-owned farms especially during the 1930s "when depression and drought threatened to overwhelm the farming sector" (ibid., 96). As a result, special reserves were created by the government to preserve 'tribal' life, to invent traditions, and hence to prevent landless Africans from urbanization and local chiefs from losing political control, making ethnicity a central concept in South African politics.

The making of ethnicity as a category of classification, peopling, and governmentality by Boer administrators resembles in many ways how British rule in India transformed the notion of caste as a traditional system of social and religious hierarchy into a model of social stratification and caste associations which continued to be a powerful identification marker long after the colonizer had left the sub-continent (Bayly 1999; Hirschhausen 2015, 732). Being part of India's postcolonial legacy, such tools of social classification and historiographical (mis-)representations were still instrumental during national awakening when indigenous colonialist elites took over their 'master's role' in governing the multinational country while turning parts of India and Pakistan (e.g. Bengali populated Bangladesh) into internal colonies (Guha 1982, 4–8; Chakrabarty 1992).[5] This strange kind of mimesis where mechanisms of colonial governance are mirrored back on minorities by the postcolonial independent state has often been highlighted in recent colonial studies.

Pre-colonial India was a continental empire well-known for its expansion in Indochina from ancient to modern times with a multiethnic, religious, and polyglot legacy influential until today and beyond Hindu ideology (Bayly 2000, 600–2). The indigenous tribes (Adivasi) of Jharkhand in Northeast India, for instance, living in a rural, hilly, poor, and underdeveloped forest area with rich mineral resources that "represents the industrial heart of India" are marginalized ethnic minorities deprived of their lands and "exploited by the developed areas as colonies" (Roy [1982] 2003, 79, 81) and by a Hindu-speaking, upper-caste elite. These Adivasi together with the Harijans (Dalit), also referred to as scheduled castes and scheduled tribes, made up almost 50% of Jharkhand's population in the 1980s. They demanded a separate state within the Union of India as early as 1954 (achieved in 2000) to contain this exploitation, which displays a mixture of dependencies: caste, class, regional disparity, and ethno-racial inequality (Corbridge 1987, 251; Dey 2010, 2015).

But tribal communities were always an easy target for state intervention and non-state actors in other parts of postcolonial Asia, like

[5] For Bangladesh see Das (1978, 101); for Bihar, the southern part of which became the new state of Jharkhand in November 2000, see Sinha (1973).

some Mon-Khmer speaking peoples of the Central Highlands in post-1975 Vietnam (Evans 1992) or Negrito minorities in the Andaman and Nicobar Islands. The Andamanese represent an indigenous people colonized by the British since 1789 and displaced by Indian settlers after 1947 in the course of their "postcolonial zeal to transform these 'backward' islands through planned development" (Sen 2017, 945). The Semang (Sakai) in southern Thailand find themselves in a similar colonial situation when they saw "their traditional lands handed over to outsiders or new immigrants [...] and find themselves repeatedly removed from place to place in accordance with whatever need is currently asserted by the national government" (Hamilton 2002, 79). The Sakai are a small minority that had lived in their forest villages for centuries differing significantly from a Thai-, Malay-, and Chinese-speaking neighborhood in terms of ethno-racial, social, and cultural belonging. Trapped between two nation-states, they are pressured to fit the Thai model of the citizen-subject including compulsory education, the "inculcation of Thai values and the teaching of Thai language" (ibid., 88).

Farther north we see Qing China (1644–1911) expanding into vast parts of East and Inner Asia. Establishing Qing rule in Mongolia, Xinjiang, Tibet, and Kökenuur (Qinghai) after the mid-seventeenth century has often been regarded as another case of continental colonialism (Di Cosmo 1998, 2012; Perdue 1998, 2005, 2010). However, to consider China an active player under the *colonial paradigm* has been much disputed over recent years by Chinese academia (cf. Wang Hui 2014, 17–21) that seemingly lacks "a skeptical spirit when faced with new historical sources," being rather guided by "national interests or political factors [...] in the compilation of history" (Li Aiyong 2016, 24). Even innocuous notions, such as 'Chinese Empire' or 'China proper,' are now suspected to be political catchwords invented by New Qing History scholars only to pinpoint "the 'imperialist' and 'colonial' nature of the Qing" (ibid., 16). Thongchai Winichakul would have characterized this controversy as "a disagreement between the two historiographies" (2014, 882), i.e. between Western and Chinese official history. Embracing debates on historical memory (politics of history), on Manchu ethnic identity, and Sinicization (Zhang Jian 2016), this controversy was particularly fanned by misleadingly comparing the effects of Chinese continental expansion with European overseas colonialism in the world. In addition, the specific dialectics of China's historical experience with imperialism and colonialism—the 'national trauma'—has often been ignored. China was a colonizing empire since Ming times, for instance in Guizhou (Goodman 1983; Oakes 1995; Herman 2007), but was colonized by the West, Russia, and Japan in the late nineteenth century. However, colonial rule imposed by foreign powers was very much limited to particular areas of the empire, and "China was never entirely subject to coherent colonial cultural policies" (Meinhof et al. 2017, 5).

By contrast, the Mongol-, Turkic-, and Tibetan-speaking groups of Inner Asia, who were brought under central control by the Manchu political elite and later dominated by the Han-Chinese population, show all characteristics of internal colonialism as has been stressed many times (Perdue 2005, 542; Schorkowitz and Ning 2017). Despite significant participation of local elites in central agencies, like the Qing Lifanyuan[6] or the Communist State Nationality Affairs Commission, the indigenous communities—initially objects of indirect rule—were progressively deprived of their homelands, legal traditions, political institutions, rights of cultural self-determination, and freedom of belief until the recent past (Israeli 1981; Goldstein 2004). The change in Qing internal colonial politics was particularly felt when in 1906 the Lifanyuan was dissolved. It transformed into another office, the Lifanbu, no longer expected "to administer the outer dependencies but to 'resettle Chinese to strengthen the frontier' (*Yimin shibian*) and to dismantle Inner Asian administrations in order to integrate them into the Chinese system" (Bulag 2017, 358). Uradyn Bulag thus rightly argues that the "Manchu-promoted Chinese expansion through county and province building was a settler colonialism *par excellence*" (ibid.).

China today is still a multinational empire keeping almost all its territorial acquisitions with the exemption of Taiwan, conquered in 1683 and lost to Japan in 1895, and Outer Mongolia which gained independence in 1911, but became separated from its co-nationals in Inner Mongolia with the formation of the Mongolian People's Republic in 1924. While Inner Mongolia was always under heavy Chinese influence "of stringent divide-and-rule policies" (Bulag 2004, 86) and suffered

---

[6]A translation of this Chinese term is difficult because the result is not a precise rendering of the proper meaning either in the original Manchu—Board for the Administration of the Outer Regions (Provinces)—or in the Mongolian—Court of Administration (Procedures dealt with) of the Autonomous Mongolian State (Outer Mongolian Government). The term has been subject to quite a variety of interpretations, some of them with a political undercurrent, not accepted by everyone (e.g. 'colonial office').

much from assimilation policies particularly under Mao's cultural revolution in the 1960s and 1970s, its northern counterpart—following the decline of the Qing dynasty—experienced first strong Russian and then Soviet influence being a "product of two imperial environments" (Perdue 2010, 273). Though Moscow's authority was not always as effective over Mongolia as it was at home, Soviet politics did have a significant impact on Mongolian society as a "form of colonialism" (crypto-colonialism), preserving such political, military, and economic control that Mongolia was transformed into a socialist satellite ally and "functioned as a subjugated state" for over seven decades (Myadar 2017, 5, 10). Regarding Xinjiang, whose northern part was homeland to the Western Mongols (Oirat) until their destruction in the 1750s and which became a regular Chinese province in 1884 with a majority of indigenous Turkic-speaking Muslims, the colonial situation resembles that of Inner Mongolia. Qing China's late expansion into Dzungaria and Eastern Turkestan was followed by massive in-migrations of Mandarin-speaking Chinese (merchants, peasants, workers, military), by Uyghur (Hui) resettlement programs, and by "colonization through army-led agricultural projects" (Kowalski 2017, 49). Notwithstanding the occasional critique against colonial labeling (Sautman 2000), Xinjiang—literally 'new frontier'—thus seems to be another prominent example of China's internal colonialism—political, economic, and cultural hegemony over different ethno-racial groups in Inner Asia. As usual, this colonial pattern has resulted in various forms of resistance—from evasiveness to irredentist movements and even open revolt (Israeli 1981; Goodman 1983, Gladney 1998; Bachmann 2004; Côté 2011).

THE CHAPTERS

In this book scholars explore the shifting forms of continental colonialism in Asia, Africa, Europe, and the Americas from the early modern period to the present, addressing a broad readership in the humanities and social sciences. Though it was tempting to have the book structured geographically and chronologically, given the diversity of regions, we deliberately have chosen a thematic arrangement, a subject-based orientation that brings into closer focus the phenomenon of colonialism itself. A geographical lens, though convenient, would always leave areas uncovered and raise questions of worldwide representation. While it is important to place our ideas about continental and internal colonialism in as broad a context as possible, there are limitations. It is not our intention to address all the kinds of colonialism that exist equally in depth. Neither can we cover all places and times. However, though focused on the modern era, the volume illustrates that the *colonial paradigm* is a framework of theories and concepts that can be applied globally and deeply into the past.

Besides a global, comparative perspective the volume offers an interdisciplinary approach that brings together historians, anthropologists, and sociologists to contribute to a "critical historical anthropology" of colonialism as Nicholas Dirks suggested (1992, 11), based on a fuller range of variations than hitherto considered. This cross-fertilization reflects an ethno-historical ethic that feels obliged to the perspectives of the *locals*, an approach likely to unveil hidden dependencies beyond the legacy of overseas colonialism. The chapters engage with a wide range of topics and disciplinary approaches from the theoretical to the empirical, deepening our understanding of under-researched areas of colonial studies and stressing the relevance of the continental and internal forms for a much neglected chapter in the history and anthropology of colonialism. Internal colonial theory can be applied as deeply in terms of time as widely in terms of space. We look into colonial agency and practices from past and contemporary perspectives examining forms of resilience and resistance among the colonized. This includes trajectories from indirect to direct rule, the homogenization of ethnic diversity or marginalization (segregation, apartheid), the persistence of colonial agencies, and contradictions between profit-making and geopolitical gains. The different positions and legacies of continental, internal, and overseas colonialism thus come under scrutiny.

Chapters are arranged into five parts. In **Colonialism as Discourse in Social Anthropology and History** *Stefan Krotz* argues that the colonial discourse developed in different directions creating regional traditions of its own and counter-discourses in a hegemonic attempt to react to processes of ongoing colonization or failed decolonization. Persistent debates in Latin America about Third World anthropologies have extensively used the concepts of cultural imperialism and internal colonialism, fostering de-colonial perspectives and strategies. Ongoing colonization and exploitation of indigenous societies by the American and Canadian settler states has received much public attention spurring indigenous de-colonial activism against the colonialism–capitalism nexus and scholarship on the longue durée of appropriation of indigenous land, labor, and local social relations as *Ingo Schröder* illustrates. Given Russia's continental expansion in Central Asia, Siberia, and the Caucasus, the discourse about 'Russia's internal colonialism' has always been controversial and is politically charged even today. While the empire was missing a proper 'colonial office' comparable to those of Western colonial powers, it established and procured analogous institutions to set up 'colonies of rule' within its imperial confines. At times, the exploitation of non-Russian peoples was admitted even by Russian historians, but its colonial nature remained highly disputed. *Dittmar Schorkowitz* enters into this debate, which resembles in some respects the controversies observed over China, which today as in the past dislikes being labeled a colonial empire and always expresses this objection ideologically.

The opening chapter of **The Empire's Colonialism 'at home'** informs more deeply about agency, practices, and traditions of empire making in Russia's Orient. Focusing on military intelligence *David Schimmelpenninck van der Oye* characterizes the role of the Imperial Russian Geographical Society as a handmaiden of conquest and rule in Central and Inner Asia. Referring back to China's historical experience with various forms of colonialism, *Lili Zhu* discusses the relevance of the *colonial paradigm* for Qing China. Arguing that Manchu rule over Han cannot be understood as colonial, her chapter questions the applicability of the internal colonial concept for 'China Proper,' thus contrasting with Qing governance over multiethnic Inner Asia. In another test, this time against the European background of the Austro-Hungarian Empire and its Communist legacies in Czechoslovakia, *David Scheffel* in his ethnographic study takes the case of the Slovak Roma, subject to various forms of state domination in many parts of Europe until today. The Roma came to be seen as a special minority that required the imposition of controls that drew on an inner-European loathing of vagabondage and added a 'colonizing' mission following Orientalist assumptions and goals. While literature on European colonialism in Africa is widespread, colonialism of Africans by Africans is less known though it predated the European model as *James Olusegun Adeyeri* illustrates for the Old Oyo Empire in West Africa. Prior to modern imperialism, various African groups established empires formed on the basis of economic and geo-strategic considerations of varying sizes that held dominion over peoples of diverse ethnic origins.

Part three on **Co-opted Elites, Local Brokers, and Go-betweens in Nation-Building** deals with typical forms of co-optation of indigenous elites whose motives were guided by their disposition to maintain traditional order and their interest in self-integration. Always playing a cross-epochal role in colonial management, the post-independence Indian elite, as illustrated by *Dipankar Dey*, turned Bharat (rural India) into a colony, a classic example of the overlapping of internal colonialism with class and caste dependencies. While early Indo-Aryan groups and later Indian states, such as the Mughal Empire, had engaged in continental colonialism in their expansion into the surrounding territories of distinct peoples, later Portuguese and British expansion exemplified overseas colonialism. The widening divide between the Hindu dominated metropolis and indigenous tribes in rural India relates back to the nineteenth-century British Empire whose exploitive patterns continued after the formal departure of the British colonizers in 1947 through clientele groups and western-educated elites. This critique of local elites leads over to other forms of co-optation in colonial and postcolonial Mexico and in other parts of Latin America. In her discussion *Ute Schüren* questions the widely assumed dichotomy between colonizers and colonized showing that the relationships between local brokers and state agents were manifold and ranged from friendship to violence and from cooperation to resistance. Comparing processes of state expansion into the Yucatán peninsula in colonial and revolutionary times, she finds similarities in the forms and means by which the state attempted to extend its domination and control over time.

In **Postcolonial Dependencies: Internal Legacies of External Colonialism**, essays tackle the long durée of colonial legacies that create specific forms of internal exploitation and hegemony after decolonization. The struggles of Mexicans in the United States, for example, have had historically much to do with claims to homeland, including issues of borders and immigration. The concepts of and the connections between internal colonialism and indigeneity in the United States are thus essential to colonial theory. These links, argues *John Chávez*, using DNA and family tree analyses, help define the colonized and establish their historic rights to place, such as residency and citizenship. In another chapter on the intersections of the two Americas *Wolfgang Gabbert* considers the contradictions between cultural heterogeneity, class cleavages, the needs of emergent export-oriented economies, and the projects of nation-building. Internal colonialism revealed major trends and regional variations in mainland Latin America where formal Spanish colonial rule had already drawn to a close in the mid-1820s. Independence did not result in the self-rule of hitherto colonized people, but in domination by a new elite of American-born Spaniards responsible for probably more collective violence than had happened during much of the formal colonial era. Legacies of colonial rule in Africa persist through a framework of related practices, strategies, and mechanisms of 'political control'. *John Githigaro* analyzes these legacies in post-independence East Africa in light of their contributions to 'ethnicizing' the political space, their impact on the Rwandan genocide of 1994, and their effect on the Kenyan electoral violence of 2007–2008. His comparison of British and Belgian colonial practices reveals the imprint they left in terms of reinforcing ethnic differences with all their consequences for ethnic policy and violence. Postcolonial developments in countries hitherto under Soviet hegemony are still very much understudied. Perceiving Soviet politics in Mongolia as a form of continental colonialism, *Orhon Myadar* theorizes the legacies of Soviet control, deploying postcolonial tools typically reserved for critiquing European control of 'distant' lands, both in temporal and spatial dimensions. She grounds her analysis in her own first-person experience of growing up during the period to illuminate the various material, symbolic, and embodied implications and manifestations of Soviet political influence in Mongolia.

The volume's final part is on **Modes of Resistance and Decolonization**. It looks into cases of internal colonialism that developed various forms of resistance leading to attempts at decolonization that either succeeded or failed. Tellingly, when the United Nations General Assembly adopted the Declaration on the Rights of Indigenous Peoples in 2007 Canada voted against it, as did the United States, Australia, and New Zealand. In the opening chapter *Carole Blackburn* examines the Canadian government's approach to the negotiation of aboriginal rights and self-government with particular attention to the Nisga'a Treaty—a land claim and self-government agreement concluded in 2000 after more than twenty years of negotiation. For imperial Russia *Willard Sunderland* discusses the abolition of serfdom, an emancipation from above by Tsar Alexander II, one of the great legislative acts of world history. Rather than a national problem, Russian serfdom was an imperial one, an institution of bondage that existed alongside many other forms of servitude within the Russian Empire and whose effects touched numerous ethnic groups from Estonians and Latvians in the Baltic region, to Georgians in the South Caucasus, Kazakh slaves on the steppe frontiers of Central Asia, and Kalmyk nomads on the Southern

Volga. Indeed, servitude can thus be discussed under the national (Russian), the imperial, and the colonial frameworks imposed on non-Russians. Trajectories of related developments in the Baltics since the 1860s are analyzed by *Epp Annus*. The Soviet era initiated a completely different political, economic, and socio-cultural situation that at first glance could be opposed to the colonial rule of the Tsarist era. However, political and rhetorical continuities between the tsarist and Soviet rule persisted. Stressing historical continuities over different periods, de-colonial movements of the Soviet era are portrayed as strategies borrowed from nineteenth-century German romanticism and introduced into the Baltic cultural realm during the 1860s–1880s.

Without duplicating common wisdom, this volume builds on an earlier critique of colonialism understood in terms of structural inequalities installed politically or invented economically. Sources of inspiration include studies of continental and internal colonialism in North America, Canada, Hispanic America, China, India, Europe, and South Africa. In an attempt to push colonial studies beyond the postcolonial turn, this book offers an overview of colonialism in various parts of the world from continental and emic perspectives capable of challenging widely held assumptions based on overseas colonialism that have generically shaped, but also limited our understanding of colonial patterns.

REFERENCES

General

Asad, Talal. [1973] 1998. "Introduction." In *Anthropology & the Colonial Encounter*, edited by Talal Asad, 9–19. Amherst, NY: Humanity Books.

Balandier, Georges. [1951] 1966. "The Colonial Situation: A Theoretical Approach." In *Social Change: The Colonial Situation*, edited by Immanuel Wallerstein, 34–61. New York: Wiley.

Bateman, Fiona, and Lionel Pilkington. 2011. "Introduction." In *Studies in Settler Colonialism: Politics, Identity and Culture*, edited by Fiona Bateman and Lionel Pilkington, 1–9. New York: Palgrave Macmillan.

Bayly, Christopher Alan. 2004. *The Birth of the Modern World, 1780–1914: Global Connections and Comparisons*. Malden, MA: Blackwell.

Bhabha, Homi K. 1984. "Of Mimicry and Man: The Ambivalence of Colonial Discourse." *October* 28: 125–33.

Bitterli, Urs. [1976] 2004. *Die 'Wilden' und die 'Zivilisierten': Grundzüge einer Geistes- und Kulturgeschichte der europäisch-überseeischen Begegnung*. 3rd ed. München: Beck.

Blaschke, Jochen. 1985. *Volk, Nation, interner Kolonialismus, Ethnizität: Konzepte zur politischen Soziologie regionalistischer Bewegungen in Westeuropa.* Berlin: Express-Edition.

Burbank, Jane, and Frederick Cooper. 2010. *Empires in World History: Power and the Politics of Difference.* Princeton: Princeton University Press.

Chaloult, Norma Beatriz, and Yves Chaloult. 1979. "The Internal Colonialism Concept: Methodological Considerations." *Social and Economic Studies* 28(4): 85–99.

Cooke, Philip. 1984. "Recent Theories of Political Regionalism: A Critique and an Alternative Approach." *International Journal of Urban and Regional Research* 8(4): 549–71.

Cooper, Frederick. 2005a. *Colonialism in Question: Theory, Knowledge, History.* Berkeley: University of California Press.

Cooper, Frederick. 2005b. "Postcolonial Studies and the Study of History." In *Postcolonial Studies and Beyond*, edited by Ania Loomba, Suvir Kaul, Matti Bunzl, Antoinette Burton, and Jed Esty, 401–22. Durham: Duke University Press.

de L'Estoile, Benoît. 2008. "The Past as It Lives Now: An Anthropology of Colonial Legacies." *Social Anthropology/Anthropologie Sociale* 16(3): 267–79.

Dey, Dipankar. 2015. "Internal Colonialism." In *The Encyclopedia of Political Thought*, edited by Michael T. Gibbons, vol. IV, 1846–48. Chichester: Wiley-Blackwell.

Dimier, Véronique. 2002. "Direct or Indirect Rule: Propaganda Around a Scientific Controversy." In *Promoting the Colonial Idea: Propaganda and Visions of Empire in France*, edited by Tony Chafer and Amanda Sackur, 168–83. Basingstoke: Palgrave.

Dirks, Nicholas B. 1992. "Introduction: Colonialism and Culture." In *Colonialism and Culture*, edited by Nicholas B. Dirks, 1–25. Ann Arbor: The University of Michigan Press.

Docker, John. 2008. "Are Settler-Colonies Inherently Genocidal? Re-reading Lemkin." In *Empire, Colony, Genocide: Conquest, Occupation, Subaltern Resistance in World History*, edited by A. Dirk Moses, 81–101. New York: Berghahn.

Edmonds, Penelope. 2016. *Settler Colonialism and (Re)conciliation: Frontier Violence, Affective Performances, and Imaginative Refoundings.* London: Palgrave Macmillan.

Fieldhouse, David K. [1965] 1982. *The Colonial Empires: A Comparative Survey from the Eighteenth Century.* London: Macmillan.

Finley, Moses I. 1976. "Colonies: An Attempt at a Typology." *Transactions of the Royal Historical Society* 26: 167–88.

Gabbert, Wolfgang. 2007. „Vom (internen) Kolonialismus zum Multikulturalismus – Kultur, Ethnizität und soziale Ungleichheit." In *Achsen der Ungleichheit. Zum Verhältnis von Klasse, Geschlecht und Ethnizität*, edited by Cornelia Klinger, Gudrun-Axeli Knapp, and Birgit Sauer, 116–130. Frankfurt am Main: Campus.

Gabbert, Wolfgang. 2015. "Ethnicity in History." In *Ethnicity as a Political Resource: Conceptualizations Across Disciplines, Regions, and Periods*, edited by University of Cologne Forum "Ethnicity as a Political Resource", 183–200. Bielefeld: Transcript Verlag.

Gagné, Natacha. 2012. "The Study of Colonial Situations: The Emergence of a New General Approach?" *Reviews in Anthropology* 41(2): 109–135.

Hall, Catherine. 2002. *Civilising Subjects: Metropole and Colony in the English Imagination, 1830–1867.* Cambridge: Polity Press.

Hechter, Michael. 1983. "Internal Colonialism Revisited." In *Internal Colonialism: Essays Around a Theme*, edited by David Drakakis-Smith and Stephen Wyn Williams, 29–41. Edinburgh: University of Edinburgh.

Herzfeld, Michael. 2009. "The Absent Presence: Discourses of Crypto-Colonialism." In *Enchantments of Modernity: Empire, Nation, Globalization*, edited by Saurabh Dube, 341–71. London: Routledge.

Hind, Robert J. 1984. "The Internal Colonial Concept." *Comparative Studies in Society and History* 26(3): 543–68.

Hirschhausen, Ulrike von. 2015. "A New Imperial History? Programm, Potenzial, Perspektiven." *Geschichte und Gesellschaft* 41(4): 718–57.

Hodder-Williams, Richard. 2001. "Colonialism: Political Aspects." In *International Encyclopedia of the Social and Behavioral Sciences*, edited by Neil J. Smelser and Paul B. Baltes, vol. 4, 2237–40. Amsterdam: Elsevier.

Horvath, Ronald J. 1972. "A Definition of Colonialism." *Current Anthropology* 13(1): 45–57.

Howe, Stephen. 2002. *Empire: A Very Short Introduction.* Oxford: Oxford University Press.

James, Wendy. [1973] 1998. "The Anthropologist as Reluctant Imperialist." In *Anthropology & the Colonial Encounter*, edited by Talal Asad, 41–69. Amherst, NY: Humanity Books.

Jansen, Jan C., and Jürgen Osterhammel. 2017. *Decolonization: A Short History.* Translated by Jeremiah Riemer. Princeton: Princeton University Press.

Levene, Mark. 2008. "Empires, Native Peoples, and Genocide." In *Empire, Colony, Genocide: Conquest, Occupation, Subaltern Resistance in World History*, edited by A. Dirk Moses, 183–204. New York: Berghahn.

Lewis, Diane. 1973. "Anthropology and Colonialism." *Current Anthropology* 14(5): 581–602.

Love, Joseph L. 1989. "Modeling Internal Colonialism: History and Prospect." *World Development* 17(6): 905–22.

Lüthi, Barbara, Francesca Falk, and Patricia Purtschert. 2016. "Colonialism Without Colonies: Examining Blank Spaces in Colonial Studies." *National Identities* 18(1): 1–9.

Memmi, Albert. [1957] 1974. *The Colonizer and the Colonized*. Introduction by Jean-Paul Sartre. London: Souvenir Press.

Osterhammel, Jürgen. [1995] 2010. *Colonialism: A Theoretical Overview*. Translated by Shelley L. Frisch. 3rd ed. Princeton, NJ: Markus Wiener Publishers.

Pels, Peter. 1997. "The Anthropology of Colonialism: Culture, History and the Emergence of Western Governmentality." *Annual Review of Anthropology* 26: 163–83.

Pels, Peter. 2008. "What Has Anthropology Learned from the Anthropology of Colonialism?" *Social Anthropology/Anthropologie sociale* 16(3): 280–99.

Pinderhughes, Charles. 2011. "Toward a New Theory of Internal Colonialism." *Socialism and Democracy* 25(1): 235–56.

Reinhard, Wolfgang. 2010. "Kolonialgeschichtliche Probleme und kolonial-historische Konzepte." In *Kolonialgeschichten: Regionale Perspektiven auf ein globales Phänomen*, edited by Claudia Kraft, Alf Lüdtke, and Jürgen Martschukat, 67–91. Frankfurt am Main: Campus Verlag.

Reinhard, Wolfgang. 2011. *A Short History of Colonialism*. Manchester: Manchester University Press.

Reinhard, Wolfgang. 2015. "Colonization and Colonialism, History of." In *International Encyclopedia of the Social and Behavioral Sciences*, edited by James Wright. 2nd ed., vol. 4, 223–27. Amsterdam: Elsevier.

Said, Edward W. [1978] 2008. "Introduction to Orientalism, 1978." In *The Routledge Critical and Cultural Theory Reader*, edited by Neil Badmington and Julia Thomas, 213–33. London: Routledge.

Said, Edward W. 1989. "Representing the Colonized: Anthropology's Interlocutors." *Critical Inquiry* 15(2): 205–25.

Schlee, Günther. 2018. "Introduction: Difference and Sameness as Modes of Integration." In *Difference and Sameness as Modes of Integration: Anthropological Perspectives on Ethnicity and Religion*, edited by Günther Schlee and Alexander Horstmann, 1–32. New York: Berghahn.

Schorkowitz, Dittmar. 2012. "Historical Anthropology in Eurasia '… and the Way Thither'." *History and Anthropology* 23(1): 37–62.

Schorkowitz, Dittmar. 2015. *Imperial Formations and Ethnic Diversity: Institutions, Practices, and Longue Durée Illustrated by the Example of Russia* (Max Planck Institute for Social Anthropology Working Paper 165). Halle/ Saale: Max Planck Institute for Social Anthropology.

Schorkowitz, Dittmar. 2017. "Dealing with Nationalities in Imperial Formations: How Russian and Chinese Agencies Managed Ethnic Diversity in the 17th to 20th Centuries." In *Managing Frontiers in Qing China: The Lifanyuan and Libu Revisited*, edited by Dittmar Schorkowitz and Chia Ning, 389–434. Leiden: Brill.

Schorkowitz, Dittmar, and Chia Ning. 2017. "Introduction." In *Managing Frontiers in Qing China: The Lifanyuan and Libu Revisited*, edited by Dittmar Schorkowitz and Chia Ning, 1–42. Leiden: Brill.

Scott, David. 1995. "Colonial Governmentality." *Social Text* 43: 191–220.

Scott, David. [2001] 2015. "Colonialism, Anthropology of." In *International Encyclopedia of the Social and Behavioral Sciences*, edited by James Wright, 2nd ed., vol. 4, 218–22. Amsterdam: Elsevier.

Spivak, Gayatri Chakravorty. [1985] 2006. "Can the Subaltern Speak?" In *The Post-colonial Studies Reader*, edited by Bill Ashcroft, Gareth Griffiths, and Helen Tiffin. 2nd ed., 28–37. London: Routledge.

Stoler, Ann Laura. 1992. "Rethinking Colonial Categories: European Communities and the Boundaries of Rule." In *Colonialism and Culture*, edited by Nicholas B. Dirks, 319–52. Ann Arbor: The University of Michigan Press.

Stoler, Ann Laura. 2009. *Along the Archival Grain: Epistemic Anxieties and Colonial Common Sense*. Princeton: Princeton University Press.

Stoler, Ann Laura, and Frederick Cooper. 1997. "Between Metropole and Colony: Rethinking a Research Agenda." In *Tensions of Empire: Colonial Cultures in a Bourgeois World*, edited by Frederick Cooper and Ann Laura Stoler, 1–56. Berkeley: University of California Press.

Stone, John. 1979. "Introduction: Internal Colonialism in Comparative Perspective." *Ethnic and Racial Studies* 2(3): 255–59.

Thomas, Nicholas. 1994. *Colonialism's Culture: Anthropology, Travel and Government*. Cambridge: Polity Press.

Twitchett, Kenneth J. 1965. "Colonialism: An Attempt at Understanding Imperial, Colonial, and Neo-colonial Relationships." *Political Studies* 13(3): 300–23.

United Nations List of Non-Self-Governing Territories. 2017. https://en.wikipedia.org/wiki/United_Nations_list_of_Non-Self-Governing_Territories#cite_ref-Non-Self-Governing_Territories_26-0. Last modified 29 June 2017, accessed July 5, 2017.

Veracini, Lorenzo. [2010] 2014. *Settler Colonialism: A Theoretical Overview*. Basingstoke: Palgrave Macmillan.

Veracini, Lorenzo. 2011. "Telling the End of the Settler Colonial Story." In *Studies in Settler Colonialism: Politics, Identity and Culture*, edited by Fiona Bateman and Lionel Pilkington, 204–18. New York: Palgrave Macmillan.

Williams, Stephen Wyn. 1983. "The Theory of Internal Colonialism: An Examination." In *Internal Colonialism: Essays Around a Theme*, edited by David Drakakis-Smith and Stephen Wyn Williams, 5–28. Edinburgh: University of Edinburgh.

Africa

Comaroff, Jean, and John Comaroff. 1991. *Of Revelation and Revolution: Christianity, Colonialism, and Consciousness in South Africa*. Chicago: The University of Chicago Press.

Comaroff, John. 2002. "Governmentality, Materiality, Legality, Modernity: On The Colonial State in Africa." In *African Modernities: Entangled Meanings in Current Debate*, edited by Jan-Georg Deutsch, Peter Probst, and Heike Schmidt, 107–34. Portsmouth, NH: Heinemann.

Harries, Patrick. 1991. "Exclusion, Classification and Internal Colonialism: The Emergence of Ethnicity Among the Tsonga-Speakers of South Africa." In *The Creation of Tribalism in Southern Africa*, edited by Leroy Vail, 82–117. Berkeley: University of California Press.

Marquard, Leo. 1957. *South Africa's Colonial Policy*. Johannesburg: South African Institute of Race Relations.

Salih, M.A. Mohamed. 1993. "Indigenous Peoples and the State: An Unaccomplished Colonial Legacy and the Dilemma of Internal Colonialism in Africa." In *"... Never Drink from the Same Cup": Proceedings of the Conference on Indigenous Peoples in Africa, Tune Denmark 1993*, edited by Hanne Veber, Jens Dahl, Fiona Wilson, and Espen Wæhle, 271–90. Copenhagen: IWGIA & CDR.

Wai, Dunstan M. 1984. "Internal Colonialism and Political Engineering in the Sudan." In *International Perspectives on Affirmative Action. A Bellagio Conference (Lake Como, Italy, August 16–20, 1982)*, edited by U.S. Department of Education, 154–75. New York: Rockefeller Foundation.

Whyte, Christine. 2016. "Between Empire and Colony: American Imperialism and Pan-African Colonialism in Liberia, 1810–2003." *National Identities* 18(1): 71–88.

Wolpe, Harold. [1975] 2013. "The Theory of Internal Colonialism: The South African Case." In *Beyond the Sociology of Development: Economy and Society in Latin America and Africa*, edited by Ivar Oxaal, Tony Barnett, and David Booth, 229–52. London: Routledge.

Zureik, Elia T. 1979. *The Palestinians in Israel: A Study in Internal Colonialism*. London: Routledge & Kegan Paul.

America (Latin)

Cotler, Julio. 1967. "The Mechanics of Internal Domination and Social Change in Peru." *Studies in Comparative International Development* 3(12): 229–46.

Epstein, Erwin H. 1971. "Education and Peruanidad: 'Internal' Colonialism in the Peruvian Highlands." *Comparative Education Review* 15(2): 188–201.

Frank, André Gunder. 1969. *Latin America: Underdevelopment or Revolution: Essays on the Development of Underdevelopment and the Immediate Enemy.* New York: Monthly Review Press.

González-Casanova, Pablo. 1965. "Internal Colonialism and National Development." *Studies in Comparative International Development* 1(4): 27–37.

Havens, Arthur Eugene, and William L. Flinn. 1970. *Internal Colonialism and Structural Change in Colombia.* New York: Praeger Publishers.

Maldonado-Torres, Nelson. 2016. "Colonialism, Neocolonial, Internal Colonialism, the Postcolonial, Coloniality, and Decoloniality." In *Critical Terms in Caribbean and Latin American Thought: Historical and Institutional Trajectories*, edited by Yolanda Martínez-San Miguel, Ben Sifuentes-Jáuregui, and Marisa Belausteguigoitia, 67–78. New York: Palgrave Macmillan.

Stavenhagen, Rodolfo. 1965. "Classes, Colonialism, and Acculturation: Essay on a System of Inter-Ethnic Relations in Mesoamerica." *Studies in Comparative International Development* 1(6): 53–77.

America (USA, Canada)

Blauner, Robert. 1969. "Internal Colonialism and Ghetto Revolt." *Social Problems* 16(4): 393–408.

Cairns, Alan C. [2002] 2008. "Citizenship and Indian Peoples: The Ambiguous Legacy of Internal Colonialism." In *Handbook of Citizenship Studies*, edited by Engin F. Isin and Bryan S. Turner, 209–30. Los Angeles: Sage.

Chávez, John R. 2011. "Aliens in Their Native Lands: The Persistence of Internal Colonial Theory." *Journal of World History* 22(4): 785–809.

Churchill, Ward. 2002. *Struggle for the Land: Native North American Resistance to Genocide, Ecocide and Colonization.* San Francisco: City Lights.

Goldstein, Alyosha. 2014. "Toward a Genealogy of the U.S. Colonial Present." In *Formations of United States Colonialism*, edited by Alyosha Goldstein, 1–30. Durham: Duke University Press.

Green, Robyn. 2015. "The Economics of Reconciliation: Tracing Investment in Indigenous-Settler Relations." *Journal of Genocide Research* 17(4): 473–93.

Hicks, Jack. 2004. "On the Application of Theories of 'Internal Colonialism' to Inuit Societies." In *Presentation for the Annual Conference of the Canadian Political Science Association, Winnipeg*, June 5. https://www.cpsa-acsp.ca/papers-2004/Hicks.pdf. Accessed November 21, 2017.

Logan, Tricia. 2015. "Settler Colonialism in Canada and the Métis." *Journal of Genocide Research* 17(4): 433–52.

MacDonald, David B. 2015. "Canada's History Wars: Indigenous Genocide and Public Memory in the United States, Australia and Canada." *Journal of Genocide Research* 17(4): 411–31.

McRoberts, Kenneth. 1979. "Internal Colonialism: The Case of Quebec." *Ethnic and Racial Studies* 2(3): 293–318.

Moore, Joan W. 1970. "Colonialism: The Case of the Mexican Americans." *Social Problems* 17(4): 463–72.

Niezen, Ronald. 2013. *Truth and Indignation: Canada's Truth and Reconciliation Commission on Indian Residential Schools.* North York, ON: University of Toronto Press.

Oropeza, Lorena. 2014. "Becoming Indo-Hispano: Reies López Tijerina and the New Mexican Land Grant Movement." In *Formations of United States Colonialism*, edited by Alyosha Goldstein, 180–206. Durham: Duke University Press.

Ritter, Kathleen V. 1979. "Internal Colonialism and Industrial Development in Alaska." *Ethnic and Racial Studies* 2(3): 319–40.

Smyth, Steve. 2005. "Responses to Internal Colonialism in the Yukon Territory: 1959–2004." In *Studies in Folk Culture, Vol. V: The Northern Peoples and States. Changing Relationships*, edited by Art Leete and Ülo Valk, 184–202. Tartu: Tartu University Press.

Taylor, Alan. 2013. *Colonial America: A Very Short Introduction.* Oxford: Oxford University Press.

Wildcat, Matthew. 2015. "Fearing Social and Cultural Death: Genocide and Elimination in Settler Colonial Canada—An Indigenous Perspective." *Journal of Genocide Research* 17(4): 391–409.

Woolford, Andrew, and Jeff Benvenuto. 2015. "Canada and Colonial Genocide." *Journal of Genocide Research* 17(4): 373–90.

Asia

Bachman, David. 2004. "Making Xinjiang Safe for the Han? Contradictions and Ironies of Chinese Governance in China's Northwest." In *Governing China's Multiethnic Frontiers*, edited by Morris Rossabi, 155–85. Seattle: University of Washington Press.

Bayly, Susan. 1999. *Caste, Society and Politics in India from the Eighteenth Century to the Modern Age.* Cambridge: Cambridge University Press.

Bayly, Susan. 2000. "French Anthropology and the Durkheimians in Colonial Indochina." *Modern Asian Studies* 34(3): 581–622.

Brown, David. [1994] 2001. *The State and Ethnic Politics in South-East Asia.* London: Routledge.

Bulag, Uradyn E. 2004. "Inner Mongolia: The Dialectics of Colonization and Ethnicity Building." In *Governing China's Multiethnic Frontiers*, edited by Morris Rossabi, 84–116. Seattle: University of Washington Press.

Bulag, Uradyn E. 2017. "Clashes of Administrative Nationalisms: Banners and Leagues vs. Counties and Provinces in Inner Mongolia." In *Managing*

Frontiers in Qing China: The Lifanyuan and Libu Revisited, edited by Dittmar Schorkowitz and Chia Ning, 349–88. Leiden: Brill.

Chakrabarty, Dipesh. 1992. "Postcoloniality and the Artifice of History: Who Speaks for 'Indian' Pasts?" *Representations* 37: 1–26.

Corbridge, Stuart. 1987. "Industrialisation, Internal Colonialism and Ethnoregionalism: The Jharkhand, India, 1880–1980." *Journal of Historical Geography* 13(3): 249–66.

Côté, Isabelle. 2011. "Political Mobilization of a Regional Minority: Han Chinese Settlers in Xinjiang." *Ethnic and Racial Studies* 34(11): 1855–73.

Das, Mitra. 1978. "Internal Colonialism and the Movement for Bangladesh: A Sociological Analysis." *Contributions to Asian Studies* 12: 93–104.

Dey, Dipankar. 2010. "Inclusive Growth and Sustainable Development in India: A Case of Internal Colonialism." August 27, 2010, http://dx.doi.org/10.2139/ssrn.1648744. Accessed December 5, 2017.

Di Cosmo, Nicola. 1998. "Qing Colonial Administration in Inner Asia." *The International History Review* 20(2): 287–309.

Di Cosmo, Nicola. 2012. "From Alliance to Tutelage: A Historical Analysis of Manchu-Mongol Relations Before the Qing Conquest." *Frontiers of History in China* 7(2): 175–97.

Evans, Grant. 1992. "Internal Colonialism in the Central Highlands of Vietnam." *Sojourn: Journal of Social Issues in Southeast Asia* 7(2): 274–304.

Gladney, Dru C. 1998. "Internal Colonialism and the Uyghur Nationality: Chinese Nationalism and Its Subaltern Subjects." *Cahiers d'Études sur la Méditerranée Orientale et le monde Turco-Iranien* 25: 1–12.

Goldstein, Melvyn C. 2004. "Tibet and China in the Twentieth Century." In: *Governing China's Multiethnic Frontiers*, edited by Morris Rossabi, 186–229. Seattle: University of Washington Press.

Goodman, David S.G. 1983. "Guizhou and the People's Republic of China: The Development of an Internal Colony." In *Internal Colonialism: Essays Around a Theme*, edited by David Drakakis-Smith and Stephen Wyn Williams, 107–24. Edinburgh: University of Edinburgh.

Guha, Ranajit. 1982. "On Some Aspects of the Historiography of Colonial India." In *Subaltern Studies I: Writings on South Asian History and Society*, edited by Ranajit Guha, 1–8. Oxford: Oxford University Press.

Hamilton, Annette. 2002. "Tribal People on the Southern Thai Border: Internal Colonialism, Minorities, and the State." In *Tribal Communities in the Malay World: Historical, Cultural, and Social Perspectives*, edited by Geoffrey Benjamin and Cynthia Chou, 77–96. Singapore: Institute of Southeast Asian Studies.

Herman, John E. 2007. *Amid the Clouds and Mist: China's Colonization of Guizhou, 1200–1700*. Cambridge, MA: Harvard University Press.

Israeli, Raphael. 1981. "The Muslim Minority in the People's Republic of China." *Asian Survey* 21(8): 901–19.

Kowalski, Bartosz. 2017. "Holding an Empire Together: Army, Colonization and State-building in Qing Xinjiang." In *Ming Qing Studies*, edited by Paolo Santangelo, 45–70. Rome: Aracne Publishers.

Li, Aiyong. 2016. "New Qing History and the Problem of 'Chinese Empire'—Another Impact and Response?" *Contemporary Chinese Thought* 47(1): 13–29.

Meinhof, Marius, Junchen Yan, and Lili Zhu. 2017. "Postcolonialism and China: Some Introductory Remarks." *InterDisciplines: Journal of History and Sociology* 8(1): 1–25.

Myadar, Orhon. 2017. "In the Soviet Shadow: Soviet Colonial Politics in Mongolia." *Inner Asia* 19(1): 5–28.

Oakes, Timothy S. 1995. "Tourism in Guizhou: The Legacy of Internal Colonialism." In *Tourism in China: Geographic, Political, and Economic Perspectives*, edited by Alan A. Lew and Lawrence Yu, 203–22. Boulder, CO: Westview Press.

Perdue, Peter. 1998. "Comparing Empires: Manchu Colonialism." *The International History Review* 20(2): 255–62.

Perdue, Peter. 2005. *China Marches West: The Qing Conquest of Central Eurasia.* Cambridge, MA: Harvard University Press.

Perdue, Peter. 2010. "War Qing-China ein koloniales Empire?" In *Kolonialgeschichten: Regionale Perspektiven auf ein globales Phänomen*, edited by Claudia Kraft, Alf Lüdtke, and Jürgen Martschukat, 259–81. Frankfurt am Main: Campus Verlag.

Roy, A.K. [1982] 2003. "Jharkhand: Internal Colonialism." In *The Jharkhand Movement: Indigenous Peoples' Struggle for Autonomy in India*, edited by Ram Dayal Munda and S. Bosu Mullick, 79–85. Copenhagen: IWGIA.

Sautman, Barry. 2000. "Is Xinjiang an Internal Colony?" *Inner Asia* 2(2): 239–71.

Sen, Uditi. 2017. "Developing *Terra Nullius*: Colonialism, Nationalism, and Indigeneity in the Andaman Islands." *Comparative Studies in Society and History* 59(4): 944–73.

Sinha, Sachchidanand. 1973. *The Internal Colony: A Study in Regional Exploitation.* New Delhi: Sindhu Publications.

Thongchai Winichakul. 2014. "Asian Studies Across Academies." *Journal of Asian Studies* 73(4): 879–97.

Wang Hui. 2014. *China from Empire to Nation-State.* Translated by Michael Gibbs Hill. Cambridge, MA: Harvard University Press.

Zhang Jian. 2016. "Manchu Sinicization: Doubts on the Ethnic Perspective of New Qing History." *Contemporary Chinese Thought* 47(1): 30–43.

Europe

Alapuro, Risto. 1979. "Internal Colonialism and the Regional Party System in Eastern Finland." *Ethnic and Racial Studies* 2(3): 341–59.

Ben-Ghiat, Ruth, and Mia Fuller. [2005] 2008. "Introduction." In *Italian Colonialism*, edited by Ruth Ben-Ghiat and Mia Fuller, 1–12. New York: Palgrave Macmillan.

Bierschenk, Thomas. 2010. "Das 'Wir-Gefühl' der Ostdeutschen." *Stern.de*, April 23, 2010. https://www.stern.de/panorama/ethnologe-widerspricht--ossi-urteil--das--wir-gefuehl--der-ostdeutschen-3099488.html. Accessed December 12, 2018.

Chafer, Tony, and Amanda Sackur. 2002. "Introduction." In *Promoting the Colonial Idea: Propaganda and Visions of Empire in France*, edited by Tony Chafer and Amanda Sackur, 1–11. Basingstoke: Palgrave.

Dümcke, Wolfgang, and Fritz Vilmar. 1995. "Was heißt hier Kolonialisierung? Eine theoretische Vorerklärung." In *Kolonialisierung der DDR: Kritische Analysen und Alternativen des Einigungsprozesses*, edited by Wolfgang Dümcke and Fritz Vilmar, 12–21. Münster: agenda Verlag.

Etkind, Alexander. 2011. *Internal Colonization: Russia's Imperial Experience.* Cambridge: Polity Press.

Fur, Gunlög. 2016. "Colonial Fantasies—American Indians, Indigenous Peoples, and a Swedish Discourse of Innocence." *National Identities* 18(1): 11–33.

Hechter, Michael. [1975] 1999. *Internal Colonialism: The Celtic Fringe in British National Development* (with a new introduction and a new appendix by the author). New Brunswick, NJ: Transaction Publishers.

Hertog, Frank den. 2004. *Minderheit im eigenen Land? Zur gesellschaftlichen Position der Ostdeutschen in der gesamtdeutschen Realität.* Frankfurt am Main: Campus.

Lafont, Robert. 1971. *Décoloniser en France. Les régions face à l'Europe.* Paris: Gallimard.

Lantto, Patrik. 2005. "Raising Their Voices: The Sami Movement in Sweden and the Swedish Sami Policy, 1900–1960." In *Studies in Folk Culture, Vol. V: The Northern Peoples and States: Changing Relationships*, edited by Art Leete and Ülo Valk, 202–34. Tartu: Tartu University Press.

Narsey, Wadan. 2016. *British Imperialism and the Making of Colonial Currency Systems.* London: Palgrave Macmillan.

Palloni, Alberto. 1979. "Internal Colonialism or Clientelistic Politics? The Case of Southern Italy." *Ethnic and Racial Studies* 2(3): 360–77.

Reece, Jack E. 1979. "Internal Colonialism: The Case of Brittany." *Ethnic and Racial Studies* 2(3): 275–92.

Verdery, Katherine. 1979. "Internal Colonialism in Austria-Hungary." *Ethnic and Racial Studies* 2(3): 378–99.

Vinkovetsky, Ilya. 2011. *Russian America: An Overseas Colony of a Continental Empire, 1804–1867*. Oxford: Oxford University Press.

Weber, Eugen. 1976. *Peasants into Frenchmen: The Modernization of Rural France, 1870–1914*. Stanford, CA: Stanford University Press.

Wendland, Anna Veronika. 2010. „Imperiale, koloniale und postkoloniale Blicke auf die Peripherien des Habsburgerreiches." In *Kolonialgeschichten: Regionale Perspektiven auf ein globales Phänomen*, edited by Claudia Kraft, Alf Lüdtke, and Jürgen Martschukat, 211–35. Frankfurt: Campus Verlag.

PART I

Colonialism as Discourse in Social Anthropology and History

Overseas, Continental, and Internal Colonialism: Responses from Latin American Anthropologies

Stefan Krotz

> *…the rising cycles of ethnology coincide, principally, with the phases of expansion of Occidental civilization.*
> Ángel Palerm (1918–1980; Mexican anthropologist)

> *The West is not in the West. It is a project, not a place.*
> Édouard Glissant (1928–2011; Martinican ethnologist)

INTRODUCTION

A colonial situation leaves a deep mark, not only on all the social and cultural relations of the groups and individuals who suffer from it, but also on those who generate, control and reproduce it. That a colonial situation similarly affects and marks the empirical analyses *of* and social-scientific reflections *on* itself has not always received sufficient

S. Krotz (✉)
Universidad Autónoma de Yucatán, Mérida, Mexico
e-mail: krotz@correo.uady.mx

Universidad Autónoma Metropolitana, Mexico City, Mexico

© The Author(s) 2019
D. Schorkowitz et al. (eds.), *Shifting Forms of Continental Colonialism*,
https://doi.org/10.1007/978-981-13-9817-9_3

consideration, and will be in the focus of this chapter.[1] In fact, we cannot consider or successfully complete decolonization without taking into account the ways the colonized analyze the colonial situation itself as part of their efforts to overcome this condition.

While true for all the social sciences and humanities, this problem is especially interesting and relevant for sociocultural anthropology due primarily to two aspects of its history. First, sociocultural anthropology's origins as a scientific discipline are interwoven in multiple ways with the nineteenth-century apogee of North Atlantic colonial expansion. That expansion was continental and internal through the compulsory formation of supposedly unitary, homogeneous national states principally in Europe and North America, but also in Latin America. The expansion was also planetary through the likewise compulsory formation of overseas colonial empires, such as the British and French, as well as informal empires with so-called spheres of influence imposed on formally independent countries as in Latin America by the United States. Second, sociocultural anthropology diffused from North Atlantic civilization to the rest of the world (including from the bourgeois urban, formally educated and patriarchal layers of industrial societies to the rural margins of Euro-North American civilization).[2] But even more important than these historical legacies is the fact that the cognitive instrument generated to systematically understand the *other* from the viewpoint of North Atlantic civilization has since been transformed, essentially in the Southern half of the planet (often called the 'Global South'). Those *others* are now using this cognitive instrument to recognize their own specific, local situation, and furthermore to explore from a Southern point of view, also more comprehensive social structures and cultural processes at national and international levels.

---

[1] Though this chapter refers specifically to sociocultural anthropology, many of its considerations can also be applied to the remaining three anthropological sub-disciplines prehistoric-historical anthropology (archaeology), linguistic anthropology (anthropological linguistics), and physical or biological anthropology.

[2] According to these two types of colonial transformation, in Central Europe, and especially in the German speaking countries, the so-called *Völkerkunde* (now almost always called social and cultural anthropology or ethnology) was concerned with non-European cultures and societies in past and present, whereas the so-called *Volkskunde* (now almost always called European ethnology) concentrated on sociocultural diversity inside European nation-states.

The geo-cultural frame of reference of this chapter is almost exclusively Latin America.[3] Its objective is to discuss some central aspects of anthropological debates over the last quarter century that describe the anthropologies that developed in Latin America as 'seconds' or dependent relative to North Atlantic civilization. Sections one and two of the paper recount the gradual visualization and consolidation of some of the main features of Latin American anthropologies, while sections three and four illustrate various current strategies to de-colonize the field in Latin America's national scientific communities. In this sense, it is true that

> the anthropology of colonialism is also always an anthropology of anthropology, because in many methodological, organizational, and professional aspects the discipline retains the shape it received when it emerged from –if partly in opposition to– early twentieth-century colonial circumstances. Studying colonialism implies studying anthropology's context, a broader field of ethnographic activity that existed before the boundaries of the discipline emerged and that continues to influence the way they are drawn. (Pels 1997, 164–65)

THE GRADUAL VISUALIZATION OF 'SECOND' ANTHROPOLOGIES IN LATIN AMERICA

Although various Latin American countries developed processes and even specialized institutions in the nineteenth century to recompile and systematize material and symbolic information on *other* societies in historical time and national spaces, modern scientific anthropology, properly speaking, developed in the region through processes of diffusion from Europe and North America in the twentieth century. Yet, these formative processes were similar to those that emerged in Europe and its North American and Russian 'margins' as the anthropological disciplines formed, and in some places these processes even exhibited a five-hundred-year history of documented interest in *internal others*, especially indigenous peoples.[4] However, so impactful was the diffusion from the

---

[3] As usual, the term 'Latin America' includes the Caribbean, but we cannot state here similarities or differences between the Latin American continent and that area which, by the way, actually still constitutes the broadest colonial region in the world.

[4] Therefore, the first general history of anthropology published in Latin America by Ángel Palerm ([1974] 2006) dedicates almost half of its first volume ("los precursores") to explorers, missionaries, and colonial administrators in Latin America, considering them forerunners of scientific anthropology.

North Atlantic that it long concealed the domestic antecedents of the discipline even from Latin American anthropologists in their respective countries. The same situation repeated itself somewhat later in African and Asian countries.

The independence of many African and Asian countries after World War II, the intensification of the Cold War between East and West, and finally the dissemination of multilateral and bilateral 'development' strategies to all areas of the world framed the historical space in which anthropology was 'planted' in those places. Gradually, the southern regions of the world—until then simply 'exotic' spaces for North Atlantic anthropological research—saw the emergence of anthropological institutions, museums, university programs, publications, and specialized anthropological events. In some areas of Latin America that process began much earlier, but today practically all countries in Latin America have anthropology departments and university programs.[5]

However, many years passed before recognition of the *distinctive anthropologies* in the South. Several generations of anthropologists considered them simply an extension or imitation of the anthropologies of the North. Indeed, anthropologies of the South were absent not only from the publications and university programs of academic institutions in the North (in many places they still are!), but also from numerous Latin American countries that for decades had no courses in their own national anthropologies. Worse yet, where such courses existed, national anthropologies often appeared as little more than imperfect copies of those in the North assumed by antonomasia to be *the* universal anthropologies. As part of the same trend, we have to understand that those courses were generally seen as belonging to the *history* of Latin American anthropology only, not to the development of Latin American anthropological theories.

Critical debates on the social character and function of Latin American anthropologies began to arise vigorously in the late 1960s. In addition to the global sociopolitical context mentioned before, other

---

[5] Perhaps the earliest and best-known antecedent is the *Escuela Internacional de Arqueología y Etnología Americana,* founded shortly before the Mexican Revolution of 1910. A century later, in 2010, undergraduate programs in social anthropology and archaeology were set up in one of the few continental countries that still had none, in Honduras, almost sixty years after the establishment of the *Instituto Hondureño de Antropología e Historia* in 1952.

important elements contributed to the formation of the three grand Latin American intellectual creations of that period. These approaches would mark the social sciences and humanities at large extending their influence even to the North, though not without obstacles and rejections.

The first was dependency theory. It is important to recall that this theory did not simply set out to correct or improve the dominant economic and social theory generically called 'modernization', but actually sought to replace it with the central theme of ongoing reproduction of worldwide inequality through the imposition of generalized unequal exchange by the industrialized countries of the North.[6] The second intellectual invention was liberation theology with the ensuing philosophy of liberation, both almost always based on dependency theory. They attempted to construct a new way of generating theological and philosophical knowledge anchored on the social and cultural results of the five hundred years of open and concealed colonialism since the first contacts between America and Europe. The vital situation of the poor constituted the starting point for reflection on liberation. The third intellectual movement to be mentioned here was the profound critique of several institutions considered usually essential for modernity (including, among others, but in an especially striking and well-known way, mandatory basic public education). The attractiveness and broad acceptance of this critical thinking were also due to the diverse practical experiments undertaken to organize alternative intellectual, ecclesiastical, and educational institutions. These alternative institutions resulted from a distinct idea of social and cultural order and provided pathways to achieving this new order.[7]

[6] The Venezuelan anthropologist Fernando Coronil called the dependency school of the 1960s and 1970s "one of Latin America's most significant contributions to postcolonial thought within this period, auguring the postcolonial critique of historicism, and providing conceptual tools for a much needed postcolonial critique of contemporary imperialism" (2004, 223).

[7] The Brazilian economist Theotonio Dos Santos, one of the founders of dependency theory, has published interesting reflections on the characteristics and the ongoing validity of dependency theory; see Dos Santos (2007) and Sader and Dos Santos (2009). In a new foreword to his famous book on liberation theology Gustavo Gutiérrez (1988) explains its origins and some of the changes that it has undergone since then. The pedagogical ideas and the related criticism of so-called modernization and development of the Brazilian Paulo Freire and of Iván Illich during his years in Mexico, regarding production and reproduction of knowledge, are still being discussed in many parts of the world; see McLaren and Leonard (1993), Bhattacharya (2011), and Hartch (2015). The recently edited volume by

Dependency and imperialism became the key concepts coined to name and problematize the colonial character of anthropology, while attempts to offer alternatives were described as 'critical' or 'new'. Some voices even advocated doing away with anthropology once and for all, deeming it a bourgeois and eurocentric ideology; their proposal was to replace it with some Marxist-tinged political economy. Paradoxically, near the end of the twentieth century, the postmodern critique of anthropology as a science contributed to directing the interests of anthropological communities once again toward the historical development of the discipline and toward certain current epistemological topics and themes in the philosophy of science in efforts to better understand that history and its effects on the present. More recent debates about postcolonial and decolonial perspectives in anthropology connect with the late 1960s and early 1970s:

> Since its emergence as a distinctive theme in anthropology in the 1970s, the problematization of colonialism has been thought of as part of an orientation towards the present at least as much as, if not more than, the past. (Scott 2001, 2236)

As a result of these motivating forces, in the 1990s several Latin American countries established their first research programs and university courses on their respective national anthropologies. This comes somewhat as a paradox, given the disappearance of bloody national security regimes during Latin America's 1980s, the 'lost decade' in terms of socio-economic development. In addition to attempts to reconstruct the exogenous and endogenous genealogical roots of their national anthropologies, the principle task—still under construction—was to analyze and comprehend their *own* peculiar character, which included, of course, studying their relations with other anthropologies worldwide but, above all, with originary anthropologies.

Peruvian sociologist Aníbal Quijano (2014) also shows the continuity and the inspiration of these ideas demonstrating its combination with the actual discussion about the idea of 'good living' which has emerged in several Latin American countries with high percentages of Indian population.

PERSPECTIVES AND TOPICS OF LATIN AMERICAN ANTHROPOLOGIES OF THE SOUTH

As often occurs with the emergence of something novel, analyzing the words used to name it may reveal a great deal about its essential quality and its degree of advancement. In general terms, we can say that Latin American anthropologies understood themselves as 'second', in both the chronological sense and as dependents of the first or originary ones that continued to be reproduced faithfully in the South and which influenced also the attempts to achieve more autonomous foundations. Among the many labels applied to the anthropologies being consolidated in Latin American countries were: 'non-Western anthropologies' or 'Third World anthropologies' as contrasted to those of the 'First World' or those of the North Atlantic nations; 'peripheral anthropologies' as contrasted to 'central' anthropologies generated in the main colonizing countries; 'indigenous' or 'local anthropologies' as contrasted to universal or world anthropologies; and 'anthropologies of the South' as contrasted to those of the North, understood less in geographic terms than in an epistemological and political-cultural sense of differentiation and dependence.[8]

Adopting here the latter term, we can say that two types or styles[9] of rootedness or embeddedness of the discipline received from the North

---

[8]For a more detailed explanation of these different though convergent concepts, see Krotz (2008). The term 'indigenous anthropology' was used for years as equivalent of local or national anthropologies in Africa and Asia, but not in Latin America, where it refers to the knowledge produced by anthropologists who belong to indigenous peoples in Latin American countries; see Mott (1982, 112). In an early attempt to visualize the beginnings of the anthropologies in the South, Kenyan born anthropologist Simeon Chilungu suggested the use of the term "Non-European-American" ("Nicht-Euro-Amerika") anthropology (1984, 314), because the notion of Third World anthropology seemed to exclude certain Southern regions, diasporas from the South in the North, and also the original populations of America. Interestingly, he considered one of the first tasks of the proposed alternative anthropology of the future—a real universal anthropology studying all societies and cultures of the planet and perhaps even of other galaxies—the strict avoidance of anthropological concepts that are seen as false, distorting, and even insulting, such as 'primitive', 'tribe', 'savage', or 'pagan' (ibid., 321). Some years earlier, the Brazilian anthropologist Darcy Ribeiro on the occasion of the XLII International Congress of Americanists in 1976 had explained (1979, 280) that the dominant anthropological theories have alienated several generations of Latin American intellectuals so strongly that they had become unable to understand the indigenous peoples of their own countries.

[9]The idea of different *styles* of the same disciplinary matrix has been discussed especially by Brazilian anthropologists Cardoso de Oliveira and Raul Ruben (1995).

co-exist in current Latin American anthropologies without major conflicts.[10] The first can be called anthropology *in the South*. This is characterized primarily as an anthropology devoted to 'applying' the theoretical and methodological currents judged the 'best' or 'most advanced' versions of the anthropology of the North available for generating knowledge on, and training professionals for, a country's own anthropology. Gaining recognition from the representatives, institutions, and publications of the first (that is the originary or Northern) anthropologies is an important aspiration for those who practice this type of anthropology in the South, which, by the way, is almost always the one adopted by the decision-makers at the summits of their scientific and educational institutions. As a matter of fact, presently almost all so-called academic evaluations of universities are based on criteria valid in the Northern countries, including publication in the English language and in journals edited in the North, often erroneously called international publications. The second type of disciplinary rootedness can be called anthropology *of the South*. This is an anthropology devoted primarily to using—sometimes rather eclectically—theoretical and methodological elements from the anthropologies of the North *and* the South that best serve to generate new knowledge, resolve critical social problems in the South, and train professionals in this perspective. The primordial aspiration of its practitioners is to make useful contributions to problem-solving without this entailing a theoretical immediateness or pragmatism. Nevertheless, the border between scientific papers and essays is often porous, and the publication of texts in a wide range of channels—academic journals, magazines, cultural supplements, blogs—aims to reach a wider readership including decision-makers.

Clearly, the first style assumes that the South is in somewhat 'underdeveloped' conditions and argues that overcoming this status requires significant efforts to reproduce correctly and adapt meticulously the received discipline of the North in the South. The second, in contrast, sees the South as a valued space through one with profound social and cultural problems, mainly originated by the forced colonial inclusion of the South into the world system dominated by the North. It sustains that anthropological analyses can provide at least glimpses of pathways

[10]This does not imply an absence of tensions, so one has heard the derogatory terms 'native Latin Americanists' or 'branch anthropologists' applied to representatives of the first type, and 'folklorists' or 'ideologists' to representatives of the second type.

that lead out of the problems, even if these analyses entail straying from the proven scientific traditions of the North or composing unorthodox combinations of his different traditions.

We might also say that the first type studies a certain sociocultural reality in the framework of habitual hegemonic ideas and teachings of anthropology, as a sequence of paradigmatic proposals in which all cognitive efforts must be situated as legitimate heirs of the original evolutionist scheme and its followers. The second type, by contrast, operates more in the mode of a Levi-Straussian '*bricoleur*', where the principle referent is a nation's own domestic academic and professional anthropological community, understood of course as linked to other social and human sciences, and concerned with improving the sociocultural situation of the country and of its citizens, especially of the poor.

In addition to the long concealment of, or amnesia regarding, their own antecedents, almost all Latin American anthropologies share[11] a national context in which

- scientific research is deemed of little importance for the country, reflected in the minuscule contribution of this activity to the Gross National Product;
- almost all universities (specially the numerous private ones, but also most public universities) are confined to teaching, leaving aside scientific research;
- university studies, primarily undergraduate, are assumed to be the highest rung on the standardized educational ladder, rather than as spaces where young people are introduced to free, innovative, critical thought; this assumption is visible in the prevalence of simple reproductive models in teaching and in the administrative systems that control the teaching faculty and evaluate only or mainly the quantitative aspects of academic performance;
- dominant neoliberal tendencies have advanced greatly in imposing so-called academic capitalism and converting knowledge and university education into merchandise;
- once and again critical social and human sciences are severely marginalized or prohibited by authoritarian regimes, and even their practitioners silenced in varied manners.

---

[11] Features discussed more broadly in Cardoso de Oliveira (1999–2000) and Krotz (1997).

Many Latin American anthropologies share another important phenomenon. For a long time *those most distant* from bourgeois, urban, university-educated cultures: the *others*—members of indigenous communities, descendants of African and Asian immigrants, sometimes also peasants in remote areas, who very often share essential social and cultural characteristics with surrounding indigenous population—have been the main segments of society subject to anthropological study, generally related to special indigenist or general nation-building strategies. While this phenomenon represents actually just one topic among many others, it still constitutes one of the discipline's widely recognized features. As such it is part of the ongoing efforts toward self-knowledge of Latin American societies.[12] It comes along with other themes like national and regional identities, their construction and reconstruction through history, and the closely related topic of 'development'. Another feature of identity of the discipline has always been 'fieldwork' in the sense of microscopic, contextual studies based on long-term participant co-existence with the members of the group under study in attempts to comprehend the so-called 'native's point of view'. Though other disciplines now use this approach too, it is apparently being abandoned in some anthropological and political-administrative institutions due to high costs, time, and other resources often required.

Being a citizen of the same country and heir to the *same hegemonic* or 'national' culture as that of the social groups studied represents another important challenge that Latin American anthropologies share. Aside from the epistemological issues involved,[13] this 'anthropology at home' entails epistemological, ethical, and political situations and problems quite distinct from those discussed in classic anthropological monographs and widely used manuals. Among others, we have to mention complications related to the sometimes unavoidable politicization of research and its results, the possibilities and problems of collaborative

[12] This aspect has been emphasized once and again by the Mexican philosopher Luis Villoro from his book on indigenism in Mexico ([1950] 1998) up to his last conversations with the Zapatista rebel movement in Chiapas.

[13] The Colombian anthropologist Myriam Jimeno (2000) and the Brazilian anthropologist Otávio Velho (2006) have studied the differences in focuses that derive from being a foreign or national researcher while the Guatemalan anthropologist Sergio Mendizábal (2007) has described and analyzed the modification of ethnic-cultural options among anthropology students through their involvement in a certain kind of participatory or engaged research.

studies, and the desire of certain groups under study to intervene actively in the research process as a function of vested interests. Also, different public, private, national, and foreign institutions seek to impose control on the results of projects that they (co-)finance, and on the concrete social and cultural conditions for the diffusion and dissemination of the results of anthropological research.

It is easy to recognize several long-lasting continuities from the beginning of the diffusion of anthropological science from the North toward the South. The North has recognized gradually the existence of Southern anthropologies in the above-mentioned sense of a complex combination of anthropologies *in* the South and anthropologies *of* the South, but supporting and promoting basically the former, and ignoring or leaving aside the latter. As already mentioned, in the countries of the South, the state administration and private universities almost always accept and favor the exogenous models. Then, anthropology was almost everywhere in Latin America, in words of the Peruvian anthropologists Carlos Iván Degregori and Pablo Sandoval being really a

> 'mestizo' anthropology, that means, a discipline which was always alert and attentive with respect to the debates that developed in the metropolitan countries, but which at the same time maintained strong links with its own intellectual traditions and with its own political dilemmas and worries with regard to the construction of the nation. (2008, 13)

In consequence, the anthropological communities required much effort to overcome the sense of inferiority regarding their own national and regional anthropologies and to reject the prejudice—although sometimes justified—that the anthropologies of the South merely evade indisputable scientific standards. This has to be seen against the background that institutional and financial support is generally very limited, particularly outside the capital cities. Especially disadvantageous for the South is the expectation that in all Latin American anthropological institutions the language of the world's most powerful country and of the largest anthropological association has to be learnt and to be used. Especially in Latin America making English *the* language of serious social and human sciences confers a clearly colonial coinage in the worldwide relationships among anthropological communities. This practice is underpinned by a kind of international division of labor that tends to assign the legitimate, innovative potential and the systematic theoretical work to the countries where anthropological science originated, and the more descriptive and applied activities to the South. With regard to this global divide and the already mentioned hegemony of the English language in international publications, it is interesting to note that almost all important Latin American anthropological journals and many books can be read online and copied free of charge, whereas anthropological journals published in Europe and North America, even when they contain articles on Latin American societies and cultures based on field studies in Latin America, are inaccessible in the South, or have to be paid dearly.

These are characteristic features of a nineteenth-century conception of progress based on the popular attraction of—then mechanical, today digital—technology,[14] which was renamed 'development' shortly after World War II, and at the beginning of political decolonization movements in Asia and Africa. From an anthropological point of view, however, this can only be understood as an enduring expression of the North Atlantic-centric paradigm of unilinear evolutionism with which modern anthropological science began to exist. Thus, Wolfgang Sachs in his introduction to the *Dictionary of Development* proposes

> … to call the age of development that particular historical period which began on 20 January 1949, when Harry S. Truman for the first time declared, in his inauguration speech, the Southern hemisphere as 'underdeveloped areas'. The label stuck and subsequently provided the cognitive base for both arrogant interventionism from the North and pathetic self-pity in the South. However, what is born at a certain point in time can die again at a later point; the age of development is on the decline because its four founding premises have been outdated by history. ([1992] 2010, XVI; see also Esteva [1992] 2010)

This conception of development was by no means limited to the humanities and social sciences of the nineteenth and twentieth centuries. It profoundly permeated the general culture and worldviews in the North and in the South, so that it has become extremely difficult for anthropology to escape from its effects. While the philosopher and historian Enrique Dussel (1993) revealed the deeply rooted, widespread, unilinear, and eurocentric model of civilizational evolution, the Haitian anthropologist Michel-Rolph Trouillot explained one of its consequences:

---

[14]This special aspect is shown and discussed by Adas (1989).

Thus, North Atlantic universals are always prescriptive inasmuch as they always suggest, even if implicitly, a correct state of affairs –what is good, what is just, what is desirable– not only what is, but what should be. Indeed, that prescription is inherent in the very projection of a historically limited experience –that of the North Atlantic– on the world stage. Thus also, North Atlantic universals are always seductive, at times even irresistible, exactly because they manage, in that projection, to hide their specific-localized, North Atlantic, and thus parochial-historical location. (2002, 220)

The Colombian anthropologist Arturo Escobar ([1995] 2011, 2004) has also shown once and again the pernicious results of this unilinear and teleological thinking in development policies ('desarrollismo') for Latin American societies and for anthropological research and teaching. On his part, Immanuel Wallerstein has shown that the

rhetoric of the leaders of the pan-European world –in particular, but not only, the United States and Great Britain– and the mainstream media and establishment intellectuals is filled with appeals to universalism as the basic justification of their policies. (2006, XIII)

STRATEGIES TO ESCAPE FROM COLONIALITY

Clearly, it is impossible to posit strategies to escape from the colonial situation and struggle against its mechanisms of reproduction if we do not first recognize its existence. Thus, the following discussion is relevant only to the second type of Latin American anthropologies outlined above. For one reason or another, these anthropologies cannot ponder the production and reproduction of anthropological knowledge, its teaching, diffusion, and dissemination without referring constantly to the major social and cultural structures and processes of which these activities and their protagonists form part. In this sense, the general situation of Latin America may provide a special historical framework for reacting against coloniality, because, as the recently deceased Peruvian sociologist and political scientist Aníbal Quijano put it fifteen years ago:

It is a time of luchas (struggles) and of options. Latin America was the original space of the emergence of modern/colonial capitalism; it marked its founding moment. Today it is, at last, the very center of world resistance against this pattern of power and of the production of alternatives to it. (cited by Escobar 2013, 392)

An insightful definition of coloniality was proposed by the Portuguese sociologist and Americanist Boaventura de Sousa Santos who characterized the South as a starting point for

> the practices of the classes and social groups that have –systematically– suffered destruction, oppression and discrimination caused by capitalism, colonialism, and all the naturalizations of inequality in which they have developed; that is, exchange value, private property in land, sacrificing Mother Earth, racism, sexism, individualism, placing the material above the spiritual, and every other monocropping of mind and society –economic, political and cultural– that seeks to stultify the emancipatory imagination and sacrifice alternatives. (2011, 16)

Setting aside for a moment the excessive tone of self-victimization, Santos' definition reminds us that coloniality is not just an academic concept, but actually a question of life and, as the famous defender of American indigenous peoples of the early Spanish colony, Bartolomé de las Casas wrote five centuries ago, an unjust and premature death for so many.

In this regard, it is important to consider the longstanding discussion of the need for a decolonial anthropology or *una antropología descolonial*,[15] in the sense of a search "for new processes of producing [and] valorizing valid, scientific and non-scientific knowledge, and for new relations among different types of knowledge" (ibid.). As mentioned above, this is not simply due to a change in the realm of objects and theories, but mainly to the fact that "new subjects joined the process of knowledge production: the 'native' anthropologists who studied their own societies" (Boivin et al. [1998] 2004, 12). This is not the place to discuss the differences between the de(s)colonial approach (which, though far from unitary, represents a set of similar focuses, and the much better known European and North American so-called 'postcolonial'

---

[15] Referring to Catherine Walsh (2009), Gabriela Veronelli explains that "to say *decolonial*, suppressing the 's' is not to promote this Anglicism, but to mark the difference from what 'des' [means] in Castilian. It is not about discarding or reversing the colonial and transiting from a colonial to a non-colonial moment, as if the traces of the former could magically cease to exist. Rather, it refers to a positioning, an attitude of thought, of living, doing, visibilizing and encouraging places of exteriority and alternative constructions" (2015, 37).

approach. However, it is clear that the 'descolonial' scheme does not assume that political independence has created a genuine postcolonial situation. The repeated overt and covert military interventions by various North Atlantic powers in many Latin American countries in the nineteenth and twentieth centuries suffice to expose the obviously relative nature of their political independence, and also the frequent compulsory programs of the International Monetary Fund and other international agencies. Rather, the 'descolonial' approach stresses the need to struggle against the still existing colonial situation expressed in and affecting— to use a well-known formula—the sociocultural dimensions of being, power, and knowing.[16] That is coloniality extends to all spheres of sociocultural reality and, therefore, strongly influences the worldviews of all social scientists and the institutions and processes that generate anthropological knowledge.[17]

This kind of reasoning spurred the aforementioned option of constructing the history of anthropology not as a sequence of theories or paradigms of North Atlantic origin with ramifications in the South, but as a three-stage sequence of the evolution of the global anthropological community. The stage was set in the second half of the nineteenth century, after a long process of incubation that dates back to the first encounters between Europe and the Americas. It eventually led to the constitution of that community of producers and reproducers of scientific anthropological knowledge whose members—almost all 'classically educated' urban white men—belonged to the North Atlantic civilization. The second stage emerged (in Latin America with some more distant antecedents) in the mid-twentieth century with the culmination of the political independence of most former African and Asian colonies and the growing incorporation of members and participants from countries

[16]On this issue see, for example, Lander (2000), Restrepo (2007), and Restrepo and Rojas (2010).

[17]Here we refer to the classical study of Ivan Illich (1973), one of the pioneers of this kind of civilizational criticism. Recently, Jafari Allen and Ryan Jobson have tried to identify a "decolonization generation – the cohort of Black, allied antiracist, feminist, and political economy-oriented scholars" (2016, 129), that gave rise to the landmark volume of Faye Harrison ([1991] 1997) on liberation anthropology. A few years before, Susan Almy had pointed out that what is understood in North America as academic freedom "is becoming known in the developing countries as 'academic imperialism'" (1977, 287).

in the South.[18] The third stage appears to be barely underway—the *other internals* of these countries are beginning to appropriate the cognitive instrument called 'anthropology' in order to, as we said above, recognize their own specific, local situations and explore from there more comprehensive social structures and cultural processes at the national and international levels.[19] Here we refer to those countries whose internally colonized members for decades served only as objects of anthropological studies conducted by scholars from national, central, or hegemonic cultures; we mean primarily members of indigenous peoples and communities and people of African descent who explicitly assume themselves as such. In this way, national anthropological communities re-discover the colonial character of generating anthropological knowledge, but now under the guise of internal colonialism. Recently, the Peruvian anthropologist Carlos Iván Degregori pointed out to the "hierarchical ladder of invisibilization and subalternation" within Latin American anthropological communities (2006, 464). This character, initially and at other times, has been misunderstood as some type of centralism, emblematically as indigenism, with the 'noble' aim of 'nation-building'. However, this internal colonial process reproduced and reproduces the same unilinear and teleological evolutionism as overseas colonialism. Recent discussions about '*Buen Vivir*' ('Good Living') in the Andean region and about communality in the Mesoamerican region imply strong criticisms of the social sciences and look for a different way of understanding life in society and human development (alternatives to development instead of alternative development).

Four interwoven strategies can be observed in attempts to respond to this challenge. The first strategy consists in reconstructing and reviewing the antecedents of the Latin American anthropologies themselves, a process that permits recognition of such complex interactions as those between endogenous and exogenous cognitive elements, between the spheres of cognition and power, and especially in the context of the

---

[18]We cannot examine here the later inclusion of anthropologies from the European Southern and Eastern periphery and of anthropologies of regions and cultures that are parts of nation-states, like Catalan anthropology in Spain or Scottish anthropology in Great Britain.

[19]The South American anthropologist Rita Segato (2015) has shown the obstacles for indigenous and black students in Brazilian universities.

beginnings of the third stage of global anthropology mentioned above, among different types of knowledge.[20]

A second key strategy entails comparisons of the multifaceted Latin American anthropologies themselves as second anthropologies. Here, current efforts to consolidate the still incipient Latin American Anthropological Association are significant. This organization could play a crucial role in introducing courses on other Latin American anthropologies for undergraduate and graduate programs where they are practically non-existent today. The Association could also promote study groups with members of different Latin American anthropological generations and national traditions.

A third strategy can be seen in current attempts to conduct, where possible, 'collaborative' forms of anthropological research, initiatives that have a long, but checkered, history in Latin America and are viable only in certain thematic areas and with certain social groups. As demonstrated recently, a three-volume edition by Xochitl Leyva and her colleagues (2015) is a markedly self-reflexive modality of anthropological research.[21] This modality has the capacity to generate interesting contributions to the understanding of anthropological knowledge production, often with explicit reference to non-scientific or pre-scientific forms of knowledge.

Finally, a fourth strategy consists in reviewing anthropological theory itself in an effort to explain the colonial situation and explore pathways that may lead to overcoming it. This approach does perceive the history of anthropology not as a sequence of anthropological paradigms, as textbooks and histories of anthropology usually do. Instead, it approaches the history of anthropology as a history of anthropological communities. In the South, these communities have their own roots and histories, but as parts of the international anthropological community, have always suffered the influences and pressures of the chronologically 'first' and now hegemonic anthropologies. So, as mentioned above, these Southern anthropological communities are under colonial pressure and, at the same time, establish colonial relations within their own national communities.

---

[20] The Mexican philosopher León Olivé (2009) has tried to establish the idea of real intercultural relations on the recognition of epistemic pluralism.

[21] In a certain sense forerunners of this kind of critique and the search for alternatives have been the Colombian sociologist-anthropologist Orlando Fals Borda (Fals Borda and Rahman 1991) and the Mexican anthropologist Rodolfo Stavenhagen (1971).

A related and interesting complementary perspective is offered by the theory of cultural control proposed by the Mexican anthropologist Guillermo Bonfil (1991). Originally elaborated as a theoretical framework for his well-known book on Mesoamerican civilization (Bonfil 1996), the concept of cultural control seems fruitful for the study of Latin American and other 'second' anthropologies, and for teaching these approaches as anthropologies in their own right as well.[22] In a clear and simple model Bonfil combines the traditional diffusionist focus with a theory of power that considers both direct domination and the construction of hegemonies, thus presenting a perspective that can be adopted by de(s)colonial studies in the sense indicated above.[23] A striking advantage of Bonfil's approach is that it not only allows us to distinguish between the exogenous and endogenous components of a national or regional anthropological theory and practice as well. His approach also implies options for using these components as a function of a given interest, in our case, that of generating anthropological knowledge that seeks to transform the existing unsatisfactory situation of society.

Two Final Comments

The multiplicity of names bestowed upon 'second' anthropologies and the range of approaches that seek to better understand and finally overcome the coloniality in which anthropology is ensconced in countries and cultures marked by colonial relations shows that elucidating the characteristics of these anthropologies and the possibilities of achieving emancipation is still very much an ongoing process. One particularly critical element of the colonial situation consists in the neoliberal transformation of the systems of scientific research and higher education, a process now underway in almost all Latin American countries. Significantly, one of the pioneering Latin American anticolonial thinkers and a founder of the concept of 'internal colonialism', Pablo González Casanova recently called our attention to the arrival of this 'new university' with its 'academic capitalism'. He perceives academia as just another aspect of the expansion of neoliberalism as a way of life throughout the

[22] On this issue see also Giglia and Krotz (2011) and Krotz (2017).

[23] Accordingly, Isabel Castro Henriques states correctly that colonization means always "the elimination of the autonomy of the colonized" (2014, 49).

world (2000, 2006; see also Palermo 2002; Krotz 2011).[24] This is why the study of academic institutions and public policies, not to mention the related collective imaginaries, has gained such importance in terms of recognizing the debts that currently weigh upon anthropology, and the cognitive potential that the discipline could develop.

Johan Galtung has asserted that "who pays the piper, tends to call the tune" (2002, 85). Thus, the 'epistemological violence' (Polo Blanco 2016) constitutes a strategic element of coloniality. And therefore it is interesting that an early contribution to a decolonized Latin American social science was precisely the conflict about a supposedly universal dictionary of social science in the 1960s and 70s, and the different positions of Spanish and of Latin America social scientists.[25] Seen from today, this debate can be understood as the beginning of a process of consciousness-raising which is now, in the midst of capitalist globalization, constructing alternative perspective on worldwide coloniality and showing ways out, that will not only benefit social science in the South, but social sciences in general.

In conclusion, it seems pertinent to reconsider the affirmation presented at the outset regarding the influence of the colonial situation on both those who benefit from it, and so strive to prolong it, and those who have recognized its distorting effects, and so seek to break it down. Responsibility for studying the colonial relations that affect the production of anthropological knowledge in the South corresponds not only to the anthropologies of the South. They are, on the one hand, an integral part of a global, but essentially diverse anthropology[26] whose potential

---

[24]Edmundo Gordon in a recent study on Nicaragua explains the situation as follows: "The social purpose of education is to discipline and train the citizenry. To train them to play the role of local citizens and workers, and to occupy the positions assigned to them in the society. This is highly problematic when the society operates under unequal conditions. In these cases, the majority, education tends to reproduce this inequality. The powers control knowledge and, with this, society" (2013, 6). The educational system has also been criticized from an African perspective as alienating and even as an important driving force behind emigration to Europe; see Kinhoun (2016).

[25]Here we refer to the publication by the Grupo de Trabajo de Desarrollo Cultural (1976) which from its beginnings has tried to 'latinamericanize' the social sciences of the Southern part of the Americas. The history of this dictionary has been reconstructed recently by Bayle and Morales (2018).

[26]This means, they are also 'world anthropologies', but 'within systems of power' (Ribeiro and Escobar 2006) which makes the recognition of anthropology's heterogeneity still difficult; see Krotz (2012, 30) and Clarac de Briceño et al. (2016).

is constrained by the fact that it maintains colonial relations in its interior. On the other hand, the exposure of the colonial situation that still exists *in* the South can be transformed into the discovery of a colonial situation that comes *from* the South, and thus provides key elements for the understanding of a multifaceted global anthropology, including the anthropologies of the North as well. It was in this sense that Jean and John Comaroff noted from an African perspective that the anthropologies of the South "are rich sites of new knowledge and ways of knowing-and-being, ways of knowing-and-being that have the capacity to inform and transform theory in the North, to subvert its universalisms in order to rewrite them in a different, less provincial register" (2013, 20).

REFERENCES

Adas, Michael. 1989. *Machines as the Measure of Men: Science, Technology, and Ideologies of Western Dominance*. Ithaca: Cornell University Press.

Allen, Jafari Sinclaire, and Ryan Cecil Jobson. 2016. "The Decolonizing Generation: (Race and) Theory in Anthropology Since the Eighties." *Current Anthropology* 57(2): 126–48.

Almy, Susan W. 1977. "Anthropologists and Development Agencies." *American Anthropologist* 79(2): 280–92.

Bayle, Paola Adriana, and Juan Jesús Morales. 2018. "Itinerario del Diccionario de Ciencias Sociales en español (UNESCO, 1952–1976)." *Revista Mexicana de Sociología* 80(1): 167–93.

Bhattacharya, Asoke. 2011. *Paulo Freire: Rousseau of the Twentieth Century*. Rotterdam: Sense Publishers.

Boivin, Mauricio, Ana Rosato, and Victoria Arribas. (1998) 2004. *Constructores de otredad: una introducción a la antropología social y cultural*. Buenos Aires: Antropofagia.

Bonfil, Guillermo. 1991. "La teoría del control cultural en el estudio de procesos étnicos." *Estudios sobre las Culturas Contemporáneas* IV(12): 165–204.

Bonfil, Guillermo. 1996. *México profundo: Reclaiming a Civilization*. Austin: University of Texas Press.

Cardoso de Oliveira, Roberto. 1999–2000. "Peripheral Anthropologies 'Versus' Central Anthropologies." *Journal of Latin American Anthropology* 4(2)–5(1): 10–30.

Cardoso de Oliveira, Roberto, and Guilhermo Raul Ruben, eds. 1995. *Estilos de antropologia*. Campinas: Editora da Unicamp.

Castro Henriques, Isabel. 2014. "Colonia, colonização, Colonial, Colonialism." In *Diccionário crítico das ciências sociais dos países de fala oficial portuguesa*, edited by Livio Sansone and Cláudio Alves Furtado, 45–58. Salvador: EDUFBA.

Chilungu, Simeon W. 1984. "Alternative Ethnologie aus der Dritten Welt." In *Ethnologie als Sozialwissenschaft* (Kölner Zeitschrift für Soziologie und Sozialpsychologie, Sonderheft 26), edited by Ernst Wilhelm Müller, René König, Klaus-Peter Koepping, and Paul Drechsel, 314–38. Opladen: Westdeutscher Verlag.

Clarac de Briceño, Jacqueline, Annel del Mar Mejías Guiza, and Albarrán Yanitza Lolaneyra. 2016. "Las Antropologías del Sur como principio para la decolonización del pensamiento." *Boletín Antropológico* 34(92): 147–63.

Comaroff, Jean, and John L. Comaroff. 2013. "Writing Theory from the South: The Global Order from an African Perspective." *The World Financial Review*, November 13, 2013. http://www.worldfinancialreview.com/?p=543. Accessed September 6, 2018.

Coronil, Fernando. 2004. "Latin American Postcolonial Studies and Global Decolonization." In *The Cambridge Companion to Postcolonial Literary Studies*, edited by Neil Lazarus, 221–40. Cambridge: Cambridge University Press.

Degregori, Carlos Iván. 2006. "Responses to 'Other Anthropologies and Anthropology Otherwise: Steps to a World Anthropologies Framework' by Eduardo Restrepo and Arturo Escobar (June, 2005)." *Critique of Anthropology* 26(4): 463–88.

Degregori, Carlos Iván, and Pablo Sandoval. 2008. "Presentación." In *Saberes periféricos: ensayos sobre la antropología en América Latina*, edited by Carlos Iván Degregori and Pablo Sandoval, 9–17. Lima: Instituto de Estudios Peruanos.

Dos Santos, Theotonio. 2007. *Del terror a la esperanza: auge y decadencia del neoliberalismo*. Caracas: Monte Ávila.

Dussel, Enrique. 1993. "Eurocentrism and Modernity (Introduction to the Frankfurt Lectures)." *Boundary 2* 20(3): 65–76.

Escobar, Arturo. [1995] 2011. *Encountering Development: The Making and Unmaking of the Third World*. Princeton: Princeton University Press.

Escobar, Arturo. 2004. "Beyond the Third World: Imperial Globality, Global Coloniality and Anti-globalisation Social Movements." *Third World Quarterly* 25(1): 207–30.

Escobar, Arturo. 2013. "Afterword." In *Globalization and the Decolonial Option*, edited by Walter Mignolo and Arturo Escobar, 391–99. London: Routledge.

Esteva, Gustavo. [1992] 2010. "Development." In *The Development Dictionary*, edited by Wolfgang Sachs, 1–23. London: Zed Books.

Fals Borda, Orlando, and Muhammad Anisur Rahman, eds. 1991. *Action and Knowledge: Breaking the Monopoly with Participatory Action-Resarch*. New York: Apex.

Galtung, Johan. 2002. "Western Deep Culture and Western Historical Thinking." In *Western Historical Thinking: An Intercultural Debate*, edited by Jörn Rüsen, 85–100. New York: Berghahn.

Giglia, Angela, and Esteban Krotz, eds. 2011. "Antropologías latinoamericanas II: la enseñanza de la antropología 'propia' en América Latina." *Alteridades* 21(41): 9–96.

González Casanova, Pablo. 2000. "La nueva Universidad." Centro de Investigaciones Interdisciplinarias en Ciencias y Humanidades – Universidad Nacional Autónoma de México, July 2000. http://www.ceiich.unam.mx/educacion/casanova.htm. Accessed September 6, 2018.

González Casanova, Pablo. 2006. "Colonialismo interno: una redefinición." In *La teoría marxista hoy: problemas y perspectivas*, edited by Atilio A. Boron, Javier Amadeo, and Sabrina González, 409–34. Buenos Aires: Consejo Latinoamericano de Ciencias Sociales.

Gordon, Edmundo. 2013. "Educación Superior y la lucha para el bienestar colectivo." In *Revista Caribe* 10(1): 6–7.

Grupo de Trabajo de Desarrollo Cultural. 1976. *Términos latinoamericanos para el Diccionario de Ciencias Sociales*. Buenos Aires: Consejo Latinoamericano de Ciencias Sociales.

Gutiérrez, Gustavo. 1988. *A Theology of Liberation: History, Politics, and Salvation* (15th Anniversary Edition with New Introduction by the Author). New York: Orbis Books.

Harrison, Faye V., ed. [1991] 1997. *Decolonizing Anthropology: Moving Further Toward an Anthropology for Liberation*. Arlington: American Anthropological Association.

Hartch, Todd. 2015. *The Prophet of Cuernavaca: Ivan Illich and the Crisis of the West*. Oxford: Oxford University Press.

Illich, Ivan. 1973. *Tools for Conviviality*. New York: Harper & Row.

Jimeno Santoyo, Myriam. 2000. "La emergencia del investigador ciudadano: estilos de antropología y crisis de modelos en la antropología colombiana." In *La formación del estado nación y las disciplinas sociales en Colombia*, edited by Jairo Tocancipá, 157–90. Popayán: Universidad del Cauca.

Kinhoun, Epiphane. 2016. "Zur Frage der Flucht von Afrika über das Mittelmeer: Eine afrikanische Perspektive." Herder Verlag: *Stimmen der Zeit*, 1.3.2016. https://www.herder.de/stz/online/zur-frage-der-flucht-von-afrika-ueber-das-mittelmeer-eine-afrikanische-perspektive/. Accessed September 6, 2018.

Krotz, Esteban. 1997. "Anthropologies of the South: Their Rise, Their Silencing, Their Characteristics." *Critique of Anthropology* 17(3): 237–51.

Krotz, Esteban. 2008. "Antropologías segundas: enfoques para su estudio." In *Presencia de José Lameiras en la antropología mexicana*, edited by José Eduardo Zárate, 41–52. Zamora: El Colegio de Michoacán.

Krotz, Esteban. 2011. "Las ciencias sociales frente al 'Triángulo de las Bermudas': una hipótesis sobre las transformaciones recientes de la investigación científica y la educación superior en México." *Revista de El Colegio de San Luis* 1: 19–46.

Krotz, Esteban. 2012. "Visibilization of the Anthropologies of the South." *Anthropology News* 53(7): 30.

Krotz, Esteban. 2017. "Ejercer el control cultural: relaciones disciplinarias 'interculturales' en la formación antropológica." In *Antropologías en América Latina: prácticas, alcances y retos*, edited by Jairo Tocancipá-Falla, 37–54. Popayán: Universidad del Cauca.

Lander, Edgardo. 2000. "Ciencias sociales: saberes coloniales y eurocéntricos." In *La colonialidad del saber: eurocentrismo y ciencias sociales. Perspectivas Latinoamericanas*, edited by Edgardo Lander and Santiago Castro-Gómez, 11–40. Buenos Aires: Consejo Latinoamericano de Ciencias Sociales.

Leyva, Xochitl, et al. 2015. *Prácticas otras de conocimiento(s): entre crisis, entre guerras*. 3 vols. San Cristóbal de las Casas: Cooperativa Editorial Retos.

McLaren, Peter, and Peter Leonard, eds. 1993. *Paulo Freire: A Critical Encounter*. New York: Routledge.

Mendizábal, Sergio, ed. 2007. *El encantamiento de la realidad: conocimientos mayas en prácticas sociales de la vida cotidiana*. Guatemala-City: Universidad Rafael Landívar.

Mott, Luiz R.B. 1982. "Indigenous Anthropology and Brazilian Indians." In *Indigenous Anthropology in Non-Western Countries*, edited by Hussein Fahim, 112–17. Durham: Carolina Academic Press.

Olivé, León. 2009. "Por una auténtica interculturalidad basada en el reconocimiento de la pluralidad epistemológica." In *Pluralismo epistemológico*, edited by Luís Tapia Mealla, 19–30. La Paz: Muela del Diablo Editores.

Palerm, Ángel. [1974] 2006. *Historia de la etnología: los precursores*. Mexico City: Universidad Iberoamericana.

Palermo, Zulma. 2002. "Políticas del mercado/políticas académicas: crisis y desafíos en la periferia." In *Indisciplinar las ciencias sociales: geopolíticas del conocimiento y colonialidad del poder*, edited by Catherine Walsh, Freya Schiwy, and Santiago Castro-Gómez, 157–74. Quito: Universidad Andina Simón Bolívar/Abya Yala.

Pels, Peter. 1997. "The Anthropology of Colonialism: Culture, History, and the Emergence of Western Governmentality." *Annual Review of Anthropology* 26: 163–83.

Polo Blanco, Jorge. 2016. "Colonialidad del poder y violencia epistémica en América Latina." *Revista Latina de Sociología* 6(1): 27–44.

Quijano, Aníbal, ed. 2014. *Des/colonialidad y bien vivir: un nuevo debate en América Latina*. Lima: Universidad Ricardo Palma.

Restrepo, Eduardo. 2007. "Antropología y colonialidad." In *El giro decolonial*, edited by Santiago Castro-Gómez and Ramón Grosfoguel, 289–303. Bogotá: Siglo del Hombre Editores.

Restrepo, Eduardo, and Axel Rojas. 2010. *Inflexión decolonial: fuentes, conceptos y cuestionamientos*. Popayán: Universidad del Cauca.

Ribeiro, Darcy. 1979. "Die Indianer und wir." In *Unterentwicklung, Kultur und Zivilisation: ungewöhnliche Versuche*, edited by Darcy Ribeiro, 255–312. Frankfurt am Main: Suhrkamp.

Ribeiro, Gustavo Lins, and Arturo Escobar. 2006. "World Anthropologies: Disciplinary Transformations within Systems of Power." In *World Anthropologies: Disciplinary Transformations Within Systems of Power*, edited by Gustavo Lins Ribeiro and Arturo Escobar, 1–25. Oxford: Berg.

Sachs, Wolfgang. [1992] 2010. "Introduction". In *The Development Dictionary*, edited by Wolfgang Sachs, XV–XX. London: Zed Books.

Sader, Emir, and Theotonio Dos Santos, eds. 2009. *A América Latina e os desafios da globalização: ensaios em homenagem a Ruy Mauro Marini*. Rio de Janeiro: Pontifícia Universidade Católica do Rio de Janeiro.

Santos, Boaventura de Sousa. 2011. "Introducción: Las epistemologías del Sur." In *Formas-Otras: saber, nombrar, narrar, hacer*, edited by Alvise Vianello and Bet Mañé, 9–22. Barcelona: Centro de Estudios y Documentación Internacionales de Barcelona.

Scott, David. 2001. "Colonialism, Anthropology of." In *International Encyclopedia of the Social and Behavioral Sciences*, edited by Neil J. Smelser and Paul B. Baltes, 2232–37. Oxford: Pergamon.

Segato, Rita. 2015. "Brechas decoloniales para una universidad nuestroamericana." In *La lucha contra la decolonialidad en ocho ensayos y una antropología a demanda*, edited by Rita Segato, 267–93. Buenos Aires: Prometeo.

Stavenhagen, Rodolfo. (1971). "Decolonizing Applied Social Sciences." *Human Organization* 30(4): 333–44.

Trouillot, Michel-Rolph. 2002. "The Otherwise Modern: Caribbean Lessons from the Savage Slot." In *Critical Modern: Alternatives, Alterities, Anthropologies*, edited by Bruce M. Knauft, 220–37. Bloomington: Indiana University Press.

Velho, Otávio. 2006. "The Pictographics of *Tristesse*: An Anthropology of Nation Building in the Tropics and Its Aftermath." In *World Anthropologies: Disciplinary Transformations Within Systems of Power*, edited by Gustavo Lins Ribeiro and Arturo Escobar, 261–79. Oxford: Berg.

Veronelli, Gabriela. 2015. "Sobre la colonialidad del lenguaje." *Universitas Humanística* 81: 33–58.

Villoro, Luis. [1950] 1998. *Los grandes momentos del indigenismo mexicano*. Mexico City: Fondo de Cultura Económica.

Wallerstein, Immanuel. 2006. *European Universalism: The Rhetoric of Power*. New York: The New Press.

Walsh, Catherine. 2009. *Interculturalidad, Estado, Sociedad. Luchas (de)coloniales de nuestra época*. Quito: Universidad Andina Simón Bolívar/Abya-Yala.

CHAPTER 4

Native Americans and Colonialism in the Longue Durée: Dancing with Incorporation

Ingo W. Schröder

INTRODUCTION

The chapter sketches a genealogy of Marxist approaches to the colonization of North American Indigenous peoples.[1] Focusing on concepts like incorporation, accumulation, and hegemony, it outlines some of the building blocks of a historical-materialist reading of North American colonial history to the present. From this point of view, colonialism refers to the introduction of a mercantile-capitalist economy, its logics, and the integration of formerly non-capitalist populations into a capitalist world-system that began with Euromerican invasion and extends to the settler colonialism of the present day. Changes in other societal realms can most likely be explained with regard to their relation to political-economic factors. John Moore notes:

---

[1] The terms Indigenous and Native American are used interchangeably in this chapter.

I. W. Schröder (✉)
Department of Cultural and Social Anthropology,
Philipps University of Marburg, Marburg, Germany

© The Author(s) 2019
D. Schorkowitz et al. (eds.), *Shifting Forms of Continental Colonialism*,
https://doi.org/10.1007/978-981-13-9817-9_4

Native American history is best understood not as a *cultural* conflict between Indians and European invaders, but as an *economic* conflict between precapitalist or communal modes of production and capitalist modes. That is, the important fact about the invasion of North America is not so much that the invaders were European foreigners, but that they were *capitalist* foreigners. It was the capitalist mode of production which determined the form of the conflict, not religion, culture, or ethnicity. (Moore 1993a, 15, emphasis in the original)

Although rarely close to the mainstream, Marxist approaches have a long history in the anthropological study of North American Indigenous societies (cf. Rose 2017). Leaving aside Lewis Henry Morgan's influence on the work of Marx and Engels (cf. Krader 1972), a first wave of scholarly studies inspired by historical materialism emerged in the 1940s and 1950s. The most influential scholar of that generation was Eleanor Leacock who studied the colonial transformation of Innu society (called Montagnais-Naskapi in her time) regarding the mode of production and gender relations (cf. Leacock 1954). A second wave, which saw a fast proliferation of research, was inspired by the Marxist turn in anthropology of the 1960s and 1970s and is represented by scholars like Patricia Albers, Richard Clemmer, Joseph Jorgensen, and John Moore. All studies from this period share a focus on the political economy of the colonial reorganization of Native American societies. The Marxist ethnohistorian's task in the study of Native American colonization has been laid out by Patricia Albers:

One of the many conundrums of modern scholarship in American Indian history is how do we get construction and condition, agency and cause, the subject and its object, to properly dance with each other without overstepping the movement of the other. How do we write histories of American Indian labor, as an example, that simultaneously give expression to the voices and memories of the workers and the forces and events surrounding their work? (2002, 107–8)

This critical reflection on the possibilities of a political-economic approach to colonialism in North America points the way to approach the transition from a "kin-ordered mode of production" (Wolf 1982, 91) to a capitalist mode of production from an anthropological perspective, acknowledging that during the colonial process, the social and the material orders of Native American societies "have coevolved historically and changed in tandem with the contradictions their relationship inevitably provokes" (Albers 2002, 111).

On the following pages I will discuss the various dimensions of the colonial restructuring of Native American societies. With the shift from overseas to continental colonialism through U. S. and Canadian independence in the eighteenth and nineteenth centuries, the pressure of political-economic transformation on Indigenous societies increased significantly, especially in terms of the colonial-capitalist nexus and the accelerated appropriation of Native lands.

ON INCORPORATION

Since the 1970s, the dominant concept employed by Marxist anthropologists in analyzing the transition of Native American societies to a capitalist mode of production is that of incorporation. The idea of incorporation is grounded on the same foundations as the modernization, dependency, and world-systems theories that dominated social-scientific approaches to the "Third World" at the time. They describe the expansion of developed states into underdeveloped regions. This description is undertaken mostly in economic terms with reference to incorporation into a colonial and later global marketplace. The degree of incorporation may range from weak to strong, from areas either outside or at the edge of the world economy, to areas shaped by a flow of influence directed primarily from core to periphery; the degree may range from that pole of the continuum where essential goods are exchanged to the peripheral area, while still underdeveloped, that provides an important flow of product and capital to the core. Local changes in social and economic relations depend on the degree to which an area is incorporated into the world system.

The classical anthropological study of Native American incorporation from a world-systems perspective is Thomas Hall's *Social Change in the Southwest, 1350–1880* (1989). While Hall's theoretical analysis is new, the comparative approach to colonialism in the Southwest had already been pioneered by Edward Spicer (1962). Hall studies the impact of four consecutive state systems on the local people of the Southwest (the Mesoamerican states, Spain, Mexico, and the United States) with the effects of incorporation becoming steadily stronger with each succeeding state. He concludes that the level of sociopolitical development of the incorporated groups played an important role in the incorporation process and that the effects also varied from sedentary (e.g. Pueblo, Pima, or Yaqui) to mobile groups (e.g. Navajo and Apache).

Standard formulations of incorporation theory have been criticized for being too static in their division of core and periphery, for paying too little attention to local agency, and finally for focusing exclusively on the past. These formulations mostly view incorporation as a finished process. The standard understanding of incorporation was clearly influenced by Marx's concept of 'primitive accumulation,' a historical phase that preceded capitalist accumulation. Thus, primitive accumulation remained in the past, a mere stepping-stone to world-economic participation, especially in terms of wage labor. From this point of view, the incorporation of Native American societies into the U.S. capitalist system appears as a process completed at a certain point as indicated by Hall's choice to limit his study to the period before 1880. Steps toward a more complex and more dialectical understanding of the process of incorporation were undertaken, for example, in the studies by Wilma Dunaway on the Cherokee (1996) and Melissa Meyer on the Anishinaabeg in Minnesota (1994). These studies put greater emphasis on indigenous agency, either in terms of resistance (i.e. preventing the achievement of complete incorporation or colonial control) or of active collaboration of individual Native American brokers who saw capitalist expansion as an opportunity for their own advancement. However, these studies still agreed in consigning incorporation to the past, as having ended around the turn of the twentieth century.

Taking the cue from post-Marxian readings of primitive accumulation—most notably Rosa Luxemburg's concept of *Landnahme* as a continuing process of capitalist encroachment into not-yet-capitalist realms, an incessant transition between non-capitalist and capitalist conditions (Luxemburg [1913] 2003)—one may now ask what is the contemporary dimension of incorporation? David Harvey (2004, 2005) has taken the notion of primitive accumulation beyond its original focus on the expansion of wage labor and the appropriation of resources, to analyze the key features of neoliberal capitalism. He introduced the concept of 'accumulation by dispossession,' which "entails the loss of rights, dignity, sustainable ecological practices, environmental rights, and the life, as the basis for a unified oppositional politics" (2005, 178). Such shifts occur through the four processes of privatization, financialization, management and manipulation of crisis, and state redistributions. These processes include elements such as the commodification of land, the conversion of other common or state property rights into private property rights, the seizure of natural resources through neocolonial processes, national debt and crisis as radical means of primitive accumulation, and the abolition or reduction of pensions, free education, or health care.

A first wave of capitalist incorporation was the fur trade (cf. Hickerson 1973). While the fur trade was a (for North America) rather atypical form of accumulation insofar as it relied primarily on the exploitation of indigenous labor by integrating Indigenous societies into a network of market relations and economic dependencies, it paved the way for later versions of colonial accumulation, all of which centered on the acquisition of indigenous land and resources. A first systematic step toward the contemporary dimension of incorporation appeared in Joseph Jorgensen's influential article "A Century of Political Economic Effects on American Indian Society, 1880–1980" (Jorgensen 1978). Proceeding from the idea that contemporary Native American societies cannot be understood without regard to the political-economic forces that have shaped them, Jorgensen focuses on the concept of "domestic dependency," a specific form of domination both political and economic at the same time. As the time frame of his study suggests, rather than viewing the nationwide establishment of the reservation system as the final step in the incorporation process, Jorgensen assumes that the condition of domestic dependency has actually intensified since the creation of reservations and persists to the present day. In this system, individual economic success is possible, if unlikely while tribal group successes are highly improbable (1978, 6). Jorgensen illustrates his argument with a historical survey of the "political economy of Indian affairs" (1978, 9) and sees contemporary agribusiness and energy development as the most recent guise of political-economic domination over Native American tribes.

Jorgensen's study had already been preceded by an article by Robert Bee and Ronald Gingerich (1977) in which the authors draw inspiration from debates on colonialism in Latin America (cf. Stavenhagen 1965) advancing the important distinction between the expropriation of natural resources through colonialism (reservation populations) and class formation through the appropriation of labor resources (urban Indigenous populations). They were the first to use the term 'internal colonialism' with regard to Native American societies, which gained wider currency among students of Indigenous political economy in the 1980s. The concept was popularized by sociologists Cardell Jacobsen (1984) and

C. Matthew Snipp. The latter suggested replacing the notion of "captive nations" with that of "internal colonies" (1986). Snipp observed that reservations had become increasingly colonial structures under the impact of recent resource exploitation, with the 'metropolis' appropriating the surplus of the 'satellite' as in other understandings of internal colonialism. Snipp also points to the interplay of private enterprise and state action in the process of the exploitation and manipulation of indigenous groups and their land. He specifically refers to the *Severalty Act (Dawes Act)* of 1887, which divided and privatized much of reservation land into 160-acre parcels, the *Tribal Leasing Act* of 1938, which authorized the U.S. Government to lease Native American mineral rights to corporations, and most prominently the *House Concurrent Resolution 108* of 1953, which initiated the Termination policy that proclaimed to end the wardship status of American Indians and robbed them of altogether 2.4 million acres of land. Notions of incorporation that rely on theoretical frameworks based on World-Systems Theory continue in more recent studies of Indigenous colonization (cf. Fenelon 1997; Hormel and Norgaard 2009) or development theory (cf. McDonald 1994; Wilkins 1993). In a recent reexamination of the incorporation concept, Caleb Bush states:

> In wanting to examine critically the process of incorporation, I argue for a fundamental reconsideration of the idea. Rather than relinquished to the past and complete, the process must be seen as ongoing and uneven. To understand world-economic expansion, the historical disconnect that has been constructed between past and present–incorporation and internal colonialism, respectively–must be torn asunder. (2005, 99)

Following Rosa Luxemburg, Bush reminds us that capital accumulation relies on the aid of non-capitalist organizations but, at the same time, it seeks to destroy them. "Disenfranchised regions" (2005, 100), such as Native American reservations, show the broken and unbalanced nature of the expansion of the capitalist world-economy and mark uneven trajectories of incorporation. The capitalist expansion onto Native American land continues today; exploitation and corporate encroachment have even increased, especially in terms of mineral leases for the mining of coal, uranium, diamonds, or bituminous sands. Such cases, however, also highlight the possibly uneven nature of incorporation. In his study of the Hopi-Navajo land dispute, Bush (2014) shows how the relocation of Hopi and Navajo people to make space for Peabody Coal's expansion of its mining activities on the Black Mesa area have revealed cleavages between tribal elites who sought to profit from the commodification of reservation land and those tribal members affected by relocation who resisted and held fast to traditional livelihoods (cf. Benedek 1999; Brugge 1994).

Aside from the proponents of the incorporation concepts, further studies have built upon other aspects of Marxist political economy by exploring changes in Indigenous organization, health, social relations and practices, and household economies in response to the introduction of the capitalist economy (cf. Moore 1993b) and the exploitation of Indigenous labor (cf. Knight 1978; Littlefield and Knack 1996).

NATIVE AGENCY, ADAPTATION, AND COLLUSION

Proponents of the concepts of incorporation and internal colonialism have been criticized for overemphasizing the goals and strategies of the colonizing and capitalist agents at the expense of the agency of the colonized. But this is, however, not quite correct, since most of these studies stress that capitalist incorporation has been a long, uneven process in which complete control over the periphery was only rarely effected. The assertion of a dominant colonial-capitalist logic precluded neither the use of the advantages of capitalist production by indigenous actors with their own agendas, nor the continuing relevance of pre-colonial social relationships and cultural ideas. It is true, however, that Indigenous agency remains comparatively undertheorized in World-Systems Theory. The latter tends to pay insufficient attention to the local appropriation of the conditions of capitalist expansion and notions of Indigenous identity and group membership that evolved at the intersection of trajectories of incorporation, appropriation, and refusal.

One concept that has the potential to link ideas of indigenous agency with the notion of incorporation is 'neo-tribal capitalism' (cf. Rose 2015; Schröder 2003). The term was coined by New Zealand sociologist Elizabeth Rata on the basis of her critical investigation of the social, political, and economic transformations of Maori communities. Rata describes the promotion of a 'neotraditionalist ideology' by the emergent tribal elite in brokerage with the government as a rhetorical strategy of legitimizing the creation of local capitalist economic structures, class formation, and the exclusion of the majority of tribal members from the full benefits that accrue on the basis of the tribal status. Such an ideology constructs a link between contemporary political relations within the tribe and an unbroken cultural heritage from pre-colonial times. In Rata's own words, neo-tribal capitalism describes "the articulation of exploitative class social relations of production within a social formation structured by a capitalist regime of accumulation" (2000, 33).

In recent decades federal policy in the United States has promoted self-determination in terms of a 'Westernization' of Native American societies played out through an increased statism in Indian Country (in terms of growing bureaucracies, professional law enforcement, and written legal codes), the reorganization of indigenous political systems as liberal representative governments, and the embracing of capitalism (in terms of tribally owned businesses, the leasing of resources for extraction by outside companies, and policies that promote the proletarization of indigenous people). The self-determination ethos that speaks from such processes can be understood as an American version of the neo-traditionalist ideology observed by Rata in New Zealand. Since the early 1970s, with stable support for tribal self-determination by U.S. administrations, and even more since the rise of neoliberalism in the 1980s, neo-tribal capitalism has become all but hegemonic in the field of Native American political economy. Samuel Rose summarizes its key features as follows:

> Accomplished and implemented through a brokerage process with settler-colonial governments, the reorganization of indigenous political economies along the lines of business corporations (and in North America also including capitalist governments resembling small liberal republics) provided indigenous peoples with a bulwark against dispossession by outside forces, However, it accomplished this through internal dispossession: It provided indigenous elites with the structural means to dispossess their own people from independent access to collective resources. It functionally dispossessed people from what they still nominally own. (2017, 26)

Neo-traditionalist ideology has been cemented by the rules of the federal recognition process, when the American state as the ultimate arbiter of indigenous identity controls which tribes are recognized and granted access to the legal, political, and economic benefits that come with tribal status. Moreover, neo-traditionalist notions of legitimacy and authenticity are apparent in the redefinition of tribal membership criteria by tribal governments, which usually means the tightening of requirements concerning the degree of blood purity as a prerequisite for tribal citizenship. Such redefinitions may be prompted by the distribution of revenue generated by tribally operated casinos, but may also occur within tribes that do not own casinos. The most widely publicized case of this kind was the disenrollment of the so-called Cherokee Freedmen (descendants of former Black slaves) from the Cherokee Nation of Oklahoma (cf. Sturm 2014). Tribal citizenship, which only recently has received increased attention from anthropologists (cf. Dennison 2012, 2014; Doerfler 2015; Sturm 2002, 2010), is a highly complex and locally contingent issue that cannot be discussed in detail here as there are numerous specific explanations for the various strategies pursued in each case. What is important, however, is that neo-tribal capitalism and its neo-traditionalist ideological legitimization represent an important element in the hegemonic discourse of Native American sovereignty which includes references to economic concepts as well as ideas related to the notion of culture.

Hegemony, in terms of William Roseberry's often-cited description, sustains "a common framework for living through, talking about, and acting on social orders characterized by domination" (1994, 361). As with hegemony in general (cf. Crehan 2002), neo-tribal capitalism not only represents the forceful imposition of a colonial model of governance and mode of thought with the colonized's acquiescence, but persists through the active, willing participation of Native American themselves. In the words of Samuel Rose,

> In practice, defenses of 'tribal sovereignty' are little more than the advocacy for and defense of neotribal power, and function to eliminate not simple criticism of neotribal governments but even discussions of alternatives. The same is true of discussions of identity and citizenship. Emphasis on 'bloodedness', authenticity, and a return to 'traditionalism' and community as natural and apolitical categories conceals the power and class relations behind them. (2015, 234)

Culture and the "identity industry" (Mason 2002, 13) have become key elements of the contemporary idiom of indigenous identities—and thus of the tribal elite's legitimizing discourse in the increasingly class-divided Native American tribes of today. As the study of Native American colonization shows, culture is by no means simply the ideational abstraction of Indigenous people's life worlds, but a highly contested and deeply controversial concept inseparable from the political context at the time of its deployment. Such observations appear most notably in Gerald Sider's long-term participant study of the Lumbees' struggle for tribal recognition. As he notes, culture is a product of colonial politics and their hegemonic rationalization. It was created and remodeled along with specific forms of social organization ('tribes') in the course of colonial incorporation but has also been sustained by indigenous elites' reproduction of such organizing narratives.

> The very same historical processes that made the context for a culture, melding together and separating increasingly distinct peoples in the colonial cauldron, also made the most pervasive and fundamental political-economic inequalities. Thus the production of culture turns out to also be the production of class – particularly as we come to see the production of class in far broader terms than those to which we have been accustomed. (2006, 278)

Such colonial creation of Native American societies obviously served first and foremost the colonizers' interest, but to a certain degree—even in the times of colonial expansion—also that of the Native peoples. "There were rewards as well for at least some of the native peoples who, while they could maneuver and negotiate between the diverse and incompatible demands upon them, had to collude with one or other kinds of use even to resist" (ibid., 280).

The social and cultural production of Native American peoples, today as in colonial times, has substantially exacerbated inequalities both within and between Indigenous societies (ibid., 282). Thus Sider points out that throughout the ongoing history of colonial domination Native American societies have been changing, on the one hand, in accordance with the imperatives of colonial accumulation, but on the other through the reproduction of a hegemonic model of social and economic relations on local terms. To quote Sider one final time,

> not only does the state produce, or intensify, inequalities–through differential education, legal protection, neighborhood services, and political representation–but the victims of these inequalities themselves often become, to a significant (if far from total) extent, active in maintaining and supporting the very state that produces and maintains their inequality. (2003, xliii)

In a similar vein, Kirk Dombrowski has investigated the contested nature of culture as the hallmark of indigenous identity among the Tlingit at the intersection of everyday experience, political-economic claims in the aftermath of the *Alaska Native Claims Settlement Act*, and the spread of Pentecostal Christianity. Culture, Dombrowski stresses, rather than being a historic collective property of Native American tribes, has been produced, affirmed, or rejected (as by Pentecostal Tlingits) in the context of political-economic opportunities. He notes, "Important social divisions exist within every group—divisions of class, age, gender, or ethnicity—and these divisions make culture or "local meaning" an issue for struggle, not something unconsciously accepted among those in a particular locality" (2001, 184).

COLONIAL CONTINUITIES AND CONTEMPORARY RESISTANCE

As sketched above, North American Indigenous societies have been entangled for centuries in a colonial situation that has altered its appearance, but never changed its fundamental goal of capitalist expansion and sociopolitical assimilation. Colonialism has mainly operated through three mechanisms: first, Indigenous societies were remade as the periphery of global capitalism by means of their economic incorporation into the colonial marketplace, the appropriation of indigenous land and labor, and the adoption of capitalist economic reasoning by Native American tribes. The most spectacular step in the direction of capitalist development arose through the revenues from tribally owned casinos (cf. Cattelino 2008; Darian-Smith 2003). Historical trajectories of the local adoption of capitalism are less well researched—several detailed studies exist only in the case of the Navajo Nation (cf. Chamberlain 2000; Francisconi [1998] 2011; Gilbreath 1973; O'Neill 2005). In recent decades, the most pressing issue of ecological colonization concerns energy development, resource exploitation, and the dumping of nuclear waste on tribal lands (cf. Fixico 1998; Grinde and Johansen 1994; LaDuke 1983; Smith and Frehner 2010).

Second, colonialism has substantially restructured Native American social relations and organizational forms. This strategy has, on the one hand, effected the separation of an increasing number of Native Americans from their land base and their incorporation into the reserve army of low-wage labor through relocation programs that have instigated a long-term shift of indigenous populations to the cities (cf. Fixico 2000). On the other hand, local inequalities have worsened as local Native bourgeoisies have appeared (cf. Mason 2002) and the local maintenance of egalitarianism has eroded. For centuries, colonialism has undermined local ways of social reproduction and processes of local anarchist resilience that used to establish clear limits for the accumulation of political and economic power in many Indigenous communities (cf. Angelbeck and Grier 2012). Finally, the promotion of the hegemonic regime of cultural sovereignty under the conditions of neo-tribal capitalism has made Native Americans accessories to their own colonization and served to depoliticize inequality and exploitation.

Since the 1980s, colonialism in Canada and the United States has shifted to a neoliberal frame of domination. Its features include the increasing commodification of nature and growing resource extraction in the name of the market, the propagation of individual rationality and the entrepreneurial subject, and the increasing financialization of the local Indigenous economy. Colonial state strategies combine the seemingly contradictory goals of an increasing political-economic oppression and social exclusion, on the one hand, and the recognition of the rights and cultural difference of disadvantaged groups, on the other. Such a strategy gives rise to a specific form of neoliberal indigeneity that aspires to autonomy while existing only with the permission of the colonial government. It also fosters a new version of incorporation—which at the same time represents a classical colonial strategy—that centers on the co-optation of indigenous elites and organizations to advocating neoliberal policies, thus wittingly or unwittingly supporting the state's interest, rather than that of their indigenous constituents. Zapotec-Canadian scholar Isabel Altamirano-Jiménez, who has published one of the few comprehensive studies of neoliberal indigeneity, summarizes the situation as follows:

> In their demands for recognition, equality, territory, and self-determination, Indigenous peoples have articulated meanings of indigeneity and cultural difference that are intelligible to the state and other transnational sites. In doing so, they have also reproduced problematic processes of differentiating between 'intelligible' and 'inauthentic' forms of indigeneity that perpetuate structural inequalities. (2013, 73)

Practices of colonial governance are nowadays mostly mediated through sub-state or civil-society bodies. The law plays a crucial role in sustaining a liberal legal and proprietary regime (cf. Goldstein 2008); another crucial strategy involves the concept of 'participation'. In her study of settler-colonial governance in Canada, Jaskiran Dhillon (2017) has investigated how state-like institutions have successfully enlisted the active participation of Indigenous people whereby the difference between Indigenous populations and the settler state are rendered as conflicts of understanding and of difficulties in need of technical intervention, rather than as conflicts of interest calling for a fundamental political realignment. The colonial situation is thus ultimately depoliticized. The Janus-faced quality of participation, which in certain cases also has the potential of pointing the way to actual community empowerment, makes it a strategy particularly difficult to critique. At the intersection of these two strategies, quasi-juridical commissions of inquiry–such as the recent Truth and Reconciliation Commission on Indian Residential Schools in Canada (cf. Niezen 2013; Regan 2010)– offer healing, reconciliation, and financial compensation at the expense of precluding further claims to political equality.

In Native America the impact of neoliberal capitalism has taken on two forms. One is typical for areas mostly outside of the capitalist core, namely the resurgence or intensification of primitive accumulation that perpetuates a history of the dispossession of Indigenous societies by means of the collusion of settler state and capital, exemplified by large-scale resource extraction in the Canadian north (cf. Black et al. 2014; Pasternak 2015, 2017; Preston 2013, 2017). The other form, typical for capitalist core areas, involves internal accumulation by cutting welfare spending and subjecting social relations to market logics, thus destroying earlier forms of local social reproduction.

The long history of acquiescence to incorporation by the colonized in Native America after military defeat has only a few times known moments of counter-hegemonic resistance–uprisings like the ones led by Pontiac or Tecumseh, religious revitalization movements like the Ghost Dance, and political movements from Red Power, to the Oka Crisis, or Idle No More in Canada, all of which, however, have failed to initiate long-term decolonization. The most recent wave of "Indigenous resurgence" (Coburn 2015) of struggles to overcome colonialism in the guise of state-sanctioned projects by private corporations or at least mitigate its disastrous effects have, not surprisingly, centered on resistance to capitalist exploitation. In a recent study, Dana Powell (2018) describes the history of such resistance by Navajo activists against the Desert Rock

Energy Project, a joint venture between the Navajo Nation and the Sithe Global Power Corporation. The project's goal was to harvest nearby coalfields to feed a new power plant on the Navajo Reservation. In the face of continuous resistance the plan was finally abandoned.

More dramatic and widely publicized instances of resistance to corporate colonialism concern the building of pipelines across Indigenous territory. In the case of the projected Northern Gateway pipeline that Enright Oil plans to build across northern British Columbia in order to connect the tar sands of northern Alberta with the harbor of Kitimat, B.C., six Indigenous communities formed the Yinka Dene Alliance to make their protest public. Following a far more radical strategy of obstruction, activists from the Unist'ot'en clan segment of the Wet'suwet'en set up a blockade along the pipeline's planned route and even stood off the Royal Canadian Mounted Police (cf. McCreary and Milligan 2014; Wood and Rossiter 2017).

Such direct action represents an extreme form of the refusal of capitalist incorporation that has gained ground in Native America. Another, possibly more long-lasting, aspect of refusal is the adoption of radical analytical schemes by a new generation of critical Indigenous intellectuals. Long frowned upon by Indigenous intellectuals and rejected as too 'Western' and narrowly materialist (cf. Churchill 1984), Marxist concepts and notions of anti-capitalism are now recognized as suitable tools for the evaluation of the colonial situation and the initiation of true decolonization. Whereas Mohawk political scientist Taiaiake Alfred ([2005] 2009) refers especially to anarchism, Yellowknife Dene scholar Glen Coulthard looks to Fanon and Marx in order to diagnose settler colonial-Indigenous relations in North America. Coulthard's recent book *Red Skin, White Masks* (2014) has been the subject of a lively debate from the perspectives of both Marxism and decolonization; his work points to concrete strategies for moving beyond colonization. Much like the Western scholars mentioned at the beginning of this chapter, Coulthard stresses that primitive accumulation must be understood not merely as the historical beginnings of capitalism, but as an ongoing process of continual dispossession that connects capitalism to colonialism. He states: "Colonial relations of power are no longer reproduced primarily through overtly coercive means, but rather through the asymmetrical exchange of mediated forms of state resistance and accommodation" (2014, 15).

The growing popularity of a political-economic frame of reference in Indigenous understandings of colonialism finds their expression in the slow rise of an Indigenous Left across North America, such as 'The Red Nation,' an Albuquerque-based, Native-led collective of Indigenous and non-Indigenous activists (cf. Heatherton 2016). Their viewpoint is succinctly expressed in their ten-point program published in the journal *Capitalism, Nature, Socialism*:

> Political possibilities for Native liberation therefore cannot emerge from forms of economic or institutional development, even if these are Tribally controlled under the guise of "self-determination" or "culture". They can only emerge from directly challenging the capitalist-colonial system of power through collective struggle and resistance. (Council of the Red Nation 2015, 6)

CONCLUSION

This chapter has diagnosed the political economy of domination and response in North America by sketching the *longue durée* of colonial domination and the forces behind it that transcend the historical minutiae of colonial practice. It has surveyed a research tradition that analyzes the past and present of Euromerican/Eurocanadian colonialism in terms of its political-economic impact on Indigenous societies. In summary, I would like to point out some key aspects of this approach that have characterized the encounter of colonizer and colonized in the long term, especially since the shift to continental colonialism and the accelerated dispossession of Indigenous land. Focus on a long historical trajectory is by itself an important aspect of colonialism: colonialism is neither a phase nor a moment in time, but a process of transformation and expropriation that is ongoing and has taken on various forms throughout its history.

As a political-economic force, colonialism represents first and foremost a strategy of capitalist accumulation. In search of an overarching explanatory framework for the capitalist penetration of the periphery, I have resurrected World-Systems Theory, which enjoyed a brief popularity among anthropologists in the 1970s and 1980s (cf. Nash 1981), as an appropriate approach to studying a globally integrated capitalist system in its processual dimension. In classical Marxist terms, colonialism aims for the appropriation of Indigenous land and the incorporation of Native groups into the capitalist realm of production and consumption.

The former aspect, which is typical for all cases of settler colonialism, points to the special relevance of continental vis-à-vis overseas colonialism. With the shift of the centers of colonial power to the American continent the demand for land became ever more salient. To a certain extent, Indigenous societies have been able to dance in tune with colonial capitalism's music quite successfully—mostly, however, the Indigenous elite has done so.

If we approach colonialism from another angle and analyze it in terms of Gramscian Marxism, it has imposed a hegemonic notion of capitalism among the colonized, with neo-tribal capitalism finally becoming established as the predominant economic form on tribal lands and the notion of a timeless Native culture as the most important currency for political claims inside and outside the tribes created by colonial administration. Historic ways of subsistence production have all but disappeared, maybe with the exception of hunting and trapping in the north. In order to secure its hegemony, capitalism has subverted the persistence of local forms of social reproduction (cf. Sider 2007), either by the coercive means of culturecide, especially through the institution of boarding schools in the not-so-distant past, or by contemporary, 'softer' sub-state strategies of legal domination and political co-optation.

Gramsci's understanding of domination, however, also entails the possibility of resistance or even revolution through the rise of political consciousness among subaltern populations. As I have sketched in the last part of the paper, after a long period of acquiescence following military defeat and severe population losses, the decades since the rebellious 1960s have seen—notwithstanding the adoption of the capitalist economy and capital-conducive forms of local governance—a shift toward what Hesketh has called a "subnational passive revolution" (2017, 5) in Native America. Aside from the acquisition of better knowledge of how to play the colonial state's legal game and how to successfully invest the gains of local enterprise based on the advantages of Indigenous status, the possibility of a popular politics of decolonizing resistance has shown up occasionally, ranging from the path-breaking Red Power activism of the 1960s and 1970s to the present-day anti-pipeline action in Canada and the United States. In the realm of theory, we have been witness to the forging of an ideology of refusal by a new generation of critical Indigenous intellectuals that envisions a Native future that is both decolonized and non-capitalist.

References

Albers, Patricia C. 2002. "Marxism and Historical Materialism in American Indian History." In *Clearing a Path: Theorizing the Past in Native American Studies*, edited by Nancy Shoemaker, 107–36. New York: Routledge.

Alfred, Taiaiake. [2005] 2009. *Wasáse: Indigenous Pathways of Action and Freedom*. Toronto: University of Toronto Press.

Altamirano-Jiménez, Isabel. 2013. *Indigenous Encounters with Neoliberalism: Place, Women, and the Environment in Canada and Mexico*. Vancouver: UBC Press.

Angelbeck, Bill, and Colin Grier. 2012. "Anarchism and the Archaeology of Anarchic Societies: Resistance to Centralization in the Coast Salish Region of the Pacific Northwest Coast." *Current Anthropology* 53: 547–87.

Bee, Robert L., and Ronald Gingerich. 1977. "Colonialism, Classes, and Ethnic Identity: Native Americans and the National Political Economy." *Studies in Comparative International Development* 12: 70–93.

Benedek, E. 1999. *The Wind Won't Know Me: A History of the Navajo-Hopi Land Dispute*. Norman: University of Oklahoma Press.

Black, Toban, Stephen D'Arcy, Tony Weis, and Joshua Kahn Russell, eds. 2014. *A Line in the Tar Sands: Struggles for Environmental Justice*. Oakland: PM Press.

Brugge, David M. 1994. *The Navajo-Hopi Land Dispute: An American Tragedy*. Albuquerque: University of New Mexico Press.

Bush, Caleb M. 2005. "Reconsidering Incorporation: Uneven Histories of Capitalist Expansion and Encroachment, Native America." *Studies in Political Economy* 76: 83–109.

Bush, Caleb M. 2014. "Subsistence Fades, Capitalism Deepens: The 'Net of Incorporation' and Diné Livelihoods in the Opening of the Navajo-Hopi Land Dispute, 1880–1970." *American Behavioral Scientist* 58: 171–96.

Cattelino, Jessica R. 2008. *High Stakes: Florida Seminole Gaming and Sovereignty*. Durham: Duke University Press.

Chamberlain, Katherine P. 2000. *Sacred Ground: A History of Navajo Oil, 1922–1982*. Albuquerque: University of New Mexico Press.

Churchill, Ward, ed. 1984. *Marxism and Native Americans*. Boston: South End Press.

Coburn, Elaine, ed. 2015. *More Will Sing Their Way to Freedom: Indigenous Resistance and Resurgence*. Halifax: Fernwood.

Coulthard, Glen. 2014. *Red Skin, White Masks: Rejecting the Colonial Politics of Recognition*. Minneapolis: University of Minnesota Press.

The Council of the Red Nation. 2015. "Native Liberation Struggles in North America: The Red Nation 10-point Program." *Capitalism, Nature, Socialism* 26 (2): 1–7.

Crehan, Kate. 2002. *Gramsci, Culture, and Anthropology*. Berkeley: University of California Press.

Darian-Smith, Eve. 2003. *New Capitalists: Law, Politics, and Identity Surrounding Casino Gaming on Native American Land*. Boston: Cengage Learning.

Dennison, Jean. 2012. *Colonial Entanglement: Constituting a Twenty-First-Century Osage Nation*. Chapel Hill: University of North Carolina Press.

Dennison, Jean. 2014. "The Logic of Recognition: Debating Osage Nation Citizenship in the Twenty-First Century." *American Indian Quarterly* 38 (1): 1–35.

Dhillon, Jaskiran K. 2017. *Prairie Rising: Indigenous Youth, Decolonization, and the Politics of Intervention*. Toronto: University of Toronto Press.

Doerfler, Jill. 2015. *Those Who Belong: Identity, Family, Blood, and Citizenship Among the White Earth Anishnaabeg*. East Lansing: Michigan State University Press.

Dombrowski, Kirk. 2001. *Against Culture: Development, Politics, and Religion in Indian Alaska*. Lincoln: University of Nebraska Press.

Dunaway, Wilma. 1996. "Incorporation as an Interactive Process: Cherokee Resistance to Expansion of the Capitalist World-System, 1560–1763." *Sociological Inquiry* 66: 455–70.

Fenelon, James V. 1997. "From Peripheral Domination to Internal Colonialism: Socio-Political Change of the Lakota on Standing Rock." *Journal of World-Systems Research* 3: 259–320.

Fixico, Donald L. 1998. *The Invasion of Indian Country in the Twentieth Century: American Capitalism and Tribal Natural Resources*. Niwot: University Press of Colorado.

Fixico, Donald L. 2000. *The Urban Indian Experience in America*. Albuquerque: University of New Mexico Press.

Francisconi, Michael J. [1998] 2011. *Kinship, Capital, Change: The Informal Economy of the Navajo, 1868–1995*. New York: Routledge.

Gilbreath, Kent. 1973. *Red Capitalism: An Analysis of the Navajo Economy*. Norman: University of Oklahoma Press.

Goldstein, Alyosha. 2008. "Where the Nation Takes Place: Proprietary Regimes, Antistatism, and U.S. Settler Colonialism." *South Atlantic Quarterly* 107: 833–61.

Grinde, Donald A., and Bruce E. Johansen. 1994. *Ecocide in Native America: Environmental Destruction of Indian Lands and People*. San Francisco: Clear Light.

Hall, Thomas D. 1989. *Social Change in the Southwest, 1350–1880*. Lawrence: University Press of Kansas.

Harvey, David. 2004. "The 'New' Imperialism: Accumulation by Dispossession." *Socialist Register* 40: 63–87.

Harvey, David. 2005. *A Brief History of Neoliberalism.* Oxford: Oxford University Press.

Heatherton, Christina. 2016. "Policing the Crisis of Indigenous Lives: An Interview with the Red Nation." In *Policing the Planet: Why the Policing Crisis Led to Black Lives Matter,* edited by Jordan T. Camp and Christina Heatherton, 109–19. London: Routledge.

Hesketh, Chris. 2017. *Spaces of Capital/Spaces of Resistance: Mexico and the Global Political Economy.* Athens: University of Georgia Press.

Hickerson, Harold. 1973. "Fur Trade Colonialism and the North American Indians." *Journal of Ethnic Studies* 1: 15–44.

Hormel, Leontina M., and Kari M. Norgaard. 2009. "Bring the Salmon Home! Karuk Challenges to Capitalist Incorporation." *Critical Sociology* 35: 343–66.

Jacobsen, Cardell K. 1984. "Internal Colonialism and Native Americans: Indian Labor in the United States from 1871 to World War II." *Social Science Quarterly* 65: 158–71.

Jorgensen, Joseph G. 1978. "A Century of Political Economic Effects on American Indian Society, 1880–1980." *Journal of Ethnic Studies* 6 (3): 1–82.

Knight, Rolf. 1978. *Indians at Work: An Informal History of Native Labor in British Columbia, 1858–1930.* Vancouver: New Star Books.

Krader, Lawrence. 1972. *The Ethnological Notebooks of Karl Marx.* Assen: Van Gorcum.

LaDuke, Winona. 1983. "The Economics of Radioactive Colonization." *Review of Radical Political Economics* 15 (3): 3–19.

Leacock, Eleanor B. 1954. *The Montagnais "Hunting Territory" and the Fur Trade* (American Anthropological Association Memoir 78). Menasha, WI: American Anthropological Association.

Littlefield, Alice, and Martha C. Knack, eds. 1996. *Native Americans and Wage Labor: Ethnohistorical Perspectives.* Norman: University of Oklahoma Press.

Luxemburg, Rosa. [1913] 2003. *The Accumulation of Capital.* London: Routledge.

Mason, Arthur. 2002. "The Rise of an Alaskan Native Bourgeoisie." *Études/Inuit/Studies* 26 (2): 5–22.

McCreary, Tyler A., and Richard A. Milligan. 2014. "Pipelines, Permits, and Protests: Carrier Sekani Encounters with the Enbridge Northern Gateway Project." *Cultural Geographies* 21: 115–29.

McDonald, James A. 1994. "Social Change and the Creation of Underdevelopment: A Northwest Coast Case." *American Ethnologist* 21: 152–75.

Meyer, Melissa L. 1994. *The White Earth Tragedy: Ethnicity and Dispossession at a Minnesota Anishinaabeg Reservation, 1889–1920.* Lincoln: University of Nebraska Press.

Moore, John H. 1993a. "Political Economy in Anthropology." In *The Political Economy of North American Indians*, edited by John H. Moore, 3–19. Norman: University of Oklahoma Press.

Moore, John H., ed. 1993b. *The Political Economy of North American Indians*. Norman: University of Oklahoma Press.

Nash, June. 1981. "Ethnographic Aspects of the World Capitalist System." *Annual Review of Anthropology* 10: 393–423.

Niezen, Ronald. 2013. *Truth and Indignation: Canada's Truth and Reconciliation Commission on Indian Residential Schools*. Toronto: University of Toronto Press.

O'Neill, Colleen. 2005. *Working the Navajo Way: Labor and Culture in the Twentieth Century*. Lawrence: University Press of Kansas.

Pasternak, Shiri. 2015. "How Capitalism Will Save Colonialism: The Privatization of Reserve Lands in Canada." *Antipode* 47: 179–96.

Pasternak, Shiri. 2017. *Grounded Authority: The Algonquins of Barriere Lake Against the State*. Minneapolis: University of Minnesota Press.

Powell, Dana E. 2018. *Landscapes of Power: Politics of Energy in the Navajo Nation*. Durham: Duke University Press.

Preston, Jen. 2013. "Neoliberal Settler Colonialism, Canada, and the Tar Sands." *Race and Class* 55 (2): 42–59.

Preston, Jen. 2017. "Racial Extractivism and White Settler Colonialism: An Examination of the Canadian Tar Sands Mega-Projects." *Cultural Studies* 31 (2–3): 353–75.

Rata, Elizabeth. 2000. *A Political Economy of Neotribal Capitalism*. Lanham: Lexington Books.

Regan, Paulette. 2010. *Unsettling the Settler Within: Indian Residential Schools, Truth Telling, and Reconciliation in Canada*. Vancouver: UBC Press.

Rose, Samuel W. 2015. "Two Thematic Manifestations of Neotribal Capitalism in the United States." *Anthropological Theory* 15: 218–38.

Rose, Samuel W. 2017. "Marxism, Indigenism, and the Anthropology of Native North America: Divergence and a Possible Future." *Dialectical Anthropology* 41: 13–31.

Roseberry, William. 1994. "Hegemony and the Language of Contention." In *Everyday Forms of State Formation: Revolution and the Negotiation of Rule in Modern Mexico*, edited by Gilbert Michael Joseph and Daniel Nugent, 355–66. Durham: Duke University Press.

Schröder, Ingo W. 2003. "The Political Economy of Tribalism in North America: Neotribal Capitalism?" *Anthropological Theory* 3: 435–56.

Sider, Gerald. 2003. *Living Indian Histories: Lumbee and Tuscarora People in North Carolina*. Chapel Hill: University of North Carolina Press.

Sider, Gerald. 2006. "The Walls Came Tumbling Up: The Production of Culture, Class, and Native American Societies." *The Australian Journal of Anthropology* 17: 276–90.

Sider, Gerald. 2007. "Remaking Marxist Anthropology." *New Proposals* 1: 12–14.

Smith, Sherry L., and Brian Frehner, eds. 2010. *Indians and Energy: Exploitation and Opportunity in the American Southwest.* Santa Fe: SAR Press.

Snipp, C. Matthew. 1986. "The Changing Political and Economic Status of the American Indians: From Captive Nations to Internal Colonies." *American Journal of Economics and Sociology* 45: 145–57.

Spicer, Edward H. 1962. *Cycles of Conquest: The Impact of Spain, Mexico, and the United States on the Indians of the Southwest, 1533–1960.* Tucson: University of Arizona Press.

Stavenhagen, Rodolfo. 1965. "Classes, Colonialism, and Acculturation." *Studies in Comparative International Development* 1(6): 53–77.

Sturm, Circe. 2002. *Blood Politics: Race, Culture, and Identity in the Cherokee Nation of Oklahoma.* Berkeley: University of California Press.

Sturm, Circe. 2010. *Becoming Indian: The Struggle Over Cherokee Identity in the Twenty-First Century.* Santa Fe: SAR Press.

Sturm, Circe. 2014. "Race, Sovereignty, and Civil Rights: Understanding the Cherokee Freedmen Controversy." *Cultural Anthropology* 29: 575–98.

Wilkins, David E. 1993. "Modernization, Colonialism, Dependency: How Appropriate Are These Models for Providing an Explanation for North American Indian 'Underdevelopment'?" *Ethnic and Racial Studies* 16: 390–419.

Wolf, Eric R. 1982. *Europe and the People Without History.* Berkeley: University of California Press.

Wood, Patricia Burke, and David A. Rossiter. 2017. "The Politics of Refusal: Aboriginal Sovereignty and the Northern Gateway Pipeline." *The Canadian Geographer* 61: 165–77.

CHAPTER 5

Was Russia a Colonial Empire?

Dittmar Schorkowitz

A STARTING POINT

Long before Russia became an empire with the end of the Great
Nordic War against Sweden and Peter the Great (1682–1725) proclaiming himself Emperor of All Russia (1721), the grand princes and
tsars of Muscovy were constantly engaged in an eastward expansion
following the decline of the Golden Horde and the power vacuum the
Turko-Mongolian rulers had left in many parts of Europe and Asia. The
famous conquest of the once mighty Kazan and Astrakhan Khanates in
1552 and 1556 by Ivan IV, first Tsar of All Russia (1547–84), represented a significant watershed in Russia's relationships with the empires
of the steppe resulting, though not without resistance and further conflict, in the submission of the Bashkirs, Volga Bulgars, and other Tatar
groups (Khodarkovsky 2002; Sunderland 2004). Equally important,
but perhaps less known, Ivan IV in 1558 commissioned the Stroganovs
to support the conquest of Siberia financially, granting the merchant
family a monopoly on the salt and fur trade in return (Martin 1986,
1995). Similar to the East India Companies of the time, the Stroganov
merchants for some years paid for the construction of fortresses along
Siberian rivers, and the Cossacks of Ataman Yermak in 1582 finally

D. Schorkowitz (✉)
Max Planck Institute for Social Anthropology, Halle (Saale), Germany
e-mail: schorkowitz@eth.mpg.de

© The Author(s) 2019   117
D. Schorkowitz et al. (eds.), *Shifting Forms of Continental Colonialism*,
https://doi.org/10.1007/978-981-13-9817-9_5

succeeded in defeating and expelling Kuchum, the last khan of the Sibir Khanate ruled by the Chingissid Shaybanid and Taibugid dynasties for centuries (Frank 1994; Forsyth 1998, 25–27).

Since then Russia "expanded in her own way of continental colonialism towards Asia" (Hildermeier 2013, 38), proceeded continuously into South and East Siberia with forts built at Okhotsk on the Pacific Coast in 1649 and in Irkutsk at Lake Baikal in 1652. It goes without saying that the land taken in the name of the tsar was, contrary to official language, no *terra nullius*, but populated—though sparsely—by indigenous groups that now experienced recurrent clashes with the expanding Cossack detachments (Collins 1991; cf. Kivelson 2007, 26–27, 35). Interestingly, despite the Stroganovs' expectation to obtain the land, the seizure of which they had financed, the Cossacks, following a different agenda and with the desire for greater recognition from the tsar, concluded all agreements with the new subjects in the name of the tsar—an absolute and autocratic monarch—who thus became sovereign over fresh tax-paying peoples and vast stretches of land. Elaborating on Muscovite colonial practices of appropriating Siberian land, Valerie Kivelson recently emphasized "the deep and consistent commitment to the kinds of legal and political claim-making that were operative in Russia at the time" (2007, 23). The conquest of Siberia was thus not so much spurred by private interest as one might assume at first glance. The Siberian fur trade became a crown monopoly based generally on tribute (*iasak*) paying indigenous peoples. The fur was then brought either to the sable treasury (*sobolinaia kazna*) of the Siberian Prikaz or to the tsar's treasury court (*kazennyi dvor*) in Moscow and sold to Western merchants outfitting European courts with fashionable furs via Arkhangelsk or Novgorod (Fisher 1943; Bakhrushin 1955b; Dmytryshyn 1991, 18; Forsyth 1998, 38–42; Aust 2000, 42; Reinhard 2011, 134–37; 2016, 677–81).

The urge to the East was, however, soon complemented by southern orientations. Peter the Great's imperial ambitions brought Russia not only into conflict with the West, but also with neighboring powers in Asia, including another war with the Ottoman Empire over Crimea and Azov in the 1680–90s, a disastrous expedition against the Khanate of Khiva (1717), a yielding war with Persia (1722–23), and clashes with Qing China over border issues leading to the treaties of Nerchinsk (1689) and Kyakhta (1727). Successes in the Russo-Turkish Wars continued under Catherine the Great (1762–96) adding the Crimean Khanate and large parts of Novorossiia to the empire. The German-born empress was also the first to bring large contingents of peasants and craftsmen from Western Europe as settlers to the Volga and Black Sea regions. The short-lived reign of her son Paul I (1796–1801) signaled a reinforced engagement in the Caucasus, particularly Georgia. Soon, the whole region turned into a fierce battlefield when Russia expanded into the southern parts and later into the lands of the northern mountain-eers culminating in the Circassian and the Murid wars of the 1850–60s (Allen and Muratoff [1953] 1999; Henze 1983; Halbach [1989] 1994; Mostashari 2001; Gammer and Kaplan 2013). As a result, the "north-west Caucasus was cleared of virtually its entire indigenous population" just to be replaced with Russian settlers (Geraci 2008, 348; cf. Comins-Richmond 2002, 63).

Entering the age of imperialism, particularly after the devastating Crimean War (1853–56), Russia increased her engagement in Central Asia which in fact had started earlier with another failed campaign against Khiva by Vasily Perovsky in 1839. Now however, Russia's com-bined efforts led to the region's final conquest within decades: Tashkent was taken in 1865, Samarkand in 1868, Khiva in 1873, and Merv in 1884. The same year when Tashkent was conquered, a 'colonial sys-tem of power' was established in Russian Turkestan by decree of the Governing Senate, a "system of internal administrative and territorial division [...] adjusted to accommodate military needs, and [...] divided into military territorial units" (Abdurakhimova 2002, 240; cf. Carrère d'Encausse 1999a, 151–53). Russia established a 'mechanism of exclu-sion', regarding the internal administration and the participation of local elites, to keep the colonial difference. The "colonial order was built on the exclusion of the native population of Turkestan from the imperial mainstream" (Khalid 2009, 415) which local intellectuals and reformers—the Jadids—sought to overcome.[1]

Significantly, all these macro-regions and some others not men-tioned, like the Baltics, survived the 1917 revolutions as integral parts of the empire and became republics of the Soviet Union. For this reason

---

[1] For more detailed accounts on colonial cooperation with the so-called 'native adminis-tration', local elders and chieftains, and changes in the legal sphere, particularly Muslim law and jurisdiction, see Pierce (1960), Brower (1997), Martin (2001), Abdurakhimova (2002), and Crews (2009). On relations and interdependencies between the Russian military and academic explorers in Central and Inner Asia, see the chapter of David Schimmelpenninck van der Oye in this volume.

Walter Kolarz employed the term 'colony' as a "common denominator for a large number of territories which enjoy either legally or factually a special status within Soviet Russia [...] similar to that of the overseas dependencies of any other power" (1952, V), while others preferred to think in terms of a 'totalitarian Soviet imperialism' because the "Soviet Communists are imposing their rule by force on nations which were once conquered by the Tsars" (Seton-Watson [1966] 1973, 115).

WHEN AND WHERE WAS COLONIALISM IN RUSSIA?

As the Russian empire expanded, its ethnic and cultural diversity also grew and the question of how to govern such a large imperial formation became a permanent concern for the authorities. In fact, the subdued nations and their governments were not permanently under direct military control, but "came *pari passu* under the authority of civil institutions of the governorate administration as the frontier advanced" (Schorkowitz 2015, 6). Their self-administration, first generously granted and subsequently more and more restricted, underwent several transitions resulting in "particularistic arrangements of rule" (Khalid 2007, 117) and in a high degree of legal and cultural forms leaving a significant imprint on Soviet times too. Though there is no doubt that "colonialism was intrinsic to the tsardom" (Hildermeier 2013, 1112) as many historians of Russia would agree, one has to bear in mind that Russian expansion and conquest, at least in Siberia, "was not a meticulously planned and carefully executed undertaking", but rather "like West European colonial adventures [...] a convulsive process propelled by many pressures and forces" (Dmytryshyn 1991, 17). Given the continental expansion in Siberia, the Caucasus, and Central Asia the question thus is not whether, but rather where, when, and how was colonialism in Russia.

The case of the Kalmyk Khanate, which had lost its independence relatively late in 1771, is telling here. Politically again upgraded by Tsar Paul in 1800, the Kalmyk administration was at first detached from the Astrakhan' governorate administration and assigned to the Collegium of Foreign Affairs, when it was brought under the control of the military governor again in 1803, due to Russia's deepening engagement in the Caucasus region. Though nominally subordinated to the Ministry of Foreign Affairs until March 1824 and, after the 1825 reforms, to the Ministry of the Interior, the dominating power remained with the military. Reformed once more in 1834, the Kalmyk administration was reassigned to the Ministry of the Interior, but the entire local administration was still controlled by the Astrakhan' military governor. With the provincial reform of 1837 responsibilities changed again when the Kalmyk administration then moved to the Ministry of State Domains for sixty-five years and was ceded once more to the Ministry of the Interior in 1902 (Schorkowitz 2015, 7).

Concerning colonial management, there is a striking contrast with Western maritime powers, most of which established a separate colonial administration whose precursors were often located in the domains either of the war, trade, or foreign ministries. This was the case with the British Colonial Office, the Spanish *Real y Supremo Consejo de Indias*, the *Ministère des Colonies* or *Ministère des Outre-mer* in France, the *Ministerie van Koloniën* in the Netherlands, the *Reichskolonialamt* of the German Empire, or the Japanese *Takumushō* (Stahl 1951, 35–37; Sunderland 2010, 127–31; Khodarkovsky 2018, 14–16). Even continental empires like Qing China and the United States of America had their colonial offices, the former represented in the *Lifanyuan* (literally: Board for the Administration of the Outer Regions), the latter in the Bureau of Indian Affairs and the Bureau of Insular Affairs, while the Russian, the Habsburg, and Ottoman Empire had none.

The tsarist government obviously felt confident in administering the newly acquired territories through its Asian Department alone, an agency of the Ministry of Foreign Affairs that became "de facto Russia's Colonial Office" (Khodarkovsky 2009, 159) coordinating all issues concerning the Orient until 1917. The department was indeed a natural outcome of Russia's foreign operations dating back to the Ambassadorial Chancellery (*Posol'skii Prikaz*) that had dealt with European and Asian affairs since 1549. In the wake of Tsar Peter's governmental reforms, the Ambassadorial Chancellery was reorganized as the Collegium of Foreign Affairs (*Kollegiia inostrannykh del*) in 1718 that included a special Department of Asian Affairs (*Departament aziatskikh del*) as early as 1797 (Rogozhin 1993; Schorkowitz 2017, 400–1). Modeled on Western European governments, the newly introduced nine Collegia replaced more or less the obsolete Muscovite *Prikaz* (office) system, various branches of which, like the *Kazanskii Prikaz* or the *Sibirskii Prikaz*, had previously been in charge of the lands conquered and annexed in the sixteenth and seventeenth centuries. Some of these offices were later simply closed when of no use anymore, some became integrated into the Ambassadorial Chancellery, others were affiliated with provincial governments or voivodships as in the case of the *Prikaz Kalmytskikh Del* whose functions were absorbed by the Astrakhan Voevodas after 1662. The *Sibirskii Prikaz*, which "might be considered as the 'Colonial Office for Siberia'" (Lantzeff 1943, 1), assumed responsibilities rather late in 1637 from the Ambassadorial Chancellery, the *Novgorodskii Prikaz*, and *Kazanskii Prikaz*, which at various times had dealt with 'Siberian Affairs' previously. Though this office even survived Tsar Peter's reforms "it was finally abolished in 1763 by the reforms of Catherine II" (ibid., 6) and its functions were taken over by the Siberian governorates.

Obviously, although missing a proper colonial office the empire established analogous institutions to set up 'colonies of rule' within its imperial confines. As the frontier advanced, previously conquered territories were annexed and changed authorities from the Foreign Affairs or War Ministry and were then governed by ministerial bureaucracies of the interior, the imperial domains, agriculture, religion, and education. Under such particularistic arrangements, these newly formed agencies faced constant challenges to build up "new competencies of their own in dealing with 'other' cultures, and to develop strategies" for their integration (Schorkowitz 2017, 401). "It matters little", Jürgen Osterhammel comments on the transformation of a 'frontier zone' to an 'imperial realm', "whether one calls the outcome an 'internal colony' or a 'borderland.' However, since it did not come under a special administration [...], there is much to be said against the term 'colony'" ([2009] 2014, 366, referring to Sunderland 2004, 223). Yet, apart from the formalistic character of his argument, Osterhammel is seemingly unaware of the many agencies that exactly served colonial ends in the Russian Empire.

The absence of a 'de jure colonial office' in the empire, whose officials preferred colonization over colonialism discourse (cf. Bakhrushin 1955a), inspired historians to think about similar institutions that could possibly come close to the functions of a colonial ministry. As a matter of fact, such agencies would have to deal with internal, not foreign affairs, thus representing administrations of internal colonialism. There are quite good candidates among Russia's nineteenth-century governmental bodies, two of which Willard Sunderland recently discussed as "proto-colonial ministries" (2010, 141)—the Ministry of State Domains (1837–94) and the Resettlement Administration (1896–1917)—parts of the Ministry of the Interior. Both bodies dealt with the administration of state lands, including the transformation and expropriation of indigenous land, its allocation to state peasants, and the latter's resettlement from European to Asiatic Russia, thus representing typical agencies of settler colonialism (cf. Fieldhouse [1965] 1982, 334). A good deal of this work was, however, also realized through the Land Department (*Zemskii otdel*) of the Ministry of the Interior and the Main Administration of Land Management and Agriculture (*Glavnoe upravlenie zemleustroistva i zemledeliia*, 1905–15), whose land reforms in Siberia were met with enmity and strong resistance by, for instance, Buriat elders and nobles (Schorkowitz 2018, 392).

Yet, there were other agencies with similar functions dealing more precisely with colonial matters at the imperial peripheries. The Ministry of State Domains, for example, which had a branch at each single governorate, directed a Bureau for Horde-Peoples (*Otdelenie ordynskikh narodov*) at Astrakhan. For many decades, this same ministry was also in charge of the Kalmyk Administration (*Kalmytskoe upravlenie*) and particularly the Commission for Street Settlement through Kalmyk Lands (*Komissii Zaseleniia Dorog chrez kalmytskiia zemli*), seated likewise in Astrakhan with representations in every single ulus where Kalmyk nobles played an ever lesser political role. The Interior Ministry conducted not only the Resettlement Administration (*Pereselencheskoe upravlenie*), but also the Department for Religious Affairs of Foreign Denominations (*Departament dukhovnykh del inostrannykh ispovedanij*) and, by the same token, supervised the department's branches for Muslims, Jews, Karaims, and Buddhists (*Departament dukhovnykh del inostrannykh ispovedanij po zakonu lamaiskomu*), exerting colonial control over shamanist practitioners as well (Schorkowitz 2001; Murray 2016).

In addition, numerous ministerial committees were created to manage imperial matters, such as the two Siberian Committees (1821–38, 1852–64) or the Caucasus Committee (1833–82). Engaging more seriously with 'population politics' in the second half of the nineteenth century, the General Staff Academy introduced military statistics and geography alongside "ethnography, anthropology, and public health" (Holquist 2001, 114; cf. Hirsch 1998) as required subjects to better understand, categorize, and govern a multiethnic colonial periphery. But "there was no single organizational venue […] for ruling over colonial matters–or colonial peoples more specifically" (Sunderland 2010, 135) perhaps, as David McDonald seems to suggest, because such a "Ministry of Asiatic Russia […] would have superseded the viceroyalties that governed the Caucasus, Central Asia, and much of Siberia" (2010, 186; cf. Geraci 2010).

After the February Revolution many of these ministerial departments transformed into agencies of the Russian Provisional Government, like the Department for Non-Slavic and Different Faith Denominations at the Ministry of Religion (*Departament po delam inoslavnykh i inovernykh ispovedanii ministerstva ispovedanii*). To bring the colonized nations more closely under central decision-making institutions and get their elite's support in difficult times the Government in September 1917 established for the first time a National Department at the Ministry of the Interior (*Natsional'nyi otdel ministerstva vnutrennykh del*). This, however, was very quickly trumped by a significantly upgraded Soviet ministry—the People's Commissariat of Nationalities (*Narodnyi komissariat po delam natsional'nostei*)—the first attempt at centralizing the particularistic arrangements of tsarist rule in internal colonial matters (Schorkowitz 2017, 402–3).

The question remains: how then was colonialism in Russia, where can we situate it among other colonial empires? We may safely say that it was continental in nature notwithstanding temporary rule of Russian America (Alaska), sold to the United States in 1867, and some short-lived presence in Hawaii and California, neither economically successful (Lincoln 1994, 141–42; Reinhard 2011, 139–40; Vinkovetsky 2011). "Unlike Russia's other colonies, [Alaska] was not contiguous to the motherland, so what happened there was of less moment" (Gibson 1991, 112); nevertheless, Beringia could be considered a transcontinental bridge. Given the arctic climate of the White Sea and Ottoman dominance over the Black Sea, tsarist Russia never developed into a maritime empire.

This continental colonialism was not, despite short-lived engagements such as the Stroganov financing of Siberian Cossacks or the Russian America Company's fur and sea otter trade in Alaska, propelled by private interest. Rather it was the state that paid for military expansion, raised taxes from the colonized, installed local bureaucracies, provided cheap mining workers by way of the exile system (*katorga*), organized peasant resettlements, and invented various ideologies to camouflage and legitimize what Michael Khodarkovsky has rightly called 'state colonialism' (2018, 2; cf. Osterhammel [2009] 2014, 367).

Yet compared with other forms of overseas colonialism, Russia's state colonialism was neither based on trade nor on a plantation economy: "Russia was an absolute monarchy with an economy based on serf agriculture; while America was a republic with an economy resting largely on free farming" (Treadgold 1952, 148). While the British Empire is characterized as a commercial empire with "liberal, diffuse maritime power", the Russian counterpart is aptly described as a military-dynastic, "autocratic, centralizing land empire" (Lieven 2004, 138). While British rule in India was geared toward extracting as much profit as possible and "the local revenues paid for a vast army of largely native troops, which made Britain a world power on land as well as on sea" (Morrison 2008, 31), the tsar's expenditure in Russian Turkestan almost amounted to twice as much as his income from that region between 1868 and 1910. In contrast to settler colonialism in Northern and Latin America, spurred by private capital and profit-making, the economic exploitation of Russia's 'internal colonies' ranked always second after territorial, geopolitical gains and the government's expectation to solve the 'peasant question'. Notwithstanding seventeenth-century runaways (*beglye*) of peasant, Cossack or Old-Believer background, agrarian settlers appeared late in Siberia, the Caucasus, and Central Asia, prompted by an ill-conceived peasant reform of 1861, which "did not remove the principle legal obstacle to freedom of movement, because peasants were still bound to the village commune" (Forsyth 1998, 191). Though formally freed from serfdom by the Emancipation Edict which Tsar Alexander II had announced in 1861, their factual emancipation was intrinsically tied to their provision with sufficient land, predominantly in Siberia and Southern Russia, a policy which became a burden for every agrarian and interior minister, particularly for prime minister Pyotr Stolypin (1906–11), from the 1880s to the October Revolution and beyond (Treadgold 1952, 149–51; Sunderland 2000, 210; Reinhard 2016, 686–90).[2]

Furthermore, to add another significant difference, maritime empires are more problematic to govern because they are located overseas and continuously separated from the metropoles. Although troops and goods may be shipped quicker and easier by sea, "a sea-borne empire's internal communications are far more subject to interdiction than that is the case with a consolidated land empire" (Lieven 2004, 139). That is why they unfold usually as 'colonies of exploitation' with commercial strongholds or as settler colonies and end up as 'colonies of rule'. The Russian Empire emerged due to the "continental expansion of the tsarist might which, by subjugating non-Russian populations, constituted

---

[2] See the chapter of Willard Sunderland in this volume.

colonial power relations sui generis" (Geyer [1977] 1987, 14). Tsarist Russia, like Qing China and Ottoman Turkey, started with continental expansion following a 'moving frontier' that resulted in 'colonies of rule' at their peripheries. Though state interference was indirect and on a lesser degree in the beginning, hence allowing for various forms of self-rule (e.g. the steppe dumas in Eastern Siberia), control increased over time with a tendency toward direct rule at a later stage (e.g. the Bashkir canton administration, the Kalmyk administration). While Russia transformed her "newly acquired frontiers step-by-step into internal colonies" (Schorkowitz 2017, 419), the shift from indirect to direct rule eventually resulted in more rigid forms of centralization, integration, and domination.

DISCOURSES ON COLONIALISM AND COLONIZATION

The discourse over Russia as a colonial empire has always been controversial as have the related connotations regarding Russia's continental or internal colonialism to this day. Though even nineteenth-century Russian historians admitted the exploitation of non-Russian peoples, its colonial nature remained either highly disputed or simply ignored. Thus, in order to euphemize colonial excesses, Soviet historiography developed a language replacing "terms such as *pokorenie* (subjugation) or *zavoevanie* (conquest) [...] using more neutral vocabulary such as *prisoedinenie* (annexation) or *osvoenie* (assimilation)" (Collins 1991, 37; cf. Khalid 2009, 416), or "the so-called *dobrovol'noe vkhozhdenie*, which literally translates as 'voluntarily joining' the Russian empire" (Schorkowitz 2012, 47). Paradoxically, politicians and intelligentsia alike "maintained that Russia's expansion avoided the violence associated with European empires and that the Russian Empire was fundamentally benevolent towards its imperial non-Christian subjects", concealing however that millions of "indigenous people were killed by Russian arms and expelled through Russian policies as the empire expanded" (Khodarkovsky 2018, 6). In other words, "Russia juxtaposed itself to the Western empires and denied the colonial character of its own" (ibid.), thus essentially denying also any colonial institutions at home.

Nevertheless, the official narrative regarding Russia's expansion and expeditions into Asia remained full of imperial pride ever since foreign minister Alexander Gorchakov sent his famous Memorandum to the European powers in 1864 legitimating general Mikhail Cherniaev's advance to Chimkent and Tashkent "by comparing Russia's behavior in Central Asia with that of 'all other civilized states' which found themselves in contact with wild, nomadic populations" (Geyer [1977] 1987, 89). The ministerial dispatch culminated in the statement that "Like the United States in America, France in Africa, Holland in her colonies, and England in East India" Russia was now being swept "less out of ambition than absolute necessity" down a path "where it is extremely difficult simply to stand pat" (ibid.; cf. Sahni 1997, 83). Such comparisons were not new for Russian intellectuals to make vis-à-vis the advances of Western European colonialism, but rather common when referring to for instance Siberia, portrayed as "'our Peru', 'our Mexico', a 'Russian Brazil', or indeed 'our little India'" (Bassin 2006, 48).

The obvious need for legitimizing the imperial expansion, combined with an attempt to catch-up with Western civilization and economy, developed into a particular Russian form of 'Orientalism' (Sahni 1997; Bassin 2006, 49; cf. Schimmelpenninck van der Oye 2010, 4–11). Conservative writer Fyodor Dostoevsky best expressed this in 1881: "In Europe we were hangers-on and slaves, while in Asia we shall be the masters. In Europe we were Tatars, while in Asia we are the Europeans. Our mission, our civilizing mission in Asia will encourage our spirit and draw us on" ([1994] 2000, 1374; cf. Sahni 1997, 71–86; Bassin 2006, 54–55; Geraci 2008, 360–61; Hofmeister 2011). To be sure, this was not an extreme position among Slavophil sentiments during Alexander III's Russocentric rule. In fact, the dictum that the "history of Russia is the history of a country that colonizes itself" (*kolonizuetsia*) was a commonplace at the turn of the century even among liberals. For example, Vasilii Kliuchevskii ([1956] 1987, 50), a historian with a significant interest in medieval history, followed his teacher Sergei Soloviev in perceiving Russia as 'frontier society' (cf. Treadgold 1952, 149; Breyfogle et al. 2007, 1–2).

However, the question remains whether the pre-modern expansion into what later became Asiatic Russia can be regarded simply as a direct continuation of the early colonization of European Russia undertaken by the grand princes of Muscovy or Novgorod. Martin Aust has pinpointed the difference between the two historical processes with the formula "'*aedificatio terrae*' versus colonialism" (2000, 40). He convincingly argues that the medieval *Landesausbau* was a European-wide settlement process arranged by feudal lords and kings, whereas Yermak's conquest of Kuchum's Sibir Khanate neither followed central planning nor improved agriculture in cooperation with indigene economies, but instead showed "basically all features of a European colonial expansion" (ibid., 42).

In fact, colonization may unfold within or beyond national borders. Regarding Russia, colonization is a rather new phenomenon starting in the late nineteenth century and pursued by socialist planning in Soviet times. It followed the conquest, annexation, and penetration of hitherto foreign lands and 'other' cultures that, over time, were transformed into integral parts of the empire. To adopt the notion of 'internal colonization' from a German background (*'Innere Kolonisation'*) used for settlement programs in East Prussia by the late German Empire as suggested by Alexander Etkind (2011, 2015) seems misleading, given the colonization of internally colonized lands in Asiatic Russia. In fact, the history of Russia and the Soviet Union is also the history of forced civilization, of a "cultural submission not implicit in colonization" (Baberowski 1999, 482; cf. Khalid 2009, 422–29).

Attempts to improve the notion of 'internal colonization' ('self-colonization') by transfer to a metaphorical level applied "onto the colonizing self", following Foucault's ideas of 'biopower' and the mechanisms of (self-)'discipline and punish', do not address in my view the hermeneutic problems involved adequately and the dialectics of the 'colonizer and colonized' either (Fournier 2012, 521–22; cf. Etkind 2001, but see Baberowski 1999, 484). And when we speak about the Russian gentry and their peasantry, dependent in legal, economic, cultural, and many other ways, why not keep time-tested notions of class structure and class dependencies. The same holds true, by the way, for later Soviet—not only Stalinist—dependencies when an urban-based elite executed central party decrees against the will and good of the people (peasantry) and when "state power by one section of society (the Control Center) [was used] to impose unfavorable rates of exchange on another part of the same society" (Gouldner 1977, 13; cf. Hind 1984, 545–46). In other words, 'internal colonization' representing a "cultural interpretation of imperial history" (Masoero 2013, 61) is not to be confused with 'internal colonialism' which, in the case of Russia and the Soviet Union, describes the colonial situation of non-Slavic, non-European groups within the imperial confines. To be sure, there are equivalents to 'internal colonialism' regarding those lands that became part of the German Empire following the three partitions of Poland.

However, while Russian publications on colonization efforts and objectives in various parts of the empire were abundant, literature on Russia as a colonial empire remained an exemption composed either by Siberian *Oblastniki* and their followers (Iadrintsev 1892; Panov 1905; Potanin 1907) or related to the colonial experience of some high-ranking Russian generals in Central Asia (e.g. Konstantin von Kaufman, Aleksey Kuropatkin) facing British imperialism in neighboring Afghanistan and Tibet. Alberto Masoero has recently called our attention again to the mushrooming literature on resettlement and colonization at the beginning of the twentieth century with an "authoritative semi-official publication" which states that "the 'lands of Asiatic Russia are an indivisible and inseparable part of our state and at the same time our only colony'" (2013, 59), thus confirming the existence of internal colonies within imperial confines. Officially, however, it was inconceivable and even risky to call the Caucasus, Siberia, Central Asia or other parts of the empire a 'Russian colony', since the "heterogeneous complexity of imperial society was accompanied by an almost obsessive concern for territorial integrity and centralization of authority" (ibid., 68). To characterize Russia as an empire of internal colonies would always challenge the cultural, hegemonic, and supranational construct of 'Russia united and inseparable' (*Rossiia edinaia i nedelimaia*), one of the basic principles of governance and 'national' identity in late imperial Russia (Frank 2003, 1659–60) and, again, today (Zorin 2013; Schorkowitz 2015, 10).

It was only in the wake of the October Revolution and for ideological purposes that colonialism was more openly addressed in order to criticize and denounce the old regime (Weinerman 1993, 430–31). Tsarist colonialism was then perceived as the outcome of mercantilism and merchant's capital rule that, according to Mikhail Pokrovsky (a student of Kliuchevskii), resulted in 'direct robbery' like everywhere else in the world (Drabkina [1930] 2014, 5). However, in contrast to Western colonial powers, Russia was a multinational empire in which "the majority of her conquered nations represented the object of colonial exploitation [...] with such an immediate closeness between colonies and metropoles" (ibid., 6; cf. Fieldhouse [1965] 1982, 334) that a borderline was sometimes hard to draw. Besides the serfdom prevailing in European Russia, the empire relied on its Asiatic peripheries that underwent colonial exploitation, performed and supported by Russia's capital, military, and bureaucracy as well as local feudal elites.

Since the economy was given a major agency in the relations between colonizer and colonized, the peasant question (resettlement) and agrarian development (colonization) dominated the colonial discourse in the 1920s and 1930s. Albeit ideologically charged and reductionist in form (Demin 2010, 86), volumes and journal articles mushroomed that detailed and applied Marxist-Leninist interpretations of tsarist colonialism for various regions of the empire, for instance Siberia (Okun 1935; Al'kor and Grekov 1936) and Transcaucasia (Petrushevskii 1936). Blaming the tsarist governments for supporting the "robbery of Kalmyk land" by landlords, peasants, and kulaks in Southern Russia, Grigorii Minkin opened his complaint in the central organ *Istorik-Marksist* (first edited by Pokrovsky): "Kalmykia before the imperialist war [World War I; D.S.] was one of Russia's colonies were Russian military-feudal imperialism ruled in full" ([1933] 1968, 30, 35). Such open criticism was, however, possible only until the late 1930s when, for obvious reasons, Marxist historiography was swiftly replaced by patriotic history, the dogma of peoples' friendship (*druzhba narodov*), and the personality cult of 'Great Leader' Stalin (Tillett 1969; Weinerman 1993, 431–33): "As the struggle for national survival against Germany fanned Russian nationalism, many Russian historians found it simply unacceptable to condemn Russian colonialism" (Weinerman 1993, 435). However, some lines of the older Marxist tradition survived and, following the Twentieth Party Congress (1956), reappeared during and after Khrushchev's short-lived thaw (cf. Gerasimova 1957; Burchinova 1968; Kamalov et al. 1971).

SOVIET DECOLONIZATION OR SOVIET COLONIALISM?

Recalling Lenin's famous dictum of 'Russia as a People's Prison', one is prone to ask whether the Soviet nationalities policy did in fact succeed in the liberation of the many nations. Were they granted sovereignty as promised by the revolutionary Bolsheviks? Walter Kolarz, a contemporary of Stalin purges, was pretty clear in his statement that "Soviet nationalities policy, instead of destroying Russian imperialism, has in reality tried to preserve and to consolidate it", and that the Soviet Union had not "solved the problem of nationalities" at all despite official claims to the contrary (1952, 303). Implementing the '*divide et impera*' principle more sophistically than the ancien regime, Soviet nationalities policy, rather promoted an ever increasing 'ethnic particularism' (Slezkine

1994) that turned the state into a 'communal apartment' (*komu-nal'ka*) with lesser room, lesser rights, and lesser power for each resident. Anyway, 'communal apartment' is but a nice metaphor for what otherwise can rightly be called 'internal colonialism', though Soviet colonialism was admittedly "markedly different from that of its tsarist predecessor" (Loring 2014, 80). The Soviet slogan 'freedom for colonial peoples' was, thus, rather meant to reach the colonized in neighboring Asia, predominantly China and India, still controlled by foreign powers, not the colonized at home.

In Soviet Central Asia, local autonomy of Bukhara, Khiva (Khwarezm), and Kokand was short-lived from 1918 to 1924, the autonomy of the Kazakh *Alash-Orda* being even shorter (Hayit 1965; Carrère d'Encausse 1999b; Sabol 2003; Kendirbai 2008). Calls for a "decolonization of the colony" (Teichmann 2016, 54) went unheard, except perhaps the 'Land and Water Reform' conducted by Mikhail Frunze in Semirechie in 1921–22, when an estimated 30,000 Slavic peasants and 10,000 more from other parts of Turkestan were forcefully resettled: "furent expulsés des terres qu'ils s'étaient appropriées, en partie lors de la répression de la révolte kazakhe et kirghize de 1916, année qui marqua le début d'une période d'extrême violence entre les colons agricoles slaves et les éleveurs centrasiatiques" (Pianciola 2008, 101). Plans for a self-determined federation based on Islamic and patriarchal traditions, brought forward in June 1923 by Kazakh born Sultanbek Khodzhanov, a multiple People's Commissar of the Turkestan Autonomous Soviet Socialist Republic, were not realized. Rather, the boundaries of the five new Central Asian republics, construed along ethnonational criteria and fixed in 1936, divided language groups and "cut across irrigation systems"; the Fergana Valley was "gerrymandered into three parts, distributed among Uzbekistan, Tajikistan and Kirghizia" (Caroe 1953, 139; cf. Teichmann 2016, 61–69).

The displacement of an indigenous peasantry by resettlements of a Slavic peasantry propelled by the Ignat'ev Commission (1884) and supervised by the Department of Agriculture and State Domains (1897) not only continued, but was purposefully increased in early Soviet times (Abdurakhimova 2002, 251–53; Fieldhouse [1965] 1982, 337). Displaced farmers and marginalized nomads (sedentarization) were turned into a proletariat, that did not exist previously, just to be merged with a small Russian proletariat based at a few factories, railways, and telegraph stations. On command and under surveillance of their senior comrades from Moscow, in private dubbed as "colonizers with party cards" (Loring 2014, 79; cf. Hayit 1965, 31), the Central Asians became first party members in their own interest, simultaneously instrumental to the Soviet modernization agenda. They built new irrigation systems and infrastructure; they planted more cotton fields. But they also took part in the genocidal collectivization drive with an estimated "1.5 million Kazakhs" who died from starvation (Olcott 1981, 122; cf. Caroe 1953, 141). Heavy industry (coal, oil, ore) and production sites arrived relatively late with the evacuation of large industry, white-collar workers, and knowledge during World War II.

Foreign trade motivated demands for an increase in Uzbek cotton production resulted in a local hunger crisis when central planning commissions were unable to secure a grain supply from other parts of Russia. It goes without saying that all economic decisions regarding "'forcing exports' and import suppression" were orchestrated in the Central Party and planning committees in Moscow, depriving "the region's inhabitants of access to basic necessities" and making "Central Asia economically dependent on the rest of the USSR for trade goods and foodstuffs" (Loring 2014, 80; cf. Weinerman 1993, 446–47; Obertreis 2017). It was the 'Control Center' that turned Central Asia into a real internal colony of the Soviet Union, and David Fieldhouse laconically noted that in 1917 "Central Asia was a typical colonial society [... and] it remained 'colonial' in all but concept" ([1965] 1982, 339; cf. Sahadeo 2007).

Central Asian scholars in postwar polemics with Muscovite colleagues on the decline of their republics were quite outspoken over tsarist and Soviet Russia's role in the "social, cultural, and political stagnation" (Weinerman 1993, 428). It was not caused by a sixteenth-century Central Asian economy, but by a colonial regime that had ruled them for over hundred years. Calls by the Party's Central Committee, reflecting a Union-wide policy (cf. Shunkov 1946; Bakhrushin 1955c), "to point out benefits Central Asia had enjoyed under Russian rule", were—though carefully worded—at the same time "outweighed by strong criticism of Russian colonialism" (Weinerman 1993, 439). Later critics, like Tajik First Secretary Bobodzhan Gafurov, argued along the lines of what Dipesh Chakrabarty has termed the 'broken promise dialog', meaning that colonialism "promised modernization, but did not deliver on it" (2009, 265, referring to Aimé Césaire; cf. Seton-Watson [1966] 1973, 116). Gafurov said in 1949 that Central Asia could have done even better and "developed capitalism without any Russian involvement [...]"

because the Russian authorities 'deliberately preserved the feudal backwardness' of Central Asia" (Weinerman 1993, 440). The question of how any regional backwardness was historically related to Russia's colonial administration and what indeed was her role in accelerating the "economic and cultural advance" (ibid., 452) in Central Asia remained a thorny political issue in historical and party debates well into the 1980s.

Resistance against collectivization and sedentarization throughout Central Asia, against the spread of cotton monoculture in Uzbekistan on the one side, attempts at economic diversification on the other, repeatedly provoked purges and harsh punishment (Carrère d'Encausse 1999b, 260–64; Hofmeister 2006, 74–77). Central Asian uprisings, like the Basmachi movement (1916–34)—in line with earlier, partly religious revolts of Andijan (1898) and Semirechie (1916)—were severely crushed (Carrère d'Encausse 1999a, 167–70; Myer 2002, 78–85; Babadzhanov 2009; Happel 2010) as were the analogous Murid uprisings in the Caucasus (Halbach [1989] 1994; Sidorko 2007). This also occurred with any other anti-Soviet movement be they organized by Slavic peasants in civil war European Russia (Brovkin 1989; Landis 2008), by indigenous peoples in Siberia in the 1930s (Leete 2005), by Ciscaucasia mountaineers (including Tatars and Kalmyks from the Ponto-Caspian steppe), or by Baltic inhabitants deported to Siberia and Central Asia in 1943–45 for alleged collaboration with Nazi Germany. It took the deported nations many years to receive political vindication and permission to return to their homelands where they faced severe opposition from a Slavic population that, fueled by Soviet propaganda, had taken their houses and settled there in the meantime (Nekrich 1978; Comins-Richmond 2002; Brandes et al. 2010; Burbank and Cooper 2010, 432; Pohl 2014; Annus 2018, 36–39).

Indeed typical for Cold War debates, it is tempting to include East Central European postwar satellites into an all Soviet list of internal colonies, especially given the "drastic tightening of Russian control over the entire bloc" (Twitchett 1965, 306). However, this seems neither appropriate nor to the point. The relationship of the Soviet Union with the German Democratic Republic, Poland, Czechoslovakia, Hungary, or Mongolia—to add another, often forgotten satellite in the Far East—was hegemonic and imperial in essence. The temporary possession of Finland, the Baltic states, and parts of Poland by the Russian Empire may define their later relationship to Russia as neo-colonial, but not more than that. Whereas "Russians' control over the Kazakhs" was colonial

(Reinhard 2011, 1). The "Soviet invasions of the Baltic states" are, as Epp Annus has repeatedly suggested, reminiscent of Russia's early expansion into other parts of the empire; the state did not arrive to colonize, but to occupy—an "occupation later developed into a period of a colonial rule" (2012, 21), which makes it "easy to classify the Soviet regime in the Baltic States as a colonial regime" (2018, 43; cf. Pohl 2014, 2–3).

In a similar way, though a genuine part of the empire, Ukraine can hardly be regarded as an 'internal colony' of the Soviet Union as students of modernization theory once thought (Biscoe 1986). Notwithstanding the exploitation of 'Little Russia' and the marginalization by 'Great Russia', the matter is more complex, given the cultural closeness between the two nations and the historical depth of their relations. Ukraine (literally: 'at the edge', borderland), also known as Kievan Rus' in medieval times, was the cradle of Russian polity, culture and economy before it gave way to the more prosperous principalities of Moscow, Vladimir-Suzdal, and Novgorod. Mongolia on the other hand, "landlocked between its two large neighbors Russia and China" (Myadar 2017, 8) was never part of the Russian Empire, but remained in the Soviet orbit and its crypto-colonial 'shadow' because of Moscow's growing political, military, economic, and cultural influence in the twentieth century.[3]

To get back to the decolonization question, the Soviet Union with the support of a Moscow influenced Comintern (1919–43) succeeded in convincing national leaders from decolonizing Asia and Africa of her good intentions to liberate their peoples from the colonial yoke while making many efforts to conceal the horrors of Communist terror at home (Baberowski 1998; Schorkowitz 2018, 412–16, 439–40). For decades, the Soviet Union and Communist China were perceived not as protagonists, but as victims of western colonialism and imperialism. This changed however, though slowly, in the mid-1950s, when "some Afro-Asians apparently distinguished between the Communist Chinese and the Soviet brands of 'colonialism'" (Twitchett 1965, 313). Fueled by the Sino-Russian conflict of the time, Moscow was blamed at the Bandung Conference (1955) for maintaining a colonial relationship with the "Eastern European countries" (Chakrabarty 2009, 269) and of "colonial practice [...], in particular when directed against its Muslim

---

[3] See also the chapters of Epp Annus and Orhon Myadar in this volume.

minorities in Central Asia" (Tarling 1992, 76; cf. Burbank and Cooper 2010, 441). Nikita Khrushchev in his speech at the United Nations in 1960 had to admit that the "colonial policy of the tsarist government did not differ essentially from the actions of Western powers in their colonies" (Weinerman 1993, 452).

IMPERIAL LEGACIES—POSTCOLONIAL OR NEO-COLONIAL?

Despite the global 'Third Wave' decolonization drive after World War II, succeeded by the 'Fourth Wave' triggered by the disintegrating Soviet Union, the colonial situation after *perestroika* did not always end with the new nations' declarations of independence. Moreover, scholars have not adequately addressed their 'colonial period' to date. As Frederick Cooper mentioned, "Nineteen eighty-nine is not celebrated here as a milestone of decolonization: Central Asian Muslims conquered by the czars and subjected to the violent modernizing project of the Soviets are not the object of analogous moral and political attention as North African Muslims colonized by the French" (2005, 410; cf. Reinhard 2011, 265–66). Though all eight republics of Central Asia and South Caucasia, as well as Belorussia, Ukraine, and the Baltic States have left the Soviet Union and become independent, others remain. They still represent relics from a not so distant colonial past, particularly the once autonomous republics of Siberia, the Volga region, Karelia, North Caucasia, and Kalmykia. The Russian Federation today is still a multinational state with a peculiar colonial legacy, rarely the focus of the "Western discourse of postcolonial studies" (Annus 2012, 23; cf. Myadar 2017, 6) (Fig. 5.1).

In fact, many unfinished struggles and tensions between adjacent nations over territorial, political, and cultural issues that are rooted in a tsarist and Soviet colonial past came only to the fore with or shortly after *perestroika* with an estimated "76 ethnic conflicts in the USSR in 1991" alone (Reinhard 2016, 1241–42). Clashes over boundaries or resources with repeated ethnic cleansing witnessed in Central Asia and the Caucasus until very recently are the obvious result of imperial gerrymandering and a divide-and-rule policy once meant to keep the imperial balance at a vulnerable periphery (Schorkowitz 2010; Huttenbach 1993; Chamberlain [1985] 1999, 109–15). While Armenia, Georgia, Azerbaijan, Moldova, and Ukraine represent states independent now for almost three decades, their status is still precarious given the frozen conflicts over Nagorno-Karabakh, South Ossetia, Abkhazia, Transnistria,

Fig. 5.1   Russia's Ethnic Republics, 1994. U.S. Central Intelligence Agency. https://www.ecoi.net/en/file/local/1058802/470_1283360485_russia-ethnic94.jpg

Crimea, and Donetsk that can rapidly turn hot at any time. Central Asia's post-socialist states "witnessed little in the way of genuine democracy", except perhaps Kyrgyzstan (and recently Armenia), exposing rather "continued traditions of authoritarianism rooted in Soviet bureaucratic practice" (Cole and Kandiyoti 2002, 199).

Other nations within the Russian Federation, which in Soviet times enjoyed a relative independence as Autonomous Soviet Socialist Republics and sought even more autonomy during *perestroika*, experienced instead a decrease in sovereignty. The First and Second Chechen Wars (1994–96, 1999–2000) exemplified the resistance to this decline. There were, of course, non-violent examples. Vladimir Putin during his first presidency (2000–2004) disempowered not only the parliament (*duma*), but also "the Federation Council as an institution of the regions and then the regions themselves" followed by another blow against federalism during his second presidency (2004–2008) when he abolished elections of regional governors and presidents (Leiße 2018, 297–98).

Thus, the head of government (*glava respubliki*) in Kalmykia, formerly called president and still elected autonomously in the early 1990s, since 2004 has been nominated by the president of the Russian Federation. Though the Tatarstan constitution stipulates that only the people can elect the president, Russian law on the nomination of governors now contradicts the constitution. The same 'election' procedure applies more or less to all eighty-three regions, such as the Buriat Republic, whose head of government was nominated or rather appointed since 2004 by the president of the Russian Federation until 2017 when an election finally took place (cf. Thompson 2008, 415; Carbonnel 2013). In addition, exclave territories with special national status became aligned. For instance, the Ust-Orda Buriat Autonomous Okrug, representing genuine Buriat homeland landlocked within Irkutsk Oblast, enjoyed autonomous status from 1993 to 2008 when it was politically downgraded and renamed Ust-Orda Buriat Okrug (Humphrey [1990] 1996, 122–23; Graber and Long 2009; Leiße 2018, 299–300).

Referring to Vladimir Putin, who in April 2005 called the fall of the Soviet Union "the greatest geopolitical catastrophe of the twentieth century" (Ukrainskaia Pravda Online 2005), Ewa Thompson thus is right in saying that "this segment of Russia's authorizing discourse [...] reflects a continuing reliance on imperial vision in the politics of historical interpretation in Russia, as well as the incompleteness of Russia's decolonization" (2008, 414; cf. Gammer and Kaplan 2013). In reaction to imperial losses at the periphery Moscow opted for even more integration, direct rule, and centralization, "stressing the importance of great power status for Russia, which [...] goes hand in hand with holding onto the remaining colonies" (Thompson 2008, 414). In fact, power structures are more streamlined, and there is a tendency to replace locally elected presidents of national republics with centrally appointed governors as in the old days, while national republics are transformed into regions. While offering an outlook on decolonization worldwide in their remarkable oeuvre, Jane Burbank and Frederick Cooper frankly admit that "Vladimir Putin revived the techniques of patrimonial power [... to] tighten control over religious institutions, bring the media to heel [... and] reenter the competition for Russia's borderlands" (2010, 455). Obviously, the "Russian empire has reappeared in yet another transmutation on its Eurasian space" (ibid.). Colonialism in Russia is not a thing of the past, and decolonization there "is thus by no means concluded" (Reinhard 2011, 266).

REFERENCES

Abdurakhimova, Nadira A. 2002. "The Colonial System of Power in Turkestan." *International Journal of Middle East Studies* 34(2): 239–62.

Al'kor, Ian Petrovich, and Boris Dmitrievich Grekov, eds. 1936. *Kolonial'naia politika Moskovskogo gosudarstva v Iakutii XVII v.: sbornik dokumentov* [Colonial Policy of the Muscovite State in Seventeenth-Century Yakutia: Collection of Documents]. Leningrad: Izdatel'stvo instituta narodov severa TsIK SSSR.

Allen, William Edward David, and Paul P. Muratoff. [1953] 1999. *Caucasian Battlefields: A History of the Wars on the Turco-Caucasian Border, 1828–1921.* Nashville, TN: The Battery Press.

Annus, Epp. 2012. "The Problem of Soviet Colonialism in the Baltics." *Journal of Baltic Studies* 43(1): 21–45.

Annus, Epp. 2018. *Soviet Postcolonial Studies: A View from the Western Borderlands.* London: Routledge.

Aust, Martin. 2000. "Rossia Siberica: Russisch-sibirische Geschichte im Vergleich zu mittelalterlichem Landesausbau und neuzeitlichem Kolonialismus." *Zeitschrift Für Weltgeschichte* 1: 39–63.

Babadzhanov, Bakhtiiar. 2009. "Andizhanskoe vosstanie 1898 goda i 'musul'manskii vopros' v Turkestane (vzgliady 'kolonizatorov' i 'kolonizirovannykh')" [The 1898 Andizhan Uprising and the 'Muslim Question' in Turkestan (Perspectives of the 'Colonizers' and the 'Colonized')]. *Ab Imperio* 2: 155–200.

Baberowski, Jörg. 1998. "Stalinismus als imperiales Phänomen: die islamischen Regionen der Sowjetunion 1920–1941." In *Stalinismus: Neue Forschungen und Konzepte*, edited by Stefan Plaggenborg, 113–50. Berlin: A. Spitz.

Baberowski, Jörg. 1999. "Auf der Suche nach Eindeutigkeit: Kolonialismus und zivilisatorische Mission im Zarenreich und in der Sowjetunion." *Jahrbücher Für Geschichte Osteuropas* 47(4): 482–504.

Bakhrushin, Sergei Vladimirovich. 1955a. "Ocherki po istorii kolonizatsii Sibiri v XVI i XVII vv" [Essays on the History of Siberia's Colonization in the 16th and 17th Centuries]. In *Nauchnye trudy, tom 3: Izbrannye raboty po istorii Sibiri XVI – XVII vv.; chast' pervaia: voprosy russkoi kolonizatsii Sibiri v XVI - XVII vv*, edited by Aleksandr Aleksandrovich Zimin, Nikolai Vladimirovich Ustiugov, Lev Vladimirovich Cherepnin, and Viktor Ivanovich Shunkov, 13–160. Moscow: Akademiia Nauk SSSR.

Bakhrushin, Sergei Vladimirovich. 1955b. "Pokruta na sobolinykh promyslakh XVII v" [Facilities for Seventeenth-Century Sable Hunting Trade]. In *Nauchnye trudy, tom 3: Izbrannye raboty po istorii Sibiri XVI – XVII vv.; chast' vtoraia: istoriia narodov Sibiri v XVI - XVII vv*, edited by Aleksandr Aleksandrovich Zimin, Nikolai Vladimirovich Ustiugov, Lev Vladimirovich Cherepnin, and Viktor Ivanovich Shunkov, 198–211. Moscow: Akademiia Nauk SSSR.

Bakhrushin, Sergei Vladimirovich. 1955c. "Polozhitel'nye rezul'taty russkoi koloni-zatsii v sviazi s prisoedineniem Iakutii k russkomu gosudarstvu" [Positive Results of the Russian Colonization in Connection with Yakutia Joining the Russian State]. In *Nauchnye trudy, tom 3: Izbrannye raboty po istorii Sibiri XVI – XVII vv.; chast' vtoraia: istoriia narodov Sibiri v XVI – XVII vv*, edited by Aleksandr Aleksandrovich Zimin, Nikolai Vladimirovich Ustiugov, Lev Vladimirovich Cherepnin, and Viktor Ivanovich Shunkov, 236–53. Moscow: Akademiia Nauk SSSR.

Bassin, Mark. 2006. "Geographies of Imperial Identity." In *The Cambridge History of Russia, vol. 2: Imperial Russia, 1689–1917*, edited by Dominic Lieven, 45–63. Cambridge: Cambridge University Press.

Biscoe, Anna. 1986. "Internal Colonialism in the USSR: The Case of Soviet Ukraine." PhD diss., The University of Alberta.

Brandes, Detlef, Holm Sundhaussen, and Stefan Troebst, eds. 2010. *Lexikon der Vertreibungen: Deportation, Zwangsaussiedlung und ethnische Säuberung im Europa des 20. Jahrhunderts*. Wien: Böhlau Verlag.

Breyfogle, Nicholas B., Abby Schrader, and Willard Sunderland. 2007. "Russian Colonizations: An Introduction." In *Peopling the Russian Periphery: Borderland Colonization in Eurasian History*, edited by Nicholas B. Breyfogle, Abby Schrader, and Willard Sunderland, 1–18. London: Routledge.

Brovkin, Vladimir N. 1989. "On the Internal Front: Bolsheviks and the Greens." *Jahrbücher für Geschichte Osteuropas* 37(4): 541–68.

Brower, Daniel R. 1997. "Islam and Ethnicity: Russian Colonial Policy in Turkestan." In *Russia's Orient: Imperial Borderlands and Peoples, 1700–1917*, edited by Daniel R. Brower and Edward J. Lazzerini, 115–37. Bloomington: Indiana University Press.

Burbank, Jane, and Frederick Cooper. 2010. *Empires in World History: Power and the Politics of Difference*. Princeton: Princeton University Press.

Burchinova, Liudmila Simbil'evna. 1968. "Kolonial'naia politika tsarizma v Kalmykii v russkoi istoriografii" [Colonial Policy of Czarism in Kalmykia in Russian Historiography]. *Vestnik Kalmytskogo Nauchno-Issledovatel'skogo Instituta Iazyka, Literatury i Istorii* 3: 5–25.

Carbonnel, Alissa de. 2013. "Putin Signs Law to Allow Him to Pick Russian Governors." Reuters World News, April 2. https://www.reuters.com/article/us-russia-elections/putin-signs-law-to-allow-him-to-pick-russian-governors-idUSBRE9310GR20130402. Accessed April 4, 2019.

Caroe, Olaf. 1953. "Soviet Colonialism in Central Asia." *Foreign Affairs* 32(1): 135–44.

Carrère d'Encausse, Hélène. 1999a. "Organizing and Colonizing the Conquered Territories." In *Central Asia, 130 Years of Russian Dominance: A Historical Overview*, edited by Edward Allworth, 151–71. Durham: Duke University Press.

Carrère d'Encausse, Hélène. 1999b. "The National Republics Lose Their Independence." In *Central Asia, 130 Years of Russian Dominance: A Historical Overview*, edited by Edward Allworth, 254–65. Durham: Duke University Press.

Chakrabarty, Dipesh. 2009. "Legacies of Bandung: Decolonization and the Politics of Culture." In *Enchantments of Modernity: Empire, Nation, Globalization*, edited by Saurabh Dube, 264–87. London: Routledge.

Chamberlain, Muriel E. [1985] 1999. *Decolonization: The Fall of the European Empires*. Malden, MA: Blackwell.

Cole, Juan R.I., and Deniz Kandiyoti. 2002. "Nationalism and the Colonial Legacy in the Middle East and Central Asia: Introduction." *International Journal of Middle East Studies* 34(2): 189–203.

Collins, David N. 1991. "Subjugation and Settlement in Seventeenth and Eighteenth-Century Siberia." In *The History of Siberia: From Russian Conquest to Revolution*, edited by Alan Wood, 37–56. London: Routledge.

Comins-Richmond, Walter. 2002. "The Karachay Struggle After the Deportation." *Journal of Muslim Minority Affairs* 22(1): 63–79.

Cooper, Frederick. 2005. "Postcolonial Studies and the Study of History." In *Postcolonial Studies and Beyond*, edited by Ania Loomba, Suvir Kaul, Matti Bunzl, Antoinette Burton, and Jed Esty, 401–22. Durham, NC: Duke University Press.

Crews, Robert D. 2009. "An Empire for the Faithful: A Colony for the Dispossessed." In *Le Turkestan russe. Une colonie comme les autres?* edited by Sergey Abashin and Svetlana Gorshenina, 79–106. Paris: IFEAC-Complexe.

Demin, M.A. 2010. "Kolonizatsiia i khoziaistvennoe osvoenie Sibiri v XVII v. v rannei Sovetskoi istoriografii" [Colonization and Economic Opening of Seventeenth-Century Siberia in Early Soviet Historiography]. *Vestnik Tomskogo gosudarstvennogo universiteta* 1(9): 86–91.

Dmytryshyn, Basil. 1991. "The Administrative Apparatus of the Russian Colony in Siberia and Northern Asia, 1581–1700." In *The History of Siberia: From Russian Conquest to Revolution*, edited by Alan Wood, 17–36. London: Routledge.

Dostoevsky, Fyodor. [1994] 2000. *A Writer's Diary: Volume Two, 1877–1881*. Translated and Annotated by Kenneth Lantz. Evanston, IL: Northwestern University Press.

Drabkina, Elizaveta Iakovlevna. [1930] 2014. *Natsional'nyi i kolonial'nyi vopros v tsarskoi Rossii* [The National and Colonial Question in Tsarist Russia]. Moscow: Lenand.

Etkind, Alexander. 2001. "Fuko i tezis vnutrennei kolonizacii: postkoloni-al'nyi vzgliad na sovetskoe proshloe" [Foucault and the Thesis of Internal Colonization: A Postcolonial Perspective on the Soviet Past]. *Novoe literaturnoe obozrenie* 49: 50–73.

Etkind, Alexander. 2011. *Internal Colonization: Russia's Imperial Experience.* Cambridge: Polity Press.

Etkind, Alexander. 2015. "How Russia 'Colonized Itself': Internal Colonization in Classical Russian Historiography." *International Journal for History, Culture and Modernity* 3(2): 159–71.

Fieldhouse, David K. [1965] 1982. *The Colonial Empires: A Comparative Survey from the Eighteenth Century.* London: Macmillan.

Fisher, Raymond H. 1943. *The Russian Fur Trade, 1550–1700.* Berkeley: University of California Press.

Forsyth, James. 1998. *A History of the Peoples of Siberia: Russia's North Asian Colony, 1581–1990.* Cambridge: Cambridge University Press.

Fournier, Anna. 2012. "Reflective Colonization: Domination, Consent, and the Self in Imperial Russia." *Russian History* 39(4): 519–37.

Frank, Allen. 1994. *The Siberian Chronicles and the Taybughid Biys of Sibir'.* Bloomington, IN: Research Institute for Inner Asian Studies.

Frank, Susi K. 2003. "'Innere Kolonisation' und *frontier*-Mythos: Räumliche Deutungskonzepte in Rußland und den USA." *Osteuropa* 53(11): 1658–75.

Gammer, Moshe, and Vera Kaplan. 2013. "Post-Soviet Narratives of the Conquest of the Caucasus." *Jahrbücher Für Geschichte Osteuropas* 61(1): 26–46.

Geraci, Robert. 2008. "Genocidal Impulses and Fantasies in Imperial Russia." In *Empire, Colony, Genocide: Conquest, Occupation, Subaltern Resistance in World History*, edited by A. Dirk Moses, 343–71. New York: Berghahn.

Geraci, Robert. 2010. "On 'Colonial' Forms and Functions." *Slavic Review* 69(1): 180–84.

Gerasimova, Kseniia Maksimovna. 1957. *Lamaizm i natsional'no-kolonial'naia politika tsarizma v Zabaikal'e v XIX i nachale XX vekov* [Lamaism and the National-Colonial Policy of Czarism in Transbaikal in the 19th and Beginning of the 20th Century]. Ulan-Ude: Buriat-Mongol'skii nauchno-issledova-tel'skii institut kul'tury.

Geyer, Dietrich. [1977] 1987. *Russian Imperialism: The Interaction of Domestic and Foreign Policy, 1860–1914.* Translated by Bruce Little. Leamington Spa: Berg.

Gibson, James R. 1991. "Tsarist Russia in Colonial America: Critical Constraints." In *The History of Siberia: From Russian Conquest to Revolution*, edited by Alan Wood, 92–116. London: Routledge.

Gouldner, Alvin W. 1977. "Stalinism: A Study of Internal Colonialism." *Telos: Critical Theory of the Contemporary* 34: 5–48.

Graber, Kathryn, and Joseph Long. 2009. "The Dissolution of the Buryat Autonomous Okrugs in Siberia: Notes from the Field." *Inner Asia* 11(1): 147–55.

Halbach, Uwe. [1989] 1994. "'Holy War' Against Czarism: The Links Between Sufism and Jihad in the Nineteenth-Century Anticolonial Resistance Against Russia." In *Muslim Communities Reemerge: Historical Perspectives on Nationality, Politics, and Opposition in the Former Soviet Union and Yugoslavia*, edited by Edward Allworth, 251–76. Durham: Duke University Press.

Happel, Jörn. 2010. *Nomadische Lebenswelten und zarische Politik: Der Aufstand in Zentralasien 1916* [Quellen und Studien zur Geschichte des östlichen Europa 76]. Stuttgart: Steiner.

Hayit, Baymirza. 1965. *Sowjetrussischer Kolonialismus und Imperialismus in Turkestan als Beispiel des Kolonialismus neueren Stils gegenüber einem islamischen Volk in Asien*. Oosterhout: Anthropological Publications.

Henze, Paul B. 1983. "Fire and Sword in the Caucasus: The 19th Century Resistance of the North Caucasian Mountaineers." *Central Asian Survey* 2(1): 5–44.

Hildermeier, Manfred. 2013. *Geschichte Russlands: Vom Mittelalter bis zur Oktoberrevolution*. München: Beck.

Hind, Robert J. 1984. "The Internal Colonial Concept." *Comparative Studies in Society and History* 26(3): 543–68.

Hirsch, Francine. 1998. "Empire of Nations: Colonial Technologies and the Making of the Soviet Union, 1917–1939." PhD diss., Princeton University.

Hofmeister, Ulrich. 2006. "Kolonialmacht Sowjetunion: Ein Rückblick auf den Fall Usbekistan." *Osteuropa* 56(3): 69–93.

Hofmeister, Ulrich. 2011. "Russische Erde in Taschkent? - Koloniale Identitäten in Zentralasien, 1867–1881." *Saeculum - Jahrbuch Für Universalgeschichte* 61 (2): 263–82.

Holquist, Peter. 2001. "To Count, to Extract, and to Exterminate: Population Statistics and Population Politics in Late Imperial and Soviet Russia." In *A State of Nations: Empire and Nation-Making in the Age of Lenin and Stalin*, edited by Ronald Grigor Suny and Terry Martin, 111–44. Oxford: Oxford University Press.

Humphrey, Caroline. [1990] 1996. "Buryatiya and the Buryats." In *The Nationalities Question in the Post-Soviet States*, edited by Graham Smith, 113–25. London: Longman.

Huttenbach, Henry R. 1993. "Nationalism in Armenia and Azerbaijan as Anti-Colonial Movements." In *In a Collapsing Empire: Underdevelopment, Ethnic Conflicts and Nationalisms in the Soviet Union*, edited by Marco Buttino, 197–202. Milano: Feltrinelli.

Iadrintsev, Nikolai Mikhailovich. 1892. *Sibir' kak koloniia v geografìcheskom, etnografìcheskom i istoricheskom otnoshenii* [Siberia as a Colony in Geographical, Ethnographical, and Historical Respect]. Sankt Petersburg: Sibiriakov.

Kamalov, Sabir Kamalovich, Zh. Ubbiniiazov, and R.K. Kosbergenov, eds. 1971. *Bor'ba trudiashchikhsia Karakalpakii protiv sotsial'nogo i kolonial'nogo gneta*

(1873 - fevral' 1917 g.) [The Struggle of Karakalpakstan Workers Against the Social and Colonial Yoke (1873–February 1917)]. Tashkent: Fan.

Kendirbai, Gulnar. 2008. "Challenging Colonial Power: Kazak Cadres and Native Strategies." *Inner Asia* 10(1): 65–85.

Khalid, Adeeb. 2007. "The Soviet Union as an Imperial Formation: A View from Central Asia." In *Imperial Formations*, edited by Ann Laura Stoler, Carole McGranahan, and Peter C. Perdue, 113–39. Santa Fe: School for Advanced Research Press.

Khalid, Adeeb. 2009. "Culture and Power in Colonial Turkestan." *Cahiers D'Asie Centrale* 17–18: 413–47.

Khodarkovsky, Michael. 2002. *Russia's Steppe Frontier: The Making of a Colonial Empire, 1500–1800*. Bloomington: Indiana University Press.

Khodarkovsky, Michael. 2009. "The Return of Lieutenant Atarshchikov: Empire and Identity in Asiatic Russia." *Ab Imperio* 1: 149–64.

Khodarkovsky, Michael. 2018. "Between Europe and Asia: Russia's State Colonialism in Comparative Perspective, 1550s–1900s." *Canadian-American Slavic Studies* 52(1): 1–29.

Kivelson, Valerie. 2007. "Claiming Siberia: Colonial Possession and Property Holding in the Seventeenth and Early Eighteenth Centuries." In *Peopling the Russian Periphery: Borderland Colonization in Eurasian History*, edited by Nicholas B. Breyfogle, Abby Schrader, and Willard Sunderland, 21–40. London: Routledge.

Kliuchevskii, Vasilii Osipovich. [1956] 1987. *Sochineniia v deviati tomakh: Kurs russkoi istorii, tom I, chast' I* [Writings in Nine Volumes: A Course of Russian History, Volume I, Part I]. Moscow: Mysl'.

Kolarz, Walter. 1952. *Russia and Her Colonies*. London: George Philip & Son Ltd.

Landis, Erik C. 2008. *Bandits and Partisans: The Antonov Movement in the Russian Civil War*. Pittsburgh: University of Pittsburgh Press.

Lantzeff, George V. 1943. *Siberia in the Seventeenth Century: A Study of the Colonial Administration*. Berkeley: University of California Press.

Leete, Art. 2005. "Anti-Soviet Movements and Uprisings Among the Siberian Indigenous Peoples During the 1920–40s." In *The Northern Peoples and States: Changing Relationships* [Studies in Folk Culture V], edited by Art Leete and Ülo Valk, 55–89. Tartu: Tartu University Press.

Leiße, Olaf. 2018. "Politisches Überleben im simulierten Föderalismus: die Republik Burjatien in Russland." In *Jahrbuch des Föderalismus 2018: Föderalismus, Subsidiarität und Regionen in Europa*, edited by Europäisches Zentrum für Föderalismus-Forschung, 297–308. Baden-Baden: Nomos.

Lieven, Dominic. 2004. "Empire on Europe's Periphery: Russian and Western Comparisons." In *Imperial Rule*, edited by Alexei Miller and Alfred J. Rieber, 133–49. Budapest: Central European University Press.

Lincoln, William Bruce. 1994. *The Conquest of a Continent: Siberia and the Russians.* London: Cape.

Loring, Benjamin. 2014. "'Colonizers with Party Cards': Soviet Internal Colonialism in Central Asia, 1917–39." *Kritika: Explorations in Russian and Eurasian History* 15(1): 77–102.

Martin, Janet. 1986. *Treasure of the Land of Darkness: The Fur Trade and Its Significance for Medieval Russia.* Cambridge: Cambridge University Press.

Martin, Janet. 1995. *Medieval Russia, 980–1584.* Cambridge: Cambridge University Press.

Martin, Virginia. 2001. *Law and Custom in the Steppe: The Kazakhs of the Middle Horde and Russian Colonialism in the Nineteenth Century.* Richmond: Curzon Press.

Masoero, Alberto. 2013. "Territorial Colonization in Late Imperial Russia: Stages in the Development of a Concept." *Kritika: Explorations in Russian and Eurasian History* 14(1): 59–91.

McDonald, David MacLaren. 2010. "Russian Statecraft After the 'Imperial Turn': The Urge to Colonize?" *Slavic Review* 69(1): 185–88.

Minkin, Grigorii Zakharovich. [1933] 1968. "Kolonial'naia politika tsarizma v Kalmykii vo vtoroi polovine XIX i nachale XX vv" [Colonial Policy of Czarism in Kalmykia in the Second Half of the 19th and Beginning of the 20th Centuries]. In *Ob obshchestvennom stroe Kalmykii i kolonial'noi politike tsarizma,* edited by A.I. Naberukhin, 30–57. Elista: Kalmytskii Nauchno-Issledovatel'skij Institut Iazyka, Literatury i Istorii.

Morrison, Alexander Stephen. 2008. *Russian Rule in Samarkand 1868–1910: A Comparison with British India.* Oxford: Oxford University Press.

Mostashari, Firouzeh. 2001. "Colonial Dilemmas: Russian Policies in the Muslim Caucasus." In *Of Religion and Empire: Missions, Conversion, and Tolerance in Tsarist Russia,* edited by Robert P. Geraci and Michael Khodarkovsky, 229–49. Ithaca: Cornell University Press.

Murray, Jesse D. 2016. "'Not Far from the Kingdom of God': Shamanism and Colonial Control in Russia's Eastern Borderlands, 1853–1917." *Journal of World History* 27(3): 535–63.

Myadar, Orhon. 2017. "In the Soviet Shadow: Soviet Colonial Politics in Mongolia." *Inner Asia* 19(1): 5–28.

Myer, Will. 2002. *Islam and Colonialism: Western Perspectives on Soviet Asia.* Richmond: Curzon Press.

Nekrich, Aleksandr M. 1978. *Punished Peoples: The Deportation and Fate of Soviet Minorities at the End of the Second World War.* New York: Norton.

Obertreis, Julia. 2017. *Imperial Desert Dreams: Cotton Growing and Irrigation in Central Asia, 1860–1991.* Göttingen: V&R Unipress.

Okun, Semen Bentsianovich. 1935. *Ocherki po istorii kolonial'noi politiki tsarizma v Kamchatskom krae* [Essays on the History of Colonial Policy of Czarism in Kamchatka Land]. Leningrad: Sotsekgiz.

Olcott, Martha Brill. 1981. "The Collectivization Drive in Kazakhstan." *The Russian Review* 40(2): 122–42.

Osterhammel, Jürgen. [2009] 2014. *The Transformation of the World: A Global History of the Nineteenth Century.* Translated by Patrick Camiller. Princeton: Princeton University Press.

Panov, Aleksandr Alekseevich. 1905. *Sakhalin, kak koloniia: ocherki kolonizatsii i sovremennogo polozheniia Sakhalina* [Sakhalin as Colony: Essays of Colonization and the Contemporary Situation of Sakhalin]. Moscow: I.D. Sytin.

Petrushevskii, Il'ia Pavlovich. 1936. *Kolonial'naia politika rossiiskogo tsarizma v Azerbaidzhane v 20-60-kh gg. XIX v* [Colonial Policy of Russian Czarism in Azerbaijan in the 1920s to 60s]. Moscow: Akademiia Nauk SSSR.

Pianciola, Niccol. 2008. "Décoloniser l'Asie Central? Bolcheviks et colons au Semirech'e (1920–1922)." *Cahiers Du Monde Russe* 49(1): 101–43.

Pierce, Richard A. 1960. *Russian Central Asia, 1867–1917: A Study in Colonial Rule.* Berkeley: California University Press.

Pohl, Otto J. 2014. "Colonialism in One Country: The Deported Peoples in the USSR as an Example of Internal Colonialism." *Journal of Race, Ethnicity, and Religion* 5(7): 1–27.

Potanin, Grigorii Nikolaevich. 1907. *Oblastnicheskaia tendentsiia v Sibiri* [Oblastnik Tendencies in Siberia]. Tomsk: Parovaia tipo-litografiia Sibirskogo tovarishchestva pechatnogo dela.

Reinhard, Wolfgang. 2011. *A Short History of Colonialism.* Manchester: Manchester University Press.

Reinhard, Wolfgang. 2016. *Die Unterwerfung der Welt: Globalgeschichte der europäischen Expansion 1415–2015.* München: C.H. Beck.

Rogozhin, Nikolai M. 1993. "Posolski Books as a Source in the Study of Political Relations of Russia with Peoples and Countries of the Orient." In *Altaica Berolinensia: The Concept of Sovereignty in the Altaic World: Permanent International Altaistic Conference, 34th Meeting, Berlin, 21–26 July 1991*, edited by Barbara Kellner-Heinkele, 191–208. Wiesbaden: Harrassowitz.

Sabol, Steven. 2003. *Russian Colonization and the Genesis of Kazak National Consciousness.* Basingstoke: Palgrave Macmillan.

Sahadeo, Jeff. 2007. *Russian Colonial Society in Tashkent, 1865–1923.* Bloomington: Indiana University Press.

Sahni, Kalpana. 1997. *Crucifying the Orient: Russian Orientalism and the Colonization of Caucasus and Central Asia.* Oslo: White Orchid Press.

Schimmelpenninck van der Oye, David. 2010. *Russian Orientalism: Asia in the Russian Mind from Peter the Great to the Emigration.* New Haven: Yale University Press.

Schorkowitz, Dittmar. 2001. "The Orthodox Church, Lamaism and Shamanism among the Buriats and Kalmyks, 1825–1925." In *Of Religion and Empire: Missions, Conversion, and Tolerance in Tsarist Russia,* edited by Robert Geraci and Michael Khodarkovsky, 201–25. Ithaca: Cornell University Press.

Schorkowitz, Dittmar. 2010. "Geschichte, Identität und Gewalt im Kontext postsozialistischer Nationsbildung." *Zeitschrift Für Ethnologie* 135: 99–160.

Schorkowitz, Dittmar. 2012. "Historical Anthropology in Eurasia '… and the Way Thither'." *History and Anthropology* 23(1): 37–62.

Schorkowitz, Dittmar. 2015. *Imperial Formations and Ethnic Diversity: Institutions, Practices, and Longue Durée Illustrated by the Example of Russia.* (Max Planck Institute for Social Anthropology Working Paper 165). Halle/Saale: Max Planck Institute for Social Anthropology.

Schorkowitz, Dittmar. 2017. "Dealing with Nationalities in Imperial Formations: How Russian and Chinese Agencies Managed Ethnic Diversity in the 17th to 20th Centuries." In *Managing Frontiers in Qing China: The Lifanyuan and Libu Revisited,* edited by Dittmar Schorkowitz and Chia Ning, 389–434. Leiden: Brill.

Schorkowitz, Dittmar. 2018. '… *Daß die Inorodcy niemand rettet und das Heil bei ihnen selbst liegt …': Quellen und Beiträge zur historischen Ethnologie von Burjaten und Kalmücken.* Wiesbaden: Harrassowitz.

Seton-Watson, Hugh. [1966] 1973. "Moscow's Imperialism." In *Crisis and Continuity in World Politics: Readings in International Relations,* edited by George A. Lanyi and Wilson C. McWilliams, 114–17. New York: Random House.

Shunkov, Viktor Ivanovich. 1946. *Ocherki po istorii kolonizatsii Sibiri v XVII - nachale XVIII vekov* [Essays on Siberia's Colonization History from the 17th to the Beginning of the 18th Centuries]. Moscow: Akademiia Nauk SSSR.

Sidorko, Clemens P. 2007. *Dschihad im Kaukasus: Antikolonialer Widerstand der Dagestaner und Tschetschenen gegen das Zarenreich (18. Jahrhundert bis 1859).* Wiesbaden: Reichert.

Slezkine, Yuri. 1994. "The USSR as a Communal Apartment, or How a Socialist State Promoted Ethnic Particularism." *Slavic Review* 53(2): 414–52.

Stahl, Kathleen Mary. 1951. *British and Soviet Colonial Systems.* London: Faber and Faber Limited.

Sunderland, Willard. 2000. "The 'Colonization Question': Visions of Colonization in Late Imperial Russia." *Jahrbücher für Geschichte Osteuropas* 48(2): 210–32.

Sunderland, Willard. 2004. *Taming the Wild Field: Colonization and Empire on the Russian Steppe.* Ithaca: Cornell University Press.

Sunderland, Willard. 2010. "The Ministry of Asiatic Russia: The Colonial Office That Never Was but Might Have Been." *Slavic Review* 69(1): 120–50.

Tarling, Nicholas. 1992. "'Ah-Ah': Britain and the Bandung Conference of 1955." *Journal of Southeast Asian Studies* 23(1): 74–111.

Teichmann, Christian. 2016. *Macht der Unordnung: Stalins Herrschaft in Zentralasien 1932–1950*. Hamburg: Hamburger Edition.

Thompson, Ewa. 2008. "Postcolonial Russia." In *A Historical Companion to Postcolonial Literatures: Continental Europe and Its Empires*, edited by Prem Poddar, Rajeev S. Patke, and Lars Jensen, 412–17. Edinburgh: Edinburgh University Press.

Tillett, Lowell. 1969. *The Great Friendship: Soviet Historians on the Non-Russian Nationalities*. Chapel Hill, NC: The University of North Carolina Press.

Treadgold, Donald W. 1952. "Russian Expansion in the Light of Turner's Study of the American Frontier." *Agricultural History* 26(4): 147–52.

Twitchett, Kenneth J. 1965. "Colonialism: An Attempt at Understanding Imperial, Colonial, and Neo-colonial Relationships." *Political Studies* 13(3): 300–23.

Ukrainskaia Pravda Online. 2005. Raspad SSSR Putin nazval samoi bol'shoi geopoliticheskoi katastrofoi [Putin Called the Breakup of the USSR the Biggest Geopolitical Catastrophe]. Ukrainskaia Pravda Online, April 25. http://www.pravda.com.ua/rus/news/2005/04/25/4387750. Accessed April 8, 2019.

Vinkovetsky, Ilya. 2011. *Russian America: An Overseas Colony of a Continental Empire, 1804–1867*. Oxford: Oxford University Press.

Weinerman, Eli. 1993. "The Polemics Between Moscow and Central Asians on the Decline of Central Asia and Tsarist Russia's Role in the History of the Region." *The Slavonic and East European Review* 71(3): 428–81.

Zorin, Vladimir Iur'evich. 2013. "Strategiia gosudarstvennoi natsional'noi politiki: Traditsionnost' i novye podkhody k ukrepleniiu edinstva mnogonatsional'nogo naroda Rossii (Rossiiskoi natsii)" [The Strategy of Governmental National Policy: Traditionalism and New Approaches for Consolidating the Unity of Russia's Multinational People (Russian Nation)]." In *X Kongress ėtnografov i antropologov Rossii: Tezisy dokladov. Moskva, 2–5 iiulia 2013 g*, edited by Marina Iur'evna Martynova, Natalina A. Lopulenko, and N.A. Belova, VII–XII. Moscow: IĖA RAN.

PART II

The Empire's Colonialism 'at home'

CHAPTER 6

Handmaidens of Continental Colonialism? The Ambiguities of the Imperial Russian Geographical Society's Central Asian Expeditions

David Schimmelpenninck van der Oye

INTRODUCTION

According to Milan Hauner, the Imperial Russian Geographical Society's "talented members played the Great Game of Central Asia with their British counterparts" (1990, 41). It was a passing remark in his book about Russian geopolitics, and he did not elaborate. Nevertheless, the statement is intriguing, for it suggests that this institution, ostensibly founded to further scientific knowledge, also engaged in military intelligence when it sent its intrepid explorers beyond Siberia's borders into 'High Asia's' uncharted wilderness during the latter half of the nineteenth century.

Hauner was hardly the only one to make this claim. Because those men who ventured into Central Asia under the society's aegis were almost invariably officers of the army's general staff, because of the

D. Schimmelpenninck van der Oye (✉)
Department of History, Brock University, St. Catharines, Canada
e-mail: dschimmelpennin@brocku.ca

© The Author(s) 2019
D. Schorkowitz et al. (eds.), *Shifting Forms of Continental Colonialism*,
https://doi.org/10.1007/978-981-13-9817-9_6

151

military's intimate ties with the organization, and because Russia engaged in a series of conquests in the region, scientific curiosity and strategic intelligence often overlapped. As the historian of Russian science, Alexander Vucinich, put it:

> The government [...] viewed the [Geographical Society] as an instrument of Russian territorial expansion and a means of collecting information in Asia. It was through the Geographical Society that the government gathered economic, ethnographic, and demographic information in the Chinese, Tibetan and Mongolian areas far beyond the boundaries of the empire. (1963, vol. 2, 87)

Indeed, the society's most famous explorer, Nikolai Przheval'skii, once described his journeys as "scientific reconnaissance" (*nauchnaia rekognostsirovka*) (1888, 56).

The argument about geography's role as a tool of colonial conquest will be familiar to readers of Edward Said's *Orientalism*. First published in 1978, the book asserted that academic knowledge about the East was a handmaiden of Western imperialism. While the author only briefly touched on the eighteenth-century voyages of James Cook and Count Louis-Antoine de Bougainville in the Pacific Ocean (1978, 117), others subsequently applied his Orientalist schema more thoroughly to Victorian Britain's explorers. Thomas Richards (1993) saw their voyages as an integral part of collecting information about far-flung territories to organize an 'imperial archive' that would help their kingdom gather and rule overseas colonies. At the same time, Paul Carter and Mary Louise Pratt read the accounts of European travelers to other continents through Said's post-colonialist lens, while Felix Driver wrote about 'geography militant' (Carter 1987; Pratt 1992; Driver 2001). And, according to *The Oxford History of the British Empire*, "Exploration and Empire sprang from the same motives and mutually supported each other in defining, exploiting and acquiring territory" (Stafford 1998, 318).

To what extent was this true for the Imperial Russian Geographical Society's Central Asian expeditions? Should this be the case, how did its 'scientific reconnaissance' fit into the machinery of tsarist colonial expansion? In short, what were the implications of the Geographical Society's role in Russian imperialism?

UNKNOWN CENTRAL ASIA

At the turn of the nineteenth century, Russians knew very little about Central Asia, the region UNESCO (2017) defines as the lands from the Caspian Sea's eastern shore to Mongolia, Xinjiang and Tibet. This became abundantly clear when Emperor Paul I ordered a host of some 22,000 Cossacks and Kalmyks to march from Western Siberia to British India on a mission of conquest in 1801.[1] As he told its commander, Cavalry General Vasilii Petrovich Orlov, "my maps only go as far as Khiva and the Amu Darya. Gathering details [about the way beyond] is your affair."[2]

The tsar did not exaggerate about Russian ignorance of the geography south of his empire's Asian frontier. In addition to the travelogue of a fifteenth-century merchant to India (Nikitin 1958), the main first-hand accounts available at the time were those of a Cossack sergeant who had escaped captivity as a slave in Bukhara in the 1770s and the peregrinations of a Greek cleric ten years later (Efremov [1811] 1995; Khrisanf 1995). Meanwhile, more recent reports about the area were highly contradictory. According to Major Egor Blankenagel, who had traveled to the Khanate of Khiva in 1793, Russian troops could easily traverse Central Asia, but seven years later Lieutenant-General Nikolai Bakhmetev, Orenburg's governor, warned that the area held 'many difficulties and dangers' (Arkhiv Gosudarstvennago Soveta 1888, 625–35; Russko-Indiiskie otnosheniia 1965, 406–9). In any event, the emperor's assassination in a coup d'état led to the quixotic campaign's cancellation before Ataman Orlov's men had even crossed the border. Paul should have known that Bakhmetev was probably closer to the mark when the general cautioned about Central Asia's hazards. The expedition his forefather, Tsar Peter I, had ordered to Khiva some eighty years earlier ended disastrously with the death of its commander, Prince Aleksandr Bekovich-Cherkasskii, and virtually all his men at the hands of the khan (Terent'ev 1906, vol. 1, 21–34).

Like the prince's ill-fated journey into Central Asia, eighteenth-century Russian explorers generally ventured at the behest of the

---

[1] For a recent overview, see Schimmelpenninck van der Oye (2014), Russian-language accounts include Bezotosnyi (2017) and Batorskii (1886).

[2] Paul I to V.P. Orlov, Rescript, 12/1/1801, Rossiiskii gosudarstvennyi voenno-istoricheskii arkhiv (hereafter: RGVIA), fond 846, opis' 16, delo 323, sheet (*list*) 1.

sovereign or the Academy of Sciences. Their missions were typically undertaken to reconnoiter the vast empire and its extremities, from Vitus Bering's Kamchatka expeditions under Peter I and his immediate successors, to Peter Simon Pallas' encyclopedic surveys of the interior under Catherine II (Lebedev and Esakov 1971). But the need to know about what lay beyond the empire's borders grew more urgent in the next century. In part, this was driven by the increasing sophistication of the army's apparatus for strategic intelligence.

MODERNIZING INTELLIGENCE

Until the Napoleonic Wars at the turn of the nineteenth century, Europe's kings and generals basically had two ways to gather details about a potential adversary: spies, including those in an official capacity (ambassadors), and battlefield reconnaissance.[3] Furthermore, they gathered such intelligence on an ad hoc basis and made no effort to set up a permanent system to analyze or keep it (Rothenberg 1992, 99). But the growing size of European armies as a result of the French Revolution's *levée en masse*, as well as more rational bureaucracies to manage them, led to some profound changes in this respect.

Already in the seventeenth-century commanders had begun to gather their assistants into a staff to look after such details as logistics, troop movements, and intelligence. Initially known as quartermasters—since their responsibilities included setting up billets, or quarters, for the men—they were organized into groups directly reporting to the commander-in-chief. Based on the model established by Sweden's King Gustav Adolphus in the early 1600s, Peter the Great had established a quartermaster's department (*kvatirmeisterskaia chast'*) during his Great Northern War in the next century's first decades. According to his regulation of 1716, the tsar defined its functions as, among other things, gathering information about the theater of operations, drawing maps, and setting up camps (Os'kin 1969, 93; Alekseev 1998, vol. 1, 29–30).

Renamed the general staff by Catherine II in 1763, this body soon became a separate corps with its own uniform.[4] However, the foreign

---

[3]For a recent comprehensive history of the 'second oldest profession' see Andrew (2018).

[4]There would be more name changes, including Main Staff (*Glavnyi shtab*) and, again, Quartermaster's Department, but the functions generally remained the same. See *Voennaia entsiklopedia* (1911–15), s.v. "General'nyi shtab."

office remained the main source of information about potential adversaries until well into the nineteenth century. Given the traditional rivalry between diplomats and soldiers, the Chorister's Bridge was not always an efficient conduit for strategic intelligence to the army (Zvonar'ev 1929, vol. 1, 32–33). There were occasional exceptions. The most notable was on the eve of the Grande Armée's invasion in 1812, when Colonel Alexander Chernyshev, the tsar's personal liaison to Napoleon, passed on the French war plans to St. Petersburg (Bezotosnyi 2005, 96–97).

Both in the Russian and other European armies, such efforts to set up a general staff were motivated by wartime exigencies and did not continue in peacetime. However, a thorough reform of the Prussian army in the wake of its humiliating defeat by Napoleon at the Battles of Jena and Auerstädt in 1806, led to a more permanent establishment in the kingdom to plan for war even in peace. According to the order in 1816 that defined its functions, the *Generalshtab* became the first permanent structure responsible for gathering, analyzing, and disseminating information about potential adversaries (Goerlitz 1985, 25–49).

In Russia, the Napoleonic Wars also saw the development of a separate body responsible for intelligence, the "Military-Scientific Committee" (*Voenno-uchenyi komitet* or VUK). Although its focus initially was on technical matters, such as artillery ballistics and engineering, the VUK's responsibilities eventually broadened to include all of the scientific requirements of the general staff and corps of topographers (Rich 1998, 57). While a step forward, the tsarist army's approach to intelligence remained rudimentary. As one historian points out, the Russian equivalent of the term, *razvedka*, was first defined in a dictionary in only 1847 (Alekseev 1996, 25).

Meanwhile, the need for officers qualified to deal with increasingly complicated work led to the establishment in 1832 of what eventually became the Nicholas Academy of the General Staff. Subjects related to geography took an important place in its curriculum from the start. Along with such subjects as strategy, tactics, and military history, the academy's students also took courses in geodesy, cartography and military statistics. David Rich points out that the latter had less to do with numbers than with more descriptive data:

The 'statistic' in the nineteenth century was a branch of political science dealing with the collection of facts bearing on the *condition of the state* or a community [… it was] in contrast to 'political arithmetic,' which was of numerical character. (Rich 1998, 43)

Turning to Asia

Before the nineteenth century, the military orientation of the Romanovs was mostly to the west. But in the decades after the Battle of Waterloo, they increasingly turned eastward. When Tsar Alexander I began to annex Georgia in 1801, he did not control the Islamic nations that inhabited the Caucasus Mountains that separated it from his empire. Their dogged resistance to tsarist rule drew the Russian army into a lengthy counter-insurgency campaign not suppressed until the 1860s. Meanwhile, that decade marked the start of a twenty-year effort to conquer Khiva, Bukhara, and Kokand in Central Asia. And the nineteenth century also saw four wars with Turkey, two with Persia, not to mention considerable tension with China.

Many of these conflicts indirectly involved Great Britain, which often viewed any Russian advances in Asia as threats to its own colonies on the Indian subcontinent. The tsarist conquests in Turkestan were particularly alarming, since they seemed to draw the formidable Eurasian empire ever closer to British India's northern frontier. The result was an intense rivalry between London and St. Petersburg for dominion over Central Asia, a conflict popularly known as the 'Great Game'.[5] Despite the sobriquet's gentlemanly connotations, it was a deadly serious confrontation that Queen Victoria saw as nothing less than "a question of Russian or British supremacy in the world" (Fromkin 1980, 951). Much like the twentieth century's Cold War between the Soviet Union and the United States, the Great Game saw practically no direct armed conflict involving the two principal players. Instead, again as during the more recent superpower confrontation, they carried out their rivalry through third parties, intrigue, and espionage. The late Peter Hopkirk, who wrote what is still the classic British account, subtitled his book *On Secret Service in High Asia*.[6]

The fact that much of Central Asia remained uncharted by Europeans made the Anglo-Russian encounter there all the more mysterious. As on the 'dark continent' of Africa, geographers were particularly keen to fill in the white spaces on their maps of the region. According to its history

---

[5] For the phrase's etymology, see Becker (2012).

[6] Hopkirk (1990), for the Russian perspective, see Khalfin (1965), Sergeev (2013). A forthcoming work by Morrison (2019) based on archival research describes Russia's advance into Western Turkestan.

of exploration, "judging by the gold medals awarded by the Royal Geographical Society, the heart of Asia between the Caspian Sea and the Great Wall of China represented the 19th century's most important arena of exploration" (Keay 1991, 76). Even if motivated more by scientific curiosity than colonial ambition, Germans were very much among them. They included, most notably, the great Prussian geographer, Baron Alexander von Humboldt, and Carl Ritter. Although more famous for his earlier South American voyage, in 1829 the baron conducted a major survey of Siberia at the invitation of Emperor Nicholas I, which resulted in the publication of *Asie Centrale*, a three-volume description of its geology and climate (Humboldt 1834; cf. Wulf 2015). Meanwhile, three of the nineteen volumes in Carl Ritter's *Erdkunde* (1822–1829) were about 'Eastern High Asia,' the region east of Iran. Humboldt and Ritter's greatest legacy was their comprehensive approach to geography. Objecting to unsystematically gathering vast data about an unknown area, as had been the practice of eighteenth-century *encyclopediste* explorers, they advocated combining topography, climatology, ethnography, and other fields into an integrated whole. According to their conception, *Erdkunde*, as geography came to be known in Germany, had a broad remit that examined all interactions between the earth and its inhabitants (Martin 2005, 107–28).

The Geographical Society

Scientists in Russia were particularly receptive to this new approach, not least because so many of them had German blood. To the annoyance of more patriotic Russians, Germans (including Baltic Germans, who were Russian subjects) had dominated the Academy of Sciences ever since its founding by Peter the Great; in 1840, out of twenty-eight full Academicians, only four were either Russian or Ukrainian (Vucinich 1963, vol. 1, 306). And when, five years later, the Russian Geographical Society was established, most of its founding members were also ethnically German. The preponderance of Germans among the Society's early members even led to friction with Russians, who within two years outnumbered them (Knight 1994, 237).

Somewhat ironically, given the future rivalry among their Central Asian explorers, the chairman of the Royal Geographical Society in London, Sir Roderick Murchison, had been one of the most enthusiastic proponents of a similar organization in St. Petersburg. During his travels in Russia in the early 1840s to write a book about its geology, Sir Roderick urged the many scientists and officials he met there to follow the British example (Vucinich 1963, vol. 1, 351). Among those enthusiastic about the idea were three veteran naval explorers, Admiral Fedor Lütke, Baron Ferdinand von Wrangel, and Karl von Baer. Their plan to establish a new learned society to promote geography in Russia gained momentum in 1845 at a banquet to honor the naturalist Alexander von Middendorff, who had just completed a long trek in northern Siberia for the Academy of Sciences (Sunderland 2014, 145).

With the enthusiastic support of Grand Duke Konstantin Nikolaevich, the tsar's second son (and the society's first president), imperial approval came quickly. At the official opening of the newly chartered Russian Geographical Society on October 7, 1845, its vice president, Admiral Lütke, stressed that studying the empire itself would get top priority. He declared that, unlike other such institutions in Europe, which focused on foreign lands, rather than their own, "the primary interest of the *Russian* Geographical Society must be promoting *Russian Geography*, using the term geography in its broadest sense" (Semenov 1896, vol. 3, 1317, italics in the original). When finalized in 1849, article eight of the charter of what was now the Imperial Russian Geographical Society confirmed that its primary goal was studying the empire itself (Vigasin et al. 1997, 87). Already a year earlier, Nikolai Nadezhdin, the president of the Ethnographic Division, had launched a major survey of European Russia's peasantry (Knight 1994, 267–76) and the young organization eagerly took over the Academy of Sciences' responsibilities for surveying Siberia (Bartol'd [1911] 1977, vol. 9, 424). But from the very start, the Society also declared its ambitions with regard to Central Asia, which eventually became "the most significant of its future tasks," according to its long-serving vice president Petr Semenov. *Raison d'état* was one of the drivers, Semenov went on to explain. As he put it, "force of circumstance drove Russia into Asia's depths," arguing that Kazakh raids on Cossack settlements and commercial caravans on the steppe frontier obligated military expansion into Turkestan (Semenov 1896, vol. 1, 27).[7]

---

[7] The Society's priorities did not meet with universal approval. In 1876, its commission charged with revising topographical maps of European Russia complained, "to make geographical discoveries, we must emerge from Asia's depths. In European Russia we will find extensive regions that require proper cartographical coverage." See Baskhanov (2014, 299).

Beginning in the early 1830s, "pioneers of Russian geographical science" (Semenov 1896, vol. 1, 27) often followed in the army's wake, and by 1846 members of the Society, including Colonel Mikhail Ivanin, as well as Lieutenants Aleksei Butakov and Aleksei Maksheev, were also leading surveys into the region. Although these expeditions were ordered by the military, the officers did not hesitate to share their findings (scrubbed of any sensitive intelligence) with the institution's scientists. It would nevertheless be a civilian member, Petr Semenov, who would lead the Central Asian expedition that brought the Geographical Society international recognition. A University of St. Petersburg student working on a master's degree on the flora of the Don River Valley, Semenov joined the organization in 1849.[8] He was an active member from the very start and would eventually serve as its vice president for four decades. At the time, despite his coursework, he was soon appointed secretary of its Physical Geography section and even agreed to translate the volumes of Ritter's *Erdkunde* dealing with southern Siberia and eastern Central Asia. Not content with sedentary scholarship, in 1855 Semenov convinced the society to sponsor his plan to explore the Tian Shan Mountains, covering, however, most of the cost from his own pocket (ibid., 95). The range, which shielded the northwestern border of the Qing Dynasty's possessions in Eastern Turkestan (now known as Xinjiang), remained virtually unknown to Europeans. Semenov's findings greatly enriched Western knowledge about the range's geology, climate, biology, and ethnography, and were eventually rewarded by the tsar's permission to add "Tian-Shanskii" to his surname (Semenov 1988). More important, the expedition marked the start of a momentous series of expeditions by the Imperial Russian Geographical Society to map Asia's unknown interior.

MILIUTIN'S NEW APPROACH

Semenov's Tian-Shan travels coincided with a critical period in Russian history.[9] In 1855, the empire was humiliated in the Crimea by a Franco-British coalition that had come to the Ottomans' defense in one of their periodic wars with the Romanovs. Defeat brought much soul searching over the coming years, which motivated the new tsar, Alexander II, to

[8] For a brief but reliable biography see Lincoln (1980).
[9] This section draws on Schimmelpenninck van der Oye (2004).

order sweeping reforms in his realm. Naturally, revitalizing the army was among them. Here the responsibility fell to his war minister, Dmitrii Miliutin. Before his appointment to Alexander's cabinet, Miliutin had been the General Staff Academy's professor of military geography. Even before he took up the post in 1845, the officer had long been interested in the subject. As a precocious young teenager, Miliutin had already written a short treatise on using mathematics to draw plans, which received a relatively favorable review in the press. He continued to publish about the subject as a young guards officer and, as a graduate of one of the General Staff Academy's first classes in 1836, had been tasked with mapping for the Guards Corps.

Miliutin was unhappy with the way his predecessor at the academy, Colonel Petr Iazykov, had taught the course. "Of all the subjects at the War Academy, the most primitive and least comprehensive was Military Geography," he recalled (Brooks 1970, 113). The new professor was particularly critical of the syllabus, which he complained "did not comprise a unified whole and had been compiled without any plan" (Miliutin 2000, 102). Therefore, he busied himself with a thoroughgoing revision of the course to make it more useful for conducting war. He wrote his brother Nikolai, "I am trying to raise Military Geography to a higher level [...] and to give it meaning – an overall evaluation of the power and might of governments in the military political sense" (Brooks 1970, 113).

Miliutin detailed his ideas in an article he published during his first year at the Academy in 1846. "Military power consists of more than just the number of troops or ships," he argued, adding, "it entails all resources and capacities a state can mobilize for war" (ibid., 174–75). Employing an anatomical metaphor, Miliutin explained that his subject should be

> like studying the body of a person, which requires first sorting out the various organs and then considering how they work together. In the same way, when we examine a political body, we begin by looking at the characteristics of each of its organs. (ibid., 172)

But, he cautioned, "science does not just consist of *describing phenomena* or *facts*. Rather, it is a logical analysis of how these phenomena or facts combine into one well-ordered, all-encompassing idea" (ibid., 158, italics in the original). To underscore his new approach, within two years he renamed his course Military Statistics, employing the more descriptive, nineteenth-century definition of the term (Miliutin 2000, 143).

Miliutin's contemporaries honored his achievements in the field with the Demidov Prize for scientific accomplishments in 1850 (ibid., 150). Historians do not typically include them among the military reforms he would subsequently carry out as war minister. Yet they were no less significant, for by developing a systematic approach to considering the martial resources of an adversary, whether real or potential, in their entirety he established a more objective, rigorous, and scientific method to strategic intelligence assessment. According to one biographer,

> Miliutin's approach was much closer to the modern concept of the general staff's role in making strategic assessments [...]. The future Minister of War had firmly grasped the significance of the new kind of warfare developing in the nineteenth century: the wars between peoples, not merely states and armies. (Miller 1968, 19)

MILITARY GEOGRAPHY

Miliutin's comprehensive system for the discipline of military statistics closely resembled the holistic approach Humboldt and Ritter had advocated for geography. It was no coincidence that Miliutin had joined the Russian Geographical Society shortly after he began teaching at the General Staff Academy. Of course, he was not the only soldier to be accepted. Along with Admiral Lütke, its first vice president, the society counted many naval and army officers among its members.

The interest of Russian military men in geography was more than purely scientific. At a time of slow, but steady expansion into Central Asia, a number of them had already explored the territory adjacent to the army's outposts there. It was only natural that those officers who were also members of the Geographical Society would combine their academic with their professional curiosity when undertaking such journeys. Moreover, the comprehensive approach to military statistics now being taught at the General Staff Academy increasingly conditioned its graduates to join the two. Admiral Lütke was well aware of the congruence between his organization's ambitions and the requirements of the empire's armed forces. In his inaugural address, he singled out the General Staff's topographical depot and the Admiralty's hydrography department as organizations with which he anticipated his members would work closely (Semenov 1896, vol. 3, 1318–19).

The Geographical Society soon put its promise to cooperate with the military to practice in Central Asia.[10] In 1847, it participated in a major expedition by Staff Captain Aleksei Maksheev and Navy Lieutenant Aleksei Butakov to chart the shores of the Northern Caspian and Aral Seas as well as the Lower Syr Darya (Rich 1998, 61). Ten years later, the organization also helped the War Ministry with three sensitive missions in 1856–58 to gather political intelligence in Khiva, Kashgar, and Herat by Colonel Nikolai Ignat'ev, Captain Nikolai Khanykov, and the Kazakh diplomat Chokhan Valikhanov, respectively (Marshall 2006, 36–37; Bailey 2008, 71–72). The foreign office also tapped the society's expertise for the commission it set up in 1862 to survey the border with China between the Altai and Tian Shan mountain ranges (Semenov 1896, vol. 1, 277–80). Meanwhile, when in 1864 General Mikhail Cherniaev was ordered to march across the Kazakh steppe with a large force to take the Kokandian city of Chimkent, the Geographical Society secured the army's permission for the zoologist Nikolai Severtsov to accompany the mission (ibid., 285). The rapid advance into Turkestan in the following years inevitably saw more joint missions to explore, survey, and map Russia's new conquests (ibid., 289–96).

The Imperial Russian Geographical Society's best known probes were to the lands east of the tsar's new Central Asian colonies, then nominally under Qing rule. While St. Petersburg had no immediate ambitions to conquer the region, the General Staff often participated in them. From Przheval'skii's first Central Asian voyage in 1870–73 to Petr Kozlov's journey to Mongolia and Xinjiang in 1907–09, the War Ministry and the Geographical Society jointly sponsored a dozen expeditions there (Baskhanov 2014, 303). Thus, nearly all of the society's leading Central Asian explorers were, as Mikhail Baskhanov calls them, "geographer generals", i.e. General Staff officers who eventually made general (ibid., 311–12), including Nikolai Przheval'skii, Mikhail Pevtsov, Bronislav Grombchevskii, and Petr Kozlov. (Baskhanov suggests that Col. Vsevolod Roborovskii would also have advanced to this rank, had it not been for his premature death).

Such journeys did provide valuable intelligence about regions of great strategic interest. However, there were also sound practical reasons for the military's involvement. In his essay "How to Explore Central Asia,"

---

[10]On the General Staff's role in organizing and financing the Geographical Society's expeditions, see Andreev (2013, 56–82).

Nikolai Przheval'skii insisted that expeditions to the region had to be led by army officers, not civilians. For one thing, he pointed out,

> The group must operate according to rigorous discipline along with the brotherly attitude of a commander to his subordinates. The entire party must live together like a single family with a single goal, headed by their leader. (Przheval'skii 1888, 3–4)

More to the point, only the military could "guarantee the safety of the scientists" in areas that "sometimes can be traversed with force rather than peacefully" (ibid.). The explorer might have added that graduates of the General Staff Academy were also well trained in geodesy, topography, and the other skills necessary for carrying out proper surveys, regardless of the objective. According to a memorandum at the General Staff Academy about the value of teaching geodesy,

> The Topographical Section's instruction is more practical: to impart the requisite skills to survey different areas, for which one must be able to examine its physical and geological characteristics [...]. To be able to employ General Staff officers not only for military reconnaissance, but also to participate in scientific expeditions, [the Academy] must combine its topography and topology courses, not to mention teach physical geography. (Esakov 2002, 19)

Przheval'skii

Nikolai Przheval'skii's extensive expeditions in the 1870s and 1880s to Eastern Turkestan, Mongolia, and Tibet are good examples of the way the military participated in the Geographical Society's activities in Central Asia. The archetypal 'geographic general,' Przheval'skii loyally served two masters—A graduate of the General Staff Academy, he held a commission in the imperial army; at the same time, his exploration of the region was always under the society's aegis.

Nature was Przheval'skii's first love. Growing up on his family's estate, he liked nothing more than to roam the surrounding countryside and hunt.[11] Indifferent to school, the lad nevertheless read voraciously.

---

[11] The definitive biography is Dubrovin (1890). For English language accounts of his life, see Rayfield (1976), Andreev (2018), Schimmelpenninck van der Oye (2001, 24–41).

According to one of his biographers, reading Nikolai Nekrasov's adventure novel 'The Three Lands of the World' (*Tri strany sveta*) with its tales of travels to the Arctic, Kamchatka, and Russian North America as a teenager inspired an insatiable wanderlust (Andreev 2018, 72). Eventually, he would devour the accounts of African explorers with equal zeal. As was typical for young men of the provincial gentry, upon completing secondary school Przheval'skii decided on a career in the army where he eventually joined the General Staff. He put his academy training to good use in 1867 by convincing his superiors and Admiral Lütke at the Geographical Society to allow him to survey the newly acquired Ussuri River region on Siberia's Pacific coast. The venture was a great success, which earned him a promotion to staff captain and the Geographical Society's silver medal (cf. Przheval'skii 1870).

The subaltern's real interest lay in Central Asia. Not long after returning to the capital from the Far East, he obtained Lütke's blessing for a more ambitious journey through Mongolia and Eastern Turkestan with the society's sponsorship. His case had been strengthened by the enthusiastic endorsement of the tsar's minister to Peking, Major-General Aleksandr Vlangali, who happened to be in St. Petersburg at the time. "A study of northern China [would be] of great interest to science," he told the admiral, adding "The Upper Yellow River, the Ordos country, Kuku Nor and other regions north of Tibet remain unexplored" (Dubrovin 1890, 92).

Since Przheval'skii was still in uniform, Lütke had to ask War Minister Dmitrii Miliutin's approval to second one of his officers. In his letter to Miliutin, the admiral used an entirely different rationale:

> Should [Przheval'skii] make it to northwestern China [i.e., Eastern Turkestan] […] which is currently wracked by a Muslim insurgency, we are reasonably confident that he will return with some fairly useful details about the rising. (Ryzhenkov 1990, 138)

It was an effective argument, and the minister readily granted the subaltern a three-year paid leave as well as matching Lütke's annual 1000-ruble subsidy. During the three-year journey, Przheval'skii accordingly sent separate reports about the unrest in the region and its geography to the War Ministry and the society, respectively.[12] The trek won Przheval'skii great acclaim both in his homeland and abroad, garnering among others the French government's *Ordre des Palmes académiques* and the Imperial Russian Geographical Society's Konstantin Gold Medal (Andreev 2018, 101). It also earned him the credibility to propose a second Central Asian expedition from 1876 to 1878, this time farther west, from the eastern Tian Shan range to the Himalayas. Once again, there was an intelligence component: to report on Yakub Beg's insurgent regime in Kashgaria.[13] The same was true of Przhevalskii's 1879–80 journey, which now concentrated on Tibet. "My scientific research will camouflage the political goals of the expedition," he suggested to his superiors at the general staff.[14] Colonel Aleksei Kuropatkin, then head of the General Staff's Asian Section, readily agreed. He wrote Emperor Alexander II:

> Together with the scientific aspect, [this expedition] proposes to gather [...] intelligence (*razvedka*) about the political structure of Tibet, the relations with its neighbors, not to mention the possibility of establishing and improving our relations with the Dalai Lama [...] [which] might open the path to political influence over all Inner Asia, right up to the Himalayas.[15]

To the explorer's great disappointment, Tibetan officials barred him from Lhasa. Nevertheless, as with his earlier Central Asian expeditions, upon his return to St. Petersburg the scientific community showered him with praise for his many findings, while the public greeted him as a conquering hero and the emperor granted an audience. Now a colonel, Przheval'skii in 1883 once again set off on a fourth journey to Tibet and Eastern Turkestan although by now he was skeptical about reaching the Potala Palace. In any case, his geographical goals were even more

[12] N.M. Przehval'skii, Report to the Voenno-uchenyi komitet, 26 February 1870, Nauchnyi arkhiv Russkogo geograficheskogo obshchestva (hereafter: NARGO), fond 13, opis' 3, delo 37, sheets 1–2.

[13] For his report, see N.M. Przheval'skii to Main Staff, "On the Current Situation in Eastern Turkestan," 6 June 1877, NARGO, fond 13, opis' 1, delo 26, sheet 1.

[14] N.M. Przheval'skii, Memorandum, 25 August 1878, RGVIA, fond 4000, opis' 1, delo 553, sheets 3–4.

[15] A.N. Kuropatkin to Alexander II, secret memorandum, November 1878, RGVIA, fond 4000, opis' 1, delo 553, sheet 24.

ambitious and the resources the government provided lavish, including 43,000 rubles, an escort of seventeen Cossacks, twenty rifles, a custom-made machine gun from the Nobel company, 16,000 rounds, as well as fifty-six camels and seven horses to carry it all (Semenov 1896, vol. 2, 538–39; Andreev 2013, 68). The munitions proved useful since the party came under attack by the local population several times. The mission's success encouraged Przheval'skii to undertake yet another voyage to Central Asia in 1888. Like the earlier expeditions, his goals were primarily to gather geographical details about the region. However, there still was an intelligence component, namely to spy on the intentions of the British in Sikkim regarding Tibet.[16] Now close to fifty and not in the best of health, he had barely begun his journey when he contracted typhus in the foothills of the Tian Shan and died after a short illness while still on Russian territory.

CONQUISTADOR GEOGRAPHERS?

Przheval'skii was not shy about voicing his opinions regarding Russian expansion. When a special committee at the War Ministry asked his advice about a possible war with China in May 1886, he urged aggression. According to the explorer's plan, Russia should strike with two forces, in Eastern Turkestan and Mongolia, and then, "like a threatening cloud, we will advance across the Gobi to Peking."[17] Once the Qing sued for peace, Russia could demand large swathes of territory, including Eastern Turkestan and northern Tibet. He repeated this view in an unclassified essay that was published in a leading journal. As he told its readers, "there are many scores to settle with our haughty neighbor, and we must show that Russia's spirit and courage know no match." (Przheval'skii 1888, 536).

Many were aghast at the explorer's bellicose views. Aleksei Pozdneev, a leading Mongolist, bitterly attacked the piece (Pozdneev 1884, 316–51). Meanwhile, Przhevalskii's superiors quietly relegated his proposal to the obscurity of the archive. They clearly knew the emperor's

---

[16] N.M. Przhevalk'skii to P.S. Vannovskii, report, 10 March 1888, RGVIA fond 401, opis' 4/928, delo 40, sheet 4.

[17] N.M. Przheval'skii to Main Staff, "Novoe soobrazhenie o voine s Kitaem," memorandum, 26 June 1886, RGO fond 13, opis' 1, delo 43, sheet 83 (the document is also in RGIA fond 971, opis' 1, delo 181.

opinion on the matter of a war of conquest against China. A year earlier, as he was trekking through Eastern Turkestan, Przheval'skii had wired the War Minister, Petr Vannovskii, urging him to take advantage of the unrest still plaguing the region by annexing it. Tsar Alexander III penciled in the cable's margin, "I have my doubts about the benefits of such an annexation."[18]

Because of Przheval'skii's fame, it might be easy to conclude that his aggressive views were typical of the men who led the Imperial Russian Geographical Society's expeditions. In fact, as the reactions of his superiors at the War Ministry and the emperor suggest, he was an outlier. To be sure, as in any European army during the age of high imperialism, a number of the tsar's officers championed colonial conquest. However, in his study of the Russian General Staff during the latter half of the nineteenth century, David Rich suggested that its officers, like many intellectual elites, often showed progressive views (Rich 1998, 50–51). As for the Geographical Society, Bruce Lincoln has argued that, despite the large proportion of military men, its members were not inevitably reactionary. In his biography of Petr Semenov-Tian-Shanskii, Lincoln observed that in its earlier years the society "became perhaps the most active agency in the Empire for bringing to bear on social and economic questions the combined expertise of scientists, scholars, progressive officials and moderate intellectuals" (Lincoln 1980, 15). Indeed, many actively participated in the preparations for emancipating the empire's serfs in 1861 (ibid., 37).

Nor were they necessarily zealous imperialists. After all, the society's membership included Prince Peter Kropotkin, the 'anarchist geographer,' who strongly criticized colonialism. Despite his political activities, the prince was also a scientist who surveyed Siberia's geology and was sent by the society to examine glacial deposits in Finland and Sweden. Even when imprisoned in the Peter and Paul Fortress for subversion in 1872, he wrote a two-volume study of Asia's orography (Breitbart 1981, 143). Meanwhile, although not as illustrious as Przheval'skii, the Central Asian explorer Grigorii Potanin was arrested in 1867 for advocating Siberian separatism (Faust 1980).

[18] P.S. Vannovskii to N.K. Giers, letter, 5 November 1885. RGVIA fond 401, opis' 4/928, delo 36, sheet 124.

CONCLUSION

There is no question that the Imperial Russian Geographical Society combined scientific and military interests. Not only were many of its members officers in the tsar's army, but the General Staff and the society often worked closely together when exploring unknown lands both within the empire's borders and beyond. Meanwhile, unlike Western European geographical societies, which carried out many of their activities overseas, their Russian counterpart stayed closer to home and crossed oceans much less frequently, supporting continental colonialism instead. Indeed, the Russian Geographical Society actively explored Turkestan both before and after the army gradually conquered its khanates. And Przheval'skii's first important assignment was to map the newly absorbed Far Eastern territories on the Ussuri River.

As a result the boundaries between surveying the empire itself as well as the regions at and beyond its frontiers were far less distinct than for the other European societies when they sent their intrepid explorers overseas to Africa during the nineteenth century. Furthermore, unlike its Western counterparts, the Russian society rarely sponsored expeditions to other continents. Nikolai Miklukho-Maclay's journeys to the South Pacific and Oceania were the exception rather than the rule. In many ways, the institution was intimately linked to expanding the Russian empire's frontiers into lands directly contiguous to its own territory.

Nevertheless, none of this meant that colonial conquest was necessarily the primary goal of the men who gathered at the society's building on Chernyshev Square in St. Petersburg. In an age that championed scientific positivism, objective curiosity about the secrets of the natural world was a powerful intellectual force. As attested by the relative attention they paid both in the field and in their writings, even such ardent imperialists as Nikolai Przheval'skii undertook their expeditions primarily to study the geography of unknown lands. Gathering intelligence tended to be entirely secondary. The Geographical Society's requests to the army for financial support seemed often to invoke military intelligence as a hook to draw the war minister's attention, rather than the society's own reasons for the mission proposed.[19] There were exceptions, most notably in Western Turkestan, where the army was actively surveying regions ripe for annexation. But in the case of the more ambitious and important

[19] I am grateful to the late Robert Belknap for this thought.

exploration of Eastern Turkestan, Mongolia, and Tibet, the members ventured out of lust for knowledge, not conquest.

REFERENCES

Archives

NARGO Nauchnyi arkhiv Russkogo geograficheskogo obshchestva [Scientific Archive of the Russian Geographical Society].
RGVIA Rossiiskii gosudarstvennyi voenno-istoricheskii arkhiv [Russian State Military Archive].

Books and Articles

Alekseev, Mikhail. 1996. *Leksika russkoi razvedki (istoricheskii obzor)* [A Vocabulary of Russian Intelligence (Historical Review)]. Moscow: Mezhdunarodnye otnosheniia.
Alekseev, Mikhail. 1998. *Voennaia razvedka Rossii ot Riurika do Nikolaia II* [Russian Military Intelligence from Riurik to Nicholas II]. Moscow: Russkaia razvedka.
Andreev, Aleksandr Ivanovich, eds. 2013. *Rossiiskie ekspeditsii v Tsentral'nuiu Aziiu: organizatsiia, polevye issledovaniia, kolektsii 1870–1920-e gg* [Russian Expeditions in Central Asia: Organisation, Fieldwork, Collections]. St. Petersburg: Nestor-Istoriia.
Andreev, Alexandre I. 2018. "Nikolai Mikhailovich Przhevalskii (1839–1888)." In *The Quest for Forbidden Lands: Nikolai Przhevalskii and His Followers on Inner Asian Tracks*, edited by Alexandre I. Andreyev, Mikhail Baskhanov, and Tatyana Yusupova, 62–149. Leiden: Brill.
Andrew, Christopher. 2018. *The Secret World: A History of Intelligence*. New Haven: Yale University Press.
Arkhiv Gosudarstvennogo Soveta. 1888. *Tom vtoroi: Sovet v tsarstvovanie imperatora Pavla I-go (1796–1801 gg)* [Archive of the State Council. Volume Two: The Counctil During the Reign of Emperor Paul I]. St. Petersburg: V Gosudarstvennoi Tipografii.
Bailey, Scott C. Matsushita. 2008. "Travel, Science, and Empire: The Russian Geographical Society's Expeditions to Central Eurasia, 1845–1905." PhD diss., University of Hawai'i at Manoa.
Bartol'd, Vasilii Vladimirovich. [1911] 1977. "Istoriia izucheniia Vostoka v Evrope i Rossii: lektsii, chitannyia v Imp. S.-Peterburgskom universitete" [The History of the Study of the East in Europe and Russia: Lectures Read at the Imperial St. Petersburg University]. In *Sochineniia*, edited by A.N. Kononov, 1–282. Moscow: Nauka.

Baskhanov, Mikhail Kazbekovich. 2014. "'Ne kovrom byla postlana nam dor-oga v glub' Azii': fenomen epokhi russkikh 'geograficheskikh generalov'" ['No carpet Was Laid out for Us on the Path into the Interior of Asia': The Phenomenon of the Period of Russia's 'Geographical Generals']. In *Rossiiskie izuchenie Tsentral'noi Azii: istoricheskie i sovremennye aspekti (k 150-letiiu P.K. Kozlova)*, edited by K.V. Chistiakov, 297–318. St. Petersburg: Rossiiskaia akademii nauk.

Batorskii, A.A. 1886. "Proekt ekspeditsii v Indiiu" [The Plan for the Expedition to India]. *Sbornik geograficheskikh, topograficheskikh i statisticheskikh materialov po Azii* 23: 1–103.

Becker, Seymour. 2012. "The 'Great Game': The History of an Evocative Phrase." *Asian Affairs* 43(1): 61–80.

Bezotosnyi, Viktor Mikhailovich. 2005. *Razvedka i plany storon v 1812 godu* [Intelligence and Plans of the Combatants in 1812]. Moscow: ROSSPEN.

Bezotosnyi, Viktor Mikhailovich. 2017. *Napoleonovskie plany: proekt zavoevaniia Indii Napoleona Bonaparte* [Napoleonic Plans: Napoleon's Plan to Conquer India]. Moscow: Russkii Vitiazy.

Breitbart, Myrna Margulies. 1981. "Peter Kropotkin, the Anarchist Geographer." In *Geography, Ideology and Social Concern*, edited by David Ross Stoddart, 134–53. Oxford: Basil Blackwell.

Brooks, Edwin Willis. 1970. "D.A. Miliutin: Life and Activity to 1856." PhD diss., Stanford University.

Carter, Paul. 1987. *The Road to Botany Bay: An Essay in Spatial History*. London: Faber and Faber.

Driver, Felix. 2001. *Geography Militant: Cultures of Exploration and Empire*. Oxford: Blackwell.

Dubrovin, Nikolai Fedorovich. 1890. *Nikolai Mikhailovich Przheval'skii: bio-graficheskii ocherk* [Nikolai Mikhailovich Przheval'skii: Biographical Sketch]. St. Petersburg: Voennaia tipografiia.

Efremov, Filipp. [1811] 1995. "Stranstvovaniia Filippa Efremova" [Filip Efreimov's Wanderings]. In *Puteshestviia po vostoku v epokhe Ekateriny II*, edited by Aleksei Alekseevich Vigasin and Sergei Georgievich Karpiuk. Moscow: Vostochnaia literatura RAN.

Esakov, Vasilii Alekseevich. 2002. *Mikhail Ivanovich Veniukov 1832–1901*. Moscow: Nauka.

Faust, Wolfgang. 1980. *Russlands goldener Boden: Der sibirische Regionalismus in der zweiten Hälfte des 19. Jahrhunderts*. Köln: Böhlau.

Fromkin, David. 1980. "The Great Game in Asia." *Foreign Affairs* 58(4): 936–51.

Goerlitz, Walter. 1985. *History of the German General Staff 1657–1945*. Translated by Brian Battershaw. Boulder: Westview Press.

Hauner, Milan. 1990. *What Is Asia to Us? Russia's Asian Heartland Yesterday and Today*. Boston: Unwin Hyman.

Hopkirk, Peter. 1990. *The Great Game: On Secret Service in High Asia*. Oxford: Oxford University Press.

Keay, John, ed. 1991. *The History of World Exploration*. New York: Mallard Press.

Khalfin, Naftula Aronovich. 1965. *Prisoedinenie Srednei Azii k Rossii (60e-90e gody XIX v.)* [The Union of Central Asia to Russia (1860's–1890's]. Moscow: Nauka.

Khrisanf (Metropolitan of New Patras). 1995. "Ob"iasneniia Grecheskogo Mitropolita Khrisanfa Neopatrasskogo, byvshego v Turtsii, Persii, Armenii, Bukharii, Khive i Indii" [Explanation of the Greek Metropolitan Khransanf Novopatrasskii, Who Was in Turkey, Persia, Bukhara, Khiva and India]. In *Puteshestviia po vostoku v epokhe Ekateriny II*, edited by Aleksei Alekseevich Vigasin and Sergei Georgievich Karpiuk, 261–99. Moscow: Vostochnaia literatura RAN.

Knight, Nathaniel. 1994. "Constructing the Science of Nationality: Ethnography in Mid-Nineteenth Century Russia." PhD diss., Columbia University.

Lebedev, Dmitrii Mikhailovich, and Vasilii Alekseevich Esakov. 1971. *Russkie geograficheskie otkrytiia i issledovaniia s drevnikh vremen do 1917 goda* [Russian Geographic Discoveries and Explorations Since Ancient Times to the year 1917]. Moscow: Mysl'.

Lincoln, Bruce W. 1980. *Petr Petrovich Semenov-Tian-Shanskii: The Life of a Russian Geographer*. Newtonville, MA: Oriental Research Partners.

Marshall, Alex. 2006. *The Russian General Staff and Asia, 1800–1917*. London: Routledge.

Martin, Geoffrey J. 2005. *All Possible Worlds: A History of Geographical Ideas*. Oxford: Oxford University Press.

Miliutin, Dmitrii Alekseevich. 1846. "Kriticheskoe izsledovanie znachenii voennoi geografii i voennoi statistiki" [A Critical Consideration of the Importance of Military Geography and Military Statistics]. *Voennyi zhurnal* 1: 124–93.

Miliutin, Dmitrii Alkseevich. 2000. *Vospominaniia 1843–1856* [Memoirs 1843–1856], edited by L.G. Zakharova. Moscow: Ruskii arkhiv.

Miller, Forrestt A. 1968. *Dmitrii Miliutin and the Reform Era in Russia*. Nashville: Vanderbilt University Press.

Morrison, Alexander. 2019, forthcoming. *The Russian Conquest of Central Asia*. Cambridge: Cambridge University Press.

Nikitin, Afanasy. 1958. *Khozhenie za tri moria* [Voyage Beyond Three Seas]. Moscow: Izdatel'stvo Akademii Nauk SSSR.

Os'kin, G. 1969. "Voznikovenie i razvitie sluzhba General'nogo shtaba v Rossii" [The Establishment and Development of the General Staff Service in Russia]. *Voenno-istoricheskii zhurnal* 3: 91–97.

Pozdneev, Aleksei M. 1884. "Tretie puteshestvie v Tsentral'noi Azii" [The Third Expedition to Central Asia]. *Zhurnal Ministerstva narodnogo prosveshcheniia* 232: 316–51.

Pratt, Mary Louise. 1992. *Imperial Eyes: Travel Writing and Acculturation*. London: Routledge.

Przheval'skii, Nikolai Mikhailovich. 1870. *Puteshestvie v Ussuriiskom krae 1867–1869 gg* [Voyage to the Ussuri Region 1867–1869]. St. Petersburg: Tip. N. Nekliudova.

Przhevalskii, Nikolai Mikhailovich. 1888. *Ot Kiakhti na istoki zheltoi reki* [From Kiakhta to the Headwaters of the Yellow River]. St. Petersburg: Tip. V.S. Balasheva.

Rayfield, Donald. 1976. *The Dream of Lhasa: The Life of Nikolai Przhevalsky (1839–1888), Explorer of Central Asia*. Columbus: Ohio University Press.

Rich, David. 1998. *The Tsar's Colonels: Professionalism, Strategy, and Subversion in Late Imperial Russia*. Cambridge, MA: Harvard University Press.

Richards, Thomas. 1993. *The Imperial Archive: Knowledge and Fantasy of Empire*. London: Verso.

Ritter, Carl. 1822–1829. *Die Erdkunde im Verhältnis zur Natur und zur Geschichte des Menschen*. Berlin: Reimer.

Rothenberg, Gunther. 1992. "Military Intelligence Gathering in the Second Half of the Eighteenth Century, 1740–1792." In *Go Spy the Land: Military Intelligence in History*, edited by Keith Neilson and B.J.C. McKercher. Westport: Praeger.

Russko-Indiiskie otnosheniia v XVIII v.: Sbornik dokumentov [Russian-Indian Relations in the 18th Century: A Collection of Documents]. 1965. Edited by Redzhinal'd Vasil'evich Ovchinnikov and M.A. Sidorov. Moscow: Nauka.

Ryzhenkov, Mikhail Rafailovich. 1990. "Rol' voennogo vedomstva Rossii v razvitii otechestvennogo vostokovedeniia v XIX-nachale XX vv.: Opyt istochnikovedcheskogo issledovaniia dokumentov Tsentral'nogo gosudarstvennogo voenno-istoricheskogo arkhiva SSSR" [The Role of Russia's War Department in the Development of Orientalism in the Fatherland in the 19th and Early 20th Centuries: An Effort in the Source Analysis of Documents in the USSR's Central State Military History Archive]. PhD diss., Moscow, Akademiia Nauk, Institut vostokovedeniia.

Said, Edward W. 1978. *Orientalism*. New York: Pantheon Books.

Schimmelpenninck van der Oye, David. 2001. *Toward the Rising Sun: Russian Ideologies of Empire and the Path to War with Japan*. DeKalb, IL: Northern Illinois University Press.

Schimmelpenninck van der Oye, David. 2004. "Reforming Military Intelligence." In *Reforming the Tsar's Army: Military Innovation in Imperial Russia from Peter the Great to the Revolution*, edited by David Schimmelpenninck van der Oye and Bruce W. Menning, 133–50. Cambridge: Cambridge University Press.

Schimmelpenninck van der Oye, David. 2014. "Paul's Great Game: Russia's Plan to Invade British India." *Central Asian Survey* 33(2): 143–52.

Semenov, Petr Petrovich. 1896. *Istoriia poluvekovoi deiatel'nosti Imperatorskago Russkago Geograficheskago Obshchestva 1845–1895* [The History of Half a Century of Activities by the Imperial Russian Geographical Society 1845–1895]. 3 vols. St. Petersburg: Tip. V. Bezobrazova.

Semenov, Petr Petrovich. 1988. *Travels in the Tian'-Shan' 1856–1857.* Translated by Liudmilla Gilmour, Colin Thomas, and Marcus Wheeler. London: Hakluyt Society.

Sergeev, Evgenii Iur'evich. 2013. *The Great Game 1856–1907: Russo-British Relations in Central Asia.* Baltimore: Johns Hopkins University Press.

Stafford, Robert A. 1998. "Scientific Exploration and Empire." In *The Oxford History of the British Empire: Vol. 3, the Nineteenth Century,* edited by Andrew Porter. Oxford: Oxford University Press.

Sunderland, Willard. 2014. "Explorations in Imperial Russia." In *Reinterpreting Exploration: The West in the World,* edited by Dane Kennedy, 135–53. Oxford: Oxford University Press.

Terent'ev, Mikhail Afrikanovich. 1906. *Istoriia zavoevaniia Srednei Azii* [The History of the Conquest of Central Asia]. 3 vols. St. Petersburg: Tip-Lit V.V. Komarova.

UNESCO. 2017. "History of Civilizations of Central Asia." http://www.unesco.org/new/en/social-and-human-sciences/themes/general-and-regional-histories/history-of-civilizations-of-central-asia. Accessed September 26, 2018.

Vigasin, Aleksei Alekseevich, P.M. Shastitko, and A.P. Baziiants, eds. 1997. *Istoriia otechestvennogo vostokovedeniia s serediny XIX veka do 1917 g* [The History of Oriental Studies in the Fatherland from the Middle of the 19th Century to 1917]. Moscow: Vostochnaia literatura.

Voennaia entsiklopedia. 1911–1915. St. Petersburg: Sytin.

von Humboldt, Aleander. 1834. *Asie Centrale: Recherches sur les chaines de montagnes et la climatologie comparée.* Paris: Gide.

Vucinich, Alexander. 1963. *Science in Russian Culture.* Stanford: Stanford University Press.

Wulf, Andrea. 2015. *The Invention of Nature: Alexander von Humboldt's New World.* New York: Alfred A. Knopf.

Zvonar'ev, Konstantin Kirillovich. 1929. *Agenturnaia razvedka* [Human Intelligence]. Moscow: IV Upravlenie shtaba Rab.-Kr. Armii.

CHAPTER 7

Manchu-Han Relations in Qing China: Reconsidering the Concept of Continental Colonialism in Chinese History

Lili Zhu

Throughout Chinese history, dynasties were repeatedly overthrown and replaced by foreign powers, such as the Liao, Yuan, and Qing founded by the Manchu. In full awareness of this, traditional scholarship nevertheless focused on Han sources and applied a relatively homogenizing perspective on China, based on the assumption that foreign conquerors assimilated to Han culture once they became rulers of China. In opposition to this perspective, scholars of the New Qing History[1] introduced 'ethnic theory' into studies of Qing history. Such studies have found that the Qing frontiers were not only at the political borders, but "very often [...] located at social, economic, or cultural fissures internal to a political

---

[1] The coming into being of the school of New Qing History is marked by the debate between Evelyn Rawski (1996) and Ping-Ti Ho (1998). The label of 'New Qing History' was first coined in 2004 by Millward, Dunnell, Elliott, and Forêt (2004) and Waley-Cohen (2004), for representative works of this school see e.g. Chang (2007), Crossley ([1990] 1991), Elliott (2001). For more on this debate see Cams (2016).

L. Zhu (✉)
Faculty of History, Bielefeld University, Bielefeld, Germany
e-mail: lili.zhu@uni-bielefeld.de

© The Author(s) 2019   175
D. Schorkowitz et al. (eds.), *Shifting Forms of Continental Colonialism*,
https://doi.org/10.1007/978-981-13-9817-9_7

order" (Crossley et al. [2006] 2007, 3). Instead of seeing Qing rulers as fully Sinicized Manchus, taking over state organization from the Ming dynasty with slight changes and adopting the orthodox Confucian culture, New Qing History scholars have argued that the Manchus were—despite their partly adoption of Han culture—by no means converted into Han. On the contrary, they stress that the Manchus made efforts to maintain the purity of their own culture (Forêt 2000; Elliott 2001; Chang 2007). Manchu rule in the Qing period is no longer seen as one of the genuine Chinese dynasties, but like the Yuan rule—distinguished from other dynasties—an empire led by ethnic Manchus, which can and should be compared with colonial empires (Perdue 1998a, b; Rowe [2009] 2012).

In addition and independent of the New Qing History, students of comparative colonialism had applied the concepts of internal and continental colonialism to Qing history before.[2] Now, scholars claimed that the Manchus imposed colonialism in China, particularly in Inner Asia.[3] Applying theories of imperialism and colonialism, these studies have argued that imperial machinery and cultural suppression were devised and enforced within the Qing's frontiers. On the one hand, the Manchu are depicted within their political realm as the colonizers and other ethnic groups as the colonized. On the other hand, in respect to foreign relations, they are described as a colonial power, and thus as global player of the early-modern era, not much different from European powers at this time (Glahn 2004; Struve 2004). In other words, the Manchu rulers were practicing continental colonialism upon other ethnic groups (including Han) within the Chinese Empire by means of military expansion and cultural campaigns (Waley-Cohen 2006). In consequence, the Opium Wars are seen as wars between colonial powers (Hevia [1995] 2005), and "Asia is postcolonial not just with reference to Western powers or to Japan, but with reference to the Chinese empire" (Fiskesjö 2017, 6).

---

[2] See Di Cosmo (1998), Gladney (1998), Goodman (1983), Herman (2007), Osterhammel ([1995] 2010); on the 'Internal Colonial Concept' see Hind (1984) and the introduction to this volume.

[3] See the introduction of Crossley et al. ([2006] 2007) and other chapters to their volume; cf. also Di Cosmo (1998), Millward et al. (2004), Forêt (2000), Hostetler ([2001] 2005), Liu ([2004] 2006), Perdue (2005), Millward ([2007] 2009), Rowe ([2009] 2012), Schorkowitz and Chia Ning (2017). See also the special issue on this topic including eight articles of *The International History Review* 20, 2 (1998).

However, the question remains whether the use of 'colonialism', a term originally connected to European expansion and global domination between the late fifteenth and the twentieth centuries, is justified and reasonable for Qing China. The discussion on Qing (Manchu) colonialism loses some of its critical potential because of a tendency in popular (but less often in academic) discourse to inflate the concept of colonialism to the point when any form of domination is equated with 'colonialism'. If continental colonialism is to be a meaningful analytical concept, then we must be clear about what it is not. Hence, I will present a study of Manchu-Han relations that are marked by violent domination, but do not qualify as a form of colonialism.

More precisely, to what extent was Manchu dominance an ethnic or even racial 'othering' of the Han people to be defined as 'colonialism'? European colonialism was, after all, not simply a conquest and oppression of new groups or territories by Europeans. Rather, the various authors trying to pinpoint the character of colonialism seem to agree that it was built on ethno-racial 'othering' between colonizers and colonized who were separated not only by spatial distance, but more importantly, by a rigidly constructed distinction produced in areas as diverse as the exclusion of the colonized from citizenship (Young [2007] 2010), regimes of labor structured by racial differentiation (Quijano 2000), Orientalist and racist discourse (Said 1978, [1993] 1994), portrayal of the colonized as uncivilized backwards or even outside of history (Buck-Morss 2000), and so on. In terms of this distinction, colonized cultures were essentially constructed as 'wholes' and portrayed as inferior to the colonizers in their entirety. As Frederick Cooper argues: "Colonial conquest emphasized that the conquered remain distinct; he or she might try to learn and master the ways of the conqueror but would never quite get there" ([2002] 2009, 16). Accounts of hybridity (Bhabha [1984] 2012), mutual influences (Werner and Zimmermann 2002), or a 'middle ground' (White 1991) between colonizers and colonized should be understood against the background of these attempts to separate them. Given that colonizers tried to construct and essentialize (ethnicize, racialize) the differences between themselves and the colonized, such accounts serve as empirical proofs that the colonizers never entirely dominated all cultural expressions. Accordingly, I would argue that at least in Manchu-Han relations there was neither a clear attempt to establish a colonial order, nor a discourse to portray Han culture as inferior in its entirety during the Qing dynasty. Their relationship was one of conqueror-conquered and later dominant-subordinate, but it was not the dichotomy of colonizer-colonized that would justify calling Manchu rule over the Han colonial rule. Indeed, the military oppression of the Han people and state exertions by the Manchu rulers were not equivalent to Western colonialism. These policies were an administrative state strategy put into practice in order to underline and reinforce the Qing cultural legacy. I argue that neither the distinctions between the Manchus and the Han during Qing rule nor the conflicts between them were based on the construction of essential ethnic differences.

HAN PEOPLE AS THE COLONIZED—A BLURRED IDENTITY

One of the obvious reasons to question the notion of colonization of the Han by the Manchu is the fact that neither group was a fixed entity. Through most of Chinese history, the identity of 'Han' was unclear. We cannot ignore the interactions and mutual influences between the Han and other ethnic groups who lived together for centuries. In Chinese history conceptions of Han, dynastic, and national identities overlapped ethnic boundaries. The Han identity was much more based on culture than blood (Ge 2007; Lu 2010). Also, modes of belonging, such as consciousness of clan, family, or region were of greater importance than the much broader ethnic identity of Han (Wang 2014). For example, it was more important to belong to a specific family lineage or to share a family name than to be 'Han'. The same applied to the Manchus as well. As Edward Rhoads points out,

> the question of who the Manchus were is greatly complicated by the fact that the single English term 'Manchu' embraces a number of different Chinese terms, ranging from Manzhou, Manzhouren, Manren, and Manzu to qiren, qijiren, and qizu. (2000, 289)

The Qing Empire was founded by the Later Jin, a political entity established by Nurhaci of the Jianzhou Jurchen people in Manchuria during 1616–36. The Jianzhou Jurchen who started to call themselves 'Manchu' in 1615, were a group, living to the north of the Yalu River in the northern part of the Ming Empire. If today's concept of 'ethnic group' applies to that time at all, then the Later Jin was a multi-ethnic polity already from the early years of its conquest and expansion. The Manchu identity was intertwined with the banner system, which was not confined to one ethnic group either. Within this system, banner people (*qiren* 旗人) were the privileged ruling class of the Qing dynasty, usually standing outside of the civilian (*min* 民) society (Elliott 2001; Liu 2008; Meng 2010). As a basic framework of administration and military force, the bannermen were granted land and income, as well as social and legal privileges. Bannermen in the main consisted of Manchu, Mongol, and Han. In the course of Qing expansion these banner groups gradually included many other ethnic origins, such as the Sibe and Evenk, two Tungusic speaking peoples. Numerous people of different ethnicities were incorporated into the banners before and after the Qing's troops moved through the Shanhai Pass to the south (Spence [1990] 1991). At the beginning of the Manchu banner system, soldiers in the banners were not distinguished by ethnic identification. Later, separate Han Chinese Banners were made up of those troops who defected to the Qing up to 1644 and joined the Eight Banners. In fact, banners were full of Han people. Because many Han defected to the Qing and swelled the ranks of the Eight Banners, ethnic Manchu became a minority (Naquin and Rawski 1987). Thus, China was conquered not by the 'Manchu' but by a multi-ethnic force in which the Manchu were a leading minority. Han Chinese bannermen were in part responsible for the successful Qing conquest of China, and later they made up the majority of governors in the early Qing. Together with the Manchu ruling class, they governed and administered China after the conquest, and stabilized Qing rule over the country.

Within the system, it was possible to switch banners or raise one's ranking to a higher banner (*taiqi* 抬旗). Neither the formation nor the internal hierarchy of the bannermen were based on ethnicity. Rather, the system was based on the submission to Manchu rule. During the Mid- to Late-Qing period, some Han people from the banner (*chuqi* 出旗) were forced to leave. However, this expulsion was not based on ethnic reasons. It was mostly due to the growing costs of the large numbers of banner people. Furthermore, this exclusion was restricted to the Han people who pledged their loyalty to the Manchu regime much later, while the earlier Han followers of the regime were not affected (Ding 2000; Liu 2008). Qing rule relied greatly on the people's pledge of loyalty, whose chronologic order of enlistment was considered the evidence. This had little to do with any particular ethnic exclusion or racial discrimination as Jian Zhang concludes:

This reveals a principle of the early makeup of the Manchus, which was that political qualifications determined ethnic attributes, and ethnic attributes such as blood relations, language, and customs did not determine qualifications. (2016, 41)

In this sense, not only did the division of ethnic classification become blurred, but there were Han Chinese people among the ruling elite. In other words, Han Chinese were not excluded from the ruling class because of their ethnicity. People could even decide to change their ethnic affiliation. Such ambiguous and interchangeable classification among the rulers and between ruler and ruled is tremendously different from Western colonial situations, where ethnic or racial differences were much more stable categories.[4]

Ethnic Conflict or Political Positioning?

The complex and political character of power relations under the Qing becomes strikingly clear when looking at the resistance of Han against oppressive politics. There was a great number of uprisings by the Han against Qing rule, most of which happened either in the early or late Qing period. However, neither the oppressive politics nor the resistance against them should be reduced to ethnic-racial conflicts between the Manchu and the Han. Early Qing rulers bloodily suppressed Han revolts. However, the oppression of the Manchu against the Han, as well as the opposition of Han against Manchu, were not based on ethnic grounds even though their rhetoric sometimes seemed to indicate such.

First of all, not all the Han people in the Qing's political realm were automatically oppressed and slaughtered. Manchus had various attitudes toward the Han and implemented oppressive policies against them depending on different circumstances, particularly between the northern

---

[4]One might be tempted to use Fairbank's notion of 'synarchy' which, I think, does not fit aptly here because it not only describes Manchu-Han relations. Above all, Fairbank's concept (1957) of 'synarchy' tries to explain Chinese–European relations after the Opium Wars by which European colonialism in China is totally dismissed. In particular, by the usage of 'synarchy', the system of unequal treaties is seen as a sort of tribute instrument the Qing applied to include the West into its own power structure. This eventually neglects the fact that the unequal treaties were forced upon China by European powers and downplays its colonial feature (Barlow 1993).

and southern regions of China. After entering the Shanhai Pass, the Qing military marched from the north to the south. It received little resistance from the Han residents in the northern regions. The slogans of Qing rulers about 'revenge for your fathers' for the oppressed Han people under Ming rule were well accepted by the residents living in the newly obtained regions in the north: "Many civilians were not feeling unpleasant. They cut their hair and welcomed the comers" (Shizu zhanghuangdi shilu 1985, vol. 3, 55). This is not difficult to understand if we consider the long-term joint living and merging of various ethnic groups residing in the northern regions of China and their loose bonds to the Ming regime. In contrast, southern Han people lived in the undisputed, pivotal region of the Han Chinese world, a bastion of Ming loyalism and anti-Manchu sentiment (Chang 2007). Moreover, it was not only a north-south Han difference, but also a matter of class. In the late Ming period, peasant uprisings resulted in riots all over the country. The regional Han squires in the north, where the Ming state power was loose, especially required and expected a consolidated and powerful government. As a result, when the Manchu came to power and established the order needed to control the regions, local Han squires and literati in the northern regions were rather willing to join the Manchu than the peasant revolts (Luo 2013, 143). And the Manchu rulers welcomed them.

Furthermore, the cultural dimension of these policies consisted mainly of strategies to consolidate the Qing's claim to legitimacy. Taking the changes in clothing and hairstyle as an example, the main aim of this policy was to distinguish between the Han people who acknowledged Manchu rule and those who did not. The rule to change Han hairstyles was first implemented to distinguish obedient Han from the people who were still resisting the Qing, and to prevent the Han people who were anti-Manchu from surrendering. However, Manchu clothing and hairstyle policy was introduced already during the Later Jin period, because an increasing number of Han people lived in the regions it controlled and conducted uprisings from time to time. Later Jin rulers thus implemented this policy to strengthen their rule and to prevent the Han from running away (Bian and Li 1998). Hence, loyal Han people could be easily recognized not only by Later Jin, but also captured or even killed by Ming frontier officers who often asked Ming courts for rewards for the capture of Han from Liaodong whose Manchu loyalty was recognized by their haircuts and clothing (Lu 2010, 81–82).

Such political positioning was shared by Han people too; the 'hair-cut act' appeared to be the main flash point of Manchu-Han conflicts. Keeping the Ming haircut meant the chance to reinstate the Ming dynasty and changing to the Manchu haircut meant acknowledging the end of the former dynasty. Many southern resistant forces claiming their loyalty to Ming were strongly against changing their haircut. Cutting one's hair was seen as a punishment, a mark of humiliation (Wu 2010, 46), and "the question of the haircuts and other was merged into one" (Huang [1993] 1997, 222). Seen from this perspective, it is not surprising to see Han people positioned on both sides: against or in favor of Qing policies. Their stance was not so much determined by being Han, but by their approval or disproval of Qing claim to rule (Lu 2010; Wu 2010). The conflict line was not drawn according to cultural differences between two ethnic groups because the haircut did not aim at the oppression or elimination of one culture by another, but rather signified loyalty to different dynasties.

The second wave of Han uprisings against Qing rule happened in the Late Qing period. At the turn of the twentieth century, nationalist movements swept over China, and slogans of 'Manchu exclusion', often depicted as 'anti-Manchuism', became wide-spread once more (Lin and Li [1990] 1991; Zhang 1983). Now indeed ethnicity and in various cases even race served as categories of identification in these conflicts. However, this was not merely an outbreak of ethnic conflict between the Manchu and the Han that was dormant before, nor was it the expression of a shift in power between different ethnic groups as Edward Rhoads (2000) has argued. The revival of this conflict is related to a more complex picture of the historical context. In fact, the new Han-Manchu conflict was a consequence of Western colonial activities in China. The loss in the Opium Wars and the apparent inability of the Qing rulers to defend against Western colonizers gave rise to various claims that the Qing dynasty was unable to save China. As some scholars have argued, the Taiping rebellion (1851–64) was the most obvious turning point in the worsening of Manchu-Han relations (Yu and Liu 1995; Zuo 2005). This became anti-Manchu sentiment during the late Qing period. However, the ultimate aim to 'oppose Qing and restore Ming' (*fanqing fuming* 反清复明) was to overthrow a backward system to build a new one in order to prevent China from being colonized by foreigners.

After the Opium Wars a series of government-led reforms took place, such as the 'Self-strengthening Movement', the 'Hundred Day's

Reform', and the 'New Policies'.[5] However, they all had little influence and failed amidst the defeats in wars against foreign colonial powers, and the concessions in uneven treaties were growing. Under these circumstances, the Qing rulers were blamed for their inability to reform and strengthen the country, to prevent it from being colonized by foreign countries (Zhang 1983). Consequently, the very slogan 'Manchu exclusion' was not a reflection of ethnic antagonism, but rather a tool to isolate and address the Manchu elite that was unwilling to reform and to mobilize for the largest possible people's support to form a joint revolutionary movement to 'rescue the nation' (Sun 2008; Wang 2006). Supporters of this approach used 'Manchu exclusion' as propaganda; they also invented a Huangdi (黄帝) image as the origin of the Han nationality, in order to build a "shared origin of the Han people" (Ishikawa 2005, 52). In this second wave of uprisings it is not possible to clearly separate resistance against the Manchu from resistance to Western colonialism against which the Manchu were perceived to be helpless.

However, different from the anti-Manchuism in the Early Qing period, in Late Qing time revolutionaries started to portray the Manchu as a different ethnicity or race because 'scientific explanations', based on race theories, were introduced by Chinese intellectuals at this time (Ishikawa 2003, 2005; Zhang 1996). The construction of a clear-cut Han nationality, even a Han race, separate from a Manchu race was thus situated within an overall attempt to grapple with Western science and technology, and to rescue China from colonialism (Zhong 1981; Zhong 1991). This may be most visible in the fact that Chinese racist theories would again be mobilized in accordance with regime loyalty: Intellectuals loyal to the Qing would promote theories of a single race including both Han and Manchu, or argue that exchange between races and mixing of races was superior to racial isolation. Anti-Qing intellectuals instead talked about racial conflicts and argued that the Han had to overcome the Manchu in order to thrive (Ishikawa 2003).

---

[5] After several defeats at the hands of the Western powers the government initiated a series of reforms, the 'Self-strengthening Movement', which failed after the Qing's defeat in the First Sino-Japanese War in 1895. The 'Hundred Day's Reform' were led by the Guangxu Emperor and his reform-minded supporters. It was hardly put into practice when the Empress Dowager Cixi and the conservative elites detained Guangxu, because they were unwilling to reform. After the siege of the International Legations in Peking and the signature of the Boxer Protocol, the Empress Dowager Cixi supported the implementation of a series of reforms ('New Policies') starting from 1901.

Sun Yat-Sen, for example, was among the leaders, who believed in the exclusion of Manchus and in the overthrow of their rule in order to build a republic at this time (Wu and Yu 2014; Zhang 1996, 2011; Zhong 1981, 1991). In this sense, the new focus on race and ethnicity in Manchu-Han relations was not a sign of Manchu power over subjugated Han people, but rather a symptom of the end of the Qing rule (Guo 1999). This focus was thus a sign of a nationalist movement against Western imperialism, designed to drive out the Manchu to build up a strong nation. In these uprisings cultural differences based on ethnic antagonism were not the reason for the conflicts, but rather the means of achieving other purposes. In fact, the Manchu-Han dichotomy and the sharpening separation between the two along ethnic lines was not the cause, but rather an outcome of this second wave of resistance.

CONTROLLED CULTURAL POLICIES WITHOUT DEVALUATION

These shifting and pragmatic politics of rule not only lacked the essential characteristics of colonialism. The holistic devaluation of the dominated culture was absent in Manchu-Han relations too. Qing rulers distinguished carefully between obedient and unruly cultural practices. Recent scholarship has argued that a complete Manchu Sinicization never took place, nor was Qing rule based on the acceptance of Han standards. Relations between the Manchu and the Han majority were instead based on marking cultural boundaries (Chang 2007; Elliott 2001; Forêt 2000; Millward et al. 2004). The Manchu made efforts to intentionally maintain their distinct culture such as 'horse-riding and archery'. However, this was not based on a politics of 'othering' as we find it in Western colonialism, in which not only a total separation of the cultures of the colonizer and the colonized, but also a holistic devaluation of the latter's culture were of great importance for creating a dominant-subordinate dynamic. Although the Qing rulers instituted high-handed policies against Han culture, as visible in the haircut act, they did not construct a discourse of a 'Han culture' as backward or inferior in its entirety.

In order to consolidate their rule over the country, Qing rulers worked not only by subjugating, but often by consolidating the Han majority. In their appeasing policies, they observed Han culture and distinguished between customs that were advantageous or not for their rule. Those cultural practices that were perceived to be a hindrance to Qing rule or a source of persistent loyalty to the Ming were suppressed, as with the haircut act. However, this did not keep Qing rulers from adopting other practices seen as advantageous to their rule. They acknowledged traditions of the Ming dynasty as legitimate, and in some instances they even made them the official practices of their own imperial rule. For example, the first important measure of the Manchu government was to give an honored burial to the last Emperor of the Ming Dynasty, which created legitimacy for the transformation from the Ming to the Qing, a kind of *translatio imperii* in accordance with the Chinese tradition of a shifting 'Mandate of Heaven' (天命). As Hui Wang argues,

> The legitimacy of the Qing dynasty as a Chinese dynasty was only established as the Qing gradually took control of China proper. For a substantial period of time after the Manchu's entry into China proper, Han people and southeastern ethnic minorities living in China proper as well as neighboring states did not recognize the Manchu Qing as a Chinese dynasty. (2014, 18–19)

The burial of the Emperor Chongzhen made it possible to construct a master narrative that explained the Manchu expansion into Ming territory in 1644 as an act to help the Ming people. The Qing narrative argued that the last Ming Emperor was killed by Shun rebels, and it was the Manchus who took revenge in the name of the Ming people by killing the rebels. Burying Chongzhen was thus an act of respect for the Ming Dynasty while symbolizing its end and the new rule of the Qing. Moreover, Qing rulers also adopted and reformed the worship system for the Temple of Past Emperors (*Lidai diwang miao* 历代帝王庙).[6] They added a large number of names to the list of emperors to be worshiped, thereby confirming and integrating themselves into the narrative of a continuous inheritance of dynasties through Chinese history from the 'Three Sovereigns and Five Emperors', mythic rulers in prehistoric China (ca. 2850–2070 BCE) who were considered cultural heroes, to the Ming dynasty (Deng 2017).

---

[6]The imperial temples of emperors are located on the Fuchengmennei Dajie in Xicheng District of Beijing today. They were originally built in the early Ming period (1373) as part of the worship system for former emperors who were considered great figures in Chinese history. Qing rulers continued this tradition and paid great attention to it. The change of the name list, as well as the comments on these emperors, can help us understand the Qing rulers' view of history.

Many practices that were used under the Ming were adopted as legitimate traditions by the Qing whose emperors started to learn the Han language and became fluent in it. They developed a high esteem of Confucian culture, and many Manchu elite individuals became experts on Confucian literature themselves. It became compulsory for the sons of emperors to be educated by both Manchu and Han teachers. In 1687, Qing Emperor Kangxi expressed his admiration clearly: "I am fully aware that the Han scholarship is hundreds of times better than the Manchu's" (The First Historical Archives of China 1984, vol. 1, 1639). In the same year, Kangxi set up three stone steles with inscriptions on the same day for temples to the saints of Confucian culture: Zhougong, Kongzi, and Mengzi. This was clearly a token of respect to Confucian customs because in Manchu culture neither Confucian saints nor God were to be worshiped. Kangxi also traveled to Confucius's hometown, Qufu, to worship him personally. This visit became a tradition followed by later rulers. Similar journeys to places of symbolic value to the Confucian tradition were undertaken by other Qing emperors as well. Moreover, the essentialization of ethnic distinction was potentially harmful to Manchu rule that was supposed to be legitimized as part of the history of their dynastic succession. For instance, by illustrating the example of Emperor Yongzheng's debate with Zeng Jing on the 'Hua-Yi' debate, Zhang Yongjiang shows:

> Arguing against such a notion by which the Manchus were to be considered barbarians or beasts, Emperor Yongzheng pointed out that the only difference between *Hua* and *Yi* was in their location of residency, which had nothing to do with the quality or the social position of the two cultures. [...] He [Emperor Yongzheng] emphasized that all nations and ethnic groups should be treated equally. This implied that not only Manchu and Mongols but also all other groups inside the Qing domain should not be viewed as *Yi* but as equal citizens. (2017, 140)

The acknowledgment and partial promotion of Confucian tradition was certainly a very efficient political strategy. These practices did not necessarily imply a complete Sinicization of the Manchu. As said before, Qing rulers did not simply assimilate Ming traditions at random, but picked up those that supported their claim for legitimacy. Yet, despite the respect they showed toward Confucian traditions, they did not necessarily strive to become entirely assimilated to the Han. Often, the situation was much more ambivalent and multi-faceted. For example, between 1751 and 1784, Emperor Qianlong made six formal 'inspection tours' to Jiangnan in southern China, the heartland of commercial wealth and literate culture. These tours have often been seen as a proof of Qianlong's admiration for Han culture and the eagerness of the Manchu to become assimilated to the Han. However, some recent scholars have argued that Qianlong used these tours to mark the boundaries between the Manchu and Han, rather than to worship Han culture (Chang 2007; Elliott 2001). Rather than arguing that the Manchu wanted to assimilate to the Han, it is more appropriate to argue that they tried to establish legitimate rule and dynastic succession. They were aware of the fact that they could 'conquer China from the horseback, but not rule it from the horseback' (Sima 1959, 2699).[7]

Confucianism was functional for legitimizing and stabilizing Qing rule because the foundation of the Confucian ideology was to promote a hierarchical social structure in which every woman obeys her man, every son his father (filial piety), and every official is loyal to the Emperor. Through the imperial examination system and the administrative structure of imperial officials, Confucianism was furthermore entangled with a highly efficient, relatively centralized bureaucratic system that made rule over vast territories possible. Moreover, by promoting Confucianism, the Qing emperors stabilized their rule by making use of cultural symbols that had already been accepted before the Qing came into power. This made the claim for a legitimate change of dynasties easier to convey.

DOES DOMINATION EQUAL COLONIALISM?

Theories of colonialism, including continental and internal forms, surely constitute a two-edged sword. On the one hand, they provide new questions, as well as new insights into different forms of domination. On the other hand, theorists are at risk of over-extending the concept of colonialism until it means everything and thus nothing anymore. Scholars in China and the West, including scholars of the New Qing History, have shown that an entirely Han-centric perspective may fail to grasp

---

[7] This comes from a classic saying about a dialogue of the founder of the Han dynasty Liu Bang who despised reading ancient classics when he could conquer the world on horseback. His adviser Lu Jia answered, "You may have got it on horseback, but can you rule it on horseback?"

the complexity of Qing history. The Han were neither the sole actors in Chinese history nor the only power that singlehandedly forged ethnic relationships. The history of the Qing dynasty is a multi-centric history full of struggles among different power groups, including struggles among ethnic groups, fights over cultural domination, and the expansion into non-Han territories beyond China proper.

As I have argued in this chapter, the portrayal of "a consolidated conquest elite" versus the "objects of the conquest" (Crossley et al. [2006] 2007, 2) would oversimplify the complex relationships of that time. Manchu rulers were eager to stabilize and legitimize their rule, and they implemented fierce measures to suppress the Han people, both economically and culturally. But they also made claims to be part of a legitimate dynastic succession. Most importantly, they used elements from Han culture—Confucianism as an example—to create a strictly hierarchical society in which people should show their loyalty to the country and the emperor. The adoption of Confucian culture should indeed be seen as connected to a power strategy in the context of military conquest and the establishment of the rule through which the Manchu oppressed the Han in various ways. However, to call this a colonial situation would go too far. Different from the case of Manchu-Han relations, colonial powers in history humiliated, murdered, and enslaved other ethnic groups and legitimized such acts through racist discourses and narratives of civilizational progress. Even at times when their rule was not explicitly violent, colonizers constructed colonial master narratives of history that would place the dominated groups in their entirety, including every aspect of their race and culture into an inferior position that lagged behind. In this way, the colonizers created a colonial culture (Stoler 1992), in which "the colonizer and the colonized were two worlds apart with no passage in between" (Verma 1992, 122).[8]

In the Manchu-Han case, certainly "Manchu interests were still an important consideration of Manchu political figures" (Elliott 2006, 13), and maintaining the privilege of Manchuism was of great concern for the Qing rulers. However, this went together with an ambiguous and interchangeable

---

[8]Of course, the focus here is on Manchu-Han relations. The degree to which internal colonialism can be applied as a concept for Manchu relations with other ethnic groups, especially minorities outside China proper, is beyond the scope of this chapter.

classification among the Manchu and between the ruler and the ruled. While Western colonizers famously constructed themselves as entirely different from the backward, uncivilized, and exotically colonized (Said [1993] 1994), Qing rulers actively portrayed their rule at least in Manchu-Han relations as legitimate *within* and compatible to Confucian tradition. Furthermore, while the rule of the Manchu over the Han indeed contained various forms of political and cultural domination, a total devaluation of the dominated culture was missing. 'Colonial' elements in Manchu cultural policy were, for example, the positioning of Han in distance from the Manchu, but they did not devalue practices of the Han in their entirety. Rather, they distinguished between certain aspects that posed a problem to their rule and thus had to be oppressed—such as hairstyles that signified loyalty to the Ming—from other aspects that were useful and were thus promoted. In fact, the Qing rulers engaged with and learned from Han traditions to the point that the fundamentals of their state administration were influenced by Confucian bureaucracy. Consequently, the hybridization of Han and Manchu cultures that took place in the Qing era was not merely an accidental practice born of everyday encounters, typical for Western colonialism, but part of official Qing policy.

Thus, in the Manchu-Han case, it would be more appropriate to talk about domination that included cultural and ethnic policy—a cultural domination—rather than a colonial situation where Qing rule is labeled as 'colonial'. Both the cruel and oppressive elements of Qing rule, as well as the pragmatic way of handling culture, demand concepts of cultural entanglement more complex than the notion of the Manchu becoming entirely like the Han. It nevertheless would be a grave mistake to overlook the degree to which Qing rulers were willing to implement Han traditions into their rule and to represent themselves as successors of former dynasties. Most importantly, it would be inappropriate to describe the state coercion and government practice toward Han as 'colonial' in the sense of overseas colonialism. Qing rule greatly differed from European colonialism, especially through the absence of late nineteenth-century colonial discourses that considered oriental culture to be anything more than exotic or ancient wisdom. It would be interesting to explore whether and to what extent the absence of such colonial discourses could help explain why Qing domination, despite its cruelty, left behind a much less traumatizing memory in Han historiography than the colonization by European powers or by Japan. To raise such a question might contribute greatly to our understanding of colonialism and the strange persistence of colonial thinking even in times after de-colonialization in Chinese history. However, Qing policy toward the Han might instead serve as a counterexample than as a case of continental colonialism.

REFERENCES

Barlow, Tani E. 1993. "Colonialism's Career in Postwar China Studies." *Positions: Asia Critique* 1(1): 224–67.

Bhabha, Homi K. [1984] 2012. "Of Mimicry and Man: The Ambivalence of Colonial Discourse." In *The Location of Culture*, edited by Homi K. Bhabha, 121–31. Hoboken: Taylor and Francis.

Bian, Jiazhen, and Ziran Li. 1998. "Shi lun qingchu manzhou guizu tuixing 'tifayifu' zhengce de zhuzhi" 试论清初满洲贵族推行 '剃发易服' 政策的主旨 [A Tentative Discussion on the Aims of the Implementation of the 'Haircut and Cloth-Changing' Policy Among the Manchu Nobles in the Early Qing Period]. *Heilongjiang National Series* 55(4): 63–65.

Buck-Morss, Susan. 2000. "Hegel and Haiti." *Critical Inquiry* 26(4): 821–65.

Cams, Mario. 2016. "Recent Additions to the New Qing History Debate." *Contemporary Chinese Thought* 47(1): 1–4.

Chang, Michael G. 2007. *A Court on Horseback: Imperial Touring and the Construction of Qing Rule, 1680–1785*. Cambridge, MA: Harvard University Asia Center.

Cooper, Frederick. [2002] 2009. *Africa Since 1940: The Past of the Present*. Cambridge: Cambridge University Press.

Crossley, Pamela Kyle. [1990] 1991. *Orphan Warriors: Three Manchu Generations and the End of the Qing World*. Princeton, NJ: Princeton University Press.

Crossley, Pamela Kyle, Helen F. Siu, and Donald S. Sutton. [2006] 2007. "Introduction." In *Empire at the Margins: Culture, Ethnicity, and Frontier in Early Modern China*, edited by Pamela Kyle Crossley, Helen F. Siu, and Donald S. Sutton, 1–24. Berkeley, CA: University of California Press.

Deng, Tao. 2017. "Mingqing diwang minyuguan he lishiguan de yitong - cong lidai diwangmiao diwangjisi jiaodu chufa" 明清帝王民族观和历史观的异同— 从历代帝王庙帝王祭祀角度出发 [The Sustaining Chinese Civilization and History—The Difference and Similarities Between Emperors in Ming and Qing Dynasties Based on the Worship of the Imperial Temples of Emperors]. *Journal of Yantai University (Philosophy and Social Science Edition)* 30(4): 83–92.

Di Cosmo, Nicola. 1998. "Qing Colonial Administration in Inner Asia." *The International History Review* 20(2): 287–309.

Ding, Yizhuang. 2000. *Man Han wen hua jiao liu shi hua* 满汉文化交流史话 [A Brief Story of the Manchu-Han Cultural Exchanges]. Beijing: Zhongguo da baike quanshu chubanshe.

Elliott, Mark C. 2001. *The Manchu Way: The Eight Banners and Ethnic Identity in Late Imperial China.* Stanford, CA: Stanford University Press.

Elliott, Mark C. 2006. "Manwen dangan yu xin qing shi" 满文档案与新清史 [Manchu-Language Archives and the New Qing History]. *The National Palace Museum Research Quarterly* 24(2): 1–18.

Fairbank, John King. 1957. "Synarchy Under the Treaties." In *Chinese Thought and Institutions*, edited by John King Fairbank, 204–31. Chicago: University of Chicago Press.

Fiskesjö, Magnus. 2017. "The Legacy of the Chinese Empires: Beyond 'The West and the Rest'." *Education About Asia* 22(1): 6–10.

Forêt, Philippe. 2000. *Mapping Chengde: The Qing Landscape Enterprise.* Honolulu: University of Hawai'i Press.

Ge, Jianxiong. 2007. *Ge jian xiong yan jiang lu* 葛剑雄演讲录 [The Lecture Collection of Ge Jianxiong]. Taiyuan: Shanxi guji chubanshe.

Gladney, Dru C. 1998. "Internal Colonialism and the Uyghur Nationality: Chinese Nationalism and Its Subaltern Subjects." *Cahiers d'Études sur la Méditerranée Orientale et le monde Turco-Iranien* 25: 1–12.

Glahn, Richard von. 2004. "Foreword." In *The Qing Formation in World-Historical Time*, edited by Lynn A. Struve, xi–xvi. Cambridge, MA: Harvard University Asia Center.

Goodman, David S.G. 1983. "Guizhou and the People's Republic of China: The Development of an Internal Colony." In *Internal Colonialism: Essays Around a Theme*, edited by David Drakakis-Smith and Stephen Wyn Williams, 107–24. Edinburgh: University of Edinburgh Press.

Guo, Shiyou. 1999. "Sun Zhongshan de fanman minzu zhuyi sixiang bielun" 孙中山的反满主义思想别论 [A New Debate on Sun Yatsen's Anti-Manchu Thought]. *The Qing History Journal* 0(4): 40–49.

Herman, John E. 2007. *Amid the Clouds and Mist: China's Colonization of Guizhou, 1200–1700.* Cambridge, MA: Harvard University Press.

Hevia, James Louis. [1995] 2005. *Cherishing Men from Afar: Qing Guest Ritual and the MaCartney Embassy of 1793.* Durham: Duke University Press.

Hind, Robert J. 1984. "The Internal Colonial Concept." *Comparative Studies in Society and History* 26(3): 543–68.

Ho, Ping-Ti. 1998. "In Defense of Sinicization: A Rebuttal of Evelyn Rawski's 'Reenvisioning the Qing'." *The Journal of Asian Studies* 57(1): 123–55.

Hostetler, Laura. [2001] 2005. *Qing Colonial Enterprise: Ethnography and Cartography in Early Modern China.* Chicago: University of Chicago Press.

Huang, Ray. [1993] 1997. *Zhongguo da li shi* 中国大历史 [A Macro-history of China]. Beijing: xinzhi sanlian shudian.

Ishikawa, Yoshihiro. 2003. "Anti-Manchu Racism and the Rise of Anthropology in Early 20th Century China." *Sino-Japanese Studies* 15: 7–26.

Ishikawa, Yoshihiro. 2005. "Ershi shiji chunian zhongguo liuri xuesheng 'huangdi' zhi zaizao - paiman, xiaoxiang, xifang qiyuan lun" 二十世纪初年中国留日学生'黄帝'之再造—排满、肖像、西方起源论 [The Rebuilding of 'Huang Di' in the 20th Century: Excluding Manchu, Portraits and Western Originality Theory]. *Studies in Qing History* 0(4): 51–62.

Lin, Jiayou, and Jikui Li. [1990] 1991. *Xin hai ge ming yun dong shi* 辛亥革命运动史 [History of the Xinhai Revolution]. Guangzhou: Zhongshan daxue chubanshe.

Liu, Lydia He. [2004] 2006. *The Clash of Empires: The Invention of China in Modern World Making.* Cambridge, MA: Harvard University Press.

Liu, Xiaomeng. 2008. *Qing dai ba qi zi di* 清代八旗子弟 [The Eight Bannermen in the Qing Dynasty]. Shenyang: Liaoning minzu chubanshe.

Lu, Yong. 2010. "Qingchao hanren guojia guannian de bianqian - cong tifaling xia hanren shenfen de zhuanbian lai kaocha" 清初汉人国家观念的变迁—从"薙发令"下汉人身份的转变来考察 ['Haircuts Act' Under the Han Chinese Identity—Han Chinese National Identity Changes in the Early Qing Dynasty]. *Journal of Southwest University of Science and Technology* 27(1): 81–88.

Luo, Xiaoliang. 2013. "Shixi kangxichao zhongze dui hanzu wenhua zhengce yu dayitong zhengzhi guanxi - yi anding jiangnan weili" 试析康熙朝中叶对汉族文化政策与大一统政治关系—以安定江南为例 [On the Relationship between the Big Unification and Culture Policy to Han Nation in the Middle of Kangxi Dynasty—Taking Stabilizing Southern Yangtze as a Case]. *Journal of Huazhong Normal University (Humanities and Social Sciences)* 52(2): 139–47.

Meng, Sen. 2010. *Qing shi jiang yi* 清史讲义 [A Lecture on the Qing History]. Beijing: Zhonghua shuju.

Millward, James A. [2007] 2009. *Eurasian Crossroads: A History of Xinjiang.* Columbia University Press.

Millward, James A., Ruth W. Dunnell, Mark C. Elliott, and Philippe Forêt, eds. 2004. *New Qing Imperial History: The Making of Inner Asian Empire at Qing Chengde.* London: RoutledgeCurzon.

Naquin, Susan, and Evelyn Sakakida Rawski. 1987. *Chinese Society in the Eighteenth Century.* New Haven: Yale University Press.

Osterhammel, Jürgen. [1995] 2010. *Colonialism: A Theoretical Overview.* Translated by Shelley L. Frisch. Princeton, NJ: Markus Wiener Publishers.

Perdue, Peter C. 1998a. "Comparing Empires: Manchu Colonialism." *The International History Review* 20(2): 255–62.

Perdue, Peter C. 1998b. "Boundaries, Maps, and Movement: Chinese, Russian, and Mongolian Empires in Early Modern Central Eurasia." *The International History Review* 20(2): 263–86.

Perdue, Peter C. 2005. *China Marches West: The Qing Conquest of Central Eurasia.* Cambridge, MA: Harvard University Press.

Quijano, Anibal. 2000. "Coloniality of Power, Eurocentrism, and Latin America." *Nepantla: Views from the South* 1(3): 533–80.

Rawski, Evelyn Sakakida. 1996. "Presidential Address: Reenvisioning the Qing: The Significance of the Qing Period in Chinese History." *The Journal of Asian Studies* 55(4): 829–50.

Rhoads, Edward J.M. 2000. *Manchus & Han: Ethnic Relations and Political Power in Late Qing and Early Republican China, 1861–1928.* Seattle: University of Washington Press.

Rowe, William T. [2009] 2012. *China's Last Empire: The Great Qing.* Cambridge, MA: Harvard University Press.

Said, Edward W. 1978. *Orientalism.* New York: Pantheon Books.

Said, Edward W. [1993] 1994. *Culture and Imperialism.* New York: Vintage Books.

Schorkowitz, Dittmar, and Chia Ning, eds. 2017. *Managing Frontiers in Qing China: The Lifanyuan and Libu Revisited.* Leiden: Brill.

"Shizu zhanghuangdi shilu." 1985. 世祖章皇帝实录 [The Veritable Records of Qing Shizu]. In *Qing shilu* 清实录 [Historical Record of Qing], vol. 3. Beijing: Zhonghua shuju.

Sima, Qian. 1959. "Lisheng lujia liezhuan" 郦生陆贾列传 [Biographies of Li Sheng and Lu Jia]. In *Shiji* 史记 [Records of the Grand Historian], vol. 8. Beijing: Zhonghua shuju.

Spence, Jonathan D. [1990] 1991. *The Search for Modern China.* New York: W. W. Norton.

Stoler, Ann Laura. 1992. "Rethinking Colonial Categories: European Communities and the Boundaries of Rule." In *Colonialism and Culture,* edited by Nicholas B. Dirks, 319–52. Ann Arbor, MI: University of Michigan Press.

Struve, Lynn A. 2004. "Introduction." In *The Qing Formation in World-Historical Time,* edited by Lynn A. Struve, 1–54. Cambridge, MA: Harvard University Asia Center.

Sun, Jing. 2008. *'Man-zhou' minzu gongtongti xingcheng licheng* 满洲民族共同体形成历程 [The Formation Process of the 'Manchu' Ethnic Community]. Shenyang: Liaoning minzu chubanshe.

The First Historical Archives of China. 1984. *Kangxi qiju zhu* 康熙起居注 [The Living Notes of Kangxi], vol. 1. Beijing: Zhonghua shuju.

Verma, Rupalee. 1992. "Dirks Nicholas B., ed. 1992. *Colonialism and Culture,* 391 pp. Ann Arbor: The University of Michigan Press." *Itinerario:*

International Journal on the History of European Expansion and Global Interaction 16(2): 121–22.

Waley-Cohen, Joanna. 2004. "The New Qing History." *Radical History Review* 88: 193–206.

Waley-Cohen, Joanna. 2006. *The Culture of War in China: Empire and the Military Under the Qing Dynasty*. London: I.B. Tauris.

Wang, Hui. 2014. *China from Empire to Nation-State*. Cambridge: Harvard University Press.

Wang, Kaixi. 2006. "Qingmo manhan guanliao yu manzu yishi jianlun" 清末满汉官僚与满汉民族意识简论 [A Brief Discussion on the Manchu and Han Bureaucracy and the Consciousness of the Manchu and Han Ethnic Identity in the Late Qing Period]. *Social Science Journal* 167(6): 168–74.

Werner, Michael, and Bénédicte Zimmermann. 2002. "Vergleich, Transfer, Verflechtung: Der Ansatz der Histoire croisée und die Herausforderung des Transnationalen." *Geschichte und Gesellschaft* 28: 607–37.

White, Richard. 1991. *The Middle Ground: Indians, Empires, and Republics in the Great Lakes Region, 1650–1815*. Cambridge: Cambridge University Press.

Wu, Lei, and Chunyang Yu. 2014. "Xinhai geming zhunbei shiqi 'paiman' sichao shuxi" 辛亥革命准备时期'排满'思潮述析 [An Analysis of 'Anti-Manchuism' Thoughts During the Preparation of the Xinhai Revolution]. *Lantai World* 2: 33–34.

Wu, Zengli. 2010. "Qingchu jiangnan yimin shengcun jingkuang yanjiu" 清初江南移民生存境况研究 [A Study of the Habitation Conditions and Spiritual World of Jiangnan Old Adherents in the Beginning of the Qing Dynasty]. PhD diss., Hunan University.

Young, Crawford. [2007] 2010. "Nation, Ethnicity, and Citizenship: Dilemmas of Democracy and Civil Order in Africa." In *Making Nations, Creating Strangers: States and Citizenship in Africa*, edited by Sara Dorman, Daniel Hammett, and Paul Nugent, 241–64. Leiden: Brill.

Yu, Jiansheng, and Chunrui Liu. 1995. "Qianxi wanqing manhan guanliao jian de maodun yu douzheng" 浅析晚清满汉官僚间的矛盾与斗争 [An Analysis of the Contradictions and Struggles Among the Manchu and Han Officials in the Late Qing Dynasty]. *Journal of Teachers' College of Qingdao University* 12(3): 39–45.

Zhang, Jian. 2016. "Manchu Sinicization: Doubts on the Ethnic Perspective of New Qing History." *Contemporary Chinese Thought* 47(1): 30–43.

Zhang, Kaiyuan. 1983. "'Paiman' yu minzu yundong" '排满'与民族运动 ['Anti-Manchuism' and Nationalist Movements]. *Modern Chinese History Studies* 3: 72–93.

Zhang, Kaiyuan. 1996. "Xinhai geming shiqi de shehui dongyuan - yi 'paiman' xuanchuan wei shili" 辛亥革命时期的社会动员--以"排满"宣传为实例

[The Social Mobilization in the Xinhai Revolution—Take the Promotion of 'Anti-Manchuism' as an Example]. *Social Science Research* 5: 93–99.

Zhang, Kaiyuan. 2011. *Zhang Kaiyuan zi xuan ji* 章开沅自选集 [A Self-selection of Zhang Kaiyuan]. Beijing: Zhongguo shehui kexue chubanshe.

Zhang, Yongjiang. 2017. "The Libu and Qing Perception, Classification and Administration of Non-Han People." In *Managing Frontiers in Qing China: The Lifanyuan and Libu Revisited*, edited by Dittmar Schorkowitz and Ning Chia, 116–43. Leiden: Brill.

Zhong, Zhenwei. 1981. "Ruhe kandai xinhai geming de fanman wenti" 如何看待辛亥革命的反满问题 [How to Understand the Question of Anti-Manchuism in the Xinhai Revolution]. *Journal of South China Normal University (Social Science Edition)* 1: 104–10.

Zhong, Zhuoan. 1991. "Xinhai geming yu fanman sichao" 辛亥革命与反满思潮 [Xinhai Revolution and the Anti-Manchuism Thoughts]. *Social Sciences in Guangdong* 5: 14–19.

Zuo, Zhitao. 2005. "Wanqing manhan shili de xiaozhang ji qi yuanyin tanxi" 晚清满汉势力的消长及其原因探析 [The Growth and Decline in Regime between Manchu and Han Nationality in the Late Qing Dynasty and Their Reasons]. *Journal of Yantai College of Education* 11(1): 6–9.

CHAPTER 8

The Slovak 'Gypsy Fringe' as a Semi-colonial Entity

David Z. Scheffel

INTRODUCTION

This chapter is based on my engagement with several communities of Slovak Roma over the past twenty years. East European Roma have become a popular object of anthropological attention over the last decades, and given their undeniable domination or even subjugation by the various host societies containing Roma, other scholars have certainly touched on the themes dealt with in this chapter. In order to avoid duplication, I dwell on forms of domination and resistance that haven't received adequate or even any attention, but which provide fertile ground for conceptualizing these as variations on colonization—and resistance—practices. I am aware of gaps in the literature used to solidify some of my arguments. This is an unavoidable consequence of circumstances beyond my control, namely the confiscation of electronic

D. Z. Scheffel (✉)
Department of Sociology and Anthropology, Thompson Rivers University, Kamloops, BC, Canada
e-mail: Dscheffel@tru.ca

© The Author(s) 2019   197
D. Schorkowitz et al. (eds.), *Shifting Forms of Continental Colonialism*,
https://doi.org/10.1007/978-981-13-9817-9_8

computer files by Slovak authorities investigating the conduct of my field research.[1] I have tried to compensate for this drawback by structuring my arguments around unpublished ethnographic material assembled with the assistance of the residents of several communities of what I describe here as the Slovak 'Gypsy fringe', an obvious allusion to the 'Celtic fringe' of Michael Hechter's classic model of internal colonialism ([1975] 1999).

FORMS OF DOMINATION: THE GYPSY COLONY

The arrival of Roma in East Central Europe in the late Middle Ages resulted in the formation of more or less self-contained communities attached to towns and villages of the host society. From the very beginning, there was a concerted effort by local authorities to curb the new arrivals' perceived or genuine 'nomadic urge' that threatened the speed and effectiveness of their domestication and assimilation. Unlike the Jews, whose highly formalized cultural distinctions justified a grudgingly granted degree of autonomy—albeit within a closely guarded ghetto— the Gypsies were seen as a backward and barbaric people who had to make a choice between assimilation and expulsion. Hence in East Central Europe there has always been a close relationship between spatial and cultural aspects of the domination exercised over Roma. In order to fulfill the host society's civilizing mission, it required the implementation of management techniques that exposed the dominated subjects to effective surveillance and indoctrination. The site upon which this effort focused was the 'Gypsy colony'.

Between the second half of the nineteenth and the first half of the twentieth century the term 'Gypsy colony' became a common designation in Czech and Slovak for rural clusters of tents, wagons and huts inhabited permanently or periodically by Roma legally domiciled in the corresponding municipality. After World War II, this term gradually gave way to the word 'settlement' (*osada*). Both appellations refer to a haphazardly established community with overtones of impermanence and a general lack of history and stability. Correspondingly, such assemblages are found on the periphery of adjoining villages or towns that exercise

---

[1] "The author could not complete this chapter to his satisfaction due to his unexpected incarceration in Slovakia. The charges he faces arise from the research into sexual practices of Roma described in this contribution" (The editors on behalf of David Scheffel).

political, economic and cultural authority over them. A Romani settlement is conceptualized as a dependency fraught with poverty, disorder,
crime, and a host of other ills associated with backwardness. Although
the physical distance between the village and the settlement can be a few
meters, it has an enormous symbolic significance as a marker of ethno-
racial distinctions. Roma attempting to cross this divide and establish residence in the adjoining village encounter a myriad of problems that very
few manage to overcome. Correspondingly, villagers or other 'whites'
who move to (or even visit) a settlement become pariahs among their
own people (see Scheffel 2005, 2015).

Today, roughly one fifth of Slovakia's approximately 500,000 Roma
continue to live in such communities. There are close to a thousand of
them, ranging in size from a few dozen residents to five thousand, and
their heaviest concentration is in the eastern, least affluent, part of the
country (Mušinka et al. 2014). Although politicians and rank-and-file
Slovaks consider these enclaves as a cancer growing on the otherwise
healthy body of the nation, ever since their appearance several centuries
ago they have served as a source of values and services appreciated by
the dominant society and extracted in a quasi-colonial manner. Some of
their occupations are well-known. Roma have served their neighbors as
musicians, blacksmiths, cadaver collectors, fortune-tellers, and laborers of
various types (Horváthová 1964). Further below I consider their contribution as providers of other infrequently discussed services. But perhaps the greatest, albeit unacknowledged, benefit Roma have given their
neighbors has been their willingness to play the role of a colonized subject and thus sustain and nurture the feeling of superiority and power
of their 'white masters'. Since traditionally the majority of Roma lived
in rural settings, this type of status enhancement conferred a feeling of
moral, economic, and cultural superiority on even the poorest peasants
at the lowest rung of a village community who, thanks to the 'Gypsies',
never found themselves completely deprived of self-respect and honor.
However deep they may have fallen due to poverty, alcoholism, disease,
or simply bad luck, such social misfits found solace in the knowledge that
they remained above 'the Gypsies'. Thus, the very exclusion of Roma
helped foster solidarity and cohesion among their neighbors.

Akin to the periodic anti-Jewish pogroms in eastern and central
Europe and their role in reinforcing the bonds and values of the sur-
rounding Christian society, Slovak peasants engaged in recurrent raids on
Romani settlements whose residents had broken some important norm

of the local master–servant matrix and therefore had to be taught a lesson about their place in the local hierarchy. Such raids have continued into the modern era, and the general disinterest of local authorities in preventing such wanton acts of aggression underlines the general consensus about the legitimacy of Romani subordination and the mastery of the core—in this context the Slovak village—over the periphery, the dependent 'colony' and its inhabitants. The precariousness of their existence reached its apex under the fascist regime of the wartime Slovak Republic when scores of Gypsy colonies were destroyed and relocated to isolated sites at some distance from the parent village (Scheffel 2015). During the subsequent socialist era with its emphasis on unilineal progress, Romani settlements came to be seen as incubators of archaic ideas and a backward lifestyle that retarded emancipatory efforts pursued by the Communist Party's social engineers. Similar to North American Indian reserves, these homelands of a problematic minority were targeted for elimination and its residents for dispersal among the majority population (Zeman 1959).

Alas, by the late 1960s it had become clear that partly because of the enormous population increase among Slovak Roma, the settlement-elimination program couldn't be completed as planned. Poverty and cultural backwardness were to become a lasting legacy, and state authorities eventually adopted a policy of containment that sought to protect the neighbors of problematic settlements through improved surveillance and the dispatch of specially trained police personnel. That approach continues during the post-socialist era. While paying lip service to the integration goals of the European Union, Slovak officials tacitly accept the status quo where Romani settlements constitute de facto self-contained communities with distinctive normative systems and lifestyles that set them apart from the surrounding majority society. As I show below, the state certainly continues to interfere, but no longer because it wishes to propel 'progress' among the Roma.

ROMA AND 'REPRODUCTIVE SURPLUS'

If we accept the definition of colonialism proposed in this volume's introduction as "a set of ideas, beliefs, practices, and politics of a given people (nation, state, empire) emanating from a habitus of cultural superiority [...] and compressed as structural hegemony that builds on extractive economy, civilizing mission, and military conquest to control other ethno-racially different peoples" (this volume, p. 37), then how can we best extend it to the encounter between the Slovak state and its Roma? In some respects, Michael Hechter's model of internal colonialism ([1975] 1999) can be fruitfully adapted to fit the Slovak situation. Here, instead of an undeveloped 'Celtic fringe' inhabited by a self-contained and culturally distinct minority, we have an even more undeveloped and culturally vastly different 'Gypsy fringe' centered on dispersed, but linked settlements that constitute semi-autonomous homelands. Unlike the British case where natural resources extracted from the Celtic periphery sustained the population of the English core, the Slovak situation lacks this kind of economic exploitation. But as in most colonial settings, a type of extraction did—and still does—take place in the form of what could be termed 'demographic contribution', a topic I will consider in some detail.

Already in the late eighteenth century European observers and students of 'Gypsies' commented on their unusually high fecundity as a potential benefit for their host societies. Heinrich Grellmann wrote about the transformation of this 'nation' into desirable citizens by virtue of its extraordinary fertility—"mit seiner Fruchtbarkeit und seinen zahlreichen Nachkommen, die alle zu brauchbaren Bürgern umgeschafft sind" (1787, 183). According to some sources, the assimilation decree issued by Emperor Joseph II in 1782 foresaw the deployment of the bountiful Gypsy population of Hungary as colonists in sparsely settled parts of Transylvania (Nečas 2000). When in 1893 Austrian and Hungarian scholars carried out the first reliable ethno-demographic surveys among the country's rapidly growing population of Roma, they expressed the conviction that this largely 'unproductive' segment of the population could be transformed into soldiers, craftsmen, skilled workers—and defenders of Magyar interests in Slavic and Romanian territories—provided they were properly educated and acculturated (Jekelfalussy and Herrmann 1895).

Due to rising sentiments of xenophobia and racism, the next half century didn't provide fertile soil for this type of pragmatism; on the contrary, Roma were increasingly segregated from mainstream society and treated as misfits. But egalitarianism and socialist humanism after World War II reversed the trend, and all the newly created people's democracies promulgated policies that aimed at making Roma into fully integrated 'productive citizens' (Zeman 1959). Already in 1947 a year before the establishment of state socialism, faced with a severe shortage of workers caused by the war and its demographic consequences—especially the expulsion of most of the Sudeten Germans (Anonymous 1946)— Czechoslovak authorities singled out Roma as an untapped source of labor to be activated (Mareš 1947). This view predominated following the communist takeover and the new regime's emphasis on compulsory labor as a vehicle for individual and social transformation. In 1954 a Communist Party policy paper echoed earlier sentiments about the Roma as a "significant reserve of the workforce" (Spurný 2011, 258). Mass inoculations, improvements in natal care, public hygiene measures, and the provision of universal free health care dramatically curbed infant mortality while generous family benefits provided new incentives for bearing more children. While the majority population throughout the socialist bloc began to produce fewer and fewer children—a trend that continues into the present—the Roma experienced a population explosion with some communities doubling in number every twenty years or so. As I have claimed elsewhere on the basis of Slovak data, the socialist era saw the emergence of a new division of labor based on ethnicity. While women belonging to the white majority entered the labor force *en masse*—which, in spite of the feverish creation of thousands of crèches and kindergartens, made them reluctant to bear more than a couple of children—their Romani peers overwhelmingly chose to stay at home and give free reign to their reproductive potential (Scheffel 2005). Troubled by the prospect of a shortage of workers to man the labor-intensive heavy industry favored in post-war Czechoslovakia, the government at first welcomed the demographic surplus provided by the Roma. Bearers of multiple children received 'motherhood medals' introduced in the 1950s—following Stalin's and Hitler's example—and thousands of Romani men were encouraged to move to predominantly Czech districts experiencing labor shortages. This was the beginning of the large-scale migration of Slovak Roma to the Czech lands.

Concerns about high concentrations of 'problematic Gypsies' triggered protests from local authorities and factory managers in some areas. This prompted government officials to reconsider the contribution made by Roma to the unskilled labor pool. Simultaneously, public health experts expressed misgivings about the 'quality' of the population generated and raised in Romani households (Petro 1985; Popálená 1987; Sokolova 2005). Eugenicist theories from the pre-war era, experiencing a revival in the 1970s and 1980s, influenced a controversial sterilization program aimed predominantly at Romani women (Sokolova 2005). But these second thoughts and corresponding policies couldn't undo two decades of active encouragement of population growth in and labor extraction from Romani communities. The 'demographic threat' associated nowadays by some Slovak and Czech politicians and scholars with Roma (Šuvada 2015) can be traced to the post-war socialist view of Gypsies as a much needed generator of a reproductive surplus.

THE 'GYPSY PROBLEM' AND *KULTÚRNOSŤ* AS A COLONIAL TOOL

The reproductive surplus provided by Roma hasn't received public priority since the emergence of the 'Gypsy problem' as a significant political issue in the 1960s, but society at large has continued to depend on it. Given the dramatic fertility decline experienced by ethnic Slovaks and Czechs during most of the post-war era (Víšek 1988), the existence of innumerable schools, hospitals, rural transportation networks, and entire municipalities with their infrastructures would be threatened without the robust Romani population segment and its continued growth. One could argue that the same demographic advantage that accrues to western immigration-friendly countries from foreign migrants prevails in immigration-hostile Slovakia due to its domestic Romani minority. Such a perspective can be seen in the local public discourse that acknowledges the Roma as a legitimate segment of society while simultaneously insisting on their 'integration'. In the Slovak context this means assimilation through the acceptance and absorption of 'hegemonic culture' (see Gramsci 1999). Here we come to the self-appointed role of ethnic Slovaks as missionaries of a superior culture whose transmission is supposed to transform 'problematic Gypsies' into acceptable Slovak citizens. The tool employed in this process of re-socialization is *kultúrnosť*.

The concept of *kultúrnosť* as a hegemonic instrument for the diffusion of ideas about 'appropriate' and 'cultured' deportment, including speech and self-presentation in general, from a norm-giving segment of society to its 'backward' periphery is commonly associated with the rehabilitation and dissemination of ideas and practices previously ostracized as 'bourgeois' in the Soviet Union of the 1930s and later (Dunham 1976; Clark 1981). Little is known about its adoption in post-war people's democracies or about the role it has played in the 'integration' of Roma in those societies. When it comes to socialist-era Czechoslovakia, as well as post-socialist Slovakia, *kultúrnosť* should be seen as the most important conceptual tool employed in the tackling of the 'Gypsy problem', a task always seen as a civilizing mission aimed at a population considered backward and uncultured. By the 1960s government and Communist Party officials had adopted a tripartite approach to the acculturation of Roma, distinguishing between first, second, and third category Gypsies, based on their level of cultural advancement. In the first class we find families and entire communities that had been successfully assimilated, the second comprised people moving in the 'right direction', while the third consisted of problematic individuals who were unwilling or unable to leave behind the backward 'Gypsy way of life' (Scheffel and Mušinka 2019). It was this last group of Roma, amounting to approximately one-third of the entire population, that attracted the most intensive scrutiny and interference by authorities dedicated to the elimination of the 'Gypsy problem'. Although the tripartite division vanished together with the socialist régime, its influence continues to be felt in the contemporary use of the term 'unadaptables' (*neprispôsobivi* in Slovak) which designates members of the third class. It is this category of Roma that I am mostly concerned with here.

Bringing *Kultúrnosť* into the 'Colony'

According to John Chávez, internal colonialism prevails when "certain categories of people" inhabiting "specific spaces" are subordinated in their "own homeland within the boundaries of a larger state dominated by a different people" (2011, 786). While the Romani settlements found in Slovakia cannot be considered 'aboriginal' or 'indigenous' insofar as their founders were immigrants, in the course of several centuries these 'specific spaces' have become the homelands of culturally and socially self-contained communities of a distinctive ethno-racial group that is exposed to the same kind of cultural proselytization as we find in classical colonial situations. And as in such situations, while the apostles of the hegemonic culture appear as benign figures—teachers, medical personnel, priests, social workers, municipal bureaucrats—this corpus of seemingly well-meaning missionaries from the dominant society enters and operates on the 'Gypsy fringe' with the backing of a powerful ('colonial') state that poses an enduring threat of a much less benign intervention in the form of police raids, arrests, imprisonment, and detainment of children from uncooperative families. What follows is an examination of some of the more influential hegemonic institutions operating in Romani settlements and their inhabitants' response to their acculturative attempts. The focus is on a particular (third class) community featured in some of my previous publications (Scheffel 2005; Scheffel and Mušinka 2019), with additional illustrations from other settlements with which I am familiar (Scheffel 2015).

It was only in the 1950s that authorities began to explore, chart, and manage social conditions in the hundreds of Romani settlements dotting the Slovak countryside, what I call here the 'Gypsy fringe'. Officials were aghast at finding there a largely illiterate mass of poverty-stricken families living in primitive shelters without access to electricity, potable water, health care, and basic education. The rate of tuberculosis and other communicable diseases was staggering, and infant mortality was far above the national norm. Some officials spoke about 'colonial conditions' and conceived of the massive aide program introduced in the late 1950s and early 1960s as a form of 'decolonization'. Cadres of medical personnel travelled from settlement to settlement, performing basic examinations, mass inoculations, and de-lousing operations. But while these emergency measures brought about undeniable improvements, the officials entrusted with devising a master plan for the solution of the 'Gypsy problem' insisted from the very beginning that its root cause was not only the centuries-long oppression suffered by the Roma as de facto powerless 'colonial' subjects, but also their intellectual backwardness caused by illiteracy and a lack of awareness of alternative lifestyles. Hence formal education in the widest possible sense came to be conceptualized as the foremost innovation to be promoted. For decades to come, adult literacy campaigns, and a rich offering of public lectures on topics ranging from disease prevention all the way to table manners became the responsibility of specially trained 'cultural workers' entrusted with bringing *kultúrnosť* to even the most isolated settlements. But at the center of this campaign stood the school. Since practically all children living on the 'Gypsy fringe' were born and lived within a community of Romani speakers where Slovak was spoken infrequently and imperfectly, state authorities embarked on a massive project aimed at providing kindergartens for all settlement children as a precondition for their successful participation in grade school. In kindergarten young Roma were to be isolated from the 'backwardness' of their home environment, taught enough of the hegemonic language that they could understand their (invariably Slovak) teachers, and acquire the basic principles of hygiene and self-discipline—all of this hopefully leading to an appreciation of *kultúrnosť* as a new compass that would direct the children's steps toward assimilation. As one official of the ministry of education put it in the late 1950s, the campaign aimed at convincing Roma that "the Gypsy lifestyle is not worthy of a human being and of a citizen of a socialist state" (Baciková 1959, 41). Public authorities had to "strip gypsies of their backward way of life and teach them to live in a cultured manner benefitting society" (ibid.).

Next to formal education, full-time paid employment played an essential part in the *kultúrnosť* campaign as an instrument of regulation and self-regulation. Although unable to move above the level of unskilled laborers, settlement Roma were thought to benefit from any type of employment as long as it required punctuality, endurance, and teamwork, all qualities believed to be underdeveloped within the confines of their traditional communities. Accordingly, all persons above the age of fifteen were obliged to seek employment, and the state expended considerable effort at creating and filling suitable jobs. Faced with stiff prison sentences if they refused a placement, Romani men grudgingly complied. But, as already mentioned, Romani women refused to leave their homes by taking advantage of exceptions from the labor code accorded to mothers of young children. The combination of traditional aversion of Romani men to their spouses working outside the home, the provision of generous maternity and child subsidies, and the view of large families as a security cushion contributed to the emergence of a culture of reproductive prowess which celebrated and rewarded high fecundity as an essential ingredient of the 'Gypsy way of life'. This created a dilemma for state authorities who correctly branded Romani mothers as a formidable obstacle to the assimilation of their children, including their enrollment and indoctrination in the state-run kindergartens. Yet at the same time, the authorities' disapproval had to be muted due to the regime's encouragement of and dependence on demographic growth. Thus authorities limited their interference in the reproductive realm to the often rather lax enforcement of laws regulating the age at which sexual activity could commence, the insistence on hospital birth as a means to reducing natal mortality, and the discouragement of Romani mothers from 'traditional vices' with a harmful effect on their offspring, such as smoking and alcohol consumption. In the words of the deputy minister of the interior, "it is Gypsy women who stubbornly keep old habits and customs, maintain various survivals and superstitions, resist culture, hygiene, school, and so on" (Kotaľ 1959, 60). All these innovations, and especially the ban on 'child marriage', were couched in the language of *kultúrnosť*.

For example, until the present, women from the 'Gypsy fringe' who complain about segregated maternity wards in terms of 'racism' are told that it isn't their race but their lack of appropriate 'cultural habits' *(kultúrne návyky)*—in this context hygienic practices—that require their segregation from their Slovak peers. The same argumentation can be encountered among defenders of segregated schools and classrooms.

The third pillar of the assimilation campaign was the Catholic Church. Though certainly not recruited as an ally by the communist regime, this institution reinforced many of the ideals associated with *kultúrnost'*, especially in the domain of sexuality. Still during the socialist era, the Church began encouraging Romani children to enroll in catechism classes to gain access to First Holy Communion, a rite of passage immensely popular in Slovak Catholic circles, but rarely extended to Roma prior to World War II. In an attempt to compensate for the loss of parishioners who had turned away from organized religion due to political circumstances, the Church became more interested in Roma and began to emphasize First Communion as a test of their suitability. As I learned from several priests with a background in parishes with large Romani communities, settlement children were expected not only to fulfill the dogmatic requirements of holy communion, such as the memorization of appropriate prayers, but they also had to go through the ritual in a solemn manner and proper attire. In Slovak culture solemnity (*dôstojnost'*) is a by-product of *kultúrnost'*, and so is of course clothing befitting a festive occasion. For reasons that I have never fully grasped, even the poorest and most down-trodden 'unadaptables' among the Roma have embraced First Communion as an essential badge of their identity. In order to live up to the local standard of *dôstojnost'* and *kultúrnost'* they purchase, at great expense, white bridal dresses for the girls and miniature black suits for the boys participating in the ritual. After the ceremony the vast majority of the just anointed parishioners never again set foot in their church.

The girls undergoing First Communion are conceived of as Christ's brides, and thus of great importance that they be virgins. This may have been one of the factors behind the communist regime's tolerance of the Catholic Church's proselytization among the Roma, for both institutions opposed, albeit for different reasons, the early commencement of sexual relations characteristic of the 'Gypsy fringe'. As I show below, the age at which sexual experimentation begins has been falling during the post-socialist period, and this has necessitated some adjustments to the First

Communion ritual. For one, Romani girls undergoing this rite of passage are getting younger in order to ensure their virginity. In the past
the usual cohort ranged between twelve and fifteen years of age, now it
is likely between ten and thirteen. According to some of my informants,
certain priests have made concessions to the new status quo by allowing girls who have lost their virginity to participate, albeit not dressed in
white but in pink.

A second marker of *kultúrnosť* propagated and enforced by the
Catholic Church concerns consanguineous unions frequently found in
some Romani communities. Although often denied—in response to disapproval by members of the dominant society—the frequency of first and
second cousin marriage among Slovak Roma is much higher than in the
surrounding population, which has caused friction with both church and
state authorities. The former disapprove for canonical reasons and refuse
to consecrate the cohabitation of such couples. The latter view consanguinity as a source of genetic risk to the already precarious health situation on the 'Gypsy fringe'. In terms of daily public discourse, though,
the cohabitation of relatives is regarded as uncivilized and as a violation
of the codex of *kultúrnosť.*

SUBVERSION OF *KULTÚRNOSŤ*

To what extent has the hegemonic culture of Slovakia made inroads
into the 'Gypsy fringe'? We cannot answer this important question adequately on the basis of available empirical evidence. The Slovak archipelago of segregated settlements is large and diverse (Mušinka et al. 2014),
and although a growing stream of anthropological studies has covered
a variety of Roma-related issues, basic ethnographic works remain a rar-
ity. In fact, only one of the almost one thousand self-contained Romani
communities found in Slovakia today has been the subject of a classical
ethnographic study (Scheffel 2005). Given this paucity of empirical data,
I cannot surmise how representative the 'Gypsy fringe' is on the basis
of my own research. I am familiar with a sufficient number of Romani
communities to feel secure in advancing the claim that at least some elements of the pattern of subversion described here are widespread enough
to consider part and parcel of the adaptation of contemporary settlement
Roma to current Slovak conditions. But that is as far as I am willing to
generalize.

The ethnographic data presented here have been gathered continuously since the late 1990s during extended stationary fieldwork, as well as short field trips. Much of what I describe derives from personal observations, but some of the more intimate details pertaining to sexuality had to be secured through interviews that took part outside the informants' community in order to ensure confidentiality and minimize interference from other residents. Generally speaking, children below the age of twelve or thirteen were interviewed by female assistants recruited from the community and acquainted with the informants' personal backgrounds. Much of what the research subjects consider to be normal and acceptable within the confines of the settlement evokes displeasure and even disgust among members of the surrounding society. Some types of behavior—especially juvenile prostitution, incestuous relations, drug use, and underage sex—are prohibited by law. For this reason, information about such aspects of the local culture isn't shared with outsiders, including teachers and social workers, let alone police officers. This makes verification difficult as some upwardly mobile community members refuse to acknowledge the existence of practices disapproved of or even criminalized by the host society for fear of being stigmatized. The quest for some lofty objective reality becomes rather difficult under such circumstances. I tried hard to verify claims that seemed too outlandish—especially those concerning the prevalence of incestuous relations—by consulting several independent informants, and I feel confident that my research is congruent with local ethnographic reality. Nevertheless, there is a great deal of variability in the frequency with which certain practices may be encountered—let alone acknowledged—within a given settlement. This is influenced by internal social differentiation and the well-known universal striving of elites to distance themselves from habits associated with the 'underclass' (Scheffel 2005).

The collection of data that include intimate details about one's personal life and that extend beyond a small cluster of close informants requires familiarity with dozens of people and their experiences over many years. It is difficult to accomplish such a task in more than a single community. In my case, such a community is a settlement of some 1500 residents from which I draw the bulk of my observations. Yet, in order to substantiate my claim that the practices reported here extend beyond a single, 'atypical', location, I also draw on data collected in nearby settlements with which I am familiar in a more superficial way. This is especially true of my engagement with juvenile prostitution that I studied in a cluster of communities, all of which yielded very similar results.

ILLITERACY AS PROTEST

The Roma of the 'Gypsy fringe' are well aware of being looked down upon by members of the surrounding society. They often invoke the 'colonial' image of natives (*domorodci*) in a grass hut catered to by teachers, social workers, and other officials trying to change their lifestyle. Over the many years of this encounter, even the lowliest 'unadaptables' have adopted elements of the majority culture and undergone limited 'modernization' (Scheffel and Mušinka 2019). Yet, they have also retained, and even developed, attitudes and practices that enhance their identity as a separate people and signal their unwillingness to be subdued. This is not articulated in the language of 'liberation' or 'decolonization', partly because such language doesn't exist locally, but partly also because dependence on the surrounding society sustains the 'Gypsy fringe' and its unique lifestyle. Not having any ancestral lands to claim nor aboriginal rights to restore, settlement Roma are too intricately connected to their 'colonial' masters to imagine any benefit associated with independence (cf. Donert 2017). They are squatters on other people's land, they subsist on government handouts, and they derive numerous advantages from free medical care and passports that allow them to travel and work throughout Europe. If they think of political autonomy, their focus is limited to the municipal level where Romani mayors and councilors can effect positive changes felt in the settlement.

It is mainly through the subversion of *kultúrnosť* and the props sustaining it that settlement Roma express their disapproval of being treated as 'colonized' natives. But here, too, one must be careful not to unduly politicize acts and sentiments that are not thought of by the actors themselves as conscious protests. Instead, they ought to be considered as a disdainful show of indifference toward the core ideas and beliefs underlying *kultúrnosť*. This means that while one can recognize the value of toothpaste and deodorants, one can, at the same time, wholeheartedly reject other commandments of hygiene, such as those regulating sexual expression. This rejection, while not a deliberate and conscious protest that one talks about and carries out in a goal-oriented fashion, is an integral part of the conceptualization of ethnic Slovaks as overbearing meddlers in the 'Gypsy way of life', as domineering officials whose reach is almost omnipresent, and as ill-intentioned oppressors whom one should try to avoid. The Roma know that they are not in a position to counter this ongoing domination through open resistance to the myriad regulations that they face in school, at work, in courts, and in the offices of the state administration where they must negotiate the hand-outs which most of them require: child care, maternity benefits, pensions, and welfare payments. Outwardly they comply with the 'colonial' machinery, but they subvert it by keeping alive the 'backward Gypsy lifestyle' belittled by communist (and post-communist) apparatchiks.

The results of this strategy can be gathered by examining the literacy campaign that began in the 1950s. Hundreds of schools, crèches, and kindergartens built by the state as a concrete foundation for the *kultúrnosť* drive notwithstanding, formal literacy has not found a fertile soil within the 'Gypsy fringe'. Despite the state's strict enforcement of the legislated nine years of compulsory schooling, most people are wholly or at least partially illiterate. Even adolescents in their last years of school or immediately past them can barely type a text message on their cell phones, let alone understand the complex sentences which Slovak bureaucrats like to employ in official documents. This task is left to social workers who keep an eye on the affairs of the settlement dwellers.

The widespread illiteracy that prevails on the 'Gypsy fringe' excludes their residents from all but the most menial jobs, and justifies their dependence on government hand-outs. I have never encountered anybody, young or old, interested in improving their literacy skills. On the contrary, the lack of formal education and the knowledge that it imparts is accepted as an essential component of the 'Gypsy way of life'; it is rarely a source of embarrassment or weakness to be remedied (cf. Jaroschek 2001; Hornberg and Brüggemann 2013). Illiteracy extends beyond reading, writing, and understanding the complexity of the host society. It also entails ignorance about all kinds of information that the citizen of a modern state is expected, and in some respects required, to possess. Young Roma rarely know their birthdates, and even their parents usually cannot determine their exact age without recourse to birth certificates or medical insurance cards. A child's age is assessed on the basis of physical characteristics, such as facial hair in the case of a boy, or the size of breasts in the case of a girl. This nonchalant attitude to chronological age subverts the state's dependence on it in determining when a child must enter school, when it may commence sexual relations, or when it can get married. All these formal boundaries are regarded as artificial and insignificant, and are widely ignored—with far-reaching consequences.

Illiteracy determines also the ability, or rather the inability, to place oneself on the grid of the society beyond the 'Gypsy fringe'. Most of the Roma whom I have known for many years live within easy commuting distance of the eastern Slovak regional capital Prešov. The bus ride there takes about fifteen minutes, but it can also be reached on foot in slightly over an hour—a march many people undertake when they lack even the spare change required for the bus fare. The city is an almost daily destination for scores of garbage pickers, beggars, shoppers, and sex workers. Periodically, people must attend to all kinds of official business, such as court proceedings, welfare claims, or more recently compulsory seminars about job search strategies. The sex workers know how to reach the central bus station where they meet clients; the welfare recipients know where to apply for benefits; most adults can find the courts and the police headquarters; and the garbage pickers direct their efforts at specific districts. But these small clusters of familiarity are surrounded by the wider city which most of the settlement dwellers know nothing about. Most of them cannot identify a single street or avenue by name, and even the name of the river that winds its way through Prešov is not considered important enough to memorize. Hardly anybody is familiar with the cardinal points of the compass; directing someone to walk 'north' or 'west' of a well-known landmark—such as a shopping center or the main post office—is meaningless. This kind of topographical illiteracy reinforces the 'Gypsy fringe' dwellers' sense of the settlement as their home territory—where they cannot get lost—and of Prešov as an alien construct where they don't belong.

Taken to a higher level, topographical illiteracy factually excises settlement Roma from the state that claims their allegiance. Of the dozens of adolescents that I have interviewed in recent years, only a small handful could identify Bratislava as the Slovak capital. Košice, the country's second largest city and merely thirty kilometers from Prešov, is an unfamiliar name. Questions about the population size of Slovakia or Prešov are countered with shrugs of indifference or absurdly small figures. I face recurrent questions about whether I take the bus or the train to return to Canada.

It is worth repeating that this kind of ignorance about the basic facts and features considered essential knowledge outside the 'Gypsy fringe' doesn't bother its residents. On the contrary, it fosters the aloofness from the 'white world' that Roma must maintain in order to morally sustain and justify breeches of 'colonial order' that they commit on a daily basis. This imposed order isn't theirs, they haven't asked for it, and they feel no guilt or shame when they violate it. On the contrary, ongoing violation of that foreign order prevents alienation from and eventual demise of the 'backward Gypsy way of life' that nurtures them and gives meaning to their lives.

FLOUTING THE LAW AND PUBLIC OPINION IN THE REALM OF SEXUALITY

In view of their indifference toward the notion of *kultúrnosť* and the moral order associated therewith, settlement Roma are generally not bothered by conduct that the dominant society defines and prosecutes as criminal unless such conduct causes easily identifiable harm to a member of the local community. I could enumerate a large number of transgressions that are committed daily without any public disapproval whatsoever—ranging from the theft of firewood and agricultural produce all the way to truancy and drug use among children—but I will limit my overview to acts that evoke particular horror among ethnic Slovaks and which sometimes lead to criminal prosecution and severe sanctions. I dwell on what members of the dominant society see as serious transgressions against sexual norms because in this sphere settlement Roma define themselves particularly assertively as a separate body that refuses to be subdued by the encroaching state.

At the top of the scale of controversial mores found in segregated Romani communities that evoke disapproval from Slovak guardians of *kultúrnosť* is child sexuality. My research shows that boys and girls commence sexual experimentation around the age of five or six. They may imitate their parents and increasingly actors in pornographic movies that are watched widely, in attempting intercourse or at least kissing and fondling a child of the opposite sex. Some boys as well as girls of this young age begin to experiment with the local drug of choice, a potent paint thinner known by one of its brand names as *toluén*, inhaled through the mouth. While drug use among preschoolers is more of an exception than a rule, nine- to ten-year-old boys and girls indulging in this habit are a frequent sight in some of the more socially isolated settlements. At this age, girls know what they are expected to do when an older male addict

counters their request for the drug with the words "cunt for toluén."
While they may be too young to follow the request literally, they will
allow the older boy—or young adult—to kiss and fondle them; they
may also jerk him off and, exceptionally at this age, perform oral sex. By
the time they reach puberty, girls in need of drugs may indeed trade for
'cunt.'

Although permanent homosexuality is regarded as an abnormal
though not necessarily a reprehensible condition, a great deal of experimentation involving same-sex partners takes place during adolescence.
This includes female drug-users who come together periodically for
private dances which can escalate, under the influence of toluén, into
orgiastic encounters. Occasionally, such events are videotaped, the films
exchanged, and even posted in private accounts on YouTube. They show
wildly dancing teens and pre-teens whiffing from plastic bags filled with
the paint thinner, eventually stripping off their blouses and bras, and in
the case of younger girls even their pants and underwear. When sufficiently intoxicated, the girls start kissing, licking each other's breasts, and
fondling genitals. Some pair off and collapse onto beds where the horse-
play continues. All of this happens with much merriment and laughter.
Indeed, such events are usually dismissed as innocent entertainment, as
boisterous fun 'with the girls' from which boys and men are excluded.
A striking feature of these 'girls only' encounters is that they allow first
cousins and even sisters to indulge in a semi-public display of intimate
affections. Also noteworthy is the presence, at times, of older, heterosexual women who cheer and encourage the girls to overcome inhibitions
that some of them may feel.

Serious heterosexual relations begin to unfold around the age of
twelve. Some girls and boys commence permanent cohabitation at such
a young age through the informal local engagement ceremony, known as
mangavipen, isn't usually performed until a year or two later. That sig-
nifies that in the eyes of the community the young couple is married.
Needless to say, such arrangements are not disclosed outside the settlement for fear of criminal charges since the Slovak age of consent is fifteen. The frequency of transgressions against the law reveals itself in the
young age at which settlement girls give birth to their first child. I possess reliable data collected over many years in one of the larger settlements near Prešov, Svinia (see Scheffel 2005). There, the sizeable cohort
of women born after the demise of socialism in 1989 displays a mean
age at first birth just slightly above sixteen. Such a figure is not only

exceptionally low in the context of Slovakia (where the norm is twenty-eight years) and Europe at large, but it clearly demonstrates that many girls begin sexual relations well ahead of the legally permitted age.

Early commencement of sex, marriage, and procreation is taken for granted as the 'Gypsy way of life' since many residents of segregated settlements feel this pattern is an essential part of their identity. Consanguinity, usually defined as the marriage of first and second cousins, is a less clear-cut identity marker. In the community where I carried out a thorough genealogical reconstruction of nuptial bonds, one-third of all marriages are consanguineous (Scheffel 2005). Again, this is a much higher rate than one finds among native Europeans throughout the continent. Most settlement Roma dismiss second cousin marriage as a minor departure from the stated ideal of exogamy, but they frown upon unions between first cousins. Nevertheless, in the vast majority of cases such breeches of local norms are eventually accepted as a by-product of a strong love bond that ought not to be broken. On account of this, ethnic Slovaks, including medical personnel, tend to invoke 'inbreeding' as a dominant trait of Romani settlements that the authorities hold partly responsible for the prevalence of deafness, congenital heart disease, and retardation.

Whereas consanguinity straddles the incest boundary, full-fledged cases of incestuous relations are also publicly known and discussed. While sister-brother and mother-son incest does exist, the most frequent type is between fathers and daughters. Incest doesn't have a legitimate place in the 'Gypsy way of life', and settlement Roma agree with ethnic Slovaks that it seriously violates morality. Yet, similar to first-cousin marriage, once it has taken place, the violation doesn't exclude the perpetrator from normal community life, nor his victim from finding a respectable husband who may, depending on circumstances, adopt as his own, a child resulting from an incestuous relationship. According to notions of love and attractiveness that circulate in settlements, incest rarely happens without the cooperation of both parties. The majority society's idea of a man forcing himself onto a helpless daughter, sister, or niece is considered implausible in a society where crowded living quarters make involuntary encounters of such kind improbable. The best-known case of incest in a community with which I am well-acquainted involved a father and consecutively three—or possibly four—of his daughters. At least two reportedly were in love with him, and one even helped him survive in the woods while police searched for him. The same woman, now married with five children, had a child with her father, which the latter adopted—with the consent of his wife—and raised as his own. After reaching the age of ten, reportedly this child also became involved in an incestuous relationship with her father/grandfather, a fact known to and apparently approved of by her mother.

The muted response of the community at large to such obvious breeches of its own moral code is often justified by references to the hot-bloodedness of 'Gypsies'. Unlike white people, whose blood is supposedly lukewarm and resistant to boiling, the hot blood of Roma is said to make them prone to impulsive acts and desires that require immediate release, such as ejaculation in the case of sexual arousal. Inebriated men asked about their pubescent daughters' affairs remarkably may speak frankly in front of their wives and daughters about incestuous longings. There is even a commonly heard phrase entitling a father to 'taste' his daughter before she takes a lover. Conversely, a victim of childhood incest confided in me that her blood 'boiled with desire' every time she saw her father put on his sunglasses—which was their private signal that the father was 'horny'. In a similar vein, an exceptionally attractive girl of fourteen, courted by scores of boys and young men, described feeling giddy in the presence of her older brother, a good-looking, but mentally ruined drug addict. Several informants claimed that the brother-sister duo indulged in the 'cunt for toluén' exchange.

The degree of sexual freedom enjoyed by children and adolescents of the 'Gypsy fringe' reveals itself in the emergence of juvenile prostitution as an important institution in quite a few settlements—though absence of reliable data does not allow assessment of its extent. My own research with juvenile sex workers (see Scheffel and Mušinka 2019), which involved interviews with more than one hundred informants, leads me to postulate that while the financial gains associated with prostitution are certainly an appreciated element, the core reward is access to multiple partners in the pursuit of undisguised physical pleasure. Girls and boys as young as ten bemoan the monotony of one intimate partner, and the complaints intensify as they grow older. Prostitution, then, becomes not so much a necessary evil chosen reluctantly by poverty-stricken teens—as mainstream society wants to see it—but rather a vehicle for sexual experimentation that comes with a financial bonus. Prostitution becomes a logical extension of the active sexual lives led by settlement children and adolescents. So it becomes something of a parody of dominant ideas about juvenile prostitution as a tragic culmination of the unwanted sexualization of innocent children driven by poverty or brute external force. The Romani participants by contrast see it as a source of fun and pleasure. Always ready to subvert *kultúrnosť* and its ethnic Slovak propagators, adolescent hookers boast about alleged intimate encounters with famous hockey stars and local politicians. Asked what makes them so attractive to Slovak clients, they resort to an organic explanation that seems widespread among white men: "they claim that the Gypsy cunt is warmer than the hole of white women...".

THE EMPIRE STRIKES BACK

Prostitution, early sex and marriage, consanguinity leading to 'inbreeding', and a general disregard for sexual mores observed by 'civilized' society are all part and parcel of the dominant European stereotype of Roma as an unbridled people given to excess and 'debauchery' (Augustini ab Hortis [1775–1776] 1995; Grellmann 1787; Schwicker 1883; Jekelfalussy and Herrmann 1895). The social engineers of the socialist era documented conditions in post-war settlements that made them subsume such departures from the norms prevalent in mainstream society under the rubric 'backward Gypsy lifestyle', and they argued for the imposition of *kultúrnosť* as a precondition for their elimination. "Frequent motherhood of even thirteen-year old girls is an absolutely untenable phenomenon" wrote a leading Communist Party ideologue entrusted with the 'Gypsy agenda' (Zeman 1959, 15). He announced a "war" against such vices, including prostitution "pursued at times by children below the age of fourteen" (ibid., 16). I have argued here that much of what the socialist-era officials—and their predecessors—riled against has survived in at least some communities of the 'Gypsy fringe'; it has become some of the fuel that fires the engines of resistance to assimilation and what local Roma see as oppressive 'white rule' exercised by ethnic Slovaks. How does the post-communist Slovak state respond to such resistance?

During the first two decades of Slovakia's independence—a transitional period marked by preparations for accession to the European Union and after its attainment in 2004 implementation of EU norms and a general 'westernization' of society—residents of the 'Gypsy fringe' received relatively little attention from the post-socialist social engineers. EU funds were used for housing projects in some settlements, and police raids were conducted in settings where the maintenance of law and order seemed threatened. But the nitty-gritty of daily life escaped detailed scrutiny and significant intervention. Occasionally, police investigated circumstances leading to under-age pregnancies, but criminal charges could often be staved off by even implausible arguments, such as a pregnant under-age girl claiming to have 'raped' her unwilling older lover. Police officers turned a blind eye even to juvenile prostitution, arguing that sexual excess was in the Gypsies' blood, and that police intervention would be meaningless.

This relatively liberal era came to an end in the mid-2010s. Since then, there has been a growing political movement afoot that seeks to restore order in 'lawless' Romani settlements regarded, once again, as breeding grounds for criminals, asocials, and parasites. Although *kultúrnosť* is no longer invoked as an appropriate weapon, its perceived absence is penalized. Just how responsive the political establishment has become to complaints about the 'unadaptables' we can gather from the 'teachers' letter' affair that erupted in 2012. In June of that year, virtually every Slovak newspaper carried an open letter penned by two teachers from a small town in eastern Slovakia in which they appealed to government officials to restore order in schools attended by 'unadaptable' Romani children. The ten pages of densely typed text covered all aspects of the 'uncultured' lifestyle of these students and their parents. Here are some excerpts concerned with sexuality and reproduction:

> Unadaptable fellow-citizens have very quickly adopted the advantages offered by the state, and they have accepted the notion that they get everything for free, that they will be taken care of, [...] and that they need not move a finger [...]. They generate a heap of children starting at the age of fourteen to ensure that they are not missing out on anything. [...] Compared with that, responsible [ethnic Slovak] young couples delay parenthood until increasingly older age, waiting until they are financially [...] secure in order to provide their baby with everything it needs, which enables them to make it into a decent, educated, socialized and productive member of society. [...] Unadaptable parents [by contrast] have absolutely no job skills, they need not get up in the morning to go to work, and that's why they don't bother waking up their children and preparing them for school. [...] A problem that also needs to be tackled is the sexual exploitation of children. Not only in our school does the number of pregnant girls in lower grades increase year after year. It isn't acceptable that a sixth-grader is viewed by society as a fully competent mother capable of raising her child! Responsible state authorities fail to undertake any steps

[to halt this trend]. Is it normal that a 14-year-old girl attending a special school [for mentally retarded children] begets a child with a mentally retarded 'graduate' of a school for mentally retarded students, and within a year is pregnant with another child? How are they going to take care of their children? [...] Disabled children give birth to disabled children, and into what kind of an environment? Such children are condemned to a life in unworthy and inhuman conditions. [...] The situation is alarming! [...] We suggest limiting financial assistance to the first three children. [...] Otherwise this sickening cycle of excessive reproduction, which is used as a source of income, will never be stopped. [...] These children [of 'una-daptables'] don't have a right to dignified living conditions? [... Their] limbs are gnawed on by rats, every day they observe their parents and other members of the household copulate before their very eyes, and even they end up being sexually abused or exploited. [If you wish to help these children] start by handing out free condoms in schools–rather than flour– to prevent sex between relatives, mentally deficient people and minors, because they will never buy a preservative on their own, and [their] gargantuan fertility will increase further, but also the spread of sexually transmitted diseases among the unadaptables. It is necessary to seriously reconsider our social safety net in this area. Otherwise, there will be multiple new generations of genetically damaged, unadaptable and unproductive children who are, in their parents' eyes, merely a tool for the financing of their idle way of life. (Polgáriová and Liptáková 2012)

The letter ends with this ominous warning:

Politicians and the government have been ignoring and tolerating concrete problems, moral decay, social injustice [and other issues]. The reaction of society (including children!) is apathy, intolerance, vandalism, aggression, racism escalating into neo-Nazism, attacks and hatred on both sides. [...] You really want social unrest or civil war? We feel that to be the direction in which we are heading. (ibid.)

This letter had an enormous impact on Slovak public opinion, because its authors disregarded political correctness and vented what many others had felt like airing during the liberal era following the country's admission to the European Union. The letter triggered a tidal wave of like-minded reactions and came to be discussed at the highest political level. Of particular significance was its reception by the government's Council for the Prevention of Criminality, which gave it a favorable hearing at its very first sitting in November 2012 (Rada vlády 2012). Noteworthy is that the newly minted council's chairman was Robert Kaliňák, the minister of the interior responsible for a slate of repressive measures aimed at the 'unadaptables' of the 'Gypsy fringe'.

These measures, adopted between 2013 and 2017, put an end to the laisser-faire approach of previous years. They emphasized the need for 'law and order' in 'pathogenic' communities—for the most part Romani settlements. They involved increased police presence, including the formation of auxiliary police troops—equipped with batons and tear gas—comprised of Romani men willing and trained to provide grassroots support for the almost exclusively white regular police force. An additional measure was, the deployment of scores of community-based social workers, paid with funds provided by the European Union, to monitor 'problematic' families. The culmination of this trend toward 'securitization' was the targeting in early 2017 of two hundred "problematic Romani locations" for special police attention, described by government officials as the conclusion of the era of "political correctness" (*Sme* 2017).

When we observe the preliminary results of this new trend at the level of specific communities within the 'Gypsy fringe', we can identify some outstanding features of the abandonment of *kultúrnosť* as the main tool of colonization in favor of a constant and pervasive 'threat of force'. Nevertheless, an important material manifestation of 'culture' appeared during the socialist era in the form of 'houses of culture' built in virtually every community, ranging from the largest cities—where each district would have its own—to the smallest villages. These literally concrete edifices served, and in many locations still serve, as the intended loci for the dissemination of *kultúrnosť* among ordinary people. They housed the local library and the offices of 'cultural workers' who organized public lectures, literacy classes, poetry readings, and musical performances. Folk dance and music ensembles practiced and performed there as did the official Gypsy bands in communities with a significant presence of Roma. In order to drive home the point that Roma were expected to partake of the programs offered through these centers, Romani workers were often employed in their construction. Nowadays, although many of these structures still exist, the government has curtailed their outreach, leaving them for use in private functions, such as family celebrations, dances, and school Christmas concerts. As regards their role in fostering the integration of Roma, the houses of culture have been replaced by community centers located on the outskirts of settlements. Financed through structural funds of the European Union, these entities are supposed to provide services deemed of benefit to impoverished settlement dwellers, such as showers, washing machines, after-school activities for children, and computer stations for public use. Increasingly, though, these functions (often present on paper, but not in reality) are being replaced by more direct reminders of the omnipresent state that seeks to control local affairs. In some settlements, social workers have taken over space intended for children's activities, and in communities that lack a police detachment the center accommodates visiting police officers who conduct interrogations of suspects and meetings with informers.

Beyond the community center with its contingent of public servants tasked with supervision, control, and if need be repression, the state maintains its presence through a network of surveillance cameras. Also financed by the European Union, a 'public safety' program initiated in the early 2010s has enabled Slovak authorities to install cameras in and around most 'problematic' Romani settlements. Monitored by municipal officials and police officers, the cameras survey schoolyards and hallways, village streets frequented by Roma, and, of course, public space within the settlement itself. Private residences, the last islands of protection against the omnipresent state, are exposed to the prying eyes of social workers during their inspection rounds. Much of the 'Gypsy fringe' is thus subjected to 'legibility régimes' as described and analyzed by Michel Foucault (1977), followed by James Scott (1998). We should remember, however, that communist officials had already recognized the need for permanent supervision addressing the 'Gypsy problem'. "For the re-education of gypsies [sic] an occasional debate or lecture is of almost no practical significance. Gypsies must perceive our interest constantly, almost at every step," wrote a highly placed adviser to the ministry of culture in the 1950s (Baciková 1959, 41). She went to recommend attention to individual families by means of regular visits:

> We come to invite them to a cultural event, we come to see how children are being taken care of, how basic norms of hygiene are being followed, and so on. [...] Let gypsy families feel the interest of our public authorities [...]. (ibid.)

Aided by advanced technology, EU subsidies, swelling numbers of police officers, and a small army of social workers, what interests Slovak authorities so much? Now as before, they seek to dismantle the 'backward Gypsy lifestyle' that evoked so much irritation among their communist-era predecessors. But nowadays, 'socialist humanism' has given way to harsh interventions unhampered by western notions of political correctness. First of all, there is a clear effort to keep the children of the 'unadaptables' from the streets in order to minimize their ability to pursue begging and prostitution. This is done primarily by rigidly enforcing the truancy law, thus compelling children to attend school—which most of them find boring and irrelevant. After trying unsuccessfully to achieve this by withholding social support payments from parents who failed to ensure their children's regular attendance, government authorities have begun sending uncooperative parents to prison. Prison terms ranging from three to eight months—and, in the case of paroled individuals, even years—are becoming the new norm. Depending on family circumstances, their youngsters may then be sent to children's homes. Children found to be endangered in their moral or physical development by their family's environment face the same prospect. Instead of addressing the alarming housing situation in many settlements, the government penalizes families that live under particularly primitive conditions by removing their children. This was recommended already in the 1950s when the then deputy minister of the interior prioritized the construction of additional state-run facilities in order to absorb the swelling number of Romani children removed from families unwilling to abandon the 'Gypsy way of life' (Kotaľ 1959). Alas, EU norms proscribing the collection of statistics based on ethnicity make it impossible to verify the widely held belief that the majority of children placed in these institutions are of Romani ancestry.

The second line of attack focuses on the prevention and penalization of under-age pregnancies. Social workers in the settlement and at school conduct regular visits to households that they suspect of accommodating juvenile girls cohabiting with de facto husbands. Often the social workers rely on rumors about pregnancies of such girls, rumors that suffice to activate the vice squad of the Prešov police detachment. Police officers then appear unannounced at school, and take the suspect for a 'virginity test' at the gynecology clinic of the Prešov hospital. Interviews conducted with the subjects of these procedures reveal an atmosphere of intimidation and a reliance on degrading and internationally condemned methods, including the widely criticized 'two-finger test', often performed by a male physician (World Health Organization 2018, 10). One fourteen-year-old victim of such procedures whom I interviewed described feeling humiliated when four male assistants pinned her down on the examination table while a male doctor inserted his gloved fingers into the vagina of the screaming and shaking girl.

If a juvenile girl below the legal age of consent is found pregnant, the vice squad moves into high gear. Interrogations are conducted to identify the culprit responsible for the girl's condition, and criminal charges usually follow. Sentences ranging from three to five years are not exceptional. Since many of these cases involve cohabiting juvenile couples bound by affection, the 'Gypsy fringe' regards the imposition of such harsh prison terms as a malevolent act directed at the very core of local culture and society. Often, while the father sits in prison, the mother is confined to a facility for juvenile single mothers where she raises her child under supervision, completely isolated from her home and family.

It is difficult to predict the impact of this new, extremely punitive, approach on the 'Gypsy fringe' and the ability of its residents to retain some degree of autonomy from a society they see as oppressive at best and 'colonial' at worst. It is perhaps fitting to conclude this bitter-sweet excursion with an observation made by an astute informant. Asked about the future of his settlement, he replied: "In the past, we sensed the cannons on top of the hill above us. Now, we feel as though the cannons have come down the hill, and they surround us day and night. It's like those old movies about African villages being shot at from battleships. We are under siege."

REFERENCES

Anonymous. 1946. "Země bez lidí." *Dnešek* 1(6).

Augustini ab Hortis, Samuel. [1775–1776] 1995. *Cigáni v Uhorsku. O dnešnom stave, zvláštnych mravoch a spôsobe života, ako aj o ostatných vlastnostiach a danostiach Cigánov v Uhorsku* [Von den heutigen Zuständen, sonderbaren Sitten und Lebensart, wie auch von den übrigen Eigenschaften und Umständen den Zigeuner in Ungarn], edited by Viera Urbancová and Ján Tibenskì. Bratislava: Štúdio –dd–.

Baciková, Eva. 1959. "Kulturně výchovná práce mezi cikánským obyvatelstvem." *Práce mezi cikánským obyvatelstvem*, 38–44. Praha: Úřad předsednictva vlády.

Chávez, John R. 2011. "Aliens in Their Native Lands: The Persistence of Internal Colonialism Theory." *Journal of World History* 22(4): 785–809.

Clark, Katerina. 1981. *The Soviet Novel: History as Ritual.* Bloomington: Indiana University Press.

Donert, Celia. 2017. *The Rights of the Roma: The Struggle for Citizenship in Postwar Czechoslovakia*. Cambridge: Cambridge University Press.

Dunham, Vera. 1976. *In Stalin's Time: Middle-Class Values in Soviet Fiction*. Cambridge: Cambridge University Press.

Foucault, Michel. 1977. *Discipline and Punish: The Birth of the Prison*. New York: Vintage.

Gramsci, Antonio. 1999. *Selections from the Prison Notebooks*, edited by Quentin Hoare and Geoffrey Nowell Smith. London: ElecBook.

Grellmann, Heinrich Moritz Gottlieb. 1787. *Historischer Versuch über die Zigeuner betreffend die Lebensart und Verfassung, Sitten und Schicksale dieses Volks seit seiner Erscheinung in Europa und dessen Ursprung*. 2nd ed. Göttingen: Johann Christian Dieterich.

Hechter, Michael. [1975] 1999. *Internal Colonialism: The Celtic Fringe in British National Development* (with a New Introduction and a New Appendix by the Author). New Brunswick, NJ: Transaction Publishers.

Hornberg, Sabine, and Christian Brüggemann, eds. 2013. *Die Bildungssituation von Roma in Europa*. Münster: Waxmann Verlag.

Horváthová, Emília. 1964. *Cigáni na Slovensku*. Bratislava: Slovenská akadémia ved.

Jaroschek, Rainer. 2001.»Wer viel weiß, leidet viel «.»Zigeuner« und Schule - Ethnologische Anmerkungen zu einem Kulturkonflikt. *Der Donauraum* 40(1–2): 46–59.

Jekelfalussy, Jozsef, and Anton Herrmann. 1895. *A Magyarországban 1893 január 31-én végrehajtott czigányösszeirás eredményei 5 grafikai táblázattal* [Ergebnisse der in Ungarn am 31. Jänner durchgeführten Zigeuner-Conscription mit fünf graphischen Beilagen] (Ungarische Statistische Mittheilungen, NF, vol. IX). Budapest: Athenaeum.

Kotaľ, Jindřich. 1959. "Nejdúležitější úkoly při výchově cikánú." *Práce mezi cikánským obyvatelstvem*. Praha: Úřad předsednictva vlády.

Mareš, Josef. 1947. "Cikáni." *Paedologické rozhledy* 3: 289–304.

Mušinka, Alexander, et al. 2014. *Atlas rómskych komunít na Slovensku 2013*. Bratislava: UNDP.

Nečas, Ctibor. 2000. "Cikáni na Moravě a ve Slezsku do první třetiny 20. století." *Český lid* 87(3): 239–47.

Petro, Ján. 1985. *Dominančné faktory odlišností cigánskych rodín*. Košice: Krajské osvetové stredisko v Košiciach.

Polgáriová, Erika, and Eleonóra Liptáková. 2012. *Otvorený list učiteliek z východného Slovenska*. Dobšiná.

Popálená, M. 1987. "Sociálne problémy cigánskych detí a ich riešenie." *Zdravotnická pracovnice* 37(5): 280–83.

Rada vlády Slovenskej republiky pre prevenciu kriminality. 2012. *Záznam z 1. zasadnutia zo dňa 6. Novembra 2012*. Bratislava: Úrad vlády Slovenskej republiky.

Scheffel, David Z. 2005. *Svinia in Black and White: Slovak Roma and their Neighbours*. Peterborough, ON: Broadview Press.

Scheffel, David Z. 2015. "Belonging and Domesticated Ethnicity in Veľký Šariš, Slovakia." *Romani Studies* 25(2): 115–49.

Scheffel, David Z., and Alexander Mušinka. 2019. "Third-Class Slovak Roma and Inclusion: *Bricoleurs* vs. Social Engineers." *Anthropology Today* 35(1): 17–21.

Schwicker, Johann Heinrich. 1883. *Die Zigeuner in Ungarn und Siebenbürgen*. Wien: K. Prochaska.

Scott, James. 1998. *Seeing Like a State: How Certain Schemes to Improve the Human Condition Have Failed*. New Haven: Yale University Press.

Sme. 2017. "Kaliňák ukázal obce, v ktorých chce bojovať s rómskou kriminalitou." 10, January.

Sokolova, Vera. 2005. "Planned Parenthood Behind the Curtain: Population Policy and Sterilization of Romani Women in Communist Czechoslovakia, 1972–1989." *The Anthropology of East Europe Review* 23(1): 79–98.

Spurný, Matěj. 2011. *Nejsou jako my: Česká společnost a menšiny v pohraničí (1945–1960)*. Praha: Antikomplex.

Šuvada, Martin. 2015. *Rómovia v slovenských mestách*. Bratislava: POMS.

Víšek, Petr. 1988. "K některým novým aspektům společenské integrace Romú v socialistickém Československu." *Slovenský národopis* 36(1): 35–44.

World Health Organization. 2018. *Eliminating Virginity Testing: An Interagency Statement*. Geneva: World Health Organization.

Zeman, Otakar. 1959. "K otázkám práce mezi cikánským obyvatelstvem v ČSR." In *Práce mezi cikánským obyvatelstvem*. Praha: Úřad předsednictva vlády.

CHAPTER 9

Colonialism Within and Without: The Old Oyo Empire in West Africa

James Olusegun Adeyeri

INTRODUCTION

Old Oyo, one of the kingdoms that emerged from Ile-Ife, cradle of the Yoruba ethnic nationality, was founded between 1388 and 1431 in the forest belt of western Sudan (modern West Africa). Although the origins of Old Oyo are hazy, some evidence suggests that Prince Oranmiyan, a scion of Oduduwa, the legendary progenitor of the Yoruba, established the empire with its capital at Old Oyo, also known as Oyo-Ile or Katunga, about eighty miles north of the modern Yoruba town of Oyo (Osae and Nwabara [1968] 1980, 94).[1]

Until 1837 when the capital was relocated to present-day Oyo town, Old Oyo was a large empire and the major power in southern Nigeria. At its peak (1630–50), Oyo was bounded to the north by the River Niger, to the east by Benin, to the west by modern Togo, and to the

---

[1]For a more detailed account of the origin and establishment of Old Oyo Empire, see also Biobaku (1955) and Forde (1951).

J. O. Adeyeri (✉)
Department of History and International Studies,
Lagos State University, Lagos, Nigeria
e-mail: olusegun.adeyeri@lasu.edu.ng

© The Author(s) 2019
D. Schorkowitz et al. (eds.), *Shifting Forms of Continental Colonialism*,
https://doi.org/10.1007/978-981-13-9817-9_9

227

south by the coastal woodland savannah. The *Alaafin* (king) of Oyo was an emperor who exercised power, authority, and influence over many provincial rulers and territories (ibid.; Aderibigbe [1965] 1976, 194; Afropedea 2010). In fact, Old Oyo by that time was territorially the largest and politically the strongest Yoruba kingdom. Its most prominent subject peoples included the Nupe, Ibariba, some of the Igbomina, Ekiti and Ibarapa, Owu, Awori, Anago, Egba, Egbado, Porto Novo, Allada, and Dahomey (Udenyi 2018, 4; Atanda [1973] 1979, 13; Akinjogbin [1971] 1976, 385–90; Alimi and Adesoji 2011). Using the Oyo case, this chapter seeks to test the applicability of colonial theory beyond the Western context, and in doing so, the study will through the prism of internal and external colonialism shed more light upon the bases and legacies of Oyo hegemony in parts of West Africa between 1500 and 1821.

A NOTE ON INTERNAL COLONIALISM

The term colonialism, as used in the nineteenth and twentieth centuries, describes a phenomenon whereby a foreign power, usually European, entered a country and undermined its indigenous institutions and values with the chief purpose of extracting economic resources for the benefit of the metropole. Colonialism more generally involves the establishment of full or partial political control over another country, occupying it with settlers, and exploiting its commercial and economic potential (Douglas-Bowers 2012). But this definition does not fully embrace all forms of colonialism, for example, the continental, neo-colonial, or internal forms. Internal colonialism, according to Robert Blauner, is a form of economic exploitation that involves the conquest of one racial or ethnic group by another in order to take advantage of the former's resources. In his view, 'classical' colonialism denotes a situation where a Western industrialized country conquers a semi-peripheral or peripheral country and exploits its manpower and other resources, while internal colonialism connotes a scenario in which an industrial country exploits a racial or ethnic minority within its own borders (Blauner 1969).

Malcolm Little (Malcolm X) and Stokely Carmichael (Kwame Ture) for their part conceptualized internal colonialism from the standpoint of national liberation from European and American colonialism, drawing inspiration from the pioneering intellectual efforts of Kwame Nkrumah and Frantz Fanon. The duo of Malcolm X and Carmichael, however, agreed that internal colonialism involves the domination of oppressed people based on the violence of the colonizer, and the exploitation of their land, labor, and natural resources, in addition to the systematic attempt to destroy non-European culture in the quest for profits (Bohmer 1999). Malcolm X and Carmichael, while theorizing race relations in the United States of the 1960s and 1970s, deployed race and ethnicity as the planks of analysis. Using this approach, Malcolm X, in particular, asserted that the government of the United States had subjected 22 million blacks within the continental United States to internal colonialism (Malcolm 1965, 126; Brankamp 2015; Pinderhughes 2009, 24).

Another viewpoint sees internal colonialism as a form of colonization from within by a contiguous greater power or state. This involves oppression, racial discrimination, and economic exploitation of the colonized people (González 2005; González-Casanova 1965, 27). In the eyes of Harold Wolpe ([1975] 2013), the key distinguishing feature of internal colonialism from 'normal' colonialism is that in the former, the colonizing state or group is domiciled in the same territory as the colonized people, whereas in the latter the colony is a distinct territorial entity, spatially detached from its imperial metropolis. Wolpe argues further, in respect to internal colonialism, that the 'underdeveloped' and 'underdeveloping' condition of subordinate ethnic and racial groups and the geographical areas they occupy within the boundaries of the state, is produced and maintained by the same mechanisms of cultural domination, political oppression, and economic exploitation which, at the international level, produce the development of the advanced capitalist states through the imperialist underdevelopment of the colonial satellites (Simons and Simons 1969, 610). Internal colonialism has also been defined as

> being closely related to external colonialism based on features of subordination and oppression not on majority/minority numbers ratios, geographic distance, capital export, foreigners, legal distinctions, or even voluntary versus involuntary migration. [...] It is a system of inequality, not just an aspect or device or component of inequality. (Toward a New Theory of Internal Colonialism 2011)

This conception of internal colonialism, among other common components of the phenomenon, emphasizes the application of a class analysis for class interests and dynamics (Pinderhughes 2011, 251). Based on this short review, the dominant characteristics of internal colonialism are

subordination, inequality, oppression, discrimination, economic exploitation, and geographical contiguity between the colonizing power and the
colonized people. Thus, this study argues that although Old Oyo was
not a modern industrial state like the European colonial powers, such as
Britain, France, and Germany, but one of the most advanced civilizations
within the forest region of West Africa, the characteristic trajectory and
legacies of Oyo Empire's hegemony in Yorubaland and beyond fit into
the internal colonial and external colonial models respectively. Let us
proceed to consider some basic preconditions for Old Oyo hegemony in
West Africa.

OLD OYO HEGEMONY IN WEST AFRICA: ORIGINS AND CONSTRAINTS

The nascent Old Oyo Kingdom's conquest of other Yoruba kingdoms,
such as the Egba, Egbado, Ekiti, Awori, Sabe, Ila and Owu, Ijesha,
Igbomina, Ijebu and Ondo, to mention a few, brought about the emergence of the Old Oyo Empire. Significantly, during *Alaafin* Abiodun's
reign (1770–89), as many as 6600 towns and villages were under Oyo's
direct or indirect rule (Boahen [1966] 1979, 91; Davidson et al. [1967]
1971, 214; Ojo 1970, 61).

Oyo's transformation from a mere kingdom to an imperial power
was not smooth. The young kingdom faced repeated threats to its territorial integrity and independence from attacks by various neighboring
groups. As an illustration, under Oyo's second *Alaafin*, Ajaka, the kingdom was attacked and nearly decimated by the Owu, a pre-Oduduwa
Yoruba group currently domiciled in Kwara and Kogi, states of Nigeria.
Alaafin Sango (Oranmiyan's son) eventually rescued Oyo by subduing the Owu, after he had dethroned Ajaka, a weak ruler. But dangerous threats from other groups, particularly the Nupe (Tapa), persisted.
Ajaka, however, returned to the throne after Sango's death and turned
into a warrior king. He initially subdued the Nupe, but Oyo-Nupe warfare later dragged on over a long period without any clear victor. Around
1450, during the reign of *Alaafin* Onigbogi and after a lengthy era of
peace and prosperity in Oyo, the Nupe successfully expelled Oyo from its
capital, forcing the latter to relocate its capital to Igboho for nearly one
hundred years. In the new capital, Oyo's travails continued. The Ibariba
(Borgu), a group that was initially friendly, began to pressure the Oyo

until around 1550 under *Alaafin* Abipa's (*Oba* Amororo) reign when Oyo successfully overcame the Ibariba and Nupe threats and returned to its original capital, Oyo-Ile. It is worth noting that while in exile at Igboho, Oyo reorganized its society along military lines, thereby making the King (*Oba*) an active military leader, and not a ruler who merely sat in the palace amidst women. The institution of Eso, a corps of professional soldiers vested with state security, was probably strengthened too during this period (Akinjogbin 2002, 31–32; Osae and Nwabara [1968] 1980, 96). We shall return to Oyo's political and military reorganization later.

The Nupe and Ibariba, whom Oyo had successfully subdued by 1550, did not reclaim their independence until the 1780s. Like Oyo, Nupe too was developing rapidly and successfully such that by the late 1780s the kingdom's monarch, *Etsu* Nupe Jia, had extended its territories to their greatest point, and between 1789 and 1790 defeated an Oyo army deployed to forestall Nupe ascendancy. It is important to note that trade routes that were crucial to the economies of many kingdoms around the Niger River passed through the territories of Oyo and Nupe, to other places including Gonja, Ashanti, the Hausa states, Bornu, and beyond. Thus, while it lasted, the subjugation of Nupe and Ibariba as external colonies, though not too distant from the Oyo metropole, gave Oyo traders access to the trade route to the North. This development probably facilitated Oyo's importation of large numbers of horses, which later helped form the Oyo cavalry that further promoted and sustained Oyo imperial expansion and authority (Lewis [2004] 2013, 13; Akinjogbin 2002, 33).

Oyo expansion continued under *Alaafin* Obalokun (1561–87) who succeeded Abipa. An Oyo imperial agent was deployed at Ijanna, another internal colony, in present-day Egbado or Yewa area of Ogun State, Nigeria. Through this agent, Oyo exercised a strong influence along the coast, which facilitated the introduction of salt into Yorubaland during the period. In addition, the Oyo Empire established contacts with European slave traders along the Allada coast at the time. About 1680, Old Oyo had established external colonial control over the coastal territories around Porto-Novo (Ajase Ipo). In 1698 Oyo attacked Allada and proceeded to capture Porto-Novo (Ojo 1970, 66; Akinjogbin 2002, 33).

Oyo hegemony was established over Dahomey, another external colony, by 1724, following which Dahomey deified the reigning *Alaafin* of Oyo, Ojigi (1694–1724). To maintain dominance, Oyo invaded

Dahomey four times between 1724 and 1730. Dahomey first drew the anger of Oyo following the former's invasion of Great Adra (the Aja States) in an attempt to secure access to the sea and gain control of the slave trading stations. In an attempt to preserve its own slave labor, Dahomey had not initially been disposed to trade slaves with the Europeans. Due to the threat posed by this policy to Oyo's external trade, which depended on its ability to sell slaves to Europeans on the Slave Coast, *Alaafin* Ojigi responded by deploying an army against Dahomey. It would appear that Oyo's response was also motivated by the need to protect the interests of its traders of other items and its citizens engaged in various other occupations in the Aja area. Although Dahomey managed to repel the Oyo army, it later called for peace and delivered presents to the *Alaafin* as a sign of submission. In 1727, Oyo attacked Dahomey again, this time to aid Quidah (Whydah) which was a vassal state of Oyo, an external colony. The Oyo army destroyed many Dahomey villages, and in 1729 Dahomey again appealed for peace and agreed to pay tribute to Oyo. But in 1738, Dahomey reneged, thereby necessitating another attack. This time, Oyo armies mounted a siege of the Dahomey capital Abomey until its authorities appealed for peace. According to the armistice that followed, Dahomey consented to the payment of tribute of forty men, forty women, forty guns, and 400 loads of cowries and corals annually, retroactive to the defeat of 1728. Thus, it remained an external colony of Oyo. Although Dahomey defaulted for some years, it usually honored the peace terms due to threats of further invasion by Oyo and continued to pay until 1821 when it regained its independence (McCaskie and Fage 2018, section The Beginnings of European Activity; Akinjogbin [1971] 1976, 387; Ojo 1970, 66; Osae and Nwabara [1968] 1980, 96–97; Onwubiko 1973, 78). Meanwhile, by 1730, during *Alaafin* Ojigi's reign, available evidence suggests that Oyo forces were operating around Atakpame (modern Togo) and in contact with the Asante armies. Indeed, by this time, the Oyo kingdom appeared to have reached the apogee of its imperial expansion and attained the full status of an empire as it comprised both Yoruba and non-Yoruba groups (Akinjogbin 2002, 33–34).

Oyo's remarkable imperial expansion was made possible by a combination of geo-strategic, political, and economic factors. First came military organization. During its exile at Igboho, the Oyo undertook a reorganization of its society along military lines in response to the challenges to its survival as a state and ethnic group. The political elite introduced an improved and more efficient military organization that encompassed a large and powerful army comprised of infantry, armored cavalry units, and the Eso—professional and experienced officers. Apparently the Oyo army could not use horses previously due to lack of adequate access to the North, a region that could breed horses because it was devoid of tsetse flies. But following subjugation of the Nupe and Ibariba, Oyo gained the needed access and thus emulated their former archrival, the Nupe, by introducing cavalry into Oyo military organization. The Eso institution, a society of seventy war chiefs headed by the *Aare Ona Kakanfo* (who doubled as the generalissimo of the Oyo army), was primarily responsible for defense of the capital. It also became the chief instrument for the successful execution of Oyo colonial expansion and for control over dissident elements and rebellious vassals within the empire (Aderibigbe [1965] 1976, 194). The Eso, each of whom was an officer of the main field army, recruited men from his personal retainers, who were often slaves of northern descent. Unlike most 'traditional chieftaincy titles' in Yorubaland, the military position of Eso was non-hereditary, but based on personal ability, achievement, and merit. They were under the direct authority of the *Oyomesi*, a state council headed by the *Bashorun*. In order to stave off ascension to the throne through military force, members of Oyo royalty were prohibited from holding the Eso title (Matory 1994, 8–13). This provision helped to promote political stability of Oyo, although in the end it was the forceful claim to political authority and territory by *Aare Ona Kakanfo* Afonja that accelerated Oyo's decline and eventual collapse.

An efficient political administrative system complemented the military's role in the Oyo expansionist drive. The Old Oyo Empire operated the traditional Yoruba monarchical system of government. Under this arrangement, the town was the primary and basic political unit; thus, the evolution of Oyo into an empire necessitated the harmonization of imperial control with a monarchical administration based on the town as its fundamental unit (Atanda [1973] 1979, 14–15). Oyo administration was divided into two parts, metropolitan (Oyo proper) and provincial Oyo which consisted of Ibarapa, Egba, Egbado, Owu, Ijebu, Awori, Popo, Dahomey, and other regions. Provincial kings (*Obas*) and chiefs (*Baales*) were generally appointed with the approval of the *Alaafin* and provincial autonomy depended on his prospects and the proximity of the province to the capital.

234 J. O. ADEYERI

By and large, most Oyo colonies were administered by Oyo colonial agents: *Ilaris* (traveling messengers) and *Ajeles* (royal residents). The main duty of the former was to collect tribute and supervise the provincial administration. The *Ajeles* were the king's personal residents who observed the activities of the local rulers to ensure that provincial autonomy was not abused as to weaken loyalty to the king (Boahen [1966] 1979, 93; Atanda [1973] 1979, 25–26). It is noteworthy that these agents did not have to be of Yoruba origin; they could be Ibariba, Nupe or Hausa. Rather, the key requirement to become an Oyo imperial agent was loyalty to the *Alaafin*. This imperial administrative system gave the *Alaafin* tight political and economic control over the provinces for some time. However, in the long-run it proved to be counter-productive as the military leaders who were the chief executors of Oyo expansionist policy and the common soldiers who undertook most of the fighting became highly disenchanted because they did not get a proportionate share of the benefits from their campaigns. In addition, the imperial agents, who were mostly non-Yoruba, acted largely as predators, causing additional disaffection and disloyalty to the king, eventually resulting in revolts by many provinces (Akinjogbin 2002, 34).

Sound economy also significantly aided Oyo imperial expansion and sustenance. This economy, which was based on highly productive agriculture, trade with the Sudan, lucrative industries, and wealth from taxes and tribute made it possible for the *Alaafin* to maintain an elaborate imperial government and also equip and maintain a large and effective military force. Agriculture being the foremost occupation in traditional Yoruba society, as in most other African societies of that era, Oyo people across genders are were generally engaged in farming, in varying degrees. While it was the main occupation for some, others who had other primary professions, undertook agriculture as secondary or complimentary work. The people widely practiced mixed farming, whereby animals including sheep, fowls, and goats were raised alongside the production of crops, such as yam, cassava, maize, beans, groundnuts, cocoa, cotton, and kola. In order to sustain and improve soil and land fertility, crop rotation, mixed cropping, and fallow land practices were adopted.

Land, for agriculture as well as other purposes, was held by the *Alaafin* in trust for the community, with various portions available to different families according to the patrilineal inheritance system. The king leased pieces of land to non-indigenes for agricultural purposes, allowed them to harvest, enjoy and control their farm produce, excluding cash crops. Farm labor came from different sources like the family, and cooperative labor (*abese*) which involved seeking the services of friends, associates, or other families. However, rich individuals also used slaves to till the land and to do other farm work while slavery and the slave trade lasted.

Concerning taxation, Oyo acquired substantial wealth from a variety of taxes. The most prominent kind was the *Owo-Onibode*, a border fee charged on all goods going into and out of Oyo, collected by gate-keepers stationed at the gates of the capital and other towns within the empire. Other important sources of tax revenue were the tribute and capitation taxes. On a yearly basis, or during festival periods, each town paid its levies to Oyo either directly or via its supervisory chief. Colonial subject towns paid sundry tributes through colonial representatives. In addition, every town under Oyo jurisdiction paid death duties on their important figures whenever they died. Cowry shells, being a uniform currency in the area, served as a common form of payment for the various taxes and tributes, although such payments were also made in the form of slaves, corals, food products, or military service. The monetary value of general tribute exacted from Dahomey alone was worth about 32,000 British pounds. In addition, the *Alaafin* reserved the right to demand his subjects' services for public works, as well as other imperial projects (Okauru 2012, 68, 73, 74; Alimi and Adesoji 2011; Onwubiko 1973, 89; Aderibigbe [1965] 1976, 196).

Finally, the geographical location of Old Oyo also aided its economic and imperial growth and power. Being very close to the Niger River, and lying on the main trade route from the north to the south (one of the trans-Saharan caravan routes which reached the Guinea Coast), Oyo was in an advantageous position to control the economy across the constituent parts of the empire, with trade being the key. The empire also controlled commercial activities between the rain forest and the Sahara to the north, with transactions covering leather goods, glassware, and salt from the north in exchange for woven cloth, kola, and iron implements produced by Oyo blacksmiths. Agriculture and fishing also benefitted immensely from Oyo's favorable location. Moreover, this location, as noted earlier, enabled Oyo to import horses from the Hausa people, a development which facilitated the emergence of a formidable cavalry unit within the Oyo military (Atanda [1973] 1979, 26; Ojo 1970, 66).

IMPERIAL AND COLONIAL LEGACIES

Despite the precipitous collapse of Old Oyo around 1830 due to many factors,[2] the empire left behind enduring political and sociocultural legacies within and outside Yorubaland. Politically, Oyo imperial expansion and success ultimately contributed to the decline and eventual demise of the once legendary empire. This was as a result of an inherent weakness arising from the size and nature of the empire. Due to its extent, coupled with the location of its capital on the northern fringes of the empire, it became difficult to effectively control the provinces from the center, especially as most of the provinces lay to the south. However, after the eventual fall of the Oyo Empire, Yoruba successor states, such as Ibadan, Modakeke, and Abeokuta inherited its political system and institutions anchored upon indigenous checks, balances, and separation of powers (Adegbite 2011). This legacy may seem inconsistent with a hegemonic empire ruled by a king and military elite. However, this system was a direct result of the unique indigenous sociopolitical principles and provisions enshrined in the Oyo unwritten constitution. Oyo empire building and colonial exploitation, like European experiments, was exploitative and oppressive, but the Oyo indigenous system of checks, balances, and separation of powers governed the internal administration of the metropole, and was imbibed as a legacy by many later Yoruba kingdoms.

As Ayittey noted, this system of government was very complex and confusing to external observers. The king was selected from the local ruling families. As the natural and political head of the kingdom, in theory he wielded considerable powers, but in practice his policies were subject to confirmation by local councils comprised of heads of non-ruling families and local societies, which checked autocratic rule. The *Oyomesi* (Council of Notables), which consisted of seven councilors, who were prominent non-royal lineage chiefs of the capital as well as kingmakers, wielded judicial powers concurrently with the *Alaafin* in the capital. However, the latter had no control over the former's appointment because chiefs acquired their positions through lineage. Significantly, the *Oyomesi* had the power to sanction an autocratic king by compelling him to open the empty calabash (abdicate the throne and commit suicide). Examples of those rejected by the people and the earth-gods in this way were *Alaafin* Odarawu and *Alaafin* Jayin in the seventeenth century.

[2] For a detailed account of the fall of Old Oyo, see Boahen ([1966] 1979).

Therefore, the *Oyomesi*, particularly its head, the *Bashorun*, served as a strong check on the *Alaafin*.

The Ogboni Council (Earth Cult), also composed of lineage-appointed chiefs had judicial powers as well, however its main duty was to preserve the Ifa oracle which was positioned to confirm or nullify the *Bashorun's* proclamation for *Alaafin's* suicide. Nevertheless, the representative of the king was an influential member of the Ogboni Council, thus capable of checking ambitious *Bashoruns*. In this way, the Ogboni Council was both a check on the *Alaafin* and the *Oyomesi* Council. Lastly, the *Aare Ona Kakanfo* and his Eso war chiefs, primarily responsible for the empire's defense and security, were required to give their loyalty to the king. However, the army was answerable to the *Oyomesi* which handled the appointment and promotion of its officers. In order to isolate the *Aare Ona Kakanfo* from politics and prevent seizure of power by him, the title holder was usually of humble slave background and was prohibited by law from entering the capital (Soyoye 2014; Ayittey 2012; Stride and Ifeka 1971, 297; Boahen and Webster [1967] 1970, 90).[3] In spite of the later establishment of British colonial rule and the subsequent introduction of western political institutions, Oyo imprints remained in the indigenous administrative structures of the successor states.

Another political legacy of the fall of Oyo was instability in Yorubaland. The final collapse of Old Oyo in the wake of the Fulani conquest of Ilorin in 1817 ushered in a lengthy period (1821–93) of political disorder characterized by internecine civil wars among the various Yoruba towns. Although the wars were very frequent and complex in nature, one of the important causes was the breakdown of central authority and the army of Oyo after the successful revolt of Afonja, the *Aare Ona Kakanfo*, in 1817. Afonja's consequent creation of an independent state, Ilorin, marked the genesis of nineteenth-century internecine warfare in Yorubaland. Because the strong unifying central authority of Oyo was no longer in existence, provincial governors emulated Afonja and began to carve out territories for themselves, as the *Onikoyi* did around Ikoyi area, and Toyeje, the Otun Are-Ona-Kakanfo (second-in-command to Oyo Army General Commander) did in the Ogbomosho area. A group of untitled young men even assembled

---

[3]For a more detailed discussion of the Oyo system of checks and balances and the separation of powers, see Lloyd (1960), Smith (1969), Atanda (1973), Ayittey (2012), and Soyoye (2014).

themselves under the name Ogo Weere (Young Glories) and embarked on a looting spree across the Oyo Empire (Onwubiko 1973, 89–90; Akinjogbin 2002, 41). The overall outcome was several decades of civil wars, chaos, political insecurity, social instability, and economic underde-velopment throughout Yorubaland. While this outcome does not justify Oyo colonialism, it is a real historical consequence of the end of Oyo colonial hegemony over Yorubaland.

In terms of linguistic legacies, from the nineteenth century, the Oyo dialect became the standard linguistic form among all Yoruba people across the various towns. Many descendants of the empire's subjects now speak the Oyo dialect, partly due to pre-European Oyo hegemony. Yoruba is currently one of the dominant languages across the Nigeria-Benin borders as far as Togo and Ghana, as a result of socio-cultural and linguistic diffusion between the Oyo Yoruba and people of the aforemen-tioned West African states. Indeed, Oyo's imperial success made Yoruba language a lingua franca almost to the shores of the Volta (Babatunde 2014, 520–21; Master 2009).

Culturally, today's pervasive Sango worship in Yoruba society and its diaspora has its roots in the period of Oyo hegemony. Sango originally was a king and former *Alaafin* of Oyo, who ruled with an iron hand. Due to unbearable opposition to his authority from the people and chiefs, Sango abdicated the throne, committed suicide, and was subse-quently deified. As in Old Oyo, in contemporary Yorubaland, Sango is acknowledged as a tutelary divinity with priests and priestesses in his cult. Sango is worshipped throughout Yorubaland and in the Yoruba dias-pora in Cuba, Puerto Rico, Venezuela, Haiti, Brazil, and Trinidad where many initiation ceremonies are performed on the basis of the venerable tradition (Awolalu and Dopamu 1979, 84; Oladipo 2011). The common worship and veneration of Sango is an enhancer of Yoruba identity, cul-ture, and unity worldwide.

Lastly, Old Oyo bequeathed urbanism to Yorubaland. Today, the Yoruba are the most urbanized of all African nationalities of comparable size, hav-ing built upon their large dense cities predating British colonial rule. Old Oyo-linked towns, such as Ibadan (whose first settlement suffered repeated military and imperial pressures from Oyo), Osogbo and Ogbomoso (which were internal colonies) are some of the major urban centers that flourished as independent entities following the collapse of Oyo (Bascom 1962; New World Encyclopedia 2016; Tomori 2018). The prevalent pattern of urban-ization found in many Yoruba towns at present was inspired by early Oyo.

WESTERN AND AFRICAN COLONIALISM: THE OLD OYO CASE

Colonialism, primarily a western concept, is undoubtedly a fluid term whose meaning and content have undergone some shifts and contestations over time. Without embarking on a detailed discussion of western colonial theory, which has received ample scholarly attention,[4] it is necessary to highlight the core features of 'Western' colonialism in order to compare and contrast it with colonialism in the indigenous African context. In the Western context, colonialism involves the establishment of durable rule over an alien people different from and subordinate to the colonizing group, such as British colonial rule over the pre-colonial 'Nigerian' states from about the early to the mid-twentieth century. The colonized group is of a separate race from the colonizing people, and the former's territory is separated by sea from the metropole (Emerson 2008), reminiscent of French, British, German, Portuguese, and Belgian colonial rule over distant African peoples and territories from about the last quarter of the nineteenth to late twentieth century. Colonialism also involves the domination of a materially inferior native majority by an alien minority that asserts racial and cultural superiority over the former. Another important feature is that the colonizing power has a strong, industrialized economy, and Christian roots, unlike the colonized people (Balandier 1951, 75; Emerson 2008). In addition, the colonial situation involves the control and exploitation of the colony's economic resources, such as raw materials, mineral deposits, labor, and markets by the colonial power (Settles 1996, 8; Sharma 2018).

Here we need to note that although the Oyo Empire ruled over numerous subject peoples, Old Oyo, the colonizing power, was of African 'race' just as the peoples of the empire's colonies, contrary to the Western colonial paradigm. However, the notion of a monolithic African 'race' is controversial. This point is underscored by the claim early European explorers made of Africa during the fifteenth century that they had met a continent populated by five human species–blacks, whites, Pygmies, Khoisan, and Asians. Indeed, it is arbitrary stereotyping to lump highly diverse peoples, such as the Igbo, Zulu, and Maasai together as a single 'race' tagged 'blacks' (Diamond 1994). Thus, it may not be appropriate to conclude that Old Oyo (like many ancient indigenous

[4] See Easton (1964), Wolfe (1997), UKEssays (2013), Kohn and Reddy ([2006] 2017), Subreenduth (2018).

African Empires) and its colonies, such as Dahomey (now the Republic of Benin), Nupe, and Ibariba belonged to the same race despite their significant physical and cultural differences. Some colonies of Old Oyo Empire were peoples of various ethnic configurations different from that of the imperial center. The cultures of these subordinate groups, particularly the Nupe, Mahi, Borgu, and Dahomey, significantly differed from that of Old Oyo in some respects (Law and Lovejoy 1999, 70).

Unlike the Western colonial powers that were 'modern' economic and industrial giants, Old Oyo's economy was still largely agrarian and rudimentary. But in spite of this, Old Oyo's economy and civilization was arguably superior to those of its colonies. By the mid-eighteenth century Old Oyo's economy had become considerably stronger primarily on account of its local and external trade, especially coastal trade with the Europeans (Editors of Encyclopedia Britannica 2018). As noted earlier, Old Oyo's military organization and strength, especially its cavalry and Eso officer corps, were outstanding, as evidenced by imperial victories against numerous states, such as Dahomey, Popo, Sabe, Ketu (the last three now in modern Togo), Ijaye, Egba, and Egbado. Oyo's socio-political structure, anchored in an indigenous and intricate system of checks and balances enshrined in its unwritten constitution, was also almost unique. As an expression of pride in their military strength and socio-political structure, the Oyo were fond of describing themselves as: '*alara, Oyo mara ju ara oko lo*' (Oyo, the owner of creative force), who knows creativity more than the lesser city (Akintonde and Areo 2013, 50–51; Atanda 1980, 12). Concerning Oyo's production and use of art, Willet's observation—that Africa is greatly endowed in art, but no other ethnic group is as prolific in art as the Yoruba (Willet 1965)—is instructive, given the fact that Old Oyo was the best-known Yoruba state and in the forefront of Yoruba art and civilization. Successful expansionist wars, the huge resultant size and population of the empire, effective government, and human as well as territorial security appeared to have significantly aided artistic advancement in Oyo (Akintonde and Areo 2013, 52; Udenyi 2018, 10).

Old Oyo, though, was not separated from its imperial colonies by sea, contrary to the prescription of Western colonialist theory, some of the latter's territories were in relatively distant locations from the empire's capital; they spanned vast areas between the River Volta and the River Niger in the west and east respectively. As an illustration, Oyo's capital was about 300 km inland, while Dahomey was closer to the Atlantic coast (Udenyi 2018, 1; Smitha 2015). In a nutshell, colonialism in the African context, as in the Old Oyo case, was similar to Western colonialism in many respects. The observed differences between the two were of degree, not of kind.

Conclusion

Like the European empires, Old Oyo's remarkable imperial expansion was anchored in several geo-strategic and economic features. However, its colonial experiment elicited a rather peculiar outcome in that the relative proximity (in contrast to European empires) of the metropole to its colonies made it easier for the latter to revolt, thereby heightening the centrifugal forces in the empire during its period of internal decay. Due to their relative closeness, subject states, such as Egba, Ijebu, Nupe and Dahomey, were able to launch a series of attacks against the heartland of Old Oyo and consequently reclaim their independence. However, Old Oyo remained significant particularly among the Yoruba long after the empire's fall, due to the important postcolonial results. Old Oyo's political system built around an effective unwritten constitution with its checks, balances and separation of powers became the indigenous political model for most Yoruba kingdoms even to the present day. The Oyo dialect, still acknowledged as standard Yoruba, became the common linguistic form across Yorubaland, and among some in the diaspora in places, such as in the Republic of Benin, Togo, and Ghana. Contemporary worship of Sango, which originated in Old Oyo, and observance of Sango-related initiation ceremonies across Yorubaland has continued to strengthen Yoruba culture, identity, and unity globally. Finally, Old Oyo bequeathed urbanism to Yorubaland.

The Old Oyo Empire, because it did not totally conform to the Western colonial model, is seldom directly called a colonial power in the existing literature. This chapter avers that Oyo rule and hegemony over many of its subject states was colonial in nature, exhibiting internal colonialism within Yorubaland in contiguous states (territories) like the Osogbo, Ogbomoso, Ijanna, Egba and Egbado, and external colonialism outside Yoruba territory in relatively distant places, such as Dahomey, Porto Novo, Nupe, and Ibariba. As the essay also indicates, the motives, trajectory, and legacies of Oyo rule in West Africa attest to the similarities between African and Western colonialism.

REFERENCES

Adegbite, Adewuyi. 2011. "Osogbo War of 1840 Revisited." *Nigerian Tribune*, September 6. https://waidigbenro.wordpress.com/2013/02/26/osogbo-war-of-1840-revisited/. Accessed October 11, 2018.

Aderibigbe, A.B. [1965] 1976. "Peoples of Southern Nigeria." In *A Thousand Years of West African History: A Handbook for Teachers and Students*, edited by Jacob Festus Ade Ajayi and Ian Espie, 193–201. Ibadan: Ibadan University Press.

Afropedea. 2010. "Oyo Empire." www.afropedea.org/oyo-empire. Accessed October 11, 2018.

Akinjogbin, I.A. [1971] 1976. "The Expansion of Oyo and the Rise of Dahomey, 1600–1800." In *History of West Africa*, vol. I, edited by Jacob Festus Ade Ajayi and Michael Crowder, 373–412. London: Longman.

Akinjogbin, I.A. 2002. *Milestones and Concepts in Yoruba History and Culture: A Key to Understanding Yoruba History*. Ibadan: Olu-Akin Publishers.

Akintonde, M.A., and M.O. Areo. 2013. "Art and Craft of Old Oyo: Its Manifestation in the Present Oyo." *IOSR Journal of Humanities and Social Sciences* 15(5): 50–59.

Alimi, Shina, and A.O. Adesoji. 2011. "Oyo Empire Up Till 1893." August 24. http://alimology.blogspot.de/2011/08/oyo-empire-up-till-1893.html. Accessed October 11, 2018.

Atanda, Joseph Adebowale. 1973. "The Yoruba Ogboni Cult: Did It Exist in Old Oyo?" *Journal of the Historical Society of Nigeria* 6(4): 365–72.

Atanda, Joseph Adebowale. [1973] 1979. *The New Oyo Empire: Indirect Rule and Change in Western Nigeria 1894–1934*. London: Longman.

Atanda, Joseph Adebowale. 1980. *An Introduction to Yoruba History*. Ibadan: Ibadan University Press.

Awolalu, J. Ọmọṣade, and P. Adelumo Dopamu. 1979. *West African Traditional Religion*. Ibadan: Onibonoje Press & Book Industries.

Ayittey, George. 2012. "The Oyo Empire." February 19. https://seunfakze.wordpress.com/?s=The+Oyo+Empire&searchbutton=go%21. Accessed October 11, 2018.

Babatunde, Samuel Olufemi. 2014. "Multilingualism Across Borders: Nigeria-Republic of Benin as Case Study." *European Scientific Journal* (August) 10(10): 518–29.

Balandier, Georges. 1951. "La Situation Coloniale: Approche Théorique." *Cahiers internationaux de sociologie* XI: 44–79.

Bascom, William R. 1962. "Some Aspects of Yoruba Urbanism." *American Anthropologist* 64(4): 699–709.

Biobaku, Saburi Oladeni. 1955. *The Origin of the Yorubas*. Lagos: Federal Ministry of Information Service.

Blauner, Robert. 1969. "Internal Colonialism and Ghetto Revolt." *Social Problems* 16(4): 393–408.

Boahen, A. Adu. [1966] 1979. *Topics in West African History.* London: Longman.

Boahen, A. Adu, and James Bertin Webster. [1967] 1970. *History of West Africa: The Revolutionary Years—1815 to Independence.* New York: Praeger.

Bohmer, Peter. 1999. "African-Americans as an Internal Colony: The Theory of Internal Colonialism." In *Readings in Black Political Economy,* edited by John Whitehead and Cobie Kwasi Harris, 89–95. Dubuque, IA: Kendall/Hunt.

Brankamp, Hanno. 2015. "The Question of 'Internal Colonialism'." *Pambazuka News,* January 13. https://www.pambazuka.org/global-south/question-%E2%80%98internal-colonialism%E2%80%99. Accessed October 11, 2018.

Davidson, Basil, Francis Kwamina Buah, and Jacob Festus Ade Ajayi. [1967] 1971. *The Growth of African Civilisation: A History of West Africa 1000–1800.* London: Longman.

Diamond, Jared. 1994. "How Africa Became Black." *Discover,* February 1. http://discovermagazine.com/1994/feb/howafricabecameb331. Accessed October 11, 2018.

Douglas-Bowers, Devon. 2012. "America's Internal Colonialism." *Global Research,* July 26. https://www.globalresearch.ca/america-s-internal-colonialism/32074. Accessed October 11, 2018.

Easton, Stewart Copinger. 1964. *The Rise and Fall of Western Colonialism: A Historical Survey from the Early Nineteenth Century to the Present.* New York: Praeger.

Editors of Encyclopedia Britannica. 2018. "Oyo Empire: Historical Kingdom in Western Africa." https://www.britannica.com/place/Oyo-empire. Accessed October 11, 2018.

Emerson, Rupert. 2008. "Colonialism: Political Aspects." *International Encyclopedia of the Social Sciences.* https://www.encyclopedia.com/history/modern-europe/ancient-history-middle-ages-and-feudalism/colonialism#A. Accessed October 11, 2018.

Forde, Cyril Daryll. 1951. *The Yoruba-Speaking Peoples of South-Western Nigeria.* London: International African Institute.

González, Deena J. 2005. "Internal Colonialism." In *New Dictionary of the History of Ideas,* vol. 3, edited by Maryanne Cline Horowitz, 1130–31. Farmington Hills, MI: Thomson Gale.

González-Casanova, Pablo. 1965. "Internal Colonialism and National Development." *Studies in Comparative International Development* 1(4): 27–37.

Kohn, Margaret, and Kavita Reddy. [2006] 2017. "Colonialism". In *Stanford Encyclopedia of Philosophy,* edited by Edward N. Zalta. https://plato.stanford.edu/entries/colonialism. Accessed October 15, 2018.

Law, Robin, and Paul E. Lovejoy. 1999. "Borgu in the Atlantic Slave Trade." *African Economic History* 27: 69–92.

Lewis, Ioan Myrddin. [2004] 2013. *History and Social Anthropology*. London: Routledge.

Lloyd, P.C. 1960. "Sacred Kingship and Government Among the Yoruba." *Africa: Journal of the International African Institute* 30(3): 221–37.

Malcolm, X. 1965. *Malcolm X Speaks: Selected Speeches and Statements*. Edited with prefatory notes by George Breitman. New York: Grove Press.

Master. 2009. "The Collapse of the Old Oyo Empire." October 27. http://investingnow-babs.blogspot.com/2009/10/colapsed-of-old-oyo-empire.html. Accessed October 15, 2018.

Matory, J. Lorand. 1994. *Sex and the Empire That Is No More: Gender and the Politics of Metaphor in Oyo Yoruba Religion*. Minneapolis: University of Minnesota Press.

McCaskie, T.C., and John, D. Fage. 2018. "Western Africa." https://www.britannica.com/place/western-Africa/The-beginnings-of-European-activity. Accessed October 11, 2018.

New World Encyclopedia. 2016. "Oyo Empire." October 4. http://www.newworldencyclopedia.org/entry/Oyo_Empire. Accessed October 15, 2018.

Ojo, Adekunle. 1970. *A Textbook of West African History*. Ibadan: Educational Research Institute.

Okauru, Ifueko Omoigui. 2012. *A Comprehensive Tax History of Nigeria*. Ibadan: Safari Books Ltd.

Oladipo, Olayinka. 2011. "Sango: The God of Thunder." *TIA*, April 17. http://tia-thisisafrica.blogspot.de/2011/04/sango-god-of-thunder_17.html. Accessed October 16, 2018.

Onwubiko, K.B.C. 1973. *History of West Africa, 1800—Present Day* (Book Two). Onitsha: Africana FEP Publishers Limited.

Osae, Theodore Adjei, and Samuel Nwankwo Nwabara. [1968] 1980. *A Short History of West Africa, A.D. 1000–1800*. London: Hodder & Stoughton.

Pinderhughes, Charles. 2009. "21st Century Chains: The Continuing Relevance of Internal Colonialism Theory." PhD diss., Boston College. http://hdl.handle.net/2345/3409. Accessed October 15, 2018.

Pinderhughes, Charles. 2011. "Toward a New Theory of Internal Colonialism." *Socialism and Democracy* 25(1): 235–56.

Settles, Joshua Dwayne. 1996. "The Impact of Colonialism on African Economic Development." May 1996. https://trace.tennessee.edu/utk_chanhonoproj/182. Accessed October 15, 2018.

Sharma, Pratik. 2018. "Colonialism: Meaning and Features; Indian Economic History." http://www.historydiscussion.net/history-of-india/economic-history/colonialism-meaning-and-features-indian-economic-history/5967. Accessed October 15, 2018.

Simons, Harold Jack, and Ray E. Simons. 1969. *Class and Colour in South Africa, 1850–1950*. Harmondsworth: Penguin.

Smith, Robert S. 1969. *Kingdoms of the Yoruba*. London: Methuen & Co. Ltd.
Smitha, Frank E. 2015. "The Kingdoms of Oyo, Dahomey and Asante." http://www.fsmitha.com/h3/h28af3-4.htm. Accessed October 15, 2018.
Soyoye, Akinyode. 2014. "Governance in the Old Oyo Empire." *Feathersproject*, September 4. https://feathersproject.wordpress.com/2014/09/04/guest-blog-post-akinyode-soyoye-governance-in-the-old-oyo-empire. Accessed October 15, 2018.
Stride, G.T., and Ifeka, Caroline. 1971. *Peoples and Empires of West Africa: West Africa in History, 1000–1800*. Lagos: Thomas Nelson.
Subreenduth, Sharon. 2018. "Colonization Theory." In *Encyclopedia of Curriculum Studies*, edited by Craig Kridel. http://sk.sagepub.com/reference/curriculumstudies/n68.xml. Accessed October 16, 2018.
Tomori, M.A. 2018. "Ibadan Metropolitan Area and the Challenges to Sustainable Development." In *MACOS Urban Management Consultancy Services*. https://www.macosconsultancy.com/Ibadan%20metropolitan.html. Accessed November 22, 2018.
Udenyi, David. 2018. "Critically Discuss How the Collapse of Oyo Empire Affected the Political Equilibrium of Yoroba Land and Dahomey." http://www.academia.edu/22410575/CRITICALLY_DISCUSS_HOW_THE_COLLAPSE_OF_OYO_EMPIRE_AFFECTED_THE_POLITICAL_EQUILIBRIUM_OF_YOROBA_LAND_AND_DAHOMEY. Accessed October 16, 2018.
UKEssays. 2013. "The Theories of Colonialism History Essay." https://www.ukessays.com/essays/history/the-theories-of-colonialism-history-essay.php?vref=1. Accessed October 16, 2018.
Willet, Frank. 1965. *The Sculpture of Western Nigeria*. Ibadan: Ministry of Information.
Wolfe, Patrick. 1997. "History and Imperialism: A Century of Theory, from Marx to Postcolonialism." *The American Historical Review* 102(2): 388–420.
Wolpe, Harold. [1975] 2013. "The Theory of Internal Colonialism: The South African Case." In *Beyond the Sociology of Development: Economy and Society in Latin America and Africa*, edited by Ivar Oxaal, Tony Barnett, and David Booth, 229–52. London: Routledge.

PART III

Co-Opted Elites, Local Brokers, and Go-Betweens in Nation-Building

CHAPTER 10

India: The Context of Its Current Internal Colonialism

Dipankar Dey

INTRODUCTION

The colonial paradigm, the collection of theories seeking to explain the phenomenon of global colonization, exists in relation to a constellation of other models regarding socioeconomic exchange across time. In the modern era the theories of Adam Smith and Karl Marx placed colonialism in the context of commercial and industrial capitalism as related to imperialism and nationalism. Early empires built around national cores, such as the Spanish, British, and French, pursued markets, labor, and territory in contacts with local peoples across the world. Later multiethnic states, such as the United States and Russia, promoted contending systems around such activities. With the collapse of the Soviet model, capitalism, through multinational corporations, moved to a stage of globalization penetrating nations large and small. This new world system became detached from national states and former empires, but continued to reflect colonial aspects of its predecessors.

D. Dey (✉)
Guest Faculty, Department of Business Management,
University of Calcutta, Kolkata, India

© The Author(s) 2019
D. Schorkowitz et al. (eds.), *Shifting Forms of Continental Colonialism*,
https://doi.org/10.1007/978-981-13-9817-9_10

249

Since 1947, independent India has been incorporated by the larger global system reinforcing a colonial legacy. While early Indian states, such as the Mughal Empire, had engaged in continental colonialism in their expansion into the surrounding territories of distinct peoples, later Portuguese and British expansion exemplified overseas colonialism. After political independence, India experienced neo-colonialism due to continuing economic and cultural dependence on the English, such as the use of their language. Within the new state, Indo-Aryans, especially the urbanized, predominated, despite their own internal caste divisions, imposing regional colonialism on rural areas of similar ethnic background and internal colonialism on the homelands of tribal peoples.[1]

EARLY CONTINENTAL COLONIALISM IN THE INDIAN SUBCONTINENT: THE ARYAN FORAY

Generally, the Timurid dynasty—arriving from Central Asia, establishing the Mughal (Mogul) Empire, and ruling over most of India and Pakistan from the sixteenth to the mid-eighteenth centuries—is considered the first foreign power that expanded into adjacent territories of the Indian subcontinent populated by distinct peoples (Richards 1995; Foltz 1998).[2] This continental colonialism was only later followed by Portuguese and British (Welch 2011) overseas colonialism. However, a recent study on genetic formation reveals that expansion into the Indian subcontinent had started much earlier than the Mughal invasion. The study "identifies the populations that almost certainly were responsible for spreading Indo-European languages across much of Eurasia" (Narasimhan et al. 2018, 4). Accordingly, the Eurasian Steppe people mixed with the people in the Indus Periphery. By co-analyzing ancient DNA and genomic data from diverse present-day South Asians, the researchers have shown that Indus Periphery-related people were the single most important source of ancestry in South Asia.

---

[1] I am grateful to Dittmar Schorkowitz, John Chávez, Ingo Schröder, and Sri Suranjan Gupta for their valuable comments and suggestions on earlier versions of this chapter. Their suggestions have immensely helped to understand and address this complex issue.

[2] Before, many other conquistadors had come and plundered different parts of the country, but most of them returned home. These frequent raids include the incursions of Central Asian Hephthalites (Hunas), the Indo-Greek Kingdom, and, of course, Alexander the Great's campaigns. By contrast, the Mughals did not leave and made India their home.

There were three major migrations into the subcontinent during the last 65,000 years. The 'Out of Africa' migrants reached India around sixty-five thousand years ago. They were followed, sometime between 7000 and 3000 BCE, by nomadic groups from the Zagros region of Southwestern Iran. These herders who imported agriculturists and grain, like wheat and barley, had mixed with 'Out of Africa' migrants (a few descendants of these first Indians still live in the Andaman Islands) and created the Harappa civilization (Venkataramakrishnan 2018).

Harappa and Mohenjo-daro were the two great cities of the Indus Valley Civilization, also known as the Harappa civilization. Recent findings estimate that the beginning of the Harappa civilization dates back to 5500 BCE. Geographically it was spread to a wide area spanning from Southeastern Afghanistan and Pakistan to the North West and Western States of India (Allchin and Allchin 1982; Wright 2009; Coningham and Young 2015; Madaan 2019). This Harappa civilization, one of the oldest civilizations of the world, was destroyed by the next wave of migrants who reached the land around 1500 BCE.

According to Heine-Geldern (1956) these Indo-Aryan groups were probably driven out of their homeland in Northwestern Iran or Transcaucasia, around 1500 BCE, due to conflicts with the dominant people who destroyed the Hittite kingdom[3] by 1200 BCE. One group of these Indo-Aryan migrants might have moved south and south-west and acquired mastery over the kingdom of Mitanni and parts of Syria. These Indo-Aryans (the Eurasian Steppe people) brought with them mastery of the chariot, an early version of Sanskrit, and various cultural practices, such as sacrificial rituals, that formed the basis of early Vedic-Hindu culture. The earliest form of Sanskrit which the Indo-Aryan introduced was also spoken in the Mitanni region of Syria (Daniyal 2015; Venkataramakrishnan 2018).

The first two major migrations had thus culminated in the development of the Harappa or Indus Valley civilization. The third, Indo-Aryan migration might have caused some amount of upheaval when it encountered the Indus Valley population. Consequently, some of the latter moved farther south, joined, and mixed with South Asian hunter-gatherers, the Ancient Ancestral South Indian (AASI), to create the Ancestral South Indian (ASI) population. The Indo-Aryan steppe

---

[3]The Hittites occupied the ancient region of Anatolia, also known as Asia Minor, modern-day Turkey prior to 1700 BCE; cf. Mark (2018), Anthony (2007).

pastoralists mixed with groups of the Indus Valley periphery living in the northern fringe, to create the Ancestral North Indian (ANI) branch. More migration into the Indian subcontinent occurred in later times, though mostly from East Asia. These groups assimilated with one of the two dominant groups. Thus, most of the South Asian populations carry either the lineage of ASI or ANI or a mixture of both. To quote the historian Tony Joseph:

> the best way to understand the Indian population is to imagine it as a pizza, with the first Indians forming its base. Though the base of this rather irregular pizza is thin in some places and thick in others, it still serves as the support that the rest of the pizza is built upon because studies show that 50% to 65% of the genetic ancestry of Indians derives from the First Indians. On top of the base comes the Harappa's sauce- that is spread over the pizza, then the toppings and the cheese - the Austro-Asiatic, Tibeto-Burman and Indo-European language speakers or Aryans, all of whom found their way into the subcontinent later. (2018a; cf. Joseph 2018b)

These Indo-European language speakers who came to India around 1500 BCE still rule the nation with the help of their Vedic culture and Sanskrit-based language, Hindi. People with ANI lineage have been successful in developing a political and social structure that has helped them to retain their hegemony over the non-ANI population of India. Researchers have found Indian groups, identified as "Brahmin-Tiwari" and "Brahmin-UP", with a higher amount of Aryan ancestry compared to Harappa and Indus Valley ancestry. It has been observed that groups of priestly status have higher Aryan ancestry, suggesting those with this mixture may have had a central role in spreading Vedic culture (Venkataramakrishnan 2018; cf. Narasimhan et al. 2018, 16).

ARYANS CONSTRUCT BRAHMANISM TO EXPAND THEIR COLONY

Probably, the four Vedas—Rig, Sama, Yajur, and Atharva—were first composed by the Aryans, in the Vedic Sanskrit language, sometime between 1500 and 1000 BCE in the northwestern region of the Indian subcontinent. Initially they were transmitted orally over many generations. The Vedas are considered as the repository of knowledge on which the Aryan philosophy of colonial hegemony was built. The first indications of a Varna division, onto which the Indian caste (literally: race, breed, or lineage) system has been engineered, can be traced to the Vedas, particularly the late Rig-Vedic Purusha Sukta. It mentions a primordial deity, Purusha, who was sacrificed by the other gods. Purusha's mind became the Moon, his eyes the Sun, his head the Sky, and his feet the Earth. According to this description, (i) the Brahmans or priests came from Purusha's mouth, (ii) the Rajanyas (Kshatriyas) or the warrior class from Purusha's arm, (iii) the Vaishyas or the commoners from Purusha's thigh, and (iv) the Shudras or the laborers and servants from his feet (Basham 1989, 25; Violatti 2018).

Around the first millennium BCE, the Vedic literature and religious sermons created a new religion, Brahmanism, which emphasized the rites performed by the Brahmans—the priestly class. Over centuries Brahmanism has emerged as a political philosophy that refers to the predominant position of the Brahmans and the importance given to a *Brahman* in the sociopolitical structure of the state. One important text that has helped to establish Brahmanism as the most powerful socioeconomic and political philosophy is Manusmriti (*The Dharma Text of Manu*) written around 100 CE. It contains twelve chapters and a total of 2694 stanzas. *The Dharma Text of Manu* has influenced all aspects of Hindu thought, particularly justification of the caste system. Among these aspects, it deals with cosmogony, definition of the dharma, rituals, initiation (the sacred thread ceremony of Brahmans), study of the Vedas, marriage, hospitality, funeral rites, dietary restrictions, pollution, means of purification, conduct of women, and the law of kings (Basham 1989; Olivelle 2005; Anthony 2007; Srikantan 2014).

The spread of Brahmanism from its North Indian heartland (Punjab, Delhi) to other parts of the subcontinent was not that smooth. It faced major resistance from two prominent religious leaders, namely Mahavira (599–527 BCE) and Gautama Buddha (480–400 BCE). These founders of Jainism and Buddhism were both born in the eastern part of India and their religious thoughts challenged the hegemony of Brahmanism that was trying to colonize other territories. While Brahmanism relied on Sanskrit for the propagation of its Vedic philosophy, Jains and Buddhists relied on Pali and Ardhamagadhi Prakrit in the propagation of their thoughts. Though the influence of Jainism was restricted to a few areas of India and mostly in the Vaishya community, Buddhism was very popular across South and East Asia: "It took a thousand-year struggle between Buddhism and Brahmanism before the latter could declare a complete victory" (Desai 2016). India became a Hindu nation around the eighth century when Adi Shankaracharya (788–820), a Keralite Brahmin, revived Brahmanism by restoring belief in the Vedas and Upanishads. He founded four monasteries (mathas)—one each at the four North, South, West, and East regions of India. He is credited with building the much-needed infrastructure for the propagation of Brahmanism in the Indian subcontinent.

The millennial struggle between Brahmanism and Buddhism was aggressive by nature. Leading historian Dwijendra Narayan Jha (2018) has argued that the conflict between Brahmanical and non-Brahmanical sects was a frequent and common phenomenon in ancient India. Two Brahmanical sects, Vaishnavism and Shivism, fought against each other, and both sects were constantly at loggerheads with the followers of Jainism and Buddhism. In one of his studies Jha has documented evidence of desecration, destruction, and appropriation of thousands of Buddhist stupas, monasteries, and other structures by Brahmanical forces. Thus, the destruction of the Nalanda Mahabihara monastery was caused by Hindu fanatics who had set fire to its library. It was not destroyed, as propagandized, by Bakhtiyar Khilji, the Muslim invader (Jha 2018; UNESCO World Heritage Centre 1992–2019). New findings have also challenged the epic Ramayana where Ravana has been portrayed as a demon king of Sri Lanka. It is claimed that Ravana was a believer in Buddhism. One of his works was *Agni Tantra*, on 'How to Walk on Fire', and another on children's diseases: "Ravana civilization was a highly advanced civilization. It was a very prosperous culture and a civilization that developed centering (Sri) Lanka. That civilization was destroyed with the advent of an Aryan group headed by Rama" ("Ravana Was a Great Ruler" 2013; cf. Obeysekere 2013).

BRAHMANISM DURING THE MUGHAL PERIOD

After the decline of Buddhism, Brahmanism faced a new challenge from Islamic Central Asia. Sporadic incursions finally climaxed in the establishment of the Mughal Empire in northern India, the cradle of Brahmanism, by Emperor Babur in the early sixteenth century. However, even under Mughal rule Brahmanism managed to survive. The society continued to be organized under Hindu traditions and the caste system remained intact.

In many parts of the country, the upper-caste Hindus (Brahmin, Kshatriyas, Vaishyas) were allowed to pay concessional land rent. A Brahman Munshi (state secretary), Chandar Bhan–who, from the 1630s to the 1660 served in the Mughal court under Jahangir, Shah Jahan, and Aurangzeb, all powerful Mughal emperors—used his caste name Takhallus, a widely used Urdu pen-name (Kinra 2015). Academics believe that this could have been a deliberate act by the Munshi. The need for identification was a "sign that Chandra Bhan was secure in both worlds—a 'sacred thread wearing' man from the learned caste who also counted among his mentors the Mughal officials who happened to be Muslim and were deeply spiritual" (Kumar 2016).

Mughals thought that Sanskrit texts and ideas offered them an opportunity to understand their Indian subjects and frame appropriate laws to rule. This initiative was mainly started by Akbar the Great who invited Brahman and Jain intellectuals to the emperor's court. Arguably, these exchanges between the Persian-speaking Islamic elite of the Mughal Empire and traditional Sanskrit scholars might have "engendered a dynamic idea of Mughal rule essential to the empire's survival" (PTI 2016; cf. Truschke 2016). Though Hindu nationalists relentlessly say that Muslim rulers demolished around 60,000 Hindu temples, there is little credible evidence for the destruction of more than eighty (Jha 2018).

EUROPEAN COLONIALISM AND ENGINEERING OF HINDU RELIGIOUS IDENTITY

The Portuguese sailor Vasco da Gama became the first European to re-establish direct trade links with India since Roman times. And he was the first to reach the southern coast in 1498 by sea. Subsequently, rivalries among Europe's seafaring nations brought other powers to India. The Dutch Republic, England, France, and Denmark-Norway established trading posts in India in the early seventeenth century. The founding of the British East India Company in 1600 heightened competition. By the mid-eighteenth century a large part of eastern India had come under the control of the British and the French East India Company (*Compagnie française des Indes orientales*). The British made Calcutta (Kolkata), a flourishing port-city of Bengal, the headquarters for their expansion in India.

According to an estimate by economist Utsa Patnaik, during 1765–1938, "the East India Company and the British Raj siphoned out at least

£9.2 trillion (or $44.6 trillion; since the exchange rate was $4.8 per pound sterling during much of the colonial period)" from India (Sreevatsan 2018). This massive loot of wealth, primarily from eastern India destroyed the prosperous economy of Bengal (Mukherjee [2011] 2015) and over 13 million people were starved to death in two massive famines (rather British genocides) in 1770 and 1943 (Sen 1981; Tauger and Sen 2011; Mukherjee 2010; Chakraborty 2014).

British colonial rule in India was divided into two periods: 1757–1857, when a large part of the country was controlled by the British East India Company and 1858–1947, when India was ruled directly by the British Crown. Jyoti Mohan describes, in detail, the arguments put forward by the Europeans to justify their colonial exploitation and appropriation of resources from their colonies like India. The first part of his study narrates the dominant European and particularly French views of the eighteenth century justifying the colonial expansion. The second part deals, more specifically, with the prevailing views of nineteenth-century English academia. European colonialism was founded on two contradictory thoughts: (a) 'the colonized' possessed the capacity to become civilized and the colonizers had to make them civilized, and (b) the political and economic agenda was built on racial purity. According to Mohan, French scholars "were among the foremost proponents of race theory and racial hierarchy [...] It was the French, and not the Germans, who placed India on an Aryan pedestal" (2016, 1576).

For French scholars, the common ground between India and France lay in their shared Aryan ancestry, which Norman Britain could not share. The diffusion theory of civilization, which was extremely popular at the time, held that civilization was spread through the world by the migrating Aryans, and described the migration of various streams of Aryans from the Caucasus region to different parts of the world. The branch of Aryans who had arrived in India was obviously linked to other branches that had migrated to Europe and elsewhere. This explained the high cultural achievements of the Vedic civilization of India and the linguistic affinities between Sanskrit and other Indo-Germanic languages. Since the Aryans were the forefathers of modern Indians, they came from the same racial stock as the Europeans. The superior civilization of the Aryans in India was already proven in terms of the institutions they had created such as the caste system, as well as the advanced religion and philosophy that they had produced in the form of Brahmanism. At its core India was an Aryan nation. [...] The presence of the 'inferior' Dravidian race and centuries of intermarriage provided a cautionary tale of the dangers of race mixing. The history of India, from her glory days of Aryan civilization and the resulting downfall of a 'superior' race as a result of diluting their pure blood [...] was a perfect example of the theory of racial hierarchy. (ibid., 1614–15)

In the nineteenth century, British colonists, who had already captured vast areas of India and decided to establish their own government, manufactured the following arguments to justify their stay in India.

India had degenerated over centuries due to the invasions of foreigners, particularly of the Muslims. But its Aryan ancestry meant that India had the capability to throw off the decline of centuries and assume its place among the advanced countries of the world once more [...] Aryans had indeed accomplished great intellectual and philosophical achievements in the ancient period, but the dilution of their race over centuries of intermarriage with 'inferior' races had left them corrupt and incapable of ruling themselves. Unlike the French and German school of Indologists who posited a possible return to greatness if India embraced her Aryan past once again, the British theory–justified in large part by the need to rule India–held that the once-great capability of the Indo-Aryans was non-existent in the present time, simply because there were no extant pure Aryans left in India. (ibid., 1615–16)

British rule "would provide Indians with the necessary institutions and civilization they needed to develop." Thus, the theory that "Indo-Aryans were the originators of the Indo-Europeans" was pushed to the back seat. British colonial academics argued that the "historical 'inferiority' of India validated British colonial rule" (ibid., 1616).

[...] the Aryan race theory was mostly propagated by romantic Indologists like Williams Jones in the eighteenth century. In the nineteenth century, [...] officials focused on retrieving evidence of the dominance of 'inferior' races, like the Dravidians [...]. The use of Aryan race theory was limited to civilians, especially missionaries, who hoped to show that Christianity was the natural Aryan corollary to the degraded religion of idolatry in India. The need for an overview of Indians was certainly felt in order to strengthen British rule, and particularly to avoid a repeat of the 1857 Rebellion [led by Mangal Pandey, a sepoy of Brahman origin; D.D.]. So the government instituted a census, which collected information relating to race. The census commissioner Herbert Risley [...] instructed his juniors to collect data about the nasal and cranial indices of different groups in India. The result of this process was the institutionalization of the caste system in India. (ibid., 1616–17)

According to Kevin Hobson (n.d.) "it was not until 1872 that a planned comprehensive census was attempted in India. This was done under the direction of Henry Beverley, Inspector General of Registration in Bengal" (ibid.). Officially, the primary purpose of the census was "governmental preparedness to deal with disaster situations [...] However, the census went well beyond counting heads [...] Among the many questions were enquiries regarding nationality, race, tribe, religion and caste. Certainly none of these things were relevant to emergency measures responses by the government [...] Caste was seen as an indicator of occupation, social standing, and intellectual ability [...]. Moreover [...] British conceptions of racial purity were interwoven with these judgements of people based on caste." Inspector General Beverley commented "that a group of Muslims were in fact converted low caste Hindus." Thus the census became not just an "accounting of what existed but an active contributor in the creation and modification of the society" (ibid.). Between 1860 and 1920, the British segregated India by caste. They granted administrative jobs and senior appointments to the upper castes only. In subsequent Censuses, the four main categories of Hindus were further divided into about 3000 castes and 25,000 sub-castes, each based on their specific occupation. Outside of this Hindu caste system were the Dalits or the untouchables. One striking feature of the Indian caste system would be its influence on Non-Hindu religions. Today it also exists among Indian Christian and Muslim communities (Deshpande and Bapna 2008; What Is India's Caste System? 2017).

ENGINEERING HINDU RELIGIOUS IDENTITY

Dwijendra Narayan Jha (2014, 12–18) believes that some conceptual roots of Hindu religious identity could be traced to the 1872 Census when the British administration codified and ratified the religious and caste divisions prevalent in India. The acceptance and dissemination of the term 'Hindu' by nineteenth-century religious thinkers and reformists was another important factor in the initial construction phase of Hindu identity, Jha argues. All prominent social leaders of that period helped to shape Hindu religious identity based on Veda teachings and Aryan history, namely—Ram Mohan Roy (1772–1833), Dayananda Swaraswati (1824–83, who established Arya Samaj in 1875), Swami Vivekananda (1863–1902, who founded the Ramakrishna Mission in

1897), Rajnarayan Basu (1826–99), Chandranath Basu (1844–1910),[4] and Bankim Chandra Chattopadhaya (1838–94, author of the famous nationalist fiction Anandamath, 1882). Furthermore, Bal Gangadhar Tilak (1856–1920) who founded the Anti-Cow-Killing-Society in 1893, pushed the Vedic period from 1500 to 8000 BCE and proudly proclaimed that the 'common factor' in Indian society was the 'feeling of Hindutva'. Aurobindo Ghosh (1870–1950), who founded the Aurobindo Ashram in 1910, was a revolutionary turned Saint who believed that the Hindu religion was the eternal religion preserved by the Aryan race through centuries, and finally, Vinayak Damodar Savarkar (1883–1966, seven times President of the Hindu Mahasabha Party and founder of modern day Hindutva),[5] and Keshav Baliram Hedgewar (1889–1940, a Maharashtrian Brahmin of Tilakite association and founder of the Rāṣṭrīya Svayamsēvaka Saṅgha in 1925).

Even before the formation of the Rashtriya Swayamgsevak Sangha (RSS), the Hindi-speaking Marwari merchants of Calcutta established Gita Press in 1923 as a unit of Govinda Bhavan Karjalaya. The main objective of the society was "to promote and spread the principles of Hindu Religion amongst the general public." Over the years, the institution has made available more than 370 million copies of the Gita, Ramayana, Bhagvat, Durga Saptashati, Puranas, Upanishads, Bhakta-Gathas, and other character-building books in Sanskrit, Hindi, English, Gujarati, Tamil, Marathi, Bangla, Oriya, Telugu, Kannada, and other Indian regional languages. This massive Brahmanical literature has helped to shape 'Hinduness' among the common people of India.

But it should be noted that the membership to Gobind Bhawan Karyalaya, the trust that owns Gita Press, is open to any Sanatan Dharmi Hindu by caste Brahmin, Kshatriya, and Vishay, but not to Shudras, 'Untouchables' (Dalits), Adivasis (indigenous people), or anyone else. Gita Press also runs a Vedic school in Rajasthan that admits only children belonging to the Brahmin, Kshatriya, and Vishay castes. Sampath (2016), while quoting from Mukul's book (2015) on Gita Press, stressed that through different publications of Gita Press

[4]See the monograph Basu (1892), cf. Sen (2015).

[5]Savarkar ([1923] 1928) argues that Hindutva, which equates with Hinduness, rather than Hinduism, constituted Hindu identity. However, Hinduvta "defies all attempts at analysis [… it] is not a word but a history. Not only the spiritual or religious history of our people, but a history in full"; cf. Jha (2018).

the "Marwaris replaced the 'aristocracy and wealthy landlords' as religious patrons and changed 'the kshatriya-brahmin interface of Hindu
society' to a 'vaishya-brahmin interface' that eventually resulted in the
'Marwarization of Hinduism'" (Sampath 2016; cf. Mukul 2015).
Sampath concludes that "if kshatriya-brahmin hegemony characterized
the subcontinent's social order till the advent of British colonialism, then
bania-brahmin hegemony is equally a marker of contemporary India"
(Sampath 2016). Though both Gita Press and RSS were established with
the primary objective of spreading Hinduism, Nagpur based RSS was an
outcome of initiatives by Marathi political activists of western India. But
Gita Press was an initiative of Marwari merchants of Calcutta who made
their editorial office in Benares (Varanasi), one of the oldest cities of this
subcontinent, situated on the bank of holy river Ganges.

THE PROMOTION OF SANSKRIT SCRIPTS

To provide instructions in Indian affairs to British civil servants, the
British administration established Fort William College in Calcutta in the
early nineteenth century. Its courses included, various languages, such
as Tamil, Bengali, Marathi, Hindustani. As no suitable textual materials
existed for the vernacular, the college decided to develop its own textbooks. Although Hindustani (Khariboli) had a vibrant prose tradition, it
was essentially literary, and often Sufistic in nature. Hence it was considered quite unsuitable for administrators.

Four authors were engaged by the British government to write books
in Hindustani—in two different scripts: Persian-Arabic and Nagari. The
more formal Persian-Arabic words were replaced with Sanskrit synonyms or Sanskrit-based local words. Thus, the Hindi language (Khariboli
Hindustani in Sanskrit script), suitable for the British administration, was
manufactured at Fort William College, at Calcutta. The efforts of the
British government to popularize Khariboli Hindi were strengthened by
the Nagari-Hindi movement which had started in northern India in the
late 1860s.

Christopher King (1994) observed that Sanskritized Khariboli Hindi
went through a process of assimilation and differentiation to establish its supremacy among the languages of India. This form of Hindi
not only undermined the position of Braj Bhasha, a language spoken
in parts of present day Haryana, Rajasthan, Uttar Pradesh, and Madhya
Pradesh, but also marked it as inferior. Despite strong opposition, the

Indian Constituent Assembly decided in 1949 that Hindi in Devanagari (Sanskrit) script would be the official language of the Indian Union, and for fifteen years, English would also be used for all official purposes.

In 1956, the Indian states were established on the basis of regional languages spoken by the respective majorities, and in 1963, a three language formula was introduced to the nation. Accordingly, high school students must learn their state language (any of the twenty-two recognized languages spoken by the majority population of that state), Hindi, and English. In 1965, Hindi was made the official language of the nation, and English was given the status of an "associate official language" of the nation (Jayasundara 2014, 221). David Laitin (1989, 417) called India's language policy a 'game' between lords at the periphery and a 'ruler' at the center. Any ruler who wants to rationalize his state administration to reduce transaction costs and increase tax revenue prefers a single language with all lords proficient to take orders and send reports in that language only. According to Laitin, an equilibrium involves a "successful rationalization of state languages".

The Creation of the Indian National Congress

Interestingly, the initiative to form a political body for educated Indians, to achieve a greater share in government to create a platform for civic dialogue between them and the British Raj, came from a retired Civil Service officer, Allan Octavian Hume. In 1885 the first session of the Congress was held under the president-ship of a Bengali Brahmin, Woomesh Chandra Bonnerjee. Allan Hume became General Secretary. Seventy-two English-educated gentlemen, mostly lawyers and journalists who represented each province of India, participated in the first session. Hindu nationalist leader Bal Gangadhar Tilak joined the Congress in 1890 and became the most widely known Indian political leader. Mohandas Karamchand (Mahatma) Gandhi joined the Congress in 1920.

Like Tilak, Gandhi was a believer in the caste system though his followers later argued that "the best way to understand Gandhi's writings— where he defends and validates caste—is to see them as a part of his long-term strategy to combat caste" (Kolge 2017, 50). Recent research reveals (Sharma 2014; Kambon 2018), however, that Mahatma Gandhi was a British collaborator during World War I and encouraged Indian youths to join the British army. Moreover, he was allegedly a racist to the bone and despised black Africans!

A background check of General Secretary Allan Hume, reveals that he was deeply involved in the creation of a long thorny hedge along the Inland Customs Line (Gokhale 2018) to facilitate tax collection (mainly on salt) by the British government. In 1869 the hedge covered a distance of 2300 miles and ran from the Indus in the Punjab to the Mahanadi River in Odisha, cutting across the heart of India (Moxham 2001b). The areas to the right of the custom line are those regions of present India that are underdeveloped (Central, East, and northeastern India) compared to the Northwest and southern regions (left to the custom line). Roy Moxham (2001a) investigated the level of salt taxation between 1765 and 1878 and its effects on the retail price of salt relative to wages. He also explored the physiological necessity for salt and the peculiar nature of salt hunger, and the particular consequences of a high salt tax in times of famine. He observed that in the earlier period of British rule, especially under the Bengal presidency, the tax was much higher and the negative consequences on the life of the people were far greater.

Thus, with the Indian National Congress the British government had created a political institution by the end of nineteenth century that later would shoulder the responsibility of carrying the Indo-European colonial legacy. Two decades after the Congress was founded the British government decided to shift its capital from east India (Calcutta) to north India (Delhi)–the 'nation core' and ancient home of Indo-Aryan immigrants since 1500 BCE.

POST-EUROPEAN INDIA

After World War II most European colonies in Asia and Africa gained political independence, and the newly independent states, including India, opted for a democratic political system. However, emancipated from British rule the country became divided into two nations religious-wise. In 1947, the Hindu-dominated part formed India, and the Muslim-dominated areas, Pakistan. Hindus and Sikhs fled into India; Muslims crossed in the other direction into Pakistan causing over fifteen million refugees. The partition woes still haunt the life of the children of those refugees (Sreenivas 2017).

Decolonization is generally understood as a political process marking the end of European empires. Yet, decolonization implies a much more complicated experience for post-colonial nations like India. Old nationalisms are gradually questioned and new identities are formed—both geographically and socially. Though decolonization of India officially began in 1947, the transfer of power to the indigenous people has not been completed even after seven decades. One possible reason could be the biased structure of the national Constitution of 1950 itself. It has established internal states and made them dependent on a strong central government which is primarily ruled by people of Aryan ancestry.

The State Reorganization Act of 1956 rearranged the states on the basis of dominant languages spoken in the state, thus giving the advantage to Indo-Aryan tongues. At present, the Union of India consists of 28 states and 9 union territories (The Linguistic Reorganization of States 2015). According to a report 2018, "more than 19,500 languages or dialects are spoken in India as mother tongue [… and] there are 121 languages which are spoken by 10,000 or more people in India, which has a population of 121 crore" (More Than 19,500 Languages Spoken in India).[6]

Indian languages belong to at least four major language families: Indo-European (most of which belong to its sub-branch Indo-Aryan), Dravidian, Austro-Asiatic, and Sino-Tibetan. Almost one third of India's mother-tongues (574 languages) belonged to the Indo-Aryan family of languages spoken by 73.30% of Indians. The Dravidian languages, 153 in number, form the second major linguistic group of the country (24.47%). The languages belonging to the Austro-Asiatic family of languages, 65 in number (530 are recorded as unclassified languages) accounted for a total number of 6.19 million speakers and 0.73% of the total population of the country speaks the languages (226 in number) of the Tibeto-Burman subfamily. Of the hundreds of languages spoken in India, the Eighth Schedule to the Indian Constitution lists only 22 languages. Out of these, 15 belong to the Indo-European family, 3 are Dravidian languages, one belongs to the Austro Asian and 2 belong to the Indo-Tibetan language families. Thus, Indo-European cultural dominance, revived again during the mid-nineteenth century, is constitutionally established. And the country is thus called India as it was by the European colonial powers, yet in local literature this vast land mass of South Asia is often addressed as Bharat.

A cursory look at the demographic profile of the fifteen prime ministers India has had until 2018 gives an idea of the power distribution.

[6]https://www.ndtv.com/india-news/more-than-19-500-languages-spoken-as-mother-tongue-in-india-census-1876085 visited on July 23, 2019.

Eleven prime ministers originated in northern India, two in the West, and two in South India. Even after seven decades of independence, East and Northeast India have not had a single prime minister to date. Fourteen were Hindus, only one being a Sikh. Except for the present Prime Minister Narendra Modi, who belongs to the Shudra category, all Hindu prime ministers have belonged to the upper caste community.

As of January 2019, the Indian government has stipulated a constitutional amendment that grants a 10% reservation for 'economically disadvantaged' upper caste candidates in government jobs and educational institutions (Upper Caste Reservations 2019).[7] Though the traditional poverty line is drawn at 32 rupees per person per day, the eligibility criteria for taking advantage of the reservation, the earning limit has been raised to over 2000 rupees per day for upper-caste applicants. The aim is not to combat economic deprivation, but to extend privileges to 95% of the upper-caste population—historically representing oppressors, not victims (Aiyar 2019). Recent studies reveal that India's upper-caste households earned nearly 47% more than the national average annual household income, and the top 10% within these castes owned 60% of the wealth within the group in 2012 (Paliath 2019). The government of India has also decided to establish a Bhartiya Shiksha Board, the country's first national school board for Vedic education. Reportedly, the Board's main objectives are to standardize Vedic education. Like any school board, it will draft syllabi, conduct examinations, and issue certificates (Chopra 2019). Thus, the cultural construct of three-thousand-year-old Vedic knowledge, established for the expansion of Indo-Aryan descendants, is being reinvented.

In this context Vinayak Damodar Savarkar's views on Aryans are noteworthy. Like Tilak, he believed that Aryans had migrated into present day Punjab from where they spread to different parts of the subcontinent giving birth to a common race of Hindus by the mixing of Aryan and non-Aryans. They created new 'colonies' on their way "until the day Rāma made his triumphant entry into Ceylon, the day which was 'the real birthday of the Hindu people'" (Jha 2014, 4). Unfortunately, this colonial expansion of the Hindutva from its North and West Indian base to other parts of the subcontinent continues.

The notion of Hinduism as a religion was a colonial construct, and it remains unchallenged. The rulers of post-independent India have skillfully

[7] https://indianexpress.com/article/india/cabinet-approves-10-quota-for-upper-castes-5526839 visited on July 24, 2019.

repositioned Brahmanism as a political philosophy. There is very little difference between the Indian National Congress, which has ruled India for about six decades, and the current ruling Bharatiya Janata Party—the political face of the RSS and other right-wing Hindu groups. Noted economist Meghnad Desai (2016) has rightly observed that bogus historical constructs get accepted and unchallenged as "patronage to academia [and] can be used to commission histories to buttress the official line."

FORMS OF INTERNAL COLONIALISM IN NEOCOLONIAL INDIA

Colonialism, particularly its internal and regional variants, parallels the 'theory of dependency' that was developed after World War II (Foster 2007). Accordingly, the 'infrastructure of dependency', which was internal to the subordinate country, included industrial organization, patterns of urbanization, and social classes. The two common examples of 'infrastructure dependency' are the patterns of dependent industrialization and the formation of clientele social classes.

The characteristics of the former included foreign domination of dynamic sectors of industry, a competitive advantage of foreign monopolistic corporations over local firms, and the introduction of advanced capital-intensive technology with tacit acceptance of resulting unemployment. The clientele classes included the industrial bourgeoisie, the state bureaucracy, and the middle class whose positions were tied to foreign interests. Thus, the 'infrastructure of dependency' represents a functional equivalent of a formal colonial apparatus, though the system rests on international capitalist institutions, rather than on particular colonial empires (Dey 2015).

In this chapter we aimed to explore the forms of colonialism that still exist in India resulting in the hypothesis that India exhibits internal and regional colonialism. The social structure of the caste system, which the in-migrating Aryans had established on the Indian subcontinent thousands of years ago, still rules the society creating 'internal colonies' through the application of a racial philosophy (Brahmanism), the cultural hegemony of linguistics supremacy, and Vedic knowledge. Historical evidence suggests that the non-Aryan groups of India's East, Northeast, Center, and South, had resisted Aryan expansion into their territory. When the European colonial powers withdrew from India, the Aryan rulers of the modern North and West Indian states have subjugated East, Northeast, and Central India to exploit the natural and human resources of these 'internal colonies'. Only the South Indian states have success-fully resisted the Aryan expansion to a large extent.

'Internal colonialism' is a broadly defined term that captures the com-plexities of structural, political, and economic inequalities between regions within a nation-state. It also depicts international exploitation of distinct cultural groups. This term refers to the subordination of an ethno-racial group "in its own homeland within the boundaries of a larger state dom-inated by a different people" (Chávez 2011, 786; cf. Dey 2015). There is a basic conceptual difference between 'internal' and 'regional' colonialism, where a macroregion is economically underdeveloped and its population oppressed relative to a country's core, but the people of both regions are of the same ethno-racial stock (Stone 1979, 255). In India 'internal' colo-nialism manifested itself in three different forms:

- Subordination of ethno-racial and non-Hindu religious groups, namely indigenous people (mostly descendants of the Harappa, AASI. Tibeto-Burman and Austro-Asiatic people),[8] Dalit (outcastes or untouchables, sweepers, latrine cleaners), and Muslims (a size-able portion of whom, especially in Eastern India, are converted lower caste Hindus)[9] by descendants of Ancestral North Indians (ANI);
- Subordination of regions not dominated by the descendants of ANI of the North and West Indian states;
- Subordination of rural populations by the urban elites where Anglicized India exploits rural Bharat.

It should be stated that the complexity of India's society, with its long history of colonial dominance, does not allow for an impermeable divi-sion between internal and regional colonialism. There are overlaps and grey areas which challenge any conventional definition. Moreover, 'regional colonialism' in India should not be confused with 'political regionalism' as the Anglicized urban elites act as 'clientele classes' of the colonial state, their English ways making them as ethnically distinct and dominant.

---

[8] For a detailed discussion see Zhang et al. (2015).

[9] H. Beverley, Census Commissioner of Bengal for the 1871–72 Census, stated that the Muslims of Bengal were converted low caste Hindus, see Hobson (n.d.).

Conclusion

Common wisdom has it that the Mughal Empire was the first power to expand into adjacent territories through continental colonialism and dominate distinct peoples in the Indian subcontinent, followed later by Portuguese and British overseas colonialism. But new genetic studies (Narasimhan et al. 2018) reveal that the origin of expansion in this subcontinent started much earlier than the Mughal invasions.

Around the first millennium BCE, Vedic literature and religious texts created a new religion, Brahmanism, relying on the rites performed by a priestly class—the Brahmans. As Buddhism, Islamic rule, and European colonialism acted as deterrents to further Brahmanical expansion into peripheral regions, Brahmanism mostly remained confined to the elites of urban centers. However, during the nineteenth and early twentieth centuries, Hindu religious identity was rebuilt on Vedic philosophy and the teachings of Manusmriti with the tacit support of the British administration. The Hindu revival developed around the 'two nation theory' that pushed the Muslims to a separate land of their own. Thus, the nation was divided in 1947, and India was granted Dominion status in the British Commonwealth. After the creation of a separate nation for the Muslims in Pakistan and the simultaneous exit of British colonial power from India, the descendants of the Indo-Aryan immigrants have taken the opportunity to rule the subcontinent again. Applying the 'infrastructure of dependency' model, the functional equivalent of formal colonialism, the new rulers treated non-Aryan peoples and peripheral regions as 'internal colonies' of a Brahmanical state.

Like most colonial powers, Indo-Aryans used their own language, Sanskrit, to establish their dominance over the colonized. In the nineteenth century, these ancient colonizers in collaboration with their colonial superiors from Europe, simplifying the Sanskrit grammar created a Sanskrit script (Devanagari) based on Hindi as the administrative language. Rulers of modern, post-1947 India have spent billions to propagate Hindi at the expense of hundreds of local, genuine languages. Recently, the state has sponsored massive projects to revive and standardize ancient Vedic texts and the Sanskrit language—the two major cultural tools of Aryan colonialism. However, Brahmanical domination is increasingly questioned in India, and new identities, both geographical and social, are appearing across the country leading to an increase in conflict and a growing resistance to the Indo-Aryan colonial hegemony.

References

Aiyar, Swaminathan Anklesaria. 2019. "New Quota Will Deepen Casteism, Not Abolish It." *The Times of India*, January 13. https://timesofindia.indiatimes.com/blogs/Swaminomics/new-quota-will-deepen-casteism-not-abolish-it. Accessed February 21, 2019.

Allchin, Bridget, and Raymond Allchin. 1982. *The Rise of Civilization in India and Pakistan*. Cambridge: Cambridge University Press.

Anthony, David W. 2007. *The Horse, the Wheel, and Language: How Bronze-Age Riders From the Eurasian Steppes Shaped the Modern World*. Princeton, NJ: Princeton University Press.

Basham, Arthur Llewellyn. 1989. *The Origins and Development of Classical Hinduism*. New York: Oxford University Press.

Basu, Chandranath. 1892. *Hindutva bā hindur prakṛtaitihās* [Hindutva: An Authentic History of Hinduism]. Kalikātā: Gurudās Caṭṭopādhyāẏ.

Chakraborty, Rakhi. 2014. "The Bengal Famine: How the British Engineered the Worst Genocide in Human History for Profit." YourStory Media Pvt. Ltd., August 15. https://yourstory.com/2014/08/bengal-famine-genocide. Accessed February 20, 2019.

Chávez, John R. 2011. "Aliens in Their Native Lands: The Persistence of Internal Colonial Theory." *Journal of World History* 22(4): 785–809.

Chopra, Ritika. 2019. "To Blend Vedic and Modern Studies, HRD Body Clears Bharatiya Shiksha Board." *The Indian Express*, January 12. https://indianexpress.com/article/education/to-blend-vedic-and-modern-studies-hrd-body-clears-bharatiya-shiksha-board. Accessed February 21, 2019.

Coningham, Robin, and Ruth Young. 2015. *The Archaeology of South Asia: From the Indus to Asoka, c. 6500 BCE–200 CE*. Cambridge: Cambridge University Press.

Daniyal, Shoaib. 2015. "Fact Check: India Wasn't the First Place Sanskrit Was Recorded—It Was Syria." Scroll.in, June 30. https://scroll.in/article/737715/fact-check-india-wasnt-the-first-place-sanskrit-was-recorded-it-was-syria. Accessed February 19, 2019.

Desai, Meghnad. 2016. "Hindu Nationalist History That Calls Muslims 'Invaders' and Aryans 'Our Own' Is Bogus." Quartz Media, March 21. https://qz.com/india/643676/hindu-nationalist-history-that-calls-muslims-invaders-and-aryans-our-own-is-bogus. Accessed February 19, 2019.

Deshpande, Satish, and Geetika Bapna. 2008. "Dalits in the Muslim and Christian Communities: A Status Report on Current Social Scientific Knowledge, Prepared for the National Commission for Minorities, Government of India." January 17. Department of Sociology, University of Delhi. http://ncm.nic.in/pdf/report%20dalit%20reservation.pdf. Accessed February 20, 2019.

Dey, Dipankar. 2015. "Internal Colonialism." In *The Encyclopedia of Political Thought*, vol. IV, edited by Michael T. Gibbons, 1846–48. Chichester: Wiley-Blackwell.

Foltz, Richard. 1998. *Mughal India and Central Asia*. Karachi: Oxford University Press.

Foster, John Bellamy. 2007. "The Imperialist World System: Paul Baran's Political Economy of Growth After Fifty Years." *Monthly Review* 59(1), May 1. https://monthlyreview.org/2007/05/01/the-imperialist-world-system. Accessed February 21, 2019.

Gokhale, Aneesh. 2018. "Why British Built the Great Hedge of India." *DNAIndia*, August 12. https://www.dnaindia.com/analysis/column-why-british-built-the-great-hedge-of-india-2648602. Accessed February 21, 2019.

Heine-Geldern, Robert. 1956. "The Coming of the Aryans and the End of the Harappa Civilization." *Man* 56(151): 136–40.

Hobson, Kevin. (n.d.). "Britain and the Indian Caste System: Ethnographic Mapping and the Construction of the British Census in India." The British Empire. https://www.britishempire.co.uk/article/castesystem.htm. Accessed February 20, 2019.

Jayasundara, Niruba Sarath. 2014. "The Development of Language Education Policy: An Indian Perspective; A View from Tamil Nadu." *International Journal of Science and Research Publications* 4(11): 220–23.

Jha, Dwijendra Narayan. 2014. *Rethinking Hindu Identity*. London: Routledge.

Jha, Dwijendra Narayan. 2018. "Monumental Absence: The Destruction of Ancient Buddhist Sites." *The Caravan Magazine*, June 1. https://caravan-magazine.in/reviews-and-essays/dn-jha-destruction-buddhist-sites. Accessed February 19, 2019.

Joseph, Tony. 2018a. "How Ancient DNA May Rewrite Prehistory in India." BBC News, December 30. https://www.bbc.com/news/world-asia-india-46616574. Accessed February 19, 2019.

Joseph, Tony. 2018b. *Early Indians: The Story of Our Ancestors and Where We Came From*. New Delhi: Juggernaut.

Kambon, Ọbádélé. 2018. "Ram Guha Is Wrong. Gandhi Went from a Racist Young Man to a Racist Middle-aged Man." ThePrint, December 24. https://theprint.in/opinion/ramachandra-guha-is-wrong-a-middle-aged-gandhi-was-racist-and-no-mahatma/168222. Accessed February 21, 2019.

King, Christopher Rolland. 1994. *One Language, Two Scripts: The Hindi Movement in Nineteenth Century North India*. New Delhi: Oxford University Press.

Kinra, Rajeev. 2015. *Writing Self, Writing Empire: Chandar Bhan Brahman and the Cultural World of the Indo-Persian State Secretary*. Oakland, CA: University of California Press.

Kolge, Nishikant. 2017. "Was Gandhi a 'Champion of the Caste System'? Reflections on His Practices." *Economic and Political Weekly* 52(13): 42–50.

Kumar, Anu. 2016. "The Brahman in the Mughal Court." The Wire, November 15. https://thewire.in/books/the-brahman-in-the-mughal-court. Accessed February 19, 2019.

Laitin, David D. 1989. "Language Policy and Political Strategy in India." *Policy Science* 22(3–4): 415–36.

Madaan, Neha. 2019. "In a First, Ancient Couple Found in Harappan Grave." *Times of India*, January 9. https://timesofindia.indiatimes.com/city/pune/in-first-such-finding-couples-grave-excavated-at-harappan-site/articleshow/67445140.cms. Accessed February 19, 2019.

Mark, Joshua J. 2018. "The Hittites." Ancient History Encyclopedia, May 1. https://www.ancient.eu/Hittite. Accessed February 19, 2019.

Mohan, Jyoti. 2016. "The Glory of Ancient India Stems from Her Aryan Blood: French Anthropologists 'Construct' the Racial History of India for the World." *Modern Asian Studies* 50(5): 1576–1618.

"More Than 19,500 Languages Spoken in India: Census." 2018. NDTV, July 1. https://www.ndtv.com/india-news/more-than-19–500-languages-spoken-as-mother-tongue-in-india-census-1876085. Accessed February 21, 2019.

Moxham, Roy. 2001a. "Salt Starvation in British India." *The Economic and Political Weekly* 36(25): 2270–2273.

Moxham, Roy. 2001b. *The Great Hedge of India*. London: Constable.

Mukherjee, Janam. [2011] 2015. *Hungry Bengal: War Famine and the End of Empire*. Oxford: Oxford University Press.

Mukherjee, Madhusree. 2010. *Churchill's Secret War: The British Empire and the Ravaging of India During World War II*. New York: Basic Books.

Mukul, Akshaya. 2015. *Gita Press and the Making of Hindu India*. Noida, UP: Harper Collins Publishers India.

Narasimhan, Vagheesh M., Nick Patterson, Priya Moorjani, Iosif Lazaridis, Mark Lipson, Swapan Mallick, Nadin Rohland, et al. 2018. "The Genomic Formation of South and Central Asia." bioRxiv, March 31. https://www.biorxiv.org/content/10.1101/292581v1. Accessed February 19, 2019.

Obeysekere, Mirando. 2013. *Ravana, King of Lanka*. Sri Lanka: Vijitha Yapa Publications.

Olivelle, Patrick. 2005. *Manu's Code of Law: A Critical Edition and Translation of the Mānava-Dharmaśāstra*. Oxford: Oxford University Press.

Paliath, Shreehari. 2019. "Income Inequality Within Castes: Top 10% Among Forward Castes Own 60% Wealth." BloombergQuint, January 14. https://www.bloombergquint.com/global-economics/income-inequality-within-castes-top-10-among-forward-castes-own-60-wealth#gs.1wRN7L7H. Accessed February 21, 2019.

PTI. 2016. "Sanskrit Texts Offered Way to Mughals to Rule India." *DNA India*, April 7. https://www.dnaindia.com/india/report-sanskrit-texts-offered-way-to-mughals-to-rule-india-book-2199311. Accessed February 19, 2019.
"Ravana Was a Great Ruler, Says a New Book." News18, July 15, 2013. https://www.news18.com/news/books/ravana-was-a-great-ruler-says-a-new-book-623855.html. Accessed February 19, 2019.
Richards, John F. 1995. *The Mughal Empire*. Cambridge: Cambridge University Press.
Sampath, G. 2016. "Caste and the Battle for Secularism." *The Hindu*, October 18. https://www.thehindu.com/opinion/lead/Caste-and-the-battle-for-secularism/article10363424.ece. Accessed February 20, 2019.
Savarkar, Vinayak Damodar. [1923] 1928. *Hindutva: Who Is a Hindu*. Bombay: Veer Savarkar Prakashan.
Sen, Amartya. 1981. *Poverty and Famines: An Essay on Entitlement and Deprivation*. Oxford: Clarendon Press.
Sen, Amiya P. 2015. *"Hinduism" and the Problem of Self-Actualization in the Colonial Era: Critical Reflections* (South Asia Institute Papers 1), edited by the South Asia Institute. Heidelberg: Heidelberg University.
Sharma, Manimugdha S. 2014. "Meet Sergeant Major Mohandas Karamchand Gandhi." *The Times of India*, October 2. https://timesofindia.indiatimes.com/india/Meet-Sergeant-Major-Mohandas-Karamchand-Gandhi/articleshow/44124189.cms. Accessed February 21, 2019.
Sreenivas, Mytheli. 2017. "December 2017: India–Pakistan Partition." Origins: Current Events in Historical Perspective. http://origins.osu.edu/milestones/december-2017-india-pakistan-partition. Accessed February 21, 2019.
Sreevatsan, Ajai. 2018. "British Raj Siphoned Out $45 Trillion from India: Utsa Patnaik." *LiveMint*, November 21. https://www.livemint.com/Companies/HNZA71LNVNNVXQ1eaIKu6M/British-Raj-siphoned-out-45-trillion-from-India-Utsa-Patna.html. Accessed February 20, 2019.
Srikantan, Geetanjali. 2014. "Towards New Conceptual Approaches in Legal History: Rethinking 'Hindu Law' Through Weber's Sociology of Religion." In *Entanglements in Legal History: Conceptual Approaches, Global Perspectives on Legal History*, edited by Thomas Duve, 101–28. Frankfurt am Main: Max Planck Institute for European Legal History.
Stone, John. 1979. "Introduction: Internal Colonialism in Comparative Perspective." *Ethnic and Racial Studies* 2(3): 255–59.
Tauger, Mark B., and Amartya Sen. 2011. "The Bengal Famine." *The New York Review of Books* 58(8). https://www.nybooks.com/articles/2011/05/12/bengal-famine. Accessed February 20, 2019.
"The Linguistic Reorganization of States." 2015. SelfStudyHistory.com, January 30. https://selfstudyhistory.com/2015/01/30/the-linguistic-reorganisation-of-states. Accessed February 21, 2019.

Truschke, Audrey. 2016. *Culture of Encounters: Sanskrit at the Mughal Court.* New York: Colombia University Press.

UNESCO World Heritage Centre. 1992–2019. "Archaeological Site of Nalanda Mahavihara at Nalanda, Bihar." https://whc.unesco.org/en/list/1502. Accessed February 19, 2019.

"Upper Caste Reservations: President Ram Nath Kovind Signs Bill Into Law." 2019. Scroll.in, January 12. https://scroll.in/latest/909224/upper-caste-reservations-president-ram-nath-kovind-signs-bill-into-law. Accessed February 21, 2019.

Venkataramakrishnan, Rohan. 2018. "Who Was Here First? A New Study Explains the Origins of Ancient Indians." Quartz Media, April 3. https://qz.com/india/1243436/aryan-migration-scientists-use-dna-to-explain-origins-of-ancient-indians. Accessed February 19, 2019.

Violatti, Cristian. 2018. "The Vedas." Ancient History Encyclopedia, May 8. https://www.ancient.eu/The_Vedas. Accessed February 19, 2019.

Welch, James. 2011. "The British Raj and India: British Colonial Influence: 1612–1948." Researchgate, September 2011. https://www.researchgate.net/publication/272383606_The_British_Raj_and_India_British_Colonial_Influence_1612_-_1948. Accessed February 19, 2019.

"What Is India's Caste System?". 2017. BBC News, July 20. https://www.bbc.com/news/world-asia-india-35650616. Accessed February 20, 2019.

Wright, Rita P. 2009. *The Ancient Indus: Urbanism, Economy and Society.* Part of Case Studies in Early Societies. Cambridge: Cambridge University Press.

Zhang, Xiaoming, Shiyu Liao, Xuebin Qi, Jiewei Liu, Jatupol Kampuansai, Hui Zhang, Zhaohui Yang et al. 2015. "Y-Chromosome Diversity Suggests Southern Origin and Paleolithic Backwave Migration of Austro-Asiatic Speakers from Eastern Asia to the Indian Subcontinent." *Scientific Reports* 5(15486), October 20. https://www.nature.com/articles/srep15486. Accessed February 25, 2019.

CHAPTER 11

Patterns of Domination and State Expansion in Early Colonial and Revolutionary Mexico

Ute Schüren

INTRODUCTION

This chapter compares the responses of the indigenous Maya-speaking population on the Yucatán peninsula in southeastern Mexico to colonial and postcolonial state attempts to extend its domination into the local sphere. After the Spanish conquest in the sixteenth century a large part of the native population was economically and culturally marginalized. This did not end after independence in the early nineteenth century nor during the oligarchical rule that followed. Even the Mexican Revolution (1910–40) brought no fundamental change in this regard, at least in the opinion of some scholars. Thus, Yucatán is an interesting case for the discussion of internal colonialism. Alicia Barabas, for example, explicitly categorizes Yucatán as a typical example of internal colonialism in the late 1970s, arguing that "privileged positions were distributed according to skin color, physical traits, and culture" as in colonial times (1979, 106).

U. Schüren (✉)
Department of History, University of Münster, Münster, Germany
e-mail: schueren@online.de

© The Author(s) 2019
D. Schorkowitz et al. (eds.), *Shifting Forms of Continental Colonialism*,
https://doi.org/10.1007/978-981-13-9817-9_11

The forms and means of state expansion are closely linked to the type of government involved (strong, weak, autocratic, democratic, dictatorial, or other), its ideological orientation (liberal, socialist, conservative, or progressive), its forms of rule (direct, indirect, oppressive, or consensual), and its agents (local power brokers, bureaucrats, police officers, teachers, clerics, or cultural promoters). In colonial times the state was feudal, partly absolutist, and self-defined as Catholic. Spanish rule rested upon the oppression and segregation of the indigenous majority. In the first half of the twentieth century, in contrast, the Mexican state was autocratic and secular. During the presidency of Lázaro Cárdenas (1934–40), the government aimed at integrating the rural population into the revolutionary party and the Mexican nation. In marginal regions such as Yucatán, where semi-feudal structures had persisted and the landholding oligarchy was still powerful, peasants and Indians were envisaged as the local bases of the revolutionary project, which included educational programs, infrastructure projects, agrarian reform, and political organization.[1]

In view of their obvious differences, one might consider the state an oppressor in the first period and a liberator in the second. However, this was not generally the case. As will be shown, perceptions of the state and its agents varied considerably within the local population in both periods. Before discussing the diversity of responses to colonial rule and the Mexican Revolution, however, I will briefly address some limitations and problems related to well-established definitions of colonialism and internal colonialism that hinder an adequate analysis of state expansion into peripheral regions. By proposing a combined structural and agency approach I hope to stimulate the debate on the concept of internal colonialism in postcolonial societies. After a brief geographic and historical introduction to the Yucatán peninsula, I will look at early colonial and postcolonial state expansion into this region from three perspectives—its institutions and forms; ideology and cultural change; and responses from the indigenous, rural population.

---

[1] In the context of the Mexican Revolution the term 'agrarian reform' (without 's') is generally used being a set expression, although there were many of them indeed.

COLONIALISM, INTERNAL COLONIALISM, AND THE QUESTION OF AGENCY

Colonialism and internal colonialism denote the existence of socioeconomic and political structures characterized by the exploitation of a marginalized population in peripheral regions by a hegemonic center or core region. Formal colonialism is often defined as rule by outsiders or foreigners on behalf of external interests and as an ideology of the colonizers' cultural superiority expressed for instance in the notion of civilization (Osterhammel [1995] 2001, 21). In despising the culture of the colonized, the colonial elite legitimizes its privileged status and the economic exploitation of the subjected population or the appropriation of the land. While in formal colonialism a distant mother country (Spain for Hispanic America), which is external to the colony, pursues its interests, internal colonialism is a similar relationship within the territory of a state, such as the Mexican republic after independence in 1821.

The internal colonizers are identified with the dominant or privileged population of the core region or with people assumed to originate from the former colonial masters, such as the *creoles* or *ladinos* in Latin America. Populations in peripheral regions or indigenous people assumed to be the offspring of the conquered population are considered the colonized. As the European colonizers did before, state agents or economic power holders emphasize cultural distinction and superiority. They promote ideologies that discriminate against the marginalized culture and population and justify the political hegemony of the core and the economic subjection of the periphery. Hechter characterizes the relationship between both poles as a 'cultural division of labor' ([1975] 1999, 30). The dominant center may be political or commercial, such as Mexico City, but also a regional capital or a rural town characterized by the exploitation of rural indigenous populations by *ladino* merchants and profiteers "exercising a monopoly over Indian commerce and credit" (González-Casanova 1965, 34). In contrast to colonial times, the center is not imagined as representing a minority in the official discourse (such as the Spanish conquerors and colonists) but as the civilized majority of the nation.[2] This image of a dominant modern mass culture increases the pressure on the marginalized populations for cultural change.

---

[2] This holds true at least for the twentieth and twenty-first centuries; in the nineteenth century the elite still perceived itself as a civilized minority. See Gabbert (2015).

As in colonial times, diverse forms of discrimination remain prominent such as racist categorizations, the disdain of indigenous languages, dress or customs, unequal rights and differential treatment of people by government institutions. In addition, so-called development projects, fostering economic enhancement, often refer to the culture of the center, its status, power, or benevolence. Thus, the building of infrastructure is not represented as the state's duty but as a paternal measure to foster the integration of a backward people. The latter's low living standard, in turn, is typically explained by cultural differences (González-Casanova 1965, 35).

To summarize, internal colonialism is a concept that offers a top-down structural perspective and is often used when describing unequal relationships between different sectors of independent countries or explaining the persistence of underdeveloped, backward zones in industrial societies. The concept is inspired by dependency theory prominent in the social sciences and development studies especially in the 1960s and 1970s.[3] In Latin America it has been generally applied to explain the relationship between rural villages (societies, regions) and the non-indigenous power holders of the center, or between the underdeveloped and culturally distinct indigenous people and the national majority. It refers to a particular type of rule different from other forms of domination by its combination of racism, cultural discrimination, social and political marginalization, and economic exploitation (see also Hind 1984, 548). The multiple unequal relationships characteristic of internal colonialism are explained by the *longue durée* of colonial deep structures still operative in world views, politics, and economy.[4]

The concept of internal colonialism allows us to link existing structures of power and inequality to past experiences. It is particularly valuable when pointing to the historical conditions and structural constraints of a certain category of people, the Indians in Latin America, whose room for maneuver has been confined by negative ascriptions, economic exploitation, and political exclusion since colonial times. The unequal

---

[3] See, for example, Love (1989) for a brief discussion of the historical development of the internal colonialism concept. The dependency-concept was developed by André Gunder Frank, Fernando Henrique Cardoso, Enzo Faletto and others as a critical answer to modernization theory. For a re-evaluation, see Heller et al. (2009).

[4] For a recent debate on colonial legacies in Latin America see Adelman (1999) and Patch (1999).

economic relationship is often based on the depredation of natural resources or the production of agricultural commodities for exportation by profiting from cheap labor. Racism, the physical depreciation of people, the highlighting of cultural differences, and class ascription underpin the exploitation of workers.

However, the structural approach to colonialism and internal colonialism is also problematic since it establishes a dichotomous relationship between colonizers and colonized, or center and periphery as the main interpretative frame to understand society, economy, and politics. Additionally, internal colonialism remains a fuzzy concept posing substantial analytical problems. Like the more recent notion of the 'coloniality of power' (Quijano 2000), which owes much to the internal colonialism debate of past decades, the concept is politically charged. The essential positions of 'colonizers' and the 'colonized' are only loosely defined. While internal colonialism can partly coincide with class or rural–urban relations, or those between more or less industrialized regions, it can also cut across class as is argued in the introduction by Dittmar Schorkowitz. The colonial situation for a colonized elite may be different from a colonized peasantry although both are objects of rule and exploitation by the colonizer.[5]

Furthermore, the forms of relationships categorized as colonial seem to be quite varied.[6] Ann Stoler, for example, has warned us not to take "colonialism and its European agents as an abstract force, as a structure imposed on local practice" and points out that the "terms *colonial state, colonial policy, foreign capital,* and the *white enclave* are often used interchangeably, as if they captured one and the same thing. While such a treatment encourages certain lines of novel enquiry, it closes off others" (1992, 320). The concepts of colonialism and internal colonialism imply a package of criteria and implications. There is no clear hierarchy between the main indicators of internal colonialism, such as racism, cultural discrimination, economic exploitation, or political exclusion. In fact, these features vary considerably in their presence, intensity, and

---

[5] See also Gledhill (1988, 313): "The 'native élite' which mediated relations between Indian and Spanish sectors, with its control of resources, linguistic fluency in the colonialists' language, adoption of Hispanic cultural styles, and sometimes even inter-marriage with Spaniards, clearly differed in some orientation from the poorer strata in its communities."

[6] Pablo González-Casanova lists almost every kind of negative, discriminatory relationship as typical for internal colonialism (1965, 36–37).

structural importance between empirical cases and different periods. The persistence of one element, such as racism, often seems to be sufficient to categorize a relationship as colonial. Racism, discrimination, and economic exploitation, however, can be found even within the lower classes and colonized groups. In addition, no clear criteria for distinguishing varying degrees of 'coloniality' are provided. How then can we detect successful processes of decolonization, or political and social integration? The widespread practice in Latin America to class all those who speak an indigenous language as Indians may be misleading because this categorization by outsiders and the self-identification by group members need not necessarily coincide. Indeed it may be considered as discrimination. Beyond that, ascriptions of inferiority have been internalized and the targeted populations often perceive themselves as 'second-class citizens' as Aurora Pérez Jiménez puts it (2015, 212–13).

The structural approach has been quite influential analyzing the impact of colonialism on indigenous lives. However, since the collectives categorized as the colonized or the colonizers were rather heterogeneous in their interests and experiences as were their responses to the colonial situation, the structural approach is inadequate to grasp the dynamics of change, negotiation, and conflict resulting from state intervention on the ground. Studies often disregard the social actors and social relations at the local level and depict the indigenous populations as mere victims of Spanish colonialism, apathetic, suffering, deprived of active roles in society. This approach has been criticized since the 1980s (cf. Stoler 1992, 319–23) by students who focus on indigenous agency understood as the capacity of individuals to act independently and to make their own free choices. Yet, many of these interpretations of colonial rule tend to overdraw their argument suggesting that black is white. Some even discard the structural constraints of the colonial relationship and impute the indigenous population with an almost unrestricted agency. Everyday forms of resistance and autonomy are often seen as self-evident.[7]

Hence and in spite of their diverging interpretations, the structural and the agency perspective share a common problem. They misconceive the actors as parts of a dual society: colonizer vs. colonized, non-Indian vs. Indian, Indians vs. the state while ignoring the internal differentiation and diversity of responses. This prevents us from understanding the

---

[7]For the recent debate on indigenous agency, see Cope (2010), for a critical discussion regarding the supposedly omnipresent resistance among the natives, see Adorno (1993).

various forms of agency, interaction, and structural constraints in the colonial and postcolonial periods. The relationships between indigenous rulers and the Spanish colonial agents, for example, turned out to be manifold, and ranged from friendship to violence, and from cooperation to resistance. Since indirect rule was a major feature of European colonialism, on which pole, for example, should rich indigenous leaders profiting from colonial empowerment be placed?

In the social sciences the debate about the relation between structure and agency is legion. Anthony Giddens in his 'Theory of Structuration' (1984a) and others have discussed the interrelation between social structure and social action. The individual reproduces existing social institutions, and at the same time influences the current structure (understood by him as a system of norms) through action. Through their actions, people influence the institutional conditions of others. Since social behavior depends on others, interaction should be a prominent subject of inquiry. All societies possess a repertoire of different lifestyles, cultural forms, perceptions, and rationalities, which members use in their search for order and meaning, and in whose maintenance or change they themselves are involved, consciously or unconsciously. Individually applied strategies and cultural perceptions are selected from available (verbal and non-verbal) discourses shared to some extent by other contemporary and contemporary actors (Long 1990, 6–10; 1993, 223–25; Giddens 1984a, b). This implies the need for a historical analysis of socioeconomic action and strategies. The scope for action is limited in many ways. But in this context actors are able to choose among different alternatives and try something new (Giddens 1984a, 16–28; 1984b, 146–57, 194, 198; Long 1993, 225–26, 231–32). Therefore, both perspectives—a structural approach and an agency approach—should be combined in order to gain a deeper understanding of colonial and postcolonial processes. Beyond the identification of existing structures, such as those defining colonialism or internal colonialism, our analysis must identify perceptions, strategies, and rationalities of the actors, their origin, their effectiveness, and structural consequences. In the following, I intend to combine a structural approach with the meso- and micro-perspective of practices and perceptions in the regional and local spheres.

The Yucatán Peninsula: A Historical Sketch

The Yucatán peninsula extends over a large area in southeastern Mexico, northern Guatemala, and Belize. It rests in the tropics far away from the central Mexican highlands, the core area of New Spain and Mexico, where the former colonial and modern capital Mexico City lies. Today the Mexican part of the Yucatán peninsula, on which I will focus my discussion, is politically divided into the states of Campeche, Yucatán, and Quintana Roo.

The conquest of Yucatán began in 1527 six years after the Spaniards vanquished the Aztec empire. The conquest was an arduous enterprise lasting twenty years until 1547. The area was divided into several provinces whose internal political organization varied.[8] Thus, several independent polities had to be conquered. Maya resistance declined as a result of military, political, and economic crises, such as the breakdown of trade relations, colonial exploitation, famines, and the ongoing depletion of the indigenous population. Due to the extremely violent campaigns and imported epidemic diseases, the death toll among the indigenous population was very high. According to reliable estimates, the population decline ranged between 50 and 90% from 1511 to 1550 (Gerhard 1979, 23–30; see also Farriss 1984, 57–67). The Spaniards finally succeeded thanks to the establishment of strategic alliances with leading Maya families, like the Pech and Xiu ruling lineages, by granting certain privileges and status symbols, such as Spanish clothing and other gifts. Thus, the Spanish strategy of subduing native rulers rested to a large degree upon exploiting political antagonism and status differences among the Indians (Gabbert 1995, 282–84; Restall 1998). This principle of strategic alliance building in the context of regional and local conflict had a long history in Mesoamerica and had been of crucial importance for the expansion of pre-Columbian states, such as those of the Aztec and Maya (Gunsenheimer and Schüren 2016, 282–315, 417–59).

The native inhabitants of the American colonies were defined as *indios* (Indians), a special social category (*casta*) to which one belonged by birth. Spanish law distinguished Indians in quasi-racial terms from other

---

[8]According to Sergio Quezada (1993, 19–58) the provinces can be understood as spheres of influence of prominent noble lineages with their followers and dependent populations instead of entities with fixed political or territorial borders.

groups in the colony (such as Spaniards, Blacks, *mestizos*—people of mixed blood). They were subject to specific laws and decrees. To close a legally binding contract, they needed the consent of the colonial authorities. Regarded as minors and wards of the Crown, most of them were forbidden to bear arms, ride horses, or dress like Spaniards. However, the government acknowledged estates inside the indigenous society with different rights and obligations; the authorities therefore treated the indigenous commoners (*macehualob*) and nobility (*almehenob*) differently. Many leaders were recognized and formally put into office by the Spaniards. They became *caciques* (*batabob*) of the towns their families had controlled before the arrival of the Europeans. This status not only derived from an outstanding lineage, but also from proximity to important ancestors as divine mediators.

Compared to other regions of Mexico, Yucatán was not very attractive for European colonists due to its hot and moist climate, the dense scrub and tropical forest, and the lack of gold and silver deposits. The colonists established their main settlements in the cities of Mérida, Campeche, and Valladolid in the northern, western, and eastern parts of the peninsula where a significant indigenous population could be exploited. However, due to the flight of many Indians to the uncontrolled regions in the south and east, Spanish colonial domination remained partial and precarious, especially in the regions around the open colonial frontier. Agricultural products such as corn, cotton, honey, wax, salt, and cattle, and the commerce in cotton cloth fabricated by women were the mainstay of Yucatán's economy. For a long time, labor and not land was the scarce resource. After independence in the nineteenth century, Yucatán became an important region for the export to the national and world markets of primary agricultural products, such as henequen (*Agave fourcroydes*), sugar, corn, cattle, and forest products (mahogany, cedar, and *chicle*[9]). Especially in northern, western, and central Yucatán agricultural estates (*haciendas*) expanded dramatically.

A large part of the Maya-speaking, rural lower class was forced into a dependent relationship with the local oligarchy that controlled access to land and water. The Mexican state enforced these developments by

---

[9] *Chicle* is the coagulated milky juice used mainly for the production of natural chewing gum. It is obtained by tapping the trunk and the thick branches of the Sapodilla (*Achras zapota*) during the rainy season.

means of repression and violence to break local resistance.[10] As a result of Yucatán's geographical isolation, the Mexican Revolution that ended the dictatorship of Porfirio Díaz (1884–1911) arrived with much delay (Joseph [1982] 1992). Although the revolution led to some important social and economic changes, local power relations were not seriously challenged. Isolated as it was, Yucatán remained under the political control of a few prominent families who remained the largest landowners, the most important merchants, carriers, and *chicle*-contractors. It was only during the presidency of Lázaro Cárdenas that political and agrarian reforms were pushed forward, accompanied by much social unrest.[11]

INSTITUTIONS AND FORMS OF STATE EXPANSION

As elsewhere in New Spain, the most important early Spanish colonial institutions were the *encomienda* and the Catholic mission. In Yucatán the Franciscan order mainly organized the Christianization campaign starting in 1542. The *encomienda* was a reward given by the Crown for a certain period to persons, often conquerors or their descendants, for their merits and services. It included the right to exact tribute and labor from a certain number of Indian commoners. In return, the holders (*encomenderos*) had to take care of the entrusted population, foster their Christianization, and if needed, provide military service to the Crown. After the conquest of the northern part of Yucatán, the Maya commoners were soon exploited through tribute, labor drafts, labor contracts, and forced sales. In addition, there were many instances of Spanish *encomenderos* compelling their Indians to serve as porters and auxiliaries for further conquests (Chuchiak 2007, 193). Particularly in its early phases, the native subjects must have seen colonial rule as arbitrary, chaotic, inconsistent, and barely consolidated. There was no unified Spanish actor discernible since conquerors, *encomenderos*, missionaries, and state officials all pursued their own agendas. Conflicts between them were ubiquitous. The Franciscan Provincial

---

[10]For the history of the Mayas in Yucatán in colonial and early postcolonial times see Farriss (1984), Rugeley (1996), Quezada (1997), Restall (1997), Bracamonte y Sosa (1993, 1994), Gabbert (2004), Patch (1993).

[11]See Fallaw (2001). On early revolutionary efforts to mobilize Mayan villages for agrarian reform and to foster a socialist education in Yucatán see especially Paoli and Montalvo (1987), Joseph ([1982] 1992, 129–79, 217–59), Fallaw (1997, 553–61), Eiss (2004).

and later Bishop Diego de Landa, for example, described the reactions of the Spanish *encomenderos* to the early missionary work around 1566 as follows:

> The Spaniards were displeased to see the friars were building monasteries, and drove away the sons of the Indians from the *repartimientos* [labor drafts], in order to keep them from going to learn Christianity, and twice they burned the monastery of Valladolid with its church which was of wood and straw. Things reached such a pass that the friars were obliged to go and live among the Indians. (Tozzer 1941, 70)

While the *encomenderos* and the soldiers pursued mainly short-term, economic interests and tended to ruthlessly exploit the indigenous population of commoners, the Catholic friars acting under royal authority and patronage wanted to spread the gospel, save indigenous souls, and foster cultural change. The *encomenderos* were not particularly interested in the mission and especially feared shortfalls in their tributes. Often the sole Spanish representatives at the local level, the friars were of crucial importance for the integration of the indigenous population into the colonial order. The ability to speak the indigenous language and understand the native culture was a necessary prerequisite for the fulfillment of this role. The friars relied heavily on local leaders, cantors, teachers, and children in the missionary schools to acquire this knowledge.[12] Landa describes the missionaries' methods as follows:

> The plan which they adopted to teach the religious doctrines to the Indians was to get together the little children of the lords and of the principal men of the place, and they established them around the monastery [...]. And these children [...] took care to notify the priests of acts of idolatry or of drunken orgies that occurred; and they broke the idols although they belonged to their own fathers. (Tozzer 1941, 73–74)

After this training, which took place in the convents of Mérida, Campeche, Mani, Conkal, and Izamal, these so-called *maestros cantores* went to their places of origin or other Indian settlements of the hinterland. There they should promote the acceptance of Christianity and pay

---

[12] See Chuchiak (2000, 51–73), Hanks (2010, 23–84), Quezada (1993, 72–81), Cunill (2008). As Landa pointed out the missionaries' educational program focused particularly on the sons of the indigenous nobility.

attention to the observance of the Catholic ritual. It was also their job to teach some young people to read, write, and sing. These were then to act as altars or scribes (*escribanos*). Especially in the early days of the mission when only a few Franciscans were active in the entire province, the *maestros cantores* also had priestly duties, such as religious instruction, baptism of the sick, granting of last rites, and hearing confession among the sick and the dying.[13]

The *caciques* became the mainstay for the execution of colonial rule at the local level. They were accepted in this role if they had converted to Catholicism and were of 'pure race.' Among other things, they had to organize the forced labor service, collect taxes, and chase fugitives. In return for their services, they received privileges, such as the title of *don* or *doña* and freedom from tribute, as well as from many fees and taxes. Colonial legislation granted them a status equal to members of the lower Spanish nobility called *hidalgos*. The *caciques* and other indigenous noblemen could obtain the right to ride on horseback or to carry Spanish weapons. Their status was heritable and usually taken over by a younger brother or the eldest son. *Caciques* and their wives received a certain number of personal servants from their towns, better treatment than other Indians, and the right even to wear fashionable Spanish clothes. Many learned the Spanish language and became important cultural brokers.[14]

Another important step for colonial rule was the destruction of indigenous petty states or provinces (*cuchcabalob*) through the reorganization of settlements. The Franciscans organized a devastating concentration of the indigenous population in selected or new towns under missionary control. These resettlement attempts aimed to better control the scattered extended family groups. However, the reorganization of settlement was poorly planned and violently executed. Many previous settlements were burned down, the gardens and plantations destroyed in order to move people away. As a consequence people died of hunger or fled to the eastern or southern parts of the peninsula. Spaniards, missionaries, and militias only sporadically entered these areas, for example,

[13]See Chamberlain ([1948] 1966, 315, 319–20), Collins (1977, 236, 243–44), Farriss (1984, 97, 335–36), Clendinnen (1987, 47, 52–53).

[14]On indigenous elites who enjoyed certain privileges, see Gabbert (2004, 11–12, 19, 23–25, 33–35), Roys ([1943] 1972, 131–37, 148–60), Quezada (1993, 128–38), Schüren (2017).

to supplement *encomiendas* and mission settlements that had suffered population losses (Farriss 1984, 29–31; Patch 1993, 41–66). Different semi-autonomous republics were created for rural indigenous villages and towns or indigenous wards in the Spanish cities. Each of these *pueblos* (*comunidades*) had to organize its own government, including a governor, a town council, judges, scribes, and other officials, following the Spanish model of municipal councils (*cabildos*) (Quezada 1993, 81–101).

The Spanish crown protected the indigenous communities to a certain extent. Until the liberal reforms in the nineteenth century, the lands of the *pueblos* were considered inalienable. However, arbitrary land grabbing and illegal sales had reduced the communal lands significantly already in colonial times (Simpson 1937, 1–14; Whetten 1948, 75–85; Ibarra Mendevil 1989, 79–88). After Mexican independence in 1821, the liberal and anticlerical reformers not only attacked the vast estates and other belongings of the church, but also the communal lands of the indigenous *pueblos*. Communities were exposed to campaigns against corporate property considered unproductive in a market economy as the peasant needed freedom from the "dreadful yoke of the community" (Hale 1968, 238).[15] In order to pave the way into a modern capitalist economy, land should become a commodity and privately owned. Subsequently, church and community as well as national, so-called vacant lands (*baldios*) were to be expropriated or sold. Outsiders, many of them large private landowners and national or foreign companies, acquired the commons. The landless became exploited farm workers and domestic servants in a system of debt peonage. Since in Yucatán, as elsewhere, labor shortage was a constant problem for commercial production, labor legislation was extremely repressive. It sanctioned the total control of farm workers by landowners and administrators. They had the right to administer justice and inflict sanctions. Workers wanting to leave the farm for short periods of time had to ask for permission. Corporal punishment was common. Farm workers also tilled swidden fields (*milpas*) for the subsistence production of corn, squash, and beans mainly on land now controlled by the *hacienda*-owners (Gabbert 2004, 37–101).

In the context of the revolutionary agrarian reform, the distribution of land and the restitution of village land became important issues of the

---

[15] On the effects of liberal reforms in Yucatán see Güémez Pineda (2005).

revolutionary leaders' and subsequent Mexican presidents' political agendas. In the official discourse the *pueblos* or *comunidades* were idealized as
symbols of collective survival and resistance against colonialism. Inspired
by the communal landholdings in colonial times, the government introduced a system of collective land tenure (*ejido*) for landless petitioners
in rural areas. While the land remained under the domain of the nation,
ejido membership was limited to a group of officially recognized, mostly
male usufructuaries. Members of an *ejido* (*ejidatarios*) had the right to
work the land individually or corporately and to participate in the decisions of their assembly. However, they could lose their right to use the
land in case of long absence. *Ejido* land could not be legally sold, mort-
gaged, leased, or otherwise alienated, thus preventing poor individuals
from losing their lands.[16]

The introduction of the *ejido* and the restitution of lands to rural
communities were responses to their devastating dispossession during
the concentration of land under the Porfirian regime.[17] Many took up
arms during the revolution for agrarian reform and land distribution.
Their claims could not be totally ignored. Notwithstanding their official
agrarian discourse, the first revolutionary presidents primarily promoted
agrarian entrepreneurs of the North American type; the government
did not strongly favor a reallocation to landless and small landholders.
The amount of redistributed land was not only negligible and of poor
quality, but used as a means of political control and state expansion
into rural communities. As President Plutarco Calles (1924–28) put it:
"Ejidal politics is the best means, to control these people [the peasants],
just saying to them: If you want land, you must be on the side of the
government; if you are not on the side of the government, you won't
receive land" (Tobler 1984, 523).[18] The *ejido* land would help keep the
costs for rural workers low by granting their subsistence. In remote rural
areas, however, prerevolutionary socioeconomic structures and local
power relationships continued (Cabrera [1960] 1992; Tobler 1984,
182, 269–70, 515). In the Chenes region of Campeche, for example,

---

[16]On the *ejido* system and the Cardenist agrarian reform in Mexico, Campeche, and
Yucatán see Baños Ramírez (1989), Fallaw (2001), Schüren (2003, 66–100).

[17]About 40% of the agricultural landholdings in the Mexican territory belonged to indigenous communities before independence. After the fall of Porfirio Díaz in 1911 it was only
5%; cf. Katz (1991, 94).

[18]All translations from German and Spanish are mine.

the large landholdings of local elites were not affected by agrarian reform, which concentrated on the distribution of national lands. Thus, established forms of exploitation continued (Schüren 2005).

Like his predecessors, President Lázaro Cárdenas used the discourse of the revolution and agrarian reform for his political objectives. However, following a socialist agenda, he was truly interested in bettering the lives of the exploited workers and peasants, including the indigenous population mostly living in rural areas. Under his administration, pressure from the cooperative movement, the Ejidal Bank (*Banco Nacional de Crédito Ejidal*), the National Revolutionary Party (*Partido Nacional Revolucionario*, PNR), regional supporting parties, such as the Agrarian Socialist Party (*Partido Socialista Agrario*) in Campeche, unions, and other organizations contributed to the creation of an increasingly progressive political climate and to the acceleration of agrarian reform. The Ejidal Bank, which operated at the national level beginning in 1936, emerged as a new actor in local politics. Like the consumer cooperatives, it organized peasants and workers, acting as an advocate against the arbitrary actions of tradesmen and entrepreneurs by breaking their credit monopoly. In the state of Campeche, in the western part of the peninsula, for example, many *ejidos* started to send petitions for more and better lands to the governors, so land distribution increased. Agrarian reform even affected some private *haciendas* although most landowners avoided greater losses by dividing their properties among family members, friends, and straw men. Also, large extensions of forest land were distributed to *ejidos* for the production of *chicle* and wood (Peña 1942, vol. 1, 64, 81–88; Schüren 2003, 171–203).

For the Mexican government, a socialist education was of utmost importance in order to overcome outworn power structures and the lack of revolutionary consciousness, especially in the remote rural areas. The federal Ministry of Education (*Secretaría de Educación Pública*, SEP) established so-called 'cultural missions' (*misiones culturales*). It sent promoters to the villages, organized political meetings, cultural venues, and sports events. Propagandistic plays were performed and classroom murals painted to win the affection and mobilize the rural population for the revolutionary cause (Fallaw 2007, 208). Party circles in the capital put pressure on state and municipal committees to carry out the official policy. In 1935, for example, the state committee of Campeche's PNR issued national committee orders to the municipalities for the performance of cultural events for peasants and workers. As in the early colonial period, the rural communities became a focus for cultural and political change. While in earlier times, Spanish missionaries and state agents had addressed especially the *caciques* and the young as local agents and cultural brokers, the revolutionary state now tried to coopt high ranking *ejidal* authorities and mobilize rural teachers who often spoke the Maya language for the revolutionary project. Many of them became quite radical.[19]

IDEOLOGY AND CULTURAL CHANGE

In colonial times the Franciscan missionaries played a central role in the establishment of the colonial order in the rural areas by introducing a new ideology and religion in a more or less violent manner. They called indigenous norms into question and depreciated pre-Hispanic religious practices and beliefs as idolatry.[20] While missionizing, the Franciscans aimed at civilizing and controlling the rural population, which affected all aspects of the local culture, including religion, politics, economy, housing, as well as family and private lives. Settlements had to be redesigned according to the Spanish pattern and households split up into nuclear families. The missionaries also worried about clothing, body jewelry, table manners (for example, a tablecloth was prescribed), and the separation of males and females during frequent bathing. Polygamy among the *caciques* appeared another problem, and they were forced to opt for a single spouse. The abolition of slavery also affected *cacique* interests since the number of workers had provided the basis of their power. Caretaking of widows and orphans was emphasized. The practice of bride price, multi-year work for the bride's parents, and rejection of women in case of childlessness were banished. Also, the church forbade the imprisoning of women in homes where they were forced to make woven fabrics, the main tribute item. According to the missionaries, local

---

[19]On the political movement of the *maestros rurales* on the Yucatán peninsula see Peña (1942, vol. 2, 180–81); Raby (1968, 1974, Chapter VII); Gabbert (2004, 226–53); Schüren (2005); Fallaw (2001, 2004, 2007), and my interviews with Ramón Berzunza Pinto (1995, 1996).

[20]Responding to the frequent absence of the missionaries, many *caciques* had already included Christian priestly practices in their repertoire. Some *caciques* had even founded their own 'Christian church' (López Medel 1983).

authorities should also ensure that wives and daughters had rights to inheritance.[21]

The colonial state thus brought fundamental changes to the socio-political, religious, and economic organization of the indigenous population, changes affecting settlement patterns, family structures, and gender relations. Since the Franciscans focused on youth, the generations clashed over different norms and value systems. The missionaries' often draconian punishments for alleged idolatry of converted Indians showed not only their disappointment over their own shortcomings, but also their frustration over the figurative father–son relationship. The Franciscan fathers saw their *indios* as infants, for whom they wanted the right education and divine edification. They considered the persistence of idolatry as personal betrayal by their wards (Clendinnen 1982; Chuchiak 2005).

After independence, the colonial understanding of Indians as minors and ignorant people continued as a key ideological concept in order to justify the ongoing exploitation of the rural lower classes. Although the legal category *indio* was abolished, it remained the standard term for the Maya-speaking population perceived as descendants of the colonized natives of Yucatán (Gabbert 2004, 60–73). Revolutionary governments generally aimed at the assimilation and integration of the indigenous population into national society. Only during his brief administration (1922–24) did Yucatecan socialist Governor Felipe Carrillo Puerto decidedly promote indigenous culture, language, and Maya ethnic consciousness as an integral part of official policies (Joseph [1982] 1992, 246, 252–56; Fallaw 1997, 555–57).

Theoretical debates in the social sciences shaped government activities in Mexico. Anthropology had become particularly influential since the 1920s contributing much to the formulation of the political and cultural concept of '*indigenismo*,' on which most government programs based their assistance to the indigenous population. Until the 1970s, it was assumed that only education, modernization, and assimilation into the national society could overcome the supposed backwardness of the indigenous rural communities. The revolution had defined the nation as consisting of people of mixed blood with a blended common culture

---

[21] Many of these regulations were repeated in the ordinances of Doctor Diego García de Palacio in the early 1580s, showing that their effect was apparently quite small and the fight against idolatry and celebrations of the *caciques* far from won (García Bernal 1985, 23–39).

(*mestizos*). Consequently, governmental activities aimed at the intro-duction of Western scientific, medical, and technical skills (Caso 1950; Aguirre Beltrán and Pozas Arciniega 1954; Aguirre Beltrán 1967, 1971; Hewitt de Alcántara 1984). Indians were generally excluded from these government programs' planning and realization. Although often truly wanting to improve the lives of the rural population, government agents continued to reproduce the stereotypes referring to the indigenous pop-ulation as ignorant and quasi-minors. However, their culture and low social status were seen as legacies of colonialism and capitalist exploita-tion, rather than of race as before.[22]

Lázaro Cárdenas, who shared these views, was the first president to draft a specific Indian policy when he founded a federal Department of Indian Affairs (*Departamento de Asuntos Indígenas*) in 1936 and encour-aged the establishment of separate organizations for Indians. However, Cárdenas and his successors, did not intend to establish an autonomous political or societal project for Indians to strengthen their consciousness of ethnic separateness. He was rather interested in mobilizing the indig-enous population for his reform agenda and for their long-term integra-tion into the nation (Aguirre Beltrán 1971, 1015–17). Cárdenas wanted to make the modern "world culture accessible to the *indio*, to bring his potentials and skills to their full deployment and to improve his liv-ing conditions" while respecting his "personality, his consciousness and character" (Cárdenas 1972, 173). On another occasion he declared that "our problem does not consist in preserving the Indian as an Indian or to Indianize Mexico but to Mexicanize the Indian" (Medin 1975, 176). He considered Indians and *mestizos* as an oppressed class. This was their prime characteristic while skin color, handicraft, or special forms of social organization had only secondary importance (Cárdenas 1972, 172; Aguirre Beltrán 1971, 1008). Cárdenas essentially defined the Indians in negative terms, stressing what they lacked instead of what they were:

The greatest dearth in education and economy exists in the remote villages. [...] A huge concentration of the indigenous population cannot speak our language and destroys the forests as a result of their insufficient knowledge of cultivation systems. There are many among them who are dominated by the vice of alcohol and narcotized by fanaticism. (Cárdenas 1972, 167–68)

[22]For Latin America see Barre (1983, 29–100), for Mexico see Gabbert (1992, 35–43; 2007, 111–17).

However, during Cárdenas' presidency mobilization of the *indios* did not progress much, and their movements did not interest his successors. Existing organizations remained small in membership and distant from the rural population. Activists for their main social bases were mostly recruited from an emerging stratum of students, teachers, government employees, and professionals of indigenous background. Their demands focused on educational and cultural issues. Political activists generally fought for their local or class interests rather than for a specifically indigenous project. Village Indians became organized as peasants in the National Peasant Confederation (Sarmiento Silva 1985, 199–200; Gabbert 1992, 37–39). Most programs were in fact measures to enhance assimilation, although some aspects of indigenous culture, such as handicrafts, music, dance, and folklore, were preserved. These symbolized the Mexican nation's independence from Spain and the United States of America to the north. Beyond this, they enriched the national folklore providing an exotic attraction for the emerging tourist industry (see Cárdenas 1972, 179). Even programs of bilingual education, held to be progressive, did not succeed much in the preservation of the indigenous languages since their key objective was to facilitate the acquisition of the national language—Spanish.

Anthropologists investigating the indigenous heritage focused mainly on cultural relics of a glorious pre-Hispanic past. When dealing with contemporary Indians their preferred unit of study was the village or community, which they considered an integrated functional system—a relatively closed, autonomous, and homogeneous universe. Local communities thus came to the fore of development programs. Ideas of socialism, collectivism, and corporatism were introduced among the peasants or Indians. Consequently, many *ejidatarios* had to organize as credit and working groups in order to be eligible for governmental aid although they preferred to work individually or with family members.

In Campeche teachers and members of the governmental cultural missions perceived their actions to bring cultural change to the countryside as another 'spiritual conquest' of the suppressed indigenous population. The Ministry of Education hoped to 'convert' the rural population through socialist education, and many of its employees displayed a radical anticlericalism. Campaigns were carried out against the Catholic Church and folk religion. In 1934 federal teachers began to close the local fiestas. Churches and convents were nationalized, shut, or converted to granaries and revolutionary schools. Authorities banned religious celebrations and replaced church songs with peasant hymns. Instead of patron saints, villages and cooperatives were named after patriotic heroes, after important thinkers such as 'Carlos Marx,' or with political catchwords like 'Fight' or 'Liberty.' As Ben Fallaw has shown, many promoters held highly discriminatory views. Samuel Pérez, for example, head of the *misión cultural* supported by the teachers' college in Hecelchakan, an important center for ideological radicalization, complained in 1934 about the "infantile mentality of the Indian" (2007, 208). As Fallaw puts it:

> Federal teachers followed national policy in rejecting bilingual education and considering the spread of Spanish as a form of nationalist modernization. Replacing indigenous languages, teaching Mexican history and geography, and spreading Western norms of housing, clothing, and recreation were also plan of SEP doctrine. (205–6)

In the early 1940s, Maya-speaking children were even physically punished if they spoke their own language: "They had to leave the classroom to look for small stones, on which they had to kneel in front of their fellow pupils."[23] Many of these measures and rhetoric to modernize the Indians remind us of the Franciscan efforts to extirpate idolatry. There were also generational conflicts, because the radicals attracted the young, especially teachers who promoted their ideas. While in the early colonial period, Christianity was promoted to overcome pre-Hispanic cultural traits, the socialist movement and their campaigns concentrated on the abolishment of religion and folk culture, seen as relics of colonial and Porfirian mentalities and power structures. Strikingly, in both periods the missionaries' and revolutionaries' success and frustration were reflected in violent attitudes and disrespectful views of their respective target groups.

RESPONSES FROM LOCAL ACTORS

(A) Processes of conversion and local leaders: In debates on colonialism in Latin America, the pre-Hispanic period is often idealized as a time of justice and self-determination, not yet contaminated by European influences. Whether colonialism could have brought about some

---

[23] Author's interview with Nicolás Kantún (1995).

improvements for parts of the indigenous societies is thus often seen as a cynical question. In my opinion the question of relative advantages and disadvantages for certain native groups is, however, entirely justified. The point here is not a normative assessment of the precolonial and colonial systems, but rather an explanation for the often close and well-documented, intense cooperation with the colonial power, as well as for the varying perceptions of the colonial representatives by the indigenous people. All this cannot be entirely explained by coercion. Although the idealization of the pre-Hispanic era is understandable in view of the extreme exploitation and arbitrariness of early colonial times, power relations had been quite disadvantageous for certain social groups, such as orphans and slaves, well before any European had set foot on American soil. The sources also show that loyalties and identities were not stable even in colonial times. The conversion to Christianity, for example, can be regarded as simply resulting from the use of force. However, the early Franciscan mission often became a haven for vulnerable social groups and thus played an ambivalent role in the colonial context.

Control was very patchy at the beginning. Density and processes of cultural change differed widely between regions. In the Spanish inspection reports of settlements, for example, the spectrum ranges from seemingly submissive, mission-drilled Indians to savage or barbarian *indios*, who had responded to Christian teaching only rudimentarily, faultily, or not at all. The effects of colonialism were also far from uniform within indigenous communities. Regional and local rulers faced diverse restraints as well as new opportunities. Indian *caciques* not only acted vis-à-vis colonial institutions, some were actually part of the system and followed the colonial norms, boasting personal deeds and achievements—such as fighting idolatry, pacifying regions, being loyal, practicing Christianity, and being of 'pure blood.'

As has been mentioned before, conflicts between indigenous rulers impeded collective action against the Spanish invaders even during the conquest. Members of noble families became Spanish allies and cooperated in the establishment and consolidation of colonial rule at the local level in Yucatán, as in other parts of Mesoamerica. However, it is seriously misleading to consider indigenous conquerors, colonial agents, and middlemen traitors of their 'Indian race,' as has often been done, because they never imagined this type of community as their own. The dichotomy of Spaniards and Indians results from a projection of modern thinking about nationalism and ethnic consciousness on precolonial and colonial actors. In reality, the memory of the pre-Columbian era soon faded. Indigenous people were raised and educated in the context of Spanish rule, and their perceptions were oriented to their contemporary environment. It is misleading therefore to assume that the modern perception of a breach between the precolonial and colonial epoch was relevant for everyday interaction in colonial times. The pre-Columbian era has been frequently idealized in view of the atrocities of the conquest. However, there were continuities between these periods.

In fact, we are dealing here with feudal systems, which had a long, but different tradition in Spain and in Mesoamerica. Social identities and status were bound to the estate, membership being defined by descent (Gabbert 2004, 33–35). This explains, for example, why indigenous elites often felt much closer to the Spaniards, than to native commoners even in their own communities. It also makes understandable why many indigenous nobles were so anxious to obtain Spanish status symbols, such as clothes and arms. *Caciques* aimed primarily at maintaining and expanding the power of their lineages and did not pursue the interests of a larger ethnic community. Thus, we should better imagine Indians and Spaniards interacting in "indefinitely stretchable nets of kinship and clientship" (Anderson [1983] 1991, 6). Though agency existed on both sides, indigenous actors had to adapt to compulsion and the changing realities of Spanish colonial expansion (cf. Cooper and Stoler 1989, 613–14). Neither Indians nor Spaniards were unified as the conflicts between missionaries and *encomenderos* show. Indeed, relations between Spaniards and native leaders changed through time. Quite a few *caciques* experienced a painful change in their way of life and curtailment of their power and status including the erosion of their economic bases and political autonomy. Those, who resisted were forcefully excluded or disempowered by the Spanish who supported more acceptable figures and installed secondary leaders or newcomers. Others fled with their followers to regions outside Spanish control. However, many utilized their positions successfully to gain personal wealth and status.

(B) Local responses to Cardenism: Although the missionaries experienced many setbacks in colonial Yucatán, Catholicism became generally accepted in the course of time. Especially in rural areas and villages with large Maya-speaking populations, adaptations of Christian saints, churches, rituals, and feasts often led to a syncretism of Christian and Maya beliefs and practices, described as folk religion. Thus, believers saw no problem in making offerings to Christian saints as well as to Mayan rain gods when celebrating agrarian rituals for their swidden fields. Throughout the colonial period and thereafter, the Catholic religion became important for social and political organization in the villages and even on the *haciendas*, which often had their own chapels for resident workers and the *hacienda*-owners' families. Local identities and social life often centered on regular church services and rituals, such as baptism, marriage, and burial. The patron saints' annual feasts including bull-fights, dances, eating, drinking, and processions were often prepared by local committees. Their membership and religious expenditure reflected, as did the system of political offices, the social and political hierarchies within and between rural towns and villages.

While the missionaries had fought idolatry by persuasion or force, anticlerical revolutionaries followed their example in the twentieth century and tried to wipe out folk religion through their educational campaigns. Like pre-Columbian 'idols' in early colonial times, Catholic objects and rituals came under attack in the period of the Mexican Revolution. Churches were closed, priests exiled, and Catholic statues burned or smashed by iconoclasts. Patron–client relationships between *hacienda*-owners, *chicle*-contractors, merchants, rural workers, and peasants were to be dissolved. Radicals condemned capitalism and oligopoly in political meetings and during cultural events. While many peasants, mobilized by revolutionary agitators, participated in so-called 'defanaticization campaigns', others opposed the anticlerical crusades, rejected teachers, or sheltered visiting priests in private homes, supported less radical politicians, joined anti-revolutionary forces to save their saints, and received the sacraments (Fallaw 2004, 70–73, 157–61; 2007, 214–18).

Responses to agrarian reform also varied as organizational and technical problems encumbered their execution frequently. The demarcation of *ejido* lands sometimes even led to conflicts between neighboring villages. As one contemporary observer put it: "This [...] is creating a state of enmity and problems between neighboring peoples, which never existed, and it is not at all remote that things go further if such an anomaly persists" (Peña 1942, vol. 1, 88). In other cases, the population was less interested in the reform than expected. In Hopelchén (Chenes, Campeche), for example, the partition of land among the beneficiaries became a political problem in the late 1930s "for the lack of cooperation not only material, but even moral of the interested parties" as the engineer in charge reported, complaining that no more than four or five individuals had appeared ever at the necessary meetings.[24]

The situation was similar in other *ejidos* in the center and south of the municipality.[25] Although many *ejidos* formally existed for years, there was still no effective organization of the peasants. It seems that at this stage the distribution of land was often not so much the result of autonomous peasant mobilization, but rather at least partially due to the initiatives of the agrarian delegation in Campeche. No wonder that the collective organization of the *ejidos* was also troublesome since most communal land was worked individually or by means of family labor, not collectively.

The lack of cooperation in land demarcation in Hopelchén was partly due to the fact that 60% of the population had left their fields and already started to collect *chicle* in the jungle during the rainy season.[26] The relatively high income made *chicle*-production the most important economic strategy for many *ejidatarios*, especially since the 1930s (Schüren 2003, 13–155, 235–89). They farmed on a small scale only during times of rest to complement the diet and income. Consequently, interest in land was limited (Peña 1942, vol. 2, 141–42). Since the population exposed to agrarian reform, *ejido* organization and socialist education was quite heterogeneous in its socioeconomic composition, interests, and perception of the state, its support for governmental projects varied considerably. Thus, a similar diversity of responses to state agency can be found as in the colonial period.

[24]Acta que se levanta para hacer constar los motivos que impiden la ejecucion del fallo presidencial que concedio ampliacion de ejidos al poblado de Hopelchén, 11.7.1938, ASRAC, Caja 31, Exp. No. 23/25/031, Primera ampliación, Hopelchén. See also the telegrams of Ing. Gilberto Esparza Castillo to the agrarian delegate in Campeche, Hopelchén, from 7.7. and 8.7. 1938 and of the agrarian delegate A. Rivas Rojo to Ing. G. Esparza, Campeche, 8.7. 1938, ASRAC, Caja 31, Exp. No. 23/25/031, Primera ampliación, Hopelchén.

[25]See the letter from Ing. Miguel Martínez Sánchez to the delegate of the agrarian department in Campeche, Xcupilcacab, 17.11. 1943, ASRAC, Caja 42, Exp. No. 23/25/042.

[26]See Acta que se levanta para hacer constar los motivos que impiden la ejecucion del fallo presidencial que concedio ampliacion de ejidos al poblado de Hopelchén, 11.7. 1938, ASRAC, Caja 31, Exp. No. 23/25/031, Primera ampliación, Hopelchén.

CONCLUSION

Concepts of internal colonialism are influenced by debates in colonial studies that favor a top-down and ex-post line of thought. While hinting at important structural features of postcolonial societies, they tend to limit the analysis of the highly complex processes of domination and exploitation in colonial and postcolonial societies to the apparently clear-cut division between colonizers and colonized while neglecting the internal class and other contradictions in each of these categories. Based on research in Yucatán I question this approach, since it is insufficient to understand colonial relationships on the ground.

By combining a structural approach with the historical study of practices and perceptions in the regional and local spheres, I have looked at early colonial and postcolonial state expansion from three perspectives—institutions and forms of state expansion; ideology and cultural change; and responses from the indigenous, rural population. The structural perspective describes the historically constituted constraints, such as socio-economic inequality, racism, and exploitation, as well as state policies; in addition, this perspective delineates the cultures and power relations of local societies. The agency perspective observes the varied perceptions, responses, and activities of the rural indigenous population in the context of these constraints.

In colonial Yucatán structural constraints and state policies were significantly shaped by the colonialist hunger for economic gain through the subjection and exploitation of the indigenous population. Independence from Spain did not fundamentally change the fate of the marginalized indigenous and non-indigenous lower classes. It was only during the presidency of Lázaro Cárdenas that profound social change was brought to remote areas, such as Yucatán. The economic advancement of the rural indigenous populations and their integration into the nation was to be achieved by political self-organization, the implementation of educational programs, and the intensification of agrarian reform.

Though the amount of committed violence, as well as the types of rule and political orientation, differed fundamentally in the colonial and revolutionary state, certain similarities existed regarding the implementation of state norms and policies as well as patterns of local resistance and adaptation. In both periods the state aimed at profoundly changing the local cultures and ways of life, even by means of physical force, while ideologies of superiority and inferiority shaped the relationship between state agents and the rural population.

In colonial times legal regulations separated the *indios* from the rest of the society. Cultural change served mainly to adjust their labor force to the needs of a colonial economy and to erase the Mayan religion. In revolutionary times, cultural programs also aimed at extinguishing folk culture, religion, and individualized swidden agriculture—all seen as colonial legacies and drawbacks to the creation of a modern socialist nation. The colonial categorizing of Yucatáns' population as *indios* and inferior to the Spaniards was institutionalized by a set of criteria (legal, spatial, cultural, ancestral) that reinforced each other. Domination and exploitation continued to be legitimized by reference to race and culture even after independence. This illustrates the *longue durée* of colonial deep structures operative even in current economies and world views and shows that Pérez Jiménez's (2015) postulate of a mental and social decolonization remains valid.

In both cases the indigenous elite played an important role. In colonial times alliances with local leaders were built to a large extent on the exploitation of political antagonisms among them. In the context of regional and local conflict during the Mexican Revolution, the co-optation and installation of local leaders was of crucial importance for the expansion of the state. Since indigenous communities were socially and politically heterogeneous inner conflicts were frequent in both the colonial and revolutionary eras. In the colonial *pueblos* the population was socially differentiated according to descent, class, gender, age, and access to political and religious offices. Spanish colonialism and the severe demographic decline, caused by conquest and epidemics, deeply shattered indigenous social structures and power systems. The form and extent of these changes were, of course, far from uniform and differed between regions and periods. While the colonial regime exploited existing social differentiations among the Indians and created new divisions, the revolutionary government tried to end exploitation within and beyond the village, thus confronting existing patron–client relations, local power holders, and the regional oligarchy. The relationship between the state and the local population was always complex and indigenous reactions to colonial policies were manifold depending on the position in the social fabric and local power structure. Since indirect rule left considerable room for maneuver, much depended on the interests and agency of local power brokers.

Mobilization and political control of the *indios* rested on their corporative organization, either in colonial Christianized indigenous towns and villages, or in postrevolutionary agrarian communities. The revolutionary state claimed many more functions than the colonial regime, including projects of social welfare and community development, such as the organization of women's groups. Various Maya villages ignored or boycotted such projects. Even agrarian reform was met with considerable resistance not only by the regional oligarchy, but also by the supposed beneficiaries for various reasons: alternative economic strategies, such as *chicle*-production, as well as opposition to cooperatives and anticlericalism. However, other groups participated, and many, especially local power brokers, benefitted from the educational and agrarian programs.

It has been shown that elements considered essential for the definition of both overseas and internal colonialism—such as an ideology of cultural superiority—also apply to seemingly progressive projects of state intervention and expansion aimed at the socioeconomic enhancement and political empowerment of the rural indigenous population during the Mexican Revolution and especially during the presidency of Lázaro Cárdenas. Those unwilling or unable to participate in the economic model or join the political and educational programs experienced discrimination as dumb Indians ignoring the benefits of civilization. In fact, even after the Mexican Revolution, the demeanor towards the poor of government officials, as well as large parts of the urban population and the Spanish-speaking rural elites, resembled colonial relationships. Not surprisingly, most speakers of indigenous languages did not adopt the term *indio* as a self-designation. Many tried to pass as non-Indians looking for social advancement by refusing to use their own language (Gabbert 2004, 96–99, 158–62; Schüren 2015).

In the long run, however, the national *indigenista* discourse, the economic development, as well as the social, educational, and agrarian reforms of Cardenism contributed to a process of social inclusion and *mestizaje* (cultural and phenotypical mixing) in Yucatán. Governmental organizations and the educational system created opportunities for more members of rural communities on the peninsula to integrate into national society and climb the social ladder. Many educated Maya-speakers thus became teachers, engineers, and government officials, and some even started to marry into the local elite. Of course, this does not mean that racism has disappeared from Yucatán today. Although the group of people denoted disrespectfully as *indios* has changed, and social exclusion and discrimination are less severe as compared, for example, to Guatemala, the use of this term in informal contexts continues today.[27] As before, the term *indio* is used as a synonym for poor, rustic, undeveloped, backward, and powerless. Thus, it often relates to class. This negative image, shared by large sectors of Mexican society, has also determined the position of those who culturally differ from the mainstream. This image still evokes at best pity and paternalism, and at worst racism and violent discrimination preventing *indios* from getting equal rights and participation in the national society.

REFERENCES

Interviews and Archives

Ramón Berzunza Pinto, Dzitbalché, 14.4. 1995 and 15.3. 1996.
Nicolás Kantún, Crucero San Luís, Campeche, 24.3. 1995.
ASRAC Archivo de la Secretará de la Reforma Agraria, Campeche.

Books and Articles

Adelman, Jeremy. 1999. "Introduction: The Problem of Persistence in Latin American History." In *Colonial Legacies: The Problem of Persistence in Latin American History*, edited by Jeremy Adelman, 1–13. New York: Routledge.
Adorno, Rolenda. 1993. "Reconsidering the Colonial Discourse for Sixteenth- and Seventeenth-Century Spanish America." *Latin American Research Review* 28(3): 135–45.
Aguirre Beltrán, Gonzalo. 1967. *Regiones de refugio: el desarrollo de la comunidad y el proceso dominical en mestizo América*. México, DF: Instituto Indigenista Interamericano.
Aguirre Beltrán, Gonzalo. 1971. "El pensamiento indigenista de Lázaro Cárdenas." *América Indígena* 31: 1007–19.
Aguirre Beltrán, Gonzalo, and Ricardo Pozas Arciniega. 1954. *La política indigenista en México. Métodos y resultados*, vol. 2. México, DF: Instituto Nacional Indigenista.
Anderson, Benedict. [1983] 1991. *Imagined Communities: Reflections on the Origin and Spread of Nationalism*. London: Verso.

---

[27]For a discussion of the new idealization of indigenous culture and a positive connotation of the term Indian by Maya-activists and a comparison of the Maya-movement in Guatemala and Yucatán see Schüren (2015).

Baños Ramírez, Othón. 1989. *Yucatán: Ejidos sin campesinos*. Mérida: Universidad Autónoma de Yucatán.

Barabas, Alicia. 1979. "Colonialismo y racismo en Yucatán: Una aproximación histórica y contemporánea." *Revista Mexicana de Ciencias Políticas y Sociales* 25(97): 105–39.

Barre, Marie-Chantal. 1983. *Ideologías indigenistas y movimientos indios*. México, DF: Siglo XXI.

Bracamonte y Sosa, Pedro. 1993. *Amos y sirvientes: Las haciendas de Yucatán, 1789–1860*. Mérida: Universidad Autónoma de Yucatán.

Bracamonte y Sosa, Pedro. 1994. *La memoria enclaustrada: Historia indígena de Yucatán, 1750–1915*. México, DF: CIESAS.

Cabrera, Luis. [1960] 1992. "Fragmento del discurso sobre el problema agrario pronunciado el 3 de diciembre de 1912 por el diputado Luis Cabrera." In *Breve historia de la revolución mexicana: Los antecedentes y la etapa maderista*, edited by Jesús Silva Herzog, 319–39. México, DF: Fondo de Cultura Económica.

Cárdenas, Lázaro. 1972. *Ideario político: Selección y presentación de Leonel Durán*. México, DF: Ediciones Era.

Caso, Alfonso. 1950. "Definición del indio y lo indio." *La Nueva Democracia* 30: 78–85.

Chamberlain, Robert S. [1948] 1966. *The Conquest and Colonization of Yucatan, 1517–1550*. New York: Octagon Books.

Chuchiak IV, John F. 2000. "The Indian Inquisition and the Extirpation of Idolatry: The Process of Punishment in the Provisorato de Indios of the Diocese of Yucatán, 1563–1812." PhD diss., Tulane University.

Chuchiak IV, John F. 2005. "In Servitio Dei. Fray Diego de Landa, the Franciscan Order, and the Return of the Extirpation of Idolatry in the Colonial Diocese of Yucatán, 1573–1579." *The Americas* 61(4): 611–46.

Chuchiak IV, John F. 2007. "Forgotten Allies: The Origins and Roles of Native Mesoamerican Auxiliaries and Indios Conquistadores in the Conquest of Yucatan, 1526–1550." In *Indian Conquistadors: Indigenous Allies in the Conquest of Mesoamerica*, edited by Laura E. Matthew and Michel R. Oudijk, 175–225. Norman: University of Oklahoma Press.

Clendinnen, Inga. 1982. "Disciplining the Indians: Franciscan Ideology and Missionary Violence in Sixteenth-Century Yucatán." *Past and Present* 94: 27–48.

Clendinnen, Inga. 1987. *Ambivalent Conquest: Mayas and Spaniards in Yucatán, 1517–1570*. Cambridge: Cambridge University Press.

Collins, Anne C. 1977. "The Maestros Cantores in Yucatán." In *Anthropology and History in Yucatan*, edited by Grant D. Jones, 233–47. Austin: University of Texas Press.

Cooper, Frederick, and Ann Laura Stoler. 1989. "Introduction. Tensions of Empire: Colonial Control and Visions of Rule." *American Ethnologist* 16(4): 609–21.

Cope, R. Douglas. 2010. "Indigenous Agency in Colonial Spanish America." *Latin American Research Review* 45(1): 203–14.

Cunill, Caroline. 2008. "La alfabeticación de los mayas yucatecos y sus consecuencias sociales, 1545–1580." *Estudios de Cultura Maya* 31: 163–92.

de la Peña, Moisés T. 1942. *Campeche económico.* 2 vol. México, DF: Gobierno constitucional del estado de Campeche.

Eiss, Paul K. 2004. "Deconstructing Indians, Reconstructing Patria: Indigenous Education in Yucatán from the Porfiriato to the Mexican Revolution." *Journal of Latin American Anthropology* 9(1): 119–50.

Fallaw, Ben. 1997. "Cárdenas and the Caste War That Wasn't: State Power and Indigenismo in Post-Revolutionary Yucatán." *The Americas* 53(4): 551–77.

Fallaw, Ben. 2001. *Cardenas Compromised: The Failure of Reform in Postrevolutionary Yucatan.* Duke: Duke University Press.

Fallaw, Ben. 2004. "Rethinking Mayan Resistance: Changing Relations Between Federal Teachers and Mayan Communities in Eastern Yucatan, 1929–1935." *Journal of Latin American Anthropology* 9(1): 151–78.

Fallaw, Ben. 2007. "'Anti-Priests' Versus Catholic-Socialists in 1930s Campeche: Federal Teachers, Revolutionary Communes, and Anticlericalism." In *Faith and Impiety in Revolutionary Mexico,* edited by Matthew Butler, 203–23. New York: Palgrave Macmillan.

Farriss, Nancy. 1984. *Maya Society Under Colonial Rule: The Collective Enterprise of Survival.* Princeton: Princeton University Press.

Gabbert, Wolfgang. 1992. "Vom Land der Mestizen zur multi-ethnischen Nation: Staatspartei und Indianer im nachrevolutionären Mexiko." In *Die Wilden und die Barbarei,* edited by Dietmar Dirmoser, Wolfgang Gabbert, Klaus Meschkat, Urs Müller-Plantenberg, Eleonore von Oertzen, Michael Rediske, and Juliane Ströbele-Gregor, 32–47. Münster: Lit Verlag.

Gabbert, Wolfgang. 1995. "Kultureller Determinismus und die Eroberung Mexikos: Zur Kritik eines dichotomischen Geschichtsverständnisses." *Saeculum* 46(2): 274–92.

Gabbert, Wolfgang. 2004. *Becoming Maya: Ethnicity and Social Inequality in Yucatán Since 1500.* Tucson: University of Arizona Press.

Gabbert, Wolfgang. 2007. "Ethnisierung von ‚oben' und von ‚unten': Staatliche Indianerpolitik und indigene Bewegungen im postrevolutionären Mexiko." In *Ethnisierung und De-Ethnisierung des Politischen: Identitätspolitiken in Lateinamerika, Asien und den USA,* edited by Christian Büschges and Joanna Pfaff-Czarnecka, 142–65. Frankfurt am Main: Campus Verlag.

Gabbert, Wolfgang. 2015. "Imagining a Nation—Elite Discourse and the Native Past in Nineteenth-Century Mexico." In *Globalized Antiquity: Uses and Perceptions of the Past in India, Mesoamerica, and Europe,* edited by Ute Schüren, Daniel Segesser, and Thomas Späth, 189–210. Berlin: Reimer.

García Bernal, Manuela Cristina. 1985. "García de Palacio y sus Ordenanzas para Yucatán." *Temas Americanistas* 5: 1–39.

Gerhard, Peter. 1979. *The Southeast Frontier of New Spain*. Princeton: Princeton University Press.

Giddens, Anthony. 1984a. *The Constitution of Society: Outline of the Theory of Structuration*. Cambridge: Polity Press.

Giddens, Anthony. 1984b. *Interpretative Soziologie: Eine kritische Einführung*. Frankfurt am Main: Campus Verlag.

Gledhill, John. 1988. "Legacies of Empire: Political Centralization and Class Formation in the Hispanic-American World." In *State and Society: The Emergence and Development of Social Hierarchy and Political Centralization*, edited by John Gledhill, Barbara Bender, and Mogens Trolle Larsen, 302–19. London: Routledge.

González-Casanova, Pablo. 1965. "Internal Colonialism and National Development." *Studies in Comparative International Development* 1(4): 27–37.

Güémez Pineda, Arturo. 2005. *Mayas: Gobierno y tierras frente a la acometida liberal en Yucatán, 1812–1847*. Zamora: Colegio de Michoacán.

Gunsenheimer, Antje, and Ute Schüren. 2016. *Amerika vor der europäischen Eroberung*. Frankfurt am Main: Fischer Verlag.

Hale, Charles A. 1968. *Mexican Liberalism in the Age of Mora, 1921–1853*. New Haven: Yale University Press.

Hanks, William F. 2010. *Converting Words: Maya in the Age of the Cross*. Berkeley: University of California Press.

Hechter, Michael. [1975] 1999. *Internal Colonialism: The Celtic Fringe in British National Development* (with a new introduction and a new appendix by the author). New Brunswick, NJ: Transaction Publishers.

Heller, Patrick, Dietrich Rueschemeyer, and Richard Snyder. 2009. "Dependency and Development in a Globalized World: Looking Back and Forward." *Studies in Comparative International Development* 44: 287–95.

Hewitt de Alcántara, Cynthia. 1984. *Anthropological Perspectives on Rural Mexico*. London: Routledge & Kegan Paul.

Hind, Robert J. 1984. "The Internal Colonial Concept." *Comparative Studies in Society and History* 26(3): 543–68.

Ibarra Mendevil, Jorge Luis. 1989. *Propiedad agraria y sistema político en México*. México, DF: M.A. Porrúa.

Joseph, Gilbert M. [1982] 1992. *Revolución desde afuera: Yucatán, México y los Estados Unidos, 1880–1924*. México, DF: Fondo de Cultura Económica.

Katz, Friedrich. 1991. "The Liberal Republic and the Porfiriato, 1867–1910." In *Mexico Since Independence*, edited by Leslie Bethell, 49–124. Cambridge: Cambridge University Press.

Long, Norman. 1990. "From Paradigm Lost to Paradigm Regained? The Case for an Actor-Oriented Sociology of Development." *European Review of Latin American and Caribbean Studies* 49: 3–24.

Long, Norman. 1993. „Handlung, Struktur und Schnittstelle: Theoretische Reflektionen." In *Entwicklungshilfe und ihre Folgen: Ergebnisse empirischer Untersuchungen in Afrika*, edited by Thomas Bierschenk and Georg Elwert, 217–48. Frankfurt am Main: Campus Verlag.

López Medel, Tómas. 1983. "Ordenanzas de Tomás López (1552–1553), Documento Número Ocho." In *Relación de las cosas de Yucatán*, edited by Fray Diego de Landa, 218–34. Mérida: Dante.

Love, Joseph L. 1989. "Modelling Internal Colonialism: History and Prospect." *World Development* 17(6): 905–22.

Medin, Tzvi. 1975. *Ideología y praxis política de Lázaro Cárdenas*. México, DF: Siglo XXI.

Osterhammel, Jürgen. [1995] 2001. *Kolonialismus: Geschichte, Formen, Folgen*. München: C.H. Beck.

Paoli, Francisco J., and Enrique Montalvo. 1987. *El socialismo olvidado de Yucatán*. México, DF: Siglo XXI.

Patch, Robert W. 1993. *Maya and Spaniard in Yucatan, 1648–1812*. Stanford: Stanford University Press.

Patch, Robert W. 1999. "Dependency and the Colonial Heritage in Southeastern Mesoamerica." In *Colonial Legacies: The Problem of Persistence in Latin American History*, edited by Jeremy Adelman, 91–106. New York: Routledge.

Pérez Jiménez, Aurora. 2015. "Decolonizing Memory: The Case of the Ñuu Sau (Mixtec People, Mexico)." In *Globalized Antiquity: Uses and Perceptions of the Past in South Asia, Mesoamerica, and Europe*, edited by Ute Schüren, Daniel Marc Segesser, and Thomas Späth, 211–18. Berlin: Reimer.

Quezada, Sergio. 1993. *Pueblos y caciques yucatecos, 1550–1580*. México, DF: El Colegio de México.

Quezada, Sergio. 1997. *Los pies de la república: Los mayas peninsulares, 1550–1750*. México, DF: CIESAS.

Quijano, Anibal. 2000. "Coloniality of Power, Eurocentrism, and Latin America." *Nepantla: Views from the South* 1(3): 533–80.

Raby, David L. 1968. "Los maestros rurales y los conflictos sociales en México (1931–1940)." *Historia Mexicana* 18(2): 190–226.

Raby, David, L. 1974. *Educación y revolución social en México, 1921–1940*. México, DF: Secretaría de Educación Pública.

Restall, Matthew. 1997. *The Maya World: Yucatec Culture and Society, 1550–1850*. Stanford: Stanford University Press.

Restall, Matthew. 1998. *Maya Conquistador*. Boston: Beacon Press.

Roys, Ralph L. [1943] 1972. *The Indian Background of Colonial Yucatan*. Norman: University of Oklahoma Press.

Rugeley, Terry. 1996. *Yucatan's Maya and the Origins of the Caste War*. Austin: University of Texas Press.

Sarmiento Silva, Sergio. 1985. "El Consejo Nacional de Pueblos Indígenas y la política indigenista." *Revista Mexicana de Sociología* 47(3): 197–215.

Schüren, Ute. 2003. „Rationalität oder Irrationalität bäuerlichen Wirtschaftens im Kontext staatlicher Politik: Haushaltsstrategien in mexikanischen Ejidos." PhD diss., Freie Universität Berlin.

Schüren, Ute. 2005. "¿Tierras para quien las trabaje? Cambios políticos y reforma agraria en una zona fronteriza de México." In *Los buenos, los malos y los feos: Poder y resistencia en América Latina*, edited by Nikolaus Böttcher, Isabel Galaor, and Bernd Hausberger, 105–31. Madrid: Iberoamericana.

Schüren, Ute. 2015. "Heirs of the Ancient Maya: Indigenous Organisations and the Appropriation of History in Yucatán, Mexico and Guatemala." In *Globalized Antiquity: Uses and Perceptions of the Past in India, Mesoamerica, and Europe*, edited by Ute Schüren, Daniel Segesser, and Thomas Späth, 231–49. Berlin: Reimer.

Schüren, Ute. 2017. "*Caciques*: Indigenous Rulers and the Colonial Regime in Yucatán in the Sixteenth Century." In *Cooperation and Empire: Local Realities of Global Processes*, edited by Tanja Bührer, Flavio Eichmann, Stig Förster, and Benedikt Stuchtey, 33–57. New York: Berghahn.

Simpson, Eyler N. 1937. *The Ejido: Mexico's Way Out*. Chapel Hill: The University of North Carolina Press.

Stoler, Ann Laura. 1992. "Rethinking Colonial Categories: European Communities and the Boundaries of Colonial Rule." In *Colonization and Culture*, edited by Nicholas B. Dirks, 319–52. Ann Arbor: The University of Michigan Press.

Tobler, Hans Werner. 1984. *Die mexikanische Revolution: Gesellschaftlicher Wandel und politischer Umbruch, 1876–1940*. Frankfurt am Main: Suhrkamp.

Tozzer, Alfred M. 1941. *Landas Relacion de las Cosas de Yucatan: A Translation*. Cambridge, MA: Peabody Museum of American Archaeology and Ethnology.

Whetten, Nathan L. 1948. *Rural Mexico*. Chicago: The University of Chicago Press.

PART IV

Post-Colonial Dependencies: Internal Legacies of External Colonialism

CHAPTER 12

Greater Mexico: Homeland, Colonialism, and Genetics

John R. Chávez

INTRODUCTION

A U.S. citizen of Mexican descent, my 95-year-old mother, Andrea Chávez, was in her forties before she crossed the international border, traveling *south into Mexico*. People are often surprised when they hear she was born in Los Angeles, California. Indeed, her native land can be described broadly as Greater Mexico, stretching up through North America, across California, New Mexico, and Texas; unlike nation-states, homelands often lack precise definition since they include subjective feelings as well as objective elements. Her people, Mexicans regardless of citizenship, are also native to this vast northern borderland; like homeland, indigeneity (or nativity) challenges definition since it depends on space often vague as to extent, like her birthplace.[1] To understand this claim regarding indigeneity and place, we can apply colonialism as a theoretical

---

[1]For a discussion of indigeneity and related concepts regarding Latin America, see Favre (1996).

J. R. Chávez (✉)
Clements Department of History, Southern Methodist University,
Dallas, TX, USA
e-mail: jchavez@mail.smu.edu

© The Author(s) 2019
D. Schorkowitz et al. (eds.), *Shifting Forms of Continental Colonialism*,
https://doi.org/10.1007/978-981-13-9817-9_12

framework and genetics as a methodology because they permit analysis of competing claims to homeland in depth across Mexican history (Favre 1996, 6–7; Osterhammel [1995] 1997, 8–9, 15).

In the case of ethnic Mexicans, the northern boundaries of the homeland can be precisely defined as those fixed by the United States and Spain in the Adams-Onis Treaty of 1819, confirmed by the former and Mexico in the 1830s. More limited claims based on actual Mexican population centers in 1848 could include coastal California, the Santa Cruz Valley in Arizona, the Rio Grande Valley in New Mexico and Texas, as well as San Antonio, Nacogdoches, and Goliad in the latter. However, the above two definitions derive from Spanish colonialism. Relying more deeply on the Indian roots of Mexicans, the wide northern opening of the geographical funnel that became Mexico forms a homeland that poured peoples south through the continent. Between the coast of California and that of Texas, the funnel first channeled the native ancestors of later Mexicans south, but they could also return as they often did in both pre- and post-contact periods. This cornucopia would overflow in the twentieth century.

COLONIALISM AS THEORY

Theoretically, colonialism or the colonial paradigm is the collection of basic and complex ideas surrounding the concept of a colony. In 1963 Mexican social scientist Pablo González-Casanova defined it thus: "Originally [...] the term 'colony' was used to designate a territory occupied by emigrants of the mother country. [...] Then colony was understood [...] as a territory in which the [...] emigrants dominated the indigenous peoples" (González-Casanova 1963, 16, 18; my translation). Basically, colony means a land occupied by outsiders, more complexly the society resulting from the occupation. The essential elements of colonial theory are land and settlers.

Historically, land is occupied through colonization. A basic example of uninhabited territory settled by Amerindians about 11,000 BCE was Limuw (place of the sea), today Santa Cruz, one of the Channel Islands about twenty-five miles off the coast of southern California, claimed in the sixteenth century by Spain, in the nineteenth by Mexico, and then by the United States (Gamble 2011, 5–6, 37–38; United States National Park Service 2016). Surrounded by the ocean, Limuw's categorization as a single region might seem natural even though the island can be grouped mentally in an archipelago of four to eight Channel Islands based on physical features. The territorial limits of this archipelago may be perceived as natural because water divides the islands from the outside world though the sea also allows communication. Theoretically, the point is that geographical unity of Limuw itself or joined with the other Channel Islands is as much artificial as natural—social construction—a region outlined, labeled, and established by people.

Settlers colonize an uninhabited place; they claim it legitimately as when bands of the Chumash people settled in politically independent villages mostly in Limuw and three other northern Channel Islands. Though the islands may have been explored and occupied earlier by as yet unknown people—if the Chumash colonists found no residents on arrival—their children became the indigenous people of the islands by apparent precedence. People who follow, such as the Uto-Aztecan-speaking Tongva who arrived about 1200 BCE in the four southern islands, may be welcomed as immigrants and accommodated as neighbors, but their status rests on their relationship to the original population (Potter and White 2009, 164; Sutton 2005, 64–66, 70). On arrival of the Chumash, the northern Channel Islands became a cultural region similar to the larger Chumash-speaking homeland, a collection of villages on the mainland spread by migration through contiguous coastal areas—through continental, as well as overseas colonization (Gamble 2011, 276–77, 259; Johnson and Lorenz 2006, 35, 56).[2] In most cases, defining a territory and its natives is more difficult than in the case of the northern Channel Islands; moreover, for purposes of colonial theory, especially involving contiguous territory, definition is essential because control of land establishes the relationship between the colonized and colonizers.[3]

As González-Casanova points out, colonialism as theory particularly involves settlers moving onto land occupied by earlier residents, not as immigrants who benignly join the locals, but as newcomers who dominate the locals often comprised of natives by earliest descent, immigrants preceding the dominant newcomers, and mixed groups, often in

---

[2]Of course, warfare among Chumash federations existed, but was not colonial since it did not involve subordination of a different ethnic group; the intrusion of Uto-Aztecan speakers, on the other hand, may have involved conquest and been colonial.

[3]Colonization of uninhabited land may cause environmental damage, but it is not a matter of the oppression of one people over another, of one ethnic group over another.

complex hierarchies. Commonly, colonizers use force to take territory belonging to another group, as the Spanish did after their arrival on the Channel Islands. Early contact between the Chumash and Spanish was contentious, but not permanent; explorers Juan Rodríguez Cabrillo in 1542 and Sebastián Vizcaíno in 1602 described the islands for future colonial expansion, including religious conversion. Besides the theoretical paradigm, colonialism means the set of beliefs associated directly with settling while colonization means the practice of settling. In 1769 the Spanish came to stay in the Channel Islands in order to secure the coast militarily and to exploit the resources of California economically in a pattern that had expanded the empire at least since Columbus. Ultimately, the colonizer establishes dominance over the local population through warfare, political subordination, economic deprivation, servitude, rape, sociocultural erasure, religious conversion, language suppression, psychological diminishment, and other intentional and unintentional practices, ranging from the extremes of genocide to discriminatory slights. The Spanish conquered, enslaved, Christianized, and hispanicized the Natives almost to the point of extinction through the mission system and inadvertently through disease (Dartt-Newton and Erlandson 2006, 424). Over time the distinction between colonizer and colonized can disappear or simply become more complicated. Though the Chumash and other tribes survived as mission Indians, intermixture in California also produced detribalized *mestizos* still proportionally more indigenous than Spanish, but ranked as a caste between the two by the end of the formal colonial period in 1821.

Decolonizing and postcolonial movements attempt to throw off the colonizer's domination and recover the native heritage, but clear lines between the foreigner and native are hard to draw after long interaction. Recognizing the native people can be problematic, as many have mixed with the colonizer (Gandhi 1998, 4).[4] By 1821 many people of Chumash descent had become Mexican mestizos. Reconstruction of the native homeland can also be problematic. Never politically unified, the Chumash of the Channel Islands and the facing California coastline hardly achieved unity or independence with establishment of the Mexican nation-state, a much larger geopolitical entity based on the

[4]Acknowledging the indigeneity of mixed detribalized people is not an appropriation of the status of natives who retain tribal and cultural bonds, but recognition of the oft-denied physical ties of mestizos, especially of maternal lines.

colonial frontiers of New Spain. In the nominally postcolonial era after Mexican independence, both *indios* and mestizos remained colonized in the northern territories, including California and the Channel Islands, that is in the formal colonies of the new Empire, then Republic of Mexico. In such borderlands this continental colonialism remained a vestige of Spain's overseas colonialism. Residents lacked full citizenship as these territories were not full members of the new nation-state since they remained largely under the sovereignty of numerous Amerindian nations.

A second cycle of colonialism can occur when another foreign people invades to dominate the natives, benign immigrants, the first colonists, and mixed groups in a new social hierarchy. The Anglo-American conquest of California, including Santa Cruz Island, would initiate such a cycle, as the United States colonized the territories that would form its new Southwest (Mendoza 2014, 122). Internal colonialism is the domestic subset of the larger colonial paradigm, including colonization, formal colonialism, postcolonialism, and other concepts that explain broader relationships of ethnic inequality across history and geography. Internal colonial theory seeks to explain the subordinate status of a racial or ethnic group in its own homeland within the boundaries of a larger state dominated by a different people (Hechter [1975] 1999, XIV–XV; Chávez 2011, 786). The degree of domination varies by time, locale, gender, class, and other factors, such as the presence of additional ethnic groups, resulting in complex hierarchies. California's admission to statehood in 1850 transformed formal colonies, such as the Chumash homeland including the Channel Islands and mestizo Santa Barbara, into internal colonies.

My mother and I belong to an indigenous group constantly regarded as foreign and inferior—witness U.S. President Donald Trump's comments on Mexicans during his campaign: "When Mexico sends its people, they're not sending their best"; he assured that his comments were not aimed at folks like my grandparents—"some [...] are good people," but the stigma remains ("Donald Trump" 2015). The alienation and sense of inferiority impressed on ethnic Mexicans regardless of birth on either side of the border marks this group as at least psychologically colonized (Barrera 1979, 4, 193–94, 202, 212).

In the case of ethnic Mexicans defining the colonized or natives, and the colonizers or foreigners is complex. Physical descendants of native peoples—such as the Tongva of California, the Pueblos of New Mexico, the Coahuiltecans of Texas, the Huichols of Zacatecas, and the Tlaxcalans and Aztecs of central Mexico—who have retained their tribal and cultural ties would be considered indigenous in Mexico. Descendants of the Spanish would clearly be colonizers, but most Mexicans are mestizos, descendants of Indians, Spaniards, and Africans. In Mexico any claim to native status would rest on mestizos' tribal heritage—on appearance, culture, including religious icons, food, oral traditions, and such. Mestizos as the majority in Mexico would not generally be regarded as colonized though color and poverty could mark them as Indian in comparison with creoles—a social result of Spanish colonialism. In the hierarchy of U.S. Southwest, however, mestizos would generally be regarded as a non-white population, lower than Anglo Americans—a result of U.S. expansion.

NATIVITY AND COLONIALISM IN THE HISTORY OF GREATER MEXICO

Like Trump, if less stridently, the media and educational system of the United States give the general impression that Mexicans are recent arrivals to the American land of immigrants, and that unlike their worthy European predecessors, many are illegal aliens. The deep ancestral history of Mexicans in North America is completely ignored. In fact, a genetic study by Satish Kumar and his colleagues conducted in San Antonio in 2011 found that 83.3% of the Mexican Americans examined had Amerindian ancestry, based on tracking of their mitochondrial DNA. This correlated well with earlier studies of "Mexican and Mexican American populations revealing 85 to 90 of mtDNA lineages are of Native American origin" (Kumar et al. 2011, 3). Indeed, the ancestors of Mexicans were among the first people of North America, the first natives by precedent and birth on the continent.

About 23,000 years ago these ancestors spread south from Alaska along the Pacific Coast, interior valleys, and plains, peopling many previously uninhabited lands, including later California, New Mexico, and Texas (Kumar et al. 2011, 1). From there, according to archeological, anthropological, and linguistic evidence, they funneled through into central Mexico. By 5000 BCE the Cochise culture—ancestor to the Aztecs, Utes, and later peoples—appeared in southern Arizona. This would be the first distinguishable culture identified through studies of material artifacts, social organization, origin myths, and language. The hunting and gathering Cochise people likely spoke Uto-Aztecan, the parent of a language family that from 1000 BCE spread with its speakers, evolving into Tongva in southern California, Hopi in Arizona, Comanche in New Mexico and Texas, Tarahumara in Chihuahua, Huichol in Zacatecas, and Nahua around Mexico City in an almost unbroken chain from today's Southwest to Central America (Hammarström et al. 2016). Over the same time maize cultivation moved north from Mexico, spreading the fundamental Amerindian food, as cultural contact moved in multiple directions. From 200 to 1520 CE in sequence the Teotihuacanos, Toltecs, and Aztecs introduced squash, beans, cloth making, pottery, architecture, irrigation methods, and methods of government to the distant Mogollon, Hohokam, Anasazi, and Pueblos of the Southwest through indirect trade establishing the indigenous cultural foundation of Greater Mexico (Chávez [1989] 2017, 291).

The European and African elements of the Mexican heritage were added after the Spanish conquest of the Aztecs. Indian mortality due to the conquest and especially Old World diseases allowed the newcomers a greater demographic impact than would otherwise have been the case. Based on archival sources, demographers Sherburne Cook and Lesley Simpson conservatively set "the 1519 population of all central Mexico [...] at 11,000,000" when the Spanish arrived with the decline hitting bottom "as low as 1,500,000" about the mid-seventeenth century (Cook and Simpson 1948, 38, 47–48).[5] However, because few Spaniards and even fewer of their women entered Mexico, their genetic if not their cultural impact was limited. As Spaniards took Indian mistresses and wives, and introduced African slaves, intermixing produced a population designated as castes with the indigenous maternal lines noted by Kumar revealing themselves in the appearance of mestizos and others.

As the Spanish with their Nahua allies expanded northward, they continued intermixing with local peoples from central Mexico City through Guanajuato, Zacatecas, and other intermediate posts en route to New Mexico. As they went, they established an evolving colonial hierarchy based on racial perceptions. Initially, Spaniards interbred with Indian women, but the pattern changed as mates became more diverse. According to David Brading (1994, 258–60), eventually, "the Spanish married with mestizos, mulattoes with Indians, and mestizos with Spanish and Indians." In Guanajuato, the birthplace of my maternal

---

[5]For a recent overview of the inconclusive debate over the population of Mexico in 1519, see Márquez-Morfín and Storey (2017, 193–94).

grandparents, caste trumped class in terms of social prestige. As Brading notes, "racial distinctions, even though they do not by themselves indicate class distinctions, in part defined *individual status* in the estimation of companions and, more importantly, in the eyes of women."

As early as 1598, the Spanish colonized New Mexico, bringing Tlaxcalan Indians from central New Spain and interbreeding with the Pueblos and many others. Spaniards did not settle Texas successfully until the early eighteenth century, intermixing with Coahuiltecans and other peoples as well. Regarding California's natives, such as the Chumash, Cook notes "that a great deal of intermarriage with non-Indians (almost entirely Mexicans [mestizos])" occurred from "the foundation of the missions" in 1769 (1976, 162–63). Continuing *mestizaje* intermixed, not only Spaniards and Africans with local Indians, but central Mexican Indians with those in the northern borderlands. By the end of the formal colonial period, Indians and mestizos formed a significant part of the population of central New Spain: According to Cook, "a final exact conclusion cannot be reached [… but] in 1793 Negroes and mulattoes constituted from 10 to 15 per cent of the population, the predominantly white element from 20-35 per cent, the mestizo and Indian element 50 to 70 per cent" (1942, 504). Though the European and African physical and cultural imprint was foreign to the Americas, constant intermixing with native peoples resulted in a heritage that remained fundamentally indigenous, a heritage ultimately called Mexican.

MEXICAN INDEPENDENCE

After Mexican independence in 1821, despite Hispanic creole social and political leadership, nationalism built on indigeneity—at least respect for the Aztec and Mayan "high civilizations"—developed in order to keep the loyalty of the Indian and mestizo masses who began the war for independence and to distinguish Mexico from Spain (De la Peña 2006, 279–80). Indeed, even the northern borderlands of New Spain—Texas, New Mexico, and California—had become increasingly mestizo when they became officially Mexican. For example, in southern California even for those identified as Indians, according to Cook, "in the decades 1828–1847 [… the] degree of Indian blood had already decreased to a mean of 70 or 80 percent" despite relatively late Spanish colonization. Of course, he meant the amount of local Indian ancestry based on genealogical records, not DNA, since the 20–30% was from "non-Indians (almost entirely Mexicans)," meaning mestizos, not Spaniards (1976, 162–63). In the borderlands Comanches, Apaches, and other tribal peoples retained independence from the new Mexican nation, but mestizos in towns, such as Los Angeles, Santa Fe, and San Antonio retained ties to local Indian peoples because they were usually related. Thus, mestizos, whether in the center or on the frontiers of Mexico, remained native peoples, especially after the peninsular officers and missionaries directly from Spain left.

OCCUPIED MEXICO

After the United States conquered California, the area became a territory within a contiguous American empire with an English-speaking national state at its eastern core. This continental colonialism had evolved from its British overseas predecessor as Anglo-Americans pushed westward from the former thirteen English colonies that had become independent states. In 1848 the United States imposed an international border across conquered Mexico, and Anglo-American colonization of the New Southwest increased. Thus, California became a formal colony, an unorganized territory, rapidly settled by Anglos during the Gold Rush, its former Mexican citizens ruled by a military governor appointed by Washington. In 1850 California achieved U.S. statehood, formal self-government, but colonialism continued internally and informally due to the continuing socioeconomic and psychological subordination of the Mexican and Indian populations.

Anglos superimposed their own colonial racial hierarchy over the Hispanic predecessor: generally, Anglos over European ethnics (including Spaniards), mestizos, Asians, then Blacks, and Indians. In 1877 the *Milwaukee Sentinel* revealed Anglo-American opinion of the alien territory of New Mexico: "nine-tenths of the population is of the Spanish-Indian class [...] a pariah class, reared and kept in supreme ignorance" (Montgomery 2002, 62). Literally, facing extermination in the late nineteenth century, more Indians hispanicized to move up the hierarchy and merge with the remaining Mexican population. Consequently in southern California, by 1903 those identified genealogically and culturally as Indians had only 45% local ancestry, but the intermixing continued almost always with Mexicans who carried native ancestry from elsewhere in Greater Mexico (Cook 1976, 156, Fig. 13). Though some had moved south immediately after the U.S.-Mexico War, Mexicans did not decline in overall numbers. They were reduced to minority status through the late nineteenth century because of heavy Anglo colonization, but movement north from Mexico nonetheless continued attracted by mining, livestock raising, and railroad labor (Hernández 2012, 33, 46, 74, 155–56).

The Mexican Revolution of 1910 reinvigorated the Mexican population of the Southwest through massive 'migration' over the border imposed across Mexico. These mestizo 'newcomers' were perceived as foreigners, legally classified as immigrants despite their prior historic pre-contact, Spanish colonial, and Mexican national ties to the Southwest. However, in this region, Mexicans continued the traditional pattern of intermarriage with the local natives. For example, in southern California they intermarried with Indians such that by 1928, the latter had 70% Mexican mestizo ancestry and 30% local native (Cook 1976, 163).

Though fewer Mexicans came than left in the 1930s and the 1950s, waves of migrants arrived constantly throughout the rest of the twentieth century. Each wave faced the same status of non-citizen, even illegal alien, in a land native to them. But nativity was evident even among ethnic Mexicans who had long called themselves Hispanos because their ancestors had resided in the borderlands since the Spanish colonial era. In such areas as northern New Mexico and southern Colorado, where the new migrants did not penetrate in great numbers, earlier patterns of interbreeding between Hispanos, Pueblos, Utes, Comanches, and others nonetheless left an indelible mark. By the 1990s genetic studies added evidence of this indigeneity to the earlier demographic work based on census, baptismal, and other genealogical records. A 1997 genetic study in the San Luis Valley in Colorado found that "The nuclear estimates of Amerindian admixture were 33.15 ± 2.41% for the Hispanics and 9.72 ± 1.90% for the Anglos, while the strictly maternally inherited mtDNA estimates of Amerindian admixture were 85.11% for the Hispanics and 0.97% for the Anglos" (Merriwether et al. 1997, 153). Native ancestry more clearly appeared when following the maternal DNA lines that reflected overwhelming Spanish interbreeding with Indian women. Regardless of estimate, the area's ethnic Mexicans had much more native ancestry than the area's Anglos did. Another study of the same area a few years later arrived at similar results, adding that "Spanish Americans and Mexican Americans in Colorado revealed a degree of Native American admixture comparable to that of other Mexican American populations nationwide" (Bonilla et al. 2004, 139, cf. 149).[6]

METHODOLOGY

Though largely unaware of such genealogical and genetic technicalities, everyday Mexicans recognized Indian heritage and nativity through appearance, oral tradition, and basic history. Despite Anglo attempts to alienate them from their northern homeland, a Zogby poll in 2002 reported that 58% of people in Mexico in the twenty-first-century still believed the Southwest belonged to their country. 57% agreed that they had the right to enter the U.S. without permission, suggesting they thought of themselves as natives to the region (Zogby 2002).[7] Clearly the Mexicans polled felt they had rights to the Southwest, but establishing the basis for that claim is essential to judging its validity and subsequently any violation of those rights according to internal colonial theory.

In the colonial paradigm, first rights to land are defined by indigeneity. Using secondary demographic and genetic sources, I have above established Mexicans' nativity within the narrative of their ancestors' presence in the region from the pre-contact era to the present. The sources demonstrate that they are closely related to the Indians of the Southwest, once part of Mexico. Mexicans have thus been denied their rightful heritage by a dominant society that implies that they are all foreigners, a society that denies 'Mexican immigrants' the rights of natural born citizens on crossing the border that divided their homeland through conquest. Thus, following internal colonialism, ethnic Mexicans form a subordinate group in their northern homeland now within the borders of the Anglo-American nation-state (Fig. 12.1).

As I began this paper on a personal note, I tested the genetic methods on myself. In my case genealogy could tell me little; I could trace my family back to the early nineteenth century in the north central Mexican states of Zacatecas and Guanajuato, but the records said little about my own

---

[6]According to Bonilla, "The ancestral proportions of the S[an] Luis] V[alley] Hispanic population are estimated as $62.7 \pm 2.1\%$ European, $34.1 \pm 1.9\%$ Native American and $3.2 \pm 1.5\%$ West African" (2004, 139).

[7]The Zogby Poll also indicated that 68% of Americans believed U.S. troops should aid the Border Patrol, suggesting the degree to which they still saw Mexicans as a foreign threat.

Fig. 12.1   Andrea Quiroz Chávez, Pico Rivera, California, 14 September 2013 (Author's personal collection)

intermixture.[8] Of course, oral family history was replete with references to vague Spanish and Indian ancestors, with appearance suggesting the degree of descent, though my Mediterranean looks little reflected the indigenous appearance of my mother. In 2014 my individual AncestryDNA results reflected the conclusions above though in some surprising ways.[9]

[8]In 2017 I found some evidence in the death record of my great grandmother, Anastasia Robles Cosio's brother, Cenoraio [sic] de Robles, described as "of indigenous race mixed with white" (Mezquitic 1909–1924, 2, 436–37; my translation).

[9]Ancestry: Genealogy, Family Trees, and Family History Records (ancestry.com) is a commercial website available through subscription; its more limited library edition may be accessed through many academic institutions, such as through https://www-ancestryli-brary-com.proxy.libraries.smu.edu/; FamilyTree.com: Genealogy, Ancestry, and Family

Opening the report, a pie chart subdivided my "ethnicity estimate" into geographical regions—or homelands in my terminology. My heritage was enumerated and labeled, "39% Native American," "23% Iberian Peninsula," and "38% other regions."[10] The largest pie slice covered both North and South America, an undifferentiated category. Unfortunately, without explanation the report failed to subdivide this hemispheric classification; consequently, it was best interpreted in light of the history sketched above and my own genealogy. With no evidence of South Amerindian heritage, my genealogy of five generations traced my ancestors exclusively to Mexico in the 1830s. Thus, AncestryDNA reinforced my claim to partial nativity in North America. The Iberian slice clearly referred to Portugal and Spain, with the latter more likely the source of my European ancestry, given my language heritage to say the least. Apparently, this slice referred to the earliest inhabitants of the peninsula detected by genetic methods. An immediate concern regarding this slice was that Europe was already subcategorized in more regional detail than the Americas, a clear bias in the sampling. This concern deepened as the third slice would include mostly "Old World" locations, thus further complicating my claims to indigeneity and homeland (Fig. 12.2).

AncestryDNA further subdivided my heritage in the "full ethnicity estimate," a separate chart. The third slice of 38% included 26% other European regions beyond Iberia. The break down suggested that I had 11% Italian and Greek nationality, which required some historical interpretation, given that genealogically I had no ancestors from modern Italy or Greece, nation-states developed in the nineteenth century when all my ancestors were in modern Mexico. Deeper reflection proposed that because Greeks and Romans had occupied the Iberian Peninsula in classical antiquity, many present people of Spanish descent would have such ancestry. The remaining 15% of European heritage could be explained similarly—less than 5% each came from "trace regions," such as Great Britain, Ireland, continental Europe, all areas that shared Celts and Germans with Iberia in early and late antiquity. Also classified among the Europeans, despite earlier origins in the Middle East were Jews at 4%,

Tree Research is also a commercial site available through subscription; both companies offer genetic testing through ancestry.com/dna and familytreedna.com, respectively.

[10]AncestryDNA 2014; in 2017 further analysis by Family Tree DNA confirmed my Amerindian ancestry at 39%.

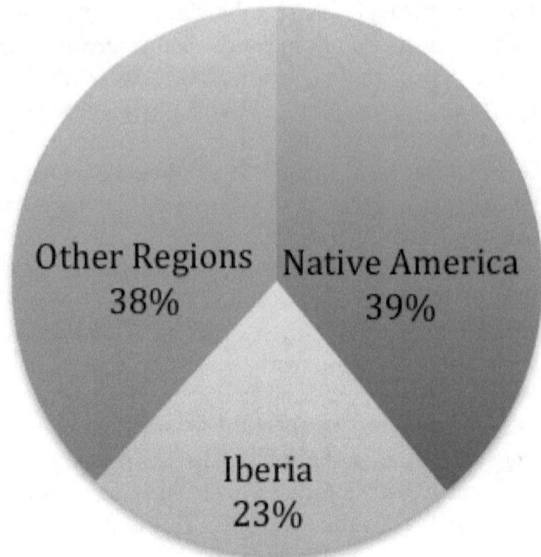

Fig. 12.2   Ethnicity Estimate for John R. Chávez (Adapted from AncestryDNA, 2014)

likely Sephardic in my case, given their presence in Iberia at least since the Roman Empire. Adding up the European ancestry totaled 49%, all likely funneled through Iberia, known as Hispania to the Romans, more specifically Spain in my case (Fig. 12.3).

This degree of European genetic ancestry would seem to make me indigenous to Spain, rather than North America or even Mexico. Other regional results strengthened this analysis. Under West Asia, the report assigned 5% of my background to the Caucasus and Middle East, possibly reflecting the Moorish occupation of Iberia in the Middle Ages if not Phoenician, Carthaginian, or even earlier migrations. Along these lines another 1% apparently came from North Africa, perhaps Berber. But since Iberia had been populated by Paleolithic Cro-Magnon people and others for thousands of years before the historic groups listed above and deeper than even genetic testing could yet reach, establishing indigeneity could become an exercise in futility with so much subsequent intermixing. It seemed the line between colonizer and colonized was relational depending on the mode of contact. Romans arrived as

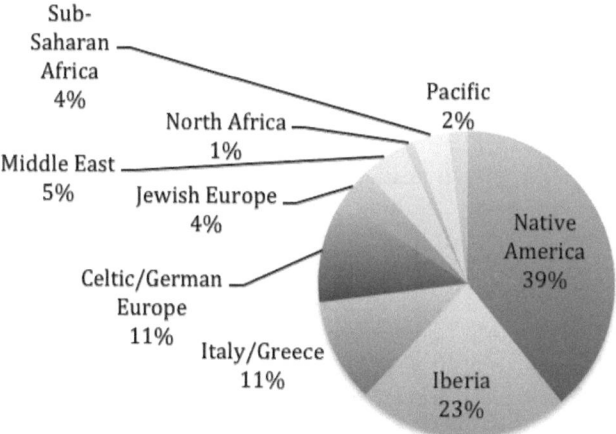

Fig. 12.3 Full Ethnicity Estimate for John R. Chávez (Adapted from AncestryDNA, 2014)

conquerors, clearly colonizers, whereas Jews arrived as refugees, both becoming indigenous as passing generations intermixed with earlier arrivals and later as when Visigoths conquered Romans and Moors conquered Visigoths.

While AncestryDNA could take me to some prehistoric depths, its other results would take me farther afield, reflecting patterns of Spanish colonialism after Columbus. To no surprise AncestryDNA revealed 4% of my genetic background derived from Africa farther south, particularly from Senegal, Benin, Togo, Mali, modern states whose lands were sources of slaves for Spanish America, people probably funneled through the Caribbean to Mexico. Though the report regarded results less than 5% as tentative, oral family history confirmed the presence of African ancestors through prior comments made by my paternal grandmother. Most surprising was the 2% suggestion of Polynesian ancestors, reflective of Spanish trade across the Pacific via the Manila Galleon, or simply erroneous as possible with other tentative findings. While these African and Pacific ancestors were not indigenous to North America, they contributed to the evolving mix based on Amerindian and Spanish ancestry to become distinctly Mexican, just as Iberians, Celts, Greeks, Romans, Jews, Germans, and Berbers had formed Spaniards.

Unlike Africa and Eurasia, however, the Americas were populated much more recently and indigeneity could be established more readily given the relative isolation of the Western Hemisphere before Columbus. Given that circumstance, in 2015 I had my mother's genetic background checked through Family Tree DNA. The results placed her in Haplogroup A, a mitochondrial line extending back at least 30,000 years and among the first, including the ancestral Chumash, to people the hemisphere (Potter and White 2009, 176–77). While this group could also be found in some parts of Eurasia, indicating a common human species in constant migration, Haplogroup A had spread throughout the Americas. Among the first arrivals in North America, Haplogroup A marked indigeneity as deeply as possible, supporting the studies of Kumar and earlier investigators regarding Mexican ancestry on the continent.

Family Tree's report on my mother's autosomal DNA confirmed my own from AncestryDNA with some variation. Like its competitor, Family Tree displayed a hemispheric map categorizing Amerindian origins though under the label, 'New World.' However, there was a broad, but significant refinement that restricted her background to western North America, thus including all of Greater Mexico. The New World classification indicated she had 51% Amerindian background, less than I had expected. (This strongly suggested my father must have had nearly 30%, more than I had thought given their appearance, an often misleading indicator.) This category included 4% attributed to South America, understandable given ancient migrations of related peoples in that direction, but excluded 4% from Asia, likely ancient Amerindian bringing the latter up to 55%. More surprising was that her 32% European roots included no Iberian, meaning her ancestors from West and Central Europe at 26% were probably early Celtic and German colonizers of the Iberian Peninsula with Greeks and Romans comprising another 6% from Southeast Europe. She had no Jewish ancestry, but the East Middle East (2%) and North Africa categories (6%) suggested Arab and Berber ancestors in Spain. West Africa contributed 4% (Family Tree DNA, My Origins 2017). Most of my mother's European background probably came from her father based on appearance, again an unreliable variable.

However, in my mother's case genealogy allowed me to trace our maternal background to the mid-nineteenth century in the central Mexican state of Guanajuato. My maternal grandmother, Anita Medina, was born in 1901 on the Hacienda de Santa Ana del Conde near the city of Leon. As a peon, she was descended from the Guachichil natives of the area, Uto-Aztecan speakers like the distant Tongva of the Los Angeles basin. Thus, my mother and I were connected to Southern California through the ancient linguistic family of the Tongva as well as the DNA of the Chumash. Still while my mother was on the whole over 50% Native, was her mDNA enough to overcome the fact that I, like other Mexicans, had overall more Spanish than Indian genetic ancestry? Defining indigeneity was obviously more complex than biology or geography.

CRITICAL RACE THEORY

Needless to say, the use of genetics to establish indigeneity and claims to homeland is controversial since such use suggests the argument rests on biological race. Critical race theory rejects the notion of biological race as scientific fact (Delgado and Stefancic 2017, 2; Winant 2000, 171). Critical race theorists argue that race is a social construction that creates categories based on superficial physical appearance, such as skin color or eye shape, rather than on biological function. Race is unlike species, a scientific classification that relies on reproduction, a biological function, to separate for example cats from dogs. Humans belong to the same species with the same origins as they all can and have interbred even if they vary in physical appearance, including degree of pigmentation.[11]

Since genes do predispose individuals to varying degrees of pigmentation, this is a biological phenomenon that has been called race, but is preferably called color. Though this may seem semantic, the social construction appears when individuals are categorized into groups based on color, raising the question of where to draw the line on a matter of degree. When there is doubt about categorization at the margins, it may seem a fair generalization to refer to the core group, as say 'white,' but any line created is artificial because society decides where to draw it. One could, for instance, argue that only albinos are white (Norwood 2013, 4–6). According to Ian F. Haney-López,

> The notion that humankind can be divided along White, Black, and Yellow lines reveals the social rather than the scientific origin of race. The idea

---

[11]For mutual respect and collaboration between historians and geneticists, see Manning (2016, 6–7); for a critique of critical race theory through class analysis, see Darder (2011, 126).

that there exist three races, and that these races are 'Caucasoid,' 'Negroid,' and 'Mongoloid,' is rooted in the European imagination of the Middle Ages, which encompassed only Europe, Africa, and the Near East. [...] Nevertheless, the history of science has long been the history of failed efforts to justify these social beliefs (1994, 13).

While AncestryDNA and Family Tree's lumping of all Amerindians into one hemispheric category reflects such earlier continental imagery, their reports utilize social geographical regions, rather than racial categories to estimate ethnicity that I in turn use to approximate indigeneity.[12] In addition to the continental definitions critiqued by Ian Haney-López, narrower but no clearer phrases such as the 'English or French race' can be deconstructed as social because they connote national, rather than physical categories. Critical race theorists would argue such labels obviously reflect changing political and cultural structures, rather than biological facts. These critics would justifiably see my Italic-Greek ethnicity as marked by AncestryDNA as a social construction. One could readily subsume it under a Spanish category depending on geography and historical period as I did above, and the company could hardly object to the new construction.

Neither the methodology of AncestryDNA nor Family Tree DNA categorizes people by race, but by ancestral place. Samples of the DNA of local people who have deep genealogies in a particular place are compared with each other. The genes that they share most become the standard to which genetic samples like my own would be compared. Of course, the way the standard samples are acquired depends on various factors, such as the definition of local natives and the definition of their areas of residence. For example, the samples could be drawn from modern Italians living in the areas of Rome, Venice, Naples, or elsewhere in the present republic that has nonetheless experienced migration and changing borders historically. This inherent imprecision contributes to the testing companies' results as estimates of ethnicity, rather than biological, racial facts.

---

[12] By 2017 AncestryDNA had subdivided the hemispheric Native American category into 'Genetic Communities,' still based on geography, rather than race or tribe. By comparison with the DNA samples of other Ancestry subscribers, my roots were placed in Zacatecas-Aguascalientes, the region of my father's family, and contiguous with Guanajuato, the region of my mother's.

However, careful not to overstate the claims of critical race theory, Haney-López clarifies its position on biological race:

Notice this does not mean that individuals are genetically indistinguishable from each other, or even that small population groups cannot be genetically differentiated. Small populations, for example the Xhosa or the Basques, share similar gene frequencies. However, differentiation is a function of separation, usually geographic, and occurs in gradations rather than across fractures (1994, 12).

Similarly, genes analyzed by AncestryDNA are biological facts that can link individuals, through scientific double-blind methods, to their ancestors in definable places even if the labels classifying them are malleable.

Moreover, though race is a not scientific fact, it remains a real social fact in that it has demonstrable consequences, such as discrimination based on color. In 1849 the few ethnic Mexican delegates at California's constitutional convention objected with limited success to a provision prohibiting Indians from voting. The delegates realized their own people could be banned based on appearance—color or even dress and customs—since mission Indians, such as the Chumash, had become Mexican. In the twenty-first century, racial profiling remains a concern for Mexican Americans in dealing with law enforcement, such as the Border Patrol, since for one thing they may appear indistinguishable from 'illegal aliens.' Though racism is now understood to apply to sociocultural as well as bodily characteristics, prejudice and discrimination based on skin color, now sometimes called 'colorism,' remain powerful social behaviors that make race appear obvious even if it is scientific fiction (Norwood 2013, 4–6).

Despite its negative associations, Haney-López stresses that "race, because it is closely tied to communities, provides an essential component of identity. In this sense, although biological race does not exist, social race is very far from being an illusion in providing a link between what we look like and who we are" (Haney-López 1994, 61, cf. 38). He believes historical processes fabricate races by assigning meaning to the morphology and heritage of groups. Indeed, he comments that U.S. expansion defined Mexicans as a race subject to discrimination for decades to follow. Though Mexican subgroups had previously existed as castes in Hispanic society, Anglo-American notions of race were superimposed on the previous social construction in a new hierarchical order.

Interestingly, the reaction to such processes could be positive for ethnic identity even as they reified race.

Even as Mexicans after independence had reacted to the Spanish caste system with pride in their pre-Columbian heritage, their descendants in the borderlands reacted to Anglo racism similarly.

> Drawing upon the new nationalist framework, the militants of the late 1960s also perceived aspects of colonial domination in U.S. race relations. [...] Often they condemned their conquest by military might, celebrated imagined homelands where they might live free, and, at least among Latinos and Native Americans, decried the continued occupation of geographically defined spaces (Haney-López 1994, 25, n. 101, cf. 38).

Significantly, Chicanos thus reconstructed the image of Aztlán, the Aztecs' mythical place of origin, and applied it to the country they would recover for themselves. Aztlán was of course a version of the Greater Mexico, the native homeland I claimed for my mother at the opening of this essay. Thus, social race can be constructed to unify a disadvantaged group ethnically.

CONCLUSION

Especially when combined with general history, archeology, linguistics, demography, and other sources of information, genetic tracking establishes that most ethnic Mexicans have an ancestral link to the U.S. Southwest that counters notions that they are foreign immigrants, let alone aliens. Despite migration across a border imposed by conquest, they remain natives in the homeland of their indigenous mothers—with rightful claims to residency and citizenship. However, they also remain alienated within an Anglo-American nation-state fenced by the colonizers—within an internal colony. As concerns internal colonialism and the colonial paradigm, the ethnic Mexican case demonstrates that the colonized land can be defined very broadly in space and time depending on both objective and subjective factors. Similarly, the colonized natives can be a complex group due to these factors. This complexity does not diminish the paradigm, but forces us to apply it more carefully to the particulars of historical reality (Chávez 2009, 202–203, 225–28).

References

AncestryDNA. 2019. "In Ancestry: Genealogy, Family Trees, and Family History Records." https://www.ancestry.com/dna. Last accessed January 2, 2018.

Barrera, Mario. 1979. *Race and Class in the Southwest: A Theory of Racial Inequality.* Notre Dame, IN: University of Notre Dame Press.

Bonilla, C., et al. 2004. "Admixture in the Hispanics of the San Luis Valley, Colorado, and Its Implications for Complex Trait Gene Mapping." *Annals of Human Genetics* 68(2): 139–53.

Brading, David A. 1994. "Grupos étnicos, clases y estructura ocupacional en Guanajuato (1792)." In *Historia y población en México: Siglos XVI-XIX*, edited by Thomas Calvo, 258–60. Lecturas de Historia Mexicana 9. Mexico City: Centro de Estudios Históricos, Colegio de México.

Chávez, John R. 2009. *Beyond Nations: Evolving Homelands in the North Atlantic World, 1400–2000.* New York: Cambridge University Press.

Chávez, John R. 2011. "Aliens in Their Native Lands: The Persistence of Internal Colonial Theory." *Journal of World History* 22(4): 785–809.

Chávez, John R. [1989] 2017. "Aztlán, Cíbola, and Frontier New Spain." In *Aztlán: Essays on the Chicano Homeland*, edited by Rudolfo Anaya, Francisco A. Lomelí, and Enrique R. Lamadrid, 289–310. Rev. ed., Albuquerque: University of New Mexico Press.

Cook, Sherburne Friend. 1942. "The Population of Mexico in 1793." *Human Biology* 14(4): 499–515.

Cook, Sherburne Friend. 1976. *The Population of the California Indians, 1769–1970.* Berkeley: University of California Press.

Cook, Sherburne Friend, and Lesley Byrd Simpson. 1948. *The Population of Central Mexico in the Sixteenth Century.* Ibero-Americana 31. Berkeley: University of California Press.

Darder, Antonia. 2011. "What's So Critical About Critical Race Theory? A Conceptual Interrogation with Rodolfo Torres: Counterpoints 418." *A Dissident Voice: Essays on Culture, Pedagogy, and Power* 6: 109–29.

Dartt-Newton, Deana, and Jon M. Erlandson. 2006. "Little Choice for the Chumash: Colonialism, Cattle, and Coercion in Mission Period California." *American Indian Quarterly* 30(3&4): 416–30.

De la Peña, Guillermo. 2006. "A New Mexican Nationalism." *Nations and Nationalism* 12(2): 279–302. http://www.gdelapen.com/Resources/%20A_New_Mexican_Nationalism.pdf. Accessed January 2, 2016.

Delgado, Richard, and Jean Stefancic. 2017. *Critical Race Theory: An Introduction*, 3rd ed. New York: New York University.

"Donald Trump Announces a Presidential Bid." 2015. *Washington Post*, 16 June. https://www.washingtonpost.com/news/post-politics/wp/2015/06/16/

full-text-donald-trump-announces-a-presidential-bid/?utm_term=.
ba3bd9541f47. Accessed June 17, 2017.

Family Tree DNA. 2019. "In FamilyTree.com: Genealogy, Ancestry, and Family
Tree Research." http://www.familytreedna.com. Last accessed January 2,
2018.

Favre, Henri. 1996. *L'indigénisme. Que sais-je?* Paris: Presses Universitaires de
France.

Gamble, Lynn H. 2011. *The Chumash World at European Contact: Power, Trade,
and Feasting among Complex Hunter-Gatherers.* Berkeley: University of
California Press.

Gandhi, Leela. 1998. *Postcolonial Theory: A Critical Introduction.* New York:
Columbia University Press.

González-Casanova, Pablo. 1963. "Sociedad Plural, Colonialismo Interno
y Desarrollo." *América Latina* 6(3): 15–32.

Hammarström, Harald, et al., eds. 2016. "Family: Uto-Aztecan." *Glottolog.* Jena,
Ger.: Max Planck Institute for the Science of Human History. http://www.
glottolog.org/resource/languoid/id/utoa1244. Accessed January 4, 2016.

Haney-López, Ian F. 1994. "The Social Construction of Race: Some
Observations on Illusion, Fabrication, and Choice." *Harvard Civil Rights-
Civil Liberties Law Review* 29(1): 1–62.

Hechter, Michael. [1975] 1999. *Internal Colonialism: The Celtic Fringe in
British National Development* (with a new introduction and a new appendix
by the author). New Brunswick, NJ: Transaction Publishers.

Hernández, José Antonio. 2012. *Mexican American Colonization During the
Nineteenth Century: A History of the U.S.-Mexico Borderlands.* New York:
Cambridge University Press.

Johnson, John R., and Joseph G. Lorenz. 2006. "Genetics, Linguistics, and
Prehistoric Migrations: An Analysis of California Indian Mitochondrial DNA
Lineages." *Journal of California and Great Basin Anthropology* 26(1): 33–64.

Kumar, Satish, et al. 2011. "Large Scale Mitochondrial Sequencing in Mexican
Americans Suggests a Reappraisal of Native American Origins." *BMC
Evolutionary Biology* 11(293): 1–17. http://www.biomedcentral.com/1471-
2148/11/293. Accessed December 27, 2015.

Manning, Patrick. 2016. "History, Science, and Community: Native American
Pasts." *Perspectives* 54(7): 6–7.

Márquez-Morfin, Lourdes, and Rebecca Storey. 2017. "Population History in
Precolumbian and Colonial Times." In *The Oxford Handbook of the Aztecs*,
edited by Deborah Nichols and Enrique Rodríguz-Alegría, 189–200. New
York: Oxford University Press.

Mendoza, Ruben G. 2014. "Indigenous Landscapes: Mexicanized Indians
and the Archaeology of Social Networks in Alta California." In *Indigenous
Landscapes and Spanish Missions: New Perspectives from Archaeology and*

Ethnohistory, edited by Lee Panich and Tsim Schneider. 2nd ed., 114–31. Tucson: University of Arizona Press.

Merriwether, D.Andrew, et al. 1997. "Mitochondrial versus Nuclear Admixture Estimates Demonstrate a Past History of Directional Mating." *American Journal of Physical Anthropology* 102(2): 153–59.

Mezquitic. 1909–1924. *Jalisco, Mexico, Civil Registration Deaths, 1856–1987*. Provo, UT: Ancestry.com Operations, 2015.

Montgomery, Charles H. 2002. *The Spanish Redemption: Heritage, Power, and Loss on New Mexico's Upper Rio Grande*. Berkeley: University of California Press.

Norwood, Kimberly Jade, ed. 2013. *Color Matters: Skin Tone Bias and the Myth of a Postracial America*. New York: Routledge.

Osterhammel, Jürgen. [1995] 1997. *Colonialism: A Theoretical Overview*. Translated by Shelley L. Frisch. Reprint, Princeton, NJ: Markus Wiener Publishers.

Potter, Amiee B., and P. Scott White. 2009. "The Mitochondrial DNA Affinities of the Prehistoric People of San Clemente Island: An Analysis of Ancient DNA." *Journal of California and Great Basin Anthropology* 29(2): 163–82.

Sutton, Mark Q. 2005. "People and Language: Defining the Takic Expansion into Southern California." *Pacific Coast Archaeological Society Quarterly* 41(2&3): 31–93.

United States National Park Service. 2016. "Channel Islands National Park, California: Santa Cruz Island." https://www.nps.gov/chis/planyourvisit/santa-cruz-island.htm. Accessed July 1, 2017.

Winant, Howard. 2000. Race and Race Theory. *Annual Review of Sociology* 26(1): 169–85.

Zogby International. 2002. "Poll: US-Mexico Border Opinions Differ." 12 June. http://www.upi.com/Poll-US-Mexico-border-opinions-differ/47571023892200/. Accessed July 3, 2017.

CHAPTER 13

The Second Conquest: Continental and Internal Colonialism in Nineteenth-Century Latin America

Wolfgang Gabbert

INTRODUCTION

The history of Latin America since the late fifteenth century is of particular interest for the comparative discussion of colonialism—overseas, continental, and internal.[1] It was the first, and for some time the only, instance of European expansion into overseas areas that implied the establishment of rule over an extended territory. Spanish domination would draw to a close in mainland Latin America in the 1820s more than half a century before Europeans even began to subdue the African interior and before 'scientific' racism emerged as the key ideology to legitimize overseas colonialism. In contrast to Africa or Asia, formal independence was gained in the Americas before nationalism and the nation-state model were fully established in Europe. Thus, processes

---

[1] Earlier versions of some of the material presented here were published in Gabbert (2012, 2015a); all translations from Spanish are mine.

W. Gabbert (✉)
Institute of Sociology, Leibniz University Hannover, Hannover, Germany
e-mail: w.gabbert@ish.uni-hannover.de

© The Author(s) 2019
D. Schorkowitz et al. (eds.), *Shifting Forms of Continental Colonialism*,
https://doi.org/10.1007/978-981-13-9817-9_13

333

of nation-building in the Americas and in Europe were contemporaneous and the former colonies could not follow a model already at hand. More than that, the independent North and Latin American countries endowed themselves with republican constitutions and advanced the principle of the sovereignty of the people while most European countries saw a conservative restoration of the nobility's privileges after the Congress of Vienna (1815). However, as will be seen, elites tried to legitimize the enduring social inequalities alluding to supposed racial differences. The dissemination of a homogenous national culture was considered a civilizing mission in both regions.

In the following I will confine myself to the former Iberian possessions in Latin America and discuss major developments in the spheres of ideology, politics, and economy in independent Latin America that can be considered dimensions of an emerging internal and continental colonialism—forms evolving from earlier overseas colonialism—particularly in respect to the colonized indigenous population collectively referred to as *indios* (Indians).[2] I will start with a brief discussion of two essential routes the European expansion to Latin America had taken that responded to fundamental sociopolitical differences among the precolonial native societies. These differences decisively shaped the forms of colonialism and the treatment of the indigenous population before and after formal independence.

LATIN AMERICAN DIVERSITY

The overall structure and dynamics of European expansion in Latin America were the result of a complex interplay between the interests, capacities, and ideology of the Iberians on the one hand, and the diversity of indigenous societies and ecological conditions on the other. The possibly 40–50 million who peopled the Americas on the eve of the conquest in the late fifteenth century differed widely in language, culture,

---

[2]While continental colonialism is related to processes of a polity's expansion into adjacent areas, internal colonialism can be seen as a particular combination of ideological, political, and economic relations combining the social exclusion, economic exploitation, and (formal or informal) political marginalization of certain groups within the boundaries of a state legitimized by ethnic or racist arguments. In contrast to class domination, both collectivities (or categories)—colonizers and the colonized—may encompass several socioeconomic strata.

economy, and social organization. They probably spoke languages belonging to more than a hundred language families, for example (Coe 1986, 42–45, 86, 156–57).

Mesoamerica in the north and the Andean highlands in the south were the most densely settled parts of the Americas. Here, complex societies, such as the Inca and Aztec empires, each with several million subjects, evolved based on the intensive cultivation of corn, potatoes, and other crops. They were characterized, among other things, by urbanism, class stratification, and state religions. The intermediate areas comprising the West Indies, Central America, and the northern parts of South America were less densely inhabited by people mostly organized in chiefdoms. Centralized leadership and inequality in the form of ranking prevailed in these mainly agricultural societies. Political and social organization, however, was less complex than in core areas. Similar structures existed in the south and southeast of the Andes and on the fertile alluvial plains along the major streams of the Latin American lowlands, such as the Amazon and Orinoco. Most of the Latin American lowlands (with the exception of the Yucatán peninsula) were populated by often highly mobile people, who combined hunting and fishing with gathering and gardening (Gunsenheimer and Schüren 2016, 107–28).

The differences between the native societies sketched above had significant consequences for the patterns of conquest and colonization in each region. Indigenous state societies were conquered in relatively short periods. The Aztec and Inca empires of central Mexico and the central Andes fell after a few years.[3] The Spaniards ousted only the top imperial leaders from offices, installing themselves at the apex of an already existent highly centralized political hierarchy. The common population, mostly composed of peasants and their families, was accustomed to relinquishing parts of their surplus product and labor to the aristocracy and the state. Thus, the Spaniards could refer to well-established institutions of government and exploitation. Consequently, Mexico and the Andean region became the core areas of the Iberian colonies. Although the enslavement of Indians played a major role during the conquest and the initial years thereafter, it was soon replaced by different forms of tribute and forced labor (Gibson 1984, 399–407; Schüren 2017). Indian tribute

---

[3]A discussion of the reasons for the Spanish success can be found in Gabbert (1995, 2010).

and the exploitation of precious metals, particularly silver, became the mainstay of the colonial economy in the core areas.

The indigenous people in the Latin American core areas were treated differently according to their social standing as were all other subjects of the Spanish crown. At first, the status of the Indian commoner estate was formally identical to that of their Spanish peers. They were legally considered free vassals of the crown. However, in light of their poverty, lack of education, and knowledge of the Spanish judicial system, they were soon compared to a special category of Spaniards, the 'rustics and miserables' (*rústicos y miserables*). This meant subjection to a regime of tutelage and protection and included certain privileges that aimed, among other things, at facilitating their access to the judicial system, such as speedy trials, reduced fees, or lesser punishments.[4] The indigenous nobles, in contrast, were treated quite differently reflecting the hierarchical world view of the Spanish elites and their fundamental role in the maintenance of colonial rule as military allies, tribute collectors, or organizers of forced labor. Consequently, their prerogatives were often respected by the Spanish crown. They held the status of the Castilian nobles and received a share of their town's tribute. Exemption from tribute, forced labor, and the legal prohibitions imposed on indigenous commoners were additional privileges. They were permitted to carry a sword and dagger, and wear European dress. A number of noblemen were granted the title of *don*, and many were allowed to ride horses. In contrast to the Indian commoners, they could acquire land individually. This allowed a certain section of the Indian nobility to own large estates, while others amassed considerable wealth in commerce. On the whole, therefore, they were often better off economically than many of the Spaniards. Hence, the indigenous nobility in the Oaxaca Valley, Mexico, for example, was closer to Spanish noblemen than to Indian commoners. The native nobles were culturally hispanicized to a high degree as a result of royal favors they had received, and in the middle of the seventeenth century Indian commoners lumped together indigenous and Spanish noblemen in their towns (see Whitecotton 1970, 379–81; Taylor 1972, 30–45; Gabbert 2004, 23–25).

---

[4] In Spanish legal thought, 'miserables' were all kinds of people in need of protection, such as orphans, minors, widows, pupils, servants, captives, paupers, and peasants or the aged; cf. Castañeda Delgado (1971, 245–48, 253–67), Zavala and Miranda (1954, 107–18).

Furthermore, in contrast to people of real or assumed African descent, there were no legal restrictions concerning the marriage between Spaniards and Indians whose origin was not considered 'vile'. In fact, in a number of cases Spaniards married Indian women, particularly if of noble descent, and Spanish women married Indian men (Mörner 1967, 36–39, 62–66; McCaa 1984, 496–97; Schüren 2017, 44). As a matter of fact, the social structure of the colonial core areas was 'bewilderingly complex', as Magnus Mörner (1967, 61) put it. While the main social categories—Spaniard and Indians—were clearly of colonial origin reflecting the dichotomy of conqueror and conquered, these categories were both internally differentiated. In addition, legal status did not necessarily match with social status. Individuals were ranked according a multiplicity of criteria, among them legal status, descent, dwelling place, and occupation. "[C]lassificatory practices derived from information on an individual's ancestral and personal social relations. Since the latter could change with the circumstances, labels could change too, and individuals could boast several through their lifetime or simultaneously" (de la Cadena 2005, 265–66). Caste labels were "simply a reflection of one's social standing, not a way to record physical descent" (Cañizares-Esguerra 2009, 320). Thus, Indians occupied a wide variety of positions in the social hierarchy and the social structure in the core areas cannot be reduced to a simple dichotomy of Spanish colonists and Indian colonized.

Conquest and the subsequent establishment of Iberian rule were more difficult in the case of less centralized native societies, where the Spaniards had to subdue each chiefdom or village individually. Spaniards and Portuguese faced the difficult task of fundamentally changing existent patterns of authority, division of labor, and distribution of surplus. Among many of the lowland tribes, stable leadership institutions had to be invented. The natives were frequently not accustomed to work for others, or to hand over their products, and submitted only to force. Personal service played a much more important role here, than in the colonial core areas (Lockhart 1984, 281–83; Garavaglia 1999, 1–2). Since gold and exploitable silver deposits were either limited or non-existent in these regions, native inhabitants constituted the sole 'commodity' of interest to Europeans. Slavery remained a key institution of colonial exploitation for a much longer period in the frontier regions and large areas that remained outside effective Spanish and Portuguese control, such as northern Mexico, parts of the Amazonian lowlands, the Pampas of Argentina, and southern Chile. The native people in such areas were subject to violent incursions by Spanish and Portuguese troops and slave raiders for the entire colonial period.[5]

On the eve of independence, the creoles, the elite of American-born Spaniards who headed the movement for autonomy, had to question the rightfulness of the Iberian conquest, to legitimize the dissolution of all bonds to the Spanish crown, and to deny or at least downplay the creoles' character as physical and cultural descendants of the conquerors. This was an especially delicate affair since the creoles, and their main adversaries, the Spaniards born on the Iberian peninsula, shared the same culture and language (Guerra 2003, 186–87). Both groups, in contrast, had little in common with the American Indians.

Thus ironically, in the struggle for independence, creole patriotism praised the indigenous pre-Columbian past and indigenous leaders who had fought against the Spanish, such as the last Aztec king, Cuauhtémoc, to legitimize their claims to autonomy. This practice was most developed in the colonial core areas where the creoles could refer to the ancient indigenous civilizations, such as the Maya, Aztec, or Inca and their monumental relics. The less complex native societies on the peripheries lent themselves less to the construction of a glorious national past since they were generally considered as 'barbarous' (Gabbert 2015a, 191–92; cf. Earle 2007, 47–78; Forment 2003, 310). While forms of internal colonialism were to develop in the colonized regions after independence, the unconquered areas would continue to suffer violent continental colonialism in the nineteenth century.

THE CHALLENGES OF INDEPENDENCE

By the mid-1820s the Latin American states had gained their independence after more than fifteen years of war with Spain.[6] Attempts at American integration failed and the greater colonial areas (viceroyalties)

---

[5] See Lockhart (1984, 283–85), Hidalgo (1984, 91–92), Hemming (1984, 503, 536–45), Wright and Carneiro da Cunha (1999, 293–95, 306, 318–50), Garavaglia (1999, 6–7), Langfur (2002).

[6] Brazil became independent in a different way. The entire Portuguese court had fled to Brazil from the French troops who occupied the Iberian Peninsula in 1807. Prince regent John elevated Brazil to a kingdom with equal rights in the monarchy in 1815. In 1821 the now King John VI returned to Portugal leaving his son Pedro in Brazil as a prince regent. The latter rejected demands for him to return to Portugal and declared independence in

disintegrated rapidly into about eighteen independent states (Rinke 2016, 51, 54). Almost all countries became republics.[7] The new states faced tremendous problems: Their territorial integrity was threatened first by the former colonial power, later by their Latin American neighbors, and the United States. Mexico, for example, lost about a half of its territory to the U.S. as a result of the war of 1846–48 (König 2006, 399–400). Peru was invaded by its neighbors several times, among others, by Chile in 1836–39 and 1879–83. The wars of independence had resulted in tremendous losses in human lives, capital, and economic infrastructure (Tutino 1986, 223–24; Bakewell 2004, 435–41; Rinke 2016, 61–62). Stable institutions could not be established for decades. The military and local, regional, or national strongmen (*caudillos*) played a major role in politics up to the mid-century and in some cases even longer. That the eighteen states produced no less than 115 constitutions in the course of the nineteenth century indicates the degree of institutional instability. Ecuador had ten constitutions, Bolivia nine, Colombia eight, and Peru seven between 1820 and 1880 (Drake 2009, 96; Rinke 2016, 51–52). Weak central governments, strong regionalism, instability, tyranny, and numerous civil wars mostly related to the conflict between centralism and federalism, haunted the countries up to the 1870s when the growth of export economies favored political stability and the establishment of oligarchic rule by the upper strata.

The wars of independence were in certain respects conservative movements intended to prevent major social changes. Thus, while the republican constitutions after independence established the formal integration of the Indians into the new polities on an equal footing with the rest of the population, the natives were often excluded by different means from effective participation as were the lower classes in general. Reality differed tremendously from what was stipulated in laws and constitutions. Governments often ruled by emergency acts, and the elections

---

1822. He became emperor of Brazil as Pedro I. The minor resistance of Portuguese troops and administrators in parts of the colony was broken in two years; see Bakewell (2004, 406–10) and König (2006, 366–73).

[7]Exceptions were Mexico during the short-lived empire of Agustin I (Iturbide) in 1822–23, the rule of emperor Maximilian (Hapsburg) in 1864–67 established during the French intervention, and Brazil ruled by descendants of the Portuguese monarchy between 1822 and 1889.

were frequently disputed and fraudulent (Forment 2003, 159–60, 181–86, 343–48, 362; Drake 2009, 99–100). Thus, independence did not bring self-rule to the colonized majority of Indians, but domination by a new elite of creoles. Let us first consider how creoles ideologically dealt with the Indian question and then look at politics and economy.

NATION-BUILDING AND THE INDIANS

The independence movement brought important changes particularly in the political system and in the dominant ideologies. In contrast to the colonial period, where the political integration of heterogeneous groups—estates or castes[8]—had been based on their shared quality as subjects of the same monarch, political legitimacy was now to be grounded, in one way or another, on 'the people' of the young republics. 'Nation' did not mean a number of kingdoms united under a common monarch any more, but a political community of individuals (Guerra 2003, 189–90, 201–5, 217). The legitimacy of political authority was no more derived 'from above' referring to the divine right of the rulers but 'from below', from the will and interest of the governed. The new elites generally accepted many aspects of liberal conceptions of society and economy, especially the creation of a free market. In contrast to Liberals, Conservatives pleaded for a stronger role for the state and opposed the separation of state and church. Constitutions stipulated regular elections as the legitimate way to transfer power and guarantee individual liberties. Colonial corporate structures and caste distinctions were abolished and the equality of male citizens before the law, but not in society, was formally established (Safford 1985, 349–51, 385–88, 395; Drake 2009, 60–61, 75–78, 89–94, 106–8, 145; Rinke 2016, 50).

However, how could the Amerindian past be claimed as part of national history without putting the contemporary Indians at the center of the nation? And how were de facto exclusionary politics and the use of extra-economic force in the relations of production to be legitimized?

We can recognize different discursive strategies in response to these questions. While a few, such as Father Velázquez in Yucatán, considered the mass of the Indians as the depository of sovereignty (Sierra

[8]The term *casta* (caste) referred to people presumed to be of mixed ancestry, such as mestizos or mulattoes, and in a wider sense to any population group including the Spanish and the Indians.

O'Reilly [1848–51] 1994, vol. 1, 285–89), most creoles flinched from such radical conclusions and claimed that they had the same rights over America as the Indians. Thus, the Dominican and Mexican congressman Fray Servando Teresa de Mier suggested that while the creoles' forefathers had come from Spain, the Indians' ancestors came from Asia. The right to America originated in being born there, cultivating the land, and building towns (de Mier 1976, 84, 324; cf. Brading 1991, 595).[9] Creoles in the former colonial peripheries in particular could argue that their Indians had always been barbarians and that the colonization of the vast hinterlands was thus a triumph of civilization and progress. The reasoning was different in the former core areas where Indians constituted the major part of the population. Here two major lines of argument can be discerned. Some authors denied that the wretched mass of contemporary Indians had any connection to the builders of the ancient empires. The Mexican writer and historian Justo Sierra O'Reilly, for example, doubted that the contemporary Indians were descended from the builders of the ancient cities: "[I]t was not the race conquered by the Spaniards that constructed those buildings" ([1848–51] 1994, vol. 1, 82–83). He subscribed to a hypothesis advanced by the Count of Friedrichsthal who suggested that Yucatán had been conquered by "a caste of superior men," probably "a Caucasian nation" (1845, 439–40), in ancient times who employed native slaves to erect the buildings that so impressed travelers later. Sierra speculated that this "race of slaves" ([1848–51] 1994, vol. 1, 84) might have been the ancestors of contemporary Indians in the peninsula. In Guatemala the archbishop and historian Francisco de Paula García Peláez made a similar argument (Earle 2007, 133–34).

Others considered contemporaneous Indians the descendants of the pre-Columbian civilizations, but argued that their forefathers had degenerated to their present deplorable state as a consequence of the conquest, the abuses of the colonial period, or other factors. These thinkers argued, for example, that the indigenous elite was responsible for the monumental ancient architecture. However, this social group had been wiped out during the conquest or assimilated into the lower class: "What was left was only an ignorant rabble" (Carrillo 1846, 62; cf. Earle 2007, 165–68 for additional examples). The contemporary Indians "would appear as

---

[9]A similar argument was made by Justo Sierra O'Reilly ([1848–51] 1994, vol. 1, 291–92).

unrecognizable animals to their emperors and caciques, were the latter to escape from the tomb," remarked the Mexican liberal Ignacio Ramírez (1889, vol. 2, 183). Spanish despotism was blamed particularly by liberals in the early decades of the nineteenth century. Conservatives, in contrast, viewed the colonial period in much brighter light and stressed misguided liberal politics as the root of the current problems. However, both agreed that the persistence of communal land tenure and the indigenous languages were factors that hindered progress (Earle 2007, 169–74).

Both lines of argument allowed the Latin American elites to claim the glorious pre-colonial past for creole nationalism without having to position contemporary Indians, considered as miserable rustics, at the center of the nation. At the same time, this history did not preclude anything regarding the legal status of Indians. The foundations of the economy, which rested to a large extent on coercion on large estates, were not questioned, and the special treatment of Indians could be justified with the argument that their lack of natural ability or education did not permit the granting of equal rights yet. Thus, the task of society was, in the liberals' view, to civilize the Indians. Besides, the promotion of private property, education, and new wants were considered important civilizing factors (see Mora [1836] 1965, vol. 1, 67; Castillo 1845, 296). The Peruvian politician and founding member of the *Sociedad Amiga de los Indios*, Miguel Zavala, stressed the need for an authoritarian state institution that could guide the Indians on their way to becoming productive citizens. Nils Jacobsen summarizes Zavala's views as follows:

> In his view, the originally vigorous and intelligent Indian had become a dim-witted, lazy brute through four-and-a-half centuries of "benevolent tutelary despotism" of the Incas and through three centuries of "slavery" under the Spaniards. [...] From the application of the democratic "principle of majorities" thus resulted "the humiliating and ridiculous absurdity that the Sovereignty of Peru was placed in the hands of an idiot race of proletarians, given that this race [the Indians] formed the overwhelming majority". [...] Society was ascending from despotism to freedom, as from childhood to adulthood. Peru's Indians were still like children, and thus it was to their own benefit to have their freedom restricted. Freedom, in any case, "ceases where it does not correspond to rational goals." Indians still needed to be taught that work was a "natural law," an existential condition imposed by the "Supreme Creator." Once Indians had been brought to

moral adulthood they could be released into the full freedom of civil society and Peru's national polity. (1997, 145–46, quotes Zavala 1868, 14–21, 33–34)

Apart from these concepts oriented to acculturation, the idea that a biological "improvement" of the indigenous population could be achieved by a "mixture of races" was common.[10] However, the intended result of the "mingling of races" was not a mixed culture and population, but the absorption of the Indians into the "prevailing mass of the white population;" there was no doubt that the center of the nation was the "white race."[11] For example, in 1828 the Peruvian deputy Pedro de Rojas y Briones expressed the opinion that miscegenation would lead to the absorption of Indians by whites (Jacobsen 1997, 133). Hopes were pinned on the immigration of Europeans to push ahead the process of "lightening" society.[12]

While the need to educate and civilize the Indian population received attention almost everywhere, extermination of those who stubbornly resisted became most important on the peripheries of the former colonies (Drake 2009, 95). In Brazil, the public debated whether to exterminate Indians as impediments to 'progress' or civilize and incorporate them into national society (Wright and Carneiro da Cunha 1999, 313). Settlers and many authorities considered the Indians who declined 'pacification' as "creatures without reason, to be hunted like wild beasts" (ibid., 333, cf. 338). Bounty hunters were hired by settlers, land speculators, railroad companies, and even the state to clear areas of Indians. In Argentina

[...] those native peoples who refused to become civilized could not participate in civil society and needed to be eliminated from the body politic. This was declared to be necessary for the survival of the very civilization that the savages rejected. As commentators observed, "The extinction of inferiors is one of the conditions of universal progress [...] It is like an

---

[10] Sierra O'Reilly ([1848–51] 1994, vol. 1, 104–5, 205, vol. 2, 278); Memoria del partido de Calkiní, Calkiní, *El Espíritu Público* [newspaper] Campeche, December 10, 1867, 2; Informe ..., Mérida, March 26, 1878, in Busto (1880, vol. 3, 266).

[11] Sierra O'Reilly ([1848–51] 1994, vol. 1, 17, 24), cf. Mora ([1836] 1965, vol. 1, 73–74), Hale (1968, 219, 223, 244).

[12] Busto (1880, vol. 3, 33, 36), Mora ([1836] 1965, vol. 1, 74), Hale (1968, 240–41; 1986, 403), Hill (1999, 714, 736).

amputation which, although painful, cures gangrene and saves the patient from death". (Earle 2007, 162)

The general public considered the native inhabitants of the South American Pampas, Amazonia, and northern Mexico barbarians who had by necessity to succumb to the irresistible forces of progress and civilization. Positivism and social Darwinism informed the thinking of Latin American elites in the latter half of the century. Thus, differential treatment, subjection, and in extreme cases extermination of the natives could be justified as the inevitable results of 'natural laws', as the necessary triumph of the stronger over the inferior race.[13]

POST-INDEPENDENCE POLITICS: THE LIMITS OF DEMOCRACY AND REPUBLICANISM

Though political authority was legitimized as the representation of the national will in the nineteenth century, still debated was who belonged to the nation and qualified for citizenship and thus the right to vote. Views that restricted membership in the nation to the 'lettered and the rich', excluding the common people or plebs, were present in Europe, as well as in Latin America.[14] Even the most famous independence leader Simón Bolivar had exposed his skepticism towards general suffrage, complaining that "the common people exhibited too much ignorance to vote correctly" (Drake 2009, 80, cf. 84)—a widespread view among independence leaders. After independence in Mexico, the historian and long-term congressman Carlos María de Bustamante put it bluntly: "The people is a ferocious and ungrateful beast which is not easy to subdue once it has lost respect for the powers that be" ([1839–43] 1963, vol. 4, 247). José María Luis Mora, a leading Liberal, criticized the Mexican federal constitution of 1824 for not limiting suffrage to property owners, and for wasting the right of citizenship by extending it in "scandalous profusion [...] even to those classes of society who are least apt to exercise it" ([1836] 1965, vol. 1, 281).

---

[13]See Drake (2009, 131), Earle (2007, 163, 168–69), Jones (1999, 176), and Larson (1999, 575, n. 3). For the mingling of acculturation and biological topics in nineteenth-century racial arguments, see also Gabbert (2015a, 203–5).

[14]For Europe see Zernatto (1944, 363).

Private property was sacrosanct according to the liberal vision of economy and society that dominated public discourse. Colonial legal privileges and corporate forms of property were regarded as obstacles to the realization of the 'natural' economic order. Society comprised an aggregation of free citizens equal before the law and unrestrained in pursuing their self-interest. Private property was thus an indispensable precondition for the development of responsible citizens. "Owners of property," said Mora, were "the only class which by the nature of things has a true interest in public order and in the repression of crime" (ibid., 280).[15] "The Indian knows no patria because he has no property," proclaimed the Peruvian liberal Manuel González Prada in the 1880s (Earle 2007, 182).

With independence the differentiation between indigenous nobility and commoners became obsolete. Wealth differences among the rural indigenous population decreased, and urban artisans, tradesmen, and wealthy individuals of indigenous descent assimilated into the mestizo population. Thus, Indians in general came to be identified with poverty, communalism, and backwardness, and were, often together with the 'plebs' in general, considered unfit for the exercise of civil rights. Ignacio Ramírez, one of the leading liberal politicians in mid-nineteenth century Mexico, for example, did not consider contemporary Indians as citizens due to their isolation and the multiplicity of native languages: "[W]e have republican institutions, but we do not have citizens, since we do not even have men" (Ramírez 1889, vol. 2, 192; see also Brading 1991, 661; Earle 2007, 179–80). Still later the administration of Porfirio Díaz, who ruled over Mexico for more than thirty years after 1876, considered indigenous people "irrational and, therefore, 'unrepresentable' as citizens" (Forment 2003, 354). In Argentina, the liberal intellectual Esteban Echeverría believed that

> only the prudent and rational part of the social community is called to exercise [...] sovereignty. Those who are ignorant remain under the tutelage and safeguard of the laws decreed by the common consent of the men of reason. Democracy, then, is not the absolute despotism of the masses or of the majority; it is the rule of reason. (Burns 1980, 21–22; see also Hill 1999, 712; Markoff 1999, 678–79)

---

[15] See ibid., 285, Hale (1968, 300–2; 1986, 378–81) and for Peru Jacobsen (1997, 133, 141–45).

In fact, Latin American elites vacillated between adhering to the principle of popular sovereignty and the fear that political participation of the lower classes might lead to chaos that had to be prevented by confining the right to manage the state to a selected few. While some elections were astonishingly inclusive,[16] voting rights were restricted by property and literary qualifications time and again, excluding the bulk of the population, Indians and non-Indians alike (Drake 2009, 61, 82–86, 94, 107–9, 119–20, 148–49; Forment 2003, 180, 357; Earle 2007, 177–78). The Ecuadorian constitution of 1845, for example, limited citizenship to those literate males above the age of twenty-one or married, and born in the country. Beyond this, property worth 200 pesos or a "scientific profession or useful trade of some mechanical or liberal art without being subjected to another one as a domestic servant or day laborer"[17] was required. Literary qualifications excluded about 90% of the population from suffrage in most Latin American states, disqualifying dependents (servants, indigents, slaves) and reducing the voters further to between 2 and 6% (Drake 2009, 84, 109, 146). Only 14% of the Mexican population above the age of six was literate in the 1890s. Literacy rates were, of course highest in the urban areas. While these restrictions on voting rights seem gross when judged from today's understanding of democracy, the Latin American political system was, in fact, often more inclusive than those of the U.S. or European countries:

> Latin Americans permitted, on paper and sometimes in practice, at least as many people-if not more-to vote than in the United States, England, or France, all of which enforced similar restrictions in the era. [...] In Mexico City's municipal elections from 1829 to 1831, approximately 27 percent of the total male population had still voted. This figure far exceeded the suffrage permitted in France and England at the same time. In France in 1831 less than 25 percent of all males over twenty-one years of age enjoyed the right to participate in municipal elections, whereas in England

[16]Almost 70% of the (male) Mexicans had the right to vote in the presidential elections in 1828, for example. Universal male suffrage was introduced for certain periods in several Latin American countries quite early (Colombia 1853, Argentina, Venezuela, Mexico 1857, Chile 1874); see Drake (2009, 62, 113–19) and Forment (2003, 157).

[17]Constitución de Ecuador 1845. For the literacy requirement in Yucatán, Mexico, see the constitutions from 1825 and 1850 (PG 1:219; APP 3:378). See also the notification on *indios hidalgos* from October 26, 1850 (AGEC, G, PY, box 15, file 1081).

in 1833 only some 4 percent of the total adult population could vote in borough council elections. (Forment 2003, 84–85, 121)

The lower class was frequently not only barred from voting, but remained also excluded from political office since considerable property was often a precondition for eligibility. In Yucatán, for example, an annual income of 400 pesos was a prerequisite to run for the office of deputy, and as much as 600 pesos in the case of senator in 1841. Regulations required an annual income of 300 pesos for eligibility as political chief heading a district (*jefe político*). A member of the municipal government (*ayuntamiento*) had to show evidence of an annual income of 200 pesos and the ability to read and write (not mentioned explicitly for higher offices).[18] Elites secured control by additional means, such as implementing systems of indirect representation (voting by electors), preying on patron–client relations, or if all this did not suffice, resorting to outright fraud (Drake 2009, 83–86, 109–13, 149).

However, discrimination against Indians and the lower classes in general was not merely the result of persisting colonial prejudice among the elites or a means to maintain political control. In fact, it provided the necessary ideological background for the new capitalist economic system that emerged after independence. Elites employed racist and acculturation-oriented arguments[19] to legitimize the appropriation of natural resources and labor, in the form of an emerging internal colonialism in the core areas, and of continental colonialism in the peripheries or in other areas not yet controlled by the Latin American governments.

[18] Constitución, March 31, 1841; Gobierno interior de los pueblos, March 31, 1841 and Convocatoria para elecciones, September 15, 1848 (APP 2:38, 96, 98–99; 3:226, 229–31); Constitución, April 6, 1825 (PG 1:234–35, 237); Requisitos para ser alcaldes auxiliares, Mérida, September 4, 1840 (AGEC, G, PY, box 1, file 41).

[19] Both kinds of arguments were often combined. This was consistent with the contemporary state of the natural sciences whose results were frequently employed by the liberals to underpin their political ideas. Even progressive biologists were unable to differentiate between changes in the behavioral repertoire of populations that were based on learning and those founded on inheritance. Lamarck's suggestion about the inheritance of acquired characteristics was accepted by many until the beginning of the twentieth century (Harris 1968, 108–28; Malik 1996, 80).

ECONOMY—CONQUEST, COLONIZATION
AND ORIGINAL ACCUMULATION

Latin America had been integrated into the overseas colonial economy as a provider of natural resources and raw materials, silver and gold being the most important. While independence ended formal colonial trade restrictions, Latin America continued supplying raw materials to Europe and now also to the United States. An export boom occurred in products, such as precious metals, copper, tin, nitrates (as a fertilizer and chemical feed stock), sugar, bananas, coffee, cocoa, grains, beef, henequen, chicle, and rubber began in the mid-nineteenth century. The exploitation of natural resources and the growing commercialization of agriculture for export, and for the expanding internal urban market, required sufficient land and labor; complaints of estate owners about the lack of hands were legion (Bakewell 2004, 444–46, 462; Hill 1999, 715). Military conquest and extermination were the major components of the republics' policies of continental colonialism where indigenous groups still existed in uncontrolled areas, such as in Chile, Argentina, Uruguay, the lowlands of Ecuador and Peru, or northern Mexico. In the former Spanish colonial core areas, by contrast, proletarianization and cultural hispanization of the Indian peasantry predominated in the form of internal colonialism. Thus, overseas colonialism evolved into continental and internal forms in the new national states (Farriss 1984, 366–88; Larson 1999; Schryer 2000, 232, 243–45).

Continental colonialism, outright conquest and dispossession of the indigenous population, became widespread in many of the former Spanish and Portuguese colonial peripheries after independence. The hitherto uncontrolled refuge areas suffered increasing attacks from the young Latin American republics, and many indigenous groups lost their independence in the second half of the nineteenth century. The Argentine state, for example, began to organize military expeditions into the Pampas and Patagonia, shortly after independence. Argentinean troops conquered and took wide fertile areas from the Mapuche Indians in the 1820s and 1830s. In a few years large farms were established in these areas particularly apt for cattle breeding. The so-called 'Indian problem'—the defiance of the state's claim to sovereignty over the country's entire territory and the repeated assaults on frontier settlements by independent indigenous groups (*malones*)—required resolution once and for all in the 1860s and 1870s when the military launched several campaigns known as "the Conquest of the Desert" (Schindler 1990, 26–28; cf. Jones 1999, 178–83). Settlers encroached on Mapuche lands south of the Biobío River in Chile to grow grain or to breed cattle and sheep by the first half of the nineteenth century. In 1867 the Chilean army started a major campaign to subdue the Indians in an effort called the 'Pacification of the Frontier'. Soldiers advanced into Mapuche territory, built forts, and began a war of scorched earth, burning Indian villages and fields, stealing their cattle, and capturing women and children. The conquest of the Mapuche lands both in Chile and in Argentina was completed in the 1880s; the defeated Indians were resettled onto reserves (called *reducciones* in Chile and *reservas* in Argentina) or employed on the cattle and sheep ranches (Hasbrouck 1935; Schindler 1990, 30–35; Jones 1999, 176, 182).

The Indian groups at the headstreams of the Amazon, in the lowlands of Venezuela, Columbia, Ecuador, Brazil, Bolivia, and Peru experienced a period of recovery due to the wars of independence and to the decades of political instability that followed as many Christian missions, colonization projects, forced relocations, and enslavements came to a temporary halt. More than fifty mission settlements were abandoned along the upper Orinoco River alone between 1830 and 1850 (Hill 1999, 706–9, 740–42). However, the growing demand for forest products, such as quinine and especially rubber, led to a renewal of the governments' interest in the refuge areas as potential sources of products for exportation in the second half of the nineteenth century. Therefore, they began to establish military fortifications, foster colonization, and grant concessions for the exploitation of huge areas to national and foreign entrepreneurs. The exploitation and repression of the indigenous population reached a new culmination, and many Indian groups suffered extermination. Rubber barons controlled vast areas with private armies securing their labor force through the enslavement of Indians or debt peonage (Hill 1999, 709–16, 742–59; Taylor 1999, 244–45; Wright and Carneiro da Cunha 1999, 355, 368–69; Karasch 2014, 199–221). Indigenous people were "harvested like other natural resources, and gangs even raided the missions in search of workers" (Hill 1999, 744). By the end of the nineteenth century, for example, the indigenous population of the Llanos de Mojos in northern Bolivia that had reached approximately 100,000 in the eighteenth century was reduced to 20,000 (Hill 1999, 710–11). The terrorizing and occasional annihilation of indigenous groups came to international attention through the

Putumayo Report of the British official Roger Casement ([1910] 1997) who detailed the widespread atrocities committed by rubber companies in the early twentieth century. Indians had been enslaved, flogged, burned, raped, and physically abused in other ways. The companies sent armed 'recruitment and vigilance commissions' to control the meeting of production quotas assigned to the indigenous labor force:

> Those indigenous persons who did not produce the required quantity of rubber were whipped, tortured, cruelly punished in stocks, or simply murdered. Disobedience was punished with such measures as mutilation or failure to provide food. (Landaburu and Camacho 1984, 31; cf. Hill 1999, 751–52)

Other hitherto unexplored indigenous territories in Brazil, such as São Paulo, the northeast and center of the country, experienced conquest and colonization by coffee farmers and cattle ranchers in the second half of the nineteenth century. Thousands of Botocudos were slain by settlers in Minas Gerais and southern Bahia, for example. Surviving Indians often experienced forced resettlement and confinement to reservations (Wright and Carneiro da Cunha 1999, 312–14, 331–34, 343–45).

In the north of Mexico colonization laws that allowed farmers, ranchers, and investors to appropriate indigenous territories passed as early as the 1820s. During the Porfiriato more than two million acres of land eventually came under the control of U.S. mining and forest firms in Chihuahua alone (Deeds 2000, 72–74). Though the Yaqui had been able to defend their independence from Spain and the Mexican Republic by intermittent war, the military defeated them in the second half of the nineteenth century. When the Yaqui rebelled against the conversion of their lands into rice and cotton plantations, they were finally subdued in the 1880s. Land and irrigation companies appropriated hundreds of thousands of acres to cultivate export products. Between 8000 and 15,000 Yaqui suffered deportation to Yucatán in the south of the country to work on henequen plantations and elsewhere (Turner [1910] 1990, 26–53; Deeds 2000, 75–76; MacLeod 2000, 27; Bakewell 2004, 464).

However, advances into hitherto uncontrolled lands on the peripheries of the new Latin American states were not always driven by economic motives, such as to acquire lands and resources. Securing the states' borders and preventing inroads from their neighbors also provided reasons (Schindler 1990, 35; Hill 1999, 710, 743). The conquest of peripheral

areas often went hand in hand with the colonization by European immigrants, such as the German colonists who settled in southern Chile and
Brazil beginning in the 1850s. About 400,000 European immigrants
came to Argentina in the 1860s and 1870s, and several millions more
arrived at the turn of the century. More than a million Europeans immi-
grated to Brazil between 1846 and 1893. The vast and sparsely settled
peripheries had to be colonized and integrated into market production
for according to the Argentinean political theorist Juan Bautista Alberdi's
dictum, "To govern is to populate" (Drake 2009, 95; cf. Wright and
Carneiro da Cunha 1999, 332, 343; König 2006, 535).

Indigenous communities in the more densely settled colonial core
areas in Mexico and the Andes had been able to keep access to communal lands to a significant degree to the end of Spanish rule. After the
mid-nineteenth century the increasing influence of liberal ideas among
the ruling elites in Latin America and the expansion of commercial agriculture for export-led to new and intense assaults on community lands,
considered major obstacles to efficient capitalist production (Hale 1986,
380–82; Larson 1999, 573–84, 623; Earle 2007, 170–72). Referring to
utilitarianism, Liberals perceived society as an aggregation of individual
citizens who, freed from corporative restrictions and bonds, would be in
a position to pursue their interests. This, Liberals argued, would automatically lead to a maximum of happiness, social harmony, and progress.

More and more Indian and non-Indian community lands were divided
into lots and supposedly unoccupied lands (*tierras baldías*) were privatized. Many peasants lost their lands to landlords or mestizo colonists and
became dependent laborers on the large cattle ranches or plantations.[20] In
Mexico land companies held one-fifth of the country's total landmass in
the early twentieth century, partly as a consequence of the law of 1883
that promised these enterprises one-third of the public lands they surveyed
"for subdivision and settlement" (MacLeod 2000, 26). The appropriators
of village lands and *tierras baldías* not only targeted property for export
production, but also aimed to undermine subsistence agriculture, and thus
force the peasants to work as field hands on haciendas and plantations.

---

[20] See Tutino (1986, 257–76), Jacobsen (1997, 147–49, 158), Larson (1999, 560–68),
and Bakewell (2004, 462). This applies also to some of the colonial borderlands, such
as the northern lowlands of South America—the lower Orinoco basin in Venezuela and
British Guyana, and the plains (*llanos*) of Venezuela and Columbia, as well as to parts of
Brazil; cf. Hill (1999, 712–14, 734–38), Wright and Carneiro da Cunha (1999, 340).

Forms of debt peonage were common not only in the rubber trade on the peripheries, but also haunted labor relations on haciendas and plantations (Turner [1910] 1990, 3–26; Katz 1959; Knight 1986; Hill 1999, 715, 742, 759). Compulsory labor (*mandamiento*) was reintroduced into Guatemala in 1877, for example.[21] Modernization projects, such as road building, made ample use of compulsory labor in Ecuador from 1850 through the 1870s. An old law that demanded four days of labor or its monetary equivalent from every citizen each year was revived in Ecuador in 1854: "By the 1860s the labor tax fell most heavily on Indian communities and smallholders, while estate-bound peons frequently found protection from their paternal landlords" (Larson 1999, 604). These projects and the numerous vagrancy laws aimed at providing cheap laborers for growing commercial agriculture and at legitimating the use of extra-economic force in the relations of production. These measures were generally directed against the Indian and non-Indian rural lower classes in general. In a number of cases, however, a special legal or administrative status for the natives reappeared in spite of the general tendency to consider Indians in principle as citizens and equal before the law.

While the colonial caste distinctions officially ended after independence in most cases, governments evidenced considerable creativity in preserving some of them in fact. When Bolivia revived the tribute under the name of personal contribution in 1827, for example, the republic defined Indians as "the persons who pay the single personal contribution, which the Spanish called tribute, their fathers, wives and children" (Irurozqui 1999, 712). In Peru and Ecuador, the Indian tribute or head-tax abolished with independence, reappeared in 1826 and 1828 and survived until 1854 and 1857, respectively. It provided 40% of the state's income in mid-nineteenth century Peru (Jacobsen 1997, 124–41; Larson 1999, 560, 596–97; Forment 2003, 178). Though the Ecuadorian census did not employ the category 'Indian' after 1876, census takers were advised, however, "to collect information about Indians to facilitate tax collection and labor conscription" (Larson 1999, 597). In Yucatán, the Indian republics (*repúblicas de indígenas*) reappeared in 1824 with the aim "to remove the obstacles for the collection of taxes, to contain the dispersion of the Indians in the forest, and to procure them an honest occupation making them useful for themselves and society" (PG 1:135). The special

---

[21] Reglamento de jornaleros (1877), Earle (2007, 167), McCreery (1986).

legal and administrative status of Indians persisted officially to the end of the 1860s. Though Yucatán abolished the Indian republics in 1868, nevertheless, the term Indian (*indígena*) continued in use in official documents.[22]

Conclusion

Considering the severe assaults on the material and cultural foundations of indigenous survival, it comes as no surprise that even in the former colonial core areas collective violence increased dramatically in the course of the nineteenth century compared to most periods of formal Spanish and Portuguese colonial rule. The expansion of haciendas and plantations, the expropriation of village holdings, and the privatization of supposedly unused national lands provoked large-scale Indian peasant rebellions all over Latin America (Coatsworth 1988). Despite this resistance, the independent states conquered the remaining Indian refuge areas, annihilating the last vestiges of native autonomy, decimating, and sometimes even exterminating entire indigenous groups. Dispossession, economic exploitation, as well as political and social exclusion were legitimized by racist and acculturation-oriented ideologies that saw the people considered Indians at the bottom of the social hierarchy supposedly lacking civilization. Thus, we can consider the nineteenth century the period of the 'second conquest' when continental and internal colonialism followed overseas colonialism. While the juxtaposition of Indian and non-Indian was particular to Latin America, reflecting the heritage of the Iberian conquest, many of the processes described above were by no means unique in the New World, but resembled developments in Europe.

First, the modern conception of colonialism as the domination of one ethnic or national group or category of people over another hardly fits the ideologies and practices of rule in estate societies, such as Spain before the nineteenth century and the pre-conquest empires in Latin America. Spain and the complex pre-conquest empires of Mesoamerica and the Andes were all highly differentiated societies. Their social

---

[22] See Suárez Molina (1977, vol. 1, 46 and vol. 2, 292). For the continued use of the term *indígena*, see, for example, a list of tax-payers from Bolonchenticul, February 17, 1873 (AGEC, G, CP, P, box 1, file 15) and documents from Hunucmá and Panabá from 1873 and 1885 (AGEY, PE, boxes 185 and 232).

structure was conceived as a pyramid of estates with a relatively small nobility ruling over a huge mass of peasants. In the contemporary European as well as in the Mesoamerican and Andean world views, it was just inconceivable to consider either the subjects of the Spanish king in Europe or the American Indians as undifferentiated masses or homogenous populations as the nationalist imaginary would suggest much later. Consequently, the indigenous people in the Latin American core areas experienced different treatment according to their social standing.

Stratification in these societies was generally based on the idea of a fundamental difference between the rulers and the ruled, from the point of view of culture and descent. Ruling dynasties were of foreign origin, often conquerors, or were at least considered as such. Social communities were not constituted on the basis of cultural or phenotypical commonalities, but rested on locality, kinship, or political vassalage. Political legitimacy was not derived from a cultural or biological tie between rulers, nobles, and commoners. On the contrary, it was based on the claim to a special relationship with God, or the gods, and on the idea of noble descent. Cultural and genealogical differences between rulers and commoners were not concealed or minimized but were stressed and openly demonstrated (see Gabbert 2015b, 184–86, 188–91).

Second, a comparative look at the history of Europe and Latin America shows that elites in both continents faced similar problems in the nineteenth century. The colonization and exploitation of peripheries, such as the Pampas in Argentina and Siberia in Russia, for example, was only one problem. Another was the challenge to develop new legitimizing ideologies for domination and inequality when confronted with the demise of the doctrine of divine right. Nationalism became the leading ideology both in Latin America and Europe; however, nationalism was exclusionary in both cases. The lower classes, not to speak of women, were generally denied full civil rights. Centrifugal tendencies, such as the deep social and cultural cleavages which characterized these societies, had to be neutralized by inculcating, by force if necessary, a national culture in all regions of the state and all classes of society. Thus, processes of continental and internal colonialism were by no means restricted to former overseas colonies, but were present in Europe as well (cf. Hechter 1975; Weber 1976).

Elite discourse in both continents shows impressive similarities in its tendency to conflate class and race: Rural and urban lower classes were despised as idle and uncivilized. Beyond this, social and biological processes often intermingled in intellectual and political discourse, causing the frequent use of the terms race (*raza*) and class (*clase*) as synonyms.[23] The meaning of both terms was by no means fixed. Race was used for descent groups of very different size—from an elite dynasty to the entire Indian people of the Americas (cf. Mora [1836] 1965, vol. 1, 64; Zernatto 1944, 361). Well into the second half of the nineteenth century, it was quite adequate among scholars, politicians and journalists, for example, to speak of the English or French poor as 'races' (Mayhew ([1861] 1968, vol. 1, 1–3; cf. Harris 1968, 101; Lorimer 1978, 101, 105; Malik 1996, 80–84). As a matter of fact, both elites and lower classes were endogamous groupings. Thus, elite rule could be seen as domination by one kind of people over another kind of people. The English journalist and social researcher Henry Mayhew (ibid., 2–3), for example, attributed the "nomadic races" of England (vagrants, mechanics on tramp, peddlers, showmen, harvest-men, and others who follow some itinerant occupation) not only "lax ideas of property" and "repugnance to continuous labor" but also cultural and physical traits such as a "slang language", 'high cheek-bones and protruding jaws'. This comes quite close to the discourses of internal colonialism widespread in the independent Latin American states as well as in Europe and that not only on the peripheries of European states, such as Wales, Scotland or Occitania. However, trajectories regarding class, race and internal colonialism diverged in the late nineteenth century.

In Latin America, the elite continued to consider upholding its separation from the American Indians essential for the legitimization of its rule and the use of force in recruiting workers for their haciendas and plantations confronted with a situation of labor shortage. A significant part of the rural population had still access to, at least some, means of production and developed only limited wants for purchased goods which limited their necessity to accept full time wage labor.

The situation in Europe was quite different. There was an excessive supply of labor force which led to massive out-migration to the U.S., Latin America or elsewhere. Many people could not even secure a minimal existence for themselves and their families in the countryside.

---

[23] See, for example, Victoriano Rivero to Secretaría General del Estado, Valladolid, April 20, 1847 (AGEY, PE, box 66); Decreto de 2 de enero de 1850 que los caciques sean de la clase de indígenas (APP 3:307–8); cf. Gabbert (2007) for the blending of race, nation, and class.

As a consequence, the use of extra-economic force was unnecessary to induce people to accept wage-work on farms or in the industries. Thus, a nationalist ideology could develop among the elites that aimed at the integration of the lower classes which themselves struggled for political and social participation. It became increasingly impossible and unnecessary to exclude the European lower classes from the national society by racist arguments. Ideologies stressing individual intelligence, capacities and merits gained importance. Thus, although social strata are still endogamous to an important extent even in contemporary Germany,[24] race was replaced by class (in the modern sense of the word as merely economic and social difference), implying the possibility of individual social mobility, as the master concept of describing social inequality.

REFERENCES

Archives and Abbreviations

AGEC   Archivo General del Estado de Campeche, Campeche
       CP   Censos y Padrones
       G   Gobernación
       P   Padrones
       PY   Período Yucateco, 1820–57
AGEY   Archivo General del Estado de Yucatán, Mérida
       PE   Poder Ejecutivo
APP   Aznar Pérez, Alonzo and Rafael Pedrera, eds. (1849–51): *Colección de leyes, decretos y órdenes o acuerdos de tendencia general del poder legislativo del estado libre y soberano de Yucatán*. 3 vols. Mérida, Yucatán.
PG   Peón, José María and Isidro Gondra, eds. (1832): *Colección de leyes, decretos y órdenes del augusto congreso del estado libre y soberano de Yucatán*. 2 vols. Mérida, Yucatán.

Books and Articles

Bakewell, Peter. 2004. *A History of Latin America: C. 1450 to the Present*. Oxford: Blackwell.
Brading, David A. 1991. *The First America: The Spanish Monarchy, Creole Patriots and the Liberal State, 1492–1867*. Cambridge: Cambridge University Press.

[24] See, for example, the material discussed in Gabbert (2007, 116–21).

Burns, E. Bradford. 1980. *The Poverty of Progress*. Berkeley: University of California Press.

Busto, Emiliano. 1880. *Estadística de la República Mexicana. Estado que guardan la agricultura, indústria, minería y comercio*. 3 vols. México: Imprenta Ignacio Cumplido.

Cañizares-Esguerra, Jorge. 2009. "Demons, Stars, and the Imagination: The Early Modern Body in the Tropics." In *The Origins of Racism in the West*, edited by Miriam Eliav-Feldon, Benjamin Isaac, and Joseph Ziegler, 313–25. Cambridge: Cambridge University Press.

Carrillo, Estanislao, Fr. 1846. "Zayi." *Registro Yucateco* 4: 61–64.

Casement, Roger. [1910] 1997. *The Amazon Journal of Roger Casement*. London: Anaconda Editions.

Castañeda Delgado, Paulino. 1971. "La condición miserable del indio y sus privilegios." *Anuario de Estudios Americanos* 28: 245–335.

Castillo, Gerónimo. 1845. "El indio yucateco: Caracter, costumbres y condicion de los indios, en el departamento de Yucatan." *Registro Yucateco* 1: 291–97.

Coatsworth, John H. 1988. "Patterns of Rural Rebellion in Latin America: Mexico in Comparative Perspective." In *Riot, Rebellion, and Revolution: Rural Social Conflict in Mexico*, edited by Friedrich Katz, 21–62. Princeton, NJ: Princeton University Press.

Coe, Michael D. 1986. *Weltatlas der Kulturen: Amerika vor Kolumbus*. München: Christian Verlag.

Constitución de Ecuador. 1845. "Expedida en Cuenca por la Convención el 3 de diciembre de 1845, Tit. 2, Secc. 2, Art. 9." http://www.cortenacional.gob.ec/cnj/images/pdf/constituciones/16%201845.pdf. Last accessed January 28, 2018.

de Bustamente, Carlos María. [1839–43] 1963. *Continuación del cuadro histórico de la revolución mexicana*. 4 vols. México: INAH.

Deeds, Susan M. 2000. "Legacies of Resistance, Adaptation, and Tenacity: History of the Native Peoples of Northwest Mexico." In *The Cambridge History of the Native Peoples of the Americas*, edited by Richard E.W. Adams and Murdo MacLeod, vol. 2, Mesoamerica, part 2, 44–88. Cambridge: Cambridge University Press.

de la Cadena, Marisol. 2005. "Are 'Mestizos' Hybrids? The Conceptual Politics of Andean Identities." *Journal of Latin American Studies* 37(2): 259–84.

de Mier, Servando Teresa. 1976. *Cartas de un americano: 1811–1812*. 2nd facs. ed. México, DF: Partido Revolucionario Institucional.

Drake, Paul W. 2009. *Between Tyranny and Anarchy: A History of Democracy in Latin America, 1800–2006*. Stanford, CA: Stanford University Press.

Earle, Rebecca. 2007. *The Return of the Native: Indians and Myth-Making in Spanish America, 1810–1930*. Durham, NC: Duke University Press.

Farriss, Nancy M. 1984. *Maya Society Under Colonial Rule*. Princeton, NJ: Princeton University Press.

Forment, Carlos A. 2003. *Democracy in Latin America, 1760–1900.* Chicago, IL: The University of Chicago Press.

Friedrichsthal, M. 1845. "Sobre las ruinas de Yucatán." *Registro Yucateco* 2: 437–43.

Gabbert, Wolfgang. 1995. "Kultureller Determinismus und die Eroberung Mexikos - Zur Kritik eines dichotomischen Geschichtsverständnisses." *Saeculum* 46(2): 276–94.

Gabbert, Wolfgang. 2004. *Becoming Maya: Ethnicity and Social Inequality in Yucatán Since 1500.* Tucson, AZ: University of Arizona Press.

Gabbert, Wolfgang. 2007. "Vom (internen) Kolonialismus zum Multikulturalismus - Kultur, Ethnizität und soziale Ungleichheit." In *Achsen der Ungleichheit: Zum Verhältnis von Klasse, Geschlecht und Ethnizität,* edited by Cornelia Klinger, Gudrun-Axeli Knapp, and Birgit Sauer, 116–30. Frankfurt am Main: Campus.

Gabbert, Wolfgang. 2010. "Warum Montezuma weinte - Anmerkungen zur Frühphase der europäischen Expansion in den atlantischen Raum." In *Atlantik: Sozial- und Kulturgeschichte in der Neuzeit,* edited by Ulrike Schmieder and Hans-Heinrich Nolte, 29–47. Wien: Promedia.

Gabbert, Wolfgang. 2012. "The longue durée of Colonial Violence in Latin America." *Historical Social Research* 37(3): 254–75.

Gabbert, Wolfgang. 2015a. "Imagining a Nation—Elite Discourse and the Native Past in Nineteenth-Century Mexico." In *Globalized Antiquity: Uses and Perceptions of the Past in South Asia, Mesoamerica, and Europe,* edited by Ute Schüren, Daniel Segesser, and Thomas Späth, 189–210. Berlin: Reimer.

Gabbert, Wolfgang. 2015b. "Ethnicity in History." In *Ethnicity as a Political Resource: Conceptualizations Across Disciplines, Regions, and Periods,* edited by University of Cologne Forum "Ethnicity as a Political Resource", 183–200. Bielefeld: Transcript Verlag.

Garavaglia, Juan Carlos. 1999. "The Crises and Transformations of Invaded Societies: The La Plata Basin (1535–1650)." In *The Cambridge History of the Native Peoples of the Americas,* edited by Frank Salomon and Stuart B. Schwartz, vol. 3, South America, part 2, 1–58. Cambridge: Cambridge University Press.

Gibson, Charles. 1984. "Indian Societies Under Spanish Rule." In *The Cambridge History of Latin America,* edited by Leslie Bethell, vol. 2, 381–419. Cambridge: Cambridge University Press.

Guerra, Francois-Xavier. 2003. "Las mutaciones de la identidad en la América Hispánica." In *Inventando la nación,* edited by Antonio Annino and Francois-Xavier Guerra, 185–220. México, DF: Fondo de Cultura Económica.

Gunsenheimer, Antje, and Ute Schüren. 2016. *Amerika vor der europäischen Eroberung.* Frankfurt am Main: Fischer.

Hale, Charles A. 1968. *Mexican Liberalism in the Age of Mora, 1821–1853.* New Haven, CT: Yale University Press.

Hale, Charles A. 1986. "Political and Social Ideas in Latin America, 1870–1930." In *The Cambridge History of Latin America*, edited by Leslie Bethell, vol. 4, 367–441. Cambridge: Cambridge University Press.

Harris, Marvin. 1968. *The Rise of Anthropological Theory: A History of Theories of Culture.* New York: Crowell.

Hasbrouck, Alfred. 1935. "The Conquest of the Desert." *Hispanic American Historical Review* 15(2): 195–228.

Hechter, Michael. 1975. *Internal Colonialism: The Celtic Fringe in British National Development, 1536–1966.* London: Routledge & Kegan Paul.

Hemming, John. 1984. "Indians and the Frontier in Colonial Brazil." In *The Cambridge History of Latin America*, edited by Leslie Bethell, vol. 2, 501–45. Cambridge: Cambridge University Press.

Hidalgo, Jorge. 1984. "The Indians of Southern South America in the Middle of the Sixteenth Century." In *The Cambridge History of Latin America*, edited by Leslie Bethell, vol. 1, 91–117. Cambridge: Cambridge University Press.

Hill, Jonathan D. 1999. "Indigenous Peoples and the Rise of Independent Nation-States in Lowland South America." In *The Cambridge History of the Native Peoples of the Americas*, edited by Frank Salomon and Stuart B. Schwartz, vol. 3, South America, part 2, 704–64. Cambridge: Cambridge University Press.

Irurozqui, Marta. 1999. "Las paradojas de la tributacion. Ciudadania politica estatal indígena en Bolivia, 1825–1900." *Revista de Indias* 59: 705–40.

Jacobsen, Nils. 1997. "Liberalism and Indian Communities in Peru, 1821–1920." In *Liberals, the State, and Indian Peasants: Corporate Lands and the Challenge of Reform in Nineteenth-Century Spanish America*, edited by Robert H. Jackson, 123–70. Albuquerque: University of New Mexico Press.

Jones, Kristine. 1999. "Warfare, Reorganization, and Readaptation at the Margins of Spanish Rule: The Southern Margin (1573–1882)." In *The Cambridge History of the Native Peoples of the Americas*, edited by Frank Salomon and Stuart B. Schwartz, vol. 3, South America, part 2, 137–87. Cambridge: Cambridge University Press.

Karasch, Mary. 2014. "Catechism and Captivity: Indian Policy in Goiás, 1780–1889." In *Native Brazil: Beyond the Convert and the Cannibal, 1500–1900*, edited by Hal Langfur, 198–224. Albuquerque: University of New Mexico Press.

Katz, Friedrich. 1959. "Plantagenwirtschaft und Sklaverei: Der Sisalanbau auf der Halbinsel Yucatan bis 1910." *Zeitschrift für Geschichtswissenschaft* 7(5): 1002–27.

Knight, Alan. 1986. "Mexican Peonage: What Was It and Why Was It?" *Journal of Latin American Studies* 18(1): 41–74.

König, Hans-Joachim. 2006. *Kleine Geschichte Lateinamerikas.* Stuttgart: Reclam.

Landaburu, Jon, and Roberto Pineda Camacho. 1984. *Tradiciones de la gente del Hacha: mitología de los indios Andoques del Amazonas*. Yerbabuena: Instituto Caro y Cuervo, UNESCO.

Langfur, Hal. 2002. "Uncertain Refuge: Frontier Formation and the Origins of the Botocudo War in Late Colonial Brazil." *Hispanic American Historical Review* 82(2): 215–56.

Larson, Brooke. 1999. "Andean Highland Peasants and the Trials of Nation Making in the Nineteenth Century." In *The Cambridge History of the Native Peoples of the Americas*, edited by Frank Salomon and Stuart B. Schwartz, vol. 3, South America, part 2, 558–703. Cambridge: Cambridge University Press.

Lockhart, James. 1984. "Social Organization and Social Change in Colonial Spanish America." In *The Cambridge History of Latin America*, edited by Leslie Bethell, vol. 2, 265–319. Cambridge: Cambridge University Press.

Lorimer, Douglas A. 1978. *Colour, Class and the Victorians: English Attitudes to the Negro in the Mid-Nineteenth Century*. New York: Leicester University Press.

MacLeod, Murdo. 2000. "Mesoamerica Since the Spanish Invasion: An Overview." In *The Cambridge History of the Native Peoples of the Americas*, edited by Richard E.W. Adams and Murdo MacLeod, vol. 2, Mesoamerica, part 2, 1–43. Cambridge: Cambridge University Press.

Malik, Kenan. 1996. *The Meaning of Race: Race, History, and Culture in Western Society*. Houndmills, Basingstoke: Macmillan.

Markoff, John. 1999. "Where and When Was Democracy Invented?" *Comparative Studies in Society and History* 41(3): 660–90.

Mayhew, Henry. [1861] 1968. *London Labour and the London Poor*. 3 vols. London: Griffin, Bohn, and Company.

McCaa, Robert. 1984. "*Calidad, Clase*, and Marriage in Colonial Mexico: The Case of Parral, 1788–90." *Hispanic American Historical Review* 64(3): 477–501.

McCreery, David. 1986. "'An Odious Feudalism': Mandamiento Labor and Commercial Agriculture in Guatemala, 1858–1920." *Latin American Perspectives* 13(1): 99–117.

Mora, José María Luis. [1836] 1965. *México y sus revoluciones*. 3 vols. México: Porrua.

Mörner, Magnus. 1967. *Race Mixture in the History of Latin America*. Boston: Little, Brown and Company.

Ramírez, Ignacio. 1889. *Obras*. 2 vols. México: Editorial Nacional.

Reglamento de jornaleros, Guatemala, April 3, 1877. http://leygt.blogspot.de/2013/11/reglamento-de-jornaleros.html. Last accessed January 19, 2018.

Rinke, Stefan. 2016. "Der Preis der Freiheit: Revolution, Krieg und Nation in Lateinamerika im atlantischen Kontext, 1760–1830." In *Revolution, Krieg und die Geburt von Staat und Nation. Staatsbildung in Europa und den Amerikas 1770–1930*, edited by Ewald Frie and Ute Planert, 46–64. Tübingen: Mohr.

Safford, Frank. 1985. "Politics, Ideology and Society in Post-independence Spanish America." In *The Cambridge History of Latin America*, edited by Leslie Bethell, vol. 3, 347–421. Cambridge: Cambridge University Press.

Schindler, Helmut. 1990. *Bauern und Reiterkrieger: Die Mapuche-Indianer im Süden Amerikas*. München: Hirmer.

Schryer, Frans J. 2000. "Native Peoples of Central Mexico Since Independence." In *The Cambridge History of the Native Peoples of the Americas*, edited by Richard E.W. Adams and Murdo MacLeod, vol. 2, Mesoamerica, part 2, 223–73. Cambridge: Cambridge University Press.

Schüren, Ute. 2017. "Caciques: Indigenous Rulers and the Colonial Regime in Yucatán in the Sixteenth Century." In *Cooperation and Empire: Local Realities of Global Processes*, edited by Tanja Bührer, Flavio Eichmann, Stig Förster, and Benedikt Stuchtey, 33–57. New York: Berghahn.

Sierra O'Reilly, Justo. [1848–51] 1994. *Los indios de Yucatán*. 2 vols. Mérida: Universidad Autónoma de Yucatán.

Suárez Molina, Victor M. 1977. *La evolución económica de Yucatán a través del siglo XIX*. 2 vols. México: Ediciones de la Universidad de Yucatán.

Taylor, Anne Christine. 1999. "The Western Margins of Amazonia: From the Early Sixteenth to the Early Nineteenth Century." In *The Cambridge History of the Native Peoples of the Americas*, edited by Frank Salomon and Stuart B. Schwartz, vol. 3, South America, part 2, 188–256. Cambridge: Cambridge University Press.

Taylor, William B. 1972. *Landlord and Peasant in Colonial Oaxaca*. Stanford, CA: Stanford University Press.

Turner, John Kenneth. [1910] 1990. *Barbarous Mexico*. Austin: University of Texas Press.

Tutino, John. 1986. *From Insurrection to Revolution: Social Bases of Agrarian Violence, 1750–1940*. Princeton, NJ: Princeton University Press.

Weber, Eugen. 1976. *Peasants into Frenchmen: The Modernization of Rural France*. Stanford, CA: Stanford University Press.

Whitecotton, Joseph. 1970. "Estamento y clase en el Valle de Oaxaca durante el periodo colonial." *América Indígena* 30(2): 375–86.

Wright, Robin M., and Manuela Carneiro da Cunha. 1999. "Destruction, Resistance, and Transformation—Southern, Coastal, and Northern Brazil (1580–1890)." In *The Cambridge History of the Native Peoples of the Americas*, edited by Frank Salomon and Stuart B. Schwartz, vol. 3, South America, part 2, 287–381. Cambridge: Cambridge University Press.

Zavala, Miguel S. 1868. *Protectorado de Indios, o sea proyecto de ley ofrecido a las consideraciones de los H. H. Representantes de la Nacion, en la presente*

Legislatura de 1868, con el fin de mejorar la deprimida condicion social del Indio, haciendo realizable sus derechos. Lima: J.M. Masias.

Zavala, Silvio, and José Miranda. 1954. "Instituciones indígenas en la colonía." In *La política indigenista en México: Métodos y resultados,* edited by Alfonso Caso, Silvio Zavala, José Miranda, and Moisés González Navarro, vol. 1, 45–206. México, DF: INI.

Zernatto, Guido. 1944. "Nation: The History of a Word." *The Review of Politics* 6: 351–66.

CHAPTER 14

Legacies of Colonial Agency in Africa: Reflections of an 'Ethnicized' Space in Kenya and Rwanda

John Mwangi Githigaro

INTRODUCTION

This chapter explores the legacies of colonialism in Africa with a focus on Kenya and Rwanda in their post-independence periods. It argues that overall colonialism in the two countries continues to be 'experienced' across the socio-political sphere and has shaped the nature of ethnic relations in the post-independence period. The essay shows how these legacies continue to shape an 'ethnicized' space in the cases of Rwanda and Kenya. The introduction sketches the wider debates on ethnicity and colonial models of control. The second part reflects on the ethnicization of the political space in Kenya, the third examines the Rwandan experience and is followed by the conclusion.

What can be observed from the onset is that the colonial agencies of political control passed intact to the new African elite that assumed power after independence. In part, this undue control over the state, as the colonial masters had exercised it, was borne out of an earlier notion of 'racial' superiority and hence their position as 'bearers of civilization'.

J. M. Githigaro (✉)
Faculty of Social Sciences, St. Paul's University, Limuru, Kenya

© The Author(s) 2019
D. Schorkowitz et al. (eds.), *Shifting Forms of Continental Colonialism*,
https://doi.org/10.1007/978-981-13-9817-9_14

363

The African elites (the educated class mainly) on assuming the reins of power also resumed this superiority complex and hence allocated for themselves an unquestioned right to govern over subjects who did not match their educational qualifications. Elitism based on class and ethnic identity became manifest and as such could be termed as internal colonialism after independence (Dey 2015). Within the ruling elite, the underlying philosophy of control was their singular perspective on the role of the state in the post-independence period. The premise of the ruling elites was a developmental and a transformative state seen through the lens of African nationalism. This envisioned state was supposed to address the challenges of poverty, ignorance, and disease. In doing so, the educated elites would thus bypass the masses owing to the former's supposedly greater appreciation of external models of development (Young 2004).

One of the enduring legacies of colonialism in the African continent has been ethnic conflict. This ethnic conflict needs to be situated in the colonial experience starting from the ways in which the colonizers encouraged ethnic diversity and consequently ethnicized the political space. Colonists would set the foundation of the soon-to-be independent African states with two styles of rule which would have an enduring legacy on the nature of ethic relations after independence. The two styles of colonial control, 'divide-and-rule' tactics and 'indirect and direct rule' used by tribal chiefs and missionaries reinforced ethnic differences (Green 2012). Indirect rule is a concept of control that emerged after the 1884 Berlin Conference. It was a practical intervention that saved on limited human and financial resources. Indirect rule thus worked through already established traditional authorities such as chiefs. Europeans, however, supervised the traditional rulers from the top (Myers 2005). While rare, direct rule brought in European 'experts' that governed the colonized territories (Cappelen and Sorens 2018). These two types of rule structurally configured the nature of ethnic relations that would follow independence.

There exists a structural model that elaborates on the contribution of the two styles of colonial rule and how they promoted ethnic strife broadly on the African continent. This model draws on the distinction between ranked and unranked systems of ethnic stratification, systems prevalent during colonial rule. The ranked system, also referred to as vertical integration, is identified by a cultural division of labor that denotes a practice of social stratification assigning specific occupations, including other social roles, on the foundation of observable cultural traits or markers (Blanton et al. 2001). This social stratification can be understood as a hierarchy of ethnic groups. One group then assumes competitive advantages over the others. It follows then that one's ethnic identity cannot be divorced from one's economic status and political interests. The alternative to the ranked system is the unranked system or the horizontally integrated structure of ethnic stratification. The unranked system is marked by a pattern of competitive ethnicity where different ethnic individuals compete with each other over resources and occupational roles in the social hierarchy. Within the unranked system, this provides an opportunity for the upward mobility of individuals of any one group without necessarily bringing conflict with outside groups. In this regard, social status is not synonymous with ethnicity. These structural variations are traceable to colonial history. The colonial administrative models adopted contributed to differences in systems of ethnic stratification and ethnic conflict that would result in the post-independence period (ibid.).

French colonialism in Africa for instance favored centralism in order to achieve cultural assimilation. This centralized system of direct rule integrated individuals from different regions and ethnic groups into a single cohesive Francophone nation. In the post-colonial states, the elite who acquired power chose to retain the centralized state of their French predecessors, but excluded other individuals or ethnic groups. The lack of meaningful leadership inclusion of varied ethnic groups in political power would have consequences for the post-colonial order. Even though it could not be generalized across the colonial divide, powers that favored direct rule such as the French 'governed' directly using the expertise of their nationals. The British on the other hand preferred indirect rule as a colonial model of control. This model entailed applying a 'divide-and-rule' policy where they emphasized traditional structures of control in efforts at preventing different ethnic groups in their colonies from forming a coalition to end British hegemony. Promoting indigenous institutions would encourage ethnic consciousness in the formal colonial era and later significantly weaken national consciousness in post-colonial Anglophone countries (Njoh 2000). The British system of indirect rule would encourage factional rivalries among different ethnic groups. It was institutionalized through the formation of ethnic governments which then ensured that various social disparities would be viewed through an ethnic lense. Colonial legacies set the stage for competitive politics founded on ethnicity, and in this case dominant groups sought to control the machinery of the state to the exclusion of minority groups (Blanton et al. 2001).

Besides colonial legacies, some African pre-colonial societies were marked by relations of dominance and dependence across gender, clan, and culture largely in a patrimonial order. Those who had wealth and larger kin networks (families and dependents) possessed power in their societies. Pre-colonial Africa thus had markers of patron–client relationships. Big-men presided over 'small' boys, other men, and women through complex linkages of reciprocal and unequal nature. These relationships would be marked by degrees of servitude and slavery. Pre-colonial societies were far from unified entities devoid of conflict and competition. Ethno-cultural constructions were present in pre-colonial conflict-ridden societies as communities tried to create order (Berman 1998).

In analyzing the evolution of ethnic identity in post-colonial Africa, the legacies of pre-colonial and colonial societies need to be contextualized. As a starting point, scholars analyzing ethnicity, such as Bruce Berman, have pointed to the need to go beyond the now often criticized models of primordialism and instrumentalism. Before 1945 primordialism as an analytical concept assumed an archaic ethnic identity that was stagnant and unchanging drawing from cultural experiences. It supposed that ethnic identity was grounded in cultural experiences and was distinct from other foundations of political identity and mobilization. Instrumentalism, on the other hand, denoted the manipulation of ethnic identities and loyalties for political and economic ends.

Now there is wide consensus that ethnicity needs to be understood from a historically grounded constructivist approach (Berman 1998; Azarya 2003, 1–4; Stone and Dennis 2003; Suzuki 2017). Ethnicity is not a fixed concept and is constantly changing. The shaping of identity is considered conflict-ridden, marked by interactions of political, economic, and cultural forces, both internal and external to the ethnic communities. In pre-colonial societies, communities existed with multiple, overlapping, and competing identities. The idea of individuals possessing a fixed, unique, and bounded identity as supposedly existed in Western societies associated with modernity did not exist until the onset of colonial rule.

According to a constructivist approach, ethnicity should not be construed as a fixed phenomenon, but rather appreciated as a historical process to be examined only within specific contexts. The contemporary ethnicities of Africa draw their origins in part from the colonial period that largely shaped their form and content through the social, economic, and cultural forces of colonialism. They are also grounded in their experiences in post-colonial societies, which would lead to the invention of a 'tribal' Africa. Tribal Africa denoted single, culturally homogenous communities that existed with indigenous institutions (Berman 1998; Lynch 2006).

It remains problematic to define what constitutes an 'ethnic community,' including membership and non-membership in an ethnic group. The commonly accepted markers of ethnicity, however, include a level of linguistic and cultural similarity, geographic concentration, self-assignment, and an accepted 'home area.' An ethnic history draws on memory and on histories whether oral or written. Lynch (2006) posits that there exists no clear formula to determine if A, B, and C belong to an ethnic group or whether X and Y do not. Given this mutability of belonging, actors on the ground contest who is a friend, foe, or cousin, including debates about group boundaries and content. This constant negotiation has in part opened the window of opportunity for multiple agents to rely on the label of ethnicity as a framework for action in different arenas over different historical periods.

'Political tribalism' would further be shaped by the actions of Europeans in the colonial era who rationalized their racial-cultural superiority over the Africans. Europeans believed they had a superior civilization and thus a right to rule over peoples of 'inferior' culture. This feeling of racial superiority, however, would signal for Africans an opportunity to reinforce their indigenous identity as a counter-claim to the Europeans' position. Furthermore, the European colonial strategy of fragmentation and isolation of different ethnic groups would promote ethnic competition and conflict (Berman 1998). Indeed scholars, such as Mahmood Mamdani (2001), have argued that one of the greatest crimes of colonialism in Africa was the politization of indigeneity because it served to reinforce differences and inter-ethnic tensions. This he asserts has continued to create clashes over such rights as access to land. This has happened in Kenya's former Rift Valley in contests not only over land, but in larger political discourses over the 'right to belong'. The so-called 'ethnic' clashes in Kenya have recurred periodically since the return to multi-partism in 1991. The logic for the violence has been to remove the outsiders and ensure that the indigenous residents of the former Rift Valley have access to their land (Klopp and Zuern 2007; Osamba 2001).

There exist at least two ways in which the colonial legacy disrupted indigenous social structures in Africa. These two ways are relevant as they give context to some of the pertinent legacies of colonialism, including ethnicization of societies in Africa. One was in the scramble for and partition of Africa. This partition did not respect the traditional boundaries of existing ethnic groups. The result of this phenomena was the dividing of multiple ethnic groups between two or more colonial entities. After independence, these boundaries assumed international legitimacy as newly founded sovereign states even though their domestic legitimacy could be questioned. Secondly, the geographic distribution of ethnic groups across state borders would lead to the additional challenges of secessionist threats including irredentist wars across borders (Blanton et al. 2001).

KENYA AND THE ETHNICIZATION OF THE POLITICAL SPACE

Kenya is a former British colony that gained independence in 1963. It is home to at least forty-two ethnic communities. A politicized ethnic space in the Kenyan context is traceable to as early as 1922 with the rise of political organizations that were agitating for a number of rights from the British colonial bureaucracy. The agitations centered on opposition to a hut-tax, the *Kipande* (pass-book), and forced labor. A key organization that advocated for African rights and was largely representative of the Kenyan communities, including Ugandans, was the East African Association, which organized the Nairobi riots in 1922 led by Harry Thuku and others. As a result, the colonial government deliberately resolved to encourage 'tribal' associations as opposed to nation-wide political organizations (Ajulu 2002). This encouragement would lead to the proliferation of tribal organizations, such as the Kikuyu Central Association and the Kavirondo Taxpayers Association, whose activities would be limited to narrow tribal issues. Not until the 1940s would the colony experience the rise of nationalist movements, and the colonial state would only fully allow the operation of nationalist movements after 1959.

With this gesture, the struggle for the control of the post-colonial state would begin in earnest. This quest for control through the formation of political outfits would witness the rise of regional and tribal outfits that even incorporated clan considerations in some respects. Heading into the first elections after independence in 1963, this would be the scenario. Such political organizations included the Akamba Peoples Party and the Taita African Democratic Union. The rise of these district-based political organizations, which the settler community tacitly endorsed, marked the politicization of ethnic cleavages in Kenyan politics. This was a continuation of their divide-and-rule tactics. Ethnic identities would thus become entrenched as different groups sought to capture state power as independence neared. Two nationalist parties would rise in this period: the Kenya African National Union (KANU) and the Kenya African Democratic Union (KADU). The former was largely comprised of the Kikuyu, Luo, Kamba, and a section of the Luhya peoples. KADU, on the other hand, was comprised of communities that considered themselves minority groups, for example, the Kalenjin, Maasai, and Coasterians. KANU would triumph in the 1963 election with Jomo Kenyatta becoming the first president of the new republic. KADU under Daniel arap Moi and Ronald Gideon Ngala advocated for a federal (*majimboist*) government owing to fears of domination by the majority communities under KANU, principally Kikuyu and Luo. *Majimboism* entailed the formation of regional governments alongside a centralized state. The advocates of *Majimboism*, largely minority groups, advocated this structure of governance owing to fears of political domination by the then-majority Luo and Kikuyu. KADU concerns would be reflected in the 1963 constitution which created eight regions with their own governments. This approach, however, changed when KADU and KANU merged in 1964 in what eventually resulted as a centralized state under Kenyatta (Ajulu 2002).

With a centralized state in sight, Kenyatta sought to neutralize the opposition that emanated from the radical wing of KANU led by Oginga Odinga and Bildad Kaggia. In 1966, following the controversies between Odinga and Kenyatta, an opportunity arose. This rivalry was based on ideological differences with Kenyatta (Kikuyu) having capitalist leanings and Odinga (Luo) leaning towards socialism. In 1966, Oginga Odinga had formed the Kenya's People Union (KPU) and defected to challenge KANU in the famous Little General Elections of 1966 (Bennett 1966; Mueller 1984). The Kenyatta regime would institute a constitutional amendment that required that if members of parliament defected from their party, they would need a fresh electoral mandate. The state would use its coercive capacity to reduce the KPU opposition mainly to Nyanza, the predominantly Luo province, and set the stage for a one-party state. In confining the KPU to the Luo homeland, the regime effectively constructed an internal colony. In the process,

Kenyatta 'constructed' the KPU as a Luo-ethnic party and even administered oaths among the Kikuyu to protect his regime ostensibly under the threat of the opposition. This would arguably mark a bitter contest for power and subsequent ethnic mistrust that persists between the Kikuyu and the Luo (Mueller 1984; Ajulu 2002).

Excluding the Luo from politics and the sharing of developmental resources thus became a larger strategy of Kikuyu strongmen who surrounded Kenyatta and were willing to exclude other ethnic groups and their regions from state benefits. With the banning of the KPU, the assassination of Tom Mboya in July 1969, and the subsequent arrest of Oginga Odinga, the rise of the Kenyatta's hegemony had begun. His regime would henceforth engage in discrimination against the Luo with demeaning language as part of their ethno-cultural exclusion. The Luo in the discourse of the Kenyatta regime became '*andu a ruguru*' (foreign westerners) (Atieno-Odhiambo 2002).

Demonstrating the superiority of Kikuyu versus Luo ethnicity, cultural discourses assumed local currency. The practice of male and female circumcision among the Kikuyu would be used as a ritual assigning superiority by granting adulthood rites. The Luo did not practice male circumcision and were ridiculed as 'small boys' not worthy of leadership. This rhetoric was applied in the 1992 general elections when Oginga Odinga was a candidate and used in 1997 when Raila Odinga (Oginga's son) was running for president. Language and cultural rituals have thus been used to ethnicize the political space in Kenya and exclude other communities from a fair electoral process (ibid.).

LAND SETTLEMENT PATTERNS AND THE RISE OF 'ETHNIC ENCLAVES' IN KENYA

Kenya's land settlement patterns in the colonial period have relevance for the ethnicization of the political space after independence. To situate this analysis, we need to investigate the process through the lense of the establishment of the colonial settler economy. This process can be categorized into four stages. The alienation and acquisition of land by the protectorate before the colonial state was formally set up and it represents the first step, the second being the imposition of English property law that sanctioned already appropriated land. The third stage is the reconfiguration of the land tenure system from customary structures of land to privatization. The fourth step that laid the groundwork for the colonial settler economy is land alienation requiring legal regulations (Kanyinga 2009).

The legal framework for this appropriation was the Crown Land Ordinance Act of 1915. It stipulated that all 'waste and unoccupied' land belonged to the crown. Additionally, this ordinance also introduced a dual structure for land administration and governance. It set the African land known as 'native reserves' apart from the Europeans' settlement land or 'scheduled land' that became known as the 'white highlands'. This law denied the Africans' rights to their land and vested them in the crown. Approximately three million hectares of arable land were ascribed to European settlers (ibid.). In addition to the Ordinance Act, the Natives Trust Bill was issued in 1926 securing specific areas (reserves) to be used by Africans. The Natives Trust Bill would also fix boundaries for the 'white highlands' including the removal of Africans from their land (Kameri-Mbote and Kindiki 2008). The 'native' reserves would lay a framework for the ethnicization of the Kenyan society as each reserve unit was reserved for a specific ethnic group. The colonial administration's strategy of having distinct ethnic reserves for the Africans thus prevented inter-ethnic political cooperation early (ibid.). These reserves would also be potential internal colonies after independence.

In the 1960s and 1970s, the government would sponsor settlement schemes and land buying companies to reallocate land in the hands of the state promoting thereby the in-migration of small scale farmers into the Rift Valley formerly part of the 'white highlands'. However, reallocating the former 'white highlands', the resettlement represented a physical extension of the 'ethnic reserves' from colonial times. The Kikuyu settlements, such as the Kinangop Plateau scheme, were hived off the eastern side of the highlands and added to the Central Province. Similarly, the Luhya, Luo, and Kisii reserves were carved out from the western highlands and allocated to respective provinces of Western (Luhya), and Nyanza (Luo and Kisii). The Kipsigis and the Nandi would also be settled separately in the Rift Valley. These policies in effect created an ethnicized land allocation pattern that was ingrained on the Kenyan map (Boone 2011). In doing so, independent Kenya was repeating the experiences of colonialism of settling different groups in geographically distinct spaces homogenously—solidifying internal colonies around the dominant Kikuyu. Over time, these ethnic reserves have created their own categorizations of 'immigrants' and 'guests' thus bringing the politics of 'belonging' into sharp focus. As a consequence, those considered 'guests' (non-natives) in a particular geographical space can be forced to leave the place during elections in times of electoral violence or may generally not be eligible to run for political office. These geographical markers of individual identity have thus served to ethnicize the political space further (Jenkins 2012) (Fig. 14.1).

Corruption and ethnic politics that supported patronage networks under the Kenyatta regime (1963–78) ensured that the dominant Kikuyu ethnic group benefited from the allocation of the most fertile areas in the Rift Valley at the expense of the Luo, Maasai, and the Kalenjin. Additionally, when the Kikuyu and the Kisii were perceived to be doing well in terms of agrarian activities, a feeling of resentment from the 'insiders' would be directed at the Kikuyu 'outsiders' leading to clashes in the 1992, 1997, and 2007 elections. Over time outsiders were labeled as '*Madoadoa*', a Kiswahili word meaning

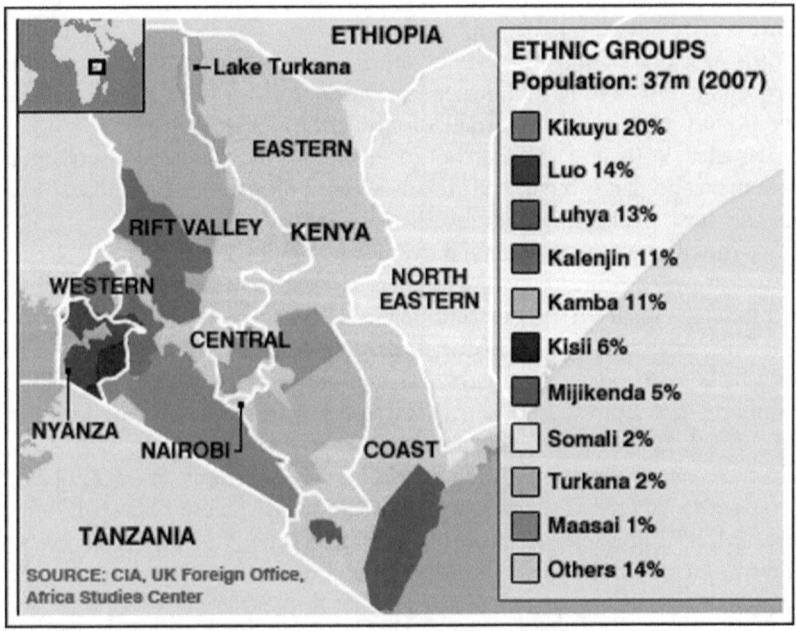

Fig. 14.1 Kenyan ethnic groups (2007)—postcolonial map of Kenya (*Source* CIA, UK Foreign Office, Africa Studies Center)

'blemishes', who needed to be evicted from the Rift Valley (Boone 2011; Kameri-Mbote and Kindiki 2008). The 2007 violence in Kenya thus developed along ethnic lines with rising anti-Kikuyu sentiments due to their perceived dominance in economic and political power. Whereas ethnicity was a mobilizing tool for violence, the unresolved land question as a core issue was responsible for triggering this violence. The 2013 elections and the controversial presidential elections of 2017 in the Rift Valley were relatively peaceful because the Jubilee Coalition and the Jubilee Party enjoyed great support in Kikuyu- and Kalenjin-dominated areas.

POLITICS OF NEO-PATRIMONIALISM IN KENYA

On the African continent 'Big-Man' politics is the point of reference in political analysis. Leaders adopt neo-patrimonialism, a structure related to elite co-optation, and state capture as a reward system to sustain their regimes (Wai 2012; Bach 2011). State capture denotes broadly the extraction of public resources for private gain (Gryzmala-Busse 2008). There remains hardly any distinction between public and private interests. Patron–client relationships are created with the provision of favors, such as public-sector jobs and business contracts, in return for clients providing political support (Bratton and van de Walle 1994, 458). What follows is control of the government in favor of one or more particular ethnic groups. The post-2013 Jubilee administration has advanced Kikuyu-Kalenjin interests in terms of patronage networks. Ethnic subjectivities thus continue to be expressed in the Kenyan context. The leadership engages in patron–client relationships often following narrow exclusivist redistribution of resources to the detriment of other ethnic groups. This has often created situations where ethnicity has a negative impact on politics, in the sense that ethnic tensions and animosities revolting against skewed development priorities increased (Bach 2011).

Thus, in the Kenyan context the Kikuyu assumed hegemonic state control after independence in 1963 using their executive and economic powers which generated resentments among other ethnic groups. Though African states—including Kenya—in their post-independence period made efforts to achieve a pan-ethnic identity with some success, such interventions did not mute ethnic identity even as they produced an ethnicized sense of national citizenship in individuals that regarded themselves as truly belonging to the nation. Each ethnic group's sole motivation centered on assuming control over the state and its resources in the interests of the group, rather than the nation. Political parties were formed on the basis of ethnic mobilization and coalitions among the elite (Ajulu 2002; Berman 2009). Gradually, ethnic patronage networks took hold with the Kikuyu at the regime's center that benefitted disproportionately at the expense of other Kenyan groups that could be regarded as internally colonized.

With the demise of Mzee Jomo Kenyatta in 1978, Daniel arap Moi assumed power and set out to dismantle the patronage networks built by the previous regime. The Kikuyu dominance in politics and in the economic sector had been detrimental to other ethnic groups. Moi, being of Kalenjin origin, embarked on 'Kalenjinising' the state, abusing his position for primitive accumulation of national resources through patronage. Ethnic identity was thus mobilized again to exclude other groups from patronage. The private accumulation of public goods and the protection of the new resources depended much on well established authoritarian control. The Moi regime thus saw the rise of competitive politics in the early 1990s with concern. It mobilized ethnicity for its survival and closed the ranks of the KAMATUSA alliance (Kalenjin, Maasai, Turkana, Samburu) to consolidate the regime. In the 1990s, the government tacitly provoked ethnic clashes (cleansing) as a way to guarantee political survival. Non-indigenous groups from the Rift Valley and parts of the Coast Province had to face this violence as a strategy to reduce political competition from such communities as the Kikuyu and the Luo in the 1990s (Ajulu 2002; Mueller 2008; Osamba 2001).

REFLECTIONS ON ETHNICIZED SPACE IN RWANDA

In reflecting on ethnicized space, it is useful to compare Kenya with Rwanda, because in both countries, colonial experiences served to reinforce ethnic differences. The case of Rwanda is particularly striking since its colonial legacy contributed to one of the most severe human atrocities on the African continent, the 1994 genocide, spurring debates on the reconstruction ethnic identities until today. Entrenching structures of governance and settlement patterns favored non-cooperation while encouraging everyday association with one's ethnic identity. A key marker that served to reinforce ethnic differences and origins was the identity card. One key contrast between the two countries was Rwanda's switching of the ethnic hierarchy previously advanced by the Germans and later the Belgians. While Kenya had multiple ethnic identities,

Rwandans in pre-colonial times shared a common language, with one's social standing providing a 'constructed' identity that was either Tutsi or Hutu. Prior to Rwanda's independence, Belgians shifted their ethnic preferences from the minority Tutsis to the majority Hutus, thus creating a new ethnicized space. After independence when not governing, each Rwandan group could consider its own homeland an internal colony within the boundaries of a larger state dominated by a different people. Thus, each could see itself as internally colonized even though both peoples shared the same country. In this way Rwanda differed from Kenya where each ethnic group usually had a more defined geographical home.

Rwanda is a small, densely populated country in Central Africa that has had a long history of tightly controlled, hierarchical government. From the mid-nineteenth century, politics were primarily organized along ethnic-class lines. The Tutsi minority approximating 14% of the population were cattle rearers and controlled the monarchical political system in the pre-colonial period. The Hutu approximating 85% of the population were mainly sedentary farmers. Both groups shared a common language, were attached to the same clans, and practiced the same religion. During the colonial era, the German and later the Belgian colonial powers favored the monarchy for obvious reasons, considering the Tutsi as a superior race and thus racializing ethnic groups that had had more experience with class than with race contradictions in pre-colonial times. After 1919, under Belgian rule, the Tutsi people got preferential treatment and access to education and employment. This unequal access to economic and political resources laid the ground for inter-ethnic tensions in the pre-independence period and would culminate in the 1994 genocide (Mann and Berry 2016; Russell and Quaynor 2017, 254) (Fig. 14.2).

Fluidity in the categorization of the Hutu and the Tutsi peoples dated back to the pre-colonial period. Indeed, in those times identities could easily be switched. For instance, if one owned many cattle even though belonging to the Hutu, one could be labeled Tutsi. Similarly, the less privileged agricultural peasants regardless of their (ethnic origin as Hutus or Tutsis, were classified as Hutus). However, the German and Belgian colonial powers then created a distorted historical account of the origin of Rwanda's three main ethnic groups (Twa, Hutu, Tutsi) pitting them against each other as part of their 'divide-and-rule' strategies (Mamdani [2001] 2002).

Fig. 14.2 Post-independence Rwanda (2015) (*Source* United Nations, Department of Field Support, Geospatial Information Section, Map No. 3717, Rev. 11)

Some scholars speculate that the Tutsi and Hutu were well on the path to a homogenous ethnic identity at the time of colonial contact. This likely amalgamation was reversed by German and Belgian authorities through their support for the pre-existing kingship, a system rooted in a rigid dichotomy between 'Tutsi lords' and 'Hutu serfs'. This gave legitimacy to an imaginary distinction between a so-called 'superior race' of Tutsi, immigrant Hamites of Egyptian or Ethiopian origin, and so-called 'primitive indigenous negroes' called Hutu and Twa (Isabirye and Mahmoudi 2001). These questions of identity and belonging in the Rwandan context are far from settled owing in part to varied explanations of their pre-colonial and colonial legacies and attendant manifestations in the post-colonial period (Uvin 1999).

In the Rwandan context, colonialism produced significant differences in terms of political, social, and economic relations skewed in favor of the

Tutsis who had privileged access to education and administrative jobs in the colonial period. The struggles for independence were thus to assume an ethnic angle and create the foundation for ethnic politics in post-independence Rwanda. In fact, it was the Rwandan revolution of 1959 that provided the Hutu elites with unfettered access to political power for the first time and led to the marginalization of the Tutsi (ibid.). This revolution had the assent of the departing colonizers who, as independence came closer, realized the need for representative structures and switched their support to the majority Hutus, a decision however informed by the fear of a radical, leftist, anti-colonial Tutsi elite (ibid.).

The Hutu thus created political, social, and economic cleavages centered on exclusive ethnic identity following their successful revolution against Tutsi power. Anti-Tutsi violence continued under the Kayibanda presidency (1962–73) and the Habyarimana regime (1973–94). A key narrative applied by both regimes to marginalize the Tutsi was the argument that Rwanda belonged to the Hutu who were its true inhabitants subjugated for centuries by colonial powers including the Tutsis. The ideology of the two Hutu governments discriminated against the Tutsi depriving them of opportunities necessary for vertical mobility in areas of education, state jobs, and political posts (Isabirye and Mahmoudi 2001; Mann and Berry 2016; Uvin 1999).

In the meantime, the generation of Tutsis that had fled the country in the violence of 1959 launched a diasporic network that later became the Rwandan Patriotic Front (RPF) under the leadership of Fred Rwigema and the current Rwandan President Paul Kagame. This movement of Tutsi refugees principally operated from Southern Uganda. Rwigema and Kagame rose to key posts in Yoweri Museveni's National Resistance Movement whose rebel army sought to oust Obote's regime in Uganda in the 1980s. This experience became instrumental in their march to Rwanda in the 1990s (Mann and Berry 2016).

The response of the Hutu government to the RPF offensive was a mass slaughter, known as the Rwandan genocide, planned by the political elite as the most viable solution to the Tutsi threat, whom the Hutu perceived as 'immigrants' to Rwanda while considering themselves as 'native' inhabitants. This plan was carried out by two Hutu death squads: the *Interahamwe* ('those who fight together') and the *Impuzamugambi* ('those with the same goal'). The RPF launched their attacks from North Rwanda on October 1, 1990 and waged a low-scale civil war over the years. It was the assassination of President Habyarimana, whose plane was shot down in Kigali in the midst of peace negotiations between his government and the RPF, that triggered the genocide of 1994. The RPF is credited with 'stopping' the genocide and initiating national reconstruction and reconciliation, a process that is still ongoing. In today's political discourse Rwanda is characterized as a 'developmental state' that shows typical structures of a patronage network where the president's confidants are benefitting disproportionately from state contracts for infrastructure development (Mann and Berry 2016).

THE RWANDAN GENOCIDE OF 1994 AS COLONIAL LEGACY

The events that culminated in the Rwandan genocide of 1994 are salient indicators of a colonial policy that spurred ethnic rivalry in this Central African nation with repercussions from the late 1950s. Estimates are that at least 937,000 Rwandans died in the genocide, including moderate Hutus. The politics of ethnic belonging and discourses of autochthony that reached their peak in 1994 have reinforced opposing categorizations, such as 'insider versus outsider', largely in a geographical sense. These categorizations excluded certain groups from access to power and resources, such as land. In the Rwandan genocidal context, government hardliners, largely Hutus, refused to acknowledge the indigeneity of Tutsi exiles when their armed detachments returned home to Rwanda in the early 1990s. The *genocidaires* responded as 'autochthons', killing 'outsiders' (Dunn 2009; Ceuppens and Geschiere 2005; Geschiere 2005).

Belgian colonial policies emphasized differences between Hutu and Tutsi identities that included the creation of hierarchies of importance and the ascription of social roles. The Belgians granted the Tutsi a superior status in society. Providing the Tutsi with leadership positions, the colonizers neglected the genuine interests of the Hutus who suffered from continued marginalization and exclusion—an experience that became deeply engrained in Rwandese ethno-politics. The 1959 revolution was particularly directed at abolishing Tutsi dominance (Alemazung 2010).

Ethnic identities across the African continent often express feelings of marginalization and political exclusion leading to 'ethnic' conflicts, partly as revenge against groups that others feel are benefiting at their expense, partly as a fight for resources (Berman 1998; Bach 2011). Identities in Rwanda were first formally entrenched with the 1933 census when Hutus, Tutsis, and Twas received cards indicating their official identities. The racialization of differences between Tutsi and Hutu was triggered both by missionaries and colonial officials. Both acted on the assumption that the Tutsis were of a 'civilized race' that justified their privileged treatment. Two institutions, the school system and the local administration, supported this narrative. From as early as the 1930s, mission schools offered different programs to Tutsi and Hutu children. The Tutsis received a 'superior' education, were trained in French, and prepared for administrative positions and citizenship. In contrast, the Hutus were provided with an education in Kiswahili considered 'inferior'. This differential education was not simply aimed at preparing the Hutus for manual labor, but at excluding them from common citizenship (Mamdani [2001] 2002, 76–102). Mahmood Mamdani is convincing in his argument that Hutu and Tutsi ethno-political identities were not static, but were changing alongside the state that enforced these identities (ibid., 34).

However, a contrasting body of literature rejects claims of ethnopolitical identities as products of European colonialism in Rwanda. While beyond the scope of this chapter, the central thesis of this debate can be briefly outlined. Scholars like Johan Pottier (2002), for instance, have argued that, given the lack of empirical research, to claim that European colonialism resulted in ethnic divisions in Rwanda is unjustified. While acknowledging that there was a colonial campaign that racialized social and economic relations, he argues that scholars also need to consider the agency of local social institutions in promoting ethnic divisions. His main point is that European colonial authorities in their attempts to racialize ethnic identities built upon existing social institutions, including ethnic divisions.

Following Pottier, failure to consider politization of ethnicity as instituted in pre-colonial times amounts to post-genocide revisionism, a narrative that was popularized by the RPF in its ascent to power in 1994. This narrative claims that the Hutu-Tutsi classification in ethnic terms was nothing, but a product of a divisive colonial construct. The RPF narrative has remained that the ethnic categories (Hutu, Tutsi, Twa) did not exist prior to colonialism (Pottier 2002). In practice, the perspective of the RPF regime is a case of ethnic amnesia to guarantee the generally Tutsi party's hold on power. Ironically, by denying the existence of the early ethnic groups, this RPF position camouflages the political instrumentalization of ethnicity that existed in colonial times (Vandeginste 2014).

Yet, there is general consensus that ethnic identity and nationalism fueled the killings and the genocide of 1994 (Straus 2006). The RPF administration of Paul Kagame has made a number of efforts at constructing national identity, but not without various criticisms. One of the administration's initiatives was to issue laws that prohibit division, ethnic ideology, and a genocide mentality in thoughts and speech acts. Ethnicity cannot be used as a means of public political expression or as a form of identification in post-1994 Rwanda. The current regime considers itself as steering the country progressively free of colonial and mental maps (Hintjens 2008). In order to reconfigure a new nation devoid of 'any ethnicized space' the government promotes a historical version stressing Rwanda's unity. Basically, this narrative stipulates that it was the Europeans who created ethnic divisions in society by importation of their 'divide-and-rule' model including racial ideology. The governmental narrative thus claims that the Rwandan people were one in pre-colonial times though researchers, such as Mahmood Mamdani and Johan Pottier, have rejected this version of national history.

How to construct a national identity in Rwanda remains challenging to the political elite as do other unsettled questions related to the new state's formation after 1994. There is concern among scholars who consider the regime's version of the Tutsis as victims and the Hutus as perpetrators of the 1994 genocide as untenable to post-conflict reconciliation. The categorization of ethnic identities even on national identity cards was banned in Rwanda after the genocide (ibid.). Another regulation banned all history lessons until an acceptable version of history was developed and finally launched in 2006 that reflected the regime's preferred narratives. Sensitive issues of pre-colonial ethnic divisions were carefully avoided. In addition, the government set up civic education camps for youth, young adults, and ex-prisoners, including university lecturers and administrators. The subjects that have been taught include the history of Rwanda, the analysis of Rwanda's problems and rights, and the obligations and duties of a citizen (Buckley-Zistel 2009). This education has continued the amnesia of history in pursuit of a new identity of 'Rwandan-ness', a new identity pushed through the ideology of Rwandani city. This ideology argues that ethnicity is nothing but a product of a divisive colonial construct. Thus, despite the banning of conversations on ethnic identity in Rwanda, ethnicity and ethnic identity continue to be manipulated by the political elite to control the state. The political largely Tutsi elite have adopted the political instrumentalization of ethnicity that was practiced under colonial rule (Vandeginste 2014).

CONCLUSION

This chapter has reflected on the colonial legacies that ethnicized political space in Kenya and Rwanda. One of the key argument is that colonialism had the effect of entrenching ethnic identities in the two countries which have led to dangerous competitive politics and the mobilization of 'ethnic' violence in both countries. Kenya's recurrent cycle of electorally related violence since the early 1990s, including the 2007 elections, and the 1994 Rwandan genocide are products of ethnicized political spaces representing partly legacies of colonialism in Africa. The political instrumentalism of ethnicity that was blamed on colonial agency was used by the new African elite as a form of internal colonial rule.

After independence in Kenya and Rwanda, the respective leaderships reinforced ethnic differences as a way to polarize and govern their citizens. In doing so, they continued their respective colonial strategies of control. This was realized through the political instrumentalization of ethnicity. The reinforcing of ethnic differences in both Rwanda and Kenya could be termed strategies of internal colonialism. In the case of Rwanda, the Tutsi identity was categorized as unworthy and 'alien' from the Hutu identity. Since the 1994 genocide, an ethnic amnesia that collapses ethnic identities into Rwandan-ness has been used as a tool of control by the mainly Tutsi people. In the case of Kenya, the Kikuyu continue to claim legitimacy to rule owing to their historical independence struggles through the Mau Mau liberation war. The Luo, on the other hand, have been aspiring to political power at the center, with the Kikuyu being their most potent competitors. In the Kenyan context, the notion of internal colonialism pitting the Luo against the Kikuyu does not project itself strongly any longer because class may now play a greater role than ethnicity in social inequality.

This study finds some differences with regard to the models of political control adopted in colonial times. Whereas both Kenya and Rwanda were governed through the 'divide-and-rule' model, there were some differences in application. In the case of Kenya, the forms of 'divide-and-rule' were geared towards creating divisions and separating the numerous communities (at least forty-two ethnic groups) to prevent them from unsettling colonial rule. In Rwanda, the 'divide-and-rule' approach was more direct in its application. It was meant to create hierarchies of identities and privileged the Tutsi over the Hutu. The Germans and later the Belgians favored the Tutsi who they felt were of superior nature to the Hutu. This discrimination was more blatant, and it created and reinforced social roles that would deeply affect the nature of ethnic relations in the country. In the Rwandan context, the Tutsi got privileged access to education and took administrative jobs to the marginalization of the Hutu. The Hutu thus early experienced a deeper sense of marginalization and had to defend their space when the opportunity arose in 1959. The Tutsi would then get an opportunity in 1994 to return and claim their 'citizenship'. The RPF administration soon after embarked on a construction of a new identity (Rwandan) and has since prohibited and criminalized the use of the earlier identity markers of Hutu, Tutsi, and Twa.

The chapter has further observed that in both countries neo-patrimonialism of varied nature has become the norm and has further continued to shape the nature of ethnic politics. In Kenya this has become more pronounced growing progressively since independence where majority groups or their narrow coalitions have sought to capture the state for the benefits that can accrue. This has had the effect of ethnicizing politics with the danger of ethnic violence. What this has meant in the long run is a dearth of nationalism and the rise of ethnic identity. In the Rwandan case, ethnic identity has been muted on account of attempts at reconstructing a new national identity. It is not absolutely clear that a national identity can be entrenched in a country that has experienced one of the worst genocides of the twentieth century, but it is critical to remain hopeful.

REFERENCES

Ajulu, Rok. 2002. "Politicised Ethnicity, Competitive Politics and Conflict in Kenya: A Historical Perspective." *African Studies* 61(2): 251–68.

Alemazung, Joy Asongazoh. 2010. "Post-colonial Colonialism: An Analysis of International Factors and Actors Marring African Socio-economic and Political Development." *The Journal of Pan African Studies* 3(10): 62–84.

Atieno-Odhiambo, Elisha Stephen. 2002. "Hegemonic Enterprises and Instrumentalities of Survival: Ethnicity and Democracy in Kenya." *African Studies* 61(2): 223–49.

Azarya, Victor. 2003. "Ethnicity and Conflict Management in Post-colonial Africa." *Nationalism and Ethnic Politics* 9(3): 1–24.

Bach, Daniel C. 2011. "Patrimonialism and Neopatrimonialism: Comparative Trajectories and Readings." *Commonwealth & Comparative Politics* 49(3): 275–94.

Bennett, George. 1966. "Kenya's 'Little General Election'." *The World Today* 22(8): 336–43.

Berman, Bruce J. 1998. "Ethnicity, Patronage and the African State: The Politics of Uncivil Nationalism." *African Affairs* 97(388): 305–41.

Berman, Bruce J. 2009. "Ethnic Politics and the Making and Unmaking of African Constitutions." *Canadian Journal of African Studies* 43(3): 441–61.

Blanton, Robert, T. David Mason, and Brian Athow. 2001. "Colonial Style and Post-colonial Ethnic Conflict in Africa." *Journal of Peace Research* 38(4): 473–91.

Boone, Catherine. 2011. "Politically Allocated Rights and the Geography of Political Violence: The Case of Kenya in the 1990s." *Comparative Political Studies* 44(10): 1311–42.

Bratton, Michael, and Nicolas van de Walle. 1994. "Neopatrimonial Regimes and Political Transitions in Africa." *World Politics* 46(4): 453–89.

Buckley-Zistel, Susanne. 2009. "Nation, Narration, Unification? The Politics of History Teaching After the Rwandan Genocide." *Journal of Genocide Research* 11(1): 31–53.

Cappelen, Christoffer, and Jason Sorens. 2018. "Pre-colonial Centralization, Traditional Indirect Rule, and State Capacity in Africa." *Commonwealth & Comparative Politics* 56(2): 195–215.

Ceuppens, Bambi, and Peter Geschiere. 2005. "Autochthony: Local or Global? New Modes in the Struggle Over Citizenship and Belonging in Africa and Europe." *Annual Review of Anthropology* 34(1): 385–407.

Dey, Dipankar. 2015. "Internal Colonialism." In *The Encyclopedia of Political Thought*, edited by Michael T. Gibbons, vol. IV, 1846–48. Chichester: Wiley Blackwell.

Dunn, Kevin C. 2009. "'Sons of the Soil' and Contemporary State Making: Autochthony, Uncertainty, and Political Violence in Africa." *Third World Quarterly* 30(1): 113–27.

Geschiere, Peter. 2005. "Autochthony and Citizenship: New Modes in the Struggle for Belonging and Exclusion in Africa." *Forum for Development Studies* 32(2): 371–84.

Green, Elliott. 2012. "Explaining African Ethnic Diversity." *International Political Science Review* 34(3): 235–53.

Gryzmala-Busse, A. 2008. "Beyond Clientism: Incumbent State Capture and State Formation." *Comparative Political Studies* 41(4–5): 638–73.

Hintjens, Helen. 2008. "Post-genocide Identity Politics in Rwanda." *Ethnicities* 8(1): 5–41.

Isabirye, Stephen B., and Kooros M. Mahmoudi. 2001. "Rwanda, Burundi and Their Tribal Wars." *Social Change* 31(4): 46–69.

Jenkins, Sarah. 2012. "Ethnicity, Violence and the Immigrant-Guest Metaphor in Kenya." *African Affairs* 111(445): 576–96.

Kameri-Mbote, Patricia, and Kithure Kindiki. 2008. "Trouble in Eden: How and Why Unresolved Land Issues Landed 'Peaceful Kenya' in Trouble." *Forum for Development Studies* 35(2): 167–93.

Kanyinga, Karuti. 2009. "The Legacy of the White Highlands: Land Rights, Ethnicity and the Post-election Violence in Kenya." *Journal of Contemporary African Studies* 27(3): 325–44.

Klopp, Jacqueline M., and Elke Zuern. 2007. "The Politics of Violence in Democratization: Lessons from Kenya and South Africa." *Comparative Politics* 39(2): 127–46.

Lynch, Gabrielle. 2006. "Negotiating Ethnicity: Identity Politics in Contemporary Kenya." *Review of African Political Economy* 33(107): 49–65.

Mamdani, Mahmood. 2001. "Beyond Settler and Native as Political Identities: Overcoming the Political Legacy of Colonialism." *Society for Comparative Study of Society and History* 43(4): 651–64.

Mamdani, Mahmood. [2001] 2002. *When Victims Become Killers: Colonialism, Nativism, and the Genocide in Rwanda*. Kampala: Fountain Publishers.

Mann, Laura, and Marie Berry. 2016. "Understanding the Political Motivations That Shape Rwanda's Emergent Developmental State." *New Political Economy* 21(1): 119–44.

Mueller, Susanne D. 1984. "Government and Opposition in Kenya, 1966–9." *The Journal of Modern African Studies* 22(3): 399–427.

Mueller, Susanne D. 2008. "The Political Economy of Kenya's Crisis." *Journal of Eastern African Studies* 2(2): 185–210.

Myers, Jason C. 2005. "On Her Majesty's Ideological State Apparatus: Indirect Rule and Empire." *New Political Science* 27(2): 147–60.

Njoh, Ambe J. 2000. "The Impact of Colonial Heritage on Development in Sub-Saharan Africa." *Social Indicators Research* 52(2): 161–78.

Osamba, Joshia. 2001. "The Dynamics of Ethnopolitical Conflict and Violence in the Rift Valley Province of Kenya." *Nationalism and Ethnic Politics* 7(4): 87–112.

Pottier, Johan. 2002. *Re-imagining Rwanda: Conflict, Survival and Disinformation in the Late Twentieth Century*. Cambridge: Cambridge University Press.

Russell, Garnett Susan, and Laura Quaynor. 2017. "Constructing Citizenship in Post-conflict Contexts: The Cases of Liberia and Rwanda." *Globalisation, Societies and Education* 15(2): 248–70.

Stone, John, and Rutledge Dennis. 2003. *Race and Ethnicity: Comparative and Theoretical Approaches*. Malden, MA: Blackwell.

Straus, Scott. 2006. *The Order of Genocide: Race, Power, and War in Rwanda*. Ithaca, NY: Cornell University Press.

Suzuki, Kazuko. 2017. "A Critical Assessment of Comparative Sociology of Race and Ethnicity." *Sociology of Race and Ethnicity* 3(3): 287–300.

Uvin, Peter. 1999. "Ethnicity and Power in Burundi and Rwanda: Different Paths to Mass Violence." *Comparative Politics* 31(3): 253–71.

Vandeginste, Stef. 2014. "Governing Ethnicity After Genocide: Ethnic Amnesia in Rwanda Versus Ethnic Power-Sharing in Burundi." *Journal of Eastern African Studies* 8(2): 263–77.

Wai, Zubairu. 2012. "Neo-patrimonialism and the Discourse of State Failure in Africa." *Review of African Political Economy* 39(131): 27–43.

Young, Crawford. 2004. "The End of the Post-colonial State in Africa? Reflections on Changing African Political Dynamics." *African Affairs* 103(410): 23–49.

CHAPTER 15

Living Under the Soviet Shadow: Postcolonial Critique of Soviet Politics in Mongolia

Orhon Myadar

INTRODUCTION

One evening in August of 1991 my family gathered around the television in our home in northern Mongolia and watched with angst as Soviet tanks rolled down the streets of Moscow in an attempted coup against Gorbachev's government before throngs of people, terrified and uncertain of the changes unfolding in front of their eyes. I vividly remember an old lady pleading to stop the madness. I also remember the nervous eyes of a soldier, perched on top his tank—seemingly as petrified as the old lady. As we watched this unsettling and terrifying event, none of us spoke. Undoubtedly this was no ordinary moment but none of us could grasp what it all really meant. And yet, we somehow knew that it would forever change our familiar way of life. As a recent high school graduate

O. Myadar (✉)
School of Geography and Development, The University of Arizona,
Tucson, AZ, USA
e-mail: orhon@email.arizona.edu

© The Author(s) 2019   387
D. Schorkowitz et al. (eds.), *Shifting Forms of Continental Colonialism*,
https://doi.org/10.1007/978-981-13-9817-9_15

a month away from starting my life as a university student, I remember wishing it was all untrue and that we could keep the life we knew then just the way it was.

I soon moved to Ulaanbaatar, the capital city of Mongolia, to begin college. As the university where I studied was located immediately next to the government palace of Mongolia, I witnessed the massive political changes and social turmoil that engulfed the city, emanating largely from the central part where I studied and lived. My life as a young adult thus was intricately tied to the ever-changing, chaotic, social, and political landscapes sharply contrasting with those of my childhood. All through my childhood, a loaf of bread, for instance, cost 1 *tugrig* 40 *mungus* (about $0.25), but the same bread all of a sudden cost hundreds of times more and became a rare commodity for which we had to stand in line for hours.

The disparity in the price of bread allegorically captured these radically different periods. Bread under the socialist regime symbolized the stability of the period. It simultaneously represented the control and confinement of an all-powerful state, which planned every aspect of life including the price of bread. The soaring price of bread during the transitional period, on the other hand, symbolized ever-changing and unpredictable social and political conditions. Also, it reflected the waning power of the totalitarian regime as we knew it.

This chapter aims to conceptualize this particular temporal juncture as a conceptual milieu to examine the weight of the Soviet role in Mongolia. Building upon my earlier work, this article suggests the Soviet politics in Mongolia should be examined within the broad colonial paradigm because "the Soviet policies that were carried out in Mongolia ideologically and practically mirrored colonial politics imposed by Europeans throughout the world" (Myadar 2017b, 7). While Spain, Britain, France, and other powers had expanded their empires overseas, the Russians had colonized Asia by land. The Soviets continued this continental colonialism both formally and informally. They incorporated countries, such as Kazakhstan, as formal political units of the USSR, but also subordinated Mongolia allowing it only nominal independence. This informal colonialism would result in the decolonization of Mongolia after the collapse of the USSR followed by a postcolonial analysis of the period.

In conversation with and as an extension to this earlier work, this chapter provides an analytical framework that is grounded in my first-person experience of growing up during the period and illuminates the various material, symbolic, and embodied implications and manifestations of the Soviet political influence in Mongolia. The work is also informed by concepts rooted in literatures on critical political geography and postcolonial studies. It is organized around several personal vignettes, which all speak to a larger theoretical framework. The vignettes are conceptually and spatially tied to my hometown, Bulgan, whence the stories emerge and through which we can situate our theoretical contestation of the everyday experience of Mongolia during the Soviet era.

The fixed price of the bread is the trope through which the chapter will explore the processes of making Mongolia into a legible society and will situate the political, social, and spatial implications of those processes on Mongolia from the time that it gained independence in 1921 to the collapse of the Soviet Union in 1991. The bread metaphor is a simple yet powerful symbol to examine the Soviet role in Mongolia. In Russian culture, bread is not only an important daily staple, but it is also a crucial cultural signifier and a mediator of harmony and peace as routinely seen in Russian 'bread and salt' greeting ceremonies (Goldstein [1983] 1999; Smith and Christian 1984). On the other hand, bread was not a traditional Mongolian staple. Yet, over the course of Mongolia's dependence on the Soviet Union through much of the twentieth century, it had become one of the most prevalent and central staples of the Mongolian diet.

Theoretically this chapter is informed by James Scott's influential work *Seeing Like a State* (1998). The work of many scholars in postcolonial studies has been shaped and enriched by the theoretical contributions of this text. With respect to Mongolia, for example, the book points to key questions about how society became ordered and standardized under the Soviet-backed regime. It gives an insight into how the bread price remained stable for an extended time and how this in turn symbolized the overall process of making Mongolia into what Scott calls a 'legible' society.

My goal here, however, is to move beyond Scott's totalizing assumption that traditional societies are mere victims of the modern state's heavy-handed policies of standardization, rationalization, and regulation. While Scott celebrates 'traditional knowledge' or *metis*, which according to him is assaulted by high-modernist policies, there is an inherent risk in Scott's approach of romanticizing and essentializing the past.

While high-modernist schemes and draconian socialist policies disrupted traditional ways of life and altered the social fabric of Mongolia, these same schemes also brought salvation from the destitution that Mongolia had been suffering. When the socialist regime took control of Mongolia, a large segment of the population had been either fully dependent on the nobility as their personal servants or barely eking out an existence in the growing urban centers. The destitution of the population became highly visible, as illustrated by historian Charles Bawden.

> In front of the high rubbish heaps in the markets and temples were poor wretches lying about, with no homes or relatives, poor and sick, without eyes or noses. Some kind people would give them a bite to eat, but most passed by on the other side disgusted, and the wretches suffered from hunger and thirst, burned by the hot sun in the summer, and frozen to the marrow in the winter, while neither the authorities nor the people, lama or lay, did a thing to help them. (1968, 155)

Such a society, with a large class of destitute poor is neither to be celebrated nor to be romanticized. Indeed, this historical background helps situate not only my own family's feelings of angst and panic at the collapse of the socialist regime of Mongolia, but also the deeply fragmented reaction of the public toward the socialist regime and its subsequent collapse in Mongolia. While the Kremlin-endorsed policies no doubt altered the traditional society of Mongolia, the gridded and legible lives of many under the socialist policies provided a sense of stability and security from which a simple interpretation is not easy to extract. This chapter rather aims to situate the dialectics between the oppressed and liberated within the socialist state introduced by Soviet informal colonialism.

Contextualizing the Soviet–Mongolian Relationship

The seventy years of Soviet–Mongolian relationship goes back to the year 1921 when Mongolia declared its independence from China with the firm backing of the Soviet Union.[1] The new Russian government played a crucial role not only liberating Mongolia from the Chinese, but also in bringing Mongolia to the world stage as a sovereign state. Upon

---

[1] This was a culmination of series of complicated historical moments. For more details see Bawden (1968), Lattimore (1986–87).

independence, Mongolia became the first formally sovereign country following in the socialist footsteps of the USSR. The ideological aspiration, however, was as new as the newly independent state, and Mongolia lacked a cohesive political apparatus that was open to this new ideological articulation.

Most probably, Mongolian revolutionary leader Damdin Sükhbaatar met Lenin who provided guidance to the newly formed regime. Sükhbaatar was a celebrated hero of the partisan war of 1921. Sükhbaatar died early in 1923 at the age of 30, but became the principal figure in the genesis of Mongolian ideological development. Whether or not the actual meeting took place, what was supposedly discussed became an official party narrative. Lenin is believed to have recommended that Mongolia bypass capitalism by forming a modest 'island of socialism' in the economy (Brasher 1971; Rupen 1979). According to Alexey Mikhalev (2013), Lenin thought that backward countries like Mongolia should skip the capitalist stage of development to build socialism and a planned economy to increase the country's productivity. A well-known poster, painted by the artist D. Amgalan, depicts a Mongolian horseman leaping over capitalism, from feudalism, straight to socialism: "The horse and rider have left the dark feudal past behind them, boldly jumped over the (equally dark) stage of capitalism, and landed square in the bright center of socialism" (Steiner-Khamsi and Stolpe 2006, 3). Anthropologist Caroline Humphrey aptly captures this peculiar political moment:

> Mongolia's adoption of socialism was difficult for Marxist theorists to account for, since the country arrived at its revolution without having undergone the due stages of social evolution [...] Thus the socialist ideology of history taught in Mongolia fudged both social evolution and chronological causation. (1992, 376)

Nevertheless, the narrative of building socialism became the base for Mongolia's political trajectory for the next seven decades during which the Soviet Union wielded enormous power over Mongolian domestic politics. The socialist regime headed by the Mongolian Revolutionary Party faithfully carried out policies that were endorsed by the Soviet regime: "In the following decades Soviet ideology was taken up almost more sincerely, more naively, more brutally than in the USSR itself" (Humphrey 1992, 375). Those who opposed this rigid ideological path were eliminated and those who unconditionally supported the Soviet blueprint began to consolidate power.

Out of these turbulent years of suspicion, purges and internal fights between the ruling members of the new independent state, Khorloogiin Choibalsan emerged as the central figure who would amass unchallenged political power. Upon his rise to the top position in the country, he would rule Mongolia for the next two decades until his death in 1952. Choibalsan's rule corresponded with Stalin's in the Soviet Union both in terms of time and style. Similar to Stalin, Choibalsan was an embodiment of the contradictory forces that defined the early years of the socialist regime in the country. Like Stalin he oversaw the massive purges that took the lives of thousands of innocent Mongolians. During World War II, he like Stalin was credited with leading the country to victory against the invading Japanese army on the Mongolian frontier. Much like Stalin, he oversaw the general rise in living standards, developed infrastructure, and increased the literacy rate of Mongolia. More importantly, like Stalin, he ruled the country with an iron fist with no tolerance for dissent or opposition.[2]

The post-Choibalsan period also replicated the post-Stalin era in the Soviet Union. Regardless of who actually was in power, Mongolian leaders came out of the same mold, the Mongolian People's Revolutionary Party (MPRP). The MPRP, as political machinery, remained unchanged in its commitment to the Soviet role in Mongolia. Under its leadership, the Mongolian social landscape changed dramatically through various radical policies that mirrored Soviet politics both in timing and scope. It was an effort to sever Mongolia from its past and remake the society from scratch: "The break is supposedly of such an order as to make it possible to see the world as a tabula rasa, upon which the new can be inscribed without reference to the past–or, if the past gets in the way, through its obliteration" (Harvey 2004, 1). The process of inscribing the new on Mongolian society meant to erase the past which included, but was not limited to, abolishing Mongolian traditional writing in favor of Russian Cyrillic, displacing traditional religion with the new communist ideology, and restructuring and eventually eliminating the traditional property regime. These elaborate, radical, colonial policies irrevocably altered Mongolian traditional social fabric (Bawden 1968).

---

[2]A prominent scholar of Mongolia and China, Owen Lattimore, in contrast, portrayed Choibalsan in a positive light and regarded him as "a great man" (see 1986–87, 13).

Despite the limitations of pre-socialist Mongolia for the majority of Mongolians who existed in an utter destitute state, many people were resistant to many of the sweeping policies that were changing their familiar way of life. Resistance, including at times violent uprisings, was widespread especially in the early years of the socialist regime: "These uprisings were manifestations of resistance against the hegemonic power of the state and colonial politics" (Myadar 2017b, 22). However, the moments of resistance were silenced by an iron fist. Edward Said's description of "the unbroken, all-embracing Western tutelage of an Oriental country" (1978, 35) could apply to the way Mongolian society evolved under these draconian politics.

By the time of my childhood, Mongolian society had become a reliable Soviet ally whose manifestation was evident in spatial, symbolic, epistemic, and material landscapes across the country. Mongolian society had arrived at the ontological intersection where the Soviet presence was woven into its very fabric. The remainder of this chapter explores these various separate, but mutually interdependent, vignettes through the juxtaposition of my gazes as a child, a young adult, and a scholar of political geography.

Spatializing Mongolia: Bulgan as a Vignette

Bulgan is a small town in north-central Mongolia. It is the administrative center of the province of the same name that borders Russia to the north. The city was established in 1938 around an old monastery site to serve as the hub and center of the province and to support the growing proletariat class. At a glance Bulgan is an archetypal Mongolian town. But precisely because of its ordinariness and its banality, Bulgan tells us a tale of the life of a typical Mongolian under the Soviet-backed regime. It serves as a site to probe and unsettle the mundane and prosaic ways Soviet influence reached into the depths of Mongolia. It is a place to revisit the ways in which Soviet politics occupied the most intimate spaces and everyday life of Mongolians.

Like most towns and cities in Mongolia, Bulgan grew over time systemically. It featured a town center from which the city radiated. The center was ornamented by a square that was the heart of the city symbolically and physically. No doubt, the square was built as a clear nod to the symbolic interventions in Soviet cityscapes: "The usual center in [Soviet] cities has a large square designed to provide room for parading troops and for throngs of people on holidays" (Fisher 1962, 253). Similarly, the central square of Bulgan became an important public site through routine rituals and ceremonies. The square was punctuated by a statue of Sandamjamts Lkhagvadorj who fought and lost his life during the Second World War against the Japanese on the Mongolian frontier.

Benjamin Forest and Juliet Johnson provide a useful conceptual framework for understanding the significance of statues as symbolic capital and public goods. According to the authors, monumental sites serve for political authors to gain "the prestige, legitimacy, and influence" derived from these sites (2011, 273). By appropriating historical figures, monuments are used "as instrumental tools in the political battle for hearts and minds" (ibid.). Relying on this view, we can thus assume that the Lkhagvadorj statue was appropriated to serve as symbolic capital appealing to the hearts and minds of Bulgan residents. The square was a reminder of the Mongolian sacrifice in the Great War under the supreme leadership of the Soviet Union—a suggestion also of a neocolonial relationship between the two countries. As Michael Shapiro relatedly asserts, "all places have a meaning that is mediated by an imaginative geography" (2012, 60). Ontologically speaking, the square was nothing more than a parcel of land that was blanketed with concrete. However, by giving meanings to the site, and animating those meanings through various mediated practices, the same space could produce an imaginary geography that wielded a profound affective power. In *Symbols and Legitimacy*, Graeme Gill examines Soviet ideological landscapes and argues that public spectacles served the Soviet regime by displaying its control of the city by instilling new symbolic meanings in it (2011, 69). He argues that Lenin specifically placed critical importance on symbolic dominance of the city: "[Lenin's] plan for monumental architecture was part of this idea of creating a city that would give voice to socialist values and thereby cease to be the locus of old regime power and symbolism and instead become the manifestation of the new" (71).

Bulgan's central square too served to appropriate new meaning for the new regime, divorced from its past and detached from its traditional identity based on nomadism and monastic Buddhism. On special occasions, including and especially October Revolution Day and May Victory Day, the residents of Bulgan gathered at the square to celebrate with much fanfare and spectacle. As celebrations of Soviet events, these festivities represented forms of neocolonialism in Mongolia. I was among generations of Bulgan children who would spend long painstaking hours perfecting their choreographed performances. Adorned with banners and flags, workers from different organizations paraded not only to showcase the success of their labor, but also to reaffirm their loyalty and support for the regime:

> By mobilizing the populace into street marches and demonstration, by transforming their essence from protest [...] into celebration, and by redirecting such activities into new routes to be taken through the city, authorities not only asserted symbolic control of the city, but invested parts of it with a new, revolutionary, symbolic significance. (ibid., 70)

By asserting symbolic control of the city as such, not only did the state produce meanings that supported and glorified the regime, but also erased and displaced meanings that were considered too archaic or contradictory to the ideals of the regime (Diener and Hagen 2013; Dwyer and Alderman 2008). Geographer David Lowenthal reminds us that the past is forever barred from us and we are confined to the present with fragmented and attenuated memories (2015, 4). Ernest Renan and others call this act of selective remembering and forgetting of the past a form of collective amnesia. The concept of collective amnesia is a useful way to understand how selective meanings were embedded within the square embodied by Lkhagvadorj and how the same meanings simultaneously purged other meanings associated with Mongolia in general and with Bulgan in particular (Myadar and Rae 2014; Myadar 2017a).

In terms of its physical geography, Bulgan is nestled in a valley surrounded by mountains, and it sprawls over rolling hills. Residential areas are built over these hills parceled by *hashaas* (fenced areas) for household use. Given Bulgan's abundance of forest, the majority of Bulgan's residents live in wooden houses. These houses are strikingly similar to wooden peasant houses that dot Russian villages, a result of Soviet informal colonial policies. The gridded development of Bulgan during the communist era paralleled the material and symbolic 'gridding' and structuring of the lives of not only Bulgan residents, but the Mongolian population in general. The gridding provided administrative and bureaucratic convenience that also facilitated the control and surveillance of the subjects of the state. Spatial legibility, to borrow from Scott (1998), also extended to the 'legibility' of Bulgan residents with each person registered within a wider population census. The 'legible' spatial order also worked "by producing and codifying a visible hierarchy" and controlling the subjects within the order (Mitchell 1988, 45). Bulgan residents' movements were carefully registered, regulated, and monitored through the wider nationwide system of formal registration and identification. They were not permitted to change jobs or to leave their home areas without official approval (Neupert and Goldstein 1994). "Regulating population movement was thus not only a spatial endeavor, but also biopolitics to control and discipline the masses" (Myadar 2017b, 20). Soviet informal colonialism was thus manifested in high-modernist policies that were antithetical to Mongolia's traditional identity based on pastoral nomadism.

Divorce from its past was not an organic outcome of Mongolia's independent pursuit of modernity and development. Per Kremlin directions, Mongolia had to move away from its past and strive to become modernized: "the Soviet's role in binding the population to territorial units was no doubt an example of gradual and slow assault on the Mongolian people, especially those who closely identified with and cherished the traditional way of life as nomadic herders" (Myadar 2017b, 20). One of the important ways the state achieved the 'gridding' of the lives of the Mongolian public in general and Bulgan residents in particular was through and by the educational system which itself had evolved to serve the greater ideological goal of the state.

EDUCATING MONGOLIA: SCHOOL AS A VIGNETTE

When I was growing up, Bulgan had three secondary schools in addition to a few elementary schools. I graduated from *School number 1* which was named after Petr Yefimovich Shchetinkin. The prominent portrait of Shchetinkin greeted me every day as I entered the school under his watchful gaze. Shchetinkin was one of the leaders of the Soviet partisan movement in the Yenisei province during Russian civil war. He led the army that defeated Baron Roman von Ungern-Sternberg's short-lived regime in Mongolia. Baron Ungern, as he was popularly known, was an anti-Bolshevik warlord who had helped Mongolia overthrow Chinese rule in the country.[3] By defeating Baron Ungern's forces, Shchetinkin personally played a critical role in securing Mongolia's independence, but also in cementing Soviet neocolonial control of Mongolia

---

[3] For an extended discussion on Baron Ungern, see Sunderland (2014).

(Lattimore 1986–87). Shchetinkin was later stationed in Mongolia to lead the Soviet party cell in the country, which he did until September 1927 when he was killed in Ulaanbaatar under unclear circumstances. In recognition of his contributions to the country's struggle for independence and to the building of a socialist state, he was honored as the Iron Hero (Timur Bator) in Mongolia.

Honoring Shchetinkin as such at a school in a remote Mongolian town thus can provide a useful framework in understanding the symbolic and material representations of the Soviet role in Mongolia. Schools are, in general, important epistemological and ontological sites to produce and nurture the ideological manifestations of the state. They are ideal places to untangle the complex legacy of Soviet informal colonialism in the country. Owing to schools, Mongolia enjoyed nearly universal literacy at the end of the seven decades of Soviet-backed regime. This trend was shared among other socialist states and is often considered, rightfully so, as one of the most progressive outcomes of the socialist, if not colonial, regimes around the world. Regardless of one's social background, the schools were not only where one learned to read and write, but also where one built a foundation to become a productive member of the society. It was also where aspiring learners started their paths to higher education at state-funded universities and colleges to become doctors, teachers, engineers, and so on. It is where I spent my tender years of childhood and where, upon graduation, I received an invitation to study at a university.

Yet, the schools were simultaneously places of conformity and production of political subjects. Michel Foucault's discussion of power, discipline, and governmentality is especially relevant to problematizing Mongolian schools as sites producing disciplined and docile subjects of the state and embryonic spaces for securing the power of the state. Foucault's several works speak to the concept of governmentality that is instrumental to unpacking the role of schools in socialist Mongolia whose spatiality and social relationships functioned to shape the everyday lives of children (Foucault [1969] 2012, [1977] 1979). Mongolian schools were structurally and conceptually modeled after the Soviet educational system of the informal colonial metropolis. The Soviet educational structure was designed not only to provide primary education to children, but also to shape the children into responsible citizens of the state in accordance with the official *Model Guide for the Upbringing of Schoolchildren* (Primernoe soderzhanie vospitaniya shkolnikov; cf. Cary 1977; Zajda 1980, 133–34). In his important work comparing citizenship training in American and Soviet schools during the height of the Cold War, Charles Cary argued that both school systems functioned not only to prepare good citizens of their respective societies, but more importantly to train school children to become politically responsible adults who would contribute to maintaining their particular political systems and perpetuating their national ideologies. Despite the fact that these two countries stood at the opposite ends of the ideological spectrum that defined the highly contentious Cold War, both placed great importance on "the inculcation in the young of certain prescribed political orientations and predispositions toward political behavior" (Cary 1977, 285). However, as Cary points out, the Soviet intervention in preparing children into responsible and desired political citizens was broader in scope and more detailed in its execution.

In Mongolia, education was highly focused on glorifying the Soviet Union and spreading the personality cult of the leaders of the Communist Party, as well as of Soviet leaders. Applauding the educational achievement of Mongolia, Shirendev and Sanjdorj noted that "due to the inculcation of Party propaganda and ideology, political and scientific education infiltrated among the public and 'revolutionary' changes took place in their consciousness" (1969, 359). Material, symbolic, and embodied manifestations of Soviet educational policy were evident in Mongolia from the most prominent to the most mundane aspects of school space. Physically, schools replicated the Soviet schools in their design and function. At the heart of any school there were classrooms of standard shapes and uniform designs. A typical classroom would consist of three rows of desks and chairs with the teacher's station positioned panoptically in the front of the classroom that commanded a complete view of the classroom and schoolchildren. From the vantage point of the children, it was "the fact of being constantly seen, of being always able to be seen, that maintains the disciplined individual in [the teacher's] subjection" (Foucault [1977] 1979, 87).

In my school, class size ranged from 30 to 40 children per teacher. Despite this ratio, by instilling respect for and obedience to the hierarchy, classrooms served to prepare the children to become self-disciplined citizens of the state: "Authority and obedience were diffused, without diminution, throughout the school, implicating every individual in a system of order. The model school was a model of the perfect society" (Mitchell 1988, 7). The design of the classroom thus provided the teachers not only a panoptican view over the children, but also afforded the type of confined space where surveillance and disciplinary actions could be achieved efficiently. Thus, we can treat a school classroom as an elementary site of social control where order was expected and power relations were internalized. While such a design was not unique to Soviet education, it served any colonial and totalitarian system especially well.

On the school premises, a hierarchy was well established, within which power relations between and within school members were well defined and the authority of those wielding greater power would not be challenged. Children learned to respect the chain of command and obey the instructions of their superiors and master the techniques of moral self-control: "The young are expected to learn that rules define good and bad, right and wrong behavior. In addition, they are expected to be able to recognize examples of each kind of behavior in their own and others' actions" (Cary 1977, 291). A challenge to the authority (e.g. teacher in the classroom) would be faced with various punitive measures, including shaming, scolding, and even physical punishments—all of which I witnessed throughout my school years.

Foucault's critical insights in *Discipline and Punish* ([1977] 1979) are applicable to the ways in which schoolchildren were disciplined and punished before witnesses. In general, an act of punishing someone (a supposedly guilty child in our case) in public is a spectacle aimed not only at punishing the accused, but also at disciplining those subjected to the spectacle. It serves to deter future transgressions through self-discipline and internalization of those punishments as the rightful outcome if one fails at self-control. Foucault discusses how the spectacular and violent punishment of the condemned body has given way to the less visible and mundane punishments designed to 'reform' the person instead of inflicting violent pain on the actual body.

Yet, schools in Mongolia continued to perform spectacular punishments (although not as violent and visceral in their form as vividly described by Foucault in his prologue). By spectacular punishment, I mean any punitive measures that were witnessed by others despite the fact that the witnesses had nothing to do with the transgression in question. The judicial power within the school thus worked to instill discipline into the moral fiber of school children. The disciplinary and punitive measures were as much about the past (the supposed transgression) as they were about the future. If all went well, due to these moral orthopedic techniques, these children would grow up to be model (docile) citizens of the state who respected the authority and obeyed the rules of the social contract.

The school day thus was the primary time when the loyalty to the state would be established and nurtured. Loyal citizens are indispensable not only for maintaining the existing political system, but also for establishing and preserving a cohesive political community (or an imagined community in Anderson's term), the basis and engine of the political system.

> Loyalty of citizens can affect the perpetuation of the political system both in war and peace. Wartime loyalty, as evidenced in patriotic service in the armed forces, may ensure the survival of the political system; peacetime loyalty, as displayed in "good citizenship," may promote the effective operation of the political system. (Cary 1977, 291)

In order to inculcate loyalty to the state, classrooms also served as the sites of epistemological interventions. In other words, classrooms were the physical spaces where children learned the ideological underpinnings of the state through various systematic and mediated practices and rituals. Even more clearly than in physical space, Soviet informal colonialism was omnipresent in the epistemology of schools across Mongolia.

As a young child, I learned about the brotherly friendship between the Soviet Union and Mongolia, known as *akh düügiin kholboo* or brothers' union to translate loosely. Like thousands of school children across Mongolia, I learned of the implicit roles within this friendship, where the Soviet Union was the older mature, and wise brother and Mongolia was the younger immature sibling (Mikhalev 2013; Myadar 2017b; Sneath 2003). In other words, Mongolia was the lesser Other or, as Billé (2014) aptly puts it, 'BrOther'. As a child, I did not question the position of each party in this fraternity, and the implications it carried. I learned to respect, admire, and love the great leaders of the communist movement, and carried the banners with their portraits proudly during parades. And I distinctly remember the pain I felt and tears I shed upon the news of Brezhnev's death. He had been the great leader of the communist world as far as I could remember, and his death meant irrevocable loss to the wide community of socialist states.

I became versed in Russian literature and loved Tchaikovsky (I thought no other was comparable to his magical music). I grew up watching Russian cartoons, with my favorite being *Nu, Pogody*, which never ceased to bring sheer bliss every time I watched it. I cheered on the Russian athletes in international competitions. As a child, I learned to love the Soviet Union and what it stood for. This profound sense of love for the Soviet empire was shared by my colonized peers. The innocence of young children's love for institutionalized frames of knowledge speaks to the extent of the epistemological power that dominated the Mongolian psyche during the Soviet era. It shows how far reaching the techniques of knowledge production were and how they generated a reservoir of carefully selected and ideologically driven episteme in Mongolia.

The primary medium by which these epistemic interventions took place was through texts (Kaplonski 1998). Mongolian children became versed in Russian culture, Soviet ideology, and communist philosophy in texts that were written in Cyrillic.[4] Until the Soviet push to abandon it, Mongolians used traditional Mongolian script which had 700 years of history prior to its condemnation by the Soviets. Replacing Mongolian script with Cyrillic took place between 1945 and 1946 (Jamyan 1962). The official basis for changing the script was that Mongolian script was archaic and too difficult to learn, and an easier script was necessary to increase the literacy rate at a sufficiently rapid pace. Anything in the indigenous writing—including signs, books, government documents, and the like—had to be discarded and replaced, and those individuals who already read traditional Mongolian script had to learn to read Cyrillic. "The primary goal was probably to use script reform to isolate Inner Mongolia and repress pan-Mongolism" as Gita Steiner-Khamsi and Ines Stolpe argue (2006, 42), and the change "served not only a practical purpose in Soviet censorship, but, perhaps more importantly, it prevented future generations from reconnecting with their past [...] The Soviets essentially burnt the bridge that connected the present to the past" (Myadar 2017b, 18).

Michael Billig's (1995) critical work on *Banal Nationalism* provides useful insights into how love for one's nation is constructed and perpetuated through routine practices and rituals in the most common everyday spaces. He argues that the constant flagging of national importance in the most unsuspecting spaces is effective in establishing people's love

---

[4]To the south of the country's border, incidentally young children in Inner Mongolia underwent a similar cultural training albeit in a Chinese context.

for their nations precisely because the affective technology of nationalism goes unnoticed and unchallenged. Benedict Anderson's (1983) seminal text on *Imagined Communities* also speaks to the subtle and prosaic ways affection for an imaginary national community is constructed. If we use these texts to understand my and others' love for the Soviet Union, we can appreciate the breadth of the Soviet role in Mongolia despite the fact the Mongolian territory stayed outside the Soviet de jure national boundaries. Even though Mongolia was not a part of the Soviet Union, the experience of Mongolians during the Soviet era suggests that the Soviets held colonial power not only over Mongolian political affairs, but also over the internal politics and everyday lives of Mongolians.

Occupying Mongolia: A Soviet Garrison as a Vignette

When I entered fourth grade, I began to study Russian as a second language. Learning Russian had long become a required component of the Mongolian educational curriculum (Steiner-Khamsi and Stolpe 2006). Though I had no choice whether to learn Russian, I very much enjoyed learning this rich language. Halfway through my first year of instruction, my school put together a large concert showcasing our Russian ability. As I was one of the two children picked from our grade to perform, I was assigned to recite a poem and sing a song with another girl. Everyone in the concert group stayed long hours after class, preparing for the big concert.

Sometime early in the spring, the much-anticipated day eventually came. All of us boarded a bus with our costumes and instruments. A bumpy country road took us to what felt like a foreign country. We were stopped by Russian soldiers in uniform who, after careful inspection, let us through into a small town of grey brick buildings. It was a territorial inscription of the Soviet heartland in the heart of Mongolia. When we arrived at a school where we would perform later that afternoon, I felt a disorienting sensation, vivid and overwhelming, *because* of the foreignness of the place and everyone we saw. It was a particular sort of space, whose existence had never registered prior to the moment and whose presence became towering at the moment of my encounter. Even though I had seen Russian people a handful of times prior to this visit, I had never been in a situation where Russians vastly outnumbered Mongolians. In that moment and space, as the subject of displacing gazes, I was the foreigner in my native land, a common sensation of the colonized.

The town I am referring to was a Russian military garrison situated about 30 km south of my hometown. Nestled in a mountain valley along the river Orkhon, the military town was one of many such settlements in Mongolia. These towns "duplicated small Soviet cities with complete infrastructure and management and [enjoyed] extra-territorial status" (Mikhalev 2013, 190). Ontologically ambiguous and territorially paradoxical, these towns functioned simultaneously inside and outside of Mongolia. The peculiar existence of these military towns across Mongolia dialectically embedded within, but detached from the rest of Mongolia helps us contextualize the colonial omnipresence of the Soviets. This presence manifested itself not only in the Mongolian epistemological field, but also ontologically, both facilitating and challenging the country's very being as an independent state.

On the one hand, as some historians argue, Mongolian national independence was facilitated by the Russian presence, including military. According to the eminent scholar of Mongolian history Charles Bawden, because of the Soviet protection, Mongolia was able to salvage its independent statehood and preserve its national purity. He argues that

> Russian involvement in Mongol affairs [was] essential to the continued existence of an undiluted Mongol race as masters in their own country: the alternative, to be swamped by colonizing Chinese, [is] clearly demonstrated in Inner Mongolia. (1968, 390–91)

Writing in the 1960s, Bawden's insight reflected Mongolia's precarious geopolitical reality very much defined and shaped by its two neighbors: "Indeed, even demarcation by means of borders, the quintessence of state territoriality, relies, to a considerable degree on the extent to which networks of association and affiliation parallel the boundaries of domination" (Agnew 2005, 443). Therefore, these military garrisons served as protectors of Mongolian territorial integrity should it become threatened and did not trigger fear of actual mass Russian settlement in Mongolia.

On the other hand, the Soviet military base can be seen as a mere manifestation of the Soviets' own geopolitical interests in using Mongolia as a buffer zone or a front line in the case of war with China. Despite their earlier alliance in the international communist movement, the USSR and China diverged and began a two-decade-long contentious split beginning in the 1960s. During this period, the tension between these two countries often became heated, and a war between them was conceivable: "By some estimates, the combined Soviet and Chinese forces facing each other across their long common border number about 1,500,000 men" (Smith 1970, 25). Naturally, the Sino-Soviet conflict had major ramifications for other countries within the greater communist bloc. Mongolia was no exception. Given Mongolia's geographic proximity and its peculiar geopolitical reality, Mongolia had to pick a side, and the choice was clear. Mongolia sided with the USSR unequivocally, and subsequently cut ties with China. As a result, Mongolia was "now squarely on the front line of the Soviet Far Eastern defense system at a time when a serious outbreak of hostilities between China and the USSR [was] a real possibility" (ibid.). During this increasingly contentious time, the USSR and Mongolia signed the Soviet–Mongolian Treaty of Friendship, Cooperation, and Mutual Assistance in 1966. The treaty included a defense clause that would facilitate the Soviet build-up of its troops and military installations in Mongolia (Mikhalev 2013; Smith 1970). Of course, this placed Mongolia within the Soviet empire's sphere of influence as an informal, military colony.

The military town I visited was a byproduct of this very treaty. Until the collapse of the Soviet Union, this town flourished supporting a community of military personnel, their support staff, and their families. The town, in architecture and in function, followed the standardized 'living space' that was a critical component of socialist city planning (Fisher 1962). Little has been written about the lives of the residents of these towns though Mikhalev's (2013) survey on *Soviet Experts in Mongolia* provides some helpful insight. According to him, in addition to the civil experts who lived in Mongolia over the course of two decades, half a million Soviet soldiers served in the country. This is a significant number given that Mongolia's population hovered between 1 million in 1960 to 1.7 million in the 1980s (World Bank).

Relying on his interviews with the former residents of military towns, Alexey Mikhalev argues that the Soviet experts (specifically the military personnel) enjoyed fairly privileged lives compared to average Mongolians. In addition to the complete support of the Soviet infrastructure and sheltered livelihoods, the Soviet experts had access to commodities of 'privilege' that were not accessible to Mongolians and the common residents in the Soviet heartland. Military stores (*voentorg*) were stocked with goods that were not available in other stores in Mongolia and the Soviet Union (Mikhalev 2013); moreover, they were strictly off limits to Mongolians. Spatial technologies of exclusion to these stores of privileged consumption were emblematic of the broader geopolitical and structural imaginations between Mongolia and the Soviet Union. These military towns thus can be seen as the embodiment of the Soviet occupation of Mongolia. With Russians as the primary population, these towns were closed off to Mongolians physically and symbolically. The biopolitics of exclusion of Mongolians can be understood within wider geopolitics of the domination of the Soviet Union over Mongolian sovereignty. As the zone of exclusion, the military towns functioned to territorialize Soviet dominion not only in the most literal, physical sense, but also in the symbolic articulations that defined the relationship between the Soviet Union and Mongolia at the time. In other words, these towns in essence enjoyed 'exceptional sovereignty'[5] within the sovereign state of Mongolia: "[T]erritoriality is only one type of spatiality or way in which space is constituted socially and mobilized politically" (Agnew 2005, 442). My encounter with the town can then be understood not only as an encounter with a particular kind of (foreign) social space, but also an encounter with Soviet hegemony. It was a type of colonial hegemony that was facilitated through and materialized by the ruling elite of Mongolia.

Photographer Eric Lusito's work, "Traces of the Soviet Empire", offers a rare window into the phantoms of these now-abandoned towns, which today lie in ruins throughout the country. *Business Insider* (2017) featured many of his photos including the one below that closely resembles the school I visited when I was about ten years old (Fig. 15.1).

RULING MONGOLIA: MIMICRY AS A VIGNETTE

As a child, I was one within many generations who looked up to this curious figure, Anastasia Tsedenbala Filatova, who headed the Mongolian Children's Fund. During special occasions, specifically on Children's Day, she would address all the country's young in televised speeches. As I came to accept, her speeches would be in Russian.[6] I also

---

[5] I borrow this term from Derek Gregory's analysis (2004) of Guantanamo Bay in which he argues that the site functioned under American 'complete authority' although the 'ultimate sovereignty' rested with Cuba.

[6] Born in Russia, Filatova spent most of her adult life in Mongolia. She spent her final years in Moscow and was survived by the couple's two children. As she was married to the

Fig. 15.1   44th Mixed Air Corps, Mongolia (Photographer: Eric Lusito)

knew to respect her, despite the distance she perpetuated through this language, as she was married to the head of the state, Yumjaa Tsedenbal. Tsedenbal led the country for four decades and was no doubt one of the most powerful figures in Mongolia.

The union of Tsedenbal and Filatova points to another important dimension of the Soviet–Mongolian relationship—co-opting elites. Relying on the Gramscian notion of hegemony, I have elsewhere argued that co-opting elites is a familiar colonial strategy: "Elites serve both to facilitate and assume hegemonic power, as they are typically positioned to induce and diffuse 'spontaneous' consent and collective consciousness

most influential figure in Mongolia, she was suspected of having an unduly influence on Mongolian political affairs.

through persuasion, coercion and power" (Myadar 2017b, 17; cf. Gramsci 1971). Homi Bhabha's article, "Of Mimicry and Man", remains one of the most critical texts in understanding the role of elites in establishing and perpetuating colonial power on subjugated territory. Bhabha argues that the elites, or 'the mimic men' in colonial discourse, were considered the most groomed and reformed 'Others', and they served as intermediaries between the colonists and the colonial subjects. According to Bhabha, colonial (in our case Soviet) mimicry could be explained by "the desire for a reformed, recognizable Other, as a subject of a difference that is almost the same, but not quite" (1984, 124). Bhabha highlights the need for an ambivalence around the discourse of mimicry which has to be produced by its slippage, its excess, its difference to be effective.

Who were the elites in Mongolia and how do we understand their position within Soviet–Mongolian relations? In the early days of socialism, Mongolia systematically purged those who wielded power and wealth or presented any challenge to the regime backed by the Soviet Union. Following the Soviet purge of its bourgeois class, Mongolia carried out an extensive campaign against those considered enemies of the state: "The first mass arrests of what was to become Mongolia's Great Terror took place on September 10, 1937, and involved about 100 people" (Kaplonski 2008, 331). To be classified as an enemy of the state was to be charged with a murky category of assaults, to be convicted on shoddy trials, and to be sentenced without due process. Of those found guilty of a range of charges, some were fined, some were demoted, and some were exiled to obscure destinations. On the gruesome end of the large-scale purges, many innocent Mongolians lost their lives. In their revealing account of these purges, Shagdariin Sandag and Harry Kendall discuss how Mongolia executed its own sons and daughters—the country's important political leaders, as well as prominent religious and intellectual figures (2000). These purges remain one of the most blatant and grotesque assaults on Mongolian society:

> This kind of annihilation cannot accurately be described merely as a 'social transformation', despite the many positive achievements of the Mongol-Soviet government, but was more like a strange apocalypse, in which ordinary people were stunned but nevertheless had to go on living. (Humphrey 1992, 380)

As a result of these purges, Mongolia systematically eradicated the former ruling class. In its place, Mongolia produced a political apparatus made up of an elite class that was reliably pro-Soviet and unequivocally loyal to the regime. Most of these elite members were educated in the Soviet Union, and many had marriage ties, including Tsedenbal. Thus Tsedenbal and Filatova's marriage was the embodiment of the elite class that was tied to the Soviet political machinery.

On the personal level, I have no doubt that Tsedenbal and Filatova's marriage was a loving union of two people. However, we can see a parallel between their union, as political figures, and Mongolia–Soviet relations. Filatova spent most of her life in Mongolia and held an important public office, but she never learned to speak Mongolian. It was not only Tsedenbal's personal choice to communicate with her in Russian, but it was our collective responsibility to learn *her* language to understand her. Children of Mongolia, whose gaze fixed on Filatova as she delivered her speeches, would internalize the subtle colonial representation beyond her speech articulating greater Soviet–Mongolian relations. They could see that they were required to learn Russian in their homeland, yet Russians never had to learn Mongolian even though they lived in Mongolia. They could see that Russian was more desirable and regarded as higher than Mongolian within the upper echelon of Mongolia, but they could not feel the contradiction.

Treating Russian as a superior language was symbolic of the ways the elite looked up to the Soviet Union not only culturally, but also ideologically and politically. The Russian language functioned as the medium through which the systemic Sovietization took place in all areas of Mongolian life. This in turn served to carry out "the dominant strategic function of colonial power" (Bhabha 1984, 126). However, there was a counter pressure to preserve the independence of Mongolia and demarcate its symbolic and material boundaries of difference. According to Bhabha, mimicry represented the ideal compromise in this context:

> Mimicry is [...] stricken by an indeterminacy: mimicry emerges as the representation of a difference that is itself a process of disavowal. Mimicry is, thus, the sign of a double articulation; a complex strategy of reform, regulation, and discipline, which "appropriates" the Other as it visualizes power (ibid.).

Mongolian elites thus became in Jacques Lacan terms 'camouflaged' or in Bhabhan terms 'mimic men' assuming the Mongolian semblance to their Russian presence.

CONCLUSION

Looking back at the moment when my family anxiously huddled in front of our television, we can appreciate that it was a symbolic moment that separated two radically different periods that have defined the contemporary history of Mongolia. Before that moment, there was a period of seven decades in the making of the Mongolian nation in the shadow of the Soviet Union. The period after that moment can be understood as the decolonizing and remaking of Mongolian society detached from the omnipresent Soviet straitjacket. I have elsewhere discussed post-Soviet Mongolia's quest for rebuilding the national identity detached from the Soviet regime (Myadar and Rae 2014).

In this essay, I have examined the period under what I called the Soviet shadow. Building upon my earlier work, I have provided a postcolonial analysis centered on and derived from my personal accounts from the period. Organized around different vignettes of my personal experiences, this essay has aimed to illuminate the experience of a typical Mongolian under the regime and to provide embodied contexts to the theoretical framework that was the basis of my earlier work on *Mongolia in the Soviet Shadow* (Myadar 2017b). While my stories are admittedly singular and unique to my own frames of knowledge and experience and my particular position, my experience growing up in a typical Mongolian town can offer a window into the Soviet reach in Mongolia in the most intimate spaces, banal encounters, and prosaic settings.

Symbolized by the fixed price of bread, the period articulated stability and predictability on the one hand, and the heavy-handed government control that ensured the very stability on the other hand. Bread also symbolized the Soviet reach in Mongolia during which time its colonized people assumed their position as lesser partners in Soviet–Mongolian brotherly relations. The newly groomed elite were central to the quest of remolding Mongolia in the interest of and at the direction of the Soviet apparatus. As a result, Soviet control in Mongolia prevailed from the political and ideological landscapes to the most intimate and tender spaces of the everyday lives of Mongolians.

From the ways the Soviets controlled Mongolia, and co-opted elites, the Soviet period in Mongolia can be seen as neocolonial. Mongolia served not only as a politically subject state, but also as a site of a social and cultural manifestation of Soviet politics as evidenced and experienced by a typical Mongolian child who grew up during the period and witnessed its collapse first hand.

References

Agnew, John. 2005. "Sovereignty Regimes: Territoriality and State Authority in Contemporary World Politics." *Annals of the Association of American Geographers* 95(2): 437–61.

Anderson, Benedict. 1983. *Imagined Communities: Reflections on the Origin and Spread of Nationalism*. London: Verso.

Bawden, Charles R. 1968. *The Modern History of Mongolia*. New York: Frederick A. Praeger.

Bhabha, Homi. 1984. "Of Mimicry and Man: The Ambivalence of Colonial Discourse." *October* 28: 125–33.

Billé, Franck. 2014. *Sinophobia: Anxiety, Violence, and the Making of Mongolian Identity*. Honolulu, HI: University of Hawai'i Press.

Billig, Michael. 1995. *Banal Nationalism*. London: Sage.

Brasher, Henry S. 1971. "The Sovietization of Mongolia." *Foreign Affairs* 50: 545–53.

Business Insider. 2017. "A Rare Look at the Abandoned Military Bases of the USSR." http://www.businessinsider.com/photos-of-abandoned-soviet-military-bases-2014-7?IR=T. Accessed on January 11, 2018.

Cary, Charles D. 1977. "The Goals of Citizenship Training in American and Soviet Schools." *Studies in Comparative Communism* 10(3): 281–97.

Diener, Alexander C., and Joshua Hagen. 2013. "From Socialist to Post-socialist Cities: Narrating the Nation Through Urban Space." *Nationalities Papers* 41(4): 487–514.

Dwyer, Owen J., and Derek H. Alderman. 2008. "Memorial Landscapes: Analytic Questions and Metaphors." *GeoJournal* 73(3): 165–78.

Fisher, Jack C. 1962. "Planning the City of Socialist Man." *Journal of the American Institute of Planners* 28(4): 251–65.

Forest, Benjamin, and Juliet Johnson. 2011. "Monumental Politics: Regime Type and Public Memory in Post-communist States." *Post-Soviet Affairs* 27(3): 269–88.

Foucault, Michel. [1969] 2012. *The Archaeology of Knowledge: And the Discourse on Language*. Translated by A.M. Sheridan Smith. New York: Vintage Books.

Foucault, Michel. [1977] 1979. *Discipline and Punish: The Birth of the Prison*. Translated by A.M. Sheridan Smith. New York: Vintage Books.

Gill, Graeme. 2011. *Symbols and Legitimacy in Soviet Politics*. Cambridge: Cambridge University Press.

Goldstein, Darra. [1983] 1999. *A Taste of Russia: A Cookbook of Russian Hospitality*. 2nd ed. Montpelier, VT: Russian Life Books.

Gramsci, Antonio. 1971. *Selections from the Prison Notebooks*. Edited and translated by Quentin Hoare and Geoffrey Nowell Smith. London: Lawrence & Wishart.

Gregory, Derek. 2004. *The Colonial Present*. Oxford: Blackwell.

Harvey, David. 2004. *Paris, Capital of Modernity*. Routledge.

Humphrey, Caroline. 1992. "The Moral Authority of the Past in Post-socialist Mongolia." *Religion, State and Society* 20(3–4): 375–89.

Jamyan, B. 1962. *Soyol Gegeerleliin Baiguullaguudyn Ajlyn Talaar Holbogdoltoi Zarlig, Togtool Zaavruudyn Systemchilsen Emhtgel* [Systematic Collection of Decrees, Resolutions and Instructions Concerning the Work of Cultural and Educational Organizations]. Ulaanbaatar: Mongolian Government.

Kaplonski, Christopher. 1998. "Creating National Identity in Socialist Mongolia." *Central Asian Survey* 17(1): 35–49.

Kaplonski, Christopher. 2008. "Prelude to Violence: Show Trials and State Power in 1930s Mongolia." *American Ethnologist* 35(2): 321–37.

Lattimore, Owen. 1986–87. "Mongolia as a Leading State." *Mongolian Studies* 10: 5–18.

Lowenthal, David. 2015. *The Past Is a Foreign Country—Revisited*. Cambridge: Cambridge University Press.

Lusito, Eric. *Traces of the Soviet Empire*. http://www.ericlusito.com/index.html. Accessed January 11, 2018.

Mikhalev, Alexey V. 2013. "Soviet Experts in Mongolia: Between International Mission and Colonial Practices." *Sensus Historiae* 10(1): 177–94.

Mitchell, Timothy. 1988. *Colonising Egypt*. Berkeley: University of California Press.

Myadar, Orhon. 2017a. "The Rebirth of Chinggis Khaan: State Appropriation of Chinggis Khaan in Post-socialist Mongolia." *Nationalities Papers* 45(5): 840–55.

Myadar, Orhon. 2017b. "In the Soviet Shadow." *Inner Asia* 19(1): 5–28.

Myadar, Orhon, and James Deshaw Rae. 2014. "Territorializing National Identity in Post-socialist Mongolia: Purity, Authenticity, and Chinggis Khaan." *Eurasian Geography and Economics* 55(5): 560–77.

Neupert, Ricardo F., and Sidney Goldstein. 1994. *Urbanization and Population Redistribution in Mongolia*. East West Center Occasional Series 122. Honolulu, HI: East West Center.

Rupen, Robert Arthur. 1979. *How Mongolia Is Really Ruled: A Political History of the Mongolian People's Republic, 1900–1978*. Stanford, CA: Hoover Institution Press, Stanford University Press.

Said, Edward. 1978. *Orientalism*. New York: Pantheon Books.

Sandag, Shagdariin, and Harry H. Kendall. 2000. *Poisoned Arrows: The Stalin-Choibalsan Mongolian Massacres, 1921–1941*. Boulder, CO: Westview Press.

Scott, James C. 1998. *Seeing Like a State: How Certain Schemes to Improve the Human Condition Have Failed*. New Haven: Yale University Press.

Shapiro, Michael J. 2012. *Discourse, Culture, Violence*. Edited by Terell Carver and Samuel A. Chambers. London: Routledge.

Shirendev, Bazar, and M. Sanjdorj. 1969. *BNMAU-iin Tuukh* [History of the Mongolian People's Republic]. Ulaanbaatar: State Printing House.

Smith, Robert A. 1970. "Mongolia: In the Soviet Camp." *Asian Survey* 10(1): 25–29.

Smith, R.E.F., and David Christian. 1984. *Bread and Salt: A Social and Economic History of Food and Drink in Russia*. Cambridge: Cambridge University Press.

Sneath, David. 2003. "Lost in the Post: Technologies of Imagination, and the Soviet Legacy in Post-socialist Mongolia." *Inner Asia* 5(1): 39–52.

Steiner-Khamsi, Gita, and Ines Stolpe. 2006. *Educational Import: Local Encounters with Global Forces in Mongolia*. New York: Palgrave Macmillan.

Sunderland, Willard. 2014. *The Baron's Cloak: A History of the Russian Empire in War and Revolution*. Ithaca: Cornell University Press.

World Bank. https://data.worldbank.org/country/mongolia. Accessed January 11, 2018.

Zajda, Joseph I. 1980. *Education in the USSR: International Studies in Education and Social Change*. Oxford: Pergamon Press.

PART V

Modes of Resistance and Decolonization

CHAPTER 16

The Treaty Relationship and Settler Colonialism in Canada

Carole Blackburn

When the United Nations General Assembly adopted the Declaration on the Rights of Indigenous Peoples in 2007, Canada was one of four countries to vote against it. The others were Australia, New Zealand, and the United States, together known as the CANZUS states. These four are prosperous liberal democracies, and Canada, in particular, has an international reputation as a peacemaker. They are also settler states and share many of the structural dimensions of settler colonialism, past and present. Settler colonialism is characterized by the acquisition of territory for permanent settlement and resource development (Wolfe 2011). Settler colonialism can be part of overseas and continental colonialisms, often consolidating into this form with the independence of the settler state from the metropolis. While the multiple forms of colonialism share many features they are likewise

C. Blackburn (✉)
Department of Anthropology, University of British Columbia, Vancouver, BC, Canada
e-mail: blcarole@mail.ubc.ca

© The Author(s) 2019
D. Schorkowitz et al. (eds.), *Shifting Forms of Continental Colonialism*,
https://doi.org/10.1007/978-981-13-9817-9_16

distinct, and in settler colonialism the critical element is territory.[1] The political and economic imperatives guiding the CANZUS states as settler states informed their refusal to ratify the Declaration. These are the UN members with the most to lose in recognizing many of the rights contained in the Declaration, like the right of Indigenous people to free, prior, and informed consent before any resource development can be undertaken on their traditional territories. Canada's Minister of Indigenous Affairs at the time argued that the right to free, prior, and informed consent amounted to a veto over all resource development, and said that in Canada "you negotiate on this," because Indigenous rights "don't trump all other rights in the country."[2]

Governments change, and in 2015 Canadians elected a Liberal government with Justin Trudeau—the son of former Prime Minister Pierre Elliot Trudeau—as prime minister. After his election the new prime minister said that there was no relationship more important to him than that between Aboriginal people and the federal government. In 2016 Canada removed its official objections to the United Nations Declaration on the Rights of Indigenous Peoples. In August 2017 the government announced that it was splitting the Department of Indigenous and Northern Affairs—which for a century has administered Canada's Aboriginal population under federal legislation known as the Indian Act—into two separate ministries. There will now be a Ministry of Crown Indigenous Relations and Northern Affairs, and a Ministry of Indigenous Services. The former is responsible for fulfilling the federal government's treaty obligations; the latter is responsible for service delivery in areas like health, housing, and education. In announcing this split Prime Minister Trudeau said that bureaucrats and the Indigenous peoples they serve "deserve an updated structure that is now much more in keeping with the true spirit of reconciliation." Carolyn Bennett, the minister responsible for Crown Indigenous Relations, said in her press conference that this is "about de-colonizing. It's about getting back to the original relationship that was the spirit and intent of the treaties" (Ivison 2017).

---

[1] "Territoriality," Patrick Wolfe reminds us, is "settler colonialism's specific, irreducible element" (2006, 388). Wolfe links this territorial imperative to the other feature of settler colonialism, which is the elimination of the Indigenous populations either through genocide or assimilation.

[2] Minister Jim Prentice, quoted in Montreal Gazette, September 14, 2007.

What is this original relationship, what does it have to do with treaties, and can returning to it be a form of decolonization in a settler state? In this chapter I argue that the original treaty relationship, as described by Elders in oral histories, by anthropologists, by historians, and invoked by my research interlocutors, was a political relationship outside of the kind of structural domination that many scholars attribute to settler colonialism. Lorenzo Veracini argues that settlers are "founders of political orders and carry their sovereignty with them" (2010, 3). This is true in many respects, but this is not the complete story because representatives of Britain, France, and other colonizing empires entered into political relationships with Indigenous peoples in North America. In so doing they occupied an alternate political order—one framed by Indigenous forms and expectations around the significance of treaties. Indigenous peoples in North America used treaties as means to secure alliances and relationships with each other well before any Europeans arrived on the continent (Williams 1999). They brought a well-defined set of protocols and expectations to bear on the process of treaty making and its aftermath. The original spirit and intent of treaties was to create relationships of mutual support and obligation between partners (Simpson 2008). Many Aboriginal people hold that treaties created Canada through their consent, meaning that their ancestors' involvement was critical for this country to take the shape it now has (Borrows 2010). Writing about pre-confederation treaties that followed the Royal Proclamation of 1763, James Tully characterizes the relationship those treaties created as "treaty constitutionalism" (1995, 111). It also means that Aboriginal people and their legal traditions have an essential part in the constitutional framework of the country (Borrows 2017). Aboriginal people in Canada do not think or accept that the political order established by treaties has necessarily faded away.[3]

[3]In Canada the term Aboriginal is used in the Constitution and is the preferred legal term. It refers to First Nations, Métis, and Inuit peoples inclusively. The term First Nations gained momentum in the 1970s and is a replacement for the term Indian or Native. It is used now in general parlance; the former National Indian Brotherhood is, for example, now called the Assembly of First Nations, while the term Indian still has legal meaning in the Indian Act. Métis refers to the people of mixed descent with historic roots in the interaction between First Nations women and European men in the fur trade. The Métis are culturally distinct, and the term Métis does not refer to all persons of mixed Aboriginal/European ancestry in Canada. Inuit refers to Aboriginal peoples of Northern Canada, who live in Nunavut, the Northwest Territories, Northern Quebec and Northern Labrador. Throughout this chapter I will use Aboriginal, First Nation, and Indigenous interchangeably.

The treaty relationship as it currently exists in Canada does not conform to the original spirit and intent of treaties as creating lasting political relationships. It has the potential, but ministerial press releases aside, it does not. In this chapter I address the failings of modern treaty implementation and highlight how much further Canadian governments need to go in order to approach the minister's stated goal of "decolonization" through a reinvigorated relationship. I do this through an analysis of the Nisga'a treaty, a modern self-government agreement concluded in 2000, involving the Nisga'a First Nation, the province of British Columbia, and the Canadian federal government. The Nisga'a are a First Nation whose traditional territories lie in the Nass River Valley on the northwest coast of British Columbia. The Nass River empties into the Pacific Ocean through Portland Inlet, near the southern tip of the Alaska Panhandle. Nisga'a elders narrate their presence in this river valley since time immemorial, and Nisga'a have lived at different village sites on the river and up the forested valley slopes throughout that time. Since 1999 I have conducted research on the Nisga'a treaty and its implementation in relation to the broader parameters of Aboriginal/state relations in Canada (e.g. Blackburn 2005, 2007).

HISTORICAL BACKGROUND AND RESEARCH CONTEXT

As early as Europeans came to North America and sought trading relationships with Indigenous people, they were obligated to enter into relational alliances that included promises of mutual support (Miller 2009). The importance of treaty making in the relationship between European newcomers and Indigenous people was legally solidified in the Royal Proclamation of 1763 issued by King George the Third after Britain defeated France in the Seven Years War and took over French possessions in North America. Sometimes referred to as the Indian Magna Carta, the Proclamation was an executive order having the force and effect of an act of Parliament; this means it has enduring legal significance as an enactment of the Crown.[4] The Proclamation dealt with multiple issues of governance then facing Britain in its new territories, including matters

---

[4]In the United States the thirteen colonies soon responded with an independence movement that removed them from British rule and the strictures of the Royal Proclamation (Calloway 2015).

concerning Indians and their land. White settlers and land speculators wanted that land and were willing to use violence to get it. The
Proclamation recognized that Aboriginal people living under the
Crown's protection "had the exclusive right to any territories they possessed that had not been ceded to the Crown" (Slattery 2006, 260).
Most importantly, it set out the guidelines that informed treaty making
in British North America and then in Canada through to and following confederation in 1867 (McNeil 2006). This included the requirement that Aboriginal people could only cede land to representatives of
the Crown in a public gathering held especially for that purpose. The
Proclamation states:

> And whereas great Frauds and Abuses have been committed in purchas-
> ing Lands of the Indians, to the great Prejudice of our Interests, and to
> the great Dissatisfaction of the said Indians: In order, therefore, to prevent
> such Irregularities for the future, and to the end that the Indians may be
> convinced of our Justice and determined Resolution to remove all reason-
> able Cause of Discontent, We do, with the Advice of our Privy Council
> strictly enjoin and require, that no private Person do presume to make any
> purchase from the said Indians of any Lands reserved to the said Indians,
> within those parts of our Colonies where We have thought proper to allow
> Settlement: but that, if at any Time any of the Said Indians should be
> inclined to dispose of the said Lands, the same shall be Purchased only for
> Us, in our Name, at some public Meeting or Assembly of the said Indians,
> to be held for that Purpose by the Governor or Commander in Chief of
> our Colony respectively within which they shall lie. (Royal Proclamation
> of 1763)

There is clearly an assumption of sovereignty here on the part of the
Crown, but also a statement that obligated its representatives to enter
into treaties in its name and to thereby participate in, and create a separate and distinct political order in North America.[5] With respect to the
assumption of sovereignty by the Crown, the courts in British Columbia
and Canada use 1846 as the date that the Crown asserted sovereignty
in British Columbia. Recently, the Supreme Court of British Columbia
found that this assertion "did not eliminate the aboriginal right of
self-government," and thereby did not eliminate the inherent lawmaking

[5] In spite of this assumption of sovereignty on the part of the Crown, Ford (2010) and
others draw our attention to how imperfect this sovereignty was.

powers that the Nisga'a assume within their treaty (Campbell et al. **2000**, §124).

After the Royal Proclamation the British Crown and then the Canadian federal government made dozens of historic treaties with Indigenous people. These included those of political alliance (sometimes called peace and friendship treaties), trading compacts, and territorial treaties. In Canada the latter became increasingly important in conjunction with settlement; through them the federal government sought to make huge tracts of land available for settlement and resource extraction (Asch **2014**; Miller **2009**). The numbered treaties are the most recent of these. Treaties 1 through 11 cover much of Canada between Alberta and Ontario and were made by the federal government, referred to as the Crown, and representatives of First Nations from 1871 to 1921.

The numbered treaties all contained a surrender clause stating that the "said Indians" surrender all their rights and title to the Crown. For the federal government this made settlement legal, and in exchange the Crown made solemn promises of protected lands, material benefits, ongoing hunting, fishing and trapping rights, and support in perpetuity. We know that the representatives of First Nations who agreed to these treaties did not understand the consequences of surrender, or extinguishment, of their title and rights. They entered into treaties, in some cases because they were resigned to some of the changes they saw coming, but nevertheless in the spirit of mutual coexistence and because they sought the support and partnership of the federal government (Asch **2014**; Craft **2013**). A brief example of the language used by Alexander Morris, Crown Treaty Commissioner, during the negotiations for Treaty 4 in 1874 is illustrative here:

> The Queen has to think of what will come long after today. Therefore, the promises we have to make to you are not for today but for tomorrow, not only for you but for your children born and unborn, and the promises we make will be carried out as long as the sun shines above and the water flows in the ocean. (quoted in Coyle **2017**, 39)

The parts of Canada settled without treaties include Quebec, Newfoundland, Labrador, parts of Ontario, much of the North, and British Columbia. Here I focus on British Columbia. James Douglas, the province's first governor, made a few small treaties on Vancouver Island, but after he left politics in 1864 provincial politicians, administrators, and settlers took the position that treaties were too costly and that Aboriginal people were too primitive to have any concept of land ownership that required a treaty process. They viewed the province as a *terra nullius*, and the Aboriginal people who inhabited it as primitive, without laws, government, or property (Tennant 1990). The Nisga'a knew about the Royal Proclamation, and they knew that other Aboriginal people in Canada had made treaties with the Crown. In the late nineteenth century the Nisga'a, along with other British Columbia First Nations, began lobbying provincial and federal governments to make treaties with them. They did so with complete confidence in their rights to the land and because they could not bear the way settlement and resource exploration occurred with no recognition of their ownership and their sovereignty. The historical record is full of Nisga'a assertions that the land is theirs, un-surrendered to any European monarch or representative of the federal government.

In 1887 a representative of the provincial government told a group of Nisga'a assembled at Gingolx that the province would always set apart land for them for their uses. Charles Russ, a Nisga'a, answered "Set it apart, how did the Queen get the land from our forefathers to set it apart for us? It is ours to give to the Queen, and we don't understand how she could have it to give it to us." At the same meeting another elderly chief, Neis Puck, jumped to his feet to say, "I am the oldest man here and can't sit still any longer and hear that it is not our father's land. Who is the chief that gave this land to the Queen? Give us his name, we have never heard it" (Papers Relating to the Commission 1888, 20).[6] At this meeting they declared unsurrendered title and asked for a treaty, saying: "We want the words and hands of the chiefs on both sides, Indian and Government, to make a promise on paper—a strong promise—that will be not only for us, but for our children forever. But we want a solemn promise—a treaty" (ibid.).

Throughout these kinds of engagements Nisga'a met consistent refusals. Politicians and the general populace applied the Lockean argument that Aboriginal people like the Nisga'a had no property rights and no notions of ownership, and wasted land that would be put to better use by settlers. The first premier of the province, William Smithe, said that

---

[6] These Nisga'a chiefs are referring to a system of land tenure whereby chiefs (*sim'oogit*) as heads of houses (*huwilp*) hold rights to House territories, known as *ango'oskws*.

the Nisga'a were like wild animals that roved about the hills when the white people first came among them (Report of Conferences 1887, 257). Smithe and others refused to honor the principles of treaty making established by the Royal Proclamation. Nisga'a were forced to watch provincial governments, settlers, and industry take up their lands and resources with no compensation or recourse while they were allotted small reserves subject to the administration of Indian agents whose job was to manage the Nisga'a according to the federal Indian Act.[7]

In spite of the intransigence of government officials, the Nisga'a continued to demand a treaty recognizing their ownership of the land. The Nisga'a Tribal Council took their case to the British Columbia Supreme Court in 1969, suing for a declaration that their title had never been extinguished. They lost, took the case to the British Columbia Court of Appeal, and then lost the appeal. In the Court of Appeal judgment Chief Justice Herbert Davey wrote that the Nisga'a "were undoubtedly at the time of settlement a very primitive people with few of the institutions of civilized society, and none at all of our notions of private property" (Asch 1984, 49). The Nisga'a Tribal Council then took the case to the Supreme Court of Canada.[8] When the court ruled in 1973, six of the seven Supreme Court justices found that the Nisga'a did have Aboriginal title in the past.[9] Three ruled that the assertion of Crown sovereignty had extinguished this title while the other three ruled that it had not. The seventh justice abstained on a technicality. Even though it was a split decision, on the issue of extinguishment the Calder ruling was enough to propel the federal government into establishing a Comprehensive Claims policy to deal with land where treaties had

---

[7] In Canada, the Indian Act applies to status Indians. These are people who are legally recognized as 'Indians' and can carry a status card.

[8] The case was known as 'Calder v. Attorney General of British Columbia' (Calder et al. 1973). It was named after Frank Calder, who at the time was the President of the Nisga'a Tribal Council. Frank Calder was a hereditary chief from Nass Harbor and for a time an elected MLA in the provincial Legislative Assembly. When he passed away in 2006 the Nisga'a honored him with the title of Chief of Chiefs.

[9] The jurisprudence on Aboriginal title in Canada continues to evolve, most notably in the cases of Delgamuukw and Tsilhqot'in (Delgamuukw v. British Columbia 1997; Tsilhqot'in Nation v. British Columbia 2014). In Delgamuukw the Supreme Court found that unceded Aboriginal title not only exists in British Columbia, it is as a right to the land itself. This means that Aboriginal title is more than just a usufructory right.

never been made, including British Columbia, Quebec, the Yukon and Northwest Territories, and parts of Newfoundland and Labrador. There are now over twenty modern treaties in place covering close to 40% of Canada's land and waters.

The Nisga'a treaty settles the extent of the Nisga'a nation's territory and jurisdiction in the Nass River Valley in northwestern British Columbia. There are currently four villages along the river, each of which was an Indian Reserve before the treaty came into effect. These are Gingolx, Laxgalts'ap, Gitwinksihlkw, and Gitlaxt'aamiks. There are over 6000 Nisga'a, approximately half of whom live in the Nass Valley. The treaty itself is just over 250 pages long, with an additional 450 pages in appendices. It sets out all of the Nisga'a peoples' rights and jurisdictional authorities in areas such as governance, lands and title, wildlife, forest resources, fisheries, justice, taxation and citizenship, and removes the Nisga'a from any Indian Act jurisdiction. The treaty recognizes the Nisga'a's right of self-government, and this right is now protected by the Canadian constitution. Nisga'a governance under the treaty includes four village governments, with elected representatives, who together also serve in the larger nation government known as the Nisga'a Lisims government. The treaty also recognizes Nisga'a ownership of 2000 square kilometers of land in the Nass Valley. These are the core treaty lands, and the Nisga'a Nation as a collective now owns them in fee simple title. Outside of these lands Nisga'a have rights of access for hunting and fishing purposes on a much larger area known the Nass Wildlife Area. This is an additional 27,000 square kilometers. The treaty also provides a cash settlement of approximately 250 million dollars. The 2000 square kilometers of land in the core area is seven percent of the claimed traditional territory of the Nisga'a people. The Nisga'a, the provincial government of British Columbia, and the federal government of Canada negotiated this treaty over the course of two decades, finally agreeing to its terms and conditions in May 1998.[10]

---

[10]Cf. *Nisga'a Final Agreement Act.* https://www2.gov.bc.ca/gov/content/environment/natural-resource-stewardship/consulting-with-first-nations/first-nations-negotiations/first-nations-a-z-listing/nisga-a-lisims-government.

IMPLEMENTATION: SEARCHING FOR THE
NATION-TO-NATION RELATIONSHIP

When the treaty came into effect in May 2000 many people said it was the beginning of a new relationship between the Nisga'a Nation and Canada, and a step toward true reconciliation. Whether or not the treaty has improved life for most Nisga'a is very difficult to answer, in part because of the difficulties of measurement. Many standard indicators linked to quality of life refer to integration into the mainstream economy and do not reflect alternative goals of cultural revitalization and well-being. Unemployment is relatively high, as it is for most Aboriginal communities in Canada and the Nisga'a are searching for ways to promote economic development on Nisga'a lands. Many people that I have spoken to over the years feel that their lives have not changed much for the better since the treaty came into effect but many others are more optimistic, and celebrate the fact that they no longer live under the Indian Act.

A treaty, whether a modern one of 250 pages or a historic one comprised of six pages and oral records, cannot achieve anything unless implemented. Implementation is everything that happens after treaties are signed, legislation is ratified, and cameras are put away. Nisga'a government officials and former treaty negotiators were not naïve about going into this treaty—they knew that the government had its own interests—but are quite critical of how the federal government now handles its relationship with the Nisga'a. Time and again, Nisga'a say that the Crown does not respect the spirit and intent of treaty making; that it does not see or understand the broader objectives of treaties; and that it does not understand them as nation-to-nation agreements that have the force of law. One administrator I talked to in Gitlaxt'aamiks complained to me that governments think of treaties as a divorce when they should be more like a marriage. He was referring first hand to a sense that the federal government saw the Nisga'a treaty as a deal that had been struck and that was the end of it. Nisga'a expect a treaty to establish an ongoing relationship between themselves and the rest of Canada. For Nisga'a, as with other Indigenous people in Canada and the United States, treaties are covenants that bind the parties in ways beyond strictly legal obligations (Miller 2009). Legal scholar Dwight Newman writes that a "covenantal conceptualization of treaties" sees them "as agreements between political communities expressing the terms of the ongoing evolution of relationships between those communities" (2011, 486). They are supposed to create relationships of mutual respect and set guidelines for coexistence. As I said earlier, this was the vision that Indigenous people brought to treaty making historically—between each other and then in their dealings with European newcomers in the encounter era—and this continues to be the vision they bring to treaties today (Williams 1999).

Instead, the ink is barely dry before the federal government stops all talk of the broad objectives of modern treaties, like reconciliation and reforming political relationships, and proceeds instead to fulfill only the narrow legal obligations set out in the agreement, like transfer payments. Even those narrow obligations are often misunderstood. Nisga'a complain that when they approach the government about implementation to make the treaty really work, they are sent off to the Department of Indigenous Affairs. But treaties, they insist, are with the Crown. They are nation-to-nation agreements, not agreements with a particular federal department, especially not the Department that was formerly charged with dealing with First Nations as wards and trustees. There is no mechanism at the federal government level for dealing with First Nations as equal partners. For First Nations like the Nisga'a this lack of equality is precisely indicative of the colonial relationship they find themselves in with respect to the rest of Canada.

Implementation is such an issue that in 2003 the Nisga'a and more than a dozen other signatories of modern treaties founded the Land Claims Agreement Coalition (Fenge 2015).[11] Based in Ottawa, this coalition brings modern treaty First Nations together to share knowledge and to advance implementation and recognition of the importance of treaties to the constitutional structure of Canada.[12] Members also use the coalition as a platform from which to lobby the federal government

---

[11] In 1975 the James Bay and Northern Quebec Agreement (JBNQA) was the first modern treaty made in Canada. See Matthew Coon Come (2015) on how the Cree struggled for more than thirty years and had to go to court against the provincial government to get their treaty implemented in any meaningful way.

[12] As of 2015 the Coalition included the Council of Yukon First Nations, Grand Council of the Crees (Eeyou Istchee), Gwichi'in Tribal Council, Inuvialuit Regional Corporation, Kwanlin Dun First Nation, Maa-nulth First Nations, Makivik Corporation, Naskapi Nation of Kawawachikamach, Nisga'a Nation, Nunatsiavut Government, Nunavut Tunngavik Incorporated, Sahtu Secretariat Incorporated, Tlicho Government, Tsawwassen First Nation, and Vuntut Gwitchin.

on matters of implementation. The reasoning is that together the members of the coalition have a stronger voice than an individual First Nation would. In addition to their domestic lobbying the coalition has made two submissions to the United Nations Human Rights Council, Universal Periodic Review of Canada, in 2007 and 2012 respectively. In 2007 Nisga'a and other members of the coalition testified before the Standing Senate Committee on Aboriginal Peoples when that committee met to examine and report on the implementation of federal obligations made in treaties and land claims agreements. Other witnesses came from the Auditor General's office and from federal departments including Indian and Northern Affairs (as it was then called).

The Senate Committee made a number of trenchant observations, including that the federal government is more concerned with concluding agreements than with implementing them. The Deputy Minister of Indian and Northern Affairs affirmed this when he appeared at the Committee hearings:

> The tendency is that once the announcement [...] is finished and the cameras have been shut off and we are on to implementation that people do not spend as much time on implementation issues. That is something that happens in government. (Senate Committee, Evidence, 12 February 2008)

The turnover rate of senior officials in the department, including ministers and deputy ministers, is high. This means that instead of sustained management attention and policy follow through there is a much greater focus on short-term initiatives and newsworthy photo opportunities (Senate Committee 2008, 14). More particularly, the federal government fails to organize, oversee, and coordinate implementation in a broad whole of government way (Papillon 2008). Time and again, people I spoke to complained that the federal government lacks coordination of its treaty obligations. Before the current split, Indigenous and Northern Affairs Canada was, at the federal level, solely tasked with implementing treaties. It had an Implementation Branch but no authority to compel other government departments to comply with responsibilities these departments often do not know they have. An executive member of Nisga'a Lisims Government told the Senate Committee that

> even when the department is trying [...] to bring about the objectives of the agreement it is often frustrated to arrive at other departments to

find that it has insufficient clout with those other departments. The other departments consider it to be the Department of Indian and Northern Affairs agreement and not theirs. In this way, they fail to acknowledge our nation-to-nation relationship with Canada, something we fought so hard to achieve through the negotiation of our Treaty. (Senate Committee, Evidence, 27 February 2008)

The Deputy Minister said much the same thing, telling the Committee that

a challenge that our department faces [...] is that [...] we are not solely responsible for implementation or in possession of all the levers and tools related to implementation. [...] We have had difficulty in the past fully engaging other government departments. [...] More often than not, these agreements are presumed by our colleagues to be the responsibility of our department. (Senate Committee, Evidence, 12 February 2008)

Treaty implementation requires working across all federal departments and the coordination of different tasks and initiatives. Administrative responsibilities written into a treaty are often joint in their structure and in their financing. The Nisga'a treaty includes provisions on fisheries management, wildlife harvesting, roads, rights of way, lands, programs, services to citizens, and environmental assessment, to name a few, all of which entail working with provincial and federal governments. The Fisheries chapter establishes a Joint Fisheries Management Board involving the Nisga'a, the province, and the federal government. The Wildlife and Migratory Birds chapter involves Nisga'a in decision making around wildlife harvesting and monitoring and establishes a Wildlife Committee. Indeed, virtually every federal organization's mandate will intersect with Aboriginal treaty rights in this and other modern and historic treaties at some point. This is why Nisga'a argue that treaty implementation, and the spirit and intent of treaties, requires a whole of government approach.

These other government departments do not understand that treaty obligations bind the government of Canada, as a whole, and not simply the Department of Indigenous Affairs. They also do not understand the constitutional nature of treaty obligations. Treaties are constitutionally protected, and the provisions in treaties are constitutional, legal obligations. The legal nature of treaty obligations is lost to many departments. Officials in all federal departments too often approach treaty implementation as a discretionary policy matter—as things that get put into the pile of what is or is not affordable in annual budget and decision making processes. Departments including the Department of Indigenous Affairs "see the implementation of treaty provisions as an aspect of [...] policy" and policy can "vary according to budgetary and other considerations. So the act of implementing treaty provisions is seen as essentially similar to other policy-making, priority-setting and program-management functions of the government" (Cree-Naskapi Commission 1986, 6). This is a fundamental misunderstanding of the nature of treaty obligations.

One of the main discrepancies in the way that governments understand treaties and First Nations understand treaties is that for governments treaties are contracts, not covenants. This interpretation is especially so for modern treaties, like the Nisga'a Final Agreement, the details of which were meticulously negotiated over twenty years by teams of negotiators and lawyers (Newman 2011). More particularly, for the federal government, a treaty is a legal mechanism that produces certainty in regards to Aboriginal rights and titles; it defines what the Section 35 rights of a First Nation are in respect to governance, territory, control over resources, and so on, outside of which there are no others. Section 35 is part of the Canadian Constitution. It recognizes the existence of Aboriginal rights, including treaty rights, and has done so since Aboriginal people across Canada forced the inclusion of this section in the Constitution in 1982.[13] Section 35 is relevant to our discussion here because it places Aboriginal rights and treaty rights within the legal protection of the Canadian Constitution. It is also consistent with Aboriginal peoples' understanding and unwavering belief that their relationship is with the Crown, and the Crown is responsible for safeguarding their rights.

---

[13] See Constitution Act (1982), Section 35:

(1) The existing aboriginal and treaty rights of the aboriginal peoples of Canada are hereby recognized and affirmed.

(2) In this Act, 'aboriginal peoples of Canada' includes the Indian, Inuit and Métis peoples of Canada.

(3) For greater certainty, in subsection (1) 'treaty rights' includes rights that now exist by way of land claims agreements or may be so acquired.

(4) Notwithstanding any other provision of this Act, the aboriginal and treaty rights referred to in subsection (1) are guaranteed equally to male and female persons.

Section 35 must be understood in the context of modern treaties for other reasons, in that it states that all Aboriginal rights and treaty rights are both recognized and protected, but the section does not state what those rights actually are. There is no list, like the UN Declaration on the Rights of Indigenous Peoples, and at the time critics said Section 35 is an empty box. Aboriginal rights must now be politically negotiated, as they were in the Nisga'a treaty, or interpreted by the courts. The courts occasionally rule on what an Aboriginal right is, in cases involving fishing or hunting rights for example, but these are single rights in isolation. In British Columbia and other parts of Canada where land surrender treaties were not made Aboriginal title is now a recognized right, although where it exists for every First Nation is not determined. This Aboriginal title is seen as 'hovering' over Crown title. Other Aboriginal rights are similarly present, but undefined and 'unknown.' This creates a situation of great uncertainty from the point of view of governments and the resource industry that has been the main economic engine in provinces like British Columbia. Logging, mining, hydroelectric development, and now pipelines transporting oil and gas from Alberta to the coast for export to China and elsewhere, are all part of the provincial economy that requires certainty around what rights and jurisdiction apply where. When I asked a provincial government representative why the province was willing to negotiate a treaty with the Nisga'a, after so many years, he immediately said it was because of "certainty on the landscape":

> Aboriginal rights and Aboriginal title are out there and it's impacting decisions government can make on the landscape. So court challenges and civil disobedience [...] and it's causing grief in the primary resource sector in what we can do. And we just need to get on with developing British Columbia. We can't with this unresolved Aboriginal rights and title issue out there. So we're looking at certainty so we know what the rules are and can get on with business, developing the province. (Interview by author)

A federal negotiator similarly described both the importance of certainty for governments and the corresponding importance of the legal model used to achieve certainty in the treaty:

> The number one thing that governments get out of treaties is certainty. If you don't have [...] certainty in a treaty, as a government you have nothing. Because what you're doing is you're setting up a new relationship

that, where you don't have to rely on court cases in the future, you don't have to rely on civil disobedience as a driving mechanism to lever governments into action. You don't have to rely on that mess of things that can happen. What you have is clear, defined, certain, rights, for the Nisga'a in this case, and everyone can rely on those. And therefore, once you have that in place for every group in the province, presuming that we can get to that point, then you genuinely have a very clear regime for managing the province. (Interview by author)

We can see here a desire for the relationship between First Nations and governments to be smoother, without the ever-present threats of court cases and civil disobedience like road blocks. This is a goal that is shared by Aboriginal people in Canada, who do not want to go to court and do not want to spend all their time in forms of civil unrest to get governments to pay attention to their rights and title. But the language around certainty also reveals a desire to legally contain Aboriginal rights. This containment both recognizes and limits Aboriginal rights while securing the kind of certainty that resource extraction industries want (Blackburn 2005). In this sense, treaty making can be aligned with neoliberal governance because it deals with Aboriginal rights to minimize the threat such rights pose to state and capital. By freeing up land and facilitating resource extraction, treaty making in these untreatied areas of Canada is consistent with the imperatives of settler colonialism, which is always to bring land into the reach of either settlement or development.

When Minister Bennett spoke to the creation of the new Ministry of Crown Indigenous Relations, she said that the dissolution and division of the former Department of Indigenous Affairs was about decolonization, and getting back to the original nation-to-nation relationship. Current Canadian government rhetoric is replete with talk of reconciliation, a new relationship, and decolonization, but there is no actual political transition to accompany this rhetoric. Decolonization means the material unsettling of the colonial state and historically has resulted in revolutions. The challenge of settler colonialism is that it is intractable; it is "resistant to decolonization" (Veracini 2011, 204). Patrick Wolfe's (2006) argument that settler colonialism is a structure and not an event is especially apt here; this structure and the underlying emphasis on lands and resource development remains, particularly around such extractive industries as logging, mining, oil, and gas. This structure also includes an ideological underpinning of entitlement and erasure that are features of everyday settler consciousness in Canada and most other settler states (Blackburn 2007; Goldstein 2008). There can be changes in the federal bureaucracy for dealing with Aboriginal people, but these occur outside of deeper structural and ideological change. Certainly most scholars and First Nations leaders who commented on the division of the Department of Indigenous Affairs were skeptical that this would really bring about much change.

Nisga'a and other members of the Land Claims Agreement Coalition had previously argued that Canada needs a Land Claims Agreement Implementation Commission, outside of the current federal organization of Departments, to coordinate and oversee implementation of treaties. They envisioned that it would report to Parliament directly and have the prominence to prioritize the relationship between Indigenous peoples and the Crown. If settler colonialism is predicated on the elimination and assimilation of Indigenous peoples, struggles against it must keep the settler/Indigenous relationship both at the forefront and ongoing (Veracini 2011, 7; Wolfe 2006).

Conclusion

Canada has recently undertaken a Truth and Reconciliation Commission on Indian Residential Schools. The TRC commissioners traveled across the country for five years of hearings and study into the effects of Canada's residential schools on Aboriginal peoples and communities. The Canadian government put residential schools in place in the late 1800s in order to assimilate Aboriginal children and eliminate what the Minister of Indian Affairs of the time called the "Indian problem." The residential school policy emerged at a time when Canada was moving away from its status as a colony of Great Britain and into existence as an independent state whose national interests were fully focused on settlement and development of its considerable natural resources. This was the juncture when the erasure of Aboriginal people, through assimilation, began to overtake previous Imperial approaches to Aboriginal peoples informed by the obligations of the Royal Proclamation. The Truth and Reconciliation Commission issued its final report in 2015. Among its many calls to action was the recommendation that Canada

> reconcile Aboriginal and Crown constitutional and legal orders to ensure that Aboriginal peoples are full partners in confederation, including the

recognition and integration of Indigenous laws and legal traditions in negotiation and implementation processes involving Treaties, land claims, and other constructive agreements. (2015, 230)

The authors of the report emphasized that treaties have an important role to play in the present: "Treaties are a model for how Canadians, as diverse peoples, can live respectfully and peacefully together on these lands we now share" (ibid.).

Most non-Aboriginal Canadians are not aware of how important treaties were and are, and are resentful when Aboriginal people cite long-standing treaty rights. Treaties are foundational to the Canadian state and an underappreciated component of the history of Canada (Coyle 2017). Through treaties Indigenous people tried to create a new kind of society with Europeans on the frontiers of North America. In Canada treaty making is now directed toward minimizing the threat that Aboriginal rights and title pose to capital, and suffers from an insufficient nation-to-nation approach. But treaty making is also a time-honored Indigenous mechanism for creating relationships, and in principle it can still stand as a tool of empowerment if state approaches to treaty making can be reformed. Treaties have the potential to enable Indigenous legal orders and governments to co-exist with non-Indigenous law and governments in Canada. Such coexistence is in keeping with the original spirit and intent of treaty making. Treaties, John Borrows writes, have the potential to build Canada on more solid ground, creating an intersocietal framework in which Indigenous laws intermingle with Imperial laws to foster peace and order across communities (2010, 21). In the original spirit and intent of treaty making, we are all treaty people.

References

Government Documents

Calder et al. v. British Columbia (Attorney General), [1973] SCR 313. https://scc-csc.lexum.com/scc-csc/scc-csc/en/item/5113/index.do. Accessed March 7, 2018.

Campbell et al v. AG BC/AG Cda & Nisga'a Nation et al, 2000 BCSC 1123 (CanLII). https://www.canlii.org/en/bc/bcsc/doc/2000/2000bcsc1123/2000bcsc1123.html?searchUrlHash=AAAAAQAPMjAwMCBCQ1NDIDExMjMgMgAAAAAE. Accessed March 7, 2018.

Canada's Residential Schools: Reconciliation. Final Report of the Truth and Reconciliation Commission of Canada, Volume 6, 2015. Montreal: McGill Queens University Press.

Constitution Act. 1982. Schedule B, Constitution Act, 1982, Part II: Rights of the Aboriginal Peoples of Canada. http://www.solon.org/Constitutions/ Canada/English/ca_1982.html. Accessed March 7, 2018.

Delgamuukw v. British Columbia, [1997] 3 S.C.R. 1010. https://scc-csc.lexum. com/scc-csc/scc-csc/en/item/1569/index.do. Accessed March 7, 2018.

Papers Relating to the Commission Appointed to Enquire into the Condition of the Indians of the North-West Coast, 1888. https://archive.org/stream/papersrela- tingto00britrich/papersrelatingto00britrich_djvu.txt. Accessed March 7, 2018.

Report of Conferences Between the Provincial Government and Indian Delegates from Fort Simpson and Naas River. B.C. Sessional Papers, 1887.

Royal Proclamation of 1763. http://www.solon.org/Constitutions/Canada/ English/PreConfederation/rp_1763.html. Accessed March 7, 2018.

Senate Committee on Aboriginal Peoples. 2008. *Honouring the Spirit of Modern Treaties: Closing the Loopholes.* Government of Canada. http://publications. gc.ca/site/eng/394531/publication.html. Accessed March 7, 2018.

Tsilhqot'in Nation v. British Columbia, 2014 SCC 44, [2014] 2 S.C.R. 256. https://scc-csc.lexum.com/scc-csc/scc-csc/en/item/14246/index.do. Accessed March 7, 2018.

Books and Articles

Asch, Michael. 1984. *Home and Native Land.* Toronto: Methuen.

Asch, Michael. 2014. *On Being Here to Stay: Treaties and Aboriginal Rights in Canada.* Toronto: University of Toronto Press.

Blackburn, Carole. 2005. "Searching for Guarantees in the Midst of Uncertainty: Negotiating Aboriginal Rights and Title in British Columbia." *American Anthropologist* 107(4): 586–96.

Blackburn, Carole. 2007. "Producing Legitimacy: Reconciliation and the Negotiation of Aboriginal Rights in Canada." *Journal of the Royal Anthropological Institute* 13(3): 621–37.

Borrows, John. 2010. *Canada's Indigenous Constitution.* Toronto: University of Toronto Press.

Borrows, John. 2017. "Introduction." In *The Right Relationship: Reimagining the Implementation of Historical Treaties,* edited by John Borrows and Michael Coyle, 17–38. Toronto: University of Toronto Press.

Calloway, Colin. G. 2015. "The Proclamation of 1763: Indian Country Origins and American Impacts." In *Keeping Promises: The Royal Proclamation of 1763, Aboriginal Rights, and Treaties in Canada,* edited by Terry Fenge and Jim Aldridge, 33–48. Montreal: McGill University Press.

Coon Come, Matthew. 2015. "Cree Experience with Treaty Implementation." In *Keeping Promises: The Royal Proclamation of 1763, Aboriginal Rights, and Treaties in Canada*, edited by Terry Fenge and Jim Aldridge, 153–72. Montreal: McGill Queens University Press.

Coyle, Michael. 2017. "As Long as the Sun Shines: Recognizing That Treaties Were Intended to Last." In *The Right Relationship: Reimagining the Implementation of Historical Treaties*, edited by John Borrows and Michael Coyle, 39–69. Toronto: University of Toronto Press.

Craft, Aimee. 2013. *Breathing Life into the Stone Fort Treaty: An Anishinabe Understanding of Treaty One*. Saskatoon: Purich Publishing.

Cree-Naskapi Commission. 1986. *Report of the Cree-Naskapi Commission*. Ottawa: K.G. Campbell Corporation.

Fenge, Terry. 2015. "Negotiation and Implementation of Modern Treaties between Aboriginal Peoples and the Crown in Right of Canada." In *Keeping Promises: The Royal Proclamation of 1763, Aboriginal Rights, and Treaties in Canada*, edited by Terry Fenge and Jim Aldridge, 105–37. Montreal: McGill Queens University Press.

Ford, Lisa. 2010. *Settler Sovereignty: Jurisdiction and Indigenous People in America and Australia, 1788–1836*. Cambridge: Harvard University Press.

Goldstein, Alyosha. 2008. "Where the Nation Takes Place: Proprietary Regimes, Antistatism, and U.S. Settler Colonialism." *South Atlantic Quarterly* 107(4): 833–61.

Ivison, John. 2017. "Is Trudeau's Cabinet Shuffle a New Dawn for Indigenous Affairs?" *National Post*, August 28. https://nationalpost.com/news/canada/john-ivison-is-trudeaus-cabinet-shuffle-a-new-false-dawn-for-indigenous-affairs. Accessed August 7, 2018.

McNeil, Kent, 2006. "Aboriginal Title and the Supreme Court: What's Happening?" *Saskatchewan Law Review* 29: 281–308.

Miller, James Rodger. 2009. *Compact, Contract, Covenant: Aboriginal Treaty Making in Canada*. Toronto: University of Toronto Press.

Newman, Dwight. 2011. "Contractual and Covenantal Conceptions of Modern Treaty Interpretation." *Supreme Court Law Review* 54: 475–91.

Papillon, Martin. 2008. "Aboriginal Quality of Life Under a Modern Treaty: Lessons from the Experience of the Cree Nation of Eeyou Istchee and the Inuit of Nunavik." *IRPP Choices* 14(9): 4–23.

Simpson, Leanne. 2008. "Looking After Gdoo-naaganinaa: Precolonial Nishnaabeg Diplomatic and Treaty Relationships." *Wicazo Sa Review* 23(2): 29–42.

Slattery, Brian. 2006. "The Metamorphosis of Aboriginal Title." *Canadian Bar Review* 85: 255–86.

Tennant, Paul. 1990. *Aboriginal People and Politics: The Indian Land Question in British Columbia, 1849–1989*. Vancouver: UBC Press.

Tully, James. 1995. *Strange Multiplicity: Constitutionalism in an Age of Diversity.* Cambridge: Cambridge University Press.

Veracini, Lorenzo. 2010. *Settler Colonialism: A Theoretical Overview.* Basingstoke: Palgrave Macmillan.

Veracini, Lorenzo. 2011. "Introducing Settler Colonial Studies." *Settler Colonial Studies* 1(1): 1–12.

Williams, Robert A. 1999. *Linking Arms Together: American Indian Treaty Visions of Law and Peace, 1600–1800.* New York: Routledge.

Wolfe, Patrick. 2006. "Settler Colonialism and the Elimination of the Native." *Journal of Genocide Research* 8(4): 387–409.

Wolfe, Patrick. 2011. "After the Frontier: Separation and Absorption in US Indian Policy." *Settler Colonial Studies* 1(1): 13–51.

CHAPTER 17

The Imperial Emancipations: Ending Non-Russian Serfdoms in Nineteenth-Century Russia

Willard Sunderland

In late July 1864, Prince Ivan Konstantinovich Bagration-Mukhranskii completed his journey to St. Petersburg. In those days, the trip from Tiflis (Tbilisi), the capital of the Caucasus, took at least a week, a meandering climb of some fourteen hundred miles up the great vertical span of European Russia, first by bouncy carriage along the Georgian Military Highway, then rutted postal roads, and, finally, the relatively straighter and smoother relay by train from Moscow.

The prince's mission was to deliver a draft of the law to free the serfs of Tiflis province to the Caucasus Committee (*Kavkazskii komitet*), the high interministerial body charged with coordinating policy for the region. In the spring of 1861, on the very day that Tsar Alexander II had announced the emancipation of the serfs in Russia, he had written to the Viceroy of the Caucasus to tell him, in effect, that the serfs of the Caucasus were

W. Sunderland (✉)
Department of History, University of Cincinnati,
Cincinnati, OH, USA
e-mail: sunderwd@ucmail.uc.edu

© The Author(s) 2019
D. Schorkowitz et al. (eds.), *Shifting Forms of Continental Colonialism*,
https://doi.org/10.1007/978-981-13-9817-9_17

next. The viceroy responded by quickly launching a process to prepare the reform. The meeting with the committee was proof that these preparations were now complete. A plan for freedom was ready for review.

The prince apparently performed his job well. We can assume this because just months after the meeting the draft that the prince had relayed to the capital became adopted as an official decree. On October 13, 1864, during a sojourn in southern France, the tsar put his signature to the law, and a little over three weeks later it was read aloud with much fanfare in Pashkevich-Erevanskaya Square (now Freedom Square [*Tavisuplebis moedani*]) in central Tiflis. The emancipation was complete.

This part of the freedom process featured well-groomed men wearing bright sashes and medals speaking in formal Russian, with a certain amount of French and Georgian mixed in. The terms were lofty, as were the expectations. The rest of the undertaking, however, was much less tidy. Just as with the reform of 1861 in Russia, the peasant reform in Tiflis province involved the labor of scores of estate stewards, local officials, and rural surveyors, descriptions and maps of hundreds of estates and villages, years of committee sessions arguing over particulars of how much would be paid by whom to whom and when, a seemingly never-ending cycle of edits and additions, howls of protest, pleas for consideration, sighs of resignation, constant intercessions from provincial officials, and directives and responses from St. Petersburg.

Much of the complexity of this process—the high-minded pronouncements as well as the more mundane calculations of acres and interests—is on display in the numerous archival files related to the emancipation in St. Petersburg and Tbilisi.[1] But some of the complexity of the question also appears in the geography of the prince's journey.

In making the long relay from Tiflis to the capital, the prince moved through the distinctive landscape of imperial servitude. Russian serfdom was concentrated overwhelmingly in the center of European Russia, largely contained within a swath of territory running north-northwest from roughly Kiev to the Upper Volga. Few serfs resided to the north of this band or, for that matter, to the south of it. Serfs lived in over 450 of the 495 districts of European Russia (excluding Poland and Finland),

---

[1] Copies of the emancipation decree and additional material appear in RGIA: fond 1268, opis' 10, delo 61a and 61b. For materials related to the Tiflis reform housed in the Georgian archives, see the holdings of STA: fond 220 and fond 221, containing close to 1150 files.

but only seven districts had a servile population of over 80%, and in many of the rest the concentration of serfs was negligible (Nafziger 2013, 9). As for the less than approximately 7% of the Russian and Ukrainian peasant population that lived outside of European Russia in 1857 (overwhelmingly in Siberia), most of these peasants were so-called state peasants rather than privately owned serfs, living on state lands administered by state officials.[2]

In sum: Russian serfs beyond the Russian heartland were few, and their presence tended to decline the farther one moved from Moscow. Imagining a trip from the Moscow Kremlin in any direction at the turn of the nineteenth century, over the first 250 miles, your stagecoach would pass numerous serf villages. Over the next 250, a few more would appear, but beyond that, Russian serfs would largely disappear.

Yet continuing the trip in multiple directions, you would still encounter forms of serfdom—they would simply be non-Russian ones, in keeping with the diversities of the empire. One found servile relations in Poland, in the Georgian lands (Tiflis as well as other Georgian provinces), elsewhere in the South and East Caucasus, and among the Kalmyks on the Lower Volga. Prior to 1816–19, serfs constituted the bulk of the population of the Baltic provinces. Serfs existed among the Roma, among Muslims.

In traveling to St. Petersburg, the prince was thus cutting his way across a variegated landscape of imperial unfreedom that had grown over the centuries as the empire expanded and was now being rolled up as the empire reformed. His journey was a reminder, in effect, that serfdom and the empire were inextricably bound together, and, therefore, that the undoing of the institution would necessarily be bound up with empire as well. Indeed, the Russian emancipation was itself part of this imperial process. Historians rarely consider it in these terms, however, because they still perform convenient sleights of hand when it comes to where and when they adopt an imperial lens to make sense of the Russian past.

When the focus falls on the Caucasus, Poland, or Turkestan, for example, there's little debate—these regions are places where Russia's history as an empire is taken as a given. But when the focus falls on regions like the Middle Volga or the Urals, the answer becomes less clear-cut. Certain topics invite the adoption of an imperial framework—the

---

[2]For the geographic distribution of the Russian peasant population within the empire, see the figures in Moon (1999, 56, Table 2.2).

history of religious policy toward Muslims in the provinces of Kazan or Orenburg, for example. But agriculture or questions of land reform in either area are more likely to be approached as domestic rather than imperial matters. One finds a similar ambiguity with regard to Siberia, which historians sometimes explore in imperial terms, other times domestic.

A comparable elision of empire occurs regarding events and turning points. The war of 1812, for example, tends to be narrated almost exclusively as a Russian national story, much like the revolutions of 1917. Or rather, while 1917 is recognized as having an imperial angle, historians generally limit their discussion of the 'imperial-ness' of the revolution to a consideration of the upheaval in the borderlands—that is, in those places where empire is *supposed* to happen. In other words for all that the 'imperial turn' in Russian historical writing over the last twenty years has shifted the study of the empire from the margins to the center of the field, the turn hasn't yet done much to integrate empire into the "grand narratives of Russian history" (David-Fox et al. 2006, 706).

The reason for this has to do at least in part with the problem of 'continental colonialism,' that is, the question of how to define and study colonial relationships in contexts where the boundaries between metropole and colony and 'colonizers' and 'colonized' are often unclear. In large, ethnically diverse states such as Russia where expansion largely occurred as a result of expansion over land rather than across seas, where does 'empire' begin? Which spaces and peoples in Russia belong to the empire, which to the nation? And following from this: Which questions should be studied from an imperial point of view? As Michael Khodarkovsky has recently suggested, given the complexities of the Russian case, it's perhaps best to simply acknowledge that the tsarist state amounted to both "a continental and a colonial empire" at the same time (2018, 3).

The study of emancipation in the Russian context raises all of these issues. On the one hand, most histories of the famous reform of 1861 connect it to the emancipations of the 1810s in the Baltic provinces, that is the freeing of Estonian and Latvian-speaking peasants from their German lords. Historians also recognize that Alexander II's directive in 1857 to Northwest Provinces Governor-General Vladimir Nazimov, his carefully orchestrated initial foray into the Russian reform, was directed at landlords who were (mostly) Polish in areas made up (largely) of Belarusian-speaking and Lithuanian-speaking peasants. Historians likewise note that influential reformers like Aleksei Levshin and Petr Semenov Tian-Shanskii were deeply influenced by their borderland experiences and were fully aware of the connections between peasant reform in 'Russia proper' and 'borderland imperial policy.'[3] Finally, historians also recognize that the Russian emancipation affected far more than just ethnically Russian peasants. The over twenty-two million serfs freed by the law of 1861 included not only several million Ukrainian and Belarusian peasants (all considered 'Russian' by the government) but also as many as 1.5 million Lithuanians and a quarter million Latvians.[4]

In other words, Russia's imperial realities indeed appear in the picture that Russian specialists provide of the Russian emancipation. Yet even accepting this, it's also clear that the dominant approach is to present emancipation as a national story. Virtually none of the analyses of 1861 offer much analysis of other emancipations, despite there being several, the Tiflis case included.[5] Even the Baltic emancipations, though customarily linked to the Russian case, are rarely analyzed as reforms within an imperial process. Indeed, the idea of viewing the Russian emancipation of 1861 as simply one component within a longer, diverse process of emancipation that extended across the nineteenth century and involved multiple non-Russian regions and peoples sounds odd. The Russian emancipation appears such a solidly national story that to regard it as anything different is barely considered. Even the most insightful literature on the subject tends to adopt a largely Russocentric view (cf. Moon 2001; Khristoforov 2011).

Leaving the empire out, however, means ignoring the full context of the liberation process. For one, it means eliding the fact that the people being freed were named not only Ivanov or Petrova, but also Jannsen and Alavidze; that they were farmers as well as nomads and semi-nomads, and Buddhists and Lutherans as well as Orthodox believers. The simple shift to adopt an imperial framework profoundly expands our appreciation for where emancipation unfolded and how it 'worked.'

---

[3]This last point is a key argument in Dolbilov (2003).

[4]On the Latvian and Lithuanian peasants emancipated by the 1861 law, see Plakans (2011, 221–22). On the ethno-confessional diversities of the serf population affected by the 1861 reform as based on the census (*reviziia*) of 1859, see Kabuzan (2002, 174–79).

[5]The most important exception is Petr Zaionchkovskii's study of the emancipation that includes a chapter focusing on the post-1861 abolitions in the South Caucasus, the Caucasus, and Bessarabia (1954, 235–51).

Just as importantly, if historians ignore the imperial context of Russian emancipation, they also risk ignoring one of the great realities of the age—the recognition that Russia in the nineteenth century was a liberating empire. The Russian state pursued liberation imperfectly, but it was nonetheless committed to emancipating people—a wide variety of people—by which I mean that the state's leaders self-consciously directed their power toward removing numerous imperial subjects from conditions of servitude. These same leaders simultaneously presided over the conquest of new territories and the establishment of new hierarchies and forms of exploitation, while the emancipations themselves were invariably drawn-out and incomplete, so to describe Russian policy as a politics of liberation is not to deny the contradictions and shortcomings of the process. It is simply to point out that Russia's engagement with what Jürgen Osterhammel has called the "tortuous imposition of free labor" (2014, 698) was imperial in scope.

This chapter will offer four broad observations related to this general thesis:

1. The various forms of imperial servitude and the emancipations that put an end to them were linked to two complicated geographies—one **external**, by which I mean the international geography of slavery and abolition that Russianists rarely engage with but that helps us see emancipation in Russia as an imperial and trans-imperial dynamic[6]; and one **internal**, in which Russian serfdom coexisted alongside numerous additional forms of unfree labor that varied from region to region, each with its own history, local conditions, and indigenous vocabulary.

2. Emancipation was a tool of imperial power. Thus, just as absorbing and modifying different serfdoms served as one of the devices of Russian 'continental colonialism,' emancipation itself became a process for furthering imperial control.

3. The process of disbanding serfdom in the empire was multifaceted and slow. This explains in part why it is easier to see individual parts of the process rather than the whole thing. Also, seemingly counterintuitively, the reform of imperial serfdoms did *not* begin in the center. Instead, it proceeded from the periphery to the center

---

[6] Recent work in the Russian field is moving in this direction, however. See, for example, Witzenrath (2015), Stanziani (2014), Farah (2013), and Kurtynova-D'Herlugnan (2010).

and then from there back out to the peripheries again. Indeed, for a variety of reasons, the center, despite its importance, was all but precluded from going first.

And finally:

4. Once launched, however, the Russian reform of 1861 immediately became the model to apply everywhere else. Thus the clear interrelationship between the Russian emancipation and emancipations and/or land reforms that followed in Poland, the South Caucasus, the Kalmyk lands of the southern Volga, and other areas. In all the post-1861 cases, the Russian reform served as the rhetorical touchstone and practical basis for imperial restructuring. But we shouldn't assume—as many historians have—that this therefore implies an all-consuming drive to pave over the differences of the empire. The Russian imperial system succeeded in part because much of the talk about uniformity and standardization, even in the late imperial era of Russification, did not, in fact, lead to uniformity in practice. A gap between word and deed was persistent, and this was very much the case with the Russian model of 1861 as well.

Here again the case of Prince Bagration-Mukhranskii and his mission are instructive. The law on the Tiflis peasants that the prince handed over to the Caucasus Committee in July 1864 was a direct consequence of the Russian reform. Without the Russian law of 1861, there would have been no law for Tiflis. This was the way Tsar Alexander had imagined things going from the start. As early as the fall of 1857, he had confided to his friend and Viceroy of the Caucasus Alexander Bariatinskii that he hoped the "general bases" for the reform laid out in the Nazimov Rescript would serve as a model for "the remainder of the empire," while at the same time conceding that every province would naturally be allowed to "elaborate [its own] details on site" (Rieber 1966, 111).[7] The critical part all along, it seemed, would be the nitty-gritty required to strike a workable balance between the insistence on general principles and the recognition of messy imperial particularities.

In the case of the serfs of Tiflis, Bagration-Mukhranskii knew exactly how he thought the balance should work. In October 1863, well before there was even a draft of an emancipation law for him to slip into his

---

[7]The letter in question dates from 22 November 1857.

travel bag, he informed Bariatinskii's successor, Viceroy Alexander Nikolai (born Alexander Freiherr von Nicolay), that the norms of the Russian emancipation could not be applied to the Georgian case because "everything here in the Trans-Caucasus has its own distinctive shape."[8] And the draft that he would later take with him to St. Petersburg indeed bears this out since it consisted of three parts, one of which offered a description of the particulars of Georgian serfdom that contrasted with the Russian situation.[9] In other words, emancipation was indeed a common imperial project, but the process of creating an emancipated empire was invariably local and diverse.

To address the points above, this chapter examines a small subset of the emancipations of the nineteenth century, tacking back and forth between them, jumping ahead in time in some cases, backtracking in others (see Table 17.1).

Among the initiatives that appear here are: The emancipations in the Baltic provinces of Estonia, Livonia, and Courland between 1816 and 1819; reforms relating to the regulation of Russian ownership of Kazakh and Kalmyk slaves along the Siberian lines in the early decades of the nineteenth century; the Russian emancipation of 1861, of course; the emancipations that followed in Tiflis and then more widely across the South Caucasus beginning in the 1860s and 1870s; the peasant land reform in Russian Poland in 1864; the anti-slavery politics of the Russian conquest of Central Asia and the Caucasus in the 1860s and 1870s; and, finally, the law of March 16, 1892, "On the Termination of Obligated Relations Between the Different Estates of the Kalmyk People."[10]

---

[8] Opinion (*mnenie*) of Prince Konstantin Mikhailovich Bagration-Murkhanskii submitted to Viceroy Aleksandr Pavlovich Nikolai, 21 October 1863. See STA, fond 221, opis' 1, delo 4, folio 19–25b, quote here from folio 19b. ("...zdes' v Zakavkazskom krae vse nosit svoi osobyi opechatok.")

[9] Viceroy Nikolai provided the titles of the three "projects" in the long cover letter that he sent with the Prince: "(I) Proekt dopolnitel'nykh pravil o krestianakh, vyshedshikh iz krepostnoi zavisimosti v Tiflisskoi gubernii; (II) Proekt mestnogo polozheniia o pozemel'nom ustroistve krest'ian, vodvorennykh na pomeshchikh zemliakh v Tiflisskoi gubernii; (III) Proekt pravil ob ustroistve krest'ianskikh obshchestv i obshchestvennogo ikh upravleniia / i ob otbyvanii simi obshchestvami kazennykh zemel' i mirskikh povinnostei v Tiflisskoi gubernii." RGIA, fond 1268, opis' 10, delo 61a, folio 134–134b.

[10] See Polnoe Sobranie Zakonov, ser. 3, vol. 12, no. 8429 (16 March 1892), 173–75: Ob otmene obiazatel'nykh otnoshenii mezhdu otdel'nymi sosloviiami kalmytskogo naroda.

Table 17.1 Decrees and treaties relating to the abolition (restriction) of serfdoms

Decrees and treaties relating to the abolition (restriction) of serfdoms and slaveries in Russia, the Atlantic, and the Black Sea

1783	Slave trade abolished in Crimea
1797	Restriction of corvée (*barshchina*) in Russia
1803	"Free agriculturalists' law" (Russia)
1804	Ban on slave trade in Georgian lands
1808	All free Russian subjects permitted to purchase Kazakh children as slaves on the Orenburg line [Same law prohibits Kazakh from selling their children to Bukharans, however]
1815	Congress of Vienna: Russia signs the "Déclaration des 8 cours, relative à l'Abolition Universelle de la Traite des Nègres"
1816	Serf emancipation in Estonia
1817	Serf emancipation in Courland (Latvia)
1818	Aix-La-Chapelle: Russia proposes joint "maritime league" to suppress the Mediterranean and North African slave trade
1819	Serf emancipation in Livonia
1819	Kazakh children purchased as slaves are restricted to lifetime rather than hereditary slavery
1821	Russian-American Company charter legalizing de facto indentured servitude for Aleuts (Aleuts' own slaves become company workers)
1825	Kazakh slaves in Russia must be freed upon reaching 25 years of age and all further purchases banned
1820s–60s	Various efforts to intercept slave and contraband trade on the Black Sea; disbanding of slave markets and freeing of slaves in Caucasus region
1841	Quintuple Treaty ["Treaty Between Great Britain, Austria, France, Prussia, and Russia, for the Suppression of the African Slave Trade"]
1842	Law on "Obliged Peasants" (Russia)
1847	Law allowing serfs to purchase their freedom upon the sale of the landlord's estate
1857	Nazimov Rescript (Lithuanian provinces)
1861	Russian serf emancipation (44 provinces; mostly central and southern European Russia but also Siberia)
1863	Emancipation of crown peasants (European Russia)
1864	Russian Poland (rural reform rather than emancipation but expressly linked to 1861)
1864	Serf emancipation in Tiflis Province (Georgia)
1865	Slavery banned in Tashkent
1865	Serf emancipation in Mingrelia (Georgia)
1866	Same in Kutaisi Province (Georgia)
1866	State peasant emancipation (parts of European Russia and western, eastern, and southern borderlands)
1868	Serf emancipation in Bessarabia

(continued)

Table 17.1   (continued)

Decrees and treaties relating to the abolition (restriction) of serfdoms and slaveries in Russia, the Atlantic, and the Black Sea

1868	Slavery and slave trade banned in Bukhara (repeated 1873)
1870–83	Serf emancipation in Armenian and Azeri areas (East and South Caucasus)
1870	Same in Abkhazia (Georgia)
1871	Same in Svanetiia (Georgia)
1873	Slavery and slave trade banned in Khiva
1890	Russia signs the Brussels Conference Act ("to put an end to the Negro Slave Trade by land as well as by sea")
1892	Kalmyk emancipation (Southern Russia)
1904	Russia signs the International Agreement for the Suppression of the White Slave Traffic
1913	Serf emancipation in Dagestan (East Caucasus)

GEOGRAPHIES OF SERFDOM AND FREEDOM

The starting point for reconsidering emancipation as a Russian imperial project is to reconsider Russian serfdom. Here I propose doing this
in two ways. One is to stress again the remarkable diversity of serfdom
as a social form. Speaking of the late eighteenth century, Jerome Blum
(1978) famously described all of Europe, from France to Russia, as a
continent of "servile lands," underscoring, much in keeping with other
Western observers, that things got progressively more servile the farther
east you went.

In truth, this would-be gradient running from a freer rural world in
the west to a less free one in the east is debatable—or at least, one could
debate numerous particulars.[11] But there is no debating the diversity of
serfdoms. Indeed, if Europe amounted to a continent of "servile lands,"
one could describe the Russian Empire as a servile continent in its own
right, with its own jumble of different servile forms.

Speaking in purely legal terms, some of these serfdoms were quite
mild, others harsh. In certain places, one found peasants who were not
serfs technically speaking but nonetheless lived in a servile status. This
was true, for example, of Baltic and Polish peasants who were emancipated forty to fifty years before peasants in central Russia and were thus

---

[11]For fresh thinking on the similarities and differences between serfdoms in Western and
Eastern Europe (and across Eurasia), see Stanziani (2014).

personally free, yet whose economic constraints were not in every case appreciably better. All across the empire's servile zones, one found myriad intricacies of obligation and submission: labor dues, cash rents, special taxes, dues in kind, possibilities for buying one's freedom in some places, no possibility elsewhere.

The other thing to do to reconceive serfdom is to break with the tendency in Russian writing to let the term stand in for unfree labor in general. Serfdom is far from the whole story of unfreedom. Rather than a stand-alone category, serfdom should be seen as merely one form within a larger gallery of servitude that would include the many variations of serfdom mentioned above as well as other servile forms such as slavery, indentured servitude, debt bondage, and penal servitude, each of which also came with its own variations.[12] Once we place Russian serfdoms within this broad context, we begin to see previously obscure connections between imperial processes, including two geographies, one external, the other internal, that haven't been examined as fully as they should in the Russian case.

The first of these geographies is the international arena of 'the Age of Abolition' that coincided with the long nineteenth century, spanning from the emergence of organized abolitionist politics in Britain in the 1780s to the Brazilian Golden Law and the suppression of Ottoman slavery of the late 1880s and early 1890s.[13]

How was Russia connected to this international process? In the first instance, through its influence as a European great power: in 1815, at the Congress of Vienna, Russia joined the other members of the anti-Napoleonic coalition (in addition to the new French government) in signing the Declaration of the Eight Courts Relative to the Universal Abolition of the [Atlantic] Slave Trade. Alexander I then played a leading role in the declaration against the trade at Aix-la-Chapelle in 1818, and Nicholas I's government signed the Quintuple Treaty of 1841 with the same purpose.[14] In 1888–89, the Baltic German jurist and legal scholar Feodor Feodorovich Martens (born Friedrich Fromhold) was a critical

---

[12]On this, see Stanziani (2014), Osterhammel (2014, 698), Bush ([1996] 2013, 2000).

[13]For a recent comprehensive account of abolitionism in the long nineteenth century, see Drescher (2009).

[14]On the Russian contribution to the declarations at Vienna and Aix-la-Chapelle, see Martinez (2012, 32–33, 44–45); for the text of the 1841 treaty, see de Martens (1898, 170–97).

player at the Brussels anti-slavery conference that produced the first comprehensive anti-slave trade treaty, while at the same time advancing European imperialism in Africa and Russian pressure on the Ottomans.[15] Meanwhile, the Russians used the same anti-slavery arguments to justify their campaigns in Central Asia and the Caucasus in the mid-to-late nineteenth century that the British used in their expansion in Afghanistan and Africa in the same period.[16]

Russia also figured in the international circulation of anti-slavery thought. *Uncle Tom's Cabin* was translated and published in "...at least 67 different editions [in Russia] between 1857 and 1917" (Mackay 2013, 8). Meanwhile, Russia's foremost literary indictment of serfdom, Ivan Turgenev's *A Hunter's Notebook*, appeared quickly in German, French, and English translations in the early 1850s (Alekseev 1955).

The most obvious proof of the influence of an external geography of emancipation on the workings of the Russian process is on the bookshelves of the Editing Commission, the high state body charged by Tsar Alexander with drawing up the law of 1861. The catalogue of the Commission's library lists some 600 foreign works, mostly in German, French, and English, including thirty-two titles relating to servile emancipations in Prussia and the Habsburg lands, donated to the Commission from the personal library of Grand Duchess Elena Pavlovna.[17]

Yet there was also an internal geography of serfdom that then helped to shape the particulars of the Russian emancipations: a servile Russian center, of course, but, in addition, concentrations of servile and quasi-servile relations in the Southern Caucasus, in parts of Russian Poland, another in the western provinces, another in the Baltic, still another form of servitude among the Kalmyks on the southern Volga. These servile areas frequently contained their own internal variations in turn.

This multiplicity of serfdoms led to multiple overlapping emancipation laws—three different emancipations, one each for Estonia,

---

[15] On the Brussels Conference, see Mulligan (2013), and Miers (1975), on Martens: Pustogarov (1999).

[16] Kurtynova-D'Herlugnan (2010), Morrison (2014), see 282–83 for Russian anti-slavery rhetoric in regards to the 1839 Khiva Expedition; and Huzzey (2012).

[17] See RGIA: fond 1180, opis' 1, delo 125, folio 1–2 (Aleksei Popel'nitskii, "Sud'ba biblioteki redaktsionnykh Kommissii po sostavleniiu zakonopolozhenii o krest'ianakh") and ibid., folio 13–14b (List of Books Donated to the Library by Grand Princess Elena Pavlovna).

Courland, and Livonia, for example, between 1816 and 1819. Multiple emancipations in different parts of the South and West Caucasus in the 1860s and 1870s, with Tiflis coming in 1864, then Kutaisi Province in 1865, Mingrelia in 1866, Abkhazia in 1870, Svanetiia in 1871, and Armenian and Azeri areas between 1870 and 1883. The last imperial echo of 1861—"On the Ending of the Dependent Relations of the Rural Residents of Dagestan Oblast' and Zakatal'skii District" (Khalifaeva 2004, 87)—was adopted by the Fourth Duma and affirmed by Nicholas II in July 1913.[18]

The Russian autocracy ruled the empire one region at a time, a fact underscored by the emancipation process, which proceeded in diversified rather than standardized fashion. In the Russian case, the regional diversities were addressed through the work of provincial committees of the nobility, whose findings and recommendations were then tidied up and smoothed out (and occasionally ignored) by the Editing Commission.

Work on the diversity of serfdom extended to places where serfdom was almost but not entirely non-existent—for example, Siberia, where, given the absence of noble assemblies, it fell to the governors-general to describe the institution.[19] Thus, playing his part in accounting for the geographic distribution of Russian serfs within the empire on the eve of the 1861 reform, the governor-general of Eastern Siberia recorded exactly one servile estate in his roughly 2.7-million-square-mile territory. The governor-general of Western Siberia meanwhile documented twenty-nine estates with a population of some 3000 agricultural serfs and close to 400 domestic servants. Still, even these tiny numbers required specific consideration, so Siberia ended up with its own "special regulations" (*osobye pravila*) (Skrebitskii 1868, 754–73).

Indeed, the emancipation of 1861 included a roster of regulations of this sort, divided according to region: special rules for different groupings of Great Russian, New Russian (*Novorossiiskie*), and Little Russian (Ukrainian) provinces, the Lands of the Don Cossacks, Stavropol' Province, and for Bessarabia, where the serfs in question were (in the language of the reports) "wandering Gypsies" as well as *tsarane*, former

---

[18] For the text of the law, see Polnoe Sobranie Zakonov, ser. 3, vol. 33, no. 39734 (7 July 1913), 733–35: O prekrashchenii zavisimykh otnoshenii poselian Dagestanskoi oblasti i Zakatal'skogo okruga k bekam i keshkelevladel'tsam i ob uchrezhdenii v sikh mestnostiakh ustanovlenii po krest'ianskim delam.

[19] On the perception of Siberia as a land without serfdom, see Hartley (2014, 47).

serfs who were still serfs of a sort and whose legal status seemed to require special clarification. The serfdoms of the empire were as diverse as the empire's rural world, so the emancipations had to be diverse, but there was also unfreedom in the towns that required sorting out.

The archive of Tobol'sk Oblast' contains multiple files on Russian merchants in the town of Tobol'sk who owned Kalmyk or Kazakh children as slaves in the early 1800s.[20] These children were sold into slavery along the Siberian line, often by their parents who traded them for flour and other staples in desperate times. Other children were simply left at trading houses along the line. The kids were then taken back to the merchants' homes in Tobol'sk where they were baptized and worked in effect as domestic servants.

This form of slavery was legal in the early nineteenth century, upheld by imperial officials in part as a means to soften the 'coarse customs' of nomads.[21] (Nomad girls were also acquired to make up for 'the lack of women' in Western Siberia.)[22] Though the law required the children to be freed by the time they reached the age of twenty-five, prior to that age they could be sold and resold, with each sale affixed in the appropriate paperwork, and this paper trail, in turn, explains why the slaves appear in the archive. The archive, for its part, makes plain that unfreedom was a highly differentiated condition that could vary from household to household and exist—even persist-in seemingly 'free' places like Siberia. The enslavement of nomadic children remained legal until the 1830s, though the interdiction did not instantly stop the practice.[23]

The intertwining of free and unfree places and categories of people then created knotty tangles for state officials to try to straighten out. One example: The Central Historical Archive in Georgia holds a list from late April 1861 compiled by the Civil Governor of Tiflis, effectively, the mayor of Tbilisi, that records the names of thirty-two household

---

[20] See GBUTO GA: fond I-361, opis' 1, delo 147 [1818]; fond I-361, opis' 1, delo 148 [1818], fond I-361, opis' 1, delo 149 [1818], fond I-361, opis' 1, delo 150 [1818]; and fond I-361, opis' 1, delo 508 [1819].

[21] For correspondence regarding legalizing this form of slavery, see RGIA: fond 1341, opis' 9, delo 2334.

[22] See Polnoe Sobranie Zakonov, ser. 1, vol. 40, no. 30224 (11.2. 1825), 62–64: O priobretenii pokupkoiu ili vymenom ot sopredel'nykh Sibiri kochuiushchikh narodov detei zhenskogo pola dlia voznagrazhdeniia nedostatka v Zapadnoi Sibiri zhenskogo pola.

[23] On slavery in these regions, see Mal'tsev (2007).

serfs in the city of "non-native origin" (*netuzemnogo proiskhozhdeniia*)—that is, thirty-two non-Georgian (presumably Russian) individuals.[24] These household serfs were freed by the 1861 law. The law did not free 'native'—that is, Georgian—household serfs owned by Georgian masters, however. The additional paperwork in the file thus includes a request from the civil governor that the viceroy's office provide him with thirty-two copies of the emancipation decree pertaining to domestic serfs so that his officials could then go door-to-door to distribute them to the 'non-native' serfs in question.

The Russian Emancipation was thus a law that affected the Russian landlord–serf relationship regardless of location. It followed that the patchy carpet of serfdom in the empire could be extremely patchy indeed. Russian serfs in Tiflis were freed by one law. Georgian serfs in Tiflis Province by another, but with a delay that created ample opportunities for confusion, if not abuse. People free in one place might wait for years before being recognized as free in another because they never learned about their freedom or their lords chose to never tell them. For example: Two years after the Russian household serfs were supposed to be freed in Tiflis, the city's civil governor was still receiving reports of servants being held illegally by their Russian owners.[25]

EMANCIPATION AS AN IMPERIAL TOOL AND THE IMPERIAL DYNAMIC OF EMANCIPATION

The predicament of 'non-native' household serfs in Tiflis is a reminder of the curious pathways of the servile order within the empire. Here, in effect, is a case of Russian serfdom operating in a region with its *own* serfdom, which then created complexities for dismantling the serfdom of the one before dismantling the serfdom of the other. Not surprisingly, one finds numerous ironies of this sort when examining how emancipation 'worked' in imperial terms.

On the face of it, the undoing of serfdom operated as a tool of imperial power much the same way that the establishment of serfdom did. The gradual consolidation of serfdom in 'Russia proper'—though influenced by a variety of factors—had the obvious consequence of linking

[24] STA, fond 220, opis' 1, kn. 2, delo 833 (1861), folio 7–7b.
[25] Ibid., folio 14–14b.

the prestige and wealth of the Russian nobility to the power of the state (which was itself a state of nobles) and underscoring a basic alliance between the two. The same interplay between noble wealth and the power of the state unfolded in the borderlands. As the Russian state expanded, it extended into territories with serfdom and, by and large, it left the serfdoms it found in place in order to secure the allegiance of the local people in charge. Thus the empire inducted the non-Russian nobles into the Russian system and, along with them, it incorporated their serfdoms.

And to a degree, just as non-Russian nobles (many, though not all) became Russified in the process, non-Russian serfdoms also acquired something of a Russian aspect. Thus as the empire expanded into the eastern Baltic under Peter the Great, the government accepted pledges of allegiance from the German nobilities of the region and promptly undid the limits on local serfdom that the Swedes had begun imposing. Russian serfdom was less regulated than the Swedish form, so as the German lords came over to the Russian side, they found themselves treated not to the status quo but rather to the status quo ante, which was, for the barons, an even better arrangement.[26]

By the same token, as the Russian state began its rule in the South Caucasus in the early 1800s it incorporated servile customs that differed from Russian norms. Georgian clerics, for example, could be enserfed. In Russia, priests were free. By the same token, various social groups could own serfs in Georgian lands, while in 'Russia proper,' the norm was that only nobles could be serf owners. Following the incorporation of Georgia, Russian decrees thus eventually worked on these differences, narrowing the gaps. Over time ownership of priests became banned in Georgia, while serf ownership in the Caucasus morphed into a purely noble privilege.[27]

Of course, myriad divergences remained. In fact, imperial officials in the borderlands were often the ones insisting on the usefulness of maintaining regional norms. But the aspiration to smooth things out was nonetheless a part of the imperial history of serfdom.

Emancipation worked in a similar way in reverse. Undoing serfdom everywhere was not so much a matter of freeing serfs—the language of

---

[26] On the ritual practice of confirming the Swedish-granted privileges of the Barons in the eighteenth century, see Laur (2005, 32).

[27] For some of these details, see RGIA: fond 1268, op. 10, delo 61a, folio 24–41.

freedom sounded rarely in most of the reform legislation. Instead, emancipation was an issue of undoing 'dependence' (*zavisimost'*) and placing the relationship between the state and the rural people of the empire on a new footing. But this of course meant creating the terms of a new relationship with the nobilities as well, securing their allegiance on new terms. Every emancipation law thus catered to differing degrees to noble concerns.

One could say, broadly speaking, that the Baltic nobles got the best deal, the Polish lords of former Congress Poland the worst (by 1864), with Kalmyk *zaisangs* faring relatively poorly as well, and Georgian lords falling somewhere in between. As for Russian lords, it's harder to generalize simply because of the enormous variation of serfdom across the area covered by the 1861 law, yet, broadly speaking, one could also say that they were less gently treated than the Baltic barons, who retained their lands, and better treated than Polish lords, some of whom lost their estates to confiscation. The reasons behind these distinctions are complicated, but they clearly reflect the shifting imperial prejudices and contexts of the different emancipations. By the same token, the emancipations themselves seem just as clearly linked by an overarching imperial dynamic.

The Baltic lords were treated well in large part because Alexander I recognized the need to favor them in the wake of the Napoleonic wars. Polish lords by contrast were punished because of their disloyalty. Following the onset of what turned out to be the most wide-sweeping of the post-partition rebellions in Russian Poland in early 1863, Alexander II famously remarked to Nikolai Miliutin, his soon-to-be top official for Polish affairs, that he—Alexander—was finished with the Polish aristocracy. Now the time had come "to raise up the common people [*narod*; i.e. the peasants], to turn to them for support" (*nado iskat' oporu v nem*) (Zakharova 2008, 386).

The Kalmyk notables—*zaisangs* and *noions*—meanwhile received somewhat less state largesse, in part at least, because they were perceived as Asian and uncivilized. As one Russian official suggested in 1884, Russian laws over the years had limited the *zaisangs'* power to buy and sell their serfs as well as the physical punishment they could inflict on them, but the Kalmyk lords had responded by maximizing the exploitation of their "commoners" (*prostoliudiny*) through whatever means they could, in the first instance, by collecting onerous taxes, all because "they [the *zaisangs*] knew that their time in power was running out."[28]

Other officials noted that emancipating the commoners needed to be linked to the reduction of Kalmyk noble land holdings in order to make more land available for Russian settlement. One way to do this was to re-categorize the domains of Kalmyk nobles (*vladel'cheskie ulusy/aimaki*) as state property, which the government pursued either by encouraging the conversion of Kalmyk owners to Orthodoxy or by expropriating their land if they died without legal heirs (this provision was in keeping with Russian inheritance law).

Another option involved the 'redemption of ownership rights' (*vykup vladel'cheskikh prav*) by effectively buying the nobles out of their property. Indeed, it was this redemption approach that ultimately provided the basis for the Kalmyk 'emancipation' law of 1892, which amounted to the state remunerating Kalmyk owners for their property loss—that is—the loss of revenue that they had earned for centuries from a special tax they levied on their 'commoners'—by paying the owners with monies the state had amassed from the commoners in the form of other taxes and land rents (Schorkowitz 2001, 98–99; 2018, 202–4, 227–29). All of this was very much in keeping with the broad drift of Russian policy over the nineteenth century, which aimed to sedentarize the Kalmyks given that their nomadic economy was considered unviable on the one hand and undesirable on the other. Dismantling the last vestiges of Kalmyk 'serfdom' was thus envisioned as part of a would-be Russian 'mission to civilize' as well.

The Kalmyk reform was also clearly identified as part of an arc of change precipitated by the Russian emancipation of 1861. Writings by officials from the 1860s to the early 1890s repeat a common refrain: how is it possible that Kalmyks could still live under serfdom when "everywhere else in European Russia" the institution had already abolished? As the chief administrator (*Glavnyi Popechitel'*) for the Kalmyks Nikolai Osipov noted bravely in an exasperated letter to the Minister of the Interior in 1885:

---

[28] RGIA: fond 1291, opis' 85, delo 22a, chast' 1, folio 30a–30b: MGI General Matters Department (Departament Obshchikh Del), Letter to Ministry of Finance, 18 August 1884.

We must act quickly to eliminate this institution, the continued existence of which serves only to reproach the government for the shameful discrepancy it upholds [between the status of Kalmyk commoners – WS] and the rights of all the other subjects of the emperor.[29]

The same logic had applied in the Georgian lands and vis-à-vis the question of land reform in Poland in the 1860s. Thus one emancipation, generally speaking, invited another, and this interregional imperial dynamic, too, is an abiding feature of the progress of emancipatory change across the nineteenth century. The law of 1861 was thus itself influenced by earlier reforms. The Baltic emancipations of the eighteen-teens, in the first instance, and the stalled inventory reforms of the 1840s in right-bank Ukraine (Kiev, Volhynia, and Podol') thereafter. In this respect, it's hard to speak of any fully self-contained serfdom within the empire. The terrain was too interconnected for that.

Conclusion

There are many historical clues that point to emancipation as an imperial and multinational rather than a purely national or "domestic" problem, but perhaps the most obvious documentary evidence of all has been hiding in plain sight since the onset of the Great Reform era. The evidence in question is the 'Historical Note' submitted by Minister of the Interior Sergei Lanskoi to Alexander II in December 1856 in which the Minister offers an overview of the evolution of 'serfdom in Russia.' The note, which has been cited by numerous historians, was composed by Lanskoi's assistant, Aleksei Levshin, a 'Kiselev man' with a sense of literary style and broad experience of the empire, from Little Russia to the Kazakh steppe. The note distills Levshin's talent for concise, evocative description, laying out the history of serfdom in three periods: The seventeenth and early eighteenth centuries when serfdom "came into being, developed, and gradually entered—or rather, insinuated itself—into law"; the remainder of the eighteenth century, when it "remained practically unchanged"; and the period from the beginning of the nineteenth century to the 1850s when "it began to decline."[30]

---

[29] RGIA: fond 1291, opis' 85, delo 22a, chast' 1, folio 58b–59: Letter to Minister of the Interior Dmitrii Tolstoi, 7 February 1885.

[30] RGIA: fond 1180, opis' 1, delo 77, folio 5–27.

Flowing across these three periods, the note ultimately rises to the conclusion that emancipation is an extremely thorny problem, too complex to jump into quickly.

> Work on a matter of such importance [...] requires thoroughness and maximum caution. Russia is so vast, and consists of regions of such economic, political and even geographic [i.e. environmental] diversity, that it would be impossible to emancipate all the serfs in a single manner everywhere at the same time, even if one devised for this purpose the very best of plans.[31]

Historians have assumed that the diversity Lanskoi (with Levshin's help) has in mind here is the diversity of 'Russia proper,' that is, the differences in the conditions of serfdom that one found between places like Tambov and Kiev, New Russia and Grodno. The document is meant to offer a context for understanding what would become the Russian law of 1861, so this is the way that historians have generally interpreted it, as the description of a national rather than an imperial process.

Yet Lanskoi also offers a wider view. He notes the first steps toward emancipation occurred in the Baltic provinces, underscoring their separateness. He also notes that the Baltic German lords called for emancipation first because of their exposure to the German states—the barons were thus open to emancipation (in Lanskoi's view) because of their physical proximity to the emancipations of Europe. The nobles of Dinaburg in Vitebsk Province then go next for the same reason: they are physically close to the German lords in Livonia. In other words, Lanskoi is describing an interconnected imperial chain. Each territory—each serfdom—has its specificities, yet each is connected to the next, and it is this chain of interconnectedness that makes each individual part relevant to the whole.

This view of an interlocking empire made up of interconnecting serfdoms comes across still more explicitly in an appendix to Lanskoi's note rarely cited by historians that appears the same archival folder immediately following the note itself, written out in the same handsome hand of the same ministerial clerk: a fifteen-page list of "Laws Pertaining to

---

[31] Ibid., folio 2b–3. The quoted passage here appears in the cover letter that Lanskoi wrote to accompany the note.

Enserfed People Issued from 1766 to 1855."[32] The list records 158 laws, and of these, twenty-eight—that is, a little less than one-fifth of the total—pertain exclusively to non-Russian peasants. Given the established narrative of the Russian Emancipation, one would expect to see the decrees that emancipated the Baltic peasants—and they indeed appear. But so, too, do laws applying to Gypsies (Roma), Jews, Tatars, and Georgians.

If Lanskoi and Levshin saw these laws as valuable for making sense of the history of Russian serfdom, it's surely because they understood serfdom as an imperial institution and emancipation as an imperial process. For them, Russia's 'continental colonialism' presupposed relatively fluid boundaries between understandings of 'national' and 'imperial' as well as still less commonly evoked divides of 'metropole' and colony'— indeed the boundaries between these would-be spaces within the empire would only start to tighten up toward the very end of the tsarist era and even then only in the thinking of certain kinds of officials and observers.[33] Lanskoi and Levshin could thus integrate the various serfdoms of the empire into a single imperial narrative. My argument in this chapter is that historians should approach the problem of emancipation in this light as well.

REFERENCES

Archives

GBUTO GA Gosudarstvennoe biudzhetnoe uchrezhdenie Tiumenskoi oblasti "Gosudarstvennyi arkhiv v gorode Tobol'ske" [State Archive of Tiumen Oblast' in the City of Tobol'sk].
Fond I-361, opis'1, delo 147 [1818]: Delo po prosheniiu Tobol'skogo kuptsa A. Lukimatushkina o vydache vladennoi vypisi na 10-letnego Kalmyka.
Fond I-361, opis'1, delo 148 [1818]: Delo po prosheniiu syna Tobol'skogo kuptsa A. Veshniakova o vydache vladennykh vypisei na Kalmykov.

---

[32] "Spisok zakonam o krepostnykh liudiakh, izdannym s 1766 po 1855 god," RGIA, fond 1180, delo 77, folio 28–43.

[33] For more on the complexities of 'colony' and 'metropole' in the late tsarist context, see Sunderland (2010).

Fond I-361, opis'1, delo 149 [1818]: Delo po prosheniiu Tobol'skogo kuptsa D. Syromiatnikova o vydache vladennoi vypisi na Kalmyka, ego doveriteliu, kolezhskomu sekretariu G. Koshevskomu.

Fond I-361, opis'1, delo 150 [1818]: Delo po prosheniiu Tobol'skogo Bukhartsa M. Niiazova o vydache vladennoi vypisi na dvorogo karakalpaka.

Fond I-361, opis'1, delo 508 [1819]: Delo po soobsheniiu Tobol'skogo gubernskogo pravleniia s chetyriami pros'bami Kalmykov ob otyskivaemoi imi iz uslug svobody.

RGIA   Rossiiskii Gosudarstvennyi Istoricheskii Arkhiv [Russian State Historical Archive].

Fond 1180: Glavnyi komitet po krest'ianskomu delu, 1839–1861 [Main Committee for Peasant Affairs].

Opis' 1, delo 77: Istoricheskaia zapiska o krepostnom sostoianii v Rossii, vsepoddanneishie predstavlennaia imperatoru Aleksandru II ministrom vnutrennykh del S.S. Lanskim v 1856 godu.

Opis' 1, delo 125: Deloproizvodstvo po kantseliarii redaktsionnykh komissii: (3) Po sobraniiu biblioteki.

Fond 1268: Kavkazskii komitet, 1833–1882 [Caucasus Committee].

Opis' 10, delo 61a and 61b: O priniatii mer k osvobozhdeniiu krepostnogo sosloviia za Kavkazom iz pomeshchich'ei zavisimosti i o sostoiavshikhsia vsledstvie sego, predpolozheniiakh k osvobozhdeniiu iz etoi zavisimosti krest'ian Tiflisskoi gubernii.

Fond 1291: Zemskii otdel MVD, 1792–1917 [Land Department of the Ministry of the Interior].

Opis' 85, delo 22a: Ob osvobozhdenii kalmykov Astrakhanskoi i Stavropol'skoi gubernii ot vlasti noionov vladel'tsev i zaisangov (v chetyrekh chastiakh), chast' 1.

Fond 1341: Pervyi departament senata, 1797–1918 [First Department of the Senate].

Opis' 9, delo 2334: Po imennomu ukazu o dozvolenii vsekh rossiiskikh poddannykh vsiakogo sostoianiia pokupat' i vymenyvat' kirgizskikh detei.

STA   Saist'orio tsent'raluri arkivi [Central Historical Archive] (Tbilisi, Georgia).

Fond 220: Kantseliariia po delam ustroistva krest'ian pri glavnom upravlenii glavnonachal'stvuiushchego grazhdanskoi chast'iu na Kavkaze [Bureau of Peasant Management within the Main Administration for Civilian Affairs in the Caucasus].

Opis' 1, kniga 2, delo 833: Perepiska o poriadke obnarodovaniia v Zakavkazskom krae manifesta i polozhenii o krest'ianakh vyshedshikh iz krepostnoi nezavisimosti v Rossii. Fond 221: Zakavkazskii tsentral'nyi komitet po delam ustroistva pomeshchich'ikh krest'ian [The South Caucasus Central Committee for the Management of Serf Affairs].

Books and Articles

Alekseev, Mikhail Pavlovich. 1955. "Mirovoe znachenie Zapisok okhotnika." In *"Zapiski okhotnika" I.S. Turgeneva (1852–1952): sbornik statei i materialov*, edited by Mikhail Pavlovich Alekseev and Muzei I.S. Turgeneva, 57–65. Orel: Orlovskaia Pravda.

Blum, Jerome. 1978. *The End of the Old Order in Rural Europe*. Princeton: Princeton University Press.

Bush, Michael L., ed. [1996] 2013. *Serfdom and Slavery: Studies in Legal Bondage*. New York: Routledge.

Bush, Michael L. 2000. *Servitude in Modern Times*. London: Polity.

David-Fox, Michael, Peter Holquist, and Alexander M. Martin. 2006. "The Imperial Turn." *Kritika: Explorations in Russian and Eurasian History* 7(4): 705–12.

de Martens, F. 1898. *Recueil des traités et conventions conclus par la Russie avec les puissances étrangères*. Tome 12, *Traités avec l'Angleterre, 1832–1895*. St. Petersburg: A. Böhnke.

Dolbilov, Mikhail. 2003. "The Emancipation Reform of 1861 in Russia and the Nationalism of the Imperial Bureaucracy." In *The Construction and Deconstruction of National Histories in Slavic Eurasia*, edited by Hayashi Tadayuki, 205–36. Sapporo: Slavic Research Center, Hokkaido University.

Drescher, Seymour. 2009. *Abolition: A History of Slavery and Anti-slavery*. New York: Cambridge University Press.

Farah, Megan Dean. 2013. "Autocratic Abolitionists: Tsarist Russian Anti-slavery Campaigns." In *A Global History of Anti-slavery Politics in the Nineteenth Century*, edited by William Mulligan and Maurice Bric, 97–116. Houndmills, Basingstoke: Palgrave Macmillan.

Hartley, Janet M. 2014. *Siberia: A History of the People*. New Haven: Yale University Press.

Huzzey, Richard. 2012. *Freedom Burning: Anti-slavery and Empire in Victorian Britain*. Ithaca: Cornell University Press.

Kabuzan, Vladimir Maksimovich. 2002. *Krepostnoe naselenie Rossii v XVIII v. – 50-kh godakh XIX v. (chislennost', razmeshchenie, etnicheskii sostav)* [The Serf Population in Russia from the 18th Century to the 1850s]. St. Petersburg: Russko-Baltiiskii informatsionnyi tsentr "BLITS".

Khalifaeva, A.K. 2004. "Agrarnaia reforma v Dagestane vo vtoroi polovine XIX veka." *Izvestiia vysshikh uchebnykh zavedenii. Severo-Kavkazskii region, Obshchestvennye nauki* 4: 82–89.

Khodarkovsky, Michael. 2018. "Between Europe and Asia: Russia's State Colonialism in Comparative Perspective, 1550s–1900s." *Canadian-American Slavic Studies* 52(1): 1–29.

Khristoforov, Igor' Anatol'evich. 2011. *Sud'ba reformy: russkoe krest'ianstvo v pravitel'stvennoi politike do i posle otmeny krepostnogo prava (1830–1890-e gg.)* [The Fate of the Reform: The Russian Peasantry and State Policy Before and After the Abolition of Serfdom (1830–1890s)]. Moscow: Sobranie.

Kurtynova-D'Herlugnan, Liubov. 2010. *The Tsar's Abolitionists: The Slave Trade in the Caucasus and Its Suppression.* Eurasian Studies Library 2. Leiden: Brill.

Laur, Mati. 2005. "Die Verortung des Baltikums im Russischen Imperium zu Beginn der Regierungszeit Katharinas II." In *Estland und Russland: Aspekte der Beziehungen beider Länder,* edited by Olaf Mertelsmann, 31–52. Hamburg: Verlag Dr. Kovač.

Mackay, John. 2013. *True Songs of Freedom: Uncle Tom's Cabin in Russian Culture and Society.* Madison, WI: University of Wisconsin Press.

Mal'tsev, Il'ia Aleksandrovich. 2007. "Legal'noe rabstvo v Sibiri i Orenburgskom krae v XVIII-pervoi polovine XIX v." *Vestnik Sankt-Peterburgskogo Universiteta, Series* 2(3): 71–77.

Martinez, Jenny S. 2012. *The Slave Trade and the Origins of International Human Rights Law.* Oxford: Oxford University Press.

Miers, Suzanne. 1975. *Britain and the Ending of the Slave Trade.* London: Longman.

Moon, David. 1999. *The Russian Peasantry, 1600–1930: The World the Peasants Made.* London: Routledge.

Moon, David. 2001. *The Abolition of Serfdom in Russia, 1762–1907.* New York: Longman.

Morrison, Alexander. 2014. "Twin Imperial Disasters: The Invasions of Khiva and Afghanistan in the Russian and British Official Mind, 1839–1842." *Modern Asian Studies* 48(1): 253–300.

Mulligan, William. 2013. "The Anti-slave Trade Campaign in Europe, 1888–90." In *A Global History of Anti-slavery Politics in the Nineteenth Century,* edited by William Mulligan and Maurice Bric, 149–70. Houndmills, Basingstoke: Palgrave Macmillan.

Nafziger, Stephen. 2013. "Serfdom, Land Inequality, and Economic Development in Tsarist Russia." *EconPapers* 14 (2013), Department of Economics Working Papers, Department of Economics, Williams College. https://econpapers.repec.org/paper/wilwileco/2013-14.htm. Accessed November 27, 2018.

Osterhammel, Jürgen. 2014. *The Transformation of the World: A Global History of the Nineteenth Century*. Princeton: Princeton University Press.

Plakans, Andrejs. 2011. *A Concise History of the Baltic States*. New York: Cambridge University Press.

Polnoe Sobranie Zakonov Rossiiskoj Imperii, Sobranie pervoe. 1830. *Complete Collection of the Laws of the Russian Empire, Series 1*. Sanktpeterburg: Gosudarstvennaia tipografiia.

Polnoe Sobranie Zakonov Rossiiskoj Imperii, Sobranie tret'e. 1885–1916. *Complete Collection of the Laws of the Russian Empire, Series 3*. Sanktpeterburg: Gosudarstvennaia tipografiia.

Pustogarov, Vladimir Vasil'evich. 1999. *Fedor Fedorovich Martens: iurist, diplomat* [Fedor Fedorovich Martens: Legal Scholar and Diplomat]. Moscow: Mezhdunarodnye otnosheniia.

Rieber, Alfred J., ed. 1966. *The Politics of Autocracy: Letters of Alexander II to Prince A.I. Bariatinskii 1857–1864*. The Hague: Mouton.

Schorkowitz, Dittmar. 2001. *Staat und Nationalitäten in Rußland. Der Integrationsprozeß der Burjaten und Kalmücken, 1822–1925*. Stuttgart: Franz Steiner.

Schorkowitz, Dittmar. 2018. '*... Daß die Inorodcy niemand rettet und das Heil bei ihnen selbst liegt ...': Quellen und Beiträge zur historischen Ethnologie von Burjaten und Kalmücken*. Wiesbaden: Harrassowitz.

Skrebitskii, Aleksandr. 1868. *Krest'ianskoe delo v tsarstvovanie imperatora Aleksandra II: materially dlia istorii osvobozhdeniia krest'ian, tom 4: Gubernskie komitety, ikh deputaty i redaktsionnye kommissii v krest'ianskom dele* [Peasant Affairs During the Reign of Alexander II: Materials Relating to the History of the Emancipation of the Serfs, vol. 4: The Provincial Committees, their Representatives, and the Editing Commissions for Peasant Affairs]. Bonn: Friedrich Krüger.

Stanziani, Alessandro. 2014. *Bondage: Labor and Rights in Eurasia from the Sixteenth to the Twentieth Centuries*. New York: Berghahn.

Sunderland, Willard. 2010. "The Ministry of Asiatic Russia: The Colonial Office That Never Was but Might Have Been." *Slavic Review* 69(1): 120–50.

Witzenrath, Christoph, ed. 2015. *Eurasian Slavery, Ransom, and Abolition in World History, 1200–1860*. Burlington, VT: Ashgate.

Zaionchkovskii, Petr Andreevich. 1954. *Otmena krepostnogo prava v Rossii* [The Abolition of Serfdom in Russia]. Moscow: Gosudarstvennoe izdatel'stvo politicheskoi literatury.

Zakharova, Larissa G. 2008. "Aleksandr II i mesto Rossii v mire" [Alexander II and Russia's Place in the World]. In *Petr Andreevich Zaionchkovskii: Sbornik stat'ei i vospominanii k stoletiiu istorika*, edited by L.G. Zakharova, S.V. Mironenko, and T. Emmons, 372–402. Moscow: ROSSPEN.

CHAPTER 18

From the Birth of Nations to the European Union: Colonial and Decolonial Developments in the Baltic Region

Epp Annus

This chapter focuses on Baltic developments from the 1860s until the present with an emphasis on historical continuities over different periods of continental colonial rule[1] and decolonial struggles. For comparative studies of colonial rule and anticolonial movements, the historical developments on the eastern shores of the Baltic Sea offer rich material: here, decolonial struggles form continuities between nineteenth-century nation-building and the late twentieth-century collapse of the Soviet Union, including also a period of independent nation-states between

---

[1] The editors consider continental colonialism as "a process and outcome of territorial expansion, land-based economic underdevelopment and center-periphery dependency within a mainland...." (see introduction). The three defining features of Russian and Soviet colonialism in the Baltics are territorial expansion, the violent privileging of the value systems of the colonizing culture, and the accompanying center–periphery difference.

E. Annus (✉)
Department of Slavic and East European Languages and Cultures,
Ohio State University, Columbus, OH, USA
e-mail: annus.1@osu.edu

© The Author(s) 2019   463
D. Schorkowitz et al. (eds.), *Shifting Forms of Continental Colonialism*,
https://doi.org/10.1007/978-981-13-9817-9_18

the two colonial eras. Paradoxes and surprises abound, especially in the Soviet-era Baltics. A colonial matrix of power is camouflaged as a friendship of nations, colonial rule is established over modern nation-states, and nineteenth-century romantic values are refabricated into a late twentieth-century decolonial agenda (Annus 2018).

Scholarly analysis of colonial rule and its impact on Baltic sociocultural developments dates back more than twenty years and has produced many volumes and a constant flow of articles, but analysis of the long durée has been scarce and rather introductory in its mode (Annus 2014, 2018, 142–71; Kalnačs 2016a, b; Kangilaski 2016). In this article, I outline the general context for Tsarist and Soviet rule, with a focus on the political and cultural continuities between the two periods. The specific angle of my inquiry deals with decolonial movements; I am interested in the similarities and continuities among decolonial processes during these two periods. We will see a paradoxical structure of repetition there, where decolonial movements of the Soviet era deployed strategies borrowed from nineteenth-century German romanticism and domesticated into the Estonian and Latvian cultural realms in the second half of the nineteenth century. This structure of repetition is most easily perceivable in the tradition of all-nation song festivals in the Baltics, a tradition that started in 1869 and continued throughout the late Tsarist era, the independence period, and the Soviet era, to culminate in the late 1980s 'Singing Revolution' and continuing to this day. The case study of Baltic song festivals as manifestations of decolonial nation-building forms the core of this article. Following the tradition of song festivals over a time span of 150 years enables us to outline the seesaw structure of decolonial movements, where relative gains in decolonizing the nation are easily lost in subsequent strengthening of colonial rule.

Latvian and Estonian national consciousness started to develop, in the mid-nineteenth century, under both Baltic German and Russian rule. The 1917 October Revolution and the subsequent War of Independence brought the establishment of the sovereign Estonian, Latvian, and Lithuanian republics. After two decades of independence, Soviet annexation in 1940 was followed by the establishment of centralized Soviet rule, a process that was interrupted by a three-year German occupation and then continued after the reannexation of the Baltic lands in 1944. Lithuania, Latvia, and Estonia shared many similar developments during the Soviet era, despite important differences in previous centuries. The story of decolonial continuities, as exemplified in the song festival culture and outlined in this chapter, is from the outset an Estonian and Latvian story, which Lithuania joins later and with a marked difference.

Tsarist-Baltic German Colonial Rule and the Prehistory of Colonialism in the Baltic Region

Since the medieval crusades, the Baltic zone has witnessed complex entanglements of different cultural developments and political regimes. Indeed, the history of colonial rule in the eastern part of the Baltic Sea can be traced to the invasions by German and Danish crusaders in the early thirteenth century when the lands of Estonian, Livonian, and Latvian tribes submitted to German and Danish rule (Tamm et al. 2011; Kaljundi 2016). Over the next centuries, these lands were divided, conquered, and reconquered by different powers, from German and Danish to Polish-Lithuanian, Swedish, and finally Russian. Nonetheless, through it all, the German ruling class, initially formed by the crusading knights, kept its privileged position. Yet a clearly colonial subordination was established perhaps only in the sixteenth and seventeenth centuries when these territories came under Swedish rule.[2]

At the beginning of the eighteenth century, treaties concluding the Nordic War between Sweden and Russia ceded these territories to the Russian Empire; by the end of the eighteenth century, Tsarist rule also extended over most of present-day Lithuania. In the nineteenth and twentieth centuries, national imaginaries developed patterns of remembering these earlier eras and, in consequence, the past became organized into hierarchies of better and worse times, such that Swedish colonial rule in the sixteenth and seventeenth centuries was collectively remembered as 'good', whereas the Tsarist era was labeled 'bad', as it was mostly remembered for its imposition of Russian language in the local schools and in the local governing bodies during the late nineteenth century.

In many ways, the Russian Empire was a rather typical colonial power, a foreign long-distance rule, established by an external force—indeed, Tsarist colonial imaginaries had themselves been shaped by colonial competition and by Tsarist tendencies to measure Russian expansionism against the British Empire. The Baltic provinces of Estonia, Livonia, and Courland received relative autonomy, with the Baltic German

---

[2]Good sources in English or German concerning the history of the region, from medieval to early modern times and beyond, include Stone (2001), Frost (2000), North (2011). Plakans (2011) provides a solid account from the eighteenth to early twentieth century period of Tsarist rule and Kasekamp (2010) offers a short and concise history of the region.

nobility retaining and strengthening its historical privileges[3] and considerable freedom of rule. Starting with the modernization efforts of Peter the Great, Russian rulers and the Baltic German nobility formed a well-functioning symbiosis of rule. Educated young Baltic Germans were employed in state positions throughout the Tsarist empire (including as cabinet ministers and governors-general), and the Baltic German nobility, having kept its privileges and finding good employment opportunities, responded with loyalty and devotion. To the dismay of Baltic German communities, Germans living in Germany started to regard the former as basically Russian—they were, after all, living in the Russian Empire and serving that state (Whelan 1999, 59). At the same time, the idea of the Baltics as the first German colonies made it possible for the Germans to assert their early participation on the prestigious international scene of colonial conquests (Saagpakk 2014; Plath 2011). Indeed, an understanding of the Baltic lands as under German colonial rule shaped the self-perception of Baltic Germans—as Bruno Erdmann writes, "The Baltic lands were always a colony, at first German, then as a colony administered by Germans under different sovereignty" (1913, 412).[4] According to Gero von Wilpert, the colonial position is among the defining features of the Baltic German literary culture, characterized by "egoism and arrogance"—"typical features of any colonial literature, oriented towards the high culture of the motherland" (2005, 26).

When Estonians and Latvians started to shape their national identities in the mid-nineteenth century, they had to position themselves in relation to two, not one dominating ideological structure. This situation might be characterized as double-layered colonialism. For the emerging national consciousness of Estonians and Latvians, the two subordinating power systems were imagined in ideological opposition, deriving from that naïve monarchism that dominated peasant value systems all over Europe—many assumed that the oppression inflicted by the local Baltic German landlords must have been unknown to the good tsar.[5]

---

[3] In addition to retaining their privileges they also regained those discarded by the earlier Swedish rule.

[4] All translations from the German and Estonian are mine.

[5] Naïve monarchism was typical of traditional peasantry not only in the Tsarist empire, but also in Western Europe; see Magocsi (2002, 79).

Estonian and Latvian peasants wrote petitions to the tsar: during the 1882 review of the administration in the Baltic provinces, Estonians and Latvians wrote 20,000 petitions, to enlighten Alexander III of the injustices of local German rule (Kasekamp 2010, 58, 83). As seems clearer in retrospect, both simple peasants and the leaders of the national movements were mistaken to place such hopes on Tsarist redress and reform (Karjahärm 2010, 331).

In the situation of double-layered colonialism, the techniques for Estonian and Latvian nation-building were mostly developed on the basis of (Baltic) German cultural models. The German language had provided an important means for advancement in Baltic society, and indeed the Germanization of the growing Estonian- and Latvian-speaking elites was seen as a major threat in the preliminary phase of nation-building in the mid-nineteenth century (Jansen 2001, 95). The vivid Baltic German cultural sphere provided useful formulae for enlightened social interaction. For example, the abundance of various Baltic German societies inspired the formation of analogous ethnically Estonian and Latvian societies. The establishment of Estonian and Latvian choral singing societies of the 1860s was followed by agricultural societies of the 1870s, and later in the 1890s, temperance societies, handicraft societies, and fire brigades—all of which required official approval from the Tsarist authorities. German tradition strongly shaped expression in nineteenth-century Estonian and Latvian literature as a massive wave of free adaptations from German popular literature reached Estonian and Latvian readers. German influence was clearly evident in the first Estonian and Latvian literary works, such as in plays by the Estonian poet Lydia Koidula and the Latvian writer Ādolfs Alunāns (Koidula 1881; Kalnačs 2016a). This has been a common practice for decolonial nation-building processes in different parts of the world—the colonized country relies on the culture of the colonizers in order to develop a vernacular identity and assert cultural independence from that very same culture (Annus 2018, 147–48; Bhabha 1994). Typically for decolonial nation-building, the emerging Estonian and Latvian cultural spheres were experienced as 'our own', notwithstanding their indebtedness to German culture. Importantly, vernacular languages became the means for building a new cultural space, instead of the German language, which was commonly spoken in educated Estonian and Latvian families. Here the Baltic situation differs greatly from decolonizing processes in many African countries, for example, where the language of European colonizers was used for the buildup of a local cultural space, so that Ngugi wa Thiong'o ([1986] 1994) could still lament the common use of English or French among African writers in the 1970s and 1980s. Each case of colonial rule and each decolonial trajectory carries its own cultural characteristics, and generalizations over colonial rules and experiences remain only partially valid on closer inspection.

The German influence was certainly crucial in the establishment and development of the modern choral song tradition in the Baltics. The German-style choral song with four-part harmonies—quite different from what prevailed in Baltic folk tradition—offered inspiration for Estonian and Latvian choral singing. The Estonian songbook of 1860, for example, included 125 songs that were all free (and sometimes quite creative) adaptations of German texts and melodies (Šmidchens 2014, 72). The German tradition of choral festivals, *Sängerfeste*, which in Germany fostered unification and a spirit of kinship (Eichner 2012, 192), also reached the Baltic provinces where Baltic German choirs organized their first song festivals in 1857 in Tallinn and 1861 in Riga. These festivals inspired Johann Voldemar Jannsen to form the first official choral society for the Estonian-speaking community, the *Vanemuise mänguselts*, in 1865 with the longer-range ambition of instituting a similar song festival tradition. In April 1867, the *Vanemuine mänguselts* sent a request to the governor-general of the Baltic provinces to hold festivities to celebrate the fiftieth anniversary of the abolishment of serfdom in the Baltic Provinces. After much delay, official permission was finally granted two years later in February 1869, just four months before the planned date of the song festival in June 1869. Rushed organization notwithstanding, fifty-one choirs and orchestras took part in the first Estonian song festival, the audience reaching 15,000 over the course of the two-day events (Põldmäe 1969, 98). The first Latvian song festival was held soon afterward in 1873 with more than a thousand singers participating. Lithuanians adopted this tradition some decades later; their first national song festival was held in 1924 several years after the collapse of Tsarist rule and featured 86 choirs, about 3000 singers, and close to 20,000 listeners (Šmidchens 2014, 86, 103).

Songs in the first Estonian and Latvian song festivals were most often based on German melodies and their words frequently adapted from German songs—yet this adapted cultural form enabled the local peoples to come together from different corners of the country, to sing together in their own language and to experience the emerging sense of a shared national belonging. Johan Reinhold Aspelin, a member of the Finnish delegation to the 1869 Estonian festival, later described the first moments when eight hundred men of different ages, social backgrounds, and regional belonging sang their first song together in the general rehearsal, a day before the opening of the festival in Tartu:

> This moment was deeply touching; the Estonian nation felt itself now united into one body, and everyone who knows the dark history of this nation and who has the least bit of heart for its severe suffering in the past, clearly understood the importance of this moment. (Põldmäe 1969, 94)

Over the two-day festival to follow, feelings of national empowerment bloomed over the festival grounds and were later communicated to friends and families back home. Lydia Koidula, one of the main organizers of the festival, wrote to an older friend and colleague that the festival experience had changed the attitudes of those ethnic Estonians, who until that time had been uncertain of their national identity:

> You should see, papa, these half-Estonians, who never before knew whether they were Germans or Russians or Livländer or Balts or something else! How they now, all of a sudden, rush to join the ranks of Estonians, into places they haven't deserved at all! (Põldmäe 1969, 153)

Indeed, the first Estonian and Latvian nationwide song festivals functioned as both manifestations and motors of the emerging sense of national unity. Through the affective feelings of togetherness, shared by more than ten thousand people, these mass events helped to consolidate the young nations and strengthen participants' sense of belonging together, their sense of sharing common aims despite all regional, educational, and class differences. As such, the song festivals were among the most powerful tools for decolonizing the attitudes of the people, in creating and disseminating the belief that a nationally shared culture in one's own vernacular language was something to cherish and protect. This is one of the most important milestones in decolonial movements—the moment when a change happens in the colonial "sphere of psycho-affective equilibrium" (Fanon [1961] 2004, 148), and the colonized culture establishes or recovers a sense of its collective agency.

FROM TSARIST TO SOVIET COLONIALISM

After the October Revolution in 1917 and the subsequent period of chaos and warfare, Soviet rule was established over most parts of the former Tsarist empire. In the Baltics, however, successful wars of independence established the nation-states of Estonia, Latvia, and Lithuania. The independence era lasted hardly two decades and ended with the 1940 annexation of these republics by the Soviet state. The initial occupation developed over the first post-World War II decade into a Soviet colonial situation. A new regime had been imposed from the outside and brought with it a violent rupture in the development of the local cultures. As compared to other Soviet borderlands, such processes in 'Pribaltika' (as the three Baltic states were now called in the Russian media) had some quite distinctive features.

First, as we have seen, Tsarist colonialism had not really accustomed Baltic cultures to a Russian presence. For Estonians and Latvians, the role of the colonial other had been principally assigned to the Baltic German nobility. The Russian cultural impact in the Baltic provinces had remained modest. The 1897 census identified only 4.5% of the provinces' population as Russian, and this included a good number of Russian factory workers (Kappeler 2009, 58). Dorpat University (now University of Tartu) provided a local Baltic option for higher education, so the Russian metropolis had not functioned as the main or most necessary educational center.[6] True, the late 1880s had witnessed a drive for Russification in Tsarist colonial strategies, with a significant effort to extend central control over the borderlands and to enforce the use of the Russian language in their education and political administration. Its impact upon Baltic cultures was mixed, however; Russian, as the official school language, turned elementary education into a farce and triggered waves of firings among local school teachers, lowering the general literacy rate in the Baltic provinces. At the same time, this political turn also brought about the extended presence of Estonians and Latvians in the civil service (Miller 2009, 39), thus clearly fostering social empowerment of ethnic Estonians. In cultural terms, Russification arrived a little too late—in an era when the basic cultural self-definitions of Estonians and Latvians had already been well established. Broadly speaking, in cultural

---

[6] However, many Baltic composers and artists were educated in St. Petersburg.

developments up to the Red October, German cultural impact far out-weighed Russian influence in the Baltic area.[7]

Second, by the time of the Baltic annexations, the official Soviet nationality policy had changed from benevolent to belligerent. The Soviet Union started out as a multiethnic state that inherited and employed a number of imperial features. After the October Revolution, Lenin and his followers endeavored to build up a new kind of a society with a clear-cut break from Tsarist rule; Lenin's government sought to eliminate Russian chauvinism and to foster national developments in the borderlands. Thus, for many smaller ethnicities within the empire, such as Mordvins and Maris, Kalmyks and Buriats (Schorkowitz 2015), the 1920s saw their first possibility to develop ethnic cultures with official state support.

After such initial developments, the Soviet state began to assume a more Russo-centric and imperial posture directed against various forms of 'national communism' (Annus 2017, 6–16). By the late 1930s, some of the initial ideals of Soviet society had been substantially revised, even though the cornerstones of Soviet society—leadership of the Communist Party, the planned economy, and state ownership of the means of production—remained in place throughout the Soviet era. In the 1930s, Russian nationalism had emerged with new force (Brandenberger 2001; Martin 2001), and for Stalin, the Tsarist empire offered a model for future annexations. The political aspirations of Peter the Great, who had regarded access to the Baltic Sea as indispensable for the development of the Tsarist empire, resurfaced in Stalinist form (Zubok 2009, 19), so that the annexations of the Baltics were now guided, not merely by the military-strategic interests of the Soviet Union, but also by Stalin's longing to recover the lost grandeur of the empire (Zubkova 2008, 94). The annexation of the Baltics was accompanied by slogans proclaiming great Russia as the leading nation in history (Annus 2017); articles with titles such as "The great Russian nation – the most outstanding nation and the leading force of the USSR" (Lebedev 1945) appeared in the borderlands' presses. The initial stage of the imposition of Soviet rule

---

[7] I am writing here about large cultural developments and leaving nuance aside for the moment. As Ivar Ijabs (2014) reminds us, members of the Young Latvia movement in the 1860s generally shared and supported the ideas of Russian Slavophiles. Still, as Ijabs also confirms, such an identification was propelled by a reaction against Baltic German cultural and administrative hegemony.

in the Baltics coincided with the era of late or "high" Stalinism (1945–53) and Russo-centrism in the USSR, which was worlds apart from the pre-existing cultural sphere of the Baltics.[8]

Third, the interwar period of independence had permitted the Baltics to foster national culture and develop a sense of identity inherently connected with their political status as nation-states. The annexation of the Baltics thus raises the question of whether it is possible to colonize a people that have adopted and internalized the norms of a nation-state. I have argued that the Soviet Union initially occupied the Baltic states and, on the basis of the initial occupation, gradually extended colonial control over different areas of the Baltic societies (Annus 2018, 88–103). The fabrication of consent in the occupied territories required massive deportations and arrests; about 200,000 people were deported from the Baltic states (Tannberg 2005, 274). In this, the Soviet regime could rely on its own extensive experience in such operations from the prewar years, as well as on the experience with the Polish deportations (Lebedeva 2001), the first waves of which preceded the Baltic deportations that stretched between 1940 and 1952. Nevertheless, in the situation of an already developed national consciousness, the local cultural imaginaries— that is, the conglomeration of shared (and partially canonized) memories and commonly accepted value systems—internalized new Soviet values and re-fabrications of national memory only partially and over the course of several decades, even as pockets of oppositional difference remained alive and active through the end of the Soviet era.

Soviet colonial rule in the Baltics included political and cultural supervision, of course, but also central regulation of local economic activities. The economy was rearranged according to the interests of the metropolis—local currencies were discontinued, previous economic ties were cut off, and all foreign trade became a monopoly of the central government. Riga, the capital of Latvia, became a disproportionately large industrial center, where the local government fought vainly against an influx of Russian-speaking settlers and the establishment of new all-Union enterprises (Grava 1993). In northeastern Estonia, a uranium plant was set up, and local inhabitants were hindered from returning to the area. Northeastern Estonia became a site of massive phosphate and oil-shale mining industries that functioned under the direct control of the central

---

[8]On post-WWII Stalinism see Fowkes (1993), McCauley (2008), Fürst (2010), Prozorov (2016).

ministries in Moscow. These recruited workers from outside the national republic and thereby, over the Soviet decades, turned the region into a Russian-speaking zone, with new settlers identifying themselves with the Soviet Union, rather than with the local republic. Most newly established industries functioned under the direct control of Moscow; in Lithuania by the 1980s, only about 15% of all industrial enterprises were under the full control of the Lithuanian government (Lane 2014, 78).

Baltic educational systems were thoroughly reorganized to produce subjects amenable to the new Soviet rule. At Tartu University in the humanities, by the end of the 1950s, 95% of the prewar academic staff had lost their jobs. Three of the five history programs were closed down; the remaining two were the program on the history of the Soviet Union and the program on general history—Estonian history was among the shuttered fields of study (Karjahärm and Sirk 2007, 545). In the field of literature in order to be published, writers, critics, and scholars had to compose texts conforming to the guidelines of socialist realism issued from Moscow. In the Estonian capital, Tallinn, and in the Latvian capital, Riga, as well as in many other smaller industrial towns all over the Baltics, the great influx of Russian-speaking settlers led to the dominance of the Russian language on the streets and in the grocery stores, in the new industries, and in the Soviet police *militsiya*.

In the late 1940s, Soviet rhetoric presented the establishment of their new rule as a benevolent and selfless act by the great Russian nation, now generously stretching forth its helping hand to aid those cultures whose social developments had not yet progressed to communism. In the context of postcolonial studies, this rhetoric is recognized as the colonial Enlightenment discourse: the establishment of colonial rule was presented as a benevolent (even sacrificial) act of selfless assistance. As is typical in colonial situations, dissenting opinions were suppressed—public enunciations were carefully screened and had to conform to the pre-given formulae established by the new regime (Annus 2017). Whereas new possibilities for national self-expression emerged after the end of High Stalinism, the foundation of colonial rule was by then firmly established and remained in place during periods of relative relaxation in central control. Even so, instead of Moscow's unquestioned hegemony in the Baltics, we see the development of entangled networks of power and endless negotiations between central authorities, their local representatives, and different strata of the borderlands' populations.

"DON'T FORGET SINGING!"—SONG FESTIVALS
UNDER STALIN'S RULE

The establishment of a new matrix of power over the first decade of Soviet rule is easily discernible in developments of the Baltic song festival tradition. This tradition, as we recall, played an important role in nineteenth-century Baltic decolonial movements and was thus still commonly associated in the Baltics with romantic ideas of nationhood. Such a decolonial heritage made it possible to interpret the tradition within the framework of an oppressed people's fight against the domination of the Baltic German bourgeoisie, a perspective which fit neatly within the Soviet ideological framework. Yet for Baltic peoples, the song festival culture primarily carried connotations of the emergence of nationhood and enshrined a canon of nineteenth-century romantic poems about attachment to the fatherland—many such poems were set to music and arranged as choral songs.

In the aftermath of the Soviet takeover, new local political leaderships were formed from among the prewar left-wing intelligentsia who were generally eager to defend local interests. Even though political arrests were widespread and the tone of public discourse had changed dramatically, local cultural processes were not instantly and fully disrupted. The first postwar song festivals, 1946 in Lithuania and 1947 in Estonia, could still carry the moods and mentalities of the prewar era. True, the Lithuanian song festival's name referred to changed circumstances: it was officially called the First Soviet Lithuanian Song Festival. Yet after the all-Soviet anthem, the traditional anthem of Lithuania, written in 1898 by Vincas Kudirka, was still performed (Šmidchens 2014, 147). In the years to come, singing pre-Soviet national anthems in the Baltics would be understood as a provocative activity and would lead to severe punitive consequences.

The 1947 Estonian festival did not perform the national anthem of the 'bourgeois' era, but it manifested its allegiance to the past in many other ways—the festival retained its numerical continuity with the prewar tradition and was officially named the 'Twelfth General Song Festival' (*Kaheteistkümnes Üldlaulupidu*). The second festival day boldly omitted Soviet anthems, opened with "Laul rõõmule" ("To Joy," Schiller's ode, set to an original Estonian composition), and presented an almost thoroughly apolitical performance. Only two songs out of thirty referred directly to Stalin and the new Soviet order (*XII Üldlaulupeo Juht* 1947).

The album produced to commemorate the 1947 festival established its continuity with prewar tradition through its selection of photographs—the image of a young girl singer is cut into the background of the photo of one of the oldest participants, the singer Liise Kiima, who had participated in the fourth festival in 1891 (*XII Üldlaulupeo Album* 1948). The festival booklet was illustrated with folk patterns, its cover featured singers in folk costumes, and its texts included touching and completely apolitical messages from conductors, such as Alfred Karindi's call for continuation: "Don't forget singing!" (Karindi 1947).[9]

Continuation was made impossible for Alfred Karindi himself, since he was imprisoned by the time of the next festival in 1950, as were the two other popular lead conductors of the 1947 festival, Tuudur Vettik and Riho Päts. In Kersti Inno's account, Vettik later told his students that in 1950 he had no idea whether the festival would happen at all—after all, the 1948 purge of the Estonian Communist Party and the 1949 mass deportations had created much general confusion and anxiety. It was only when Vettik saw the flash of passing folk skirts on the street, from the small window of his basement cell, that he knew that the song festival was being held after all (Inno 2006).

As it transpired, the tradition of all-nation song festivals continued into the subsequent era of Soviet colonial rule. Mass singing was now regarded by the Soviet authorities as an effective means to disseminate Soviet ideas and value systems. As Aleksander Kelberg, the secretary of the Estonian Communist Party, wrote: "Soviet mass singing is among the best ways to engage the active involvement of the masses and to educate them in the spirit of communism and Soviet patriotism" (1950, 8). Soviet functionaries showed great optimism in the potential to indoctrinate the people by mass singing, in which singers repeat en masse verses such as "Lenin and Stalin, zealously they fought, they created a homeland for us" (*Nõukogude Eesti* 1950, 40), over and over again, in preparation for the song festival. Such processes of Soviet education started in full intensity during preparations for the 1950 song festivals in the three Baltic republics.

The 1950 Estonian song festival exemplified new developments in local cultural and political possibilities. Indeed, the festival was a massive

---

[9]Later, in 1951, all materials of the 1947 song festival—all informational booklets for singers and local conductors, notes, the festival album—were removed from the libraries, to cleanse the libraries from ideologically harmful materials; see Torri (2008, 21, 25).

manifestation of colonial control over the public sphere.[10] The traditional numbering of song celebrations was abolished, and the sidelining of the political message seen in the previous festival was condemned in the harshest terms:

> The organization of the 1947 song festival revealed a number of important shortcomings that reduced its ideological and political importance. Bourgeois nationalists Andresen, Semper, Vettik, Karindi, and Päts tried to give the song festival an apolitical character, to detach the repertoire from the actual life, they slipped into the repertoire songs that were sung not only during the bourgeois dictatorship, but also during the fascist occupation. From the work of Soviet composers, only 2–3 pieces were included in the repertoire, and only one song of the brotherly nations of the USSR. Bourgeois nationalists continued their subversive action also after the song festival. They also intended to make the program of the 1950 song festival politically infertile and thus deprive people of an important tool for political education. Therefore, the new committee of the 1950 Song Festival of Soviet Estonia considered it necessary, after the unveiling and destruction of the bourgeois nationalists, to make significant improvements to the song festival repertoire and to change the composition of the heads of the song festival. (Kelberg 1950, 6)

Indeed, the majority of songs in the 1950 festival were selected for their ideological and political importance, so as not to "deprive people of an important tool for political education." The program also included songs in Russian; some singers, not yet familiar with Russian language, had to rewrite Russian texts for themselves in Latin script (Vainu 1994, 10). Yet even in this zealously Sovietized festival, the singers stayed on stage after the end of the program and spontaneously sang the beloved song that had been left out of the official program, 'My Fatherland is my Love' (*Mu isamaa on minu arm*), an affirmation of belonging together with one's land (Kuutma 1996, 9; Vainu 1994, 11). As Robert Young reminds us, "anti-colonialism is as old as colonialism itself" (2001, 6); from the very beginning of its establishment, Soviet colonial rule in the Baltics was accompanied by efforts to sustain pre-colonial traditions and to find ways to counterbalance the Soviet mandates of the new era.

---

[10] In Latvia, the turn towards full Sovietization of song festival tradition happened after the 1950 song festival, which still included a good number of pieces from prewar Latvian repertoire; see Šmidchens (2014).

LOCAL RESPONSES AND DECOLONIAL CONTINUITIES

Systematic decolonial efforts started in the Baltics immediately following the end of Stalinist oppression. Of course, the decades after Stalin included many fluctuations in which a loosening of central control was followed by another consolidation of centralized power, yet each advancing decolonial wave in the borderlands' cultural sphere was made possible by a relative easing of Soviet norms and values in the center. Decolonial action, then, should not be understood as resistance operating in opposition to developments from the colonial center; instead borderlands' decolonial developments often responded to reforms and changes in political attitudes in central institutions. In situations of political change within imperial ideologies, the borderlands' local elites sometimes emerged as the main obstruction to cultural change. Thus, the laudatory reaction to Baltic art exhibitions in Moscow in 1956 (Estonian art), 1959, and 1960 (Baltic art more generally) made possible a more permissive climate in the borderlands visual arts sphere (Talvoja 2017; Annus 2017)—a recalibration that ironically included new approval of pre-Soviet art that central authorities in earlier years had deemed unsuitably bourgeois. As cycles would swing back and the center would more strictly regulate the borderlands' sociocultural expressions, the decolonial tide would recede. Yet each decolonial tide would gain new ground from imperial control, and these gains, notwithstanding their cyclical setbacks, would remain within the cultural memory as something within the reach of the possible.

In the post-Stalin period, the Baltic song festivals came to function as a strong framework for fostering and sustaining decolonial attitudes on a large scale. The song festival tradition, supported by Soviet rule as a means of indoctrination, was officially acceptable as a celebration of major Soviet anniversaries—so many years from the Great October revolution, so many from the establishment of Soviet rule. In the eyes of Soviet authorities, the festival also comported with the general slogan 'nationalist in form and socialist in content'; indeed, the authorities encouraged Sovietized versions of folk traditions and the emblematic use of folk costumes. The song festivals nevertheless provided, after the easing of Stalinist pressure, an occasion to experience affective togetherness at the national level and in a decolonial mood. In mass choral song, tens of thousands could actively participate; the largest Soviet-era song festival, the 1985 Lithuanian festival, included as many as 38,856 performers. The whole audience joined in and stood up for the popular non-Soviet songs, such as the Latvian *Pūt Vējiņi* ('Blow, Winds'), and the Estonian *Mu isamaa on minu arm* ('My Fatherland is my Love'). The highlight of these celebrations was the finale with its elevated moods and follow-up songs, not included in the official program. One commentator suggests in hyperbolic terms that at the 1960 Estonian festival, the extra pieces "formed a whole second concert" (Pant 1969).[11] A participant at the 1980 Estonian festival recalls how at the end of the concert, a chant *Eesti rahvas la-va-le* ('The Estonian nation onto the stage!') started up, and the stage was flooded with both festival singers and participants, who together sang an apolitical nineteenth-century tune. This spontaneous after-event ended only when lines of militia forced the last singers from the stage (Sookruus 2014). In Latvian festivals, *Pūt Vējiņi* was cut from the official festival program after 1960, with an exception of the centennial 1973 festival, but the festival choir and the audience nevertheless sang it after the official program had concluded (Šmidchens 2014, 175).

In the context of decolonial efforts, an important part of the song festivals' impact was simply the sense of continuity, a widely shared understanding that this tradition was rooted in the pre-Soviet history of Baltic nations. This continuity was made visible and sensible by national costumes with their long ethnic histories, worn by some choirs but certainly by dancers, who would, during the singing parts of the festival, merge with the audience, thus elevating the communal sense of belonging within an ethnos. For many among the performers and audiences, the continuity was also a matter of personal experience—song festivals brought together different generations as older singers, dancers, and audience members had taken part in the pre-Soviet festivals. This essay has already mentioned the photo of the aged singer Liise Kiima included in the album for the 1947 Estonian Song Festival. For the older generations, their participation might have dated not just to the times of independent Estonia, but even as far back as the Tsarist era. This continuity was sustained throughout the Soviet years until the dissolution of the USSR. In Lithuania, the conductor Kostas Gurevičius recalled in the 1990 song festival program

---

[11] Pages are not numbered in this publication.

how he had been a conductor in Lithuania's first song festival in 1924 (Šmidchens 2014, 201); Gurevičius, born in 1898, died the same fall at the age of 92. In Estonia, Gustav Ernesaks, the beloved choir conductor of the Soviet years and the official chief conductor of several festivals, was likewise born in 1908 under Tsarist rule, had lived through the first Estonian republic and through the Soviet years, and finally died in 1993 in an Estonia that was once again independent—but not without conducting the grand finale one last time in the 1990 song festival. In one anecdote that spread among composers and choir conductors, Ernesaks had wittily responded to a complaint about the considerable presence of Soviet songs in the festival program: "Don't worry – we will sing them through quickly!" (Puderbaugh 2008, 41)— as if one could quickly dispense with the Soviet trappings of a festival event that, after all, signified so much more.

The sense of national continuity, extending beyond the Soviet era, already carried a decolonizing impact. Song festivals were not just a set of concerts, but much more: a year-long period of rehearsals all over the country, local pre-festival concerts at the regional level, the festival parade, and the special atmosphere in the festival city filled with singers, dancers, and jubilant energies. The festival also functioned as a media event broadcast on television and radio, and widely discussed in newspapers. Direct television and radio broadcasts, so rare in the highly censored Soviet era, added special possibilities. As Peeter Sookruus (2014) recalls, highly skilled radio commentators could smooth over the obligatory Soviet propaganda parts and foreground the sublime national atmosphere of these events. The festival included both material paraphernalia, such as scarves, streamers, and badges, as well as a set of associated publications—a festival album for the general public, an informational booklet for singers, and in some years semi-academic books about the history of song festivals (Tamarkin 1965; Põldmäe 1969). So, as a media event it was not limited to the festival days alone, but stretched over a lengthy period, multiplying its potential impact. The reputation of the festivals as magnificent events, not to be missed, supported the continuation of choir culture more generally, and the choirs themselves often functioned as nationally attuned mini-societies. Heinz Valk talks about his experience from the post 1956-period:

I sang in a male choir. These were fully nationally minded organizations. In all our meetings we sang forbidden songs and discussed 'the Estonian matters.' For encores in our concerts we sang […] songs which had been removed from the official song festival repertoire. (Labi 2011, 111)[12]

The sense of continuity and the extended duration of song celebration moods became especially manifest in the hundred-year celebrations of the Estonian and Latvian song festivals, in 1969 and 1973, right at the peak of the first decolonial wave. In these centennial celebrations, the final concerts were preceded by a set of introductory events. In Estonia, a symbolic festival light was lit in Tartu, by the sun's rays, in commemoration of the site of the first, 1869 festival. The torch was then carried, over a two week period, to Tallinn, and the passage of the festival light was celebrated with concerts along its way (Ratassepp 1985, 30–33).[13] New songs, commissioned for the centennial festival, commemorated the tradition of singing. In Latvia, *Manai dzimtenei* ('To my homeland'), a song by the popular composer Raimonds Pauls and the poet Jānis Peters connected the Latvian history of singing with a utopian promise of new mornings and new paths. This song included both intertextual allusions to well-known Latvian songs and a reference to the 1905 revolution and Latvian riflemen; the song was performed as the festival finale for every Soviet-era song festival thereafter (Šmidchens 2014, 178–79). Both in Estonia and Latvia, the summative structure of the jubilee festival gave occasion to include in the program a good number of songs from earlier, pre-Soviet festivals, thus creating a general mood in which a specifically national pathos dominated over the obligatory Soviet elements.

[12] 'Eesti asi' or 'Estonian matters' was a commonly used expression during the Soviet era. It signified any kind of non-Soviet, nationally tuned activity. The opposite term 'Russian stuff' was also commonly in use in everyday parlance, and referred to anything related to Soviet rule, economy, or culture.

[13] The tradition of lighting a festival light was initiated in 1960, after the construction of a new stage with a special tower for the festival light. In 1960, the torch was lit in Uku farm in Saku district, where a Communist printing house was set up during "the bourgeois era" (Allandi 2014, 195).

THE 1969 ALBUM: THE FIRST SINGERS WERE THE WIND AND THE WAVES

The Estonian centennial choral festivities of 1969 also extended into the field of print culture. A monograph was published about the first Estonian song festival (Põldmäe 1969), and an album *Laulusajand 1869–1969* (The Century of Song 1869–1969) was released for the centennial celebration. This richly illustrated hardcover book presented a remarkable collection of images accompanied by a lyrical overview of the song festival tradition (Pant 1969). In the context of a highly ideological Soviet print culture, this was a striking publication in many respects and emblematic of the special qualities of the 1969 festival. Its representational strategies included visualization of temporal parallels between the past and present, together with a poetic view of the pre-Soviet past. Even more, the album managed to minimize the obligatory Soviet-era narrative, where history was typically presented as class struggle and friendship with the Russian people was sure to be highlighted.

Indeed, the force of such a publication can be best understood in the general context of Soviet rule in the Baltics, with its heavily censored representations of culture and society. The local culture had to reproduce Soviet models for presenting socio-historical processes—the center introduced and disseminated the 'correct models' both through ideological texts translated from Russian into the local languages and through various other forms of political education. Tellingly, in the first years of Soviet rule, the mediating role of translation was generally concealed in mass media texts. Publishers did not mark translations from Russian as such, nor did they indicate the source of the text, even when the borderlands' newspapers would reproduce, after a brief delay, texts that had already appeared in central newspapers such as *Pravda* and *Izvestiya*. The result was a public media discourse not just heavily controlled by the colonial center, but to a significant extent spoken with the voice of the center, reproducing without marked difference words issued from Moscow.

The success of local authors depended on their ability to imitate and reproduce the same rhetorical models under different local thematic subheadings. Writing vernacular modern histories demanded narratives of class struggle and required both unequivocal condemnation of the earlier period of independence and a new obligatory emphasis on the 'historical friendship with the Russian people' (Annus 2017; Gruodytė 2008;

Karnes 2008). In visual representations of the Soviet era, Stalinist ico-
nography of the great leader and the jubilating masses later gave way
to images of factories and other signifiers of Soviet-era progress. Visual
imagery of the Soviet era—including photographs in mass media, general publications, and posters in public places—became heavily politicized and had to carry unambiguous markers of Sovietness. A 1965 book
about the history of Estonian song festivals, for example, stressed in its
introduction its aim to give a "Marxist interpretation to Estonian song
festivals" (Tamarkin 1965, 5) and so it diligently reproduced the canonical mode of writing such things. A strongly pejorative tone accompanied
its surveys of all festivals prior to the start of the Soviet era whereupon at
long last the people were finally free to "sing about matters that are close
to their hearts: about their bright lives, about their leader in struggles –
the Communist Party" (ibid.).[14]

In the context of such inflexible conventions, the 1969 song festival album emerges in its stunning difference. The album opens with
several pages of images of landscapes, clouds, water, birds, plants, and
insects without any written text at all. Here, readers view photographs
that are unmistakably shot in recent years, as evidenced by their up-to-
date technicalities as well as the distinctive artistic sensibilities of the
1960s. Yet, strikingly, these images of Soviet-era Estonia are purified of
any Sovietness—the first full-page panoramic image glances over forests,
fields and pre-Soviet farm homes scattered throughout the landscape. On
the facing page, four smaller images show a cloudy sky, an overgrown
forest with tall fir trees, a close-up of the sea with small waves that are
circling rocks close to the shore, and a grain field with fir trees in the
background. These are archetypical images of Estonianness that suggest
a certain inviolability of the land entirely apart from political rules and
regimes—as if the Soviet order could never have any true impact here.
On the next page, Vanemuine, the pagan god of music (invented in
the nineteenth century in Romantic Estonian neo-mythology) sits with
his harp on his lap. His graphic imprint is set against the backdrop of
another Estonian rural landscape, this time a picturesque image of a
pre-Soviet lakeside farm home—a collage-like double-layered image
where the landscape faintly shimmers through the body of the 'ancient'
god. The next pages have images of birds, plants, insects, and a close-up

---

[14]In the Estonian SSR, the more balanced way of writing about the pre-Soviet past
became slowly possible in the 1970s; see Sarapik (2015).

of a nineteenth-century farmhouse, again shot according to the rules of modern aesthetics, where the image of the main building is framed by the log wall of another building (a barn?) very close to the camera. A forest emerges behind the farm home, and signs of Soviet modernity are nowhere to be seen.

After nine full pages of images, the reader finally reaches the text. The first two lines are borrowed from *Mu isamaa on minu arm*, the nineteenth-century poem I have mentioned earlier as a much loved choral song: "My fatherland is my love / whom I have given my heart...". The text then continues with an autochthonous story of creation where the tale of the nation is intertwined with images of nature, ancient traditions, and the birth of song:

> The first singers were the wind and the waves. We have something of that pine tree in wind and something of the rocks by the sea in us. [...]

> Then Vanemuine sang. [...]

> Then the mother sang by her cradle. The spinning wheel whirred, the sparkle of light flickered in the hut and the night crept behind the window.

> Everything started from here. (Pant 1969)

Readers are presented with a poetic tale of the autochthonous birth of a song, a singing tradition, and eventually a whole nation, all as if sprouting forth from the winds and the waves, from the pines and the rocky shores, from the energies of the Earth, intertwined with the never-ending cycle of life and death—a story strikingly different, indeed worlds apart, from the typical Soviet narrative of class struggle inevitably leading toward the victory of communism. Here, the decolonial gesture points to Estonianness as rooted in nature, part and parcel with the singing tradition, something so ancient that a few years of one rule or another leave little trace on its body of forests, lakes, seas, and traditional dwellings. Poetry and mythic fantasy overtake reality, and for a brief moment the poetic imaginary erases political reality.

In the next years, Baltic cultures experienced a new tightening of control and stricter limits on the possibilities of expression. Yet the publications of the late 1960s remained on people's bookshelves, and both the singers and audiences would remember the 1969 festival atmosphere.

Moreover, the decolonial spirit continued here and there to show itself in public, both on the song festival fields and elsewhere—at rock concerts, in theaters, and in a more veiled form in print culture—to say nothing of the occasional protest movement and everyday culture with its jokes, anecdotes, and small quotidian resistances to Soviet rule.

THE LATE 1980s: THE DECOLONIAL
AS THE NEW SOCIAL DOMINANT

In 1988 the Baltic tradition of song festivals that had played a substantial role in sustaining and disseminating the decolonial mood, both in Tsarist times and during the Soviet era, emerged in its fullest decolonial potential within a set of events that have become known as the 'Singing Revolution'.[15] The use of national symbols, above all the anthems and the national flags of the pre- Soviet republics, had been strictly forbidden throughout the Soviet era. Equally proscribed were any positive endorsements of the Baltic states as political entities separate from the Soviet Union, whether in the past or in the future. The Gorbachev reforms with their increased permissibility introduced a new chance to collectively transgress these taboos. The Estonian blue-black-white tricolor was first openly displayed during the Tartu Music Days in May 1988, during a presentation of the 'Five Fatherland Songs' cycle—these creative rewritings of nineteenth-century patriotic verses, quickly became the emblematic tunes of the 'Singing Revolution'. On July 1, the tricolors of all three pre-Soviet Baltic republics were openly displayed in Vilnius, during 'Gaudeamus', the song festival of Baltic university students.[16] Later in July, the Latvian national flag publicly flew in Riga for the first time in Soviet-era Latvia, once again in the context of a song and dance celebration—this time during the folklore festival 'Baltica' (Klotiņš 2002, 123). The open display of pre-Soviet national flags was a highly symbolic act. In addition to demonstrating the continuing allegiance to pre-Soviet traditions and values after close to fifty years of Soviet occupation, this was also a gesture of defiance, the claiming of a public space formerly controlled by Soviet authorities.

[15] About the Perestroika-era developments in the Baltics, see Taagepera (1993), Smith (1996, 1999).

[16] By this time, the pre-Soviet Lithuanian flag had already been displayed once again, but in the context of a different meeting.

The Baltic decolonial movement of the late 1980s again exploited strategies that dated back to Baltic German colonial rule. The tradition of song festivals now developed into a set of peaceful demonstrations that consisted of a combination of speeches and songs, in the streets and other venues all over the Baltic states. Songs dating to the first festivals in the late nineteenth century now accrued an additional layer of decolonial critique—some nineteenth-century patriotic tunes were repurposed, with new rhythms and melodies, and with references to the present-day political situation (Annus 2018, 166–67). The historical continuity was striking—the ritual of collective singing, once again, rose into the level of political expression and helped to consolidate the nation. This time, in relation to the reform movement and in relation to political confusion in Moscow, the decolonial processes would develop their full potential and culminate in the Baltic states regaining their political sovereignty.

Conclusion: From Decolonial to New Europe

This chapter has focused on colonial regimes and particularly on decolonial continuities in the Baltic area. Both colonial regulations and decolonial efforts develop dialogical ideological structures, in which new colonial rules and new decolonial strategies borrow and rely upon earlier practices and experiences. Decolonial necessities bridge times and traditions in ways that would not make sense without the colonial context—in the Baltics, decolonial necessities kept alive the Romantic nineteenth-century tradition of national choral song festivals, all through the era of space travel, up to the emergence of postmodern sensibilities. Affective nation-building in the Baltics was successful precisely as a response to the colonial condition. At the same time, decolonial efforts did not develop in full opposition to colonial rule, but emerged in relation to new political directions from the center, and reacted to the possibilities granted by the governing regime.

In the postcolonial period from 1990 to the present, independent Estonia, Latvia and Lithuania have had to deal not only with the consequences of Soviet migration and ecological damage, but also with the necessity of rebuilding social, political, and economic systems according to local needs and interests. Decolonial nation-building tends toward essentializing attitudes and non-inclusive us-and-them oppositions; the continuing task of nation-building in post-imperial times is to overcome past traumas and provide a welcoming social atmosphere undefined by ethnic prejudices.

Joining the European Union in 2004 has allowed new possibilities, brought new responsibilities, and introduced new matrices of power into the Baltic states. In 2013, 2015, and 2017, Lithuania, Latvia, and Estonia held the presidency of the Council of the European Union—an experience that certainly strengthened the sense of national agency and contributed to the emotional and psychological distance from the Soviet colonial past. At the same time, Russia's aggressive politics of the last decades has reinforced negative image of Russia and has hindered the processes of building a civil society in the Baltics, unburdened by the fear of reliving the past. Decolonial efforts to establish national self-determination may be complete in the Baltic lands, but postcolonial struggles to construct an open and just civil society continue.

Acknowledgments Research for this chapter was supported by the research grants PUT1218 and IRG22-2 of the Estonian Ministry of Education and Research, the Centre of Excellence in Estonian Studies (CEES, European Regional Development Fond) and the Estonian Literary Museum.

REFERENCES

Allandi, Marge. 2014. "Kolm tuld: Jüriöö, Võidupüha, laulupidu" [Three Fires: *Jüriöö, Võidupüha*, song festival]. *Ajalooline Ajakiri* 2(3)/148(1): 173–206.

Annus, Epp. 2014. "Layers of Colonial Rule in the Baltics: Nation-Building, the Soviet Rule and the Affectivity of a Nation." In *(Post-) Colonialism Across Europe: Transcultural History and National Memory*, edited by Dirk Göttsche and Axel Dunker, 359–84. Bielefeld: Aisthesis.

Annus, Epp. 2017. "Ma tõstan klaasi vene rahva terviseks. Sotskolonialismi diskursiivsed alustalad" [I Propose a Toast to the Russian People: Discursive Foundations of Soviet Colonialism]. *Methis: Studia Humaniora Estonica* 16(20): 4–26.

Annus, Epp. 2018. *Soviet Postcolonial Studies: A View from the Western Borderlands*. London: Routledge.

Bhabha, Homi K. 1994. *The Location of Culture*. London: Routledge.

Brandenberger, David. 2001. "'… It Is Imperative to Advance Russian Nationalism as the First Priority': Debates Within the Stalinist Ideological Establishment, 1941–1945." In *A State of Nations: Empire and Nation-Making in the Age of Lenin and Stalin*, edited by Ronald Grigor Suny and Terry Martin, 275–99. Oxford: Oxford University Press.

Eichner, Barbara. 2012. *History in Mighty Sounds: Musical Constructions of German National Identity, 1848–1914.* Woodbridge: Boydell Press.

Erdmann, Bruno. 1913. "Einige Glossen über Baltische Lebensformen." *Baltische Monatsschrift* 55(1): 404–16.

Fanon, Frantz. [1961] 2004. *The Wretched of the Earth.* New York: Grove Press.

Fowkes, Ben. 1993. *The Rise and Fall of Communism in Eastern Europe.* Houndmills: Palgrave Macmillan.

Frost, Robert I. 2000. *The Northern Wars: War, State, and Society in Northeastern Europe, 1558–1721.* London: Routledge.

Fürst, Juliane. 2010. *Stalin's Last Generation: Soviet Post-War Youth and the Emergence of Mature Socialism.* Oxford: Oxford University Press.

Grava, Sigurd. 1993. "The Urban Heritage of the Soviet Regime: The Case of Riga, Latvia." *Journal of the American Planning Association* 59(1): 9–30.

Gruodytė, Vita. 2008. "Lithuanian Musicology in Historical Context: 1945 to the Present." *Journal of Baltic Studies* 39(3): 263–82.

Ijabs, Ivars. 2014. "Another Baltic Postcolonialism: Young Latvians, Baltic Germans, and the Emergence of Latvian National Movement." *Nationalities Papers* 42(1): 88–107.

Inno, Kersti. 2006. *Koorijuhiks sündinud. Ants Üleoja* [Born to be a Conductor. Ants Üleoja]. Tallinn: Eesti Segakooride Liit.

Jansen, Ea. 2001. "Eestlaste rahvuslik ärkamisaeg" [Estonian National Awakening]. In *Eesti identiteet ja iseseisvus*, edited by A. Betricau and Lore Listra, 89–108. Tallinn: Avita.

Kaljundi, Linda. 2016. "The Baltic Crusades and the Culture of Memory: Studies on Historical Representation, Rituals, and Recollection of the Past." Ph.D. diss., Helsinki University. http://urn.fi/URN:ISBN:ISBN978-951-51-1874-5.

Kalnačs, Benedikts. 2016a. *20th Century Baltic Drama: Postcolonial Narratives, Decolonial Options.* Bielefeld: Aisthesis.

Kalnačs, Benedikts. 2016b. "Comparing Colonial Differences: Baltic Literary Cultures as Agencies of Europe's Internal Others." *Journal of Baltic Studies* 47(1): 15–30.

Kangilaski, Jaak. 2016. "Postcolonial Theory as a Means to Understand Estonian Art History." *Journal of Baltic Studies* 47(1): 31–47.

Kappeler, Andreas. 2009. "Hiliskeiserlik Vene impeerium moderniseerumise ja traditsiooni vahel" [Late Tsarist Russian Empire Between Modernization and Tradition]. In *Vene impeerium ja Baltikum: venestus, rahvuslus ja moderniseerimine 19. sajandi teisel poolel ja 20. sajandi alguses. I*, edited by Tõnu Tannberg and Bradley Woodworth, 51–92. Tartu: Eesti Ajalooarhiiv.

Karindi, Alfred. 1947. "Ärge unustage laulu" [Don't Forget Song]. In *XII Üldlaulupeo juht*, 18. Tallinn: Ilukirjandus ja Kunst.

Karjahärm, Toomas. 2010. "Moderniseerimise strateegiad hilises Vene impeeriumis: Semstvo ja Balti maaomavalitsus 1880–1917" [Modernization Strategies in Late Russian Empire: *semstvo* and Baltic Local Self-Government 1880–1917]. In *Vene impeerium ja Baltikum: venestus, rahvuslus ja moderniseerimine 19. sajandi teisel poolel ja 20. sajandi alguses. II*, edited by Tõnu Tannberg and Bradley Woodworth, 323–59. Tartu: Eesti Ajalooarhiiv.

Karjahärm, Toomas, and Väino Sirk. 2007. *Kohanemine ja vastupanu: Eesti haritlaskond 1940–1991* [Conformity and Resistance. Estonian intelligentsia 1940–1991]. Tallinn: Argo.

Karnes, Kevin C. 2008. "Soviet Musicology and the 'Nationalities Question': The Case of Latvia." *Journal of Baltic Studies* 39(3): 283–305.

Kasekamp, Andres. 2010. *A History of the Baltic States*. Houndmills: Palgrave Macmillan.

Kelberg, Aleksander. 1950. "Nõukogude Eesti 1950. a. üldlaulupidu" [The Soviet Estonian 1950 Song Festival]. In *Nõukogude Eesti 1950. A. üldlaulupeo juht*, 5–9. Tallinn: Eesti Riiklik Kirjastus.

Klotiņš, Arnolds. 2002. "The Latvian Neo-Folklore Movement and the Political Changes of the Late 20th Century." *The World of Music* 44(3): 107–30.

Koidula, Lydia. 1881. *Saaremaa onupoeg. Naljamäng ühes waatuses* [A Cousin from Saaremaa. A One Act Comedy]. Tartu: Schnakenburg.

Kuutma, Kristin. 1996. "Laulupeod rahvusliku identiteedi kandjana" [Song Festivals as Carriers of National Identity]. *Mäetagused* 1–2: 1–10. https://doi.org/10.7592/mt1996.01/02.internet, Accessed September 5, 2018.

Labi, Kanni. 2011. "Isamaalaulud ja okupatsioonirežiim – nostalgia, utoopia ja reaalsus" [Estonian Patriotic Songs and the Occupational Regime—Nostalgia, Utopia and Reality]. *Methis: Studia Humaniora Estonica* 5(7): 109–21.

Lane, Thomas. 2014. *Lithuania: Stepping Westward*. London: Routledge.

Lebedev, V. 1945. "Suur Vene rahvas – Nõukogude Liidu silmapaistvaim rahvus ja juhtiv jõud" [The Great Russian Nation—The Most Outstanding Nation and the Leading Force of the USSR]. *Postimees* 235, October 7.

Lebedeva, N.S. 2001. "The Deportation of the Polish Population to the USSR, 1939–41." In *Forced Migration in Central and Eastern Europe, 1939–1950*, edited by Alfred J. Rieber, 28–45. London: Frank Cass.

Magocsi, Paul Robert. 2002. *Roots of Ukrainian Nationalism*. Toronto: University of Toronto Press.

Martin, Terry. 2001. *The Affirmative Action Empire: Nations and Nationalism in the Soviet Union, 1923–1939*. Ithaca, NY: Cornell University Press.

McCauley, Martin. 2008. *Stalin and Stalinism: Revised Third Edition*. 3rd ed. Harlow: Pearson Education Limited.

Miller, Alexey. 2009. "Venestus või venelased" [Russification or Russians]. In *Vene impeerium ja Baltikum: venestus, rahvuslus ja moderniseerimine 19. sajandi teisel poolel ja 20. sajandi alguses. I*, edited by Tõnu Tannberg and Bradley Woodworth, 33–50. Tartu: Eesti Ajalooarhiiv.

Ngugi wa Thiong'o. [1986] 1994. *Decolonising the Mind: The Politics of Language in African Literature*. Harare: Zimbabwe Publishing House.

North, Michael. 2011. *Geschichte Der Ostsee: Handel und Kulturen*. München: Beck.

Nõukogude Eesti 1950. a. üldlaulupeo juht [The Guide to Soviet Estonian 1950 Song Festival]. Tallinn: Eesti Riiklik Kirjastus.

Pant, Valdo. 1969. *Laulusajand 1869–1969* [The Century of Song 1869–1969], edited by Aarne Mesikäpp, Valdo Pant, and Aron Tamarkin. Tallinn: Eesti Raamat.

Plakans, Andrejs. 2011. *A Concise History of the Baltic States*. Cambridge: Cambridge University Press.

Plath, Ulrike. 2011. *Esten und Deutsche in den Baltischen Provinzen Russlands: Fremdkonstruktionen, Lebenswelten, Kolonialphantasien 1750–1850*. Wiesbaden: Harrassowitz.

Põldmäe, Rudolf. 1969. *Esimene Eesti Üldlaulupidu 1869* [First Estonian Song Festival 1869]. Tallinn: Eesti Raamat.

Prozorov, Sergei. 2016. *The Biopolitics of Stalinism: Ideology and Life in Soviet Socialism*. Edinburgh: Edinburgh University Press.

Puderbaugh, David. 2008. "How Choral Music Saved a Nation: The 1947 Estonian National Song Festival and the Song Festivals of Estonian's Soviet Occupation." *The Choral Journal* 49(4): 28–43.

Ratassepp, Arvo. 1985. *Eesti laulupeod* [Estonian Song Festivals]. Tallinn: Perioodika.

Saagpakk, Maris. 2014. "Christine Jencken's Großmutters Erzählung (Grandmother's Story) and the Aspect of Power in Baltic-German Autobiographical Writing." *Interlitteraria* 19(1): 167–76.

Sarapik, Virve. 2015. "How to Write Soviet Estonian Art History: Three Attempts, from Stalinism Through the Khrushchev Thaw and Beyond." *Kunstiteaduslikke Uurimusi* 24(3–4): 150–72.

Schorkowitz, Dittmar. 2015. *Imperial Formations and Ethnic Diversity: Institutions, Practices, and Longue Durée Illustrated by the Example of Russia*. Max Planck Institute for Social Anthropology Working Paper No. 165. Halle (Saale): Max Planck Institute for Social Anthropology.

Smith, Graham, ed. 1996. *The Baltic States: The National Self-Determination of Estonia, Latvia and Lithuania*. Houndmills: Palgrave Macmillan.

Smith, Graham. 1999. *The Post-Soviet States: Mapping the Politics of Transition*. London: Arnold.

Šmidchens, Guntis. 2014. *The Power of Song: Nonviolent National Culture in the Baltic Singing Revolution*. Seattle: University of Washington Press.

Sookruus, Peeter. 2014. "Peeter Sookruus: Ajakirjanikud muutsid 80ndate laulupidude ülekanded värvikateks ja inimlikeks" [Peeter Sookruus: Journalists Gave a Vibrant and Human Tone to Broadcasts of the 1980s Song Festivals.]

490   E. ANNUS

DELFI 29(6). http://www.delfi.ee/archive/article.php?id=68968387. Accessed September 5, 2018.

Stone, Daniel. 2001. *The Polish-Lithuanian State, 1386–1795.* Seattle: University of Washington Press.

Taagepera, Rein. 1993. *Estonia: Return to Independence.* Boulder: Westview Press.

Talvoja, Kädi. 2017. "Kammerlikust karmiks: Karm stiil Nõukogude Eesti rahvusliku kunsti delegaadina" [Soviet Severe Style as a Representative of National Particularities in Estonian Art]. *Methis. Studia Humaniora Estonica* 16(20): 141–67.

Tamarkin, Aron, ed. 1965. *Lauluga läbi aegade* [Singing Through the Ages]. Tallinn: Eesti Raamat.

Tamm, Marek, Linda Kaljundi, and Carsten Selch Jensen, eds. 2011. *Crusading and Chronicle Writing on the Medieval Baltic Frontier: A Companion to the Chronicle of Henry of Livonia.* Farnham: Ashgate.

Tannberg, Tõnu. 2005. "Hilisstalinistlik Eesti NSV" [Late Stalinist Estonian SSR]. In *Eesti ajalugu VI. Vabadussõjast taasiseseisvumiseni,* edited by Sulev Vahtre, 271–87. Tartu: Ilmamaa.

Torri, Liina. 2008. "Saaremaa rahvaraamatukogude kogude muutumine Kihelkonna, Valjala ja Orissaare raamatukogude näite põhjal 1946–1990. Lõputöö" [Changes in the Collections of Saaremaa Public Libraries Considered Through the Examples of Kihelkonna, Valjala and Orissaare Libraries 1946–1990]. Viljandi: Tartu Ülikooli Viljandi Kultuuriakadeemia.

Vainu, Herbert. 1994. "Nõukogudeaegsete üldlaulupidude köögipoolelt. Noppeid Aksel Pajupuu meenutustest" [From the Hidden Side of Soviet-era Song Festivals. Selected Recollections by Aksel Pajupuu]. *Muusikaleht* 6: 10–11.

von Wilpert, Gero. 2005. *Deutschbaltische Literaturgeschichte.* München: Beck.

Whelan, Heide W. 1999. *Adapting to Modernity: Family, Caste and Capitalism among the Baltic German Nobility.* Köln: Böhlau.

XII Üldlaulupeo album. Tallinnas 1947. 1948. Tallinn: Ilukirjandus ja Kunst.

XII Üldlaulupeo juht. 1947 [The Guide to Soviet Estonian Twelfth Song Festival]. Tallinn: Ilukirjandus ja Kunst.

Young, Robert. 2001. *Post-Colonialism: An Historical Introduction.* Oxford: Blackwell.

Zubkova, Elena. 2008. *Pribaltika i Kreml', 1940–1953* [The Baltics and the Kremlin, 1940–1953]. Moscow: Rosspen.

Zubok, Vladislav M. 2009. *A Failed Empire: The Soviet Union in the Cold War from Stalin to Gorbachev.* Chapel Hill: The University of North Carolina Press.

CONTRIBUTORS

D. Schorkowitz et al. (eds.), *Shifting Forms of Continental Colonialism*,
https://doi.org/10.1007/978-981-13-9817-9

INDEX

© The Editor(s) (if applicable) and The Author(s) 2019
D. Schorkowitz et al. (eds.), *Shifting Forms of Continental Colonialism*,
https://doi.org/10.1007/978-981-13-9817-9